MEDIA, FEMINISM, CULTURAL STUDIES

Stepping Forward: Essays, Lectures and Interviews
by Wolfgang Iser

Wild Zones: Pornography, Art and Feminism
by Kelly Ives

Global Media Warning: Explorations of Radio, Television and the Press
by Oliver Whitehorne

'Cosmo Woman': The World of Women's Magazines
by Oliver Whitehorne

Andrea Dworkin
by Jeremy Mark Robinson

Cixous, Irigaray, Kristeva: The Jouissance of French Feminism
by Kelly Ives

Sex in Art: Pornography and Pleasure in Painting and Sculpture
by Cassidy Hughes

The Erotic Object: Sexuality in Sculpture
From Prehistory to the Present Day
by Susan Quinnell

Women in Pop Music
by Helen Challis

Detonation Britain: Nuclear War In the UK
by Jeremy Mark Robinson

Julia Kristeva: Art, Love, Melancholy, Philosophy, Semiotics
by Kelly Ives

Luce Irigaray: Lips, Kissing, and the Politics of Sexual Difference
by Kelly Ives

Helene Cixous I Love You: The Jouissance of Writing
by Kelly Ives

The Poetry of Cinema
by John Madden

EROTIC ART
In the 19th century

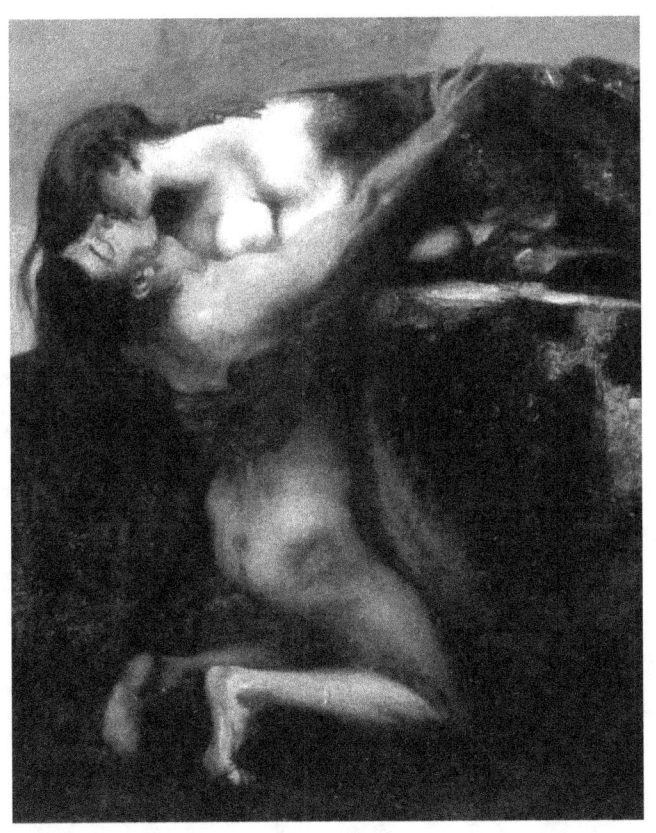

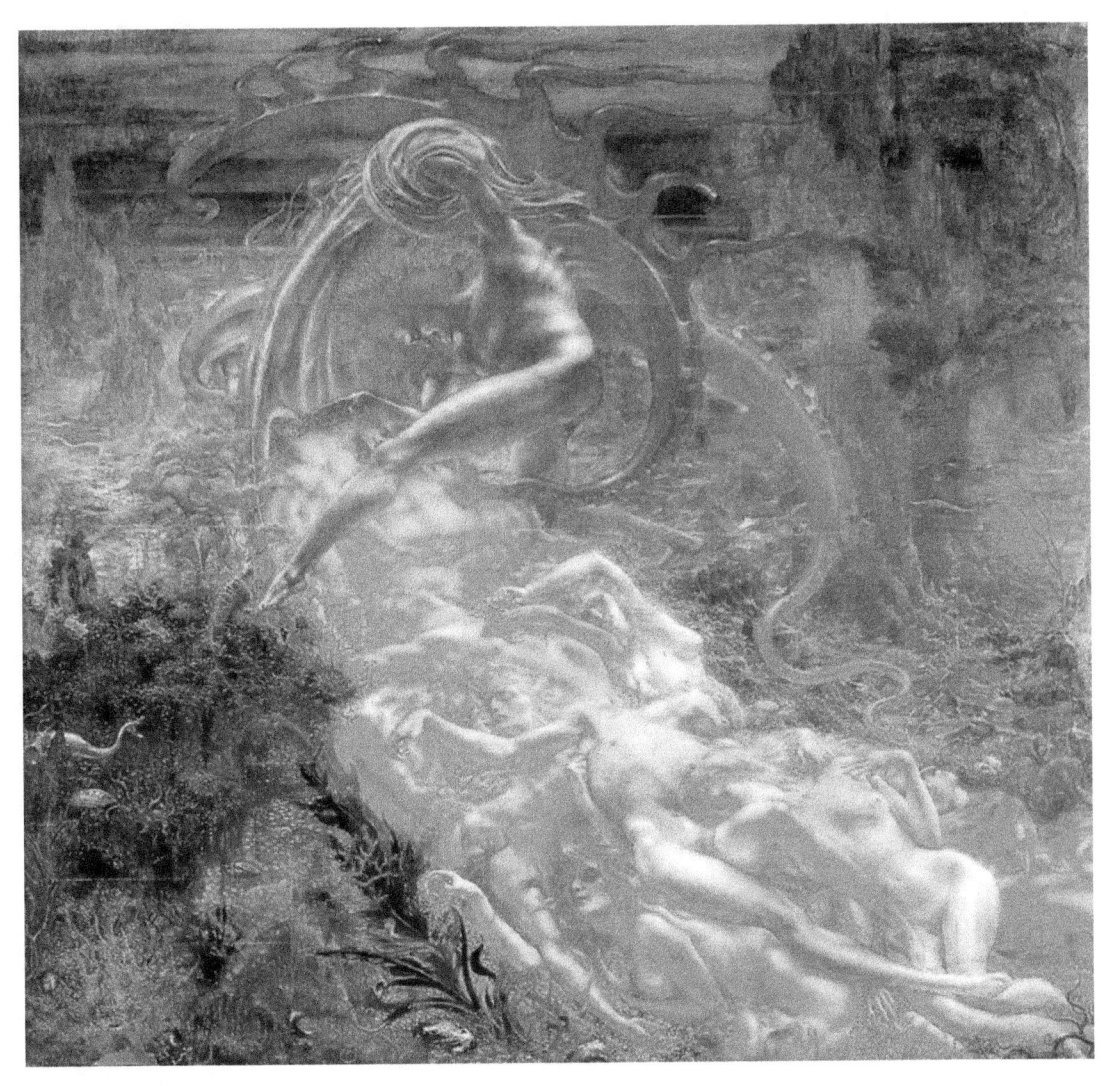

EROTIC ART
In the 19th Century

Cassidy Hughes

Crescent Moon

First published 2015.
© Cassidy Hughes 1998, 2015.

Printed and bound in the U.S.A.
Set in Book Antiqua 10 on 14pt.
Designed by Radiance Graphics.

British Library Cataloguing in Publication data

Hughes, Cassidy
Erotic Art In the 19th Century
I. Title
704.9

ISBN-13 9781861715043(Hbk)
ISBN-13 9781861715135(Pbk)

CRESCENT MOON PUBLISHING
P.O. Box 1312, Maidstone, Kent, ME14 5XU
Great Britain, www.crmoon.com

CONTENTS

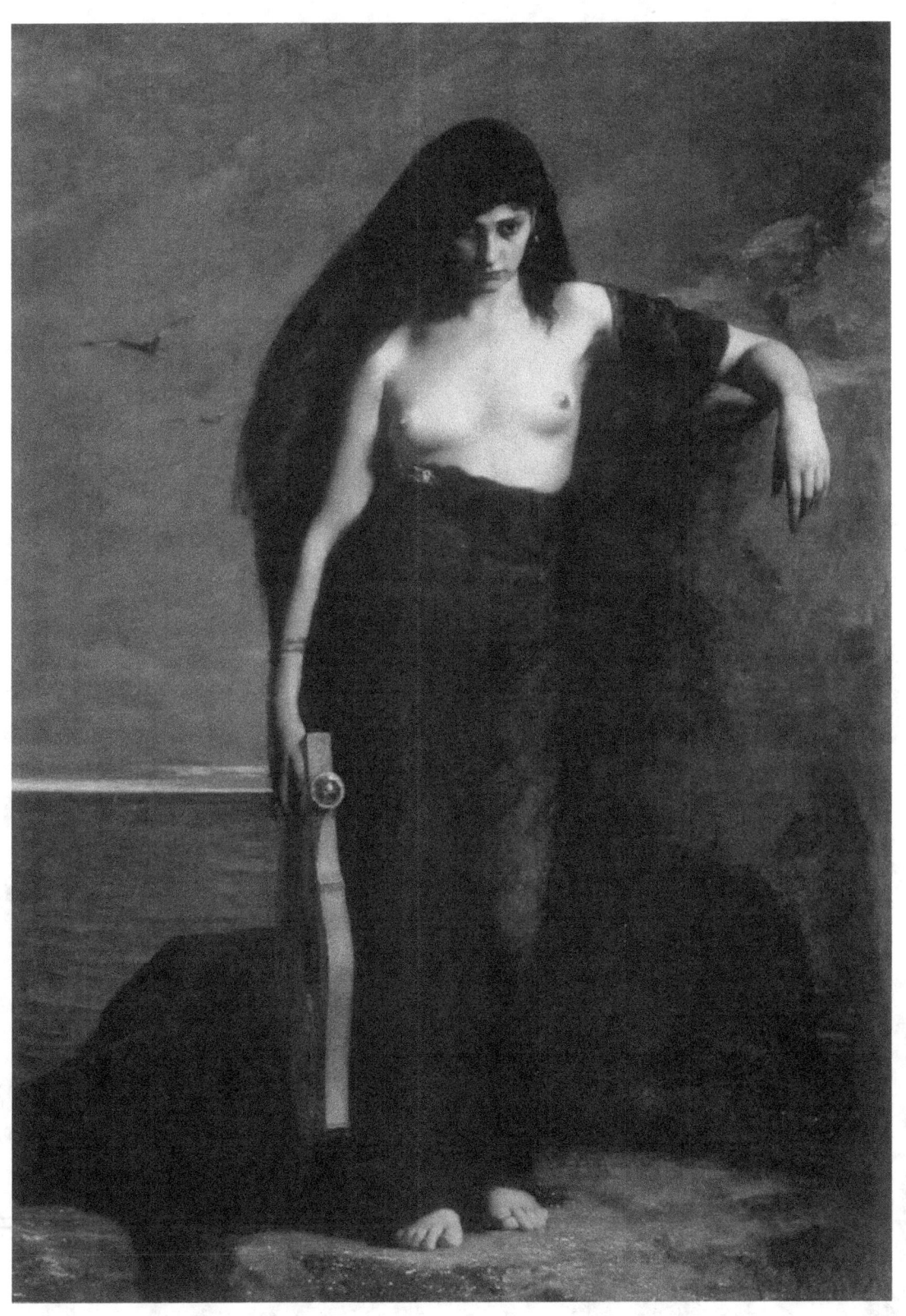

Charles Mengin, Sappho, 1867, Manchester

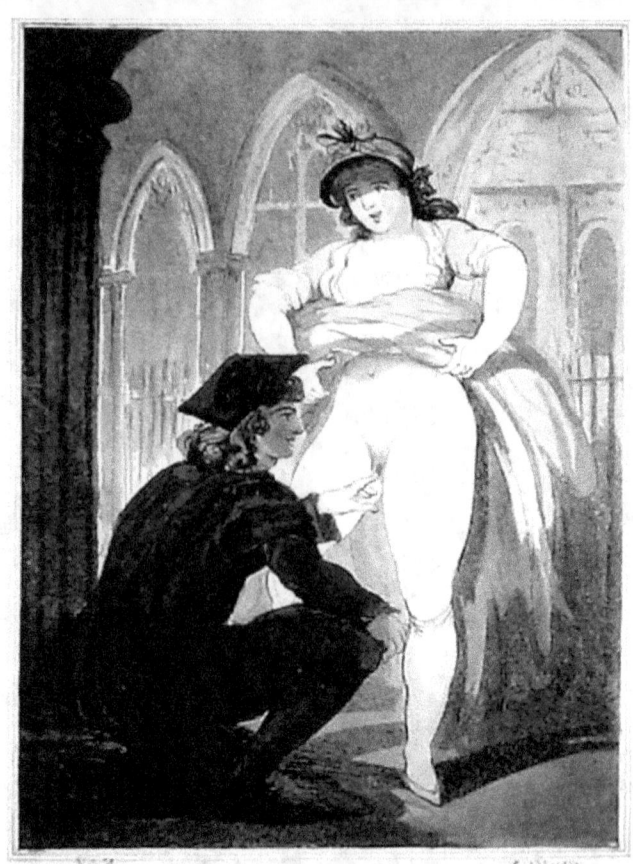

Thomas Rowlandson

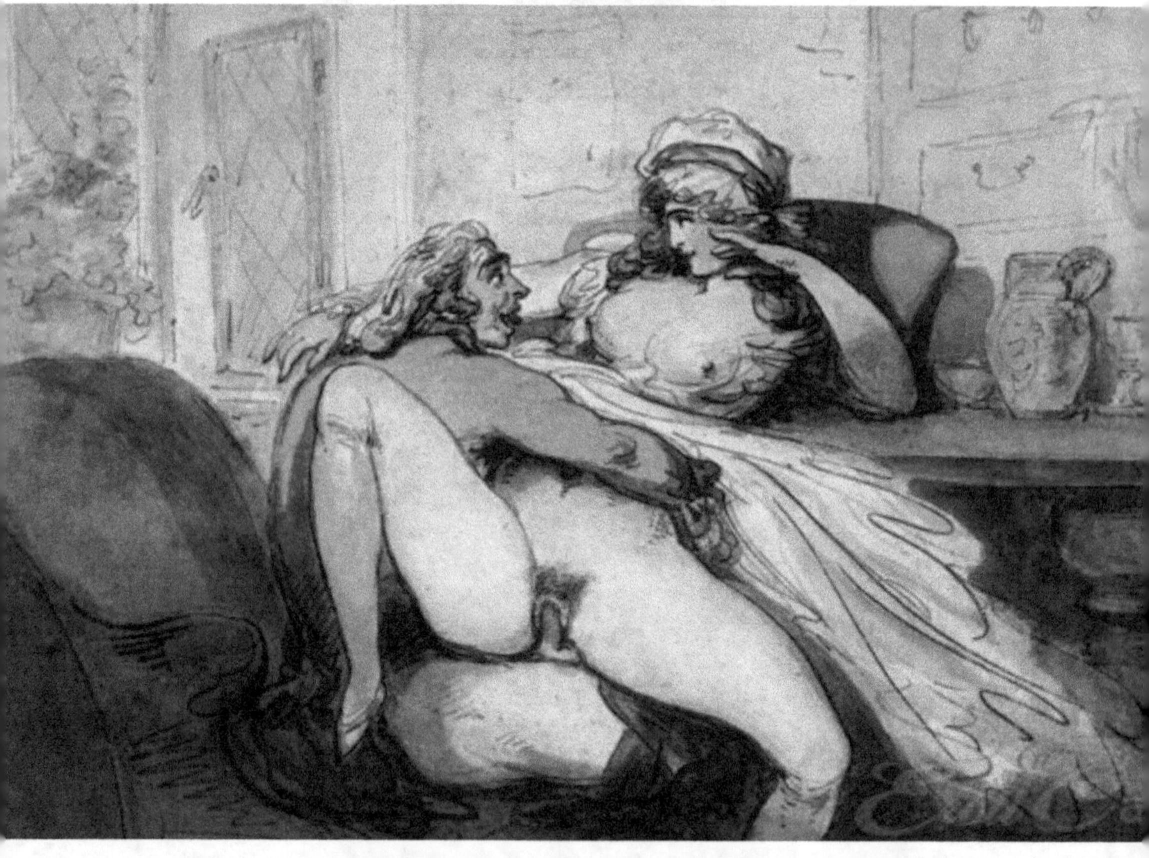

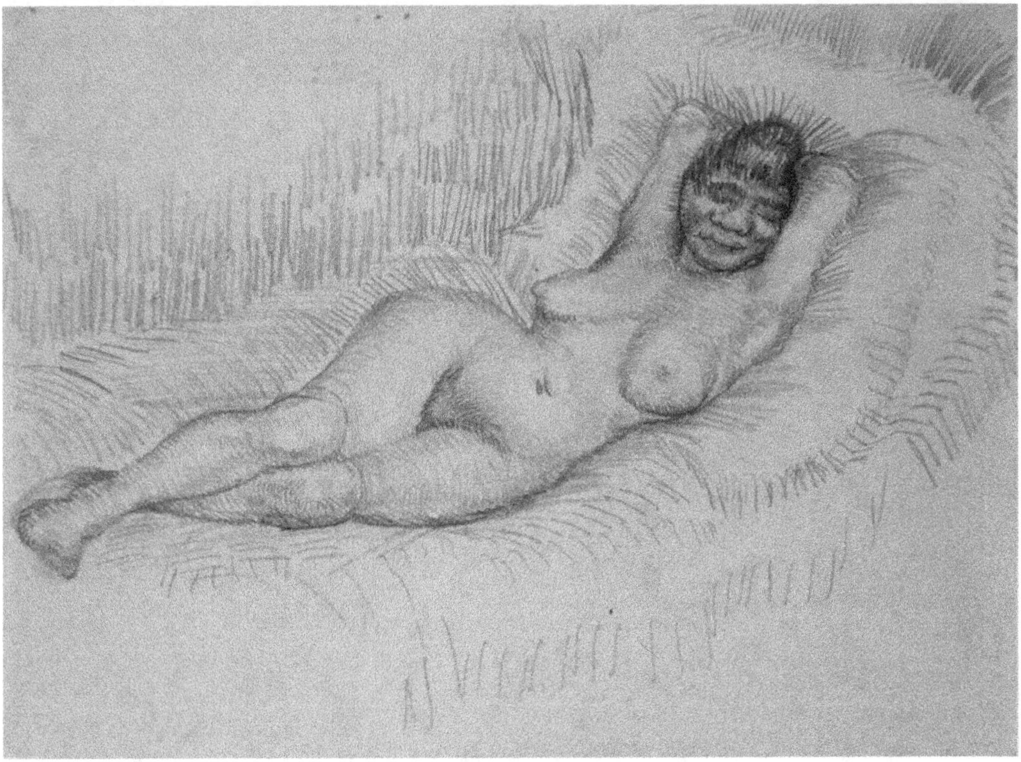

Vincent van Gogh, Reclining Nude. The Sketch (1887, Van Gogh Museum, above).
The Painting (1887, Barnes Foundation, below).

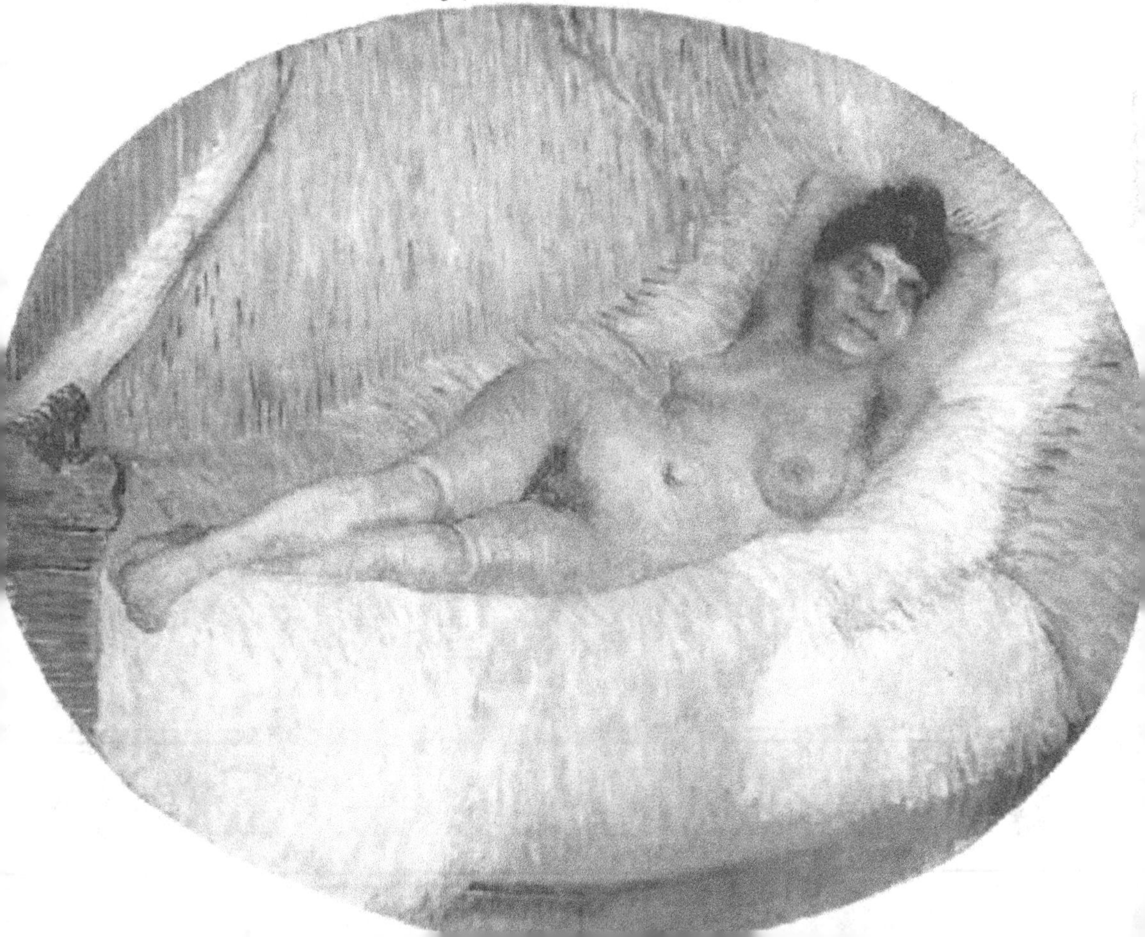

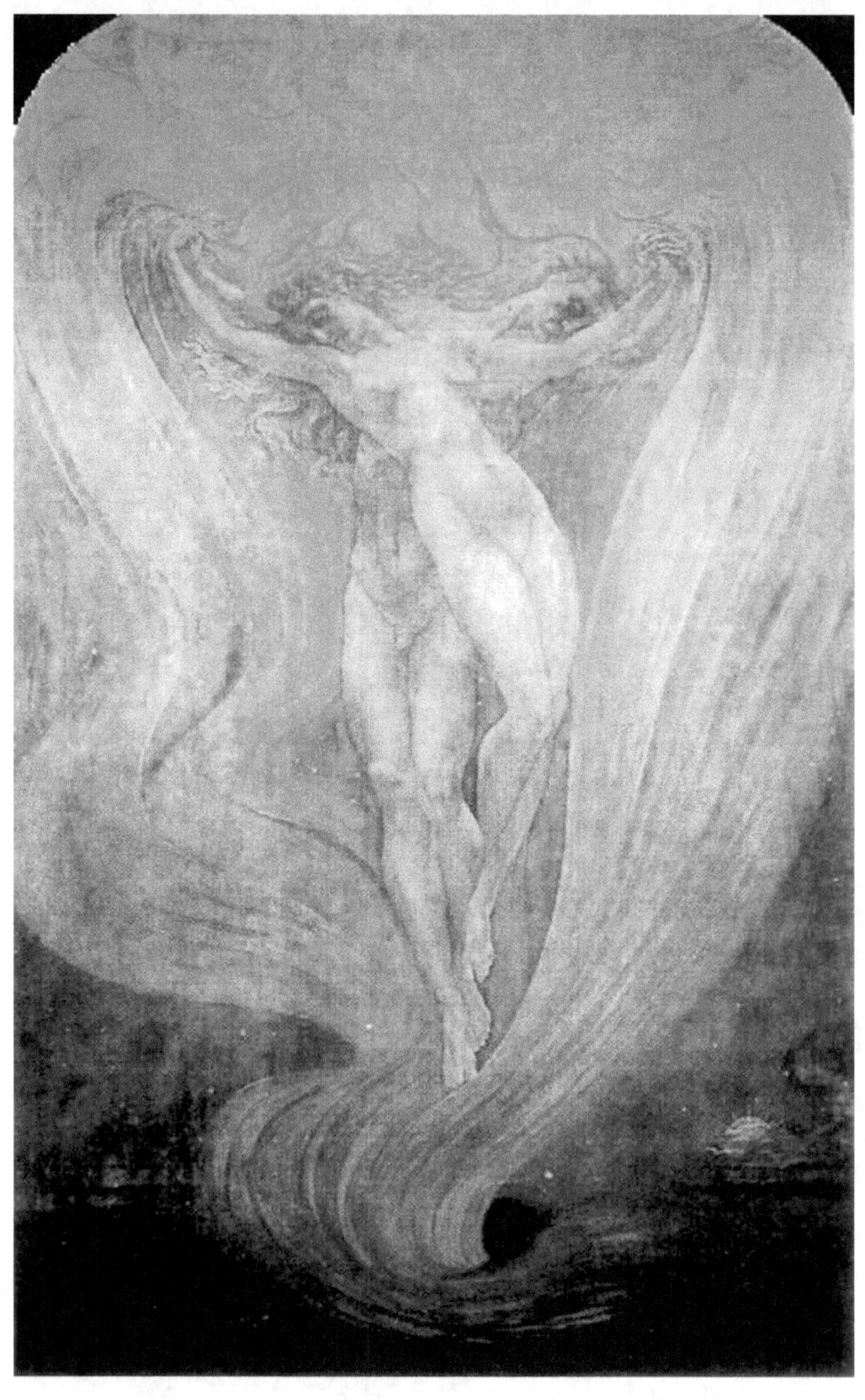

Jean Delville, The Love of Souls, 1900, Brussels

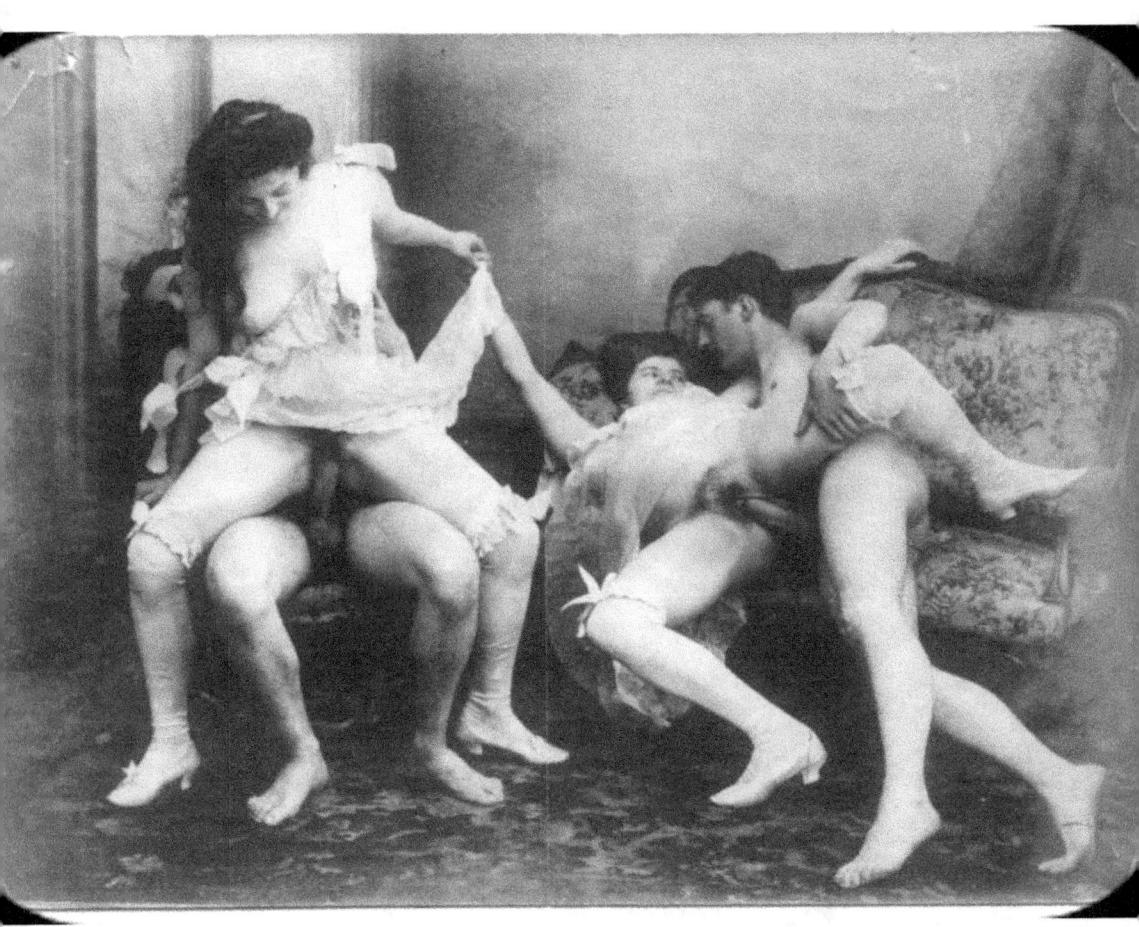

Anonymous, late 19th century

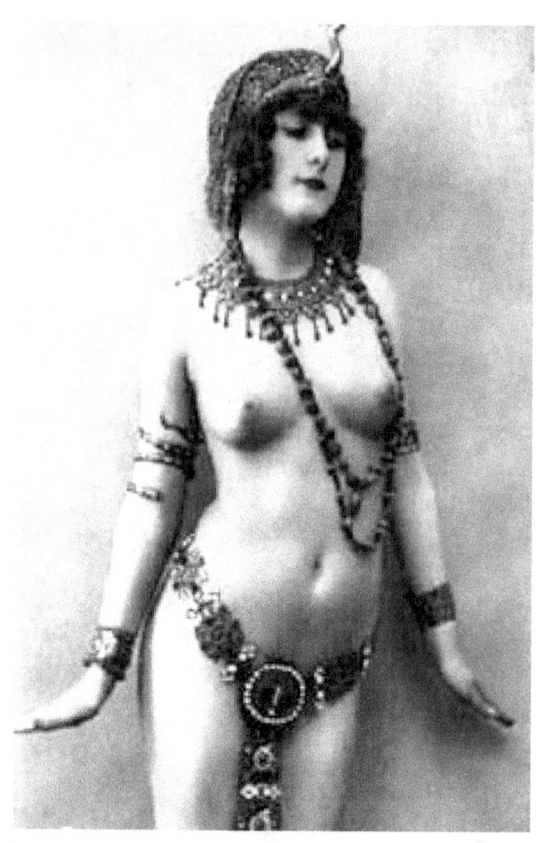

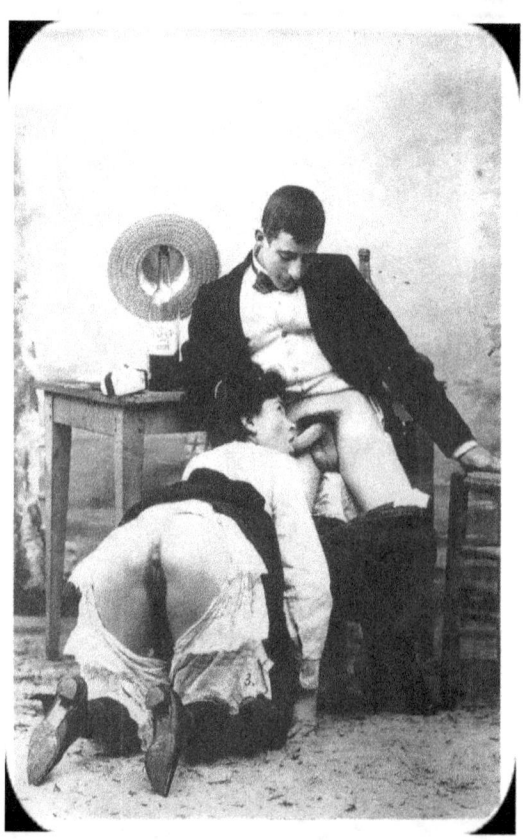

Late 19th century photographs, anonymous

The first part of this book on 19th century erotic art uses short entries about aspects of erotic art (with examples from the whole history of erotic art).

The bulk of the second part of the book focusses on the celebrated artists of the 19th century whose work is considered erotic, as well as many anonymous works. The appendices feature some more classics of erotic art of the 19th century.

Part One

Issues In Erotic Art

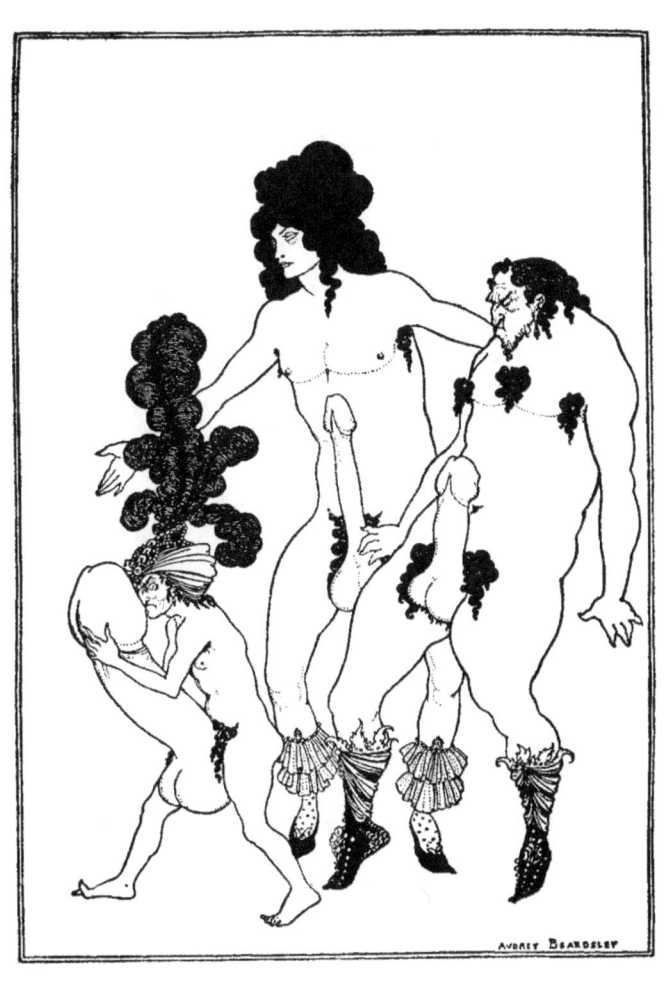

EROTIC ART AND PORNOGRAPHY

The establishment art historical view of erotic art and pornography is that true erotic or high art engenders quiet contemplation, a detached ravishing of the senses, a meditation on Platonic, Aristotlean and Kantian ideas of 'beauty' and æsthetics. 'High art', which is legitimate art, art which justifies itself by its 'genius' or obvious 'greatness', is about distance and disinterested pleasure. The high art nude, in painting or sculpture, in the patriarchal view, justifies its existence by the brilliance of its production, the sumptuousness of its colour and form, the marvel of its human touches, the grandeur of its design, the loftiness of its ambition, the dynamism of its structures, and so on. As that producer of exquisite bodies, French Neo-Classical artist J.A.D. Ingres, wrote:

> There are not two arts, there is only one: it is the one which has as its foundation the beautiful, which is eternal and natural.[1]

---

1 J.A.D. Ingres, quoted in R. Goldwater, 216

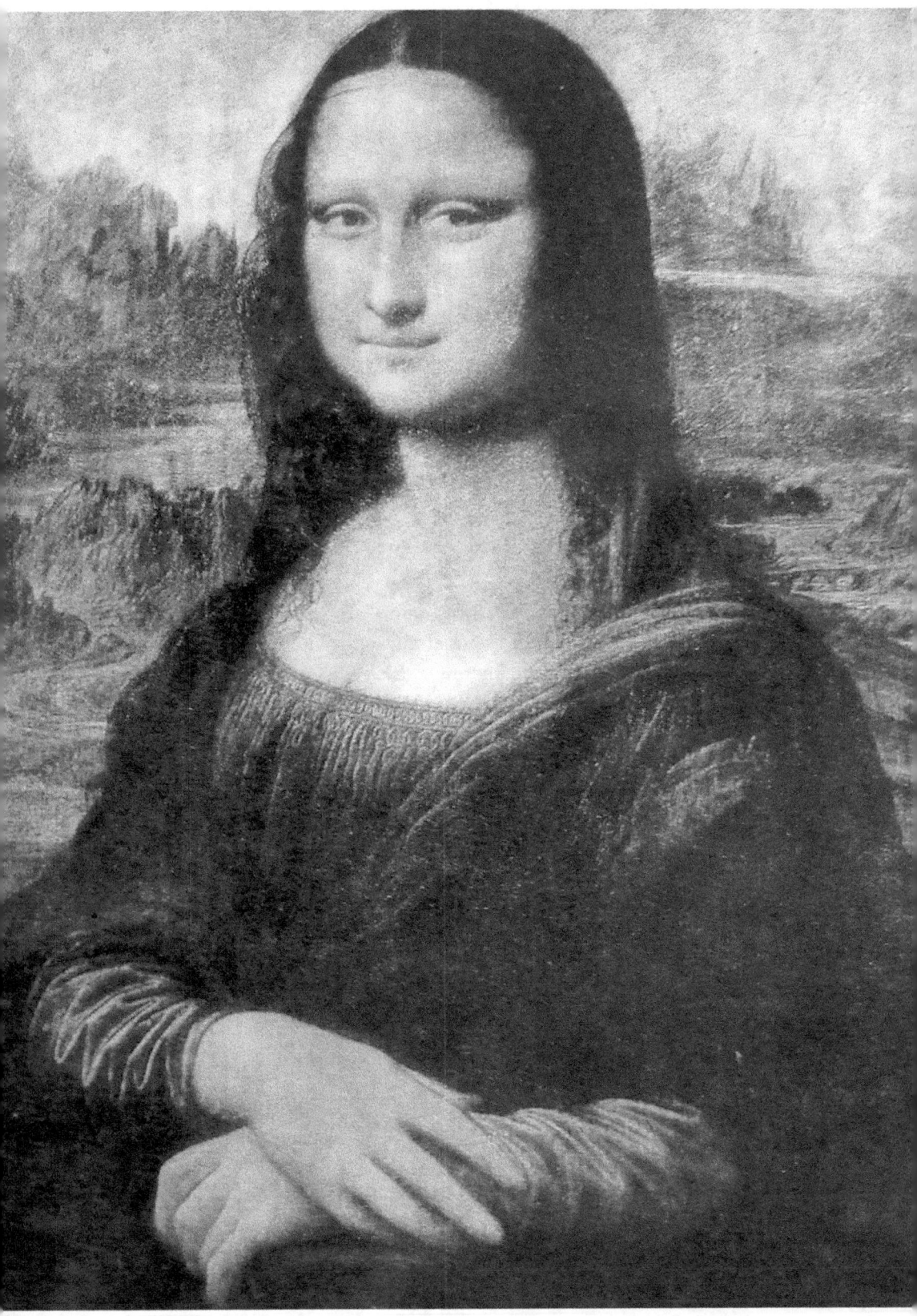

EROTIC ART VERSUS PORNOGRAPHY

We know the male/ patriarchal view of the art versus pornography debate. Eroticism is justified and good because it is 'high
art', it is superbly crafted, it is a 'work of art'. Thus the
Kronhausens, the organizers of a major exhibition of 'erotic art' (of
1968),[1] write:

> one can perhaps distinguish between pornography and art. The
> criterion would be that the more a picture contains evidence of
> interpretative, creative elaboration, the closer it is to art.[2]

For the Kronhausens, as for so many artists and philosophers
and intellectuals, erotic art is art because it is done well.
Pornography is simply bad art.

Many guardians of æsthetics, many professors of art history
and dons of 'the beautiful' go along with this view. Kenneth
Clark is a typical establishment critic who puts forward the
patriarchal view: nudes are OK provided they are æsthetically
pleasing, provided they remain 'in the realm of contemplation' as
he put it.[3]

---

1 The 'first international exhibition of erotic art' was at the Museum of Art, Lund, Sweden, and
Aarhus, Denmark, in 1968
2 Phyllis & Eberhard Kronhausen: *Erotic Art: A survey of erotic fact and fancy in the fine arts*,
W.H. Allen, 1971, 3
3 Quoted in Lord Longford: *Pornography: The Longford Report*, Coronet, 1972, 99f

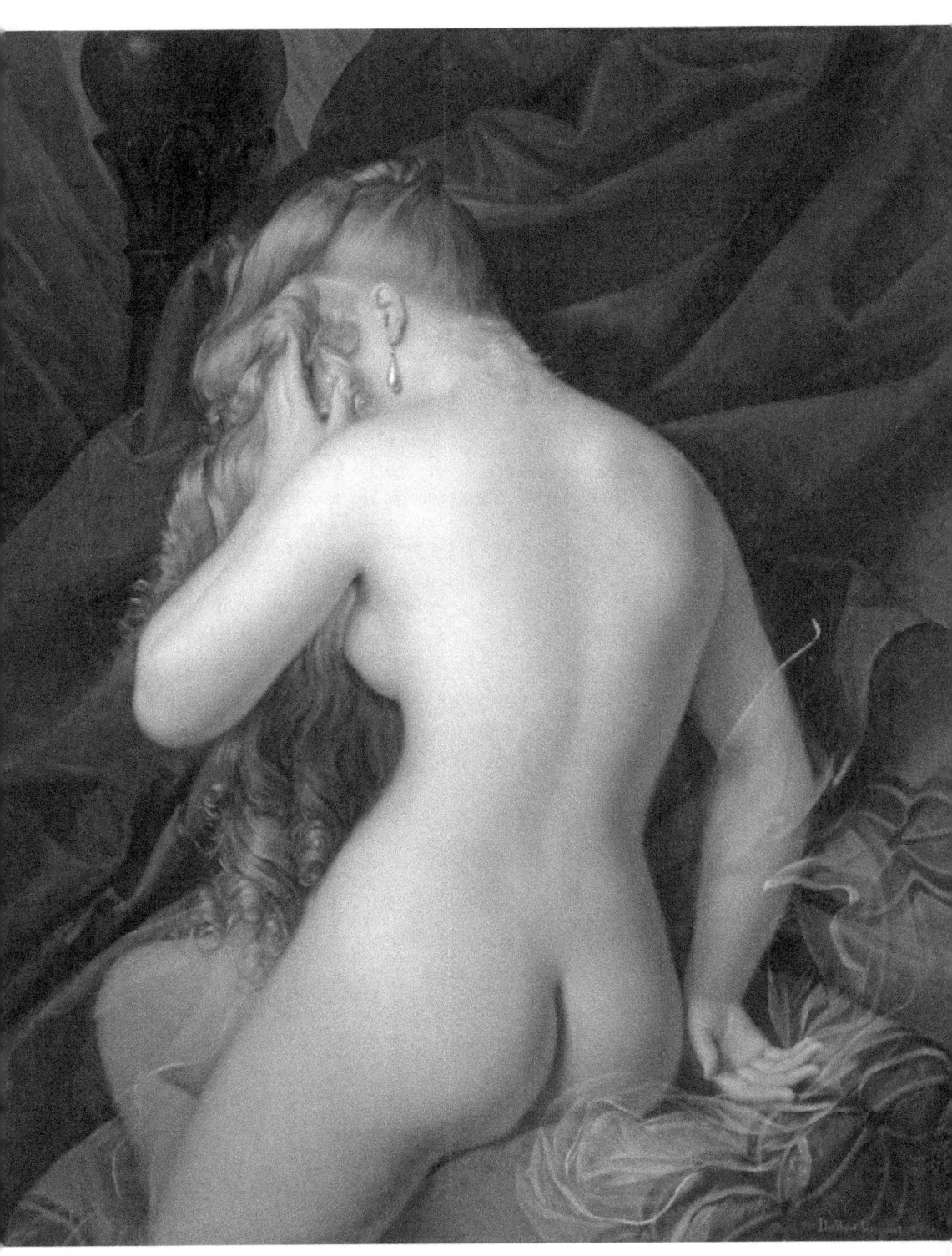

Alexandre-Jean Dubois-Drahonet,
Female Nude, 19th century

THE FEMALE NUDE

The 'sublime' qualities of high art, to use one popular adjective of art criticism, are crucial to its success, as Carol M. Armstrong notes in her essay on Edgar Degas:

> One of the things any painted object does is to resist signification at some level because of its very objecthood. And the female nude – because of *its* objecthood may be seen as almost emblematic of that level of resistance. In fact, the female nude has been linked to that stratum of painting most in tension with the work of signification – the stratum we connect to what we call, inadequately, "abstraction"; facture, the handling of paint per se, foregrounded as an obvious fact of the painting. Femaleness and facture, facture and the female nude, they go together somehow. One need only think of Titian, the first great painter of the female nude in the Western tradition.[1]

Much as worshippers properly gaze at an icon or an image of a deity with wonder, the art critic and historian kneels before 'great art' and worships it.[2] The female nude is the highest form of non-religious art, and it confers a religious awe in its æsthete consumers. The emphasis is on Neoplatonic terms such as 'purity', 'beauty', 'form' and 'symmetry'. As Aristotle puts it: '[t]he chief forms of beauty are order and symmetry and definiteness.'[3]

---

1 Carol M. Armstrong; "Edgar Degas and the Representation of the Female Body", in S. Suleiman, 223
2 See Pierre Bourdieu: *Distinction: A Social Critique of the Judgment of Taste,* tr Richard Nice, Routledge & Kegan Paul, New York 1984
3 Aristotle: *Metaphysics,* book XIII, in Albert Hofstadter & Richard Kuhns, eds: *Philosophies of Art and Beauty: Selected Readings in Aesthetics From Plato to Heidegger,* Random House, New York 1964, 96

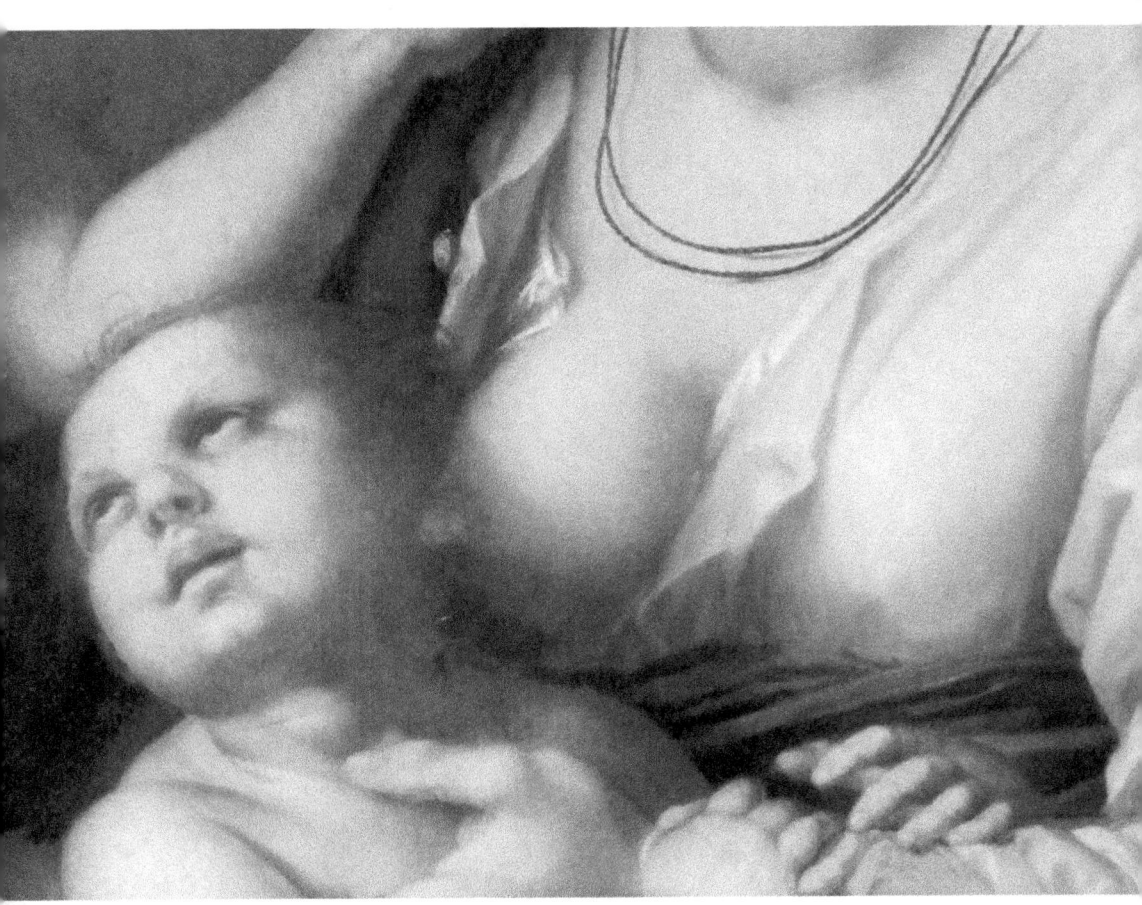

Andrea del Sarto, Madonna and Child, detail

THE FEMALE NUDE

Depictions of the female nude and of erotic gestures or acts can be problematic. The female body, for instance, is already 'objectified' even before it is painted or represented. Once painted, it becomes a cultural artifact, a mass of codes, meanings, signs and values, none of them fixed, all of them dependent on the context of consumption, dependent on the socio-political make-up of the viewer, and so on. None of this, however, has prevented erotic nudes and female nudes from being produced.

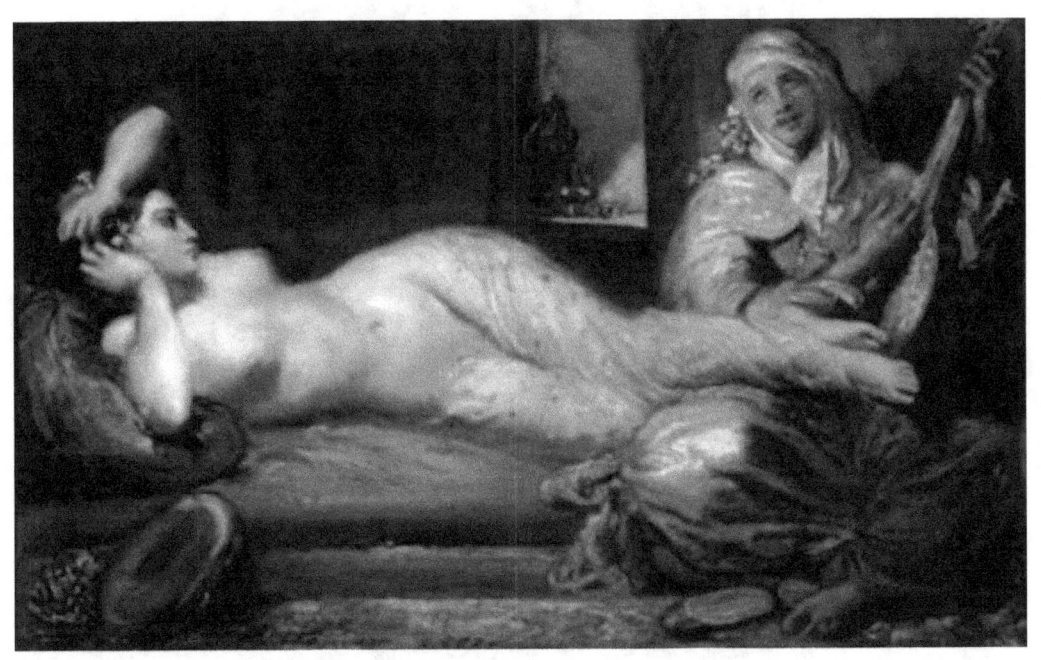

Théodore Chasséreau (1819-56)

William Bouguereau,
The Birth of Venus,
above

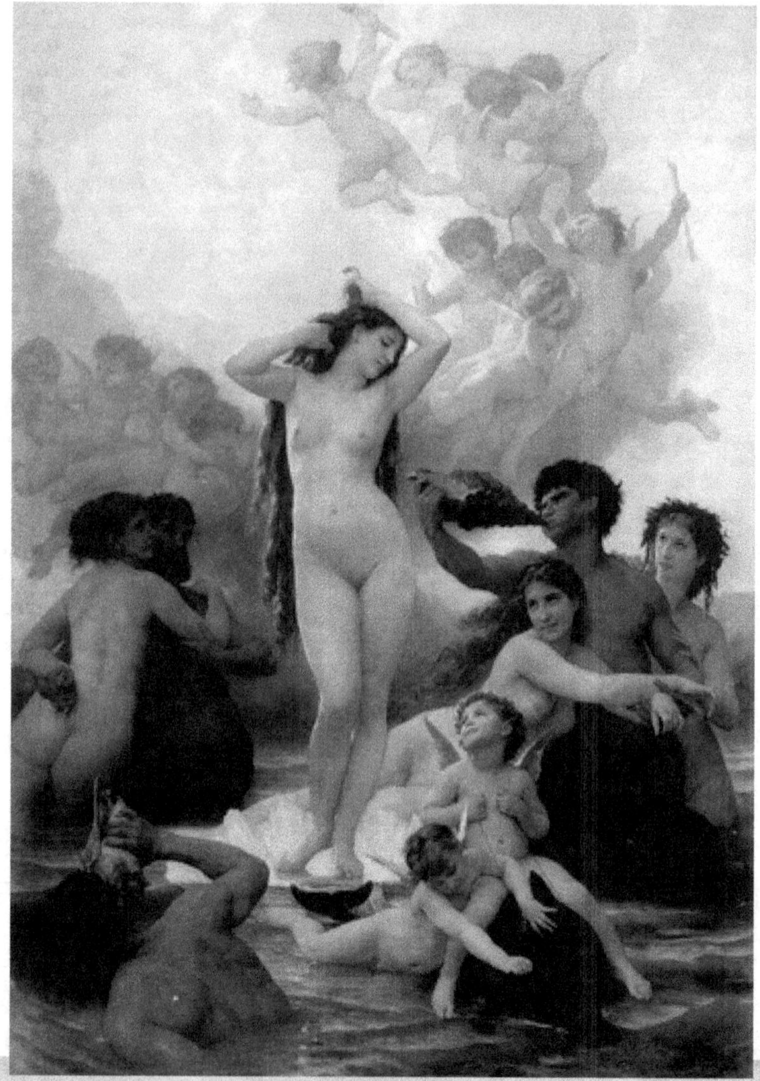

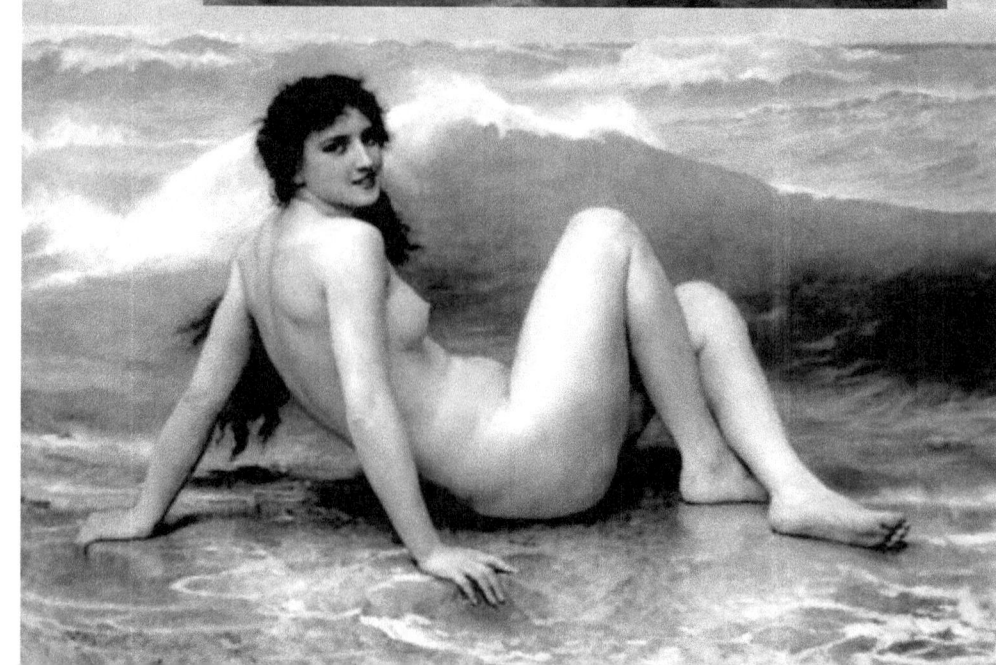

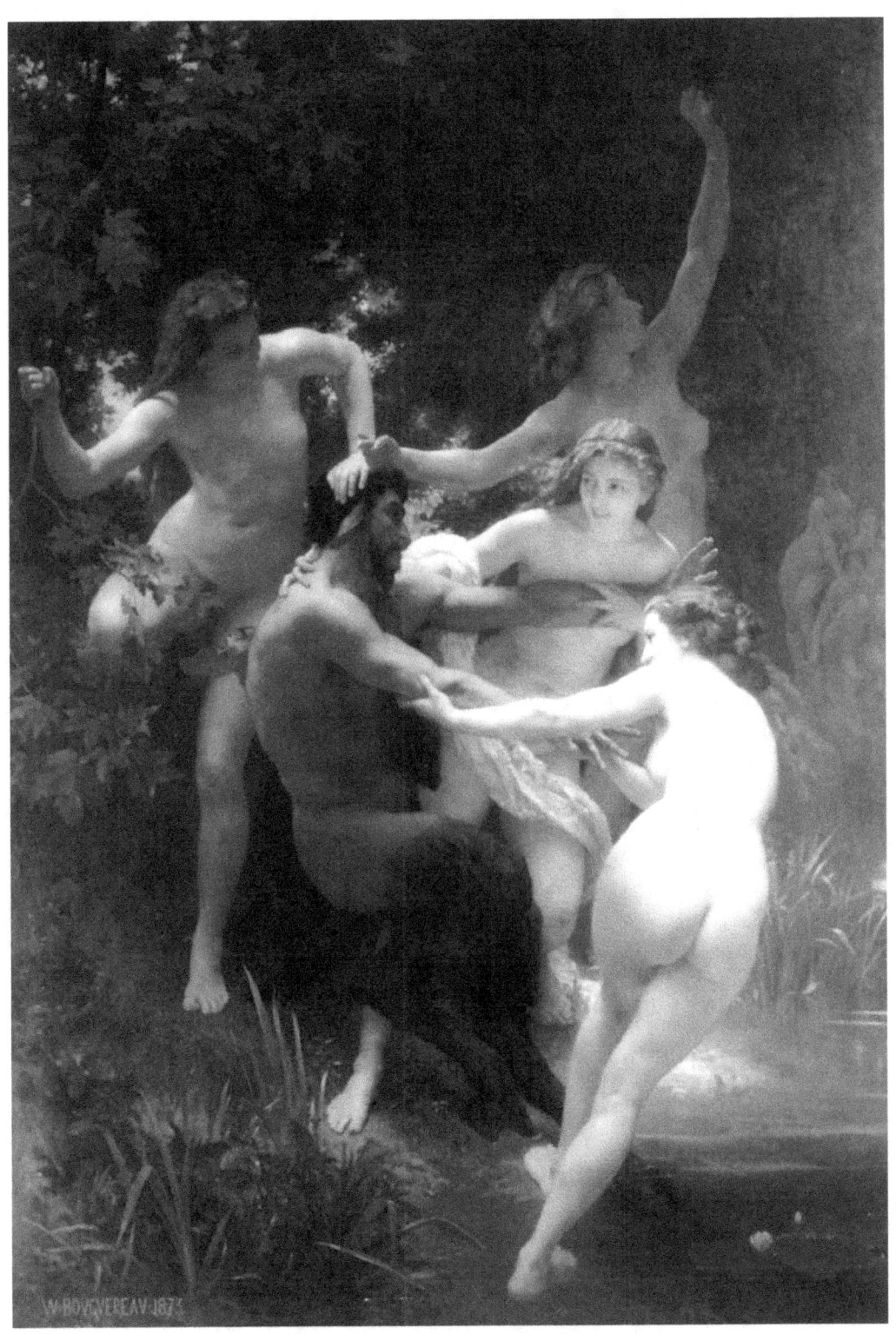

William Bouguereau, Nymphs and Satyr

THE FEMALE NUDE

Context is crucial in matters of eroticism. An image that is seen as 'erotic' in one context can easily be seen as 'pornographic' in another context. Take an image out of context, and soon a new, often ironic set of meanings are set in motion. Jacques Derrida has shown that a text may have many contexts, and is not fixed in one context forever.[1] Feminist artists have explored meanings and contexts, by placing traditional images in new contexts. Meanings are constantly in a state of flux. Nothing is fixed anymore. As Catherine Belsey writes: 'meanings circulate between text, ideology and reader' (144). Roland Barthes wrote that '[a]ll images are polysemous...they imply, underlying their signifiers, a floating chain of signifieds'. The consumer has the ability to 'choose some and ignore others'.[2] The cultural environment, socialization, economy, power relations, education, any number of factors can influence the meanings drawn from an image. With the female nude, in painting or erotica, the meanings are context-ualized as erotic. As Anne Hollander notes, the nude always has a sexual dimension to it.

For instance, men can 'possess' and yet never 'possess' a female nude painting. It remains an image. The 'possession' or consumption is of a cerebral order, which is why critics and professors such as Kenneth Clark, Bernard Berenson, Jacob Burckhardt, Walter Pater, John Ruskin, Aby Warburg, Roger Fry, Ernst Gombrich and other art critics emphasize the *intellectual* nature of enjoying art. Art for the head, not the body, art for the eyes, not the full five senses.

1 Jacques Derrida: *Eperons. Les styles de Nietzsche*, Flammarion, Paris 1978, 103f
2 Roland Barthes: *Image-Music-Text*, Hill & Wang, New York 1977, 39

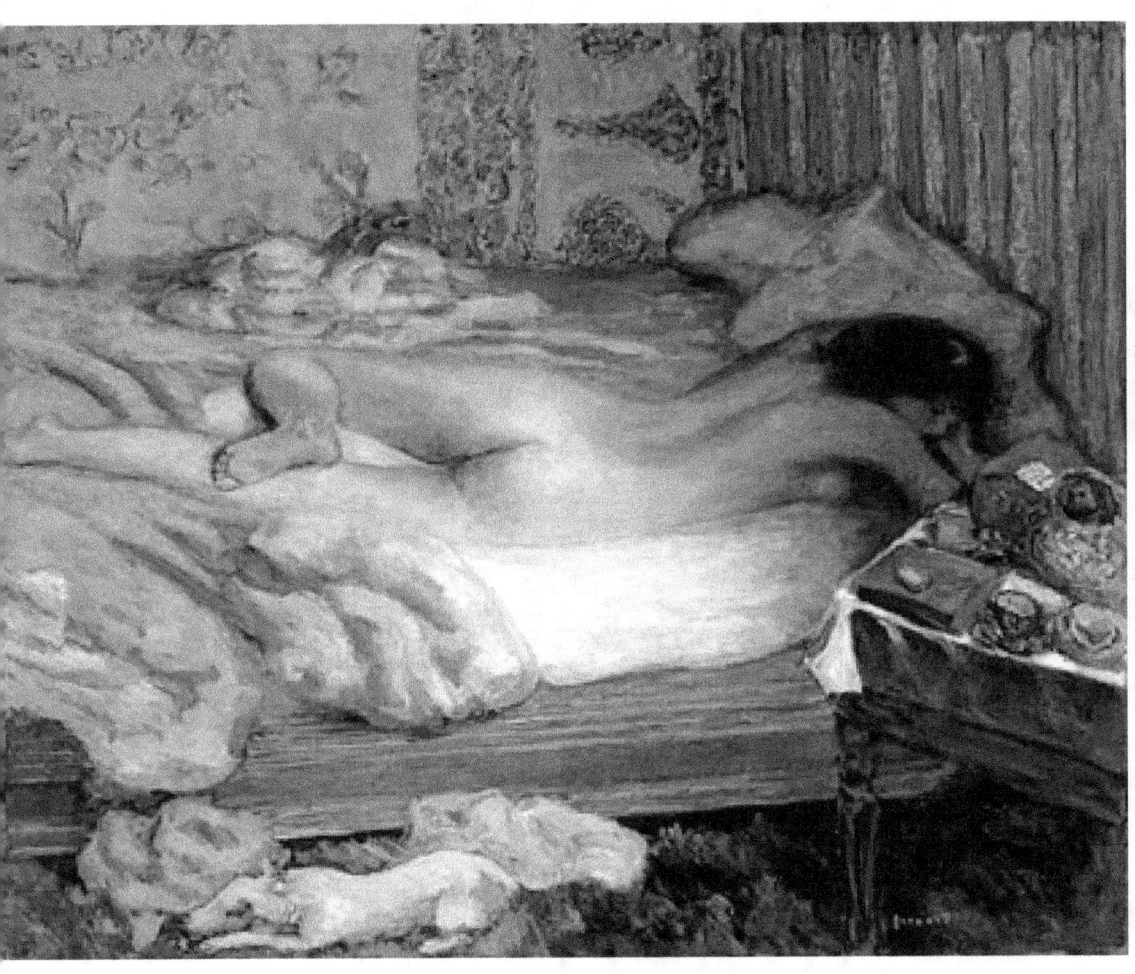

Pierre Bonnard

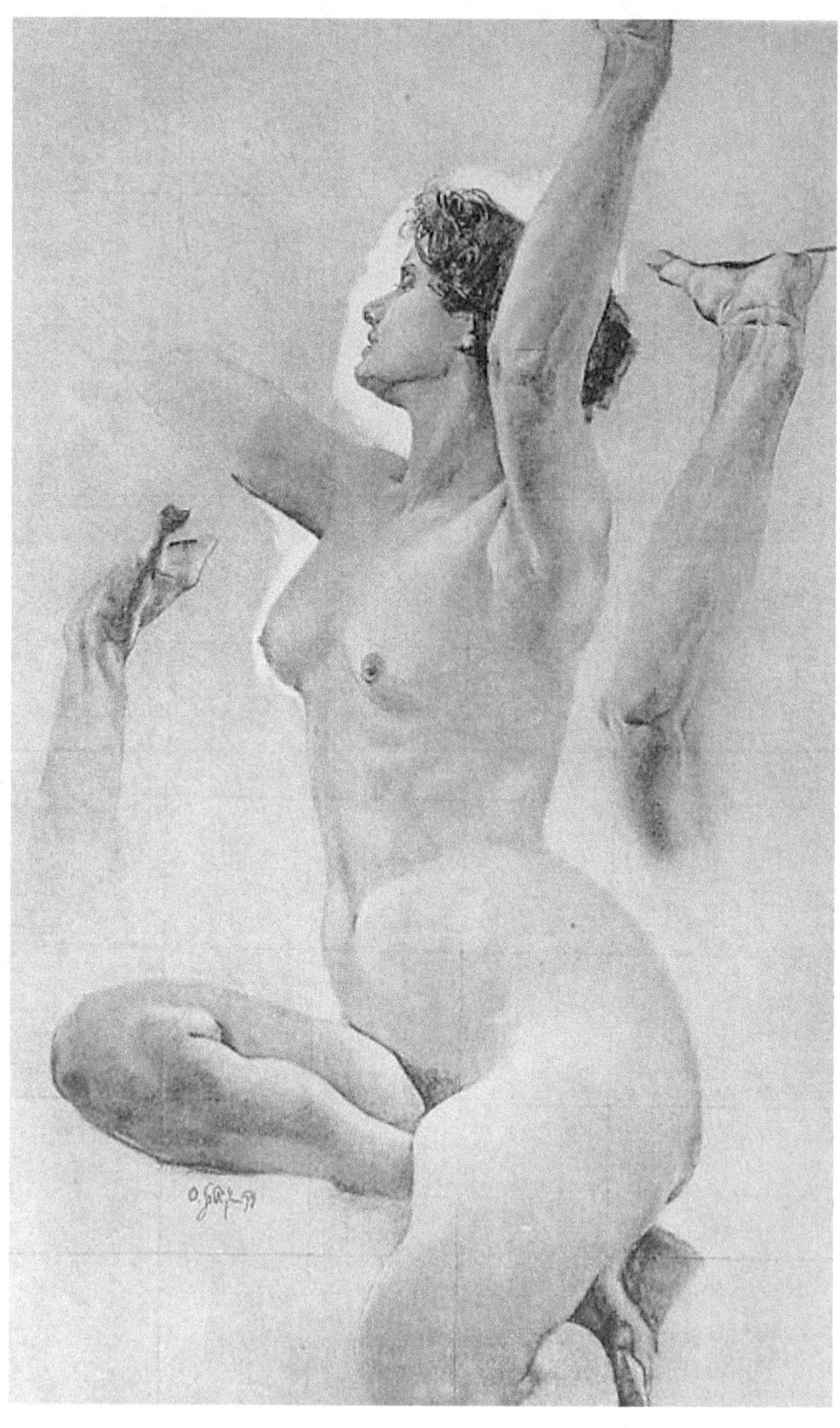

Otto Grenier, Study For Odysseus, 1912-33

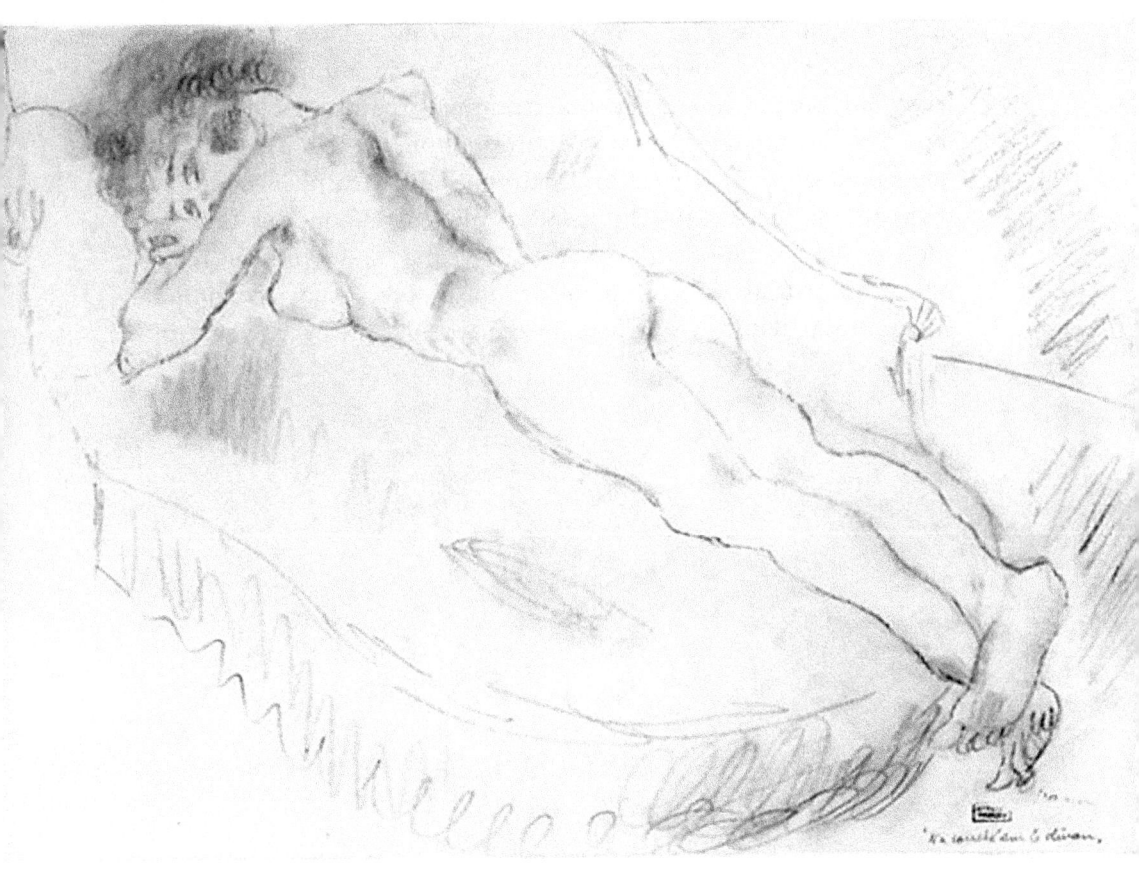

Jules Pascin

THE FEMALE NUDE

The high art nude, then, is a site of political and economic manipulation, an expression of the power relations between patron and painter, between connoisseur, artist and model. In the trinity of people linked by the painting – patron, painter and model – the model is clearly at the bottom of the pile. She is dependent on both painter and patron. She has to please both of them to be successful. The relation of artist to model thus is another manifestation, like that of husband and wife, of male power, of patriarchal culture in action, of the sexual economics which are at work everywhere in the world, and everywhere in history.

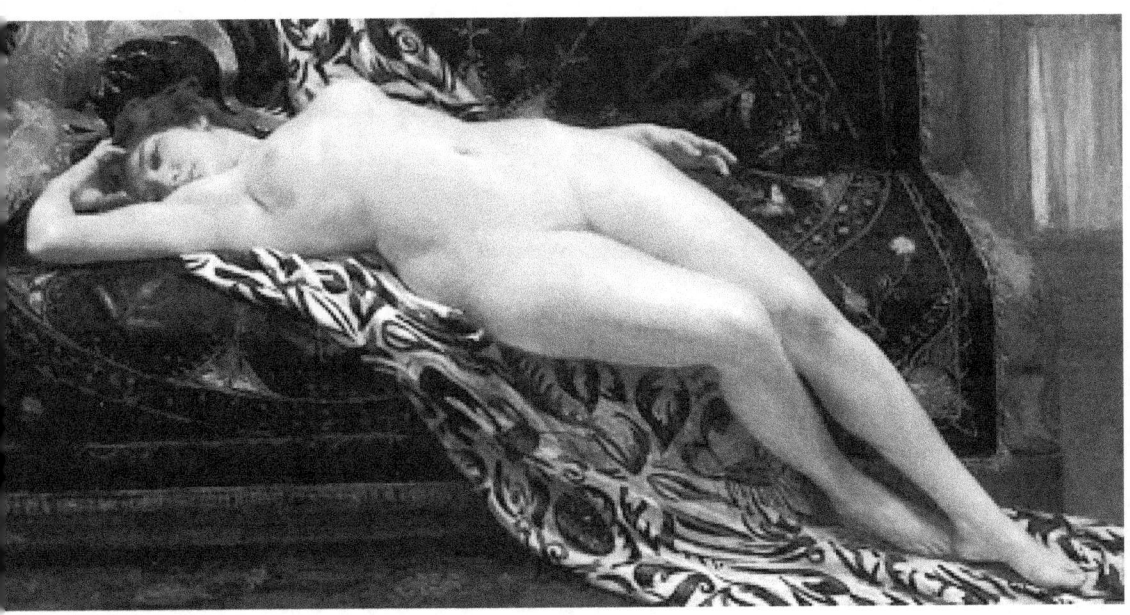

Guillaume Seignac, L'Abandon (above).
The Wave (below).

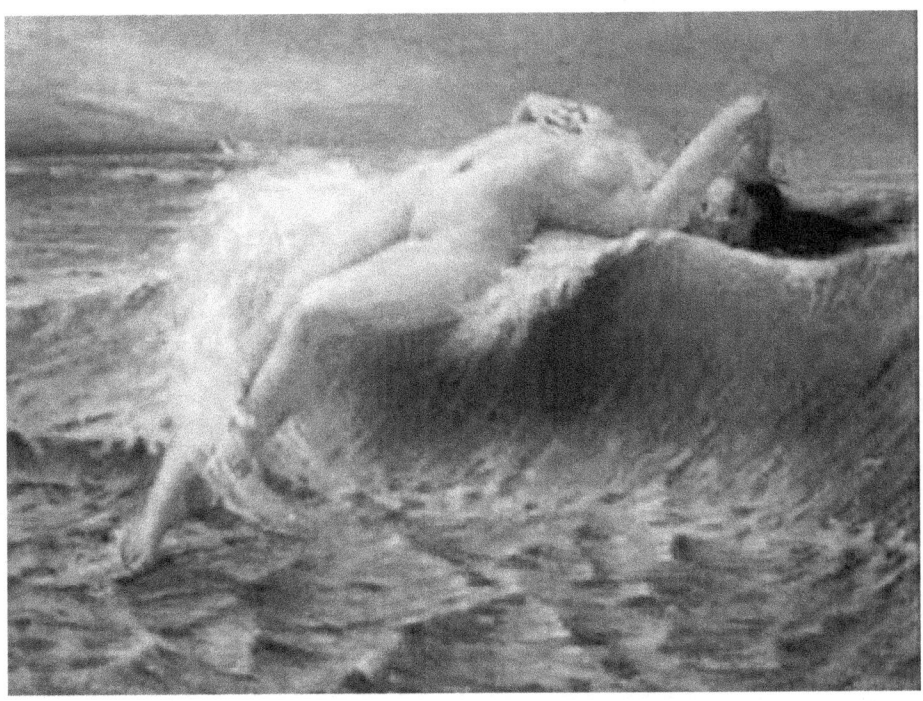

MALE NUDES

The male nude can be seen as a phallus, as Gill Saunders pointed out:

> The male body, while not constructed as the site of sexual pleasure, is often symbolic of phallic power. The whole body, muscular, potent, active, may come to represent the phallus.[1]

The penis isn't a phallus, so, to make up for the disappointing insufficiency of the penis, macho masculinity is demonstrated by bulging muscles, clenched fists, sturdy poses. The male nude poses with a body of 'rippling muscles', bizarrely exaggerated, or gripping a gun, or standing next to a motorcycle, a car, a machine, something that can connote phallic power.

---

1 G. Saunders: *The Nude*, 26.

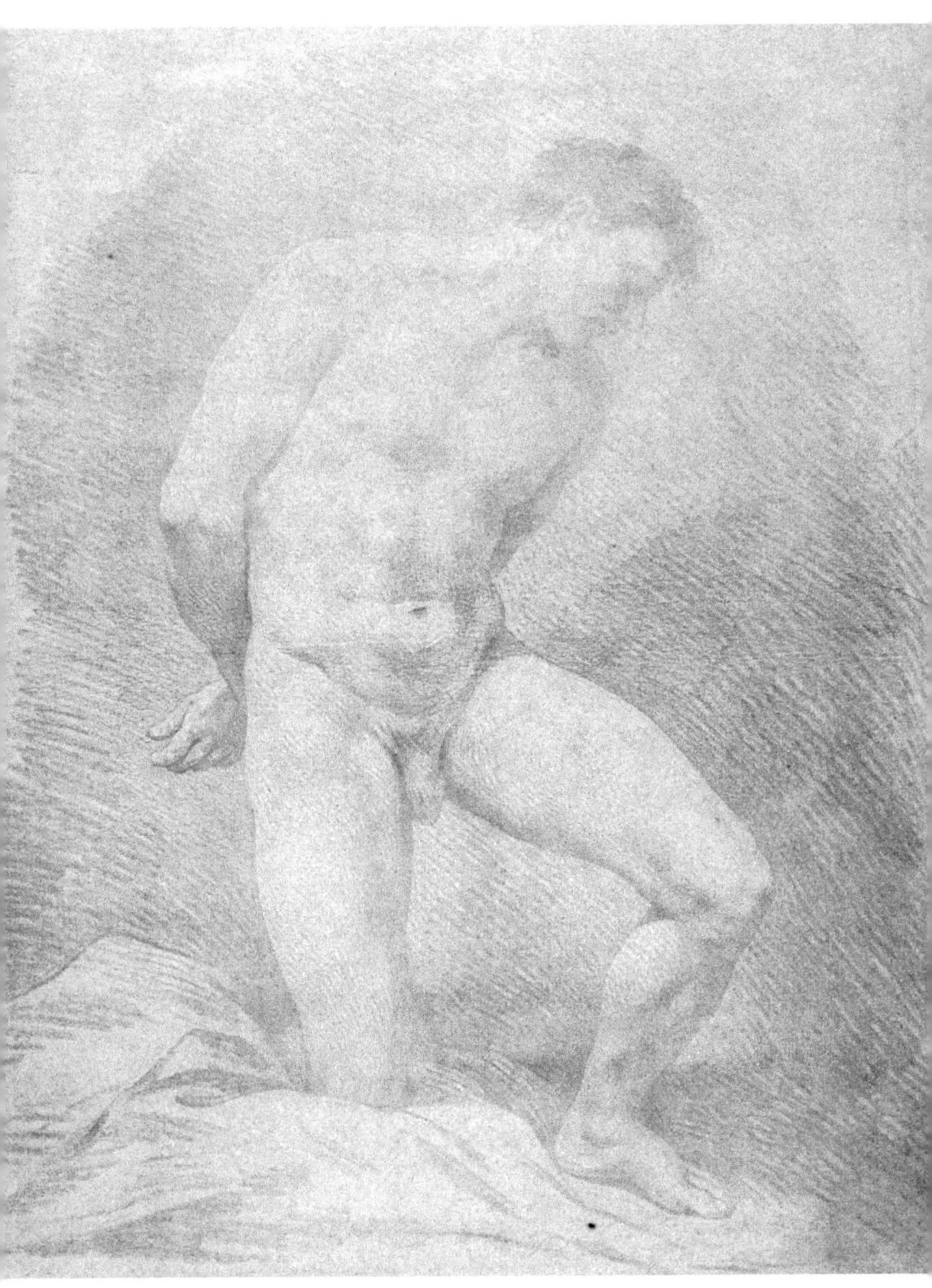

Male Nude, 19th century

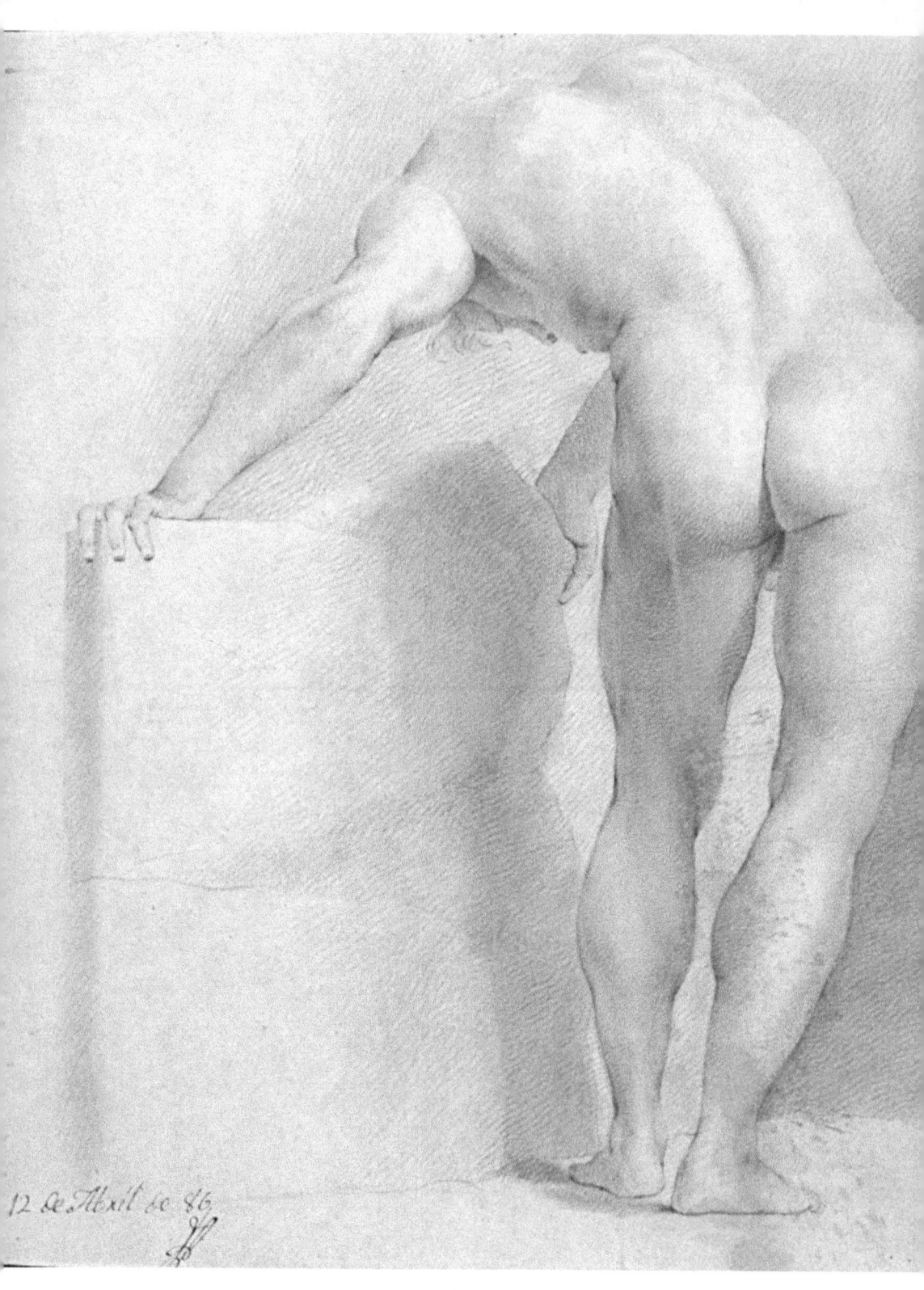

Mariano Amare, Male Nude, 1786.

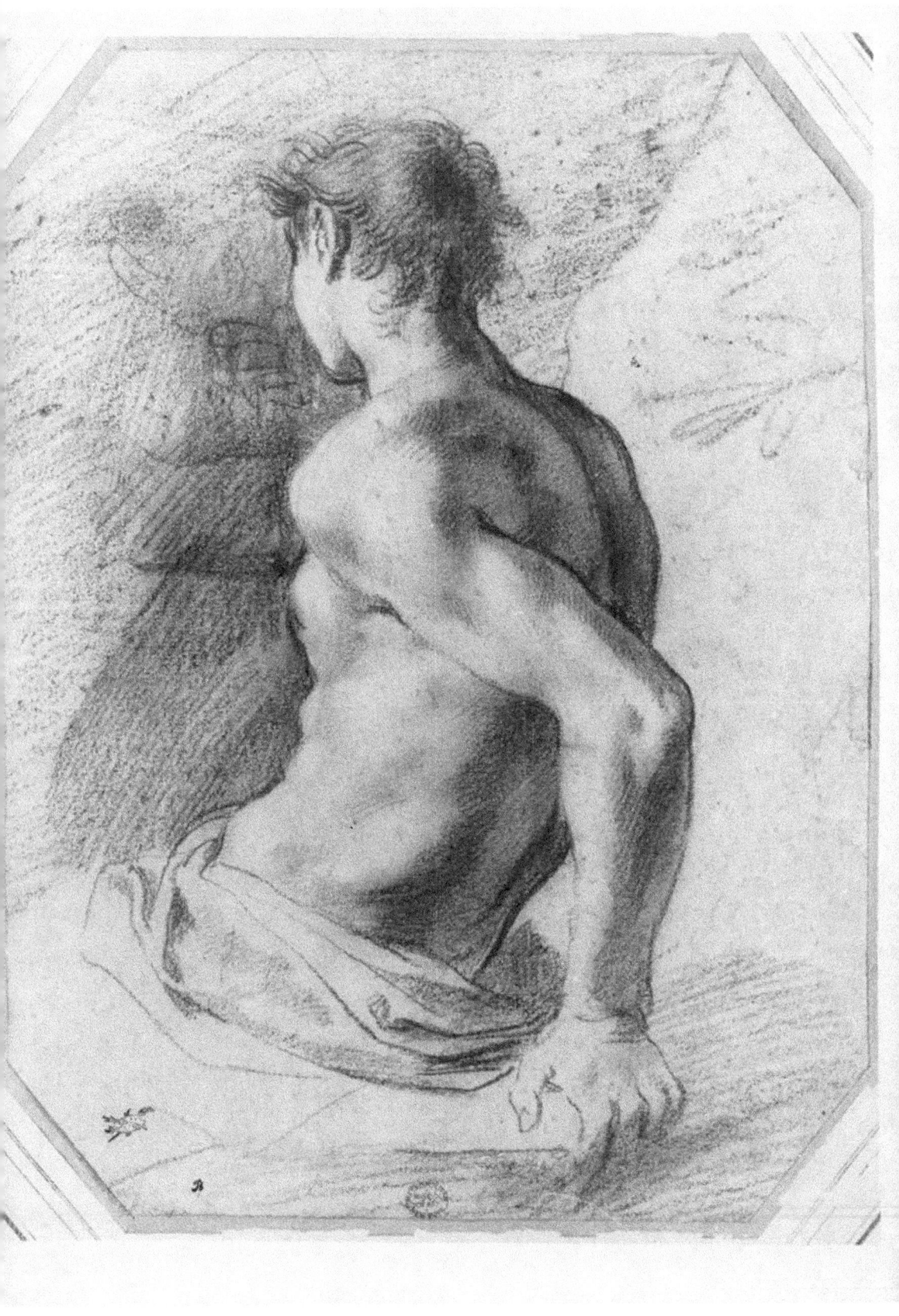

Annibale Carracci, Male Nude, Half-Figure, 16th century

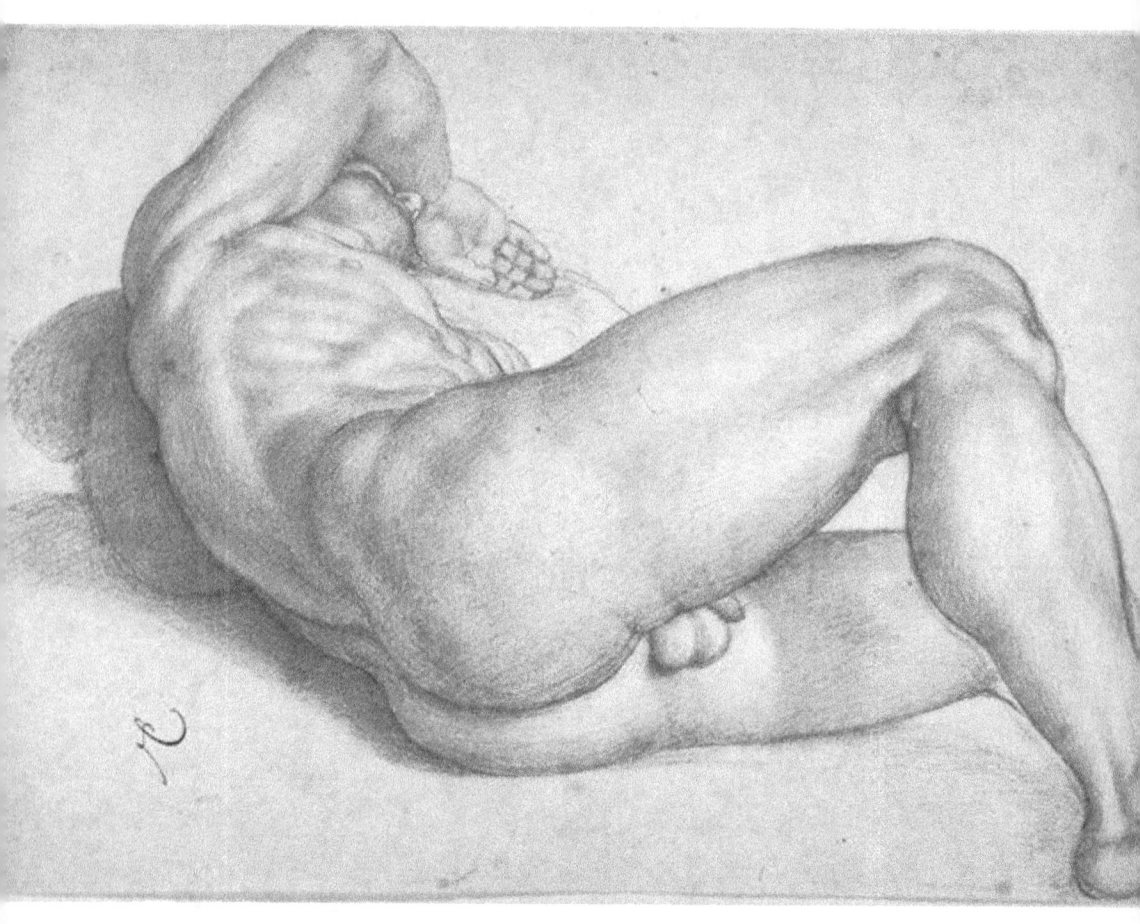

Agnolo di Cosimo (Il Bronzino),
Naked Man Lying On His Back, 16th century

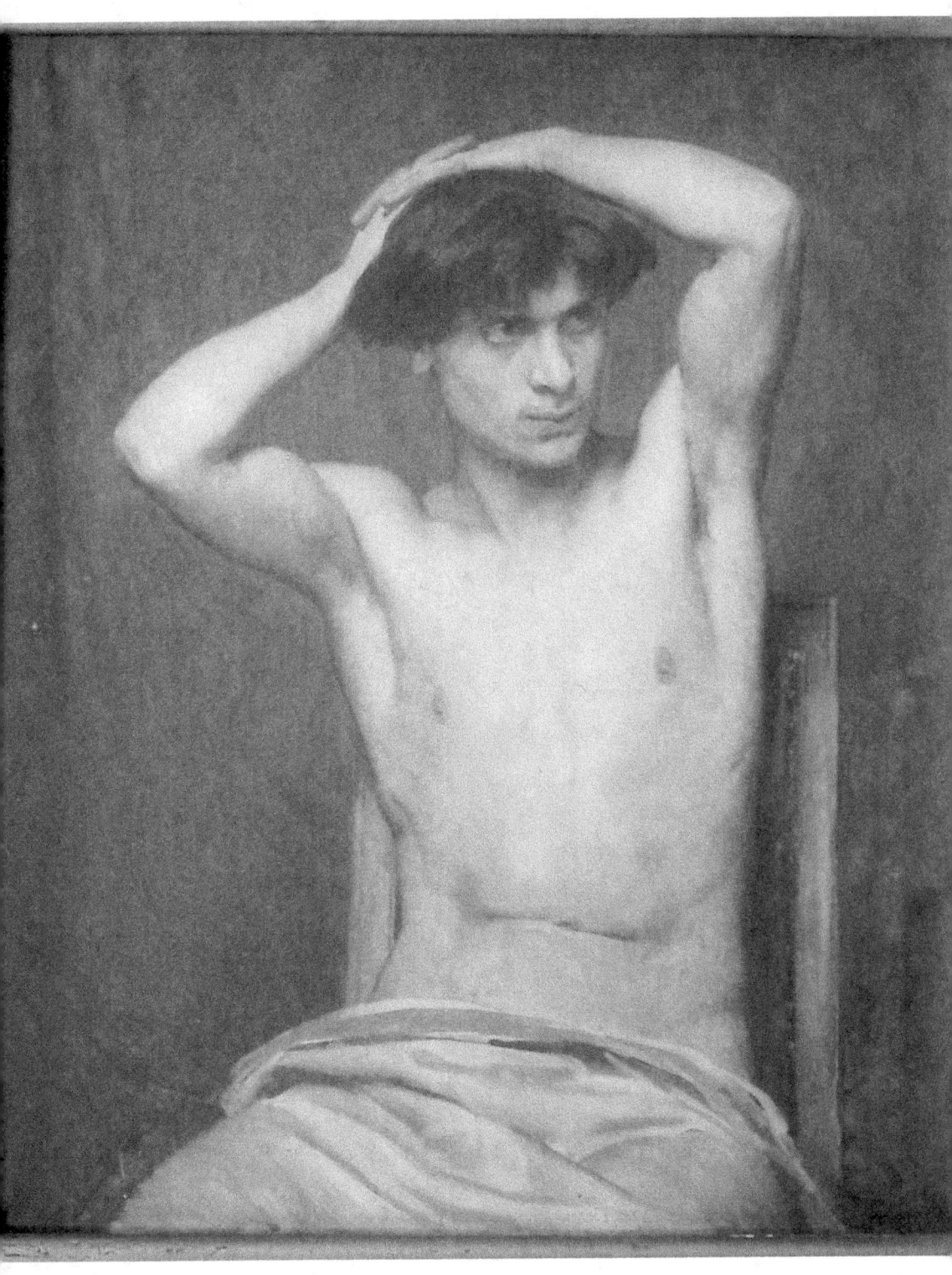

Henri-Lucien Doucet, Half-Nude Figure, 1879

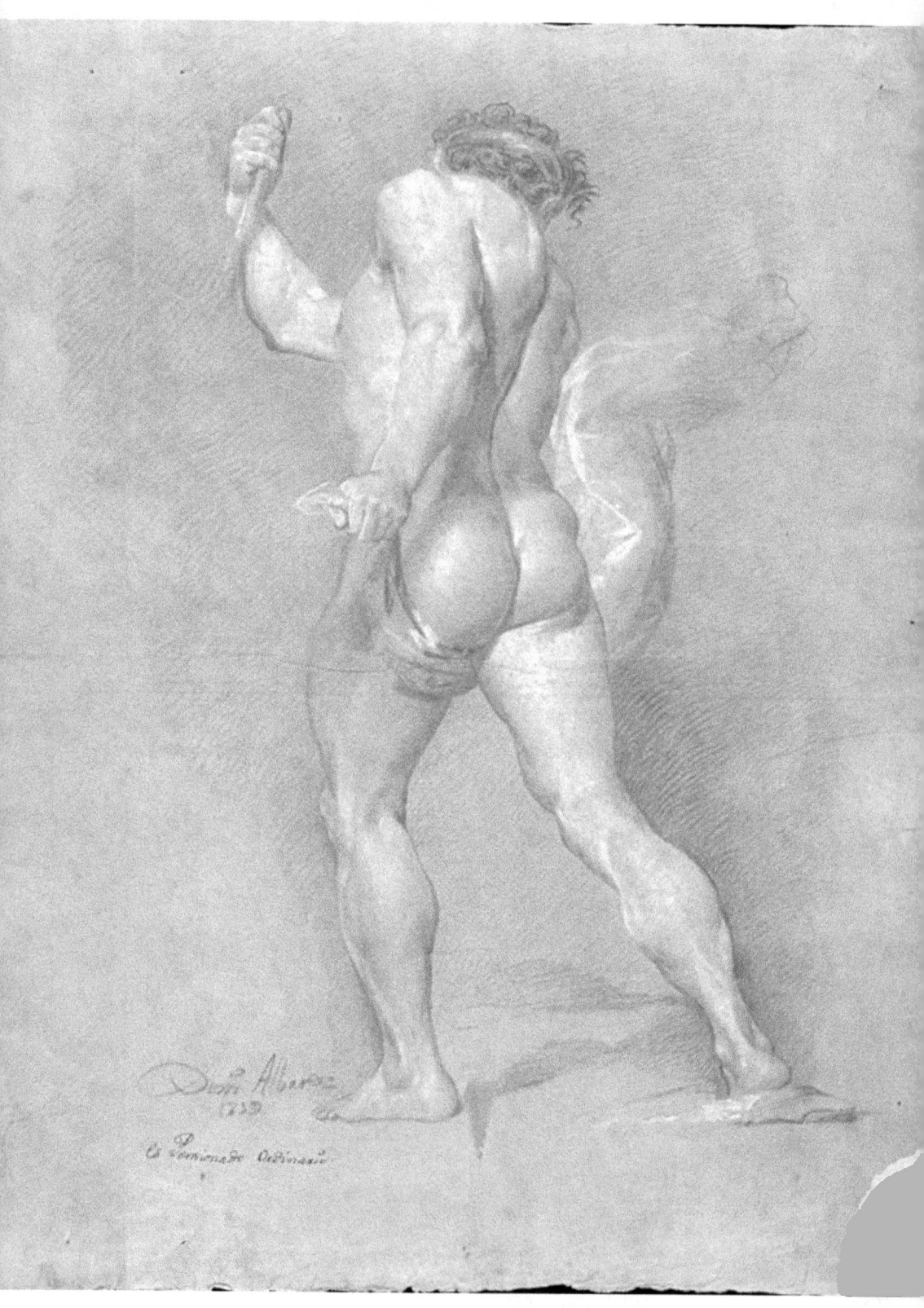

Domingo Alvarez Enciso, Male Nude, 1759

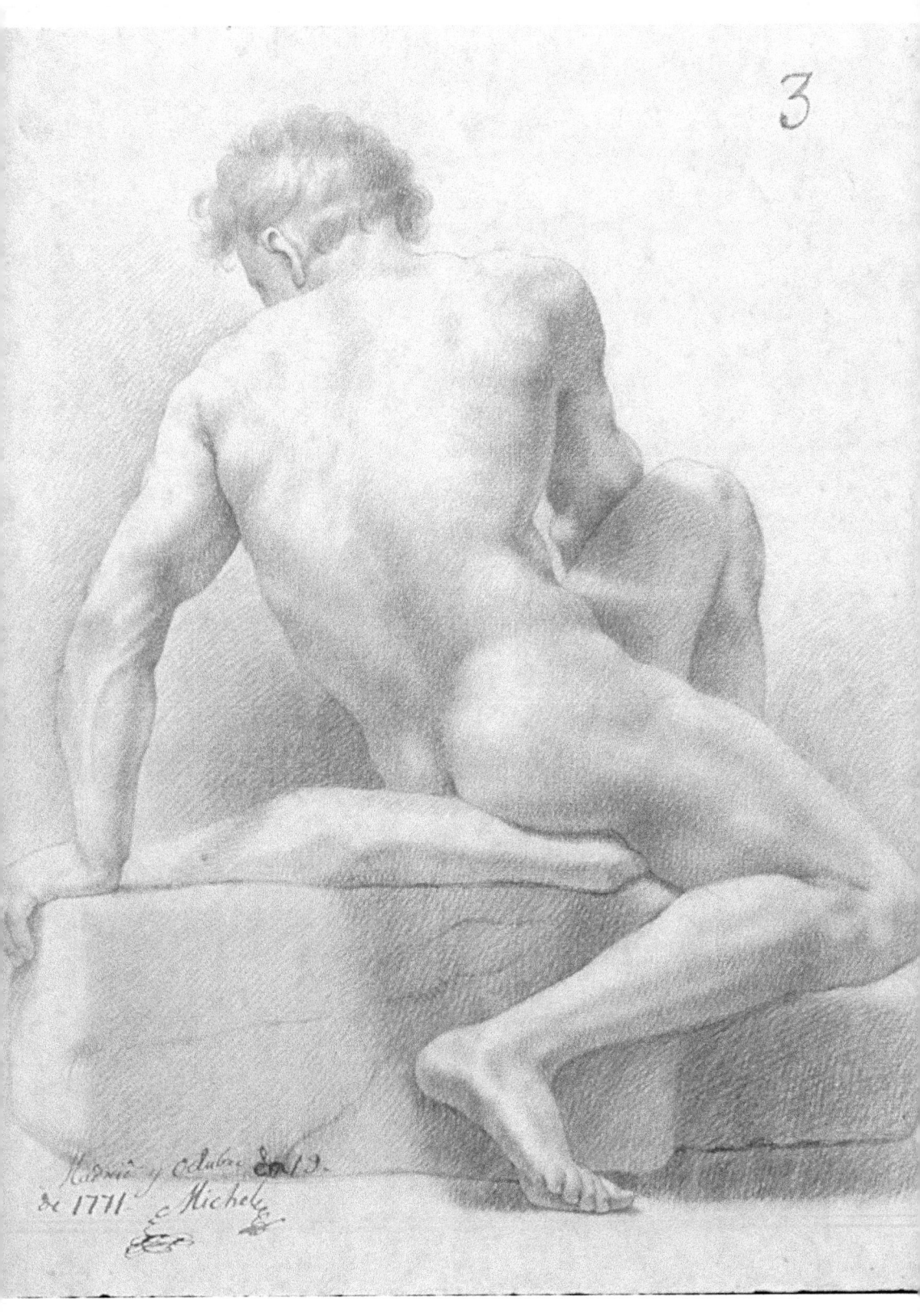

3

Pedro Pascual Munoz, Seated Male Nude, 1771

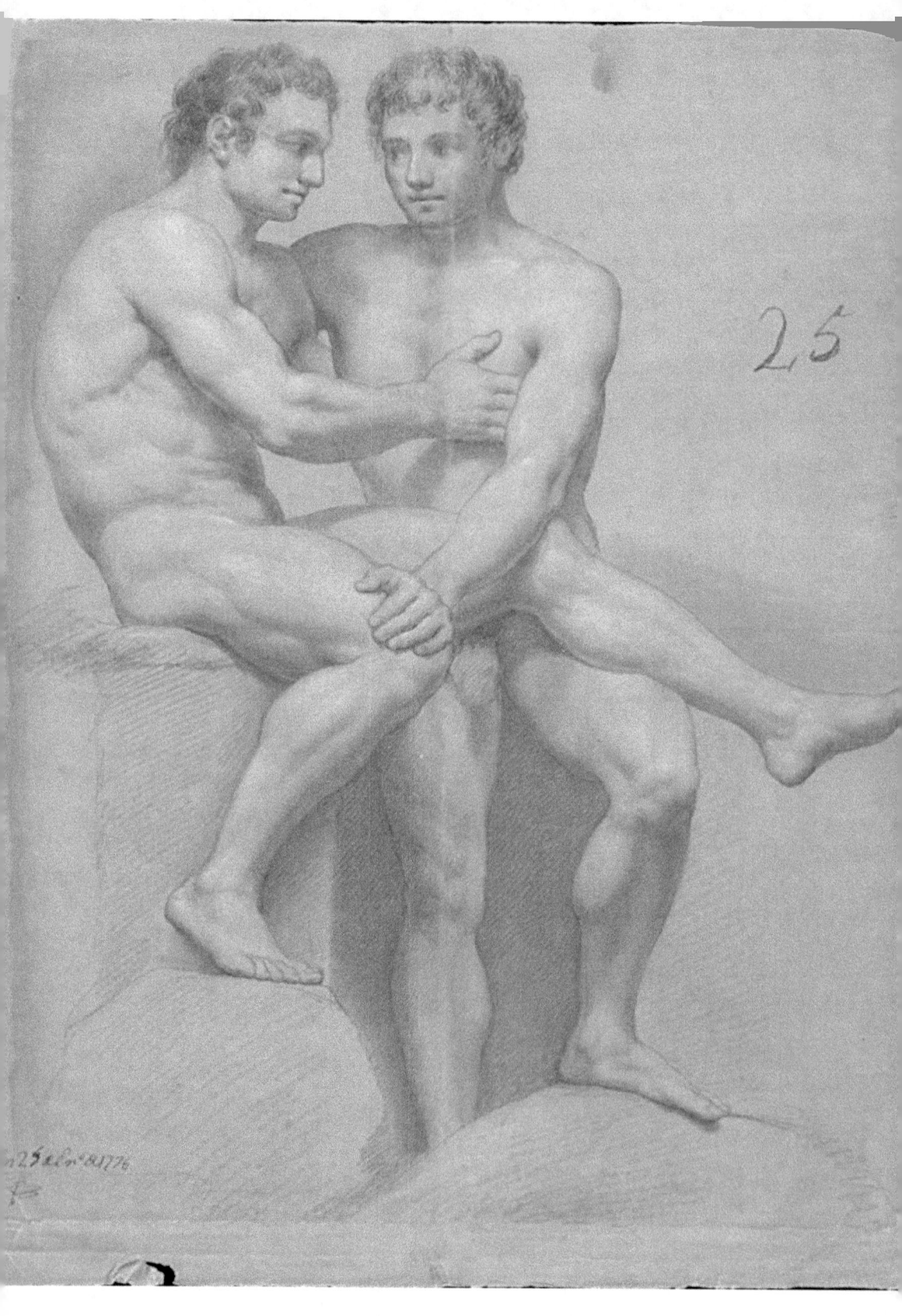

Gustin Esteve Marques, Two Male Nudes, 1776

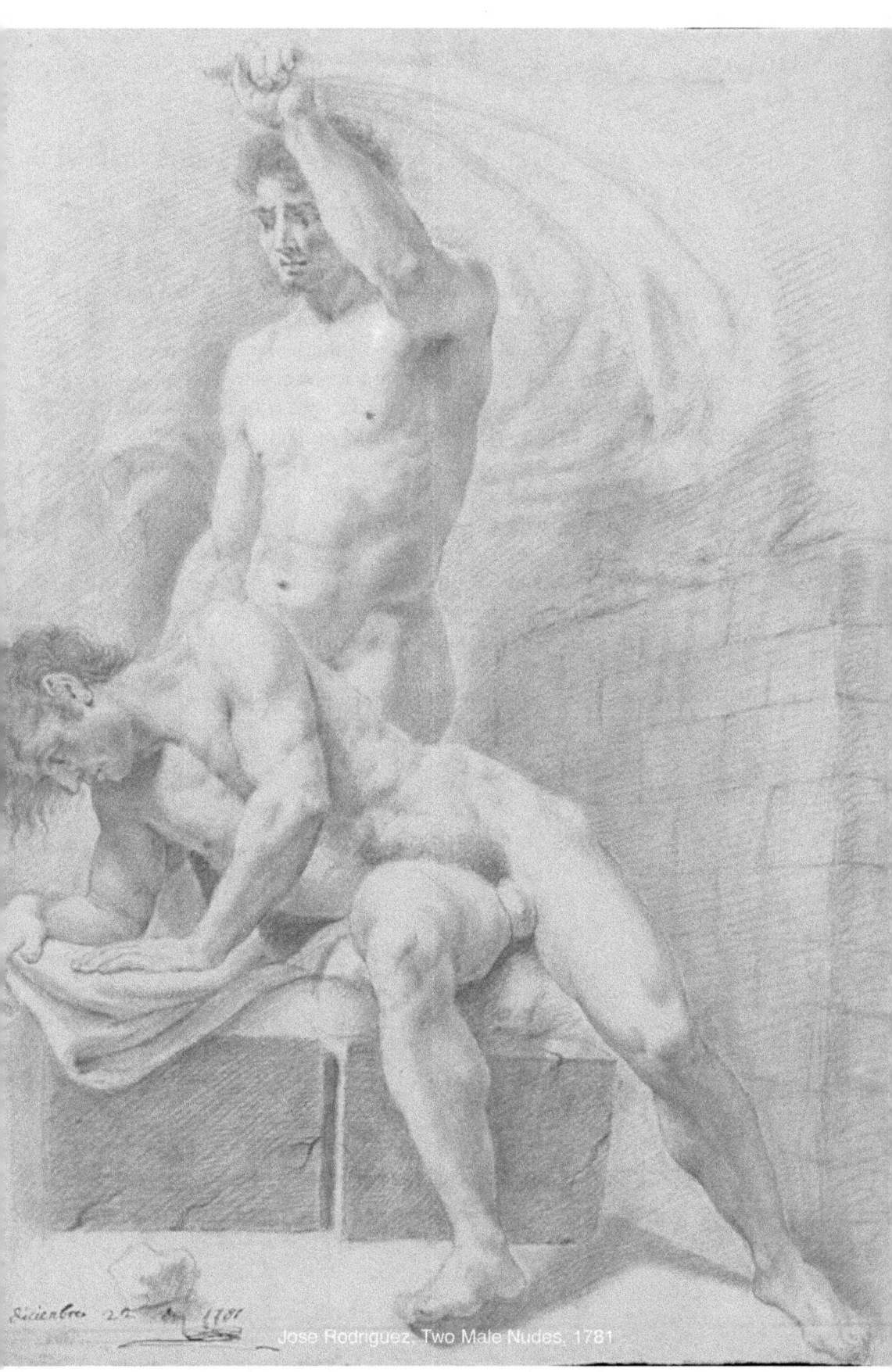

Jose Rodriguez, Two Male Nudes, 1781

MALE NUDES

The male nude can be appear uncomfortable. He doesn't like his photograph or painting or sculpture to be looked at like female nudes. He is used to being the one doing the looking. When the roles are reversed, ambiguity and confusion seeps in. The male nude is set up as spectacle, and as a passive object. To counter the awkwardness of this passivity, the male nude is shown *doing* something. Running, throwing a spear, fighting, etc. It tries to engage a position of activity, because to be the 'looked-at' one, the passive sex object, is very disquieting. Further, the activity of the male nude, which's seen everywhere – in photographs by Eadweard Muybridge,[1] in sculptures by Michelangelo Buonarroti, in movies, in gay porn – aims at portraying phallic power. 'Even in an apparently relaxed, supine pose,' Richard Dyer in 1983,

> the model tightens and tautens his body so that the muscles are emphasized, hence drawing attention to the body's potential for action. More often, the male pin-up is not supine anyhow, but standing taut ready for action.[2]

1 See L. Williams: "Film Body, an implantation of perversions", *Cinétracts*, vol. 3, no.4, Winter 1981, 19-25.
2 Richard Dyer: 'Don't Look Now", *Screen*, vol. 23, 3/ 4, 1983, 20, and in Angela McRobbie, 206

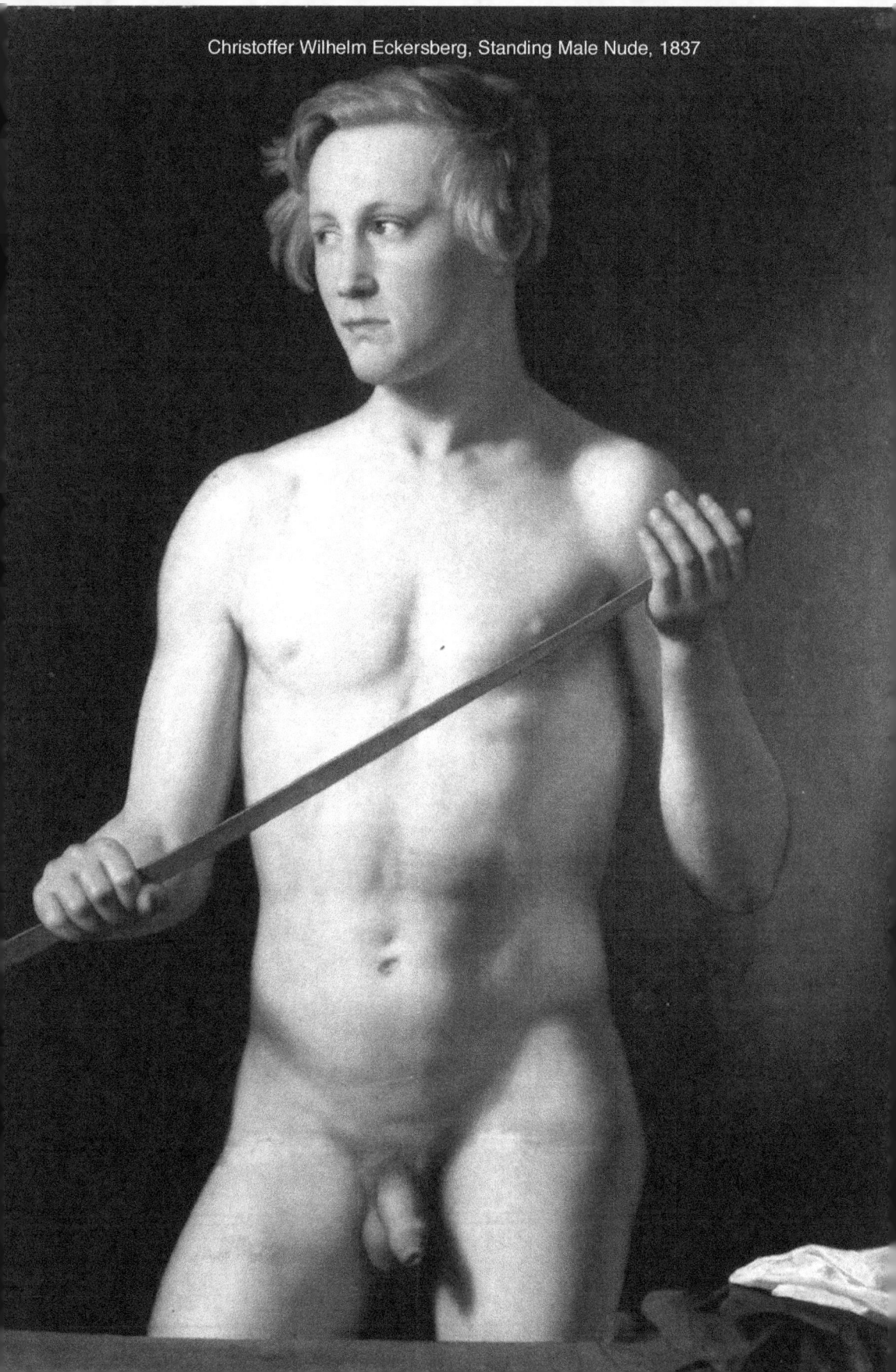
Christoffer Wilhelm Eckersberg, Standing Male Nude, 1837

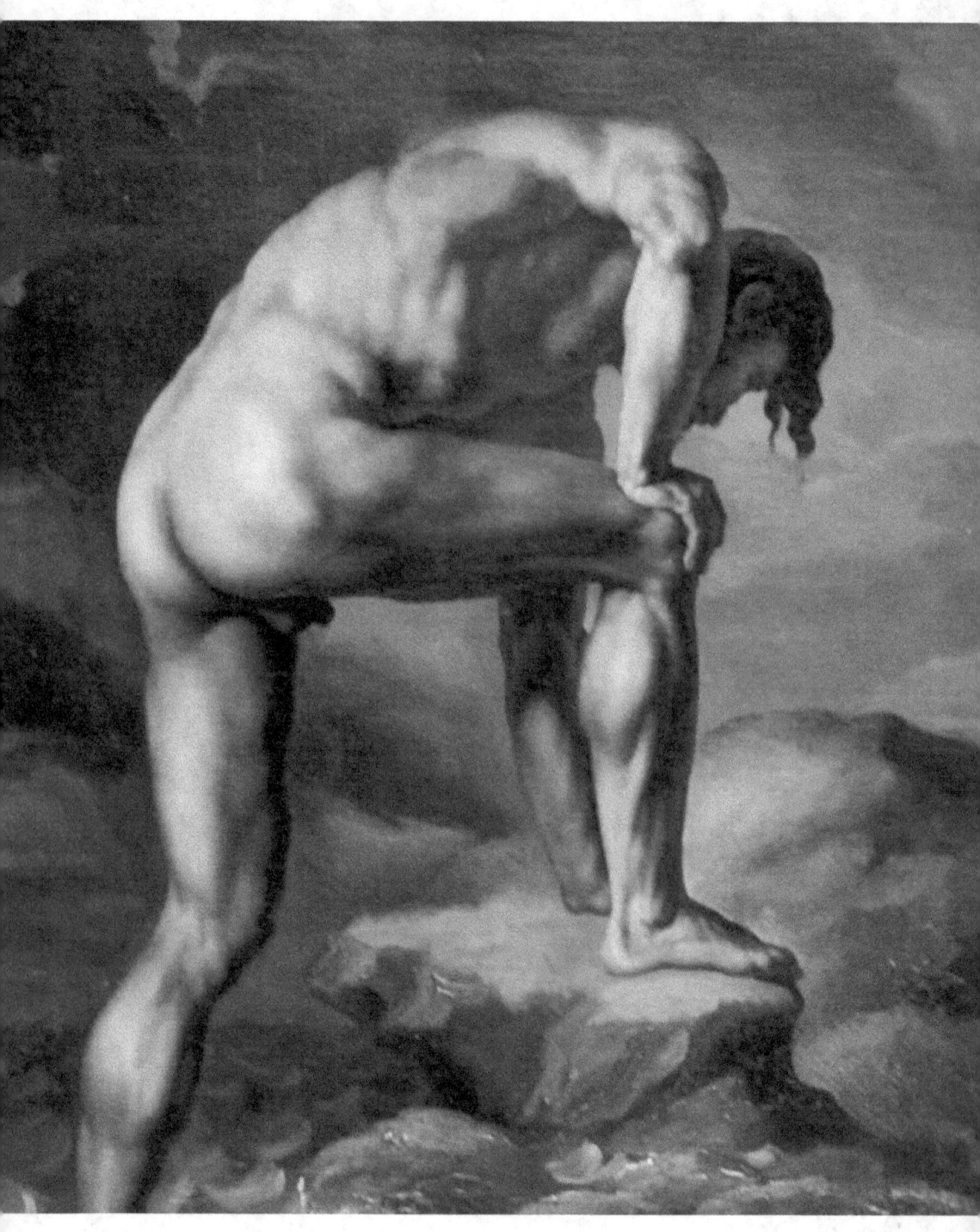

Jean-Louis Andre Theodore Géricault, A Shipwreck, c. 1819

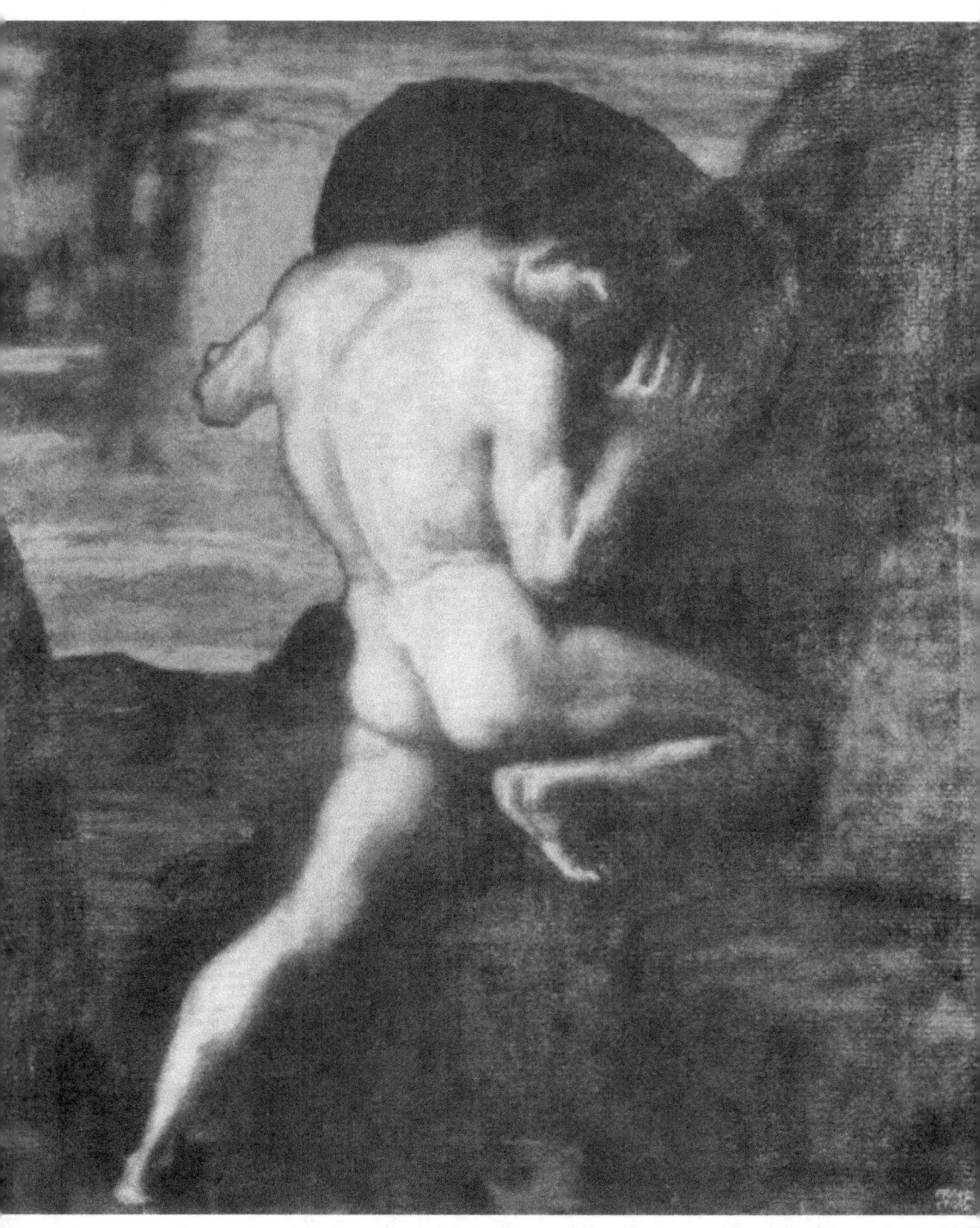

Franz von Stuck, Sisyphus

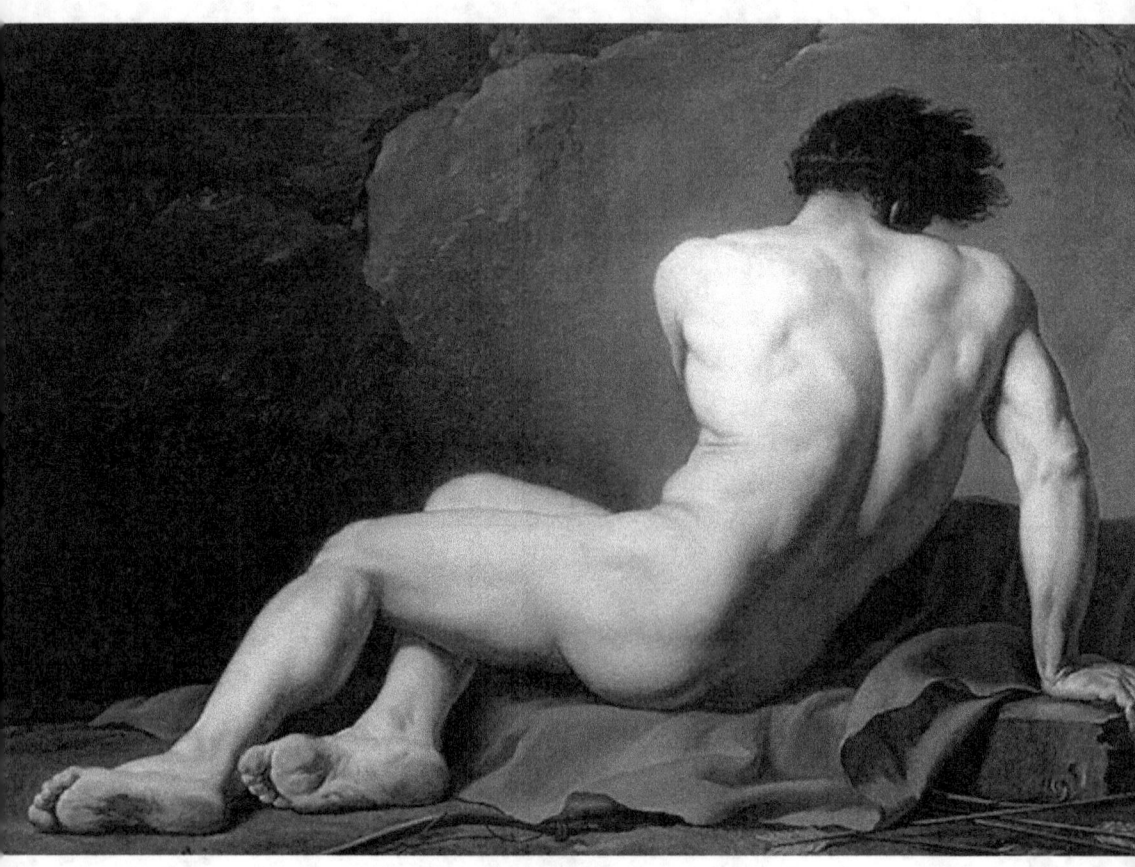

A classical French male nude painting
by Jacques-Louis David (known as Patrocles)

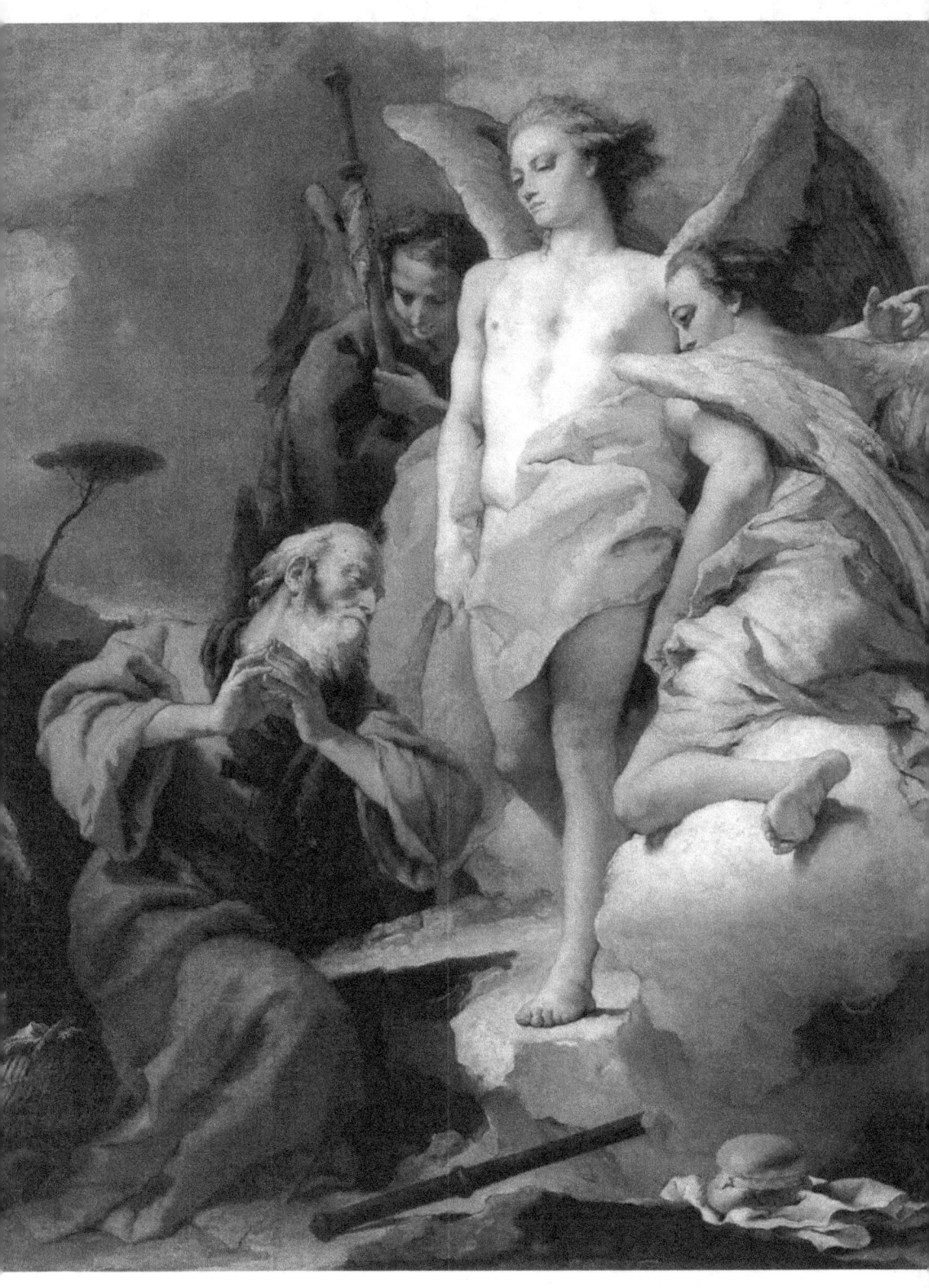

Giovanni Battista Tiepolo, Abraham and Three Angels, c. 1770

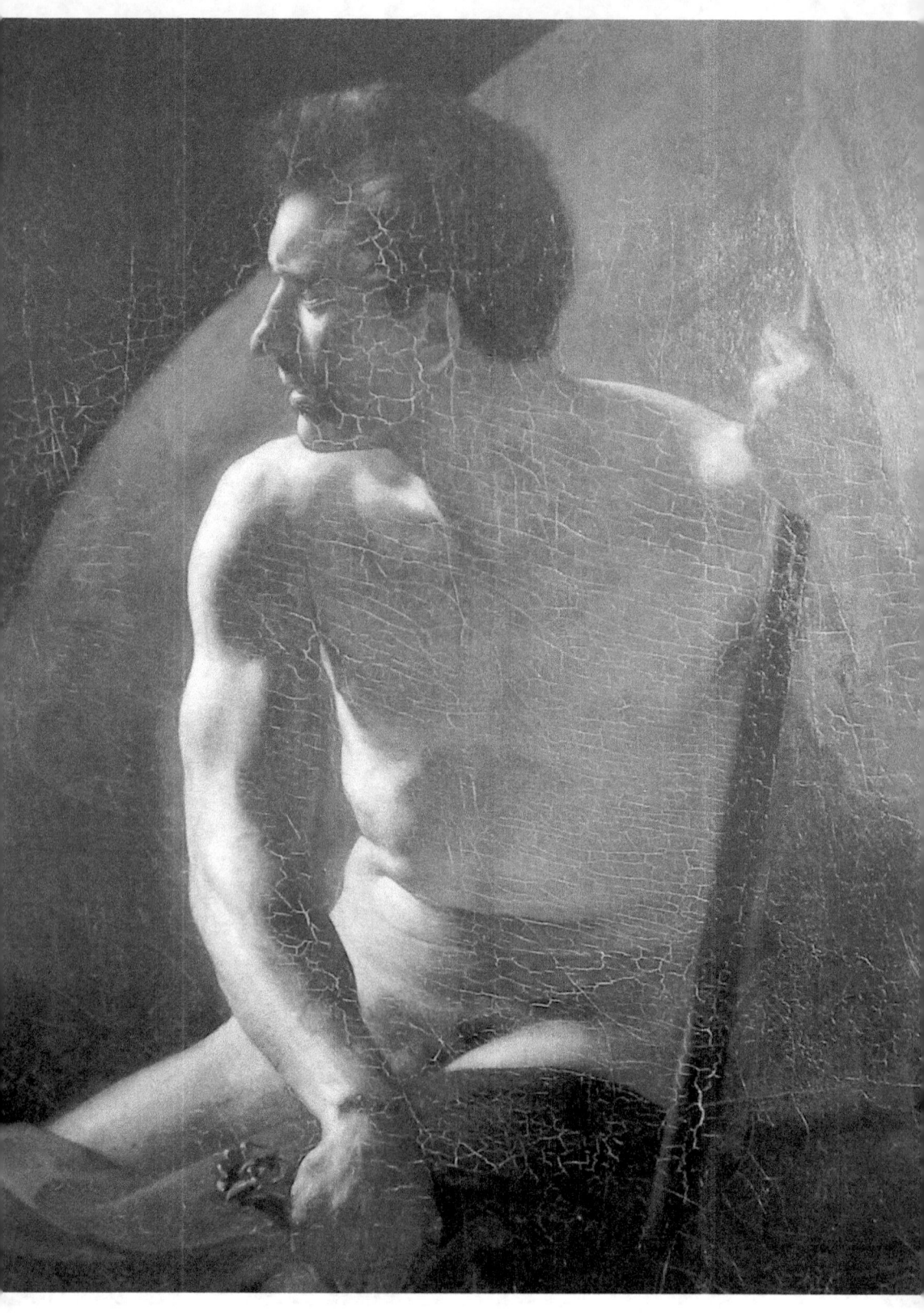

Hippolyte Dominique Holfeld, Half-Nude Figure, 1831

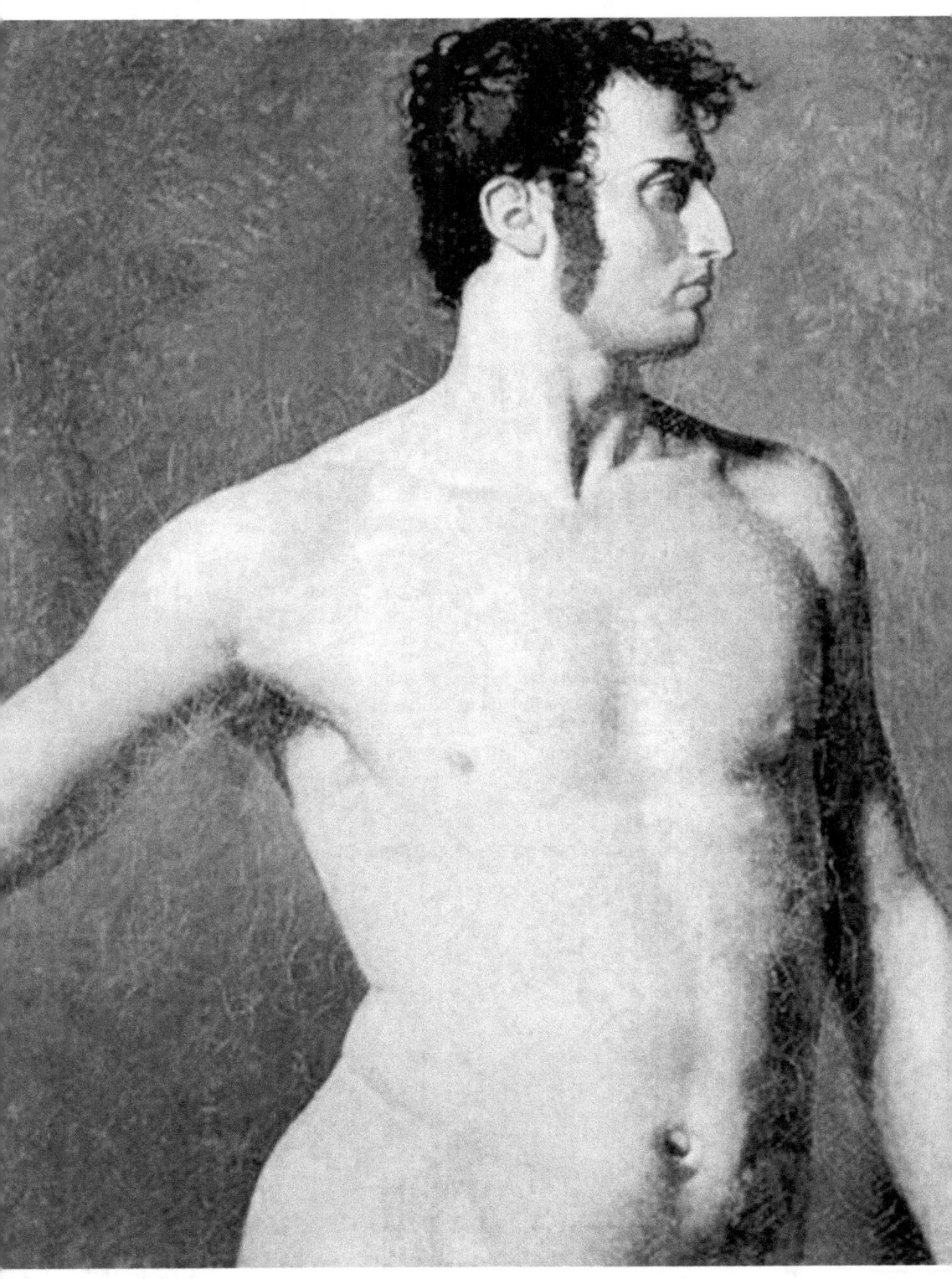

J.A.D. Ingres, Male Torso, 1801, Musée Ingres

MALE NUDES

The male nude image is subject to the same changes in culture as anything else: if you look at the nudes included here, you'll see the changes in fashion and style, at the superficial level, as well as the developments in the politics and society of the time, reflected in the nude images. Even though the body is nude, there are still numerous marks of culture upon it.

In the advanced capitalist, technological world, the body is not a 'natural' form any more, as Elizabeth Grosz explains in *Volatile Bodies*: clothing, exercise, jewellery, lifestyle, habits, negotiations of the cultural and social as well as the physical environment, and all sorts of activities alter it, inscribe it, turn it into something definitely not 'natural':

> Makeup, stilettos, bras, hair sprays, clothing, underclothing mark women's bodies, whether black or white, in ways in which hair styles, professional training, personal grooming, gait, posture, body building, and sports may mark men's. There is nothing natural or ahistorical about these modes of corporeal inscriptions. Through then, bodies are made amenable to the prevailing exigencies of power. They make the flesh into a particular type of body – pagan, primitive, medieval, capitalist, Italian, American, Australian. (142)

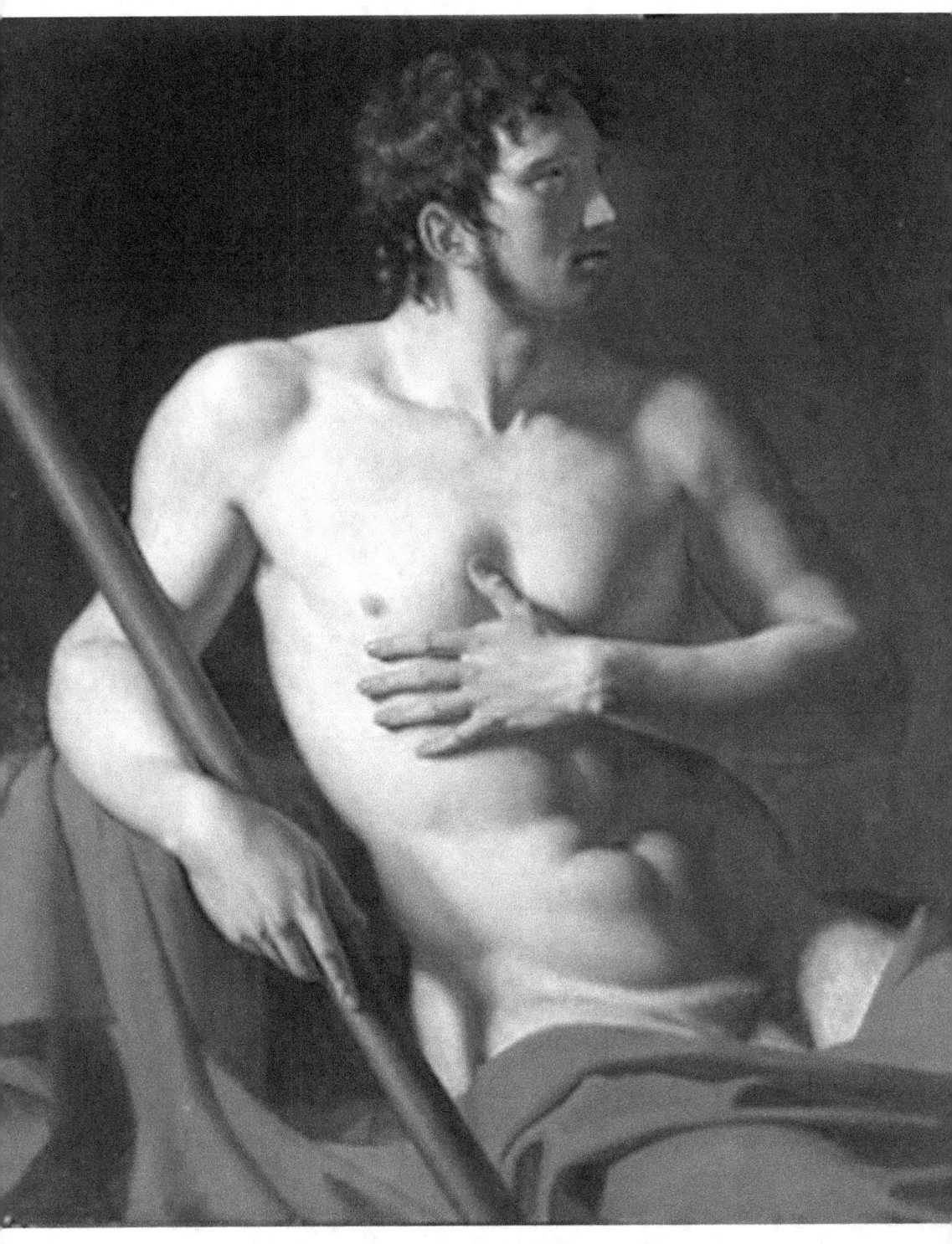

Auguste-Alphonse Gaudar de la Verdine, Male Nude, 1799

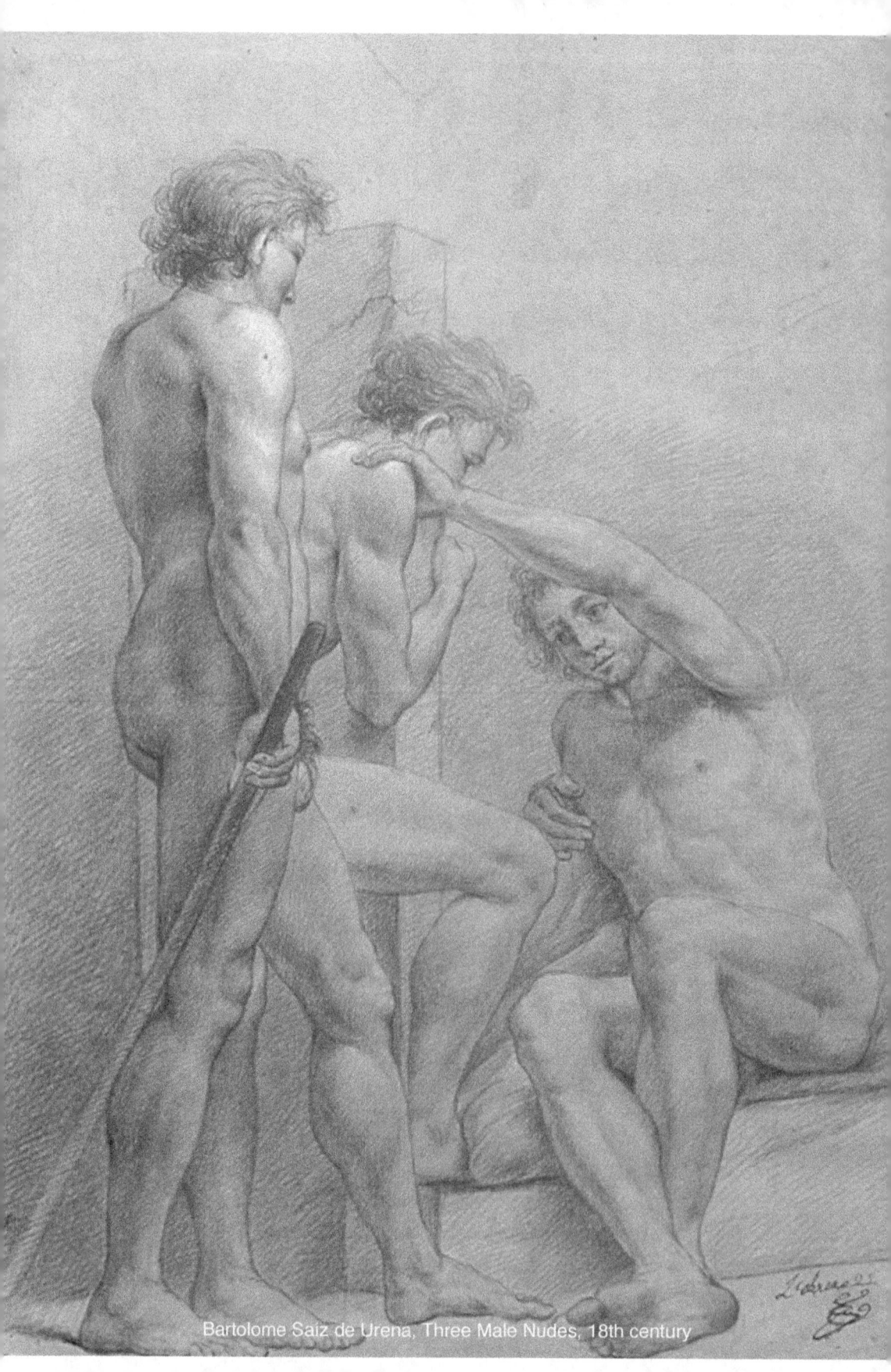

Bartolome Saiz de Urena, Three Male Nudes, 18th century

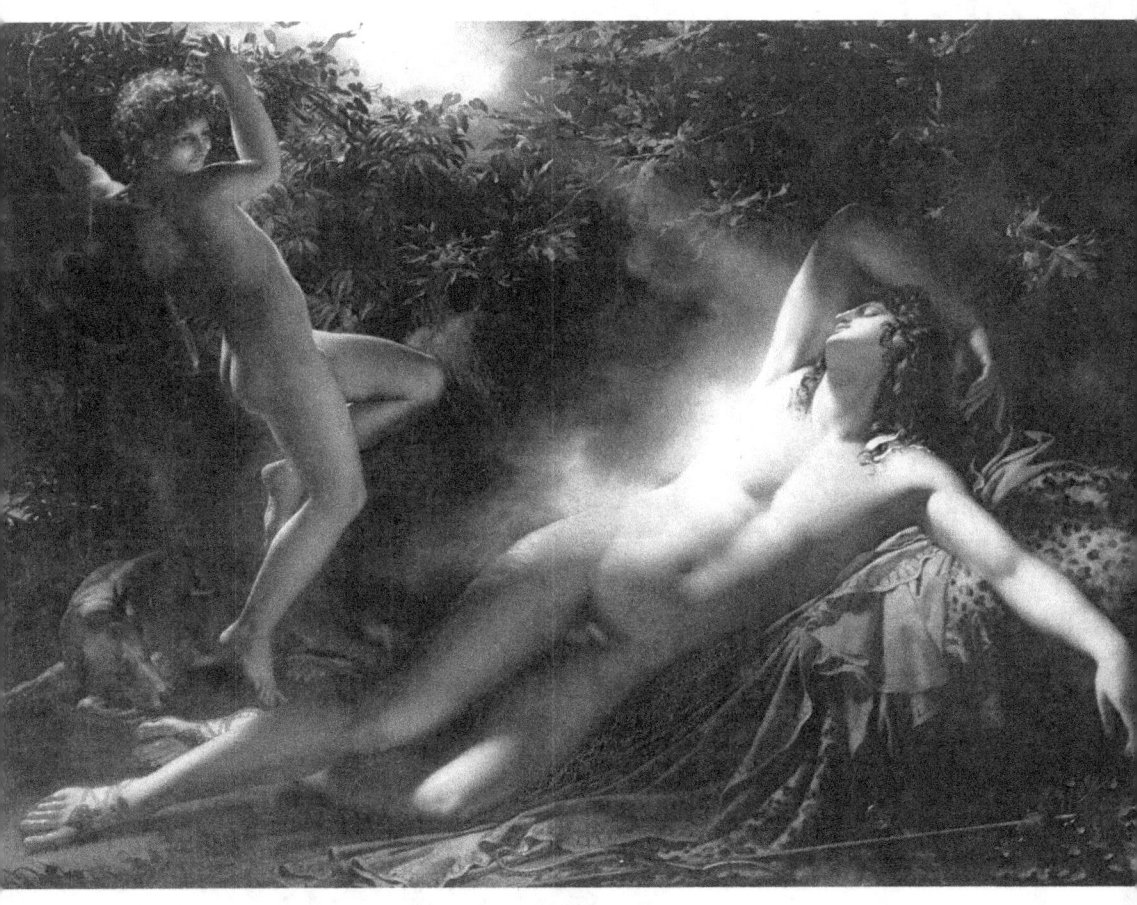

Anne-Louis Girodet-Trioson, Endymion, 1793

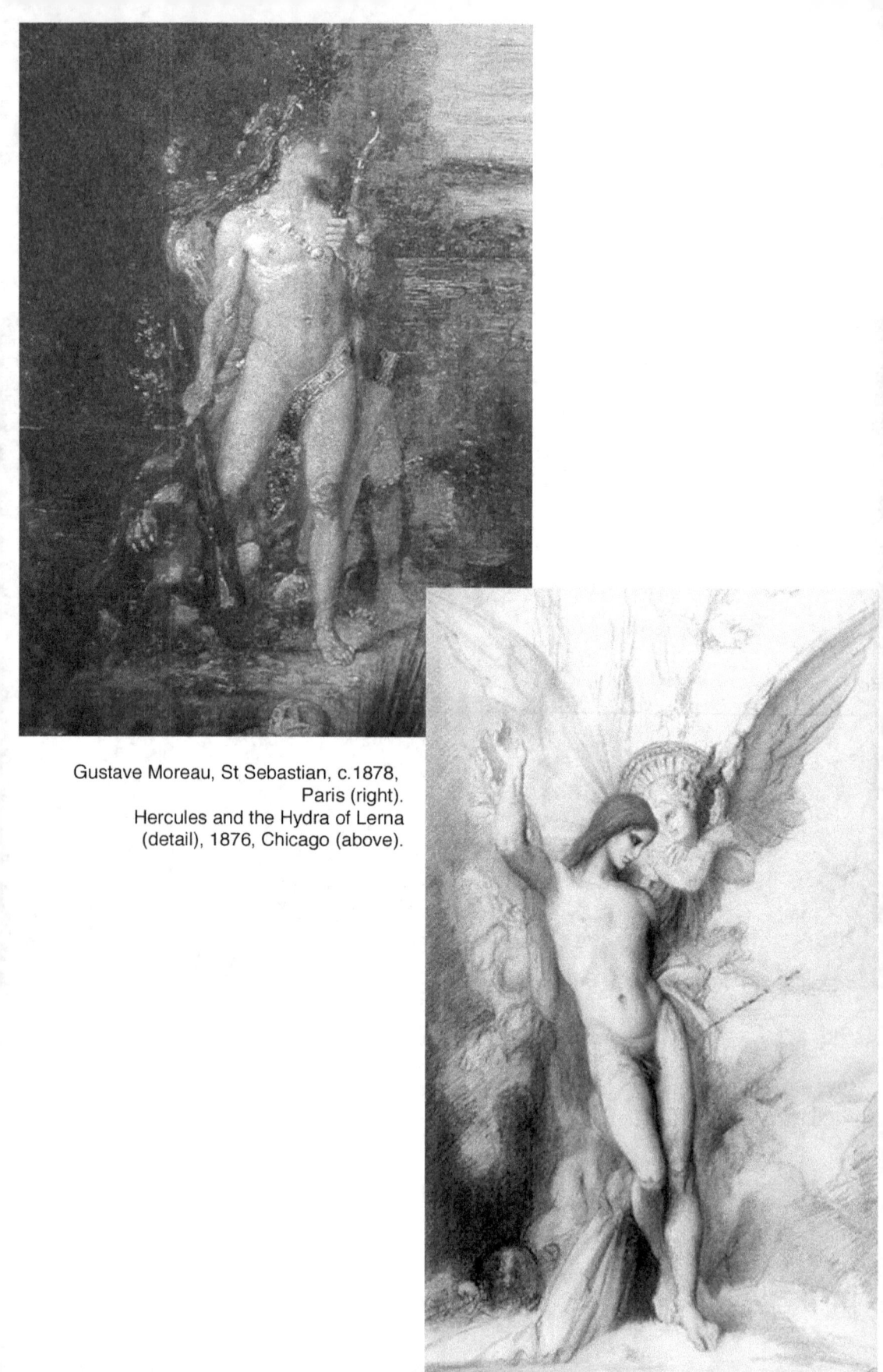

Gustave Moreau, St Sebastian, c.1878,
Paris (right).
Hercules and the Hydra of Lerna
(detail), 1876, Chicago (above).

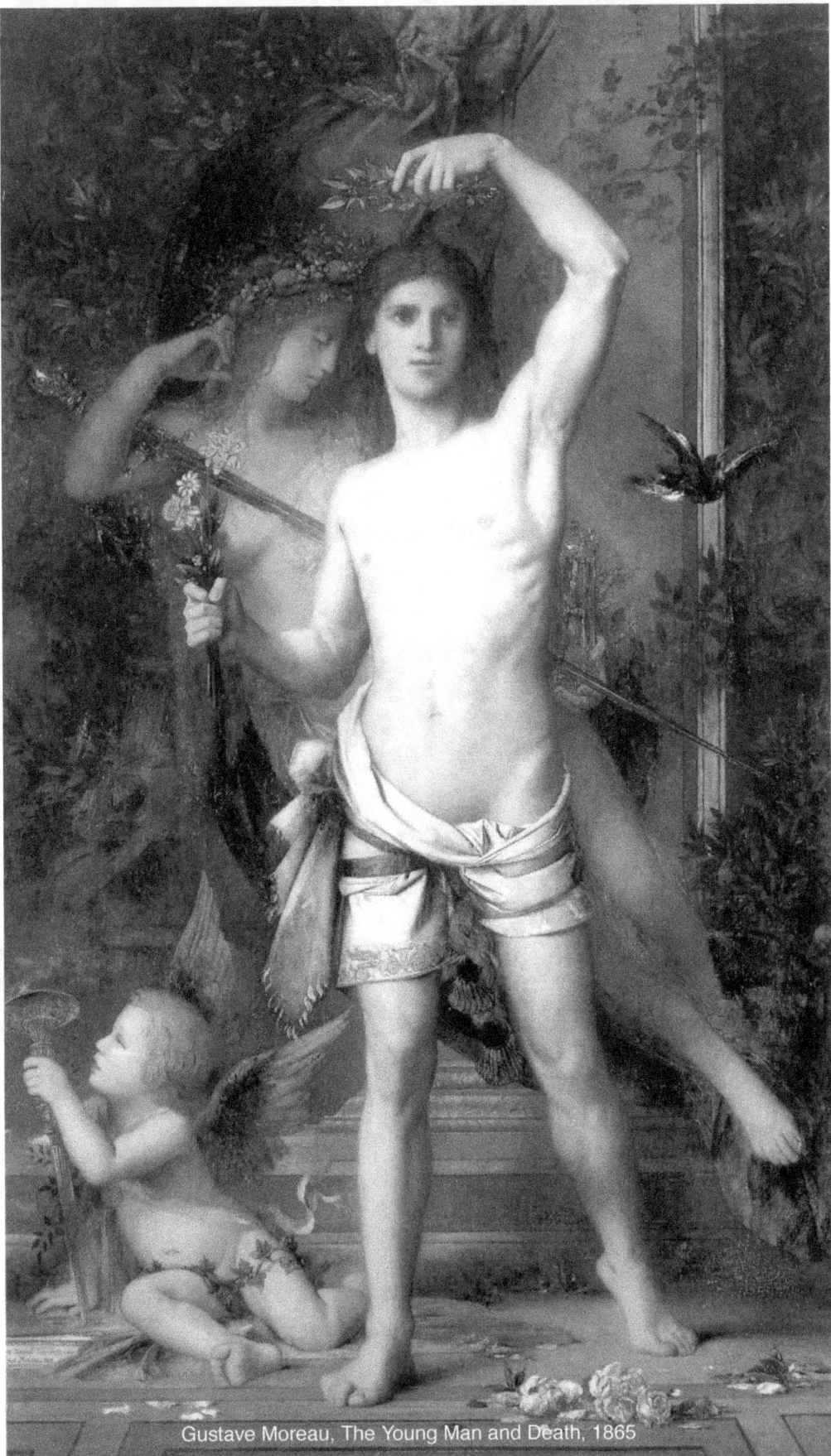

Gustave Moreau, The Young Man and Death, 1865

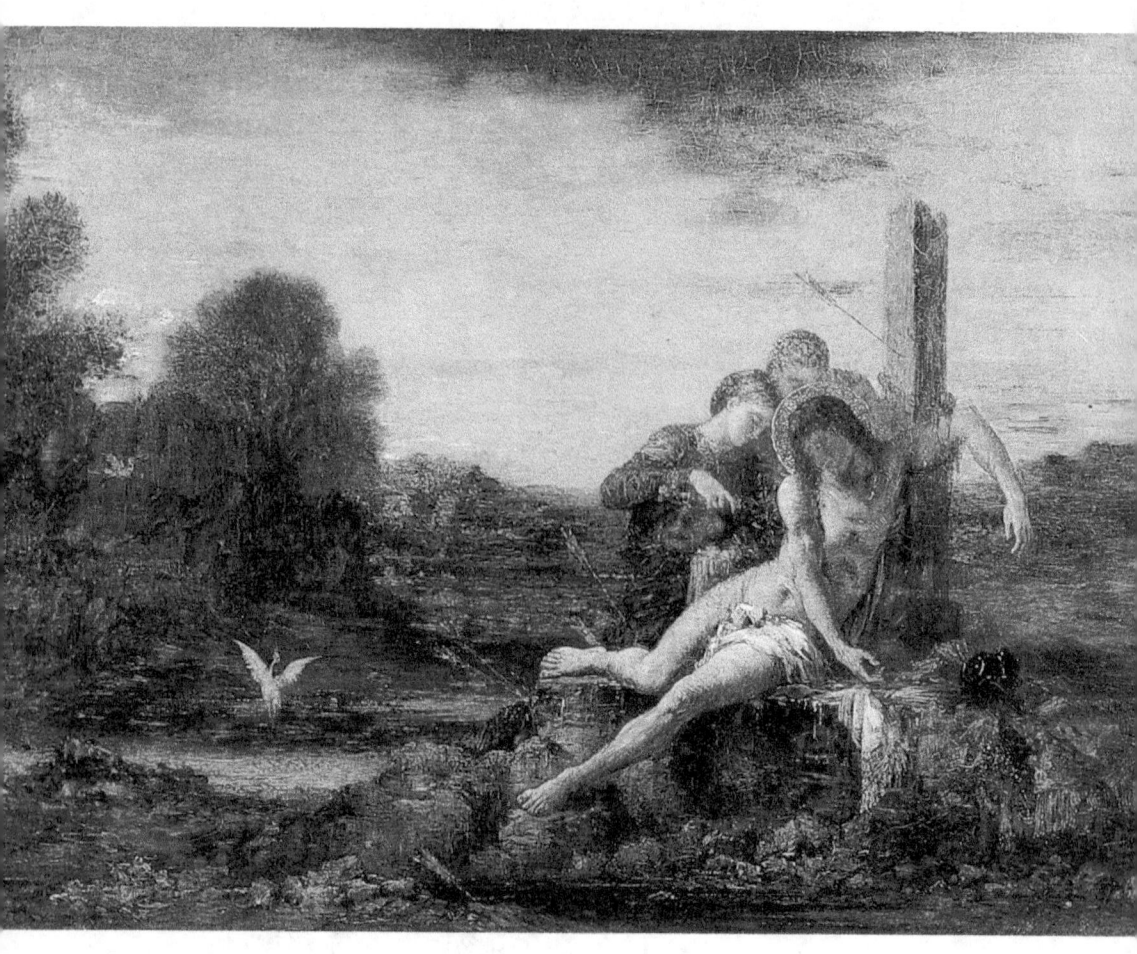

Gustave Moreau, St Sebastian, 1869

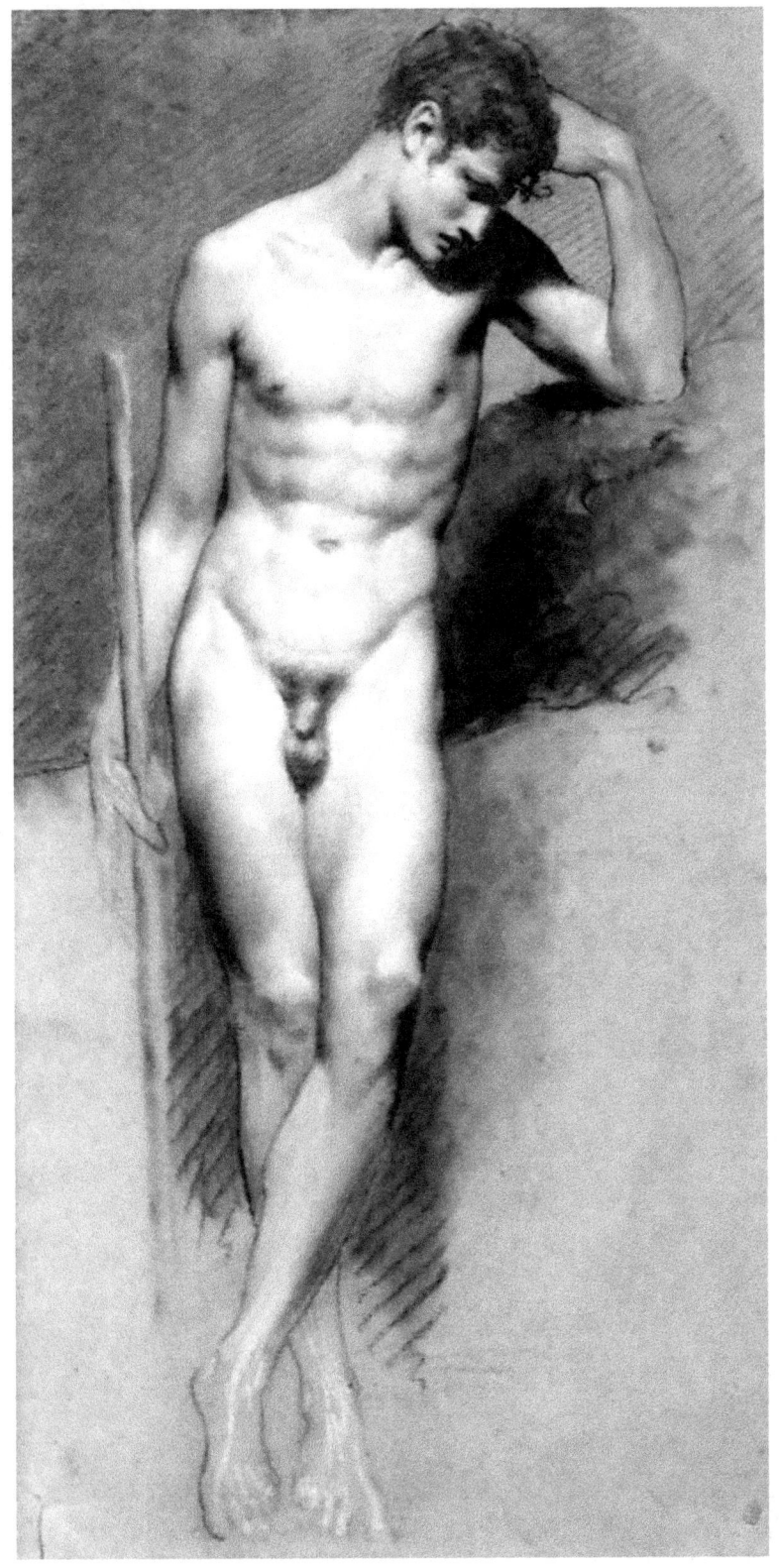

Pierre-Paul Prud'hon (1758-1823), Male Nude Standing

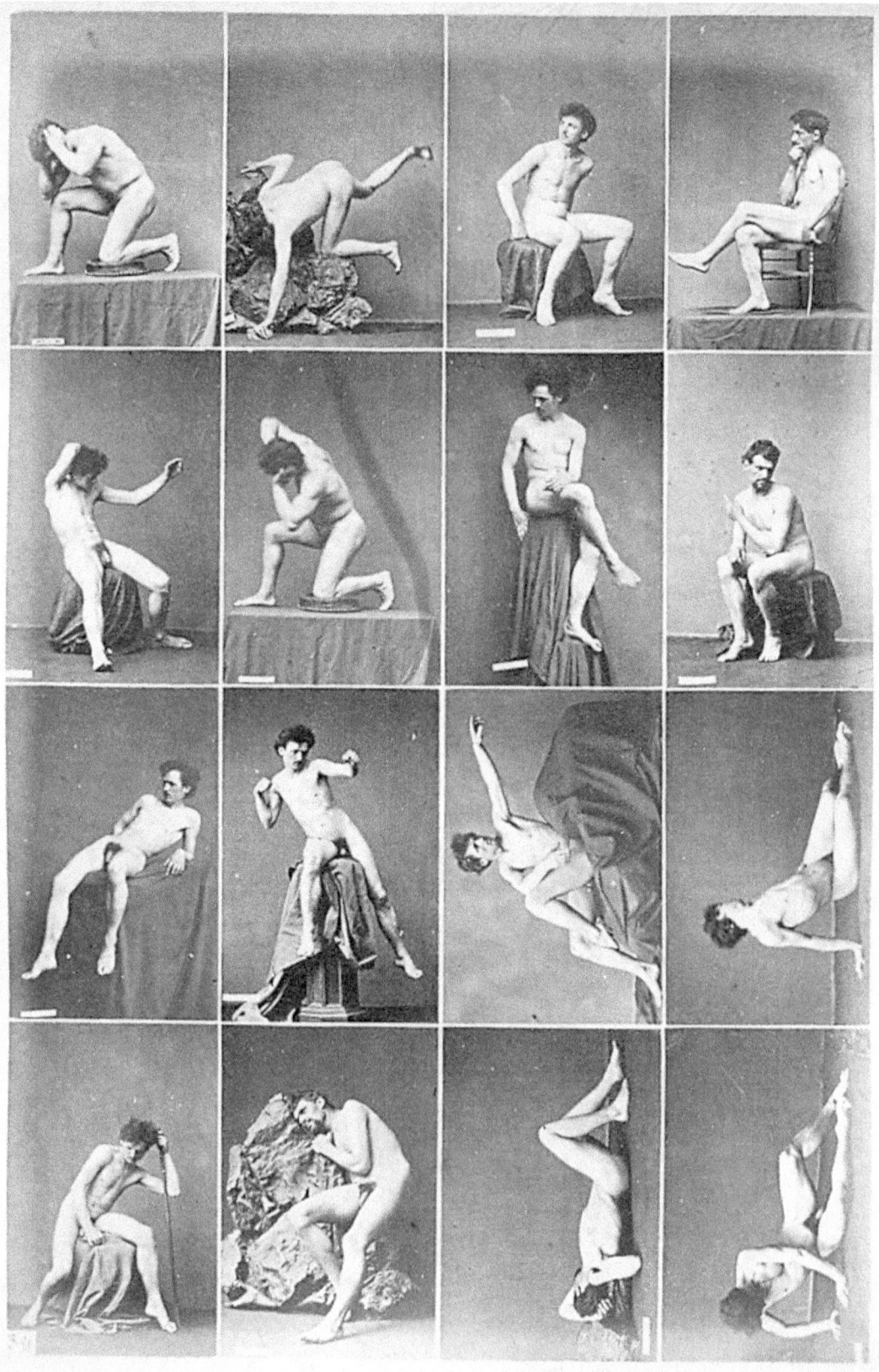

Ignout, Male Nude Studies, 1875

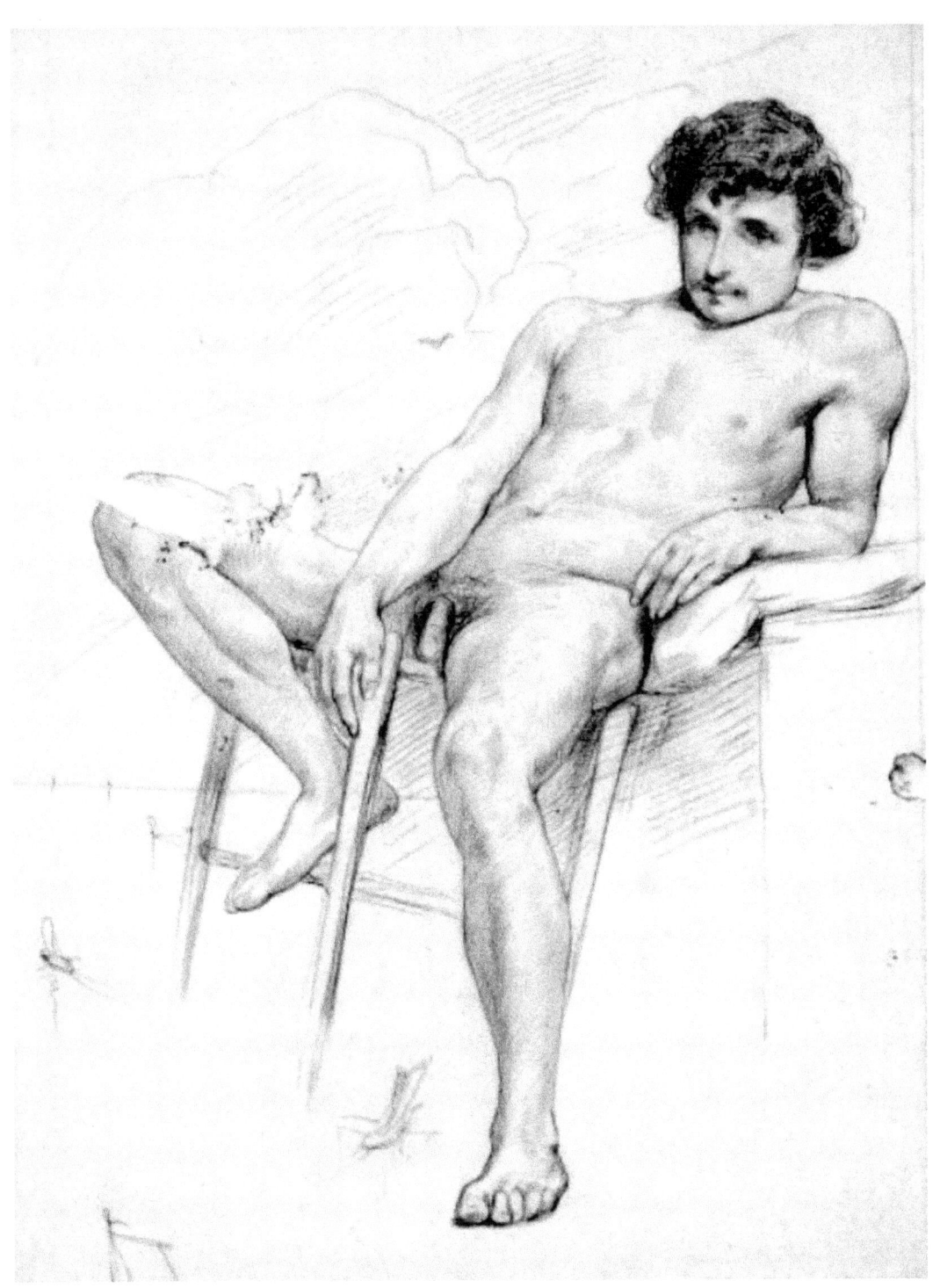

Lord Leighton, life drawing

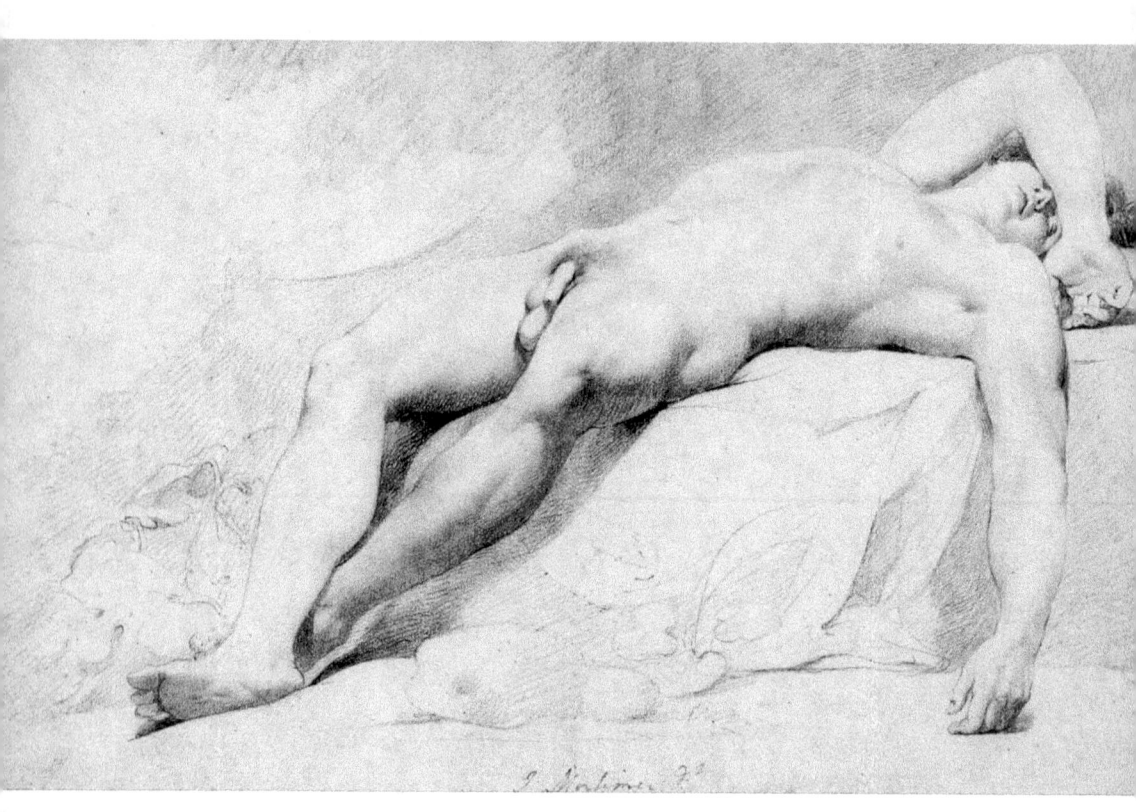

John Hamilton Mortimer, Recumbent Male Nude, c. 1773

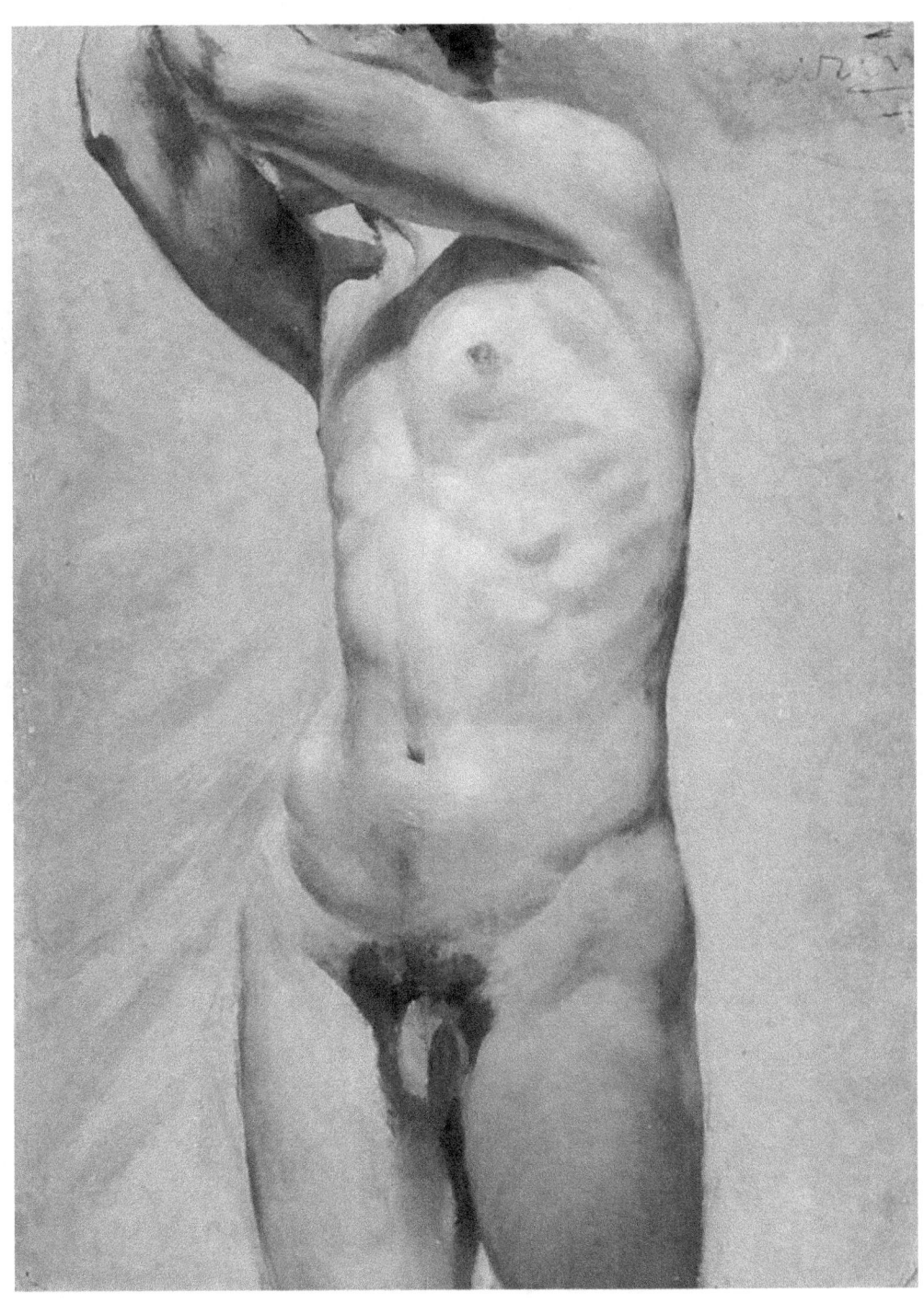

French school, c. 1890

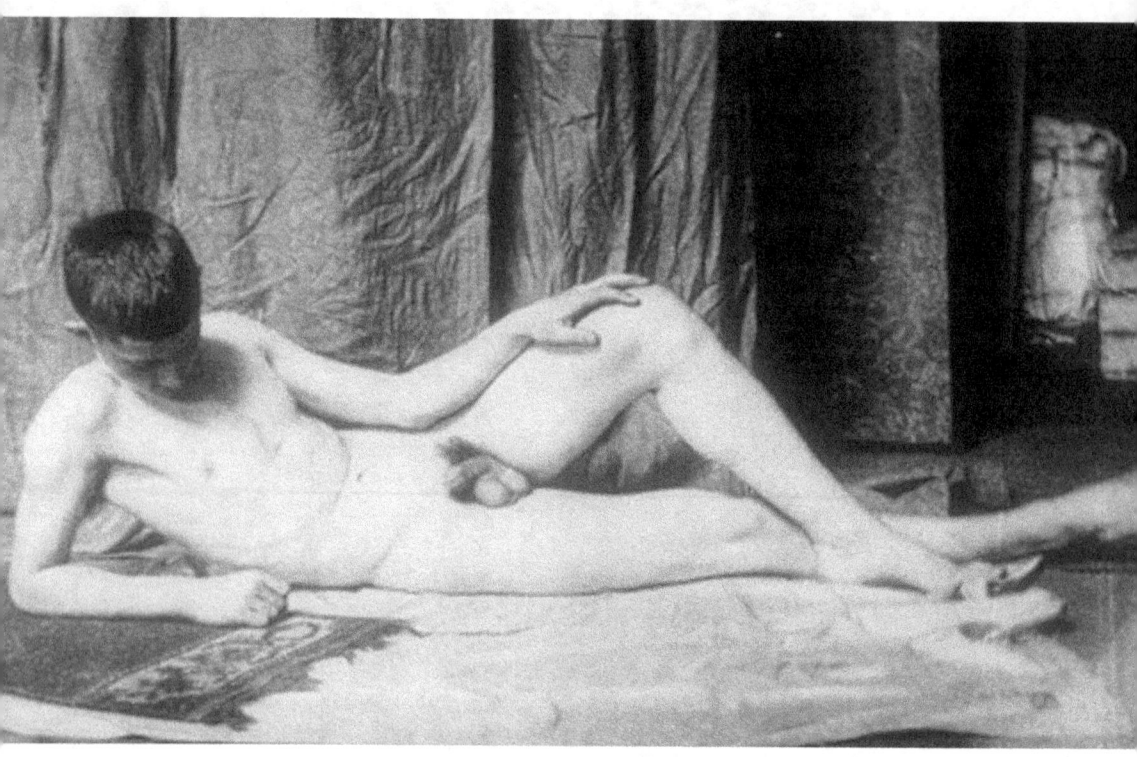

Reclining Male Nude, 1887–92,
Thomas Eakins, platinum print

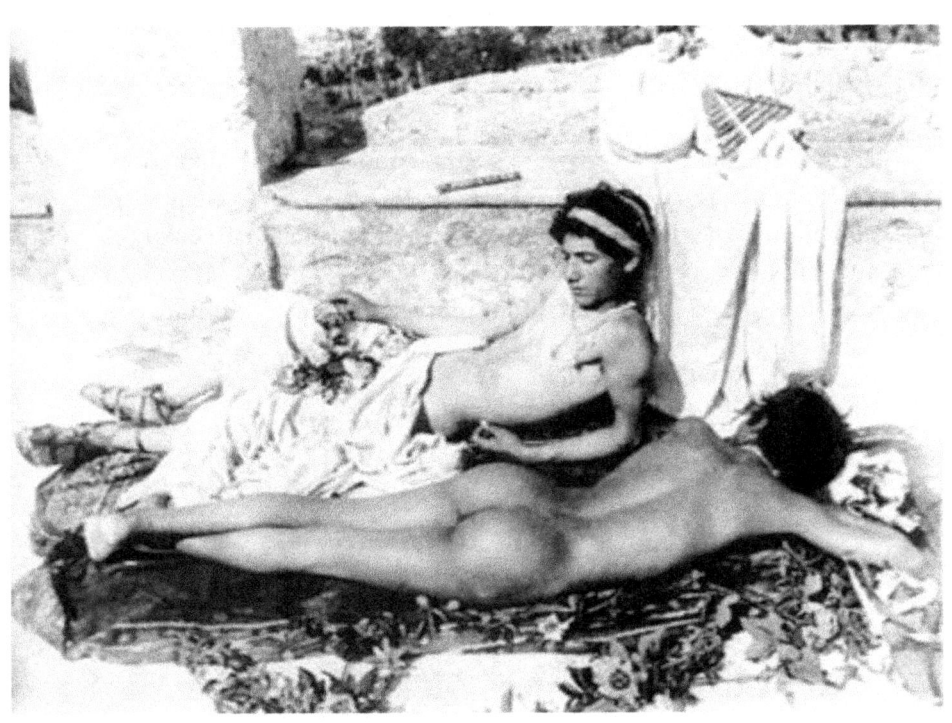

Wilhelm von Gloeden, c. 1900

PORNOGRAPHY

There are many different kinds of pornography, as there are many different kinds of art or feminism. Seen through cultural or postmodern or deconstructionist or semiological theory, pornography can be viewed as a realm of codes, meanings, contexts, signifiers, values, experiences and attitudes, which are politically controlled, manufactured by social, economic and political needs and demands. Pornography is thus the *representation* of... something; maybe certain kinds of sexuality, maybe somebody's thoughts on certain kinds of sexuality. Pornography is not *sexuality in itself*, it is mediation, representation, communication, a relic, a trace.

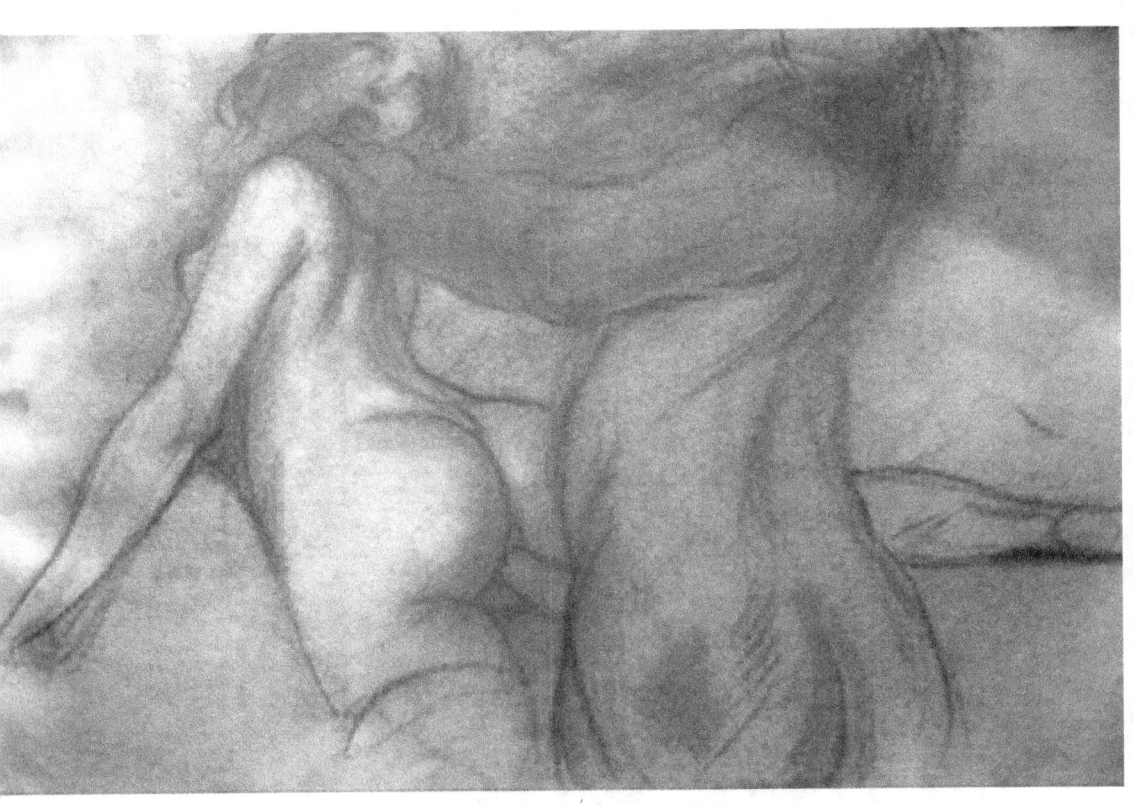

Aroldo Bonzagni

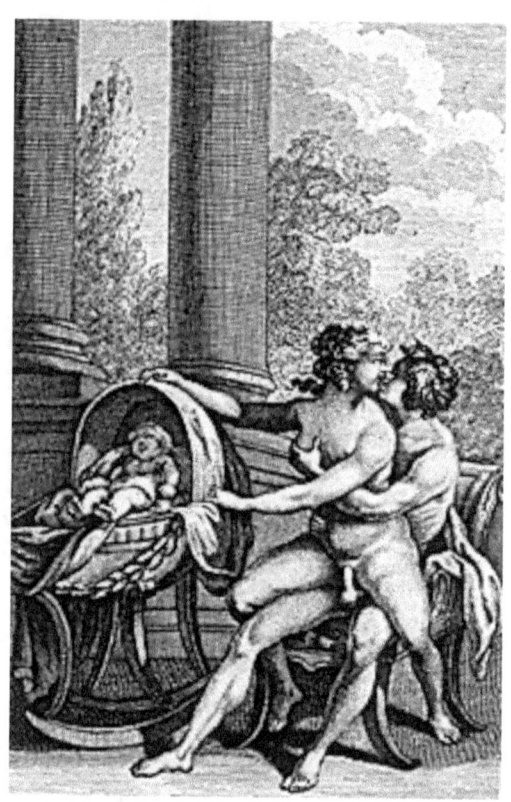

Anonymous, illustrations to
the Sonnets by Pietro Aretino

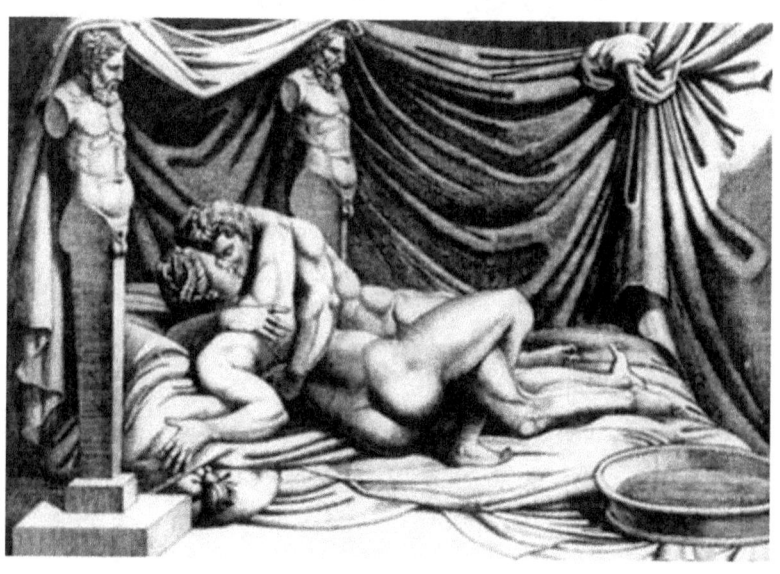

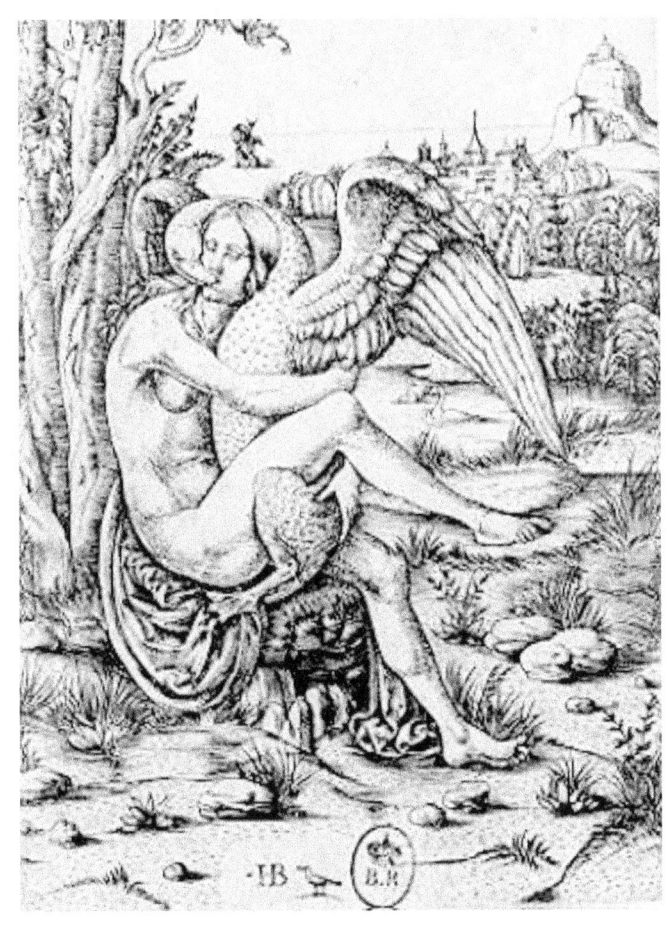

Hans Baldung (1484-1545), this page and over

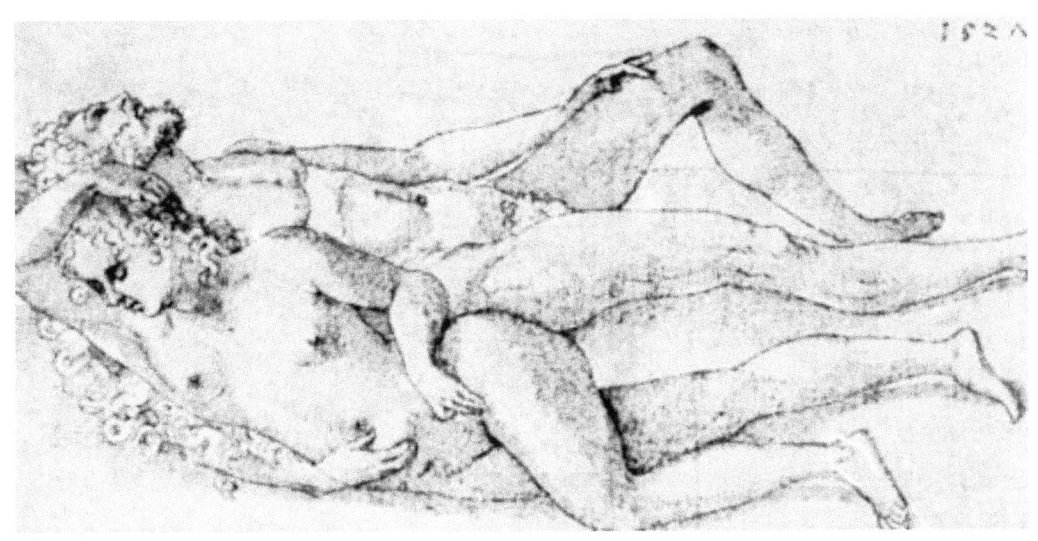

Pornography has its own 'genres' of sub-categories: there is S/M, hardcore, lesbian, gay porn, soft core, and pornography geared to any number of fetishes; rubber, leather, boots, large breasts, bondage, etc.[1] What's your fetish? Porn will have something for you!

The history of art too has its categories and forms of erotic art, with the reclining (female) nude as perhaps the most well-known, and the most celebrated in art criticism. Other forms include humans and deities, humans and animals (often gods in beast-form), sexual positions, religious subjects, mythological subjects, Venus and Cupid, etc.

---

1 These sub-genres are institutions in themselves, with their own codes and structures, but their institutionalized sexual images do not express the real eroticism that people experience (they suggest it, perhaps, or reflect parts of it).

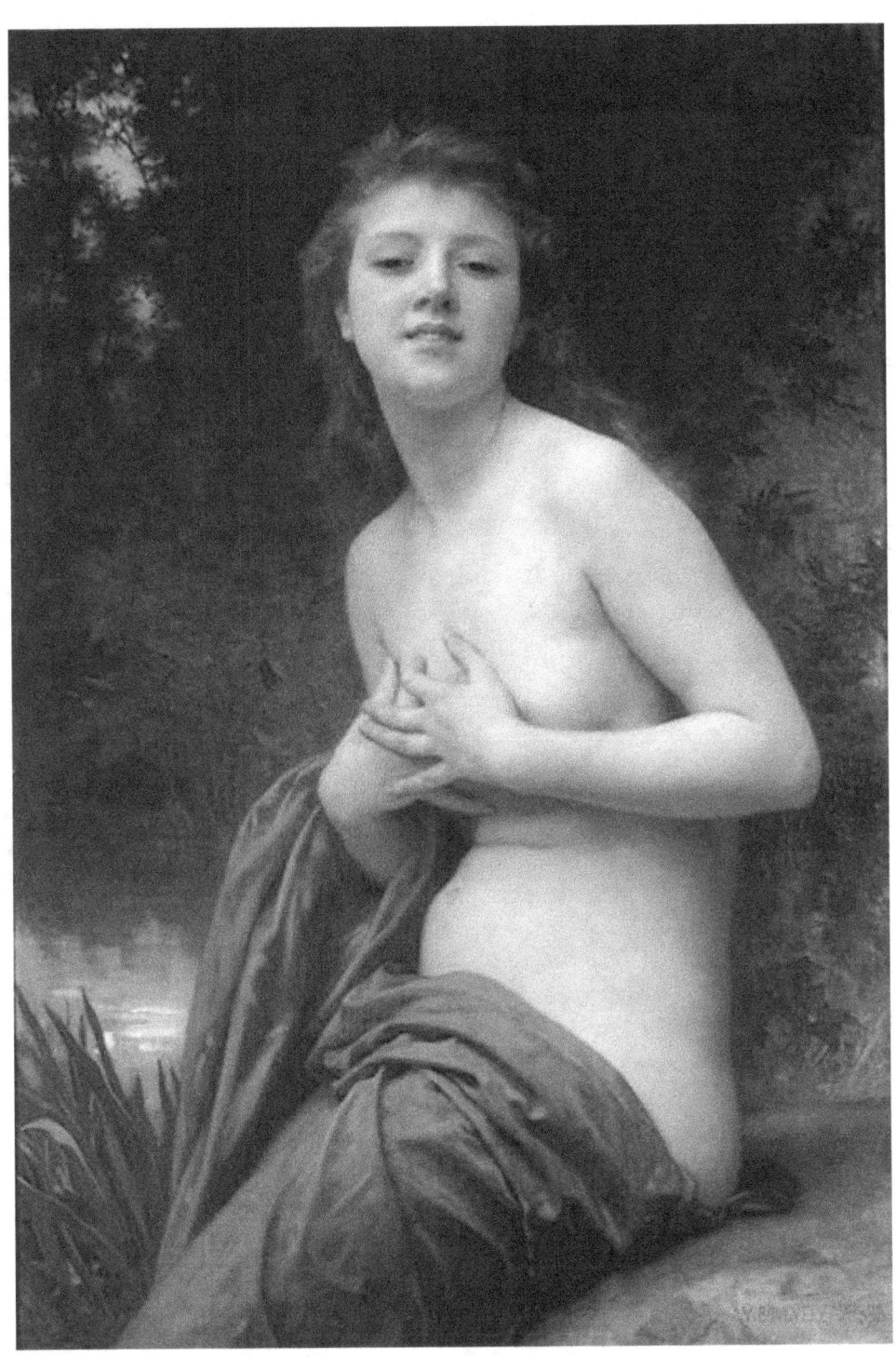

William Bouguereau, Spring Breeze, 1895

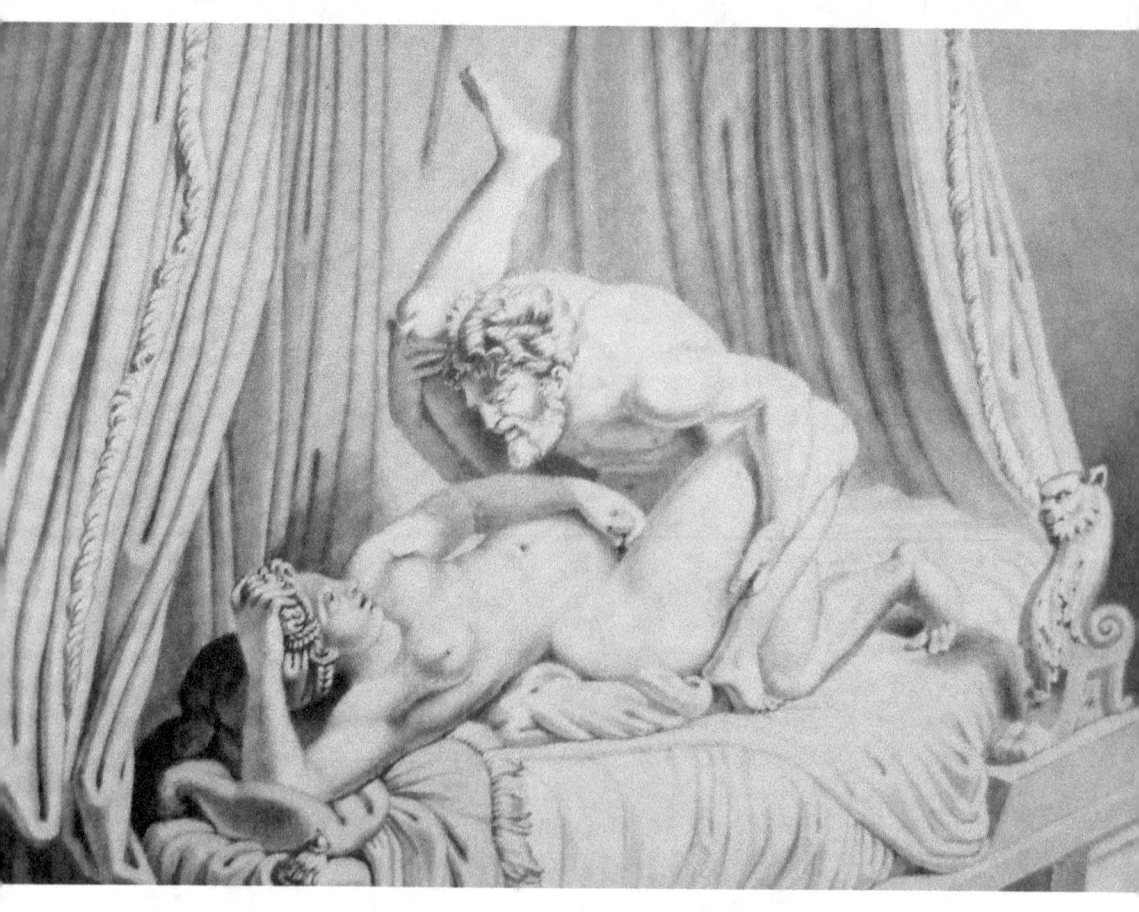

Friedrich von Waldeck, from Postures, c. 1858
(This page and following pages)

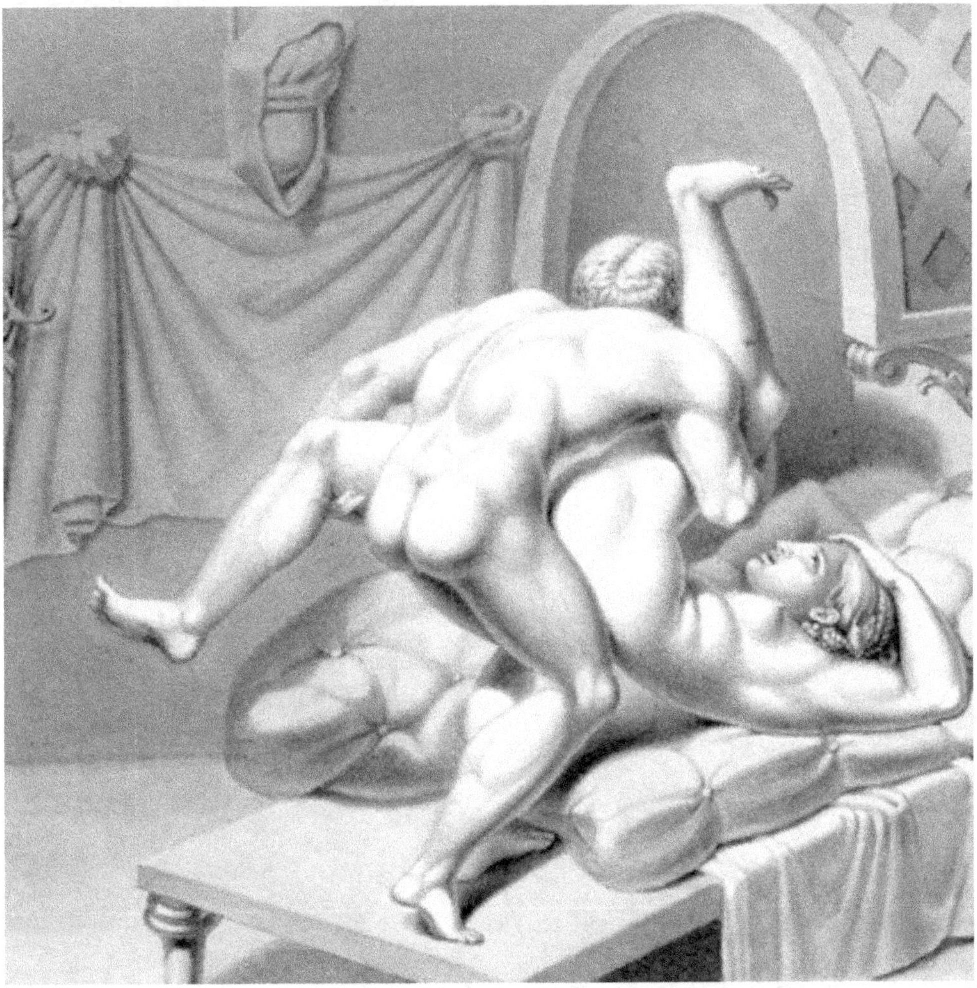

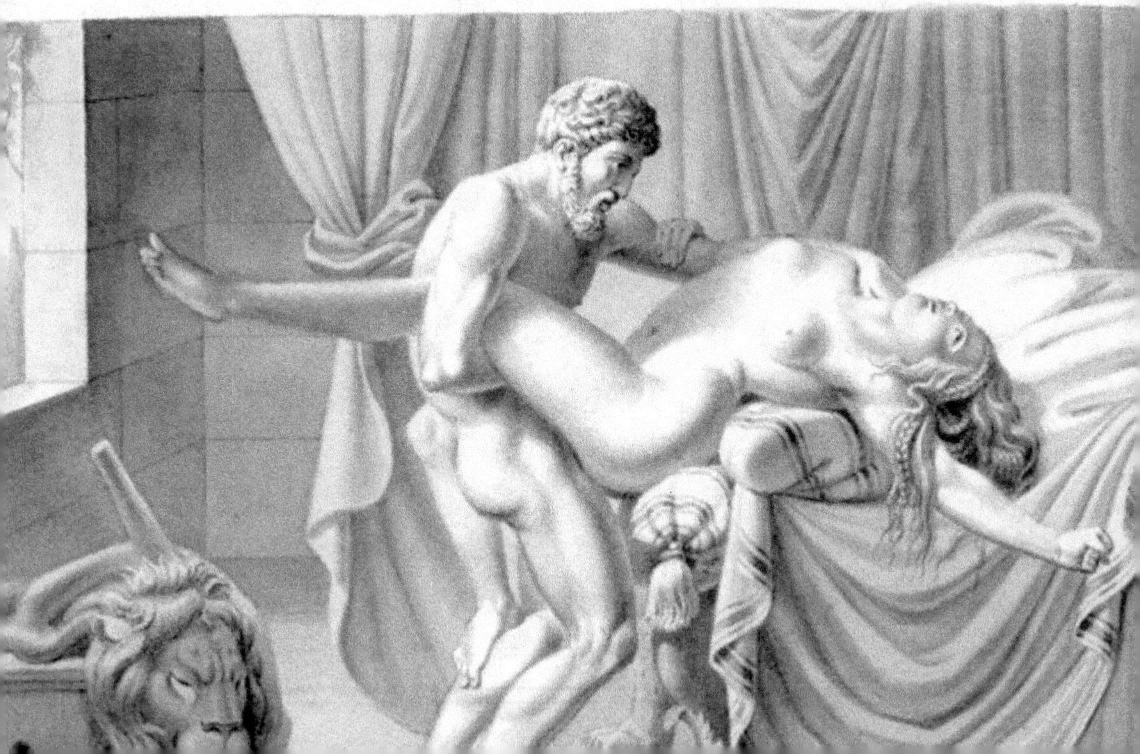

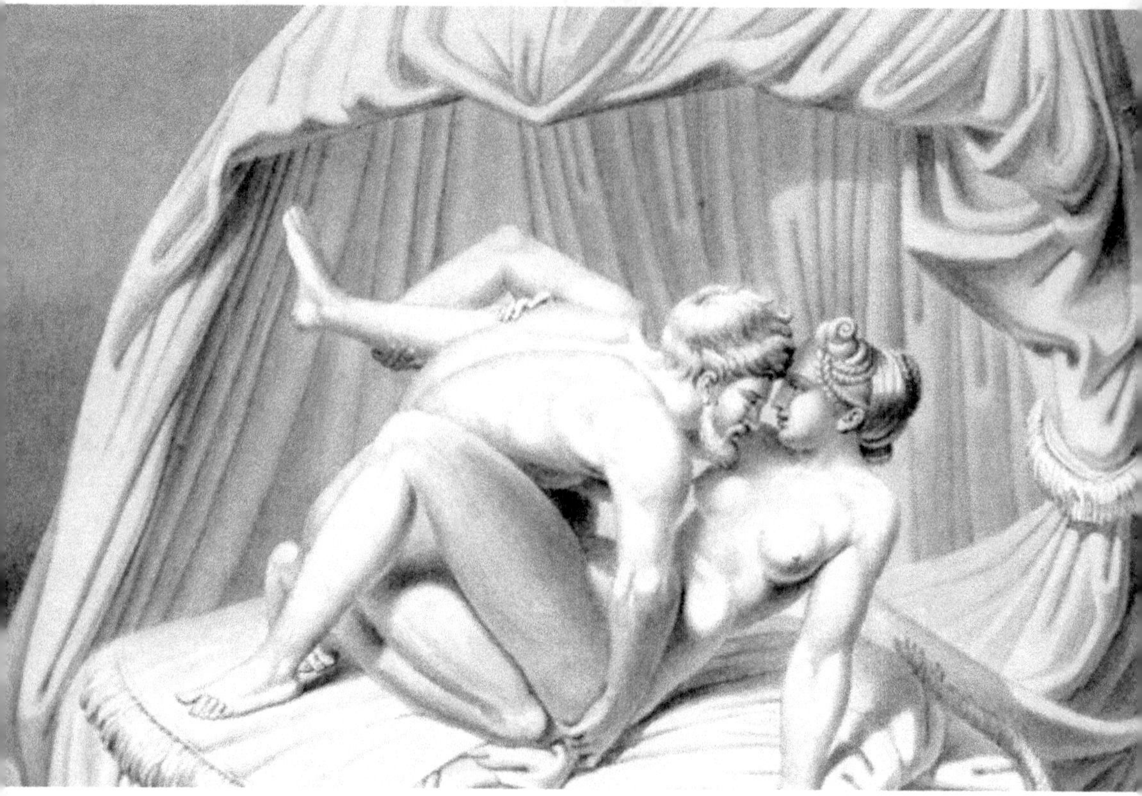

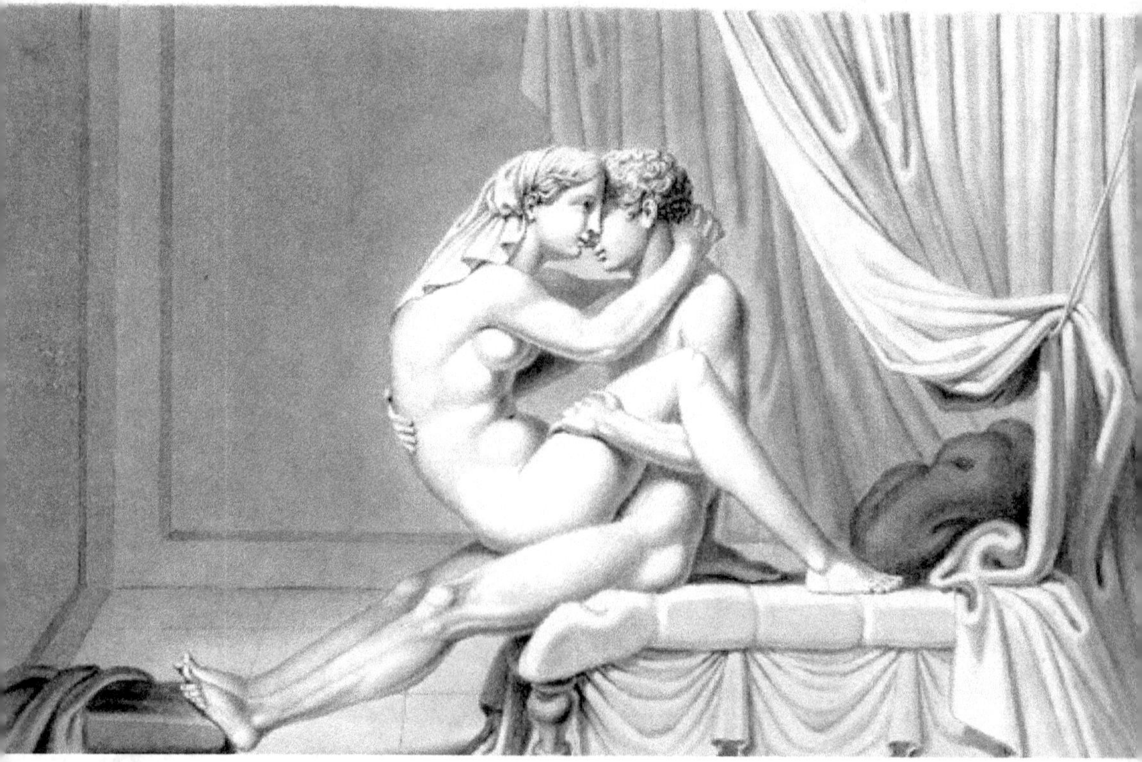

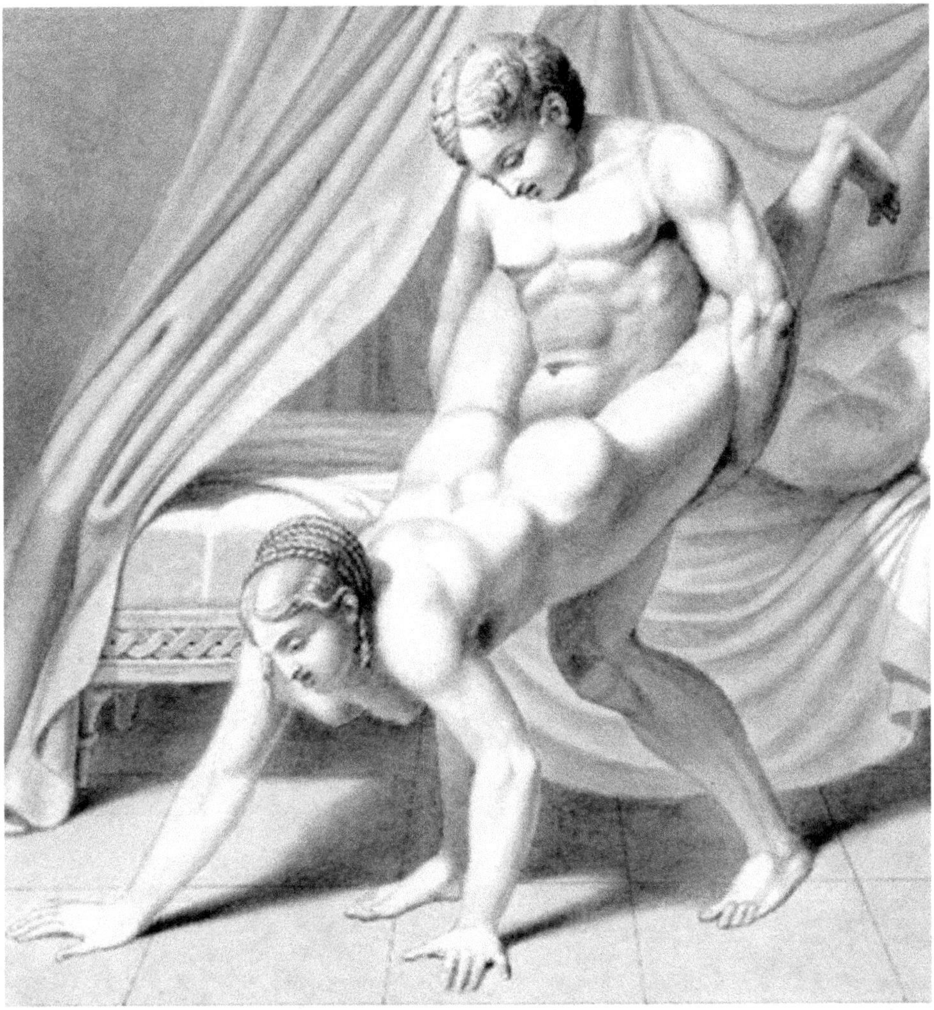

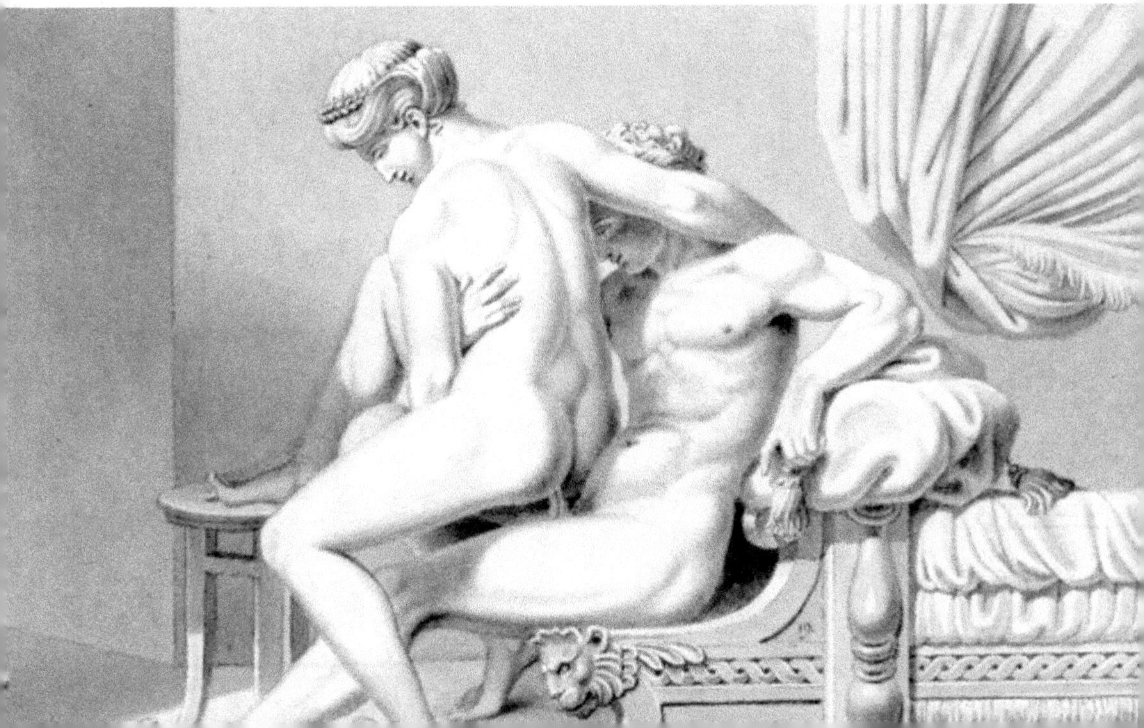

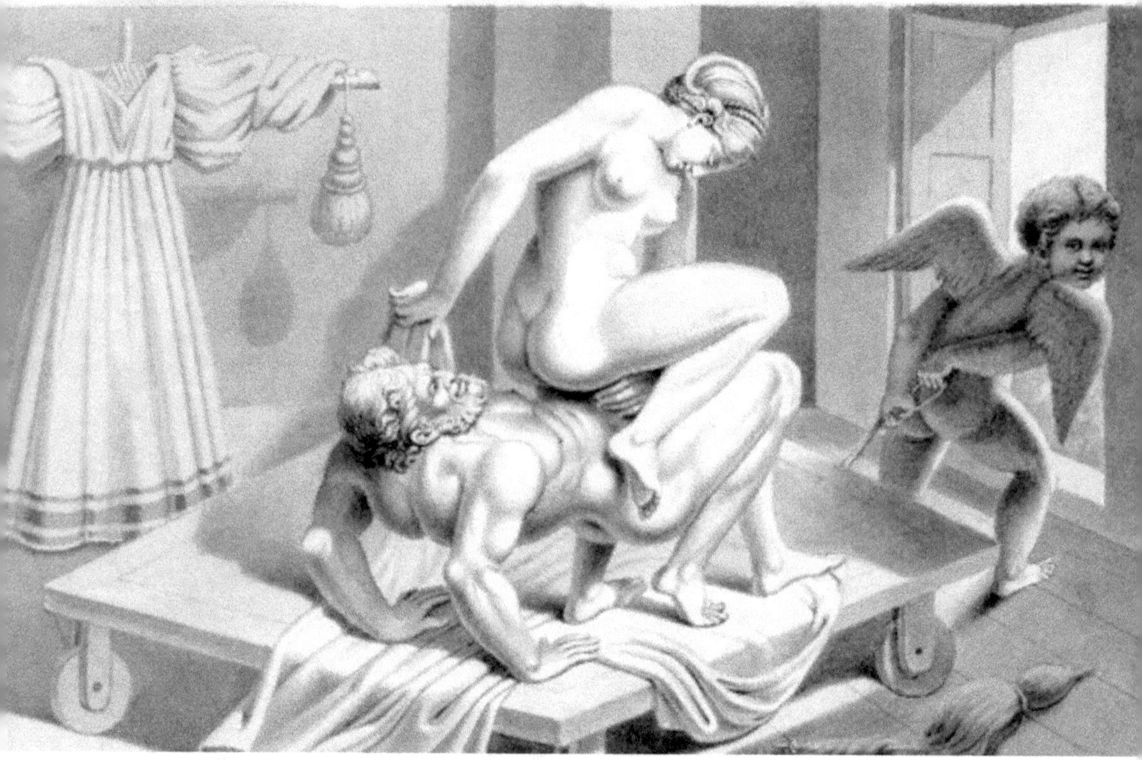

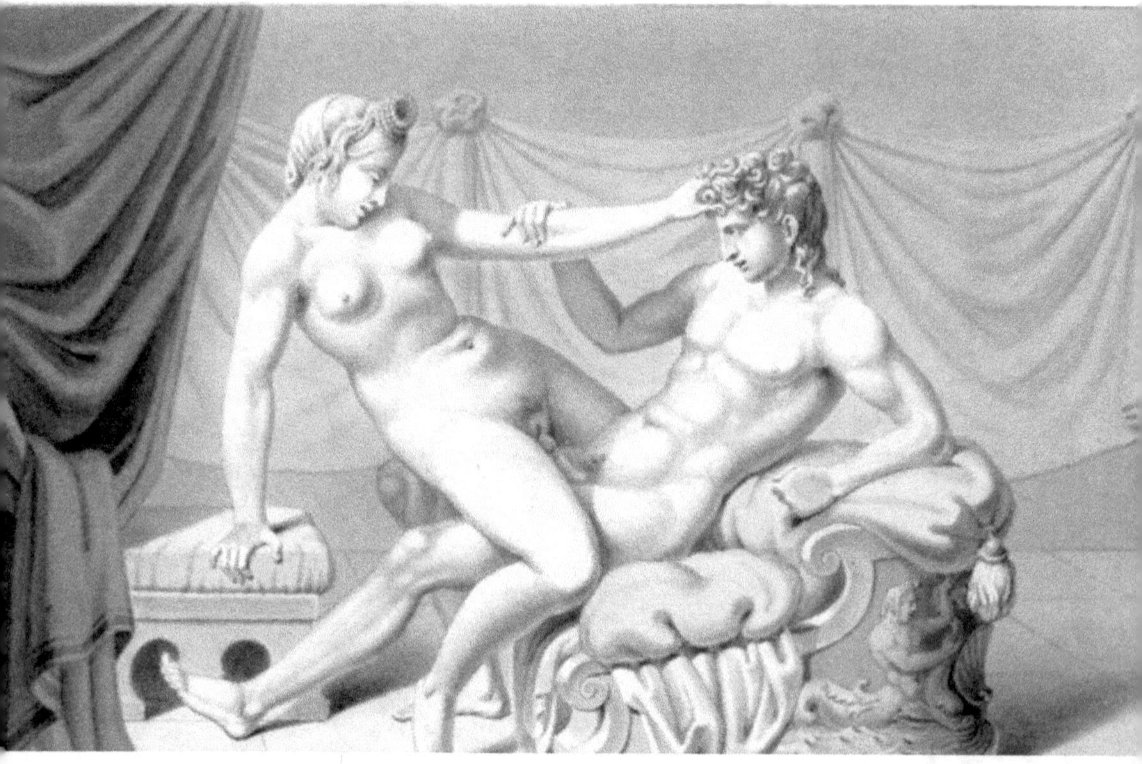

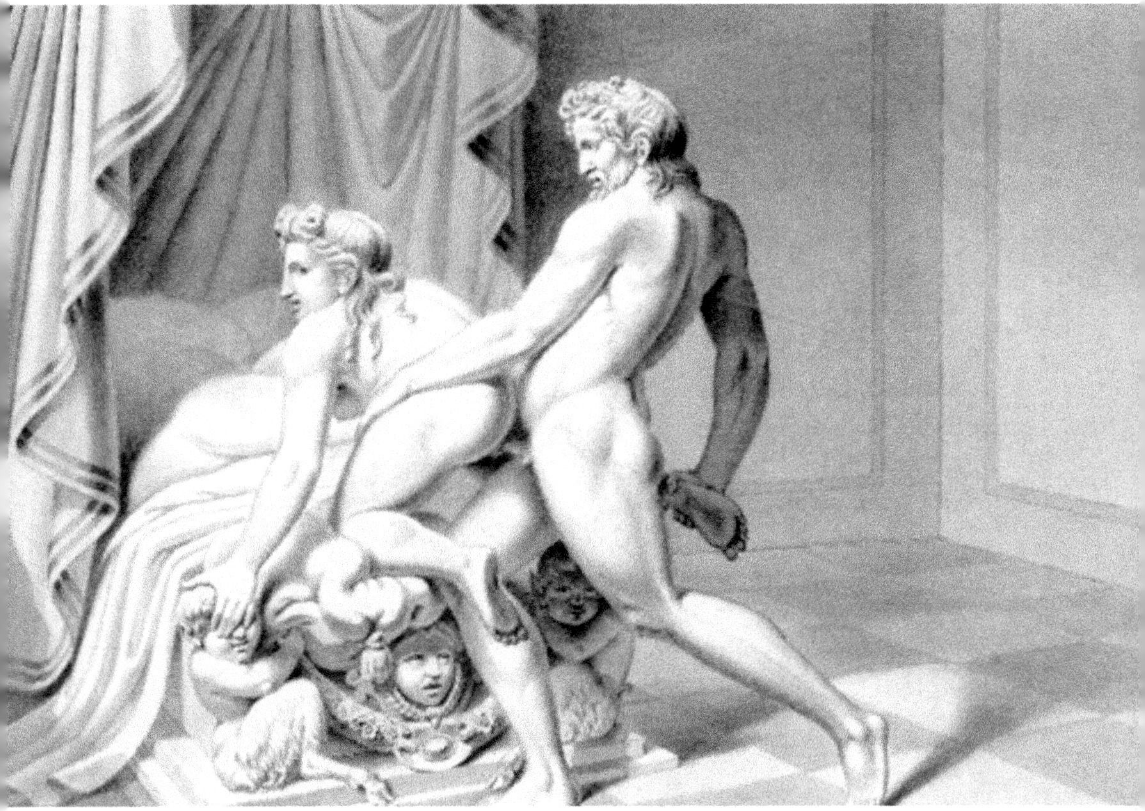

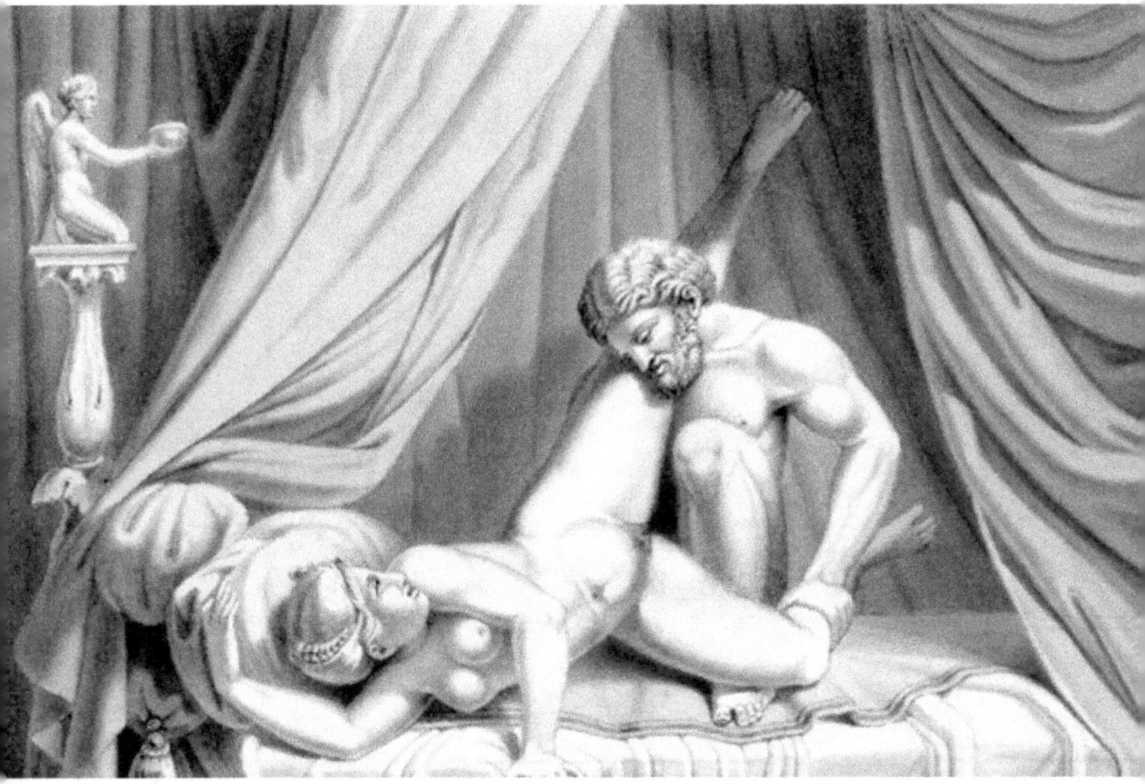

What occurs in most Western art, from Greek and Roman sculpture through the glories of the Renaissance to the latest pornography are male representations of female eroticism. Feminists say that there are no real depictions of female *jouissance* in art or literature. 'In my opinion,' wrote Marguerite Duras, 'women have never expressed themselves.'[1] What she means, perhaps, is that women have expressed themselves thus far in the terms and means and social structures defined by men. There is no 'feminine' or 'women's' writing, according to some feminists. Hélène Cixous reckons she's found only three 'inscriptions of femininity' this century: Colette, Marguerite Duras and Jean Genet.[2] In art, there are many women artists who have tackled erotic issues, but in the history of art, going back to, say, the Renaissance, the number of women artists who have survived are far fewer.

1 Duras, interview in *Signs*, Winter 1975, in E. Marks, 175.
2 H. Cixous: "The Laugh of the Medusa", *Signs*, summer 1976, in E. E. Marks, 249.

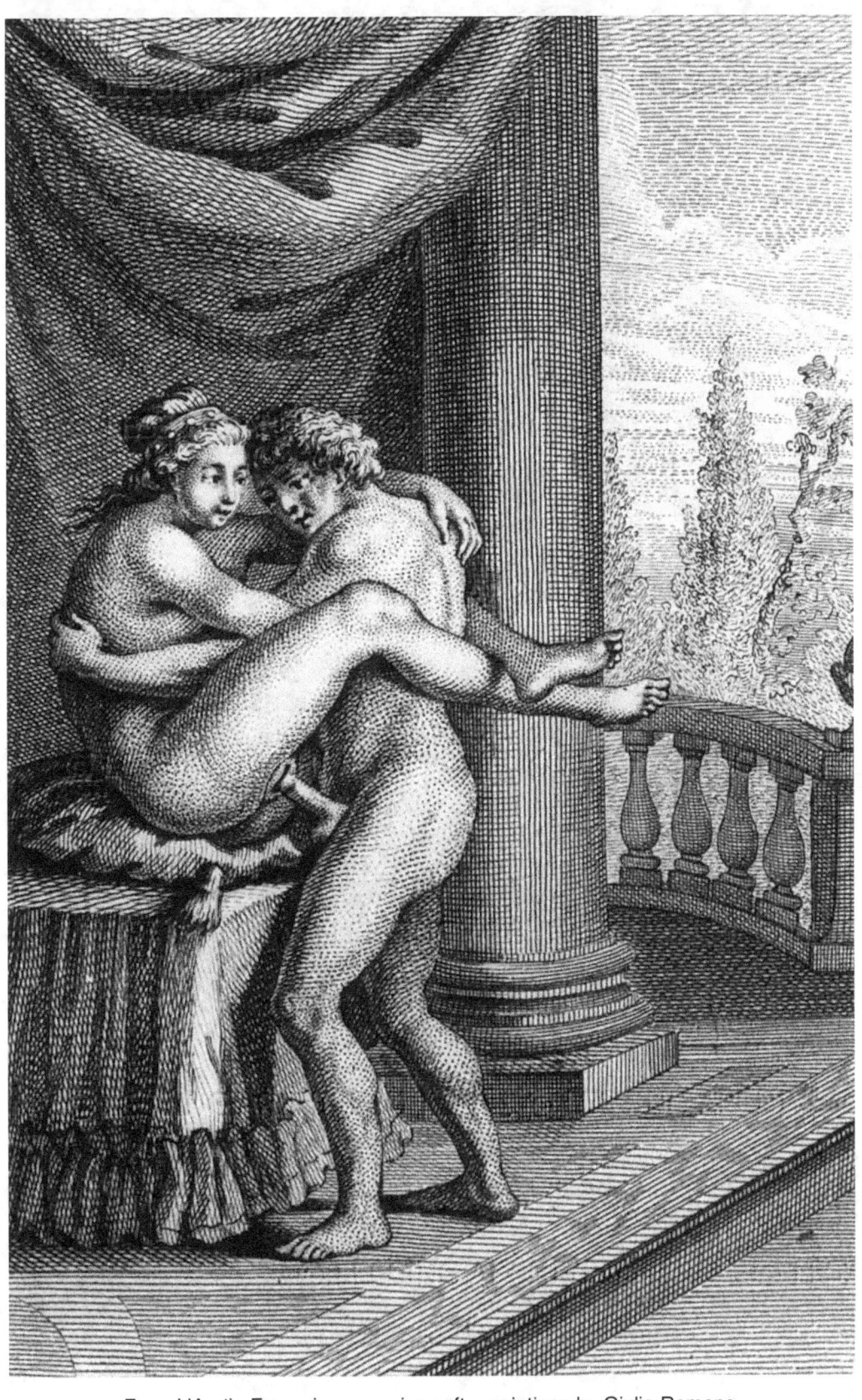

From L'Aretin Francais, engravings after paintings by Giulio Romano,
illustrating the Sonnets of Pietro Aretino
(this page and following pages)

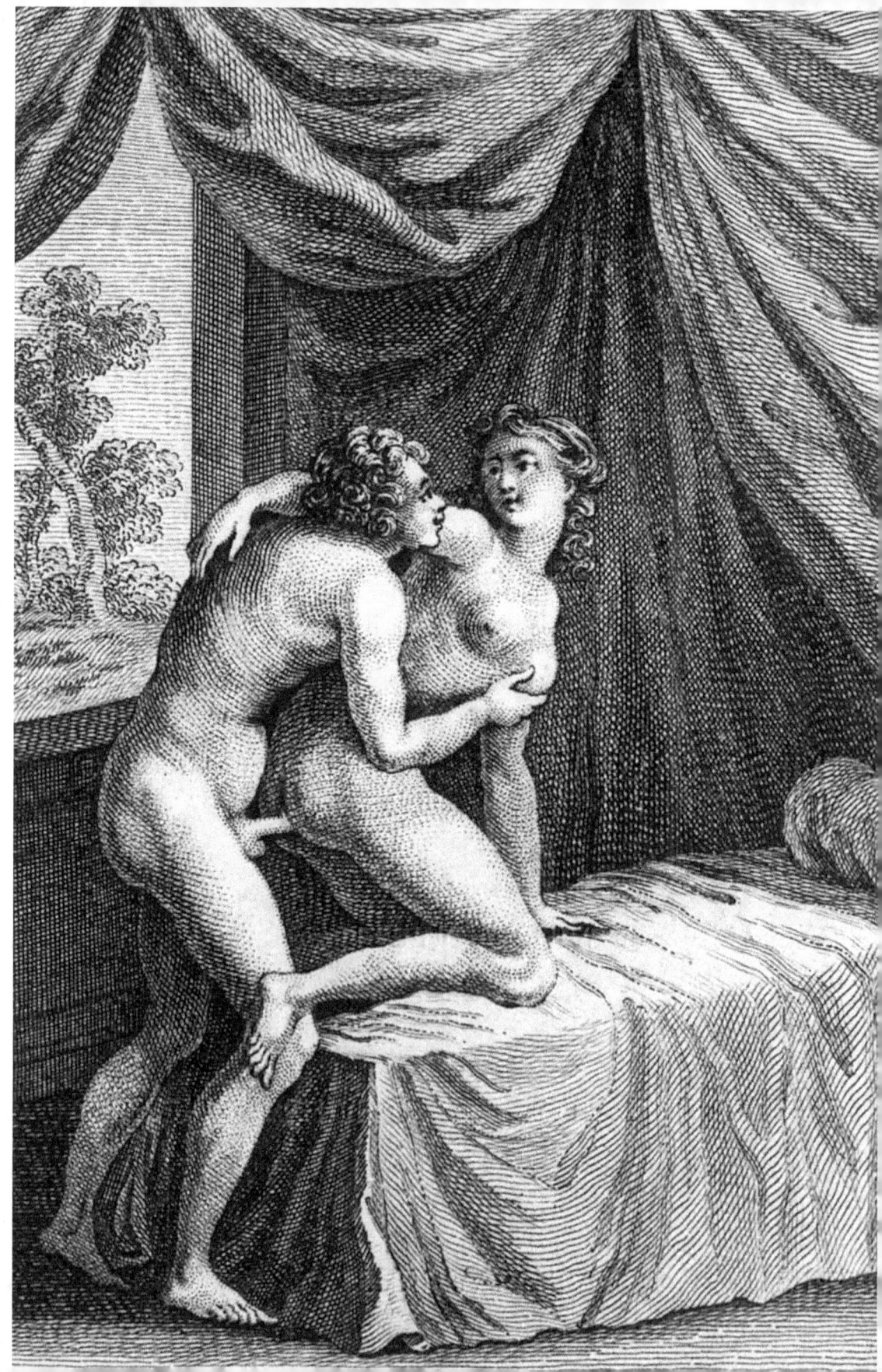

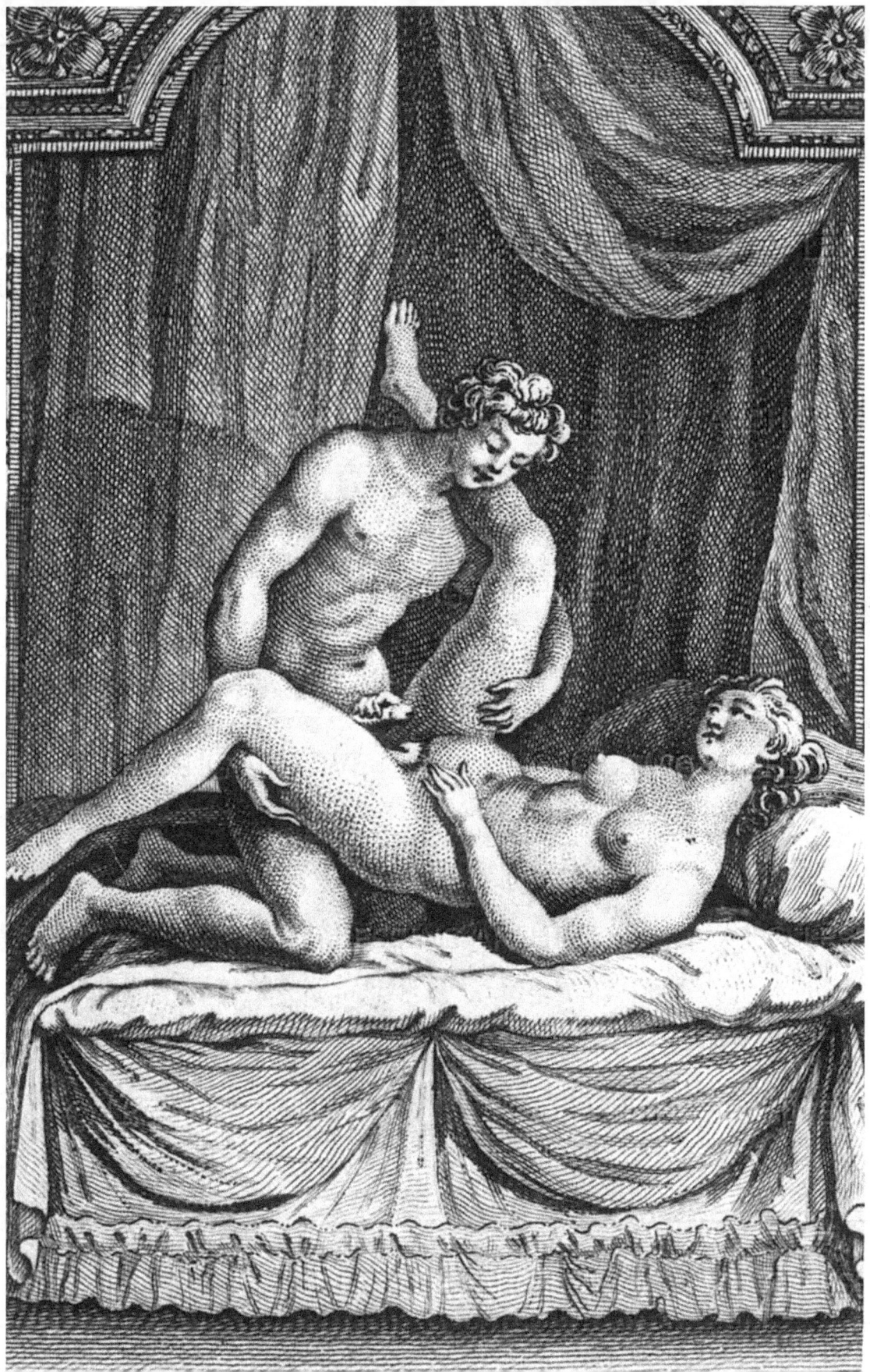

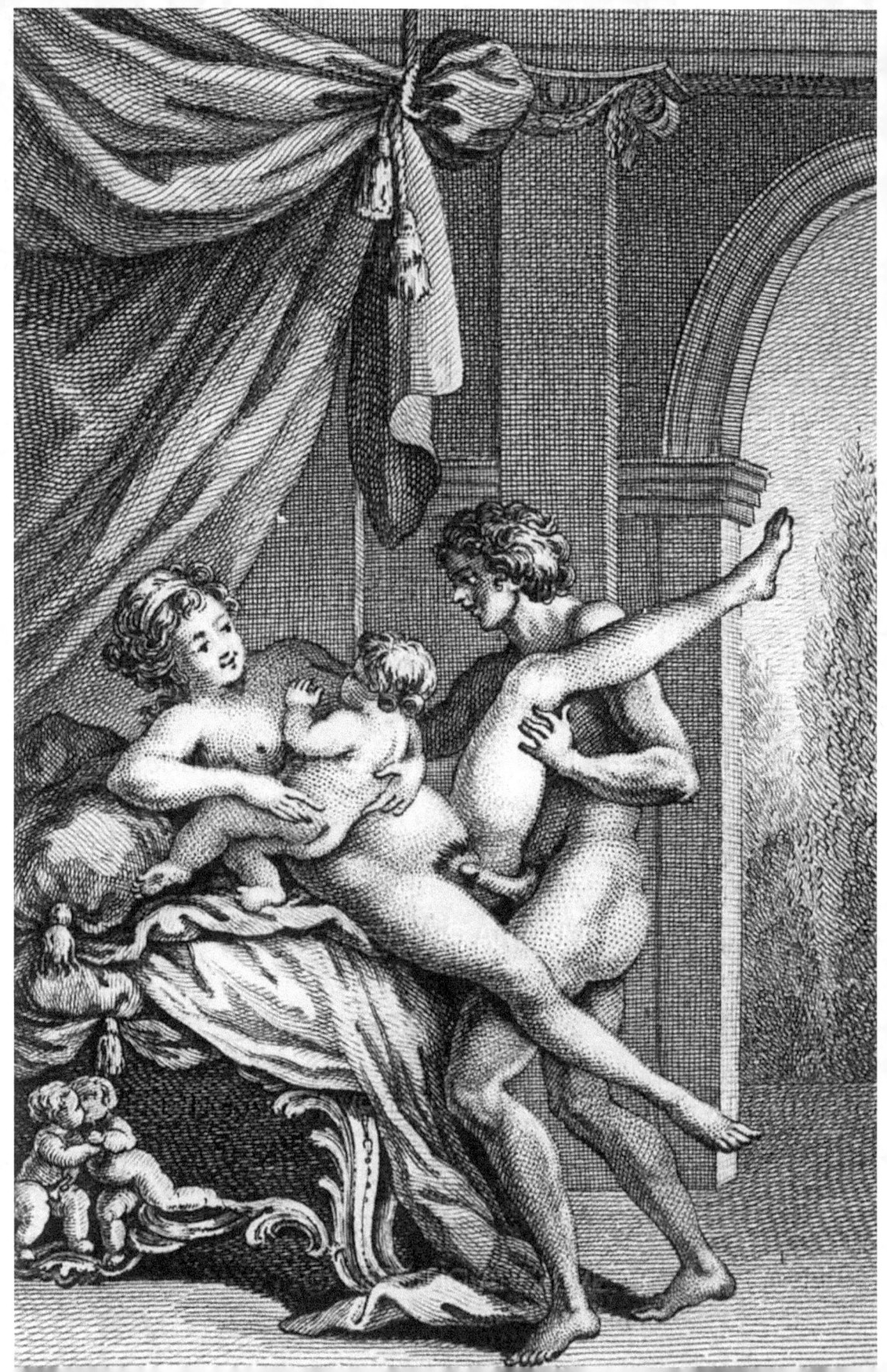

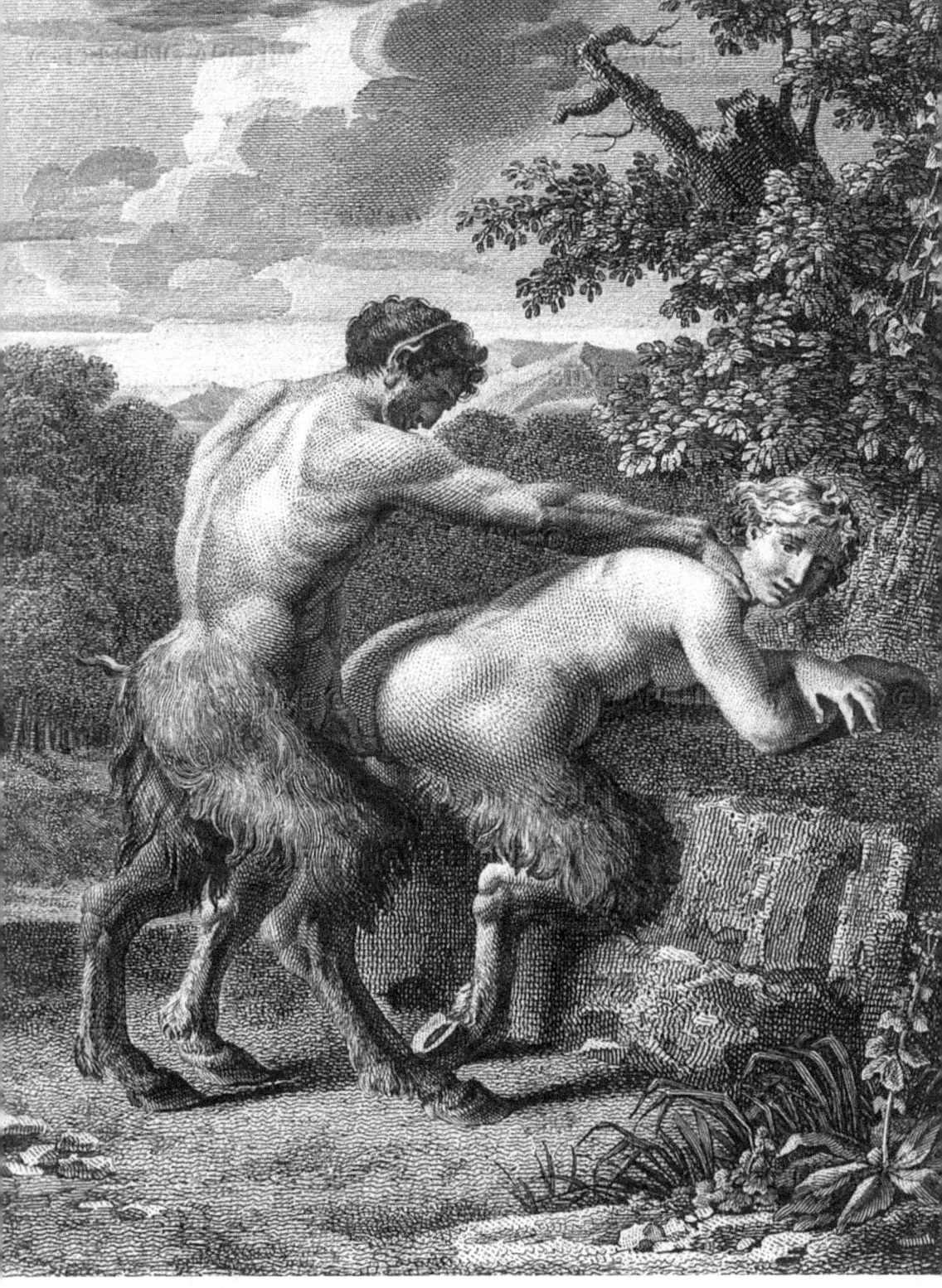

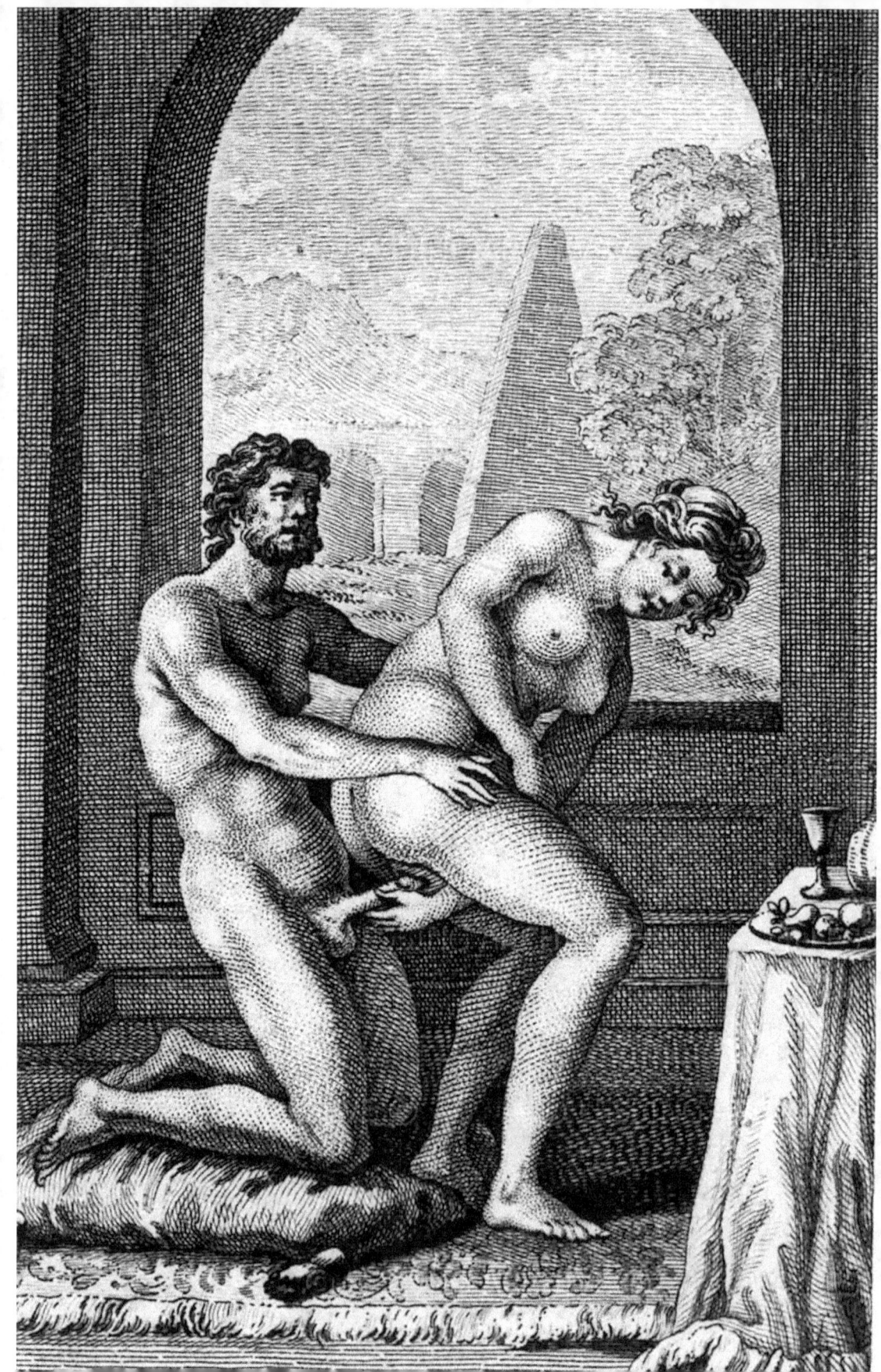

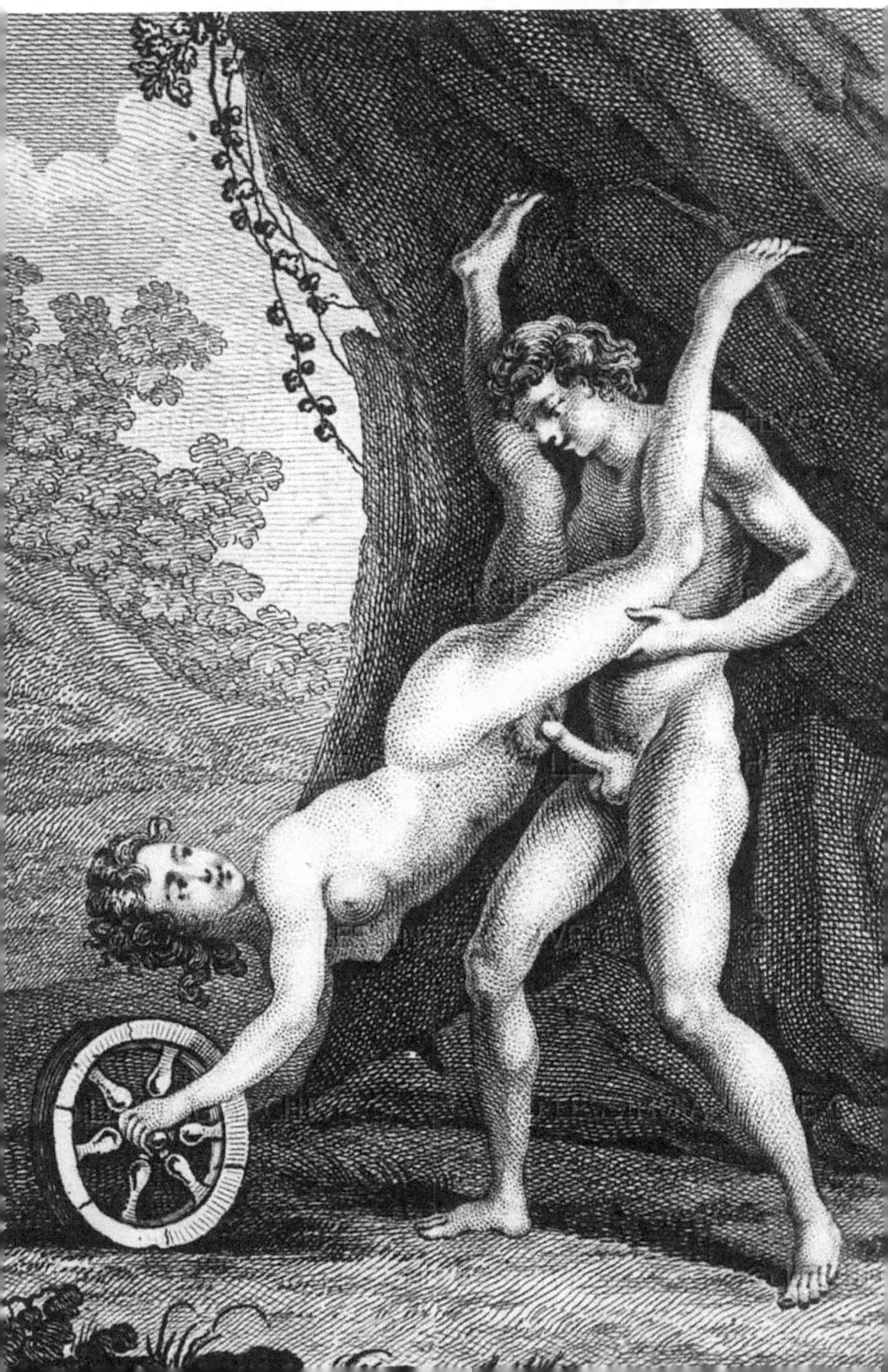

For law-abiding citizens, it seems, the 'line' has to be drawn somewhere. Somewhere between public and private, between sex and love, between visible and invisible, between freedom and control, between secrecy and publicity, between availability and censorship. Indeed, Walter Kendrick said the only definition of pornography is in terms of its forbidden or secret nature.[1]

Pornography brings the secret life of people out into the open. What the Western world holds most dear – the primacy and holiness of the individual, and the primacy and holiness of (heterosexual) love, of marriage, of the family – is cast into doubt by pornography.

Hardcore pornography, in particular, tries to make everything as clear and as visible as possible, and is thus disruptive and unsettling for the establishment. There are, thus, many close-ups of genitals in hard core pornography. Sex is ecstatic, so hard core pornography has to show this ecstasy. It does this by focussing on the genitals.

---

1 W. Kendrick: *The Secret Museum: Pornography in Modern Culture*, Viking, New York, NY, 1987.

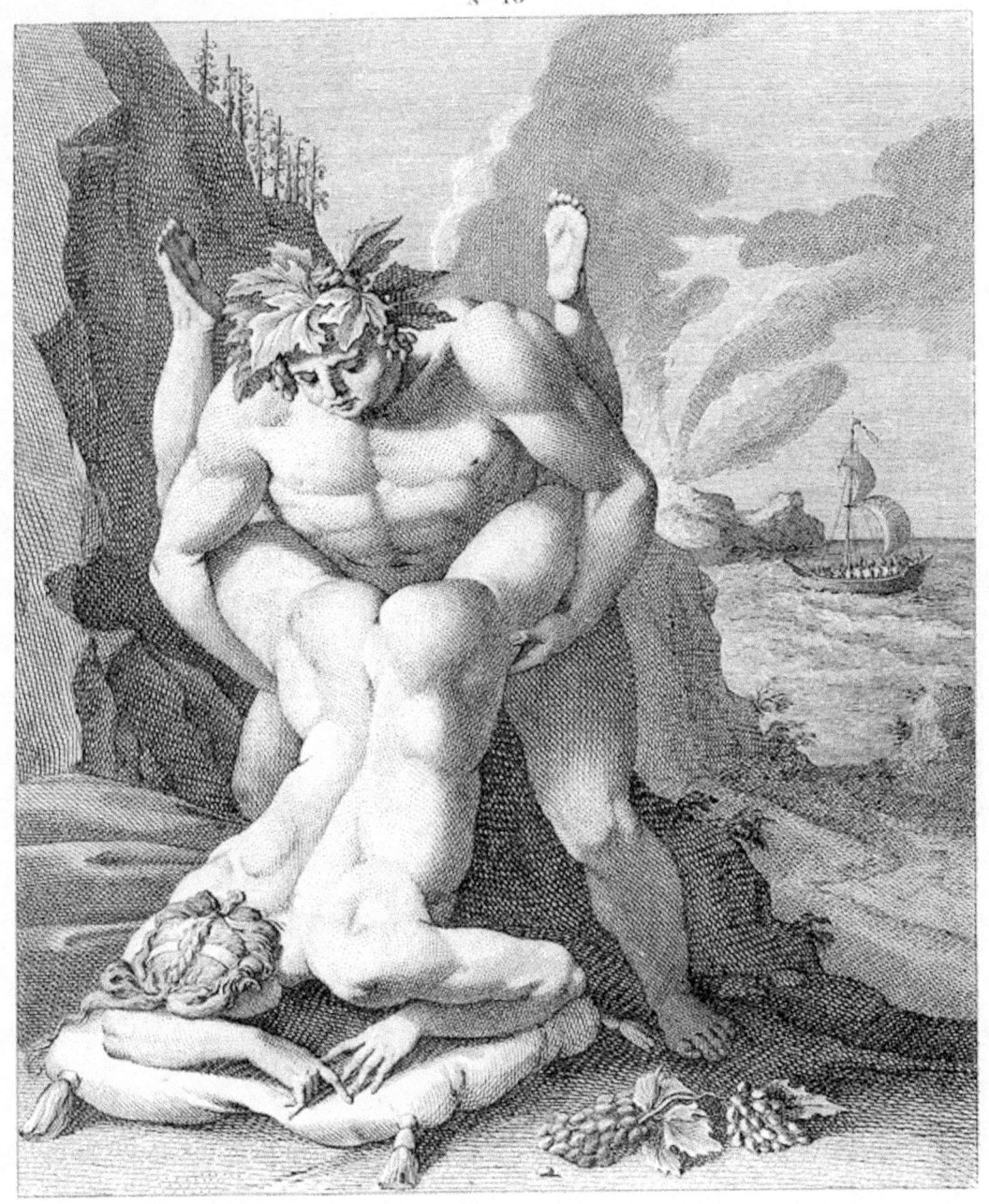

BACHUS ET ARIANE.

After Agostino Caracci, from I Modi

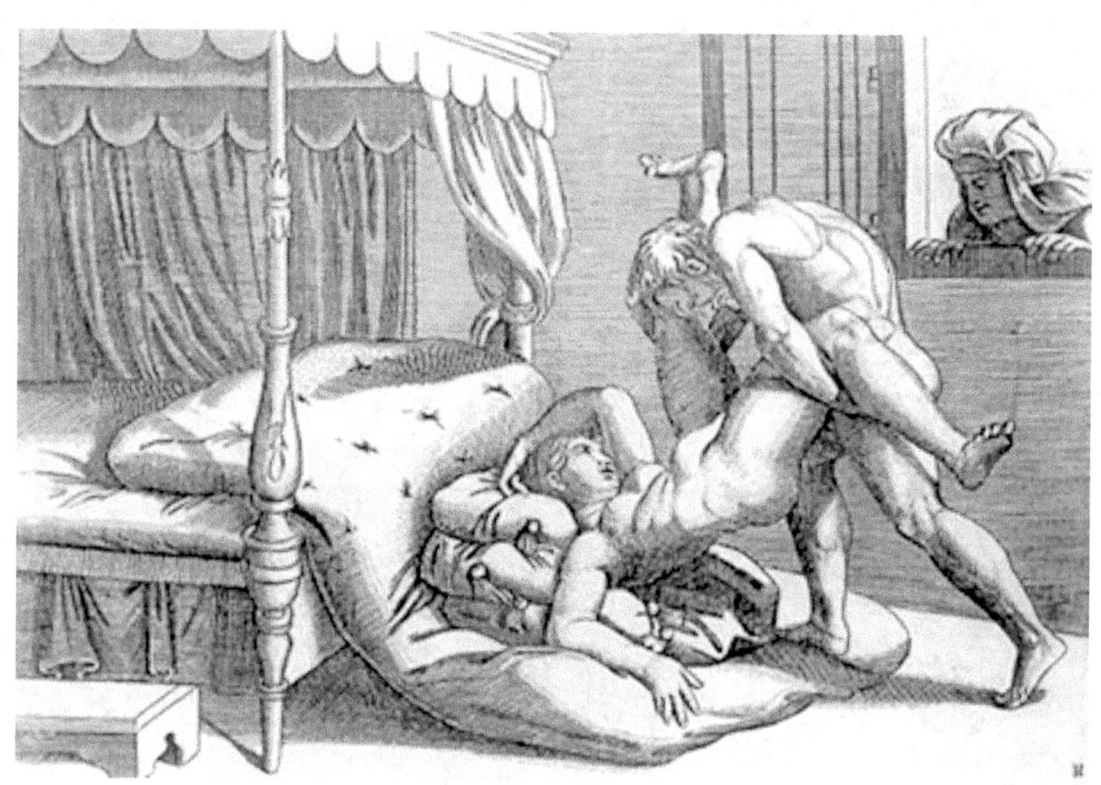

I Modi, by Pietro Aretino, illustrated by Giulio
Romano, 16th century

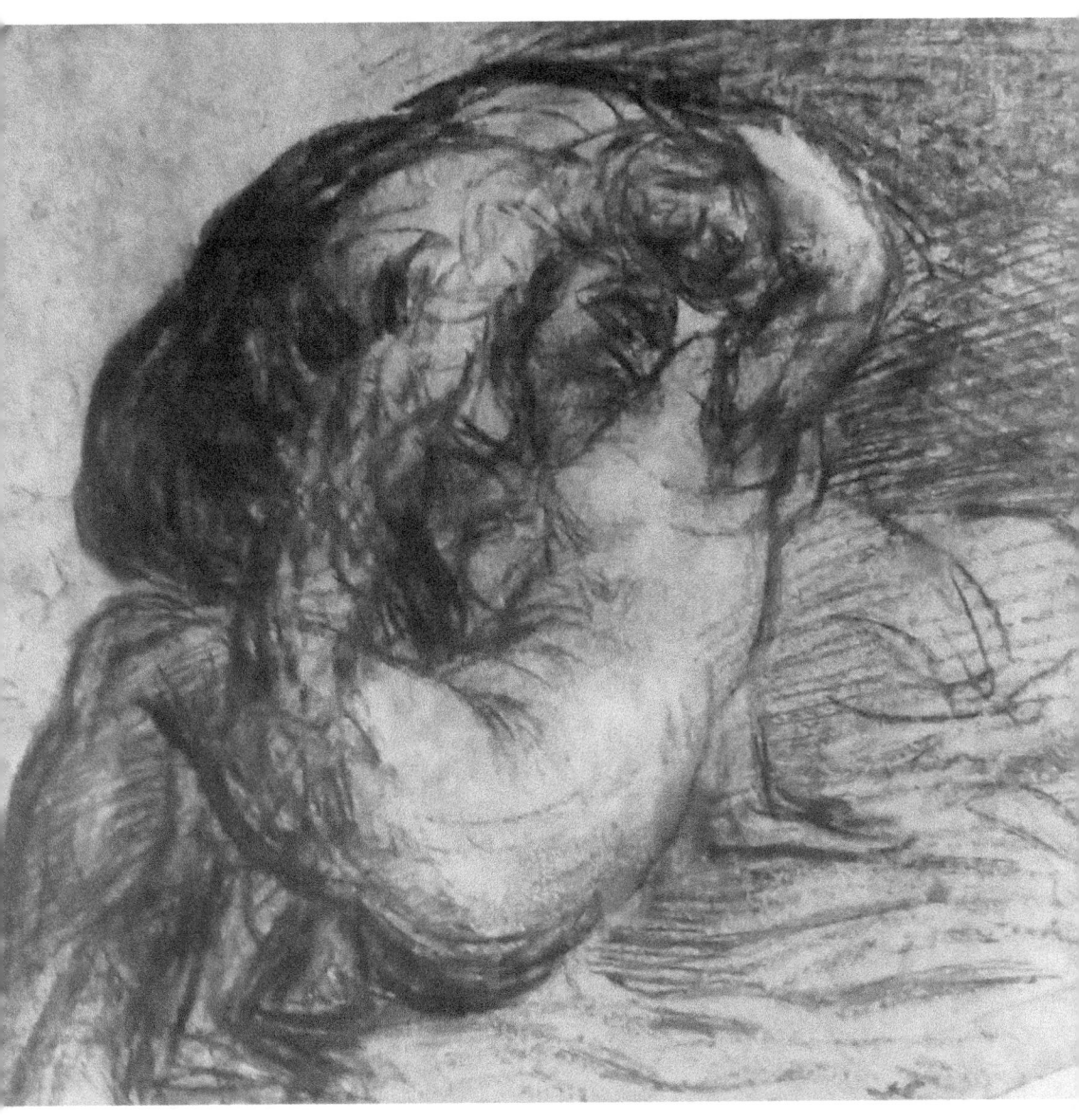

Titian, A Couple, c. 1570, Cambridge

Pornography is the culture of eroticism in the West. There is sex on TV, in fiction, in blockbuster films, in theatre, in pop music, but it is in pornography that erotic feelings are most frequently communicated. Yet pornography is commodified sex, materialist sex, sex manufactured into particular types, genres, roles and modes. There are standard pornographic encounters, standard pornographic camera angles, standard pornographic orgasms. Eroticism, as Freud knew, is powerful, whether emotionally, psychologically, culturally or politically. Pornography, then, deals with really wild eroticism by categorizing it, putting into particular genres or narratives. The visual aspect of pornography helps to deal with the wildness and passion of erotic feeling. Pornography produces images and representations, which are easier to deal with than the real thing. Jane Gallop wrote that the 'visual mode produces representations as a way of mastering what is otherwise too intense'.[1] Experiences such as orgasm and erotic desire can be too overwhelming to be communicated in words. Putting these experiences into visual representations enables them to be controlled, packaged, commodified.

---

1 J. Gallop: *The Daughter's Seduction: Feminism and Psychoanalysis*, Cornell University Press, New York, NY, 1982, 35.

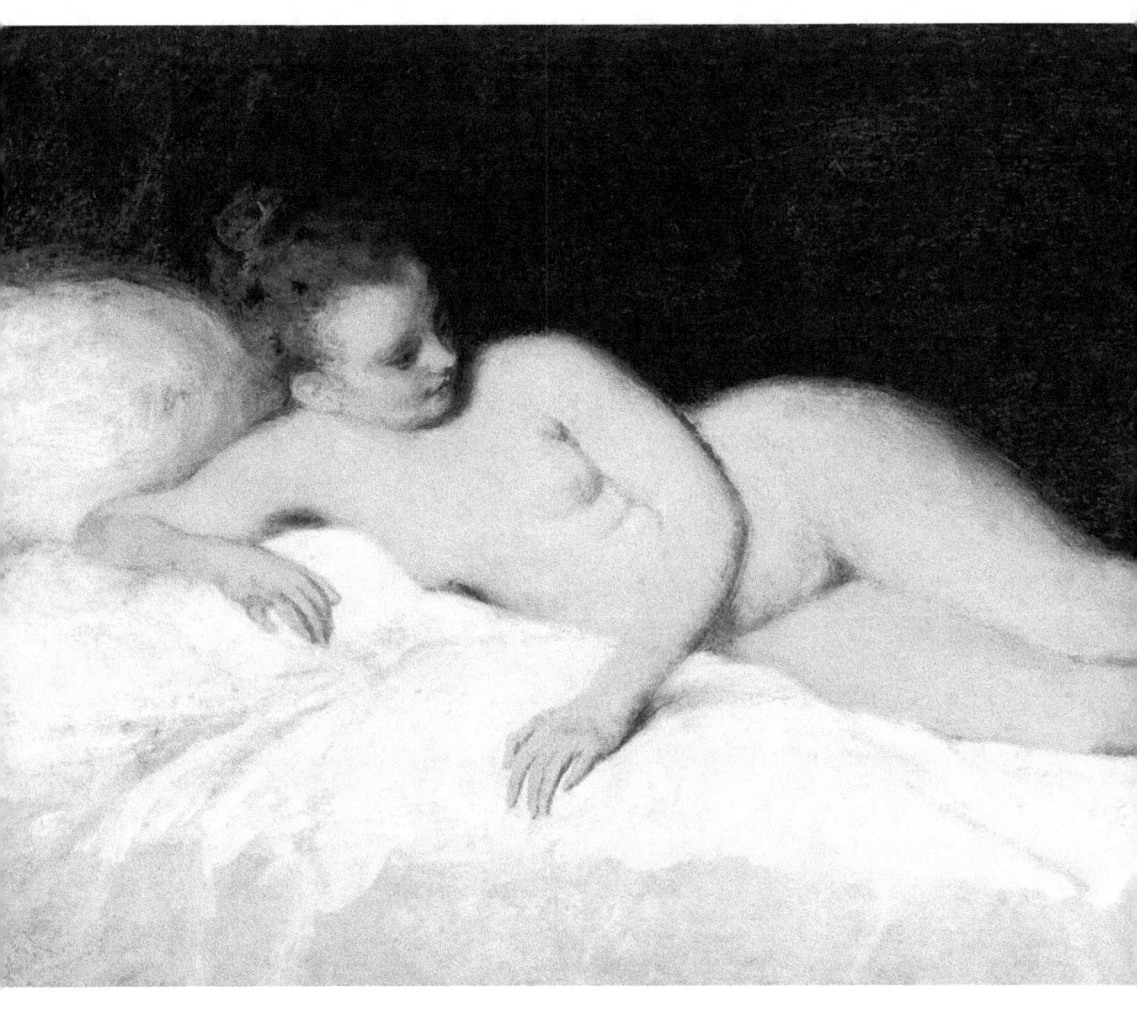

Antoine Watteau, Reclining Woman, 1713-17

Pornography is *fantasy*, as well as genre, product, system, and materialism. Pornography does not offer the consumer real people, but images, narratives, ideas, suggestions. The visual dimension of pornography helps to create certain kinds of representations of erotic feelings which the consumer can deal with, because they are communicated in recognizable forms. So now we're in an S/M narrative – masters, mistresses and slaves Or, over here we're in the narrative where a sexually frustrated male picks up a female hitchhiker. Or, here we are in the 'bored housewife' scenario: sex-starved, she humps the plumber over the washing machine. The consumer always knows where she or he is with pornography.

Pornography delivers the goods.

It delivers the goods: which's why it's bigger than the movie or pop music industries.

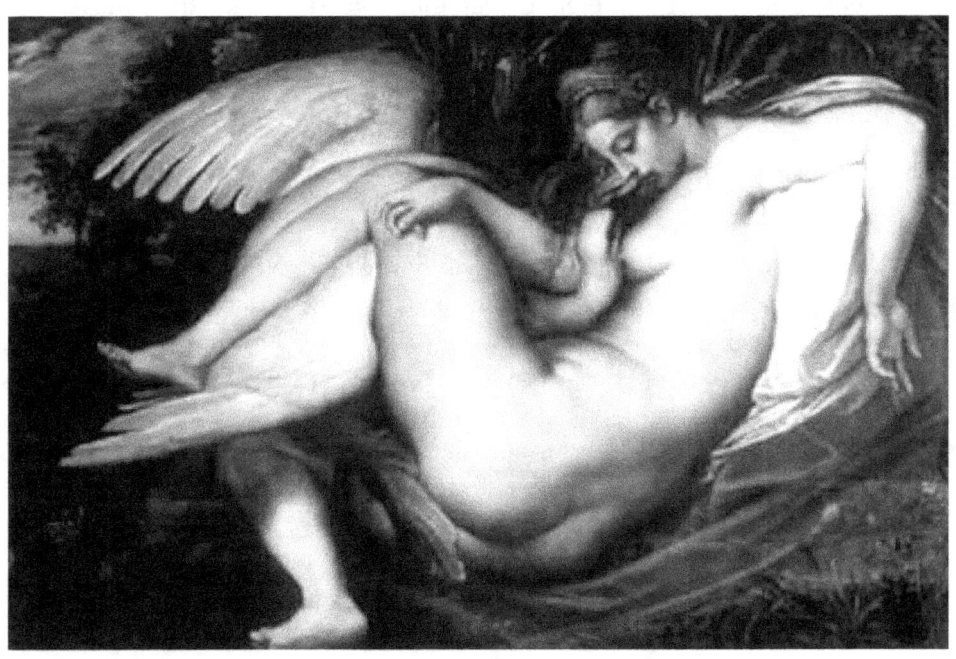

Peter Paul Rubens, Leda and the Swan

If some work is erotic – a scene on TV, a photo, a sculpture, a dance – it's because, in the opinion of some people, you don't 'see' everything. Something is hidden. The 'erotic' in art is about anticipation, waiting, yearning. It's about potential and possibility, hidden but not hidden, partially clothed. As the photographer Grace Lau, who has made many pictures of fetishism, wrote: 'I prefer images that conceal, rather than those that reveal all.'[1]

Pornography, meanwhile, has people doing it now. They undress, and start attacking each other immediately. There's nothing to get in the way, not contraception, not fear, not aversions, not menstruation, not impotence, not interruptions, not anything. In short: it's *fantasy*.

Pornography turns 'what if?' into a reality. What if somebody took their clothes off in this train carriage and started having sex? is a typical question that erotic art suggests but pornography answers. What if this woman at home turns out to be a nymphomaniac and this plumber turns out to be a superstud? What if the wedding guest who just smiled at you turns out to be the fuck of a lifetime? In pornography, people *do* rip their clothes and start mashing each other up.

Pornography presents as a normal, everyday occurrence what is hidden away, what is desired but unspoken. Pornography is the ultimate in fantasy, for in the fairy tale world of pornography, every dream comes true. And it is not only 'true', it is 'real'.

---

1 Grace Lau: "Confessions of a Complete Scopophiliac", in Gibbons, 195

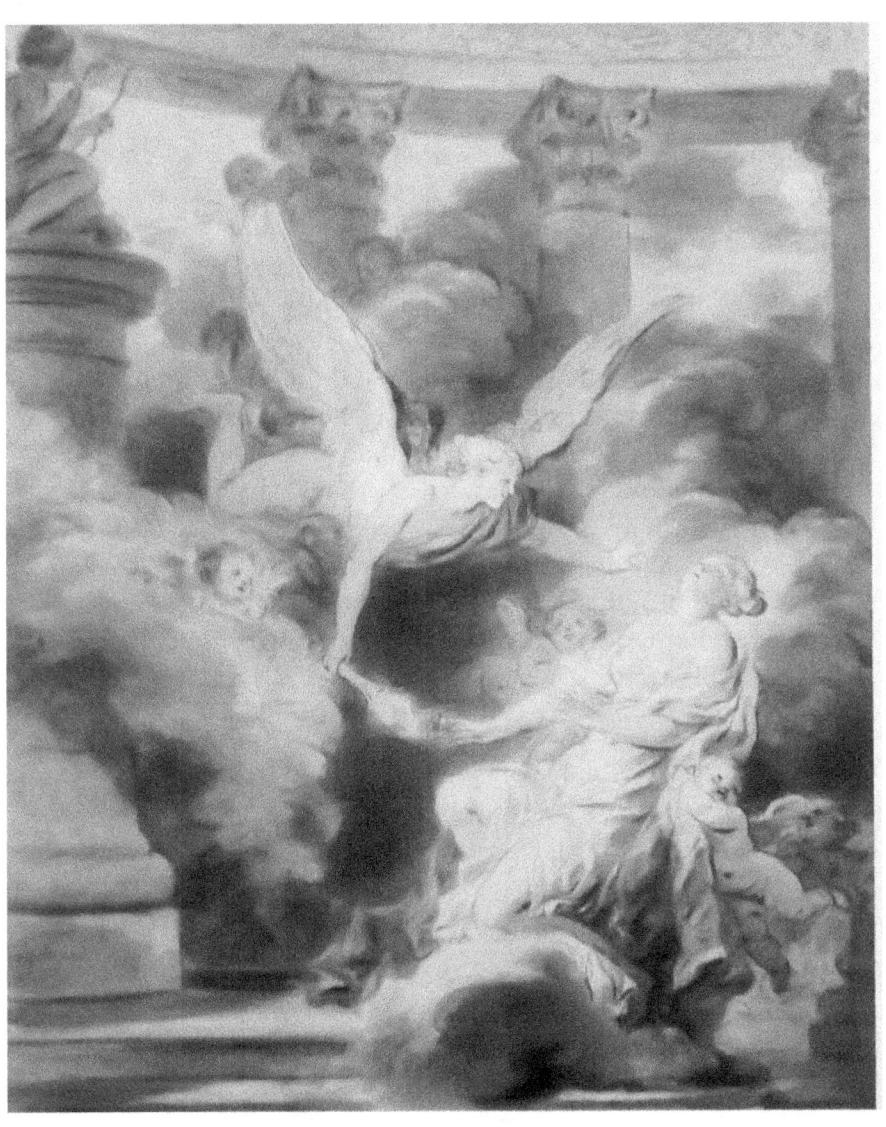

Jean-Honoré Fragonard, The Sacrifice of the Rose, c. 1780,
private collection

CENSORSHIP

One of the most contentious and fiercely debated aspects of erotic art and pornography is the issue of obscenity, taste and censorship. Throughout the history of art and pornography, different individuals or groups of people have sought to defend certain territories, whether moral, psychological, emotional, spiritual, religious, philosophical, political or ideological. There is always some line between the 'acceptable' and the 'obscene'.

The history of censorship is long and complex. In the 20th century there were many confrontations between artists and the establishment: with D.H. Lawrence's *Lady Chatterley's Lover*, with *Ulysses*, with films such as *Last Tango in Paris, Kids, Natural Born Killers, The Killing of Sister George, Performance, Trash, A Clockwork Orange* and countless others, with the *Oz* trials, with Senator Jesse Helms trying to stop NEA tax payers' money funding 'obscene' work, with reference to the photographer Robert Mapplethorpe (whose photos have created much 'controversy'),[1] with internet porn, with punk rock and gangsta rap, and so on.[2]

1 See M. Schoofs: "Robert Mapplethorpe: Exquisite Subversions", *Windy City Times*, 16 Mch, 1989; H. Kramer: "Mapplethorpe Show at the Whitney: A Big, Glossy, Offensive Exhibit", *The New York Observer*, 22 Aug, 1988; A.C. Danto: *Encounters & Reflections*, Farrar Straus Giroux, New York 1990; E. Kastor & Carla Hall: "Mapplethorpe Aftermath", *Washington Post*, 23 June 1989; T.A. Yasui: "The Mapplethorpe Bonanza", *Washington Post*, 21 Aug, 1989; P. Schjeldhal: "The Mainstreaming of Mapplethorpe: Taste and Hunger", *7 Days*, 10 Aug, 1988; R. Rooney: "The unambiguous stare of Mapplethorpe's lens", *Australian*, 25 Feb, 1986.
2 More Mapplethorpe articles: D. Dominick: "Robert Mapplethorpe's Proud Finale", *Vanity Fair*, Feb, 1989; "Robert Mapplethorpe: Aestheticizing the Perverse", *Artscribe International*, Nov/Dec 1988; J. Ribalta: "Decorative Heroism, The death of Mapplethorpe", *Lapiz*, Apl, 1989.

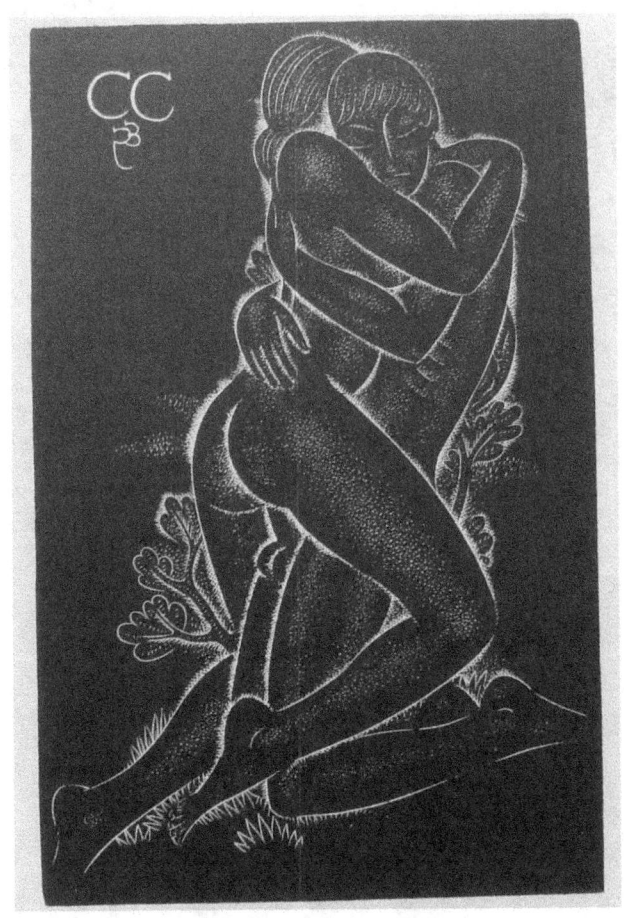

Fucking a flame into being: one of
Eric Gill's illustrations for D.H. Lawrence's book

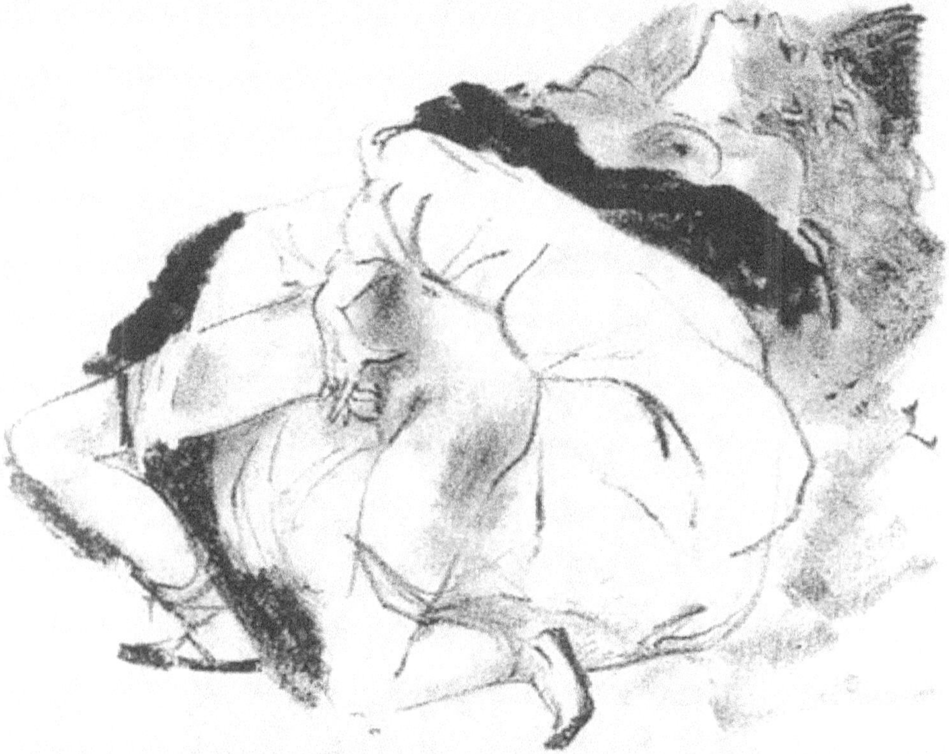

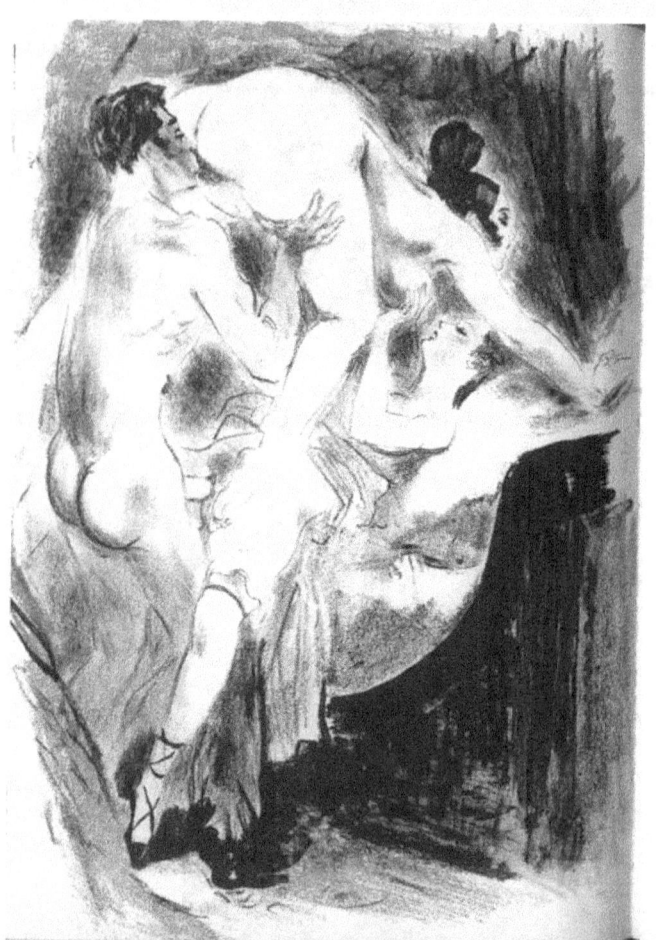

Louis-André Berthomme
Saint-André, Gamiani ou Deux Nuits
d'Excés, by Alfred de Musset

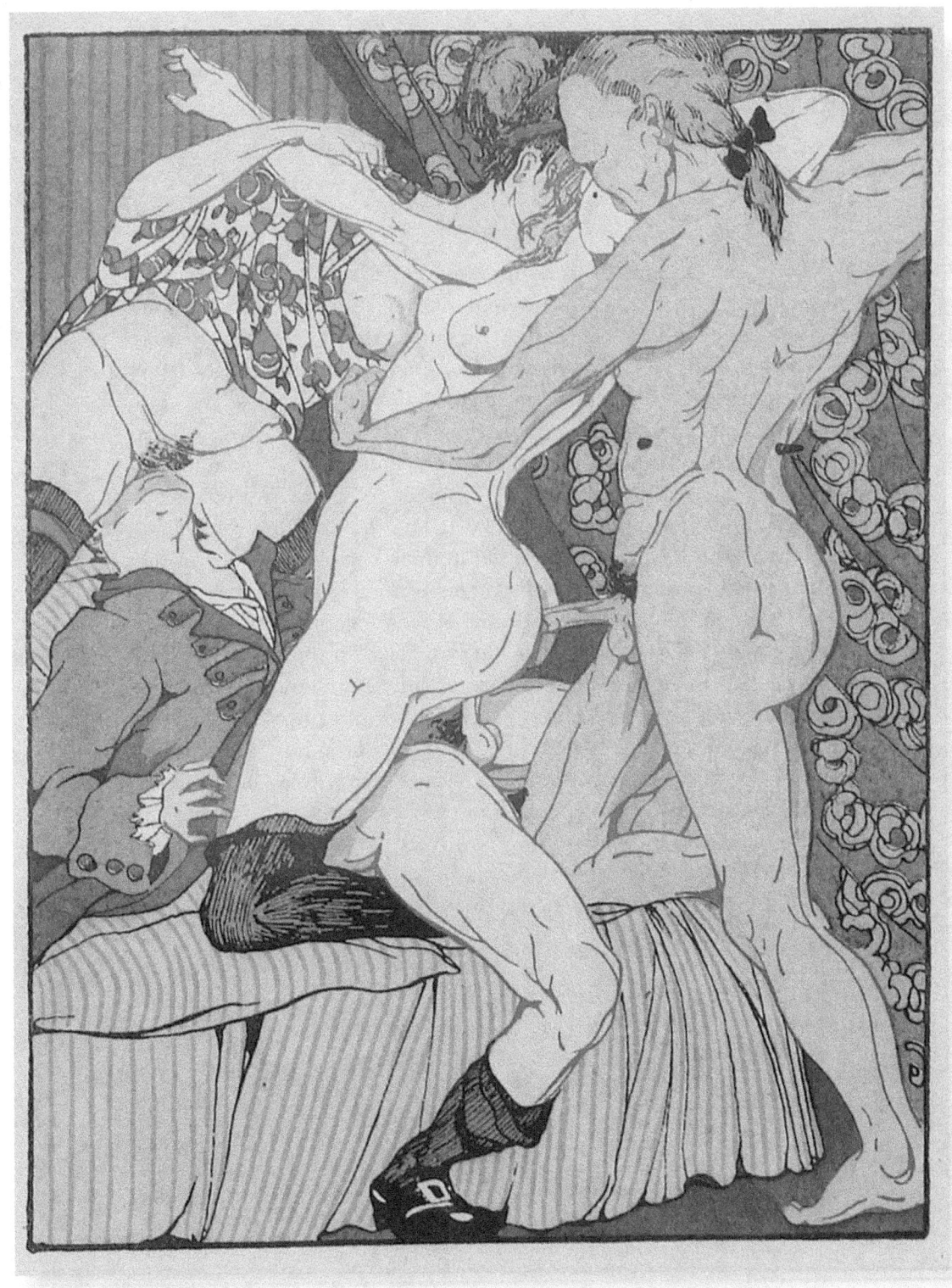

Illustration for the Marquis de Sade,
Le Bordel de Venise, 1921,
by Couperyn (a.k.a. George A. Drains), Paris

CENSORSHIP

The many debates concerning several Obscene Publications Acts and bills, the First Amendment of the American constitution, different regulatory groups, pressure groups, media organizations, publishers, and all manner of intellectuals and artists, have been intense, complex, protracted, and often a shambles. The confusions and ambiguities are at the centre of Western society. Pornography debates produce, very quickly, all manner of confusions and hypocrisies, of a moral, religious, psychological, social and ideological nature.[1] For some, though, the censorship debate is 'in fact, a little internal quibble between sections of the bourgeois community' (according to Suzanne Kappeler).

Pornography goes to the heart of what people hold dear: their identities, their feelings, their philosophical, spiritual and political views, their view of the 'quality of life'. Pornography unsettles these notions and structures. The fervour and uncertainty of the many attempts at legislation and policing show how problematic pornography is. In a case of recent years, five 'homosexual sadomasochists' were convicted in 1990 of inflicting 'injuries on each another's genitals during ritual sex' which involved 'cutting each other's genitals with surgical scalpels, sandpapering scrotums and pushing hooks into penises'. Their appeal was rejected by the courts.[2]

1 See *Art in America*, May 1990; C.H. Rolph: *The Trial of Lady Chatterley*, Penguin, London, 1961; G. Robertson: *Obscenity: an Account of Censorship Laws and Their Enforcements in England and Wales*, Weidenfeld & Nicolson, London, 1979; *The Attorney General's Commission on Pornography – the Meese Commission – Final Report*, US Government Printing Office, Washington DC, 1986; L. Lederer, ed, op. cit.
2 I. MacKinnon: "Lords reject appeals by sado-masochists", *The Independent*, 12 Mch, 1993.

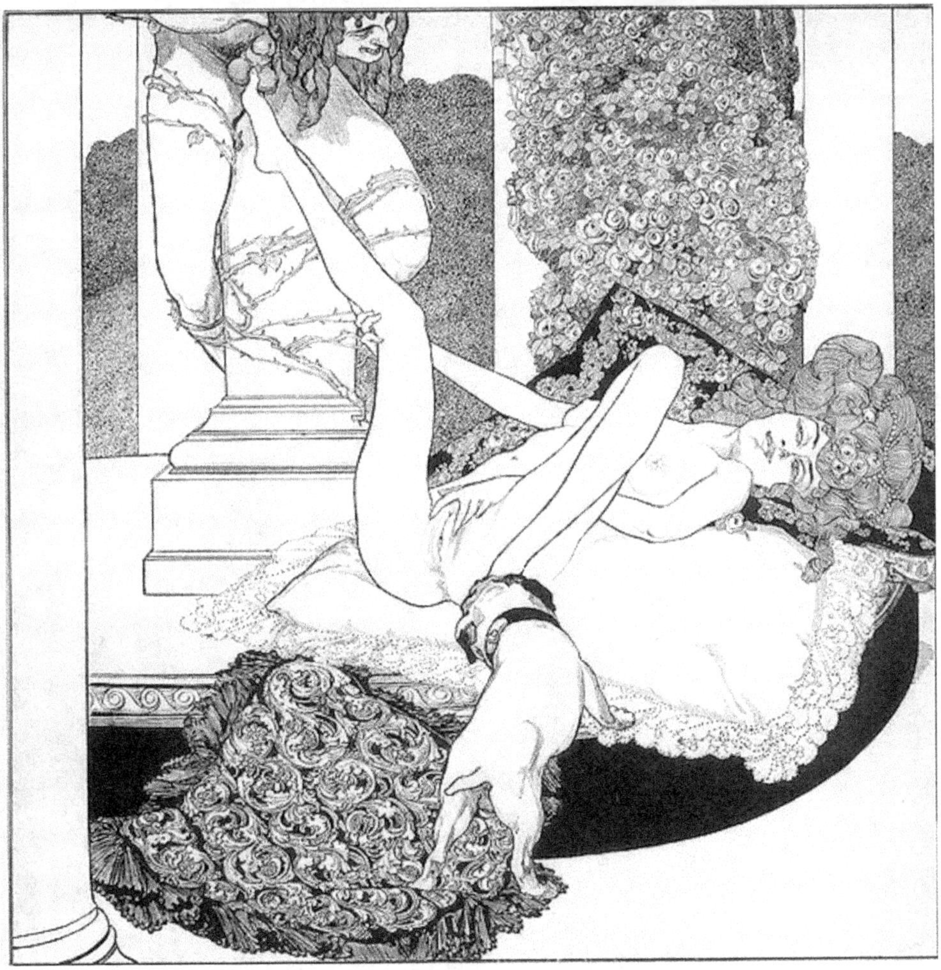

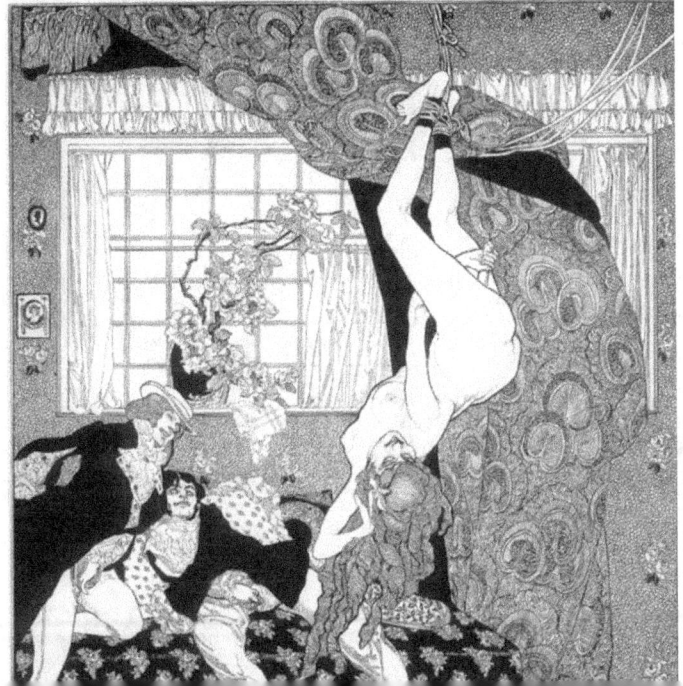

Franz von Bayros (1866-1924),
Der Toilettentisch, Tantalus, 1908

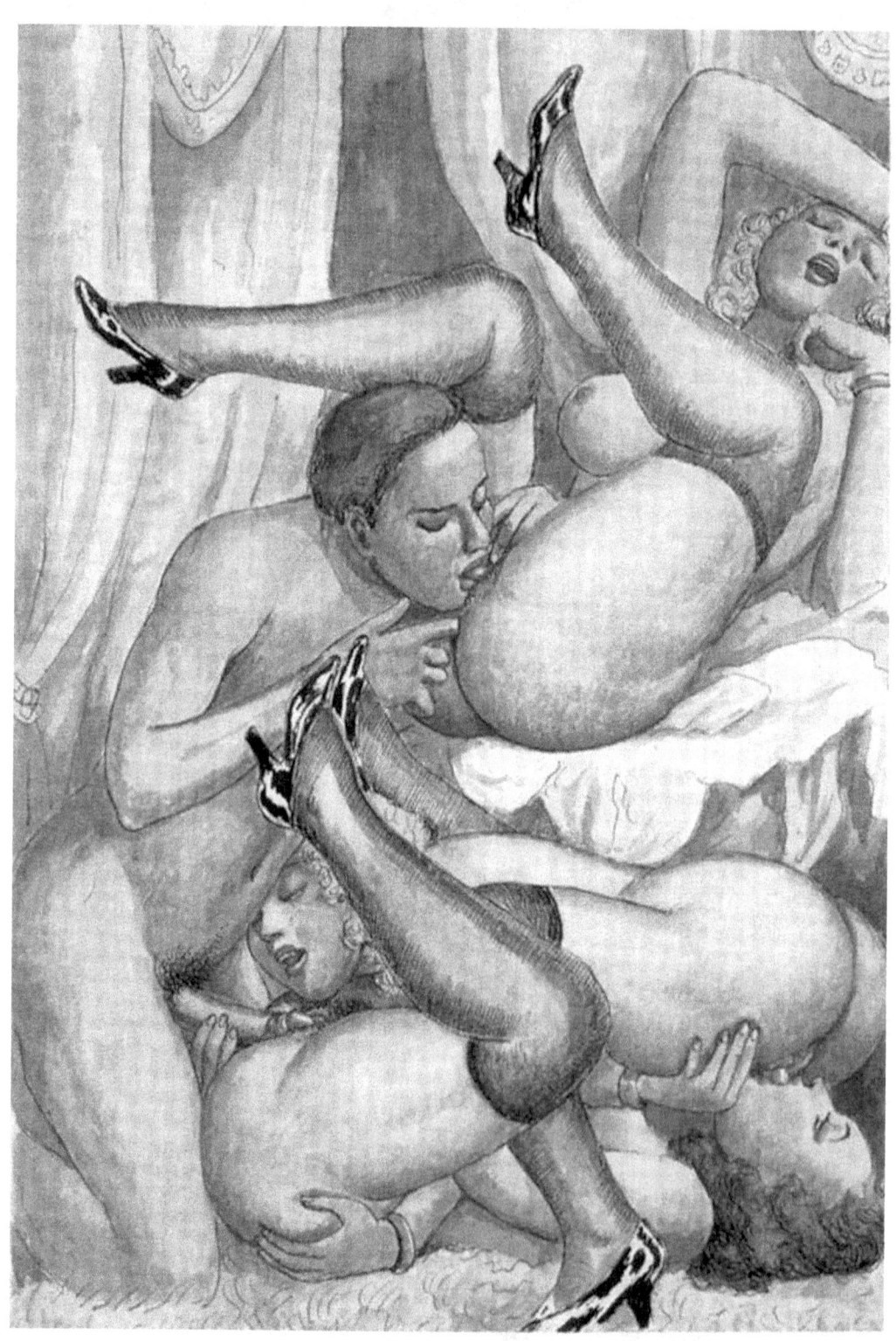

Anonymous, early 20th century

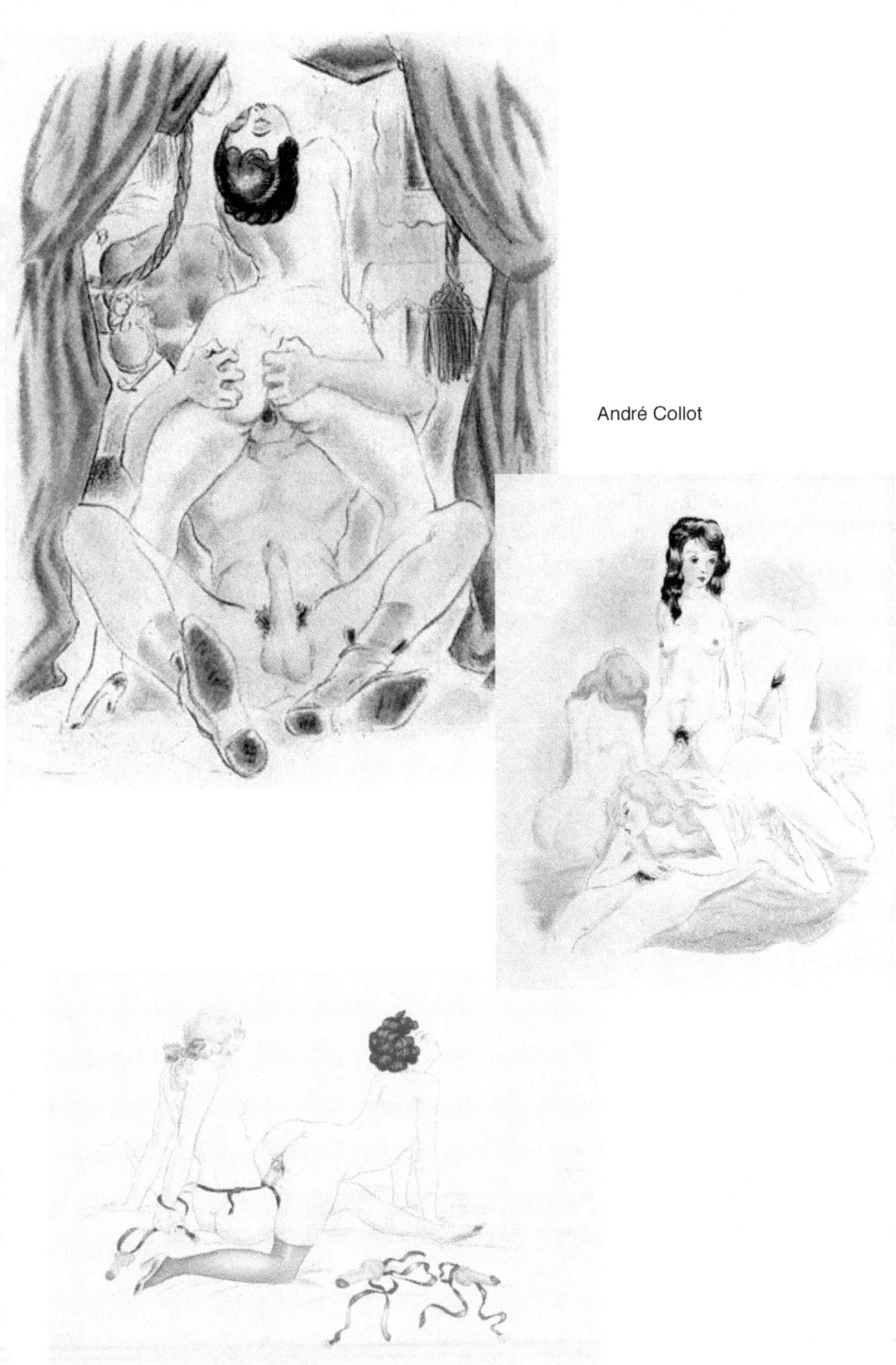

André Collot

FEMALE ORGASM

The female orgasm is 'anatomically invisible', as far as erotica is concerned. So the history of erotica and porn, for some commentators, 'is the history of visual strategies to overcome the anatomical invisibility of the female orgasm'.[1] In erotica, female orgasm is regarded with confusion and ambivalence. What actually is it? eroticists ask, what does it feel like? (Note that most eroticists throughout history have been men, forever excluded from directly experiencing the female orgasm). Thus the controversy over clitoral and vaginal orgasm, over female 'ejaculation', over 'multiple' orgasms. Female 'ejaculation' is 'visible evidence' of orgasm, yet it is censored by pornographers themselves at times.[2]

1 L. Nead, 98; see also L. Williams, 1990.
2 See S. Bell: "Feminist Ejaculations", in Arthur and Marilouise Kroker, eds: *The Hysterical Male: New Feminist Theory*, St Martin's Press, New York, 155-169; also C. Straayer: "The Seduction of Boundaries: Feminist Fluidity in Annie Sprinkle's Art/Education/Sex", in P. Gibson, ed, 168f

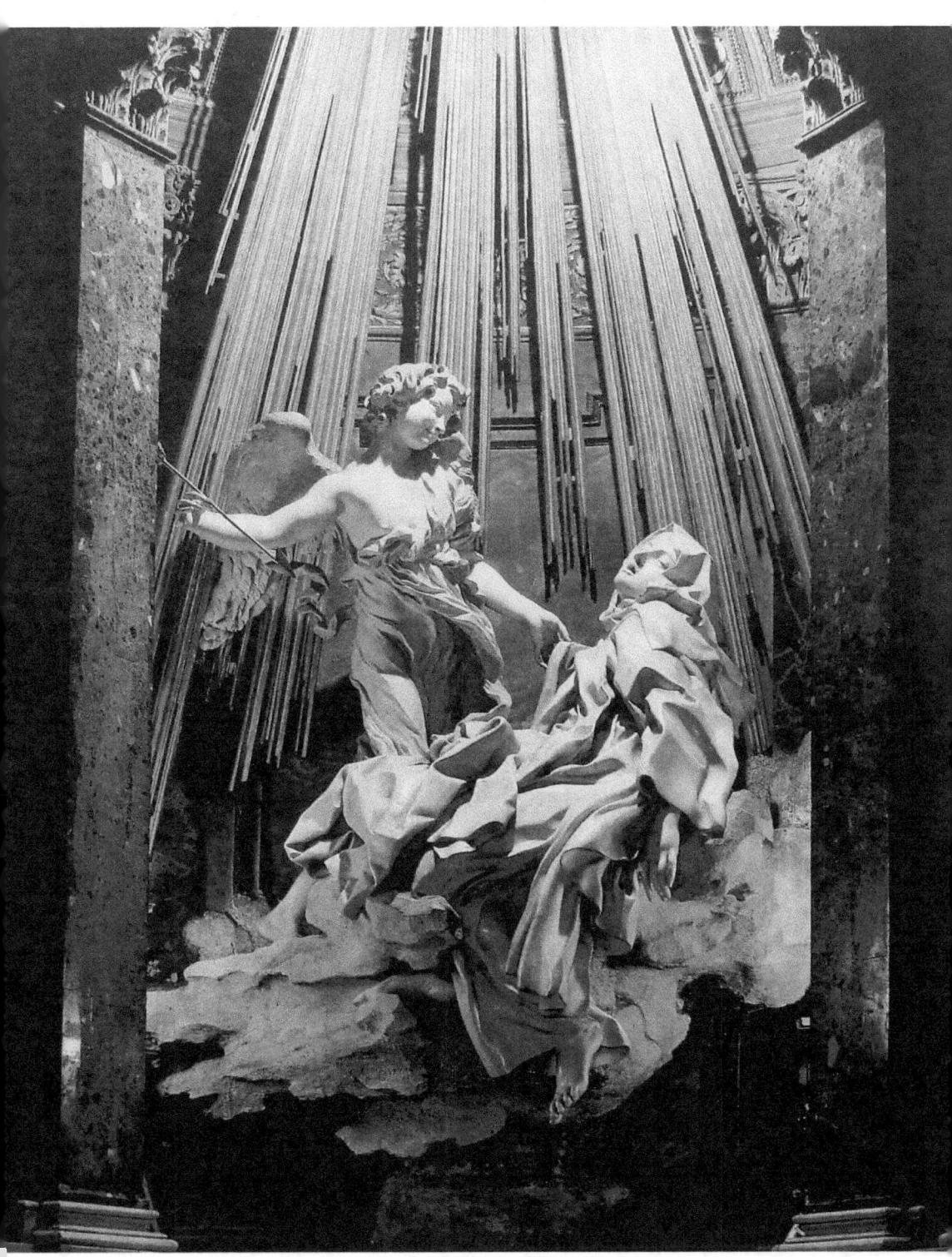

Gianlorenzo Bernini, The Ecstasy of St Theresa, 1652, Rome

ORGASM

Sexuality is not what you *are*, but what you *do*. It is not *who* is fucking *whom*, but *how*.[1] The question is *how is this fucking being done?* Never *why*, always *how*.

For patriarchal people, of either or any sex, it seems it is essential to know *who* is speaking about sex. Is the author male or female (or some other gender)? What is her/ his sexual identity? Patriarchal people are disturbed when their expectations of gender are disrupted. When, say, a male author writes of lesbian sexuality as if from the 'inside', as if in the 'character' of a lesbian. For example, who is the speaker and who is the subject of this poem:

> First, I want to make
> kiss you…
> I want to make you come
> in my mouth like a storm.[2]

It seems the speaker (Marilyn Hacker) is female and she is describing lesbian sex. But the words could just as apply hetero-sexual or homosexual eroticism. Only when parts of the body are mentioned – clitoris, nipples, penis, breasts – is it possible to decipher the gender of speaker, text or subject, and sometimes not even then.

---

1 see Valerie Traub, in V. Wayne, 83
2 Marilyn Hacker: 'Noces', from *Love, Death and the Changing of the Seasons*, Arbor House 1986

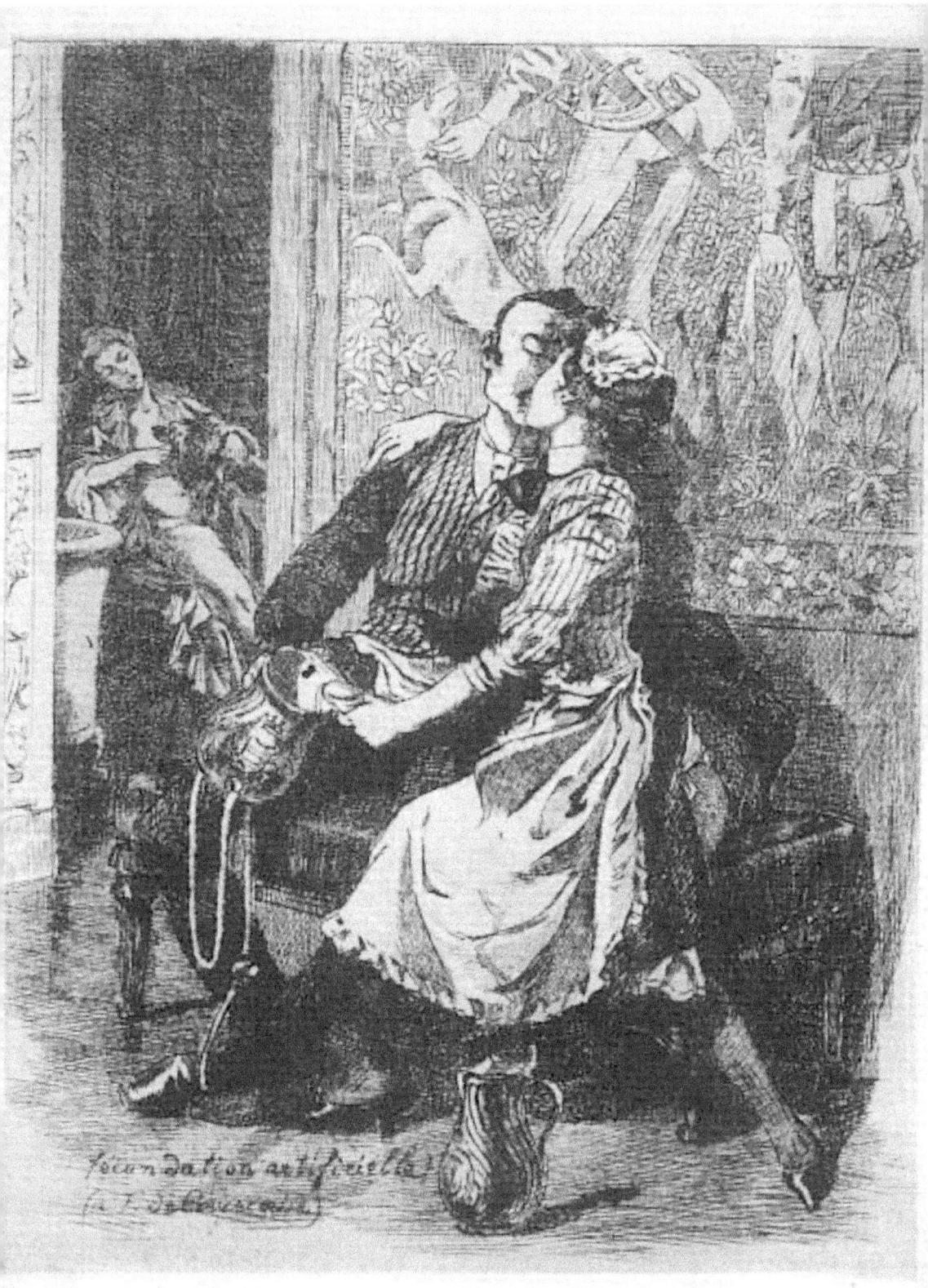

Martin van Maele

THE PHALLUS

In pornography, the great signifier is the phallus, while the site of pleasure is the woman's body. Reclining on a million couches in artists' studios, the female nude offers itself up as a country to be colonized. It is both a pleasure machine and a fantasy. The orchestrator of pleasure in this pornographic scenario is that little slip of flesh, the penis. The phallus is good, whole, true, unifying, as opposed to the bad, fragmented, impure, chaotic vagina.[1] The phallus is the emblem of male power, as many commentators, not only feminists, note: '[t]he supreme power is the power that prevails over mortality', and this power is 'reasonably equated with the phallus'.[2] For feminists, the West is a phallic/ phallocentric/ phallogocentric society, where the phallus, the sublime signifier, the most censored image in the West, is the beginning and the end of sexual pleasure. For Madeleine Gagnon, the phallus is an emblem of male narcissism:

> The phallus... represents repressive capitalist ownership, the exploiting bourgeois... The phallus means everything sets itself up as a mirror. Everything that erects itself as perfection.[3]

1 See T. Moi: *Sexual/Textual Politics*, 66f; S.M. Gilbert & S. Gubar: *The Madwoman in the Attic: The Woman Writer and the Nineteenth Century Literary Imagination*, Yale University Press, New Haven, CT, 1979.
2 L. Steinberg: *The Sexuality of Christ in Renaissance Art and in Modern Oblivion*, Pantheon, New York, 1984, 90.
3 M. Gagnon: "Corps I", *La venue à l'écriture*, UGE, 10/18, Paris 1977; in E. Marks, 180.

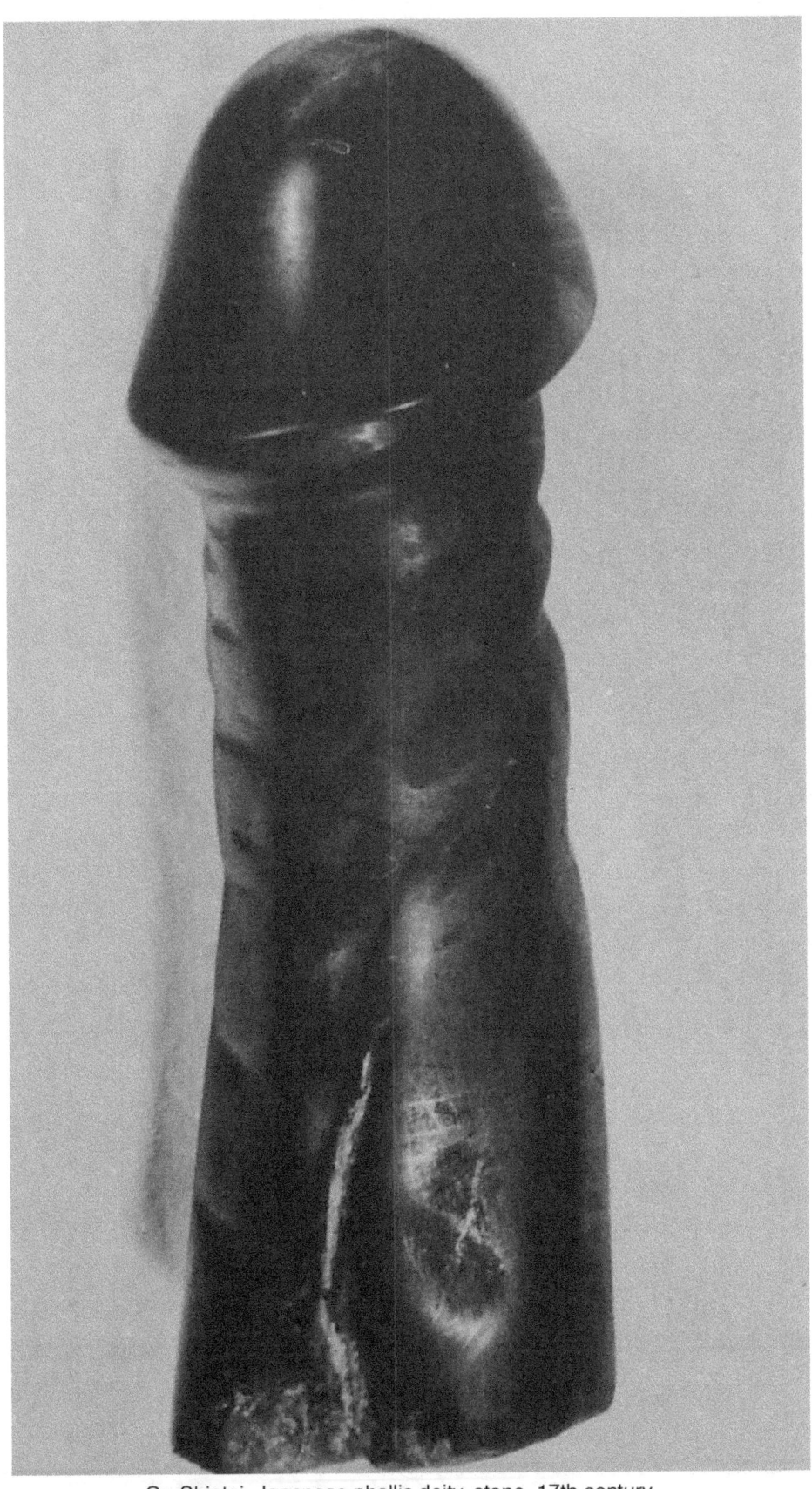

Go-Shintai, Japanese phallic deity, stone, 17th century

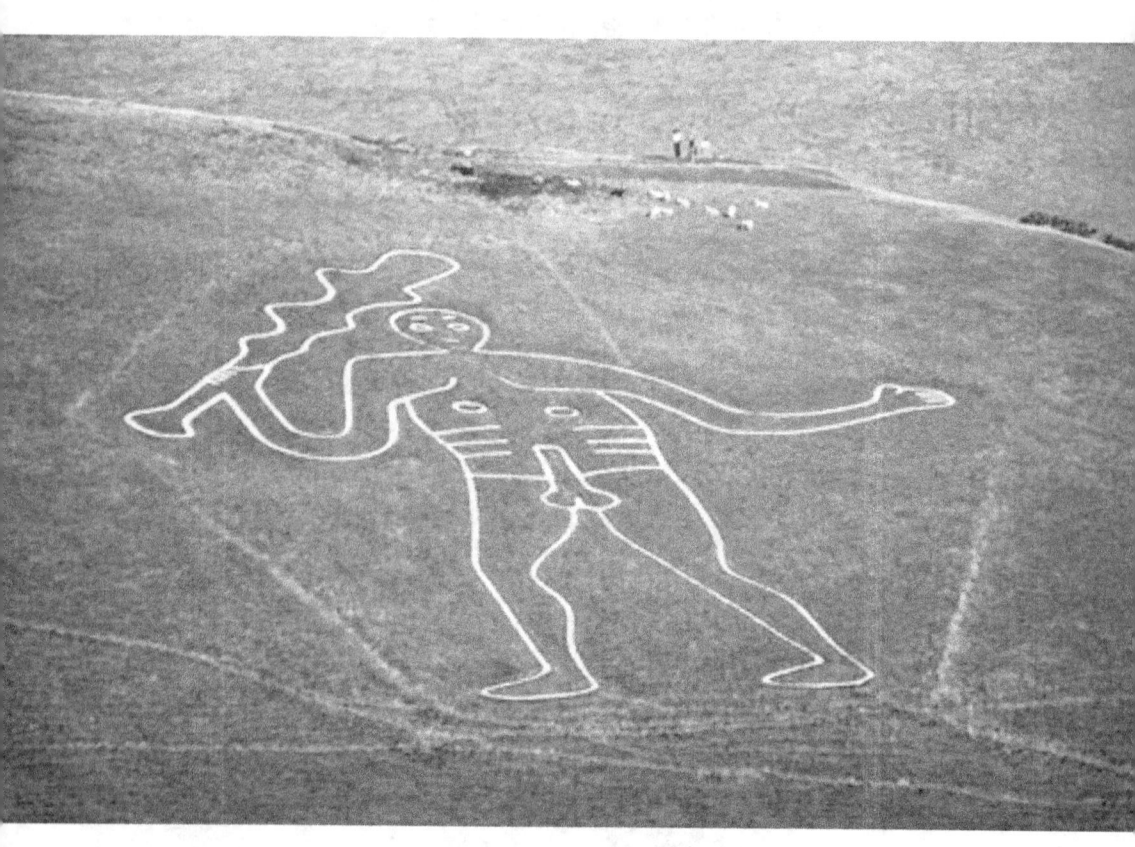

Cerne Giant, Dorset, England

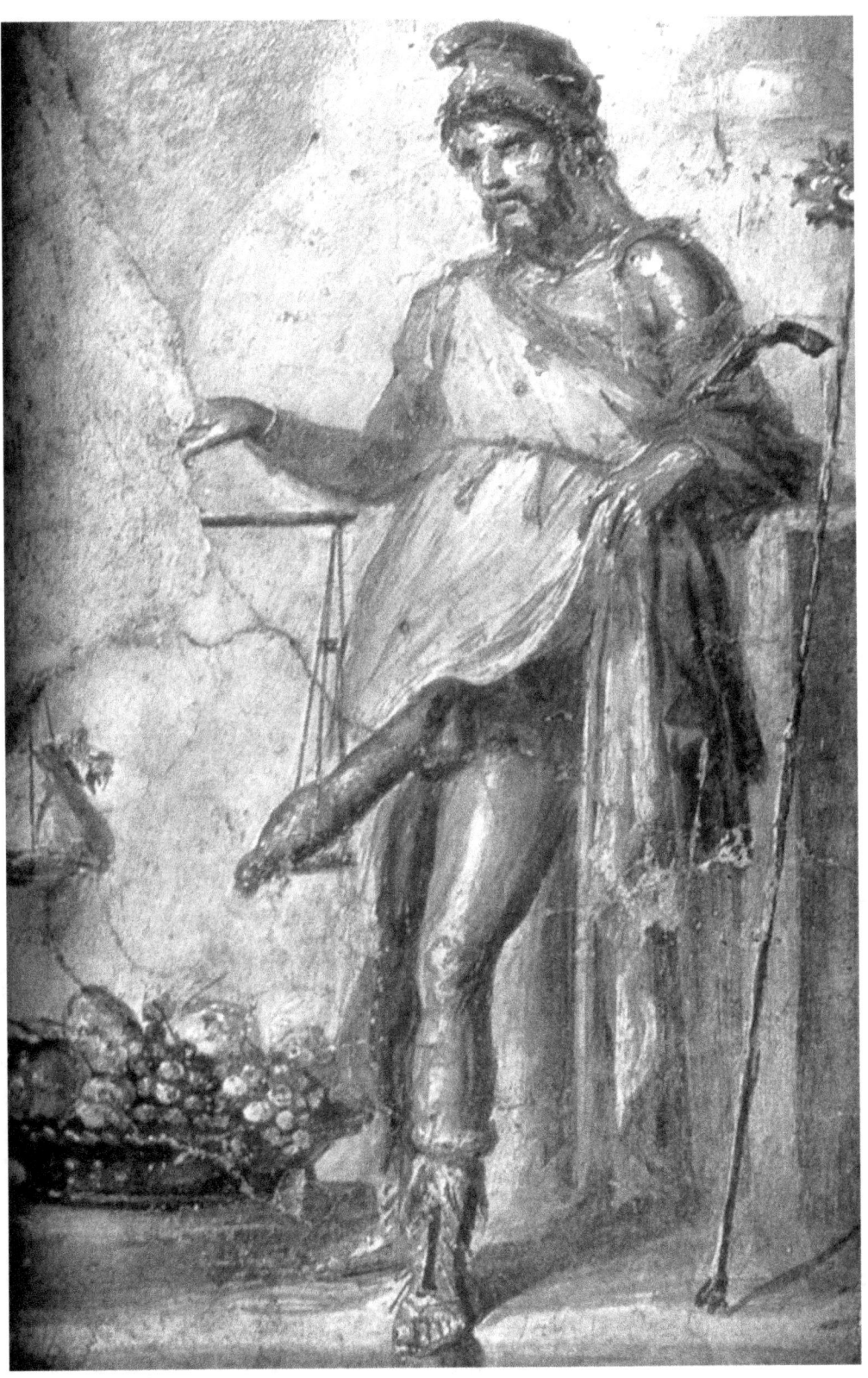

Fresco, Ancient Roman

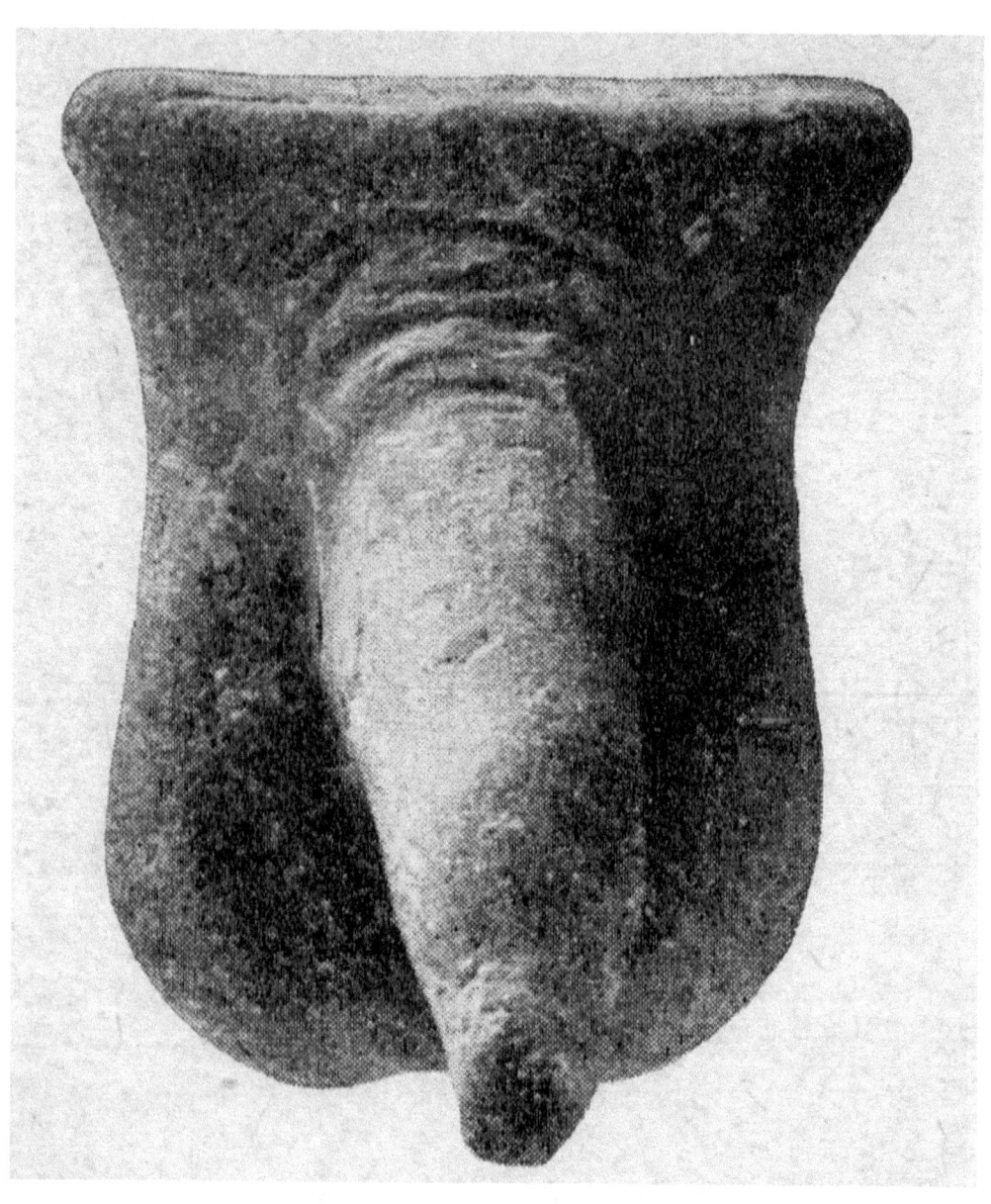

Ancient Votive Phallus, from Albert Moll, Handbuch der
Sexualwissenschaften, Verlag Von F.C. Vogel, Leipzig, 1921

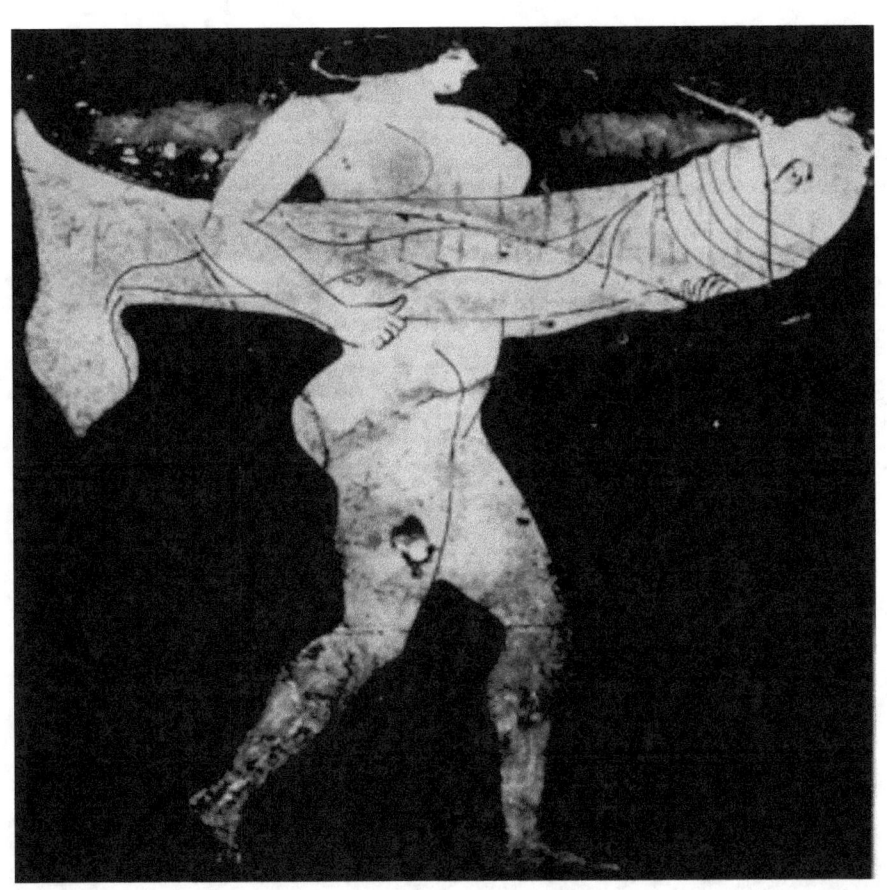

Vase, Ancient Greek

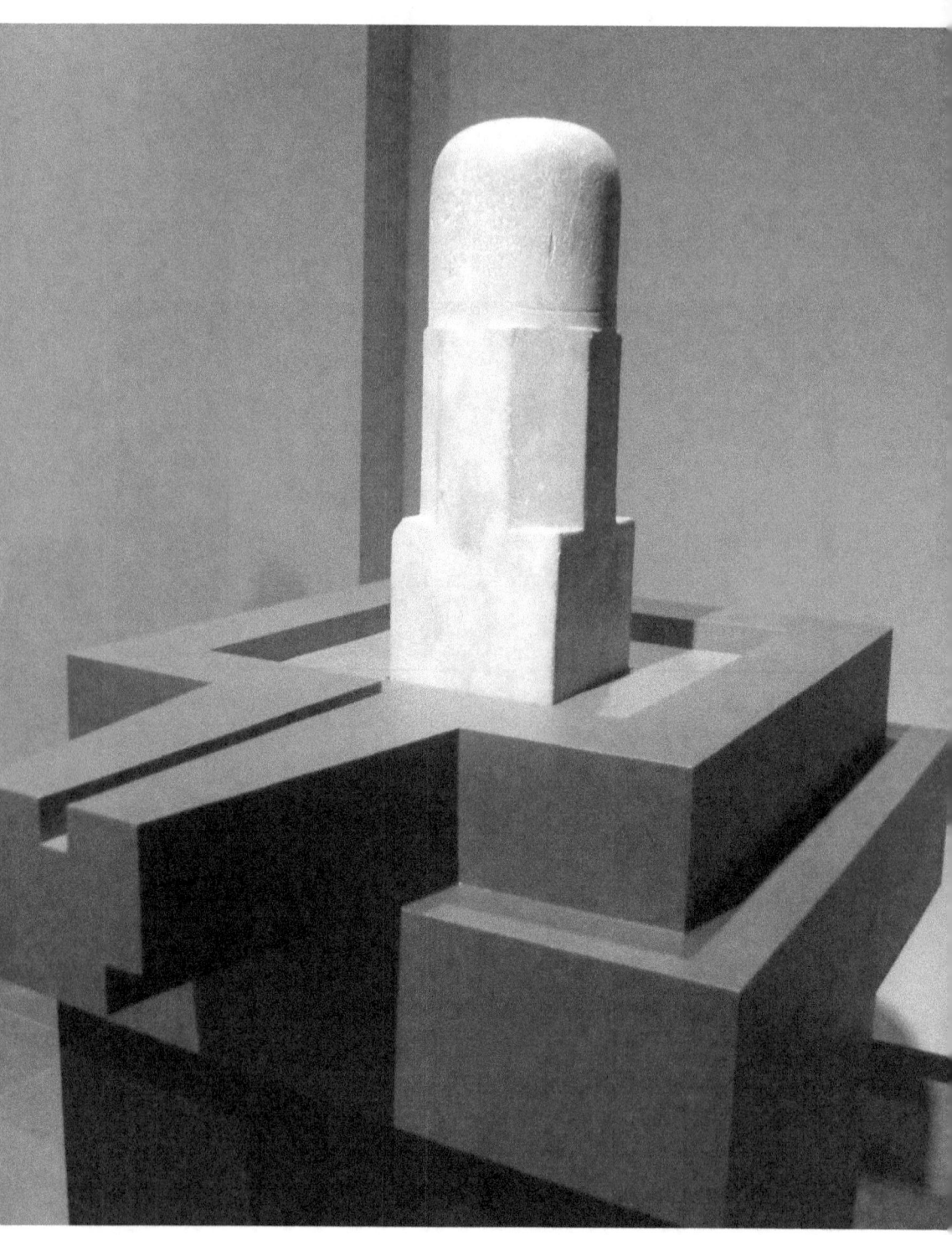

Lingam and Yoni, Cambodian, Norton Simon Museum, Pasadena, CA

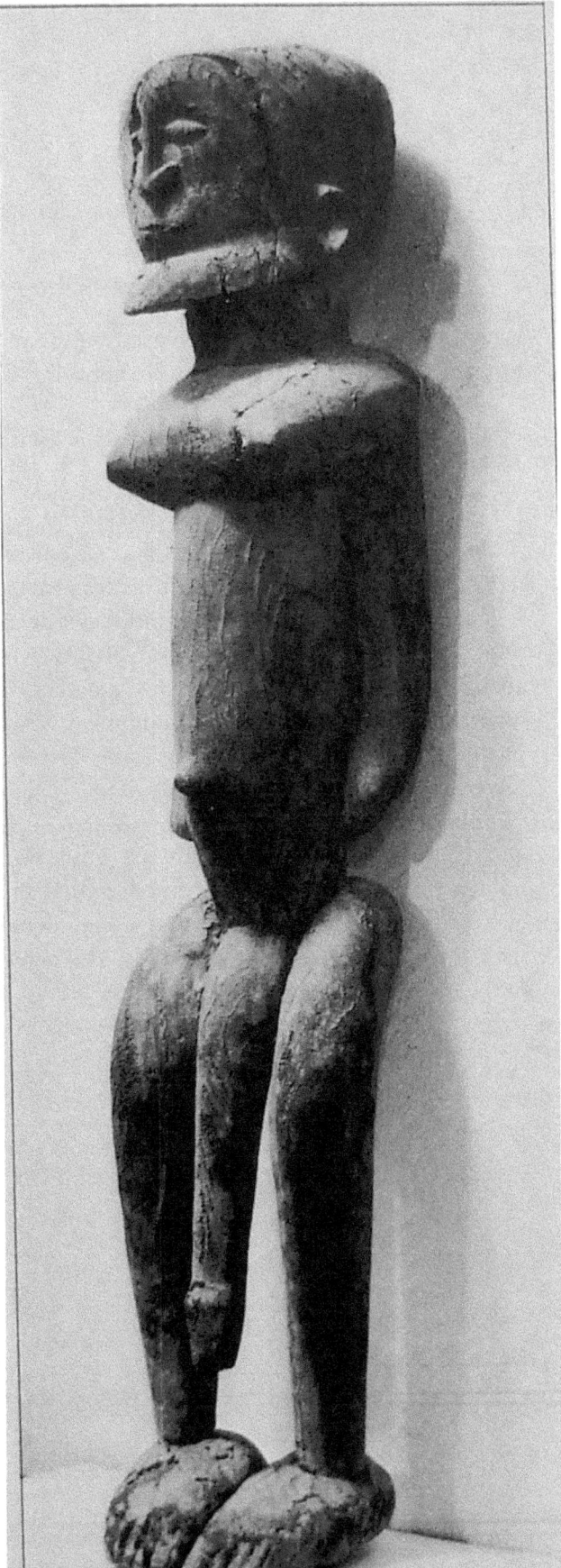

Wood figure, Ivory Coast

THE PHALLUS

Whole philosophic systems are based on the phallus, yet, as Juliet Mitchell remarked in "Feminine Sexuality':

> It's extraordinary what happens when you get rid of the centrality of the concept of the phallus. I mean, you get rid of the unconscious, get rid of sexuality, get rid of the original psychoanalytic point.[1]

If men reduce people to their sexual identities, as some feminists claim, then at the heart of this is the penis. Women are reduced to 'cunt', as Kate Millet put it, while men are all phallus. There are certainly no shortage of phallic symbols and artifacts about. The real thing, the real penis, is censored, carefully guarded – it's not much to look at anyway – so men displace their phallic sexuality onto thrusting cars, lorries, missiles, bombs, towers, cameras, computers, guitars, cigarettes, telephones, swords, guns, eyes, etc. These things abound in (patriarchal) art, and throughout the history of art (and pornography adds a million further fetishes). The trouble is that the penis ain't much of a thing, after all. As Richard Dyer commented: 'the fact is that the penis isn't a patch on the phallus. The penis can never live up to the mystique implied by the phallus'.[2]

1 J. Mitchell: "Feminine Sexuality: Interview with Juliet Mitchell and Jacqueline Rose", *m/f,* 8 (1983), 15.
2 R. Dyer: 'Don't Look Now", *Screen,* vol. 23, 3/4, 1983, and in A. McRobbie, 206.

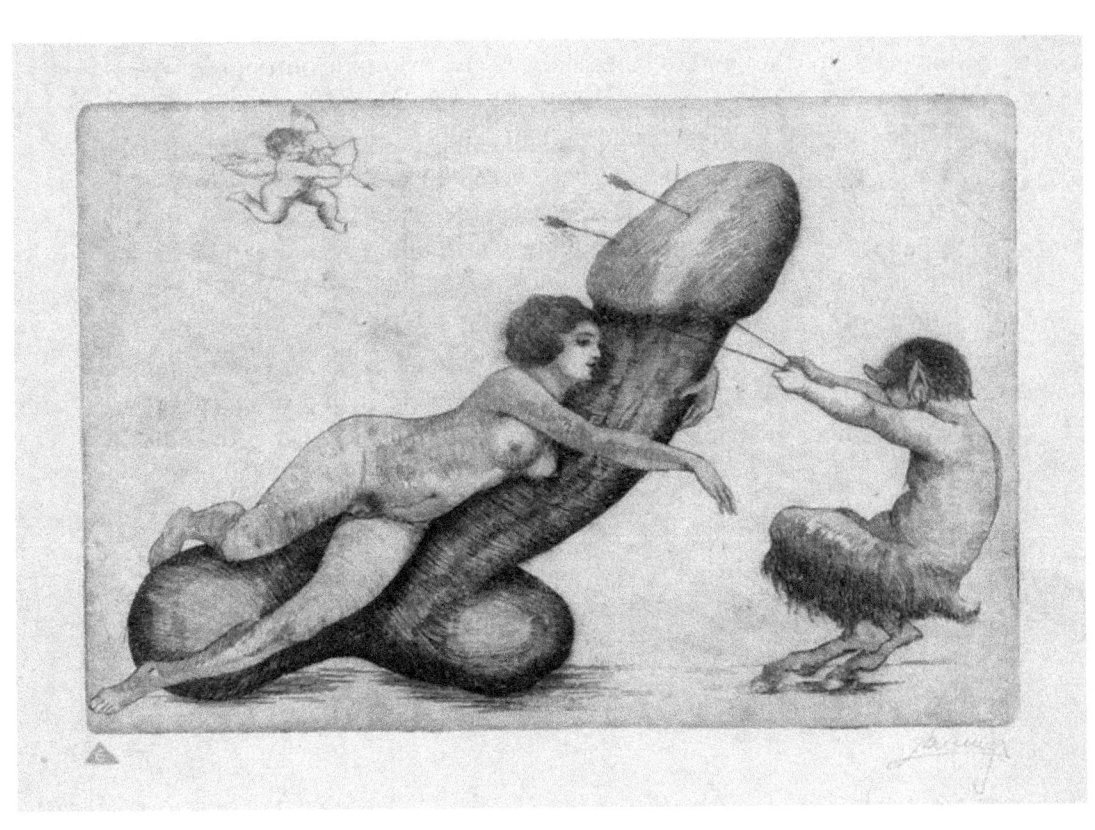

After Max Klinger (1857-1920)

In the (second wave) feminist view, the pornographer creates with his penis – the paintbrush, camera, computer or pen – these things are called 'tools', a common euphemism for the penis (there are thousands of other phallic control devices, such as game consoles, TVs, digital cameras, hi-fis, factory machinery, aeroplanes, etc). The quill, stylus or 'sharp projective' is a crucial element in the male's manufacture of art and pornography.[1] When Pierre Renoir was asked how he painted when he hands were crippled by arthritis he replied, '[w]ith my prick'.[2]

In pornography, the eye becomes the phallus, and looking is equated with caressing the obscure object of desire with the phallus (in the Lacanian system). Throughout Western art the phallus has been that visually absent but psychologically and ideologically present object. It is central in erotic art. Look at the Western art nudes – by Titian, Picasso, Ingres, Boucher: the phallus is there even though one doesn't see it. It's the same in any number of books, poems, sculptures, plays, operas, installations.

1 See J. Derrida: *Spurs: Nietzsche's Styles*, tr. B. Harlow, University of Chicago Press, Chicago 1979, 37-9; on the penis as a paintbrush, see Carol Duncan: "The Esthetics of Power in Modern Erotic Art", *Heresies*, 1, 1977, 46-50.
2 In J. Hobhouse, 135.

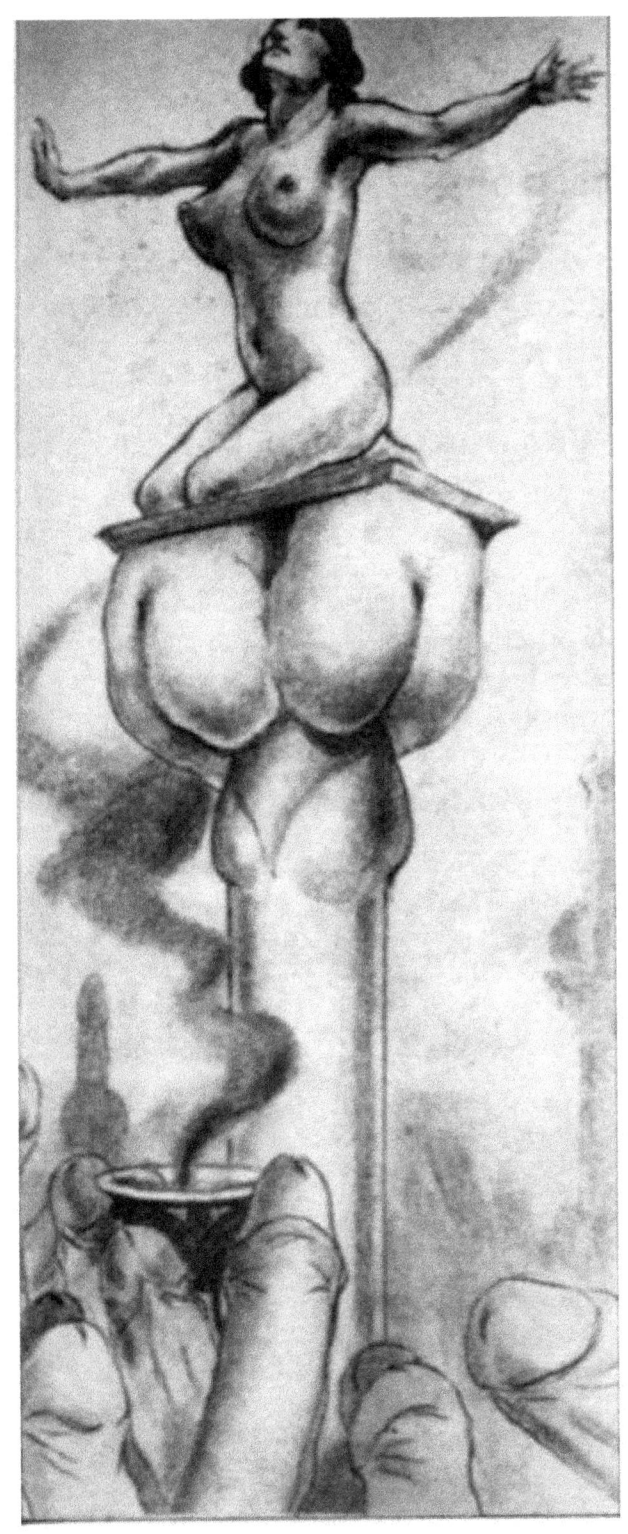

Anonymous, 19th century

LESBIAN EROTICA

In heterosexual pornography, lesbian eroticism is often introduced, but always controlled by a patriarchal force. Typically, in a soft porn scenario, two bisexual women cavort on a bed overseen by a male ('I've always wanted to see ya with another woman' drools the man to his wife/ girlfriend; or, frequently, 'I got back from work an' saw my wife and her best friend writhin' on the bed'). Towards the end of the scene, the man makes love to both women. Why? Because they needed the phallus, they needed a man to be fulfilled. Variations on this scenario occur endlessly in pornography. The male presence (the phallus) is seen as necessary for the true satisfaction for women (for valorization, for authenticity: i.e., it's not *true* sex without the phallus).

Lesbian or women's pornography, made by women for women, disappoints some feminists. Elizabeth Carola, who called herself as a 'radical feminist lesbian', described magazines such as *On Our Backs, Bad Attitude, OW! – Outrageous Women: A Journal of Woman-to-Woman SM, Yellow Silk, The Power Exchange*:

> Like all porn, this new 'woman's' porn is neither about nor for women. Like all porn it is, in a most basic sense, *against* women and *about* male fantasy – the basic male fantasy of Woman as Wholly Sexual Object whose Purpose is To Be Fucked – which feeds men's egos, fuels their violence...

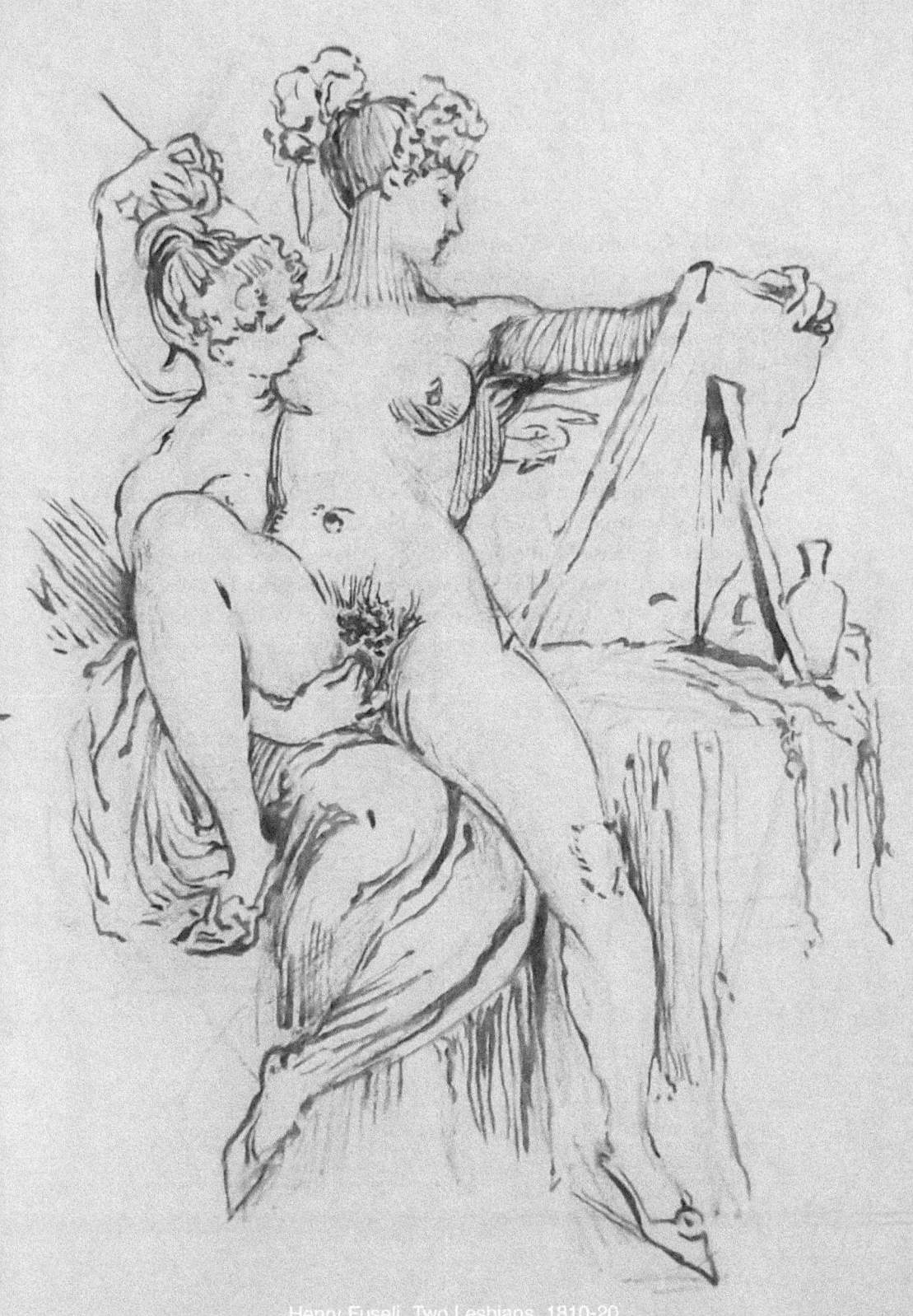

Henry Fuseli, Two Lesbians, 1810-20,
private collection

LESBIAN EROTICISM

Lesbian sex is marked in contemporary cultural theory by the *lack* of the phallus. Hence, lesbian eroticism must always be 'deviant', because it departs from the patriarchal norms which exalt the phallus. Lesbianism must always be 'other', sexually, and many feminists note that the otherness of lesbian sexuality is one of the reasons that men and their patriarchal institutions are very threatened by lesbianism.[1] Lesbian attacks patriarchy at its powerbase. Men cannot control lesbians: '[l]esbians, by loving women and not men, pose a direct threat to the very basis of male supremacy', write Alice, Gordon, Debbie and Mary.[2] The lesbian is crucial, argued Monique Wittig, because she 'is the only concept that I know of which is beyond the categories of sex (man and woman)'.[3] Wittig moved towards a view of culture that goes beyond gender, beyond 'biological dimorphism', and biology.

1 T. Atkinson: *Amazon Odyssey*, Links Books, New York 1974; Alice, Gordon, Debbie and Mary: "Separatism", in S.L. Hoagland & J. Penelope, eds: *For Lesbians Only: A separatist anthology*, Onlywomen Press 1988, 31-40; A. Rich: "Towards a woman-centred university", in *On Lies, Secrets and Silence*, Novotny, New York 1979; J. Johnston: *Lesbian Nation: The Feminist Solution*, Simon & Shuster, New York 1974; S. Rowbotham: *Beyond the Fragments: Feminism and the making of Socialism*, Merlin 1979.
2 Alice, Gordon, Debbie and Mary, op. cit., 31-40.
3 M. Wittig: "One is not born a woman", in S. Hoagland, op. cit., 446-7.

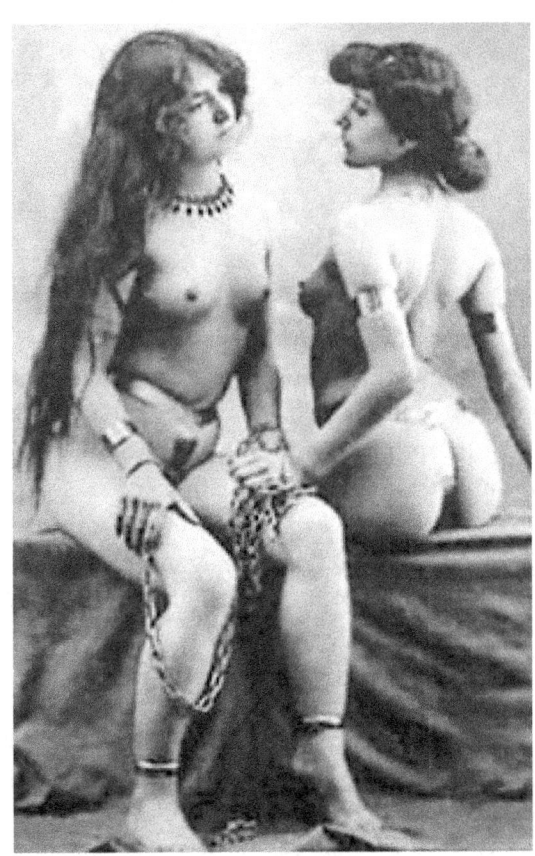

Anonymous, lesbian photograhs,
19th century

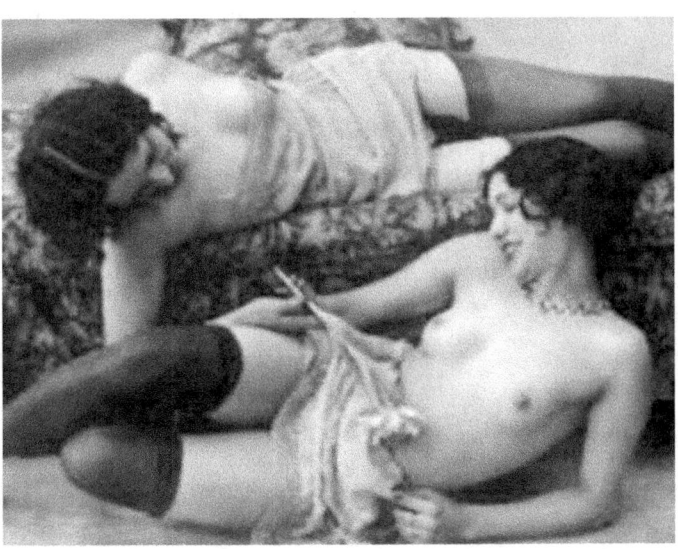

LESBIAN EROTICA

In heterosexual pornography, lesbian eroticism is often introduced, but always controlled by a patriarchal force. Typically, in a
soft porn scenario, two bisexual women cavort on a bed overseen
by a male ('I've always wanted to see ya with another woman',
drools the man to his wife/ girlfriend; or, frequently, 'I got back
from work an' saw my wife an' her best friend writhin' on the
bed'). Towards the end of the scene, the man makes love to both
women. Why? Because they needed the phallus, they needed a
man to be fulfilled. Variations on this scenario occur endlessly in
pornography. The male presence (the phallus) is seen as
necessary for the true satisfaction for women (for valorization, for
authenticity: i.e., it's not *true* sex without the phallus).

Lesbian or women's pornography, made by women for
women, disappoints some feminists. Elizabeth Carola, who called
herself as a 'radical feminist lesbian', described magazines such as
*On Our Backs, Bad Attitude, OW! – Outrageous Women: A Journal of
Woman-to-Woman SM, Yellow Silk* and *The Power Exchange* in
"Women, Erotica, Pornography":

> Like all porn, this new 'woman's' porn is neither about nor for
> women. Like all porn it is, in a most basic sense, *against* women and
> *about* male fantasy – the basic male fantasy of Woman as Wholly
> Sexual Object whose Purpose is To Be Fucked – which feeds men's
> egos, fuels their violence...[1]

1 Elizabeth Carola: "Women, Erotica, Pornography: – Learning to Play the Game", in G.
Chester, 172.

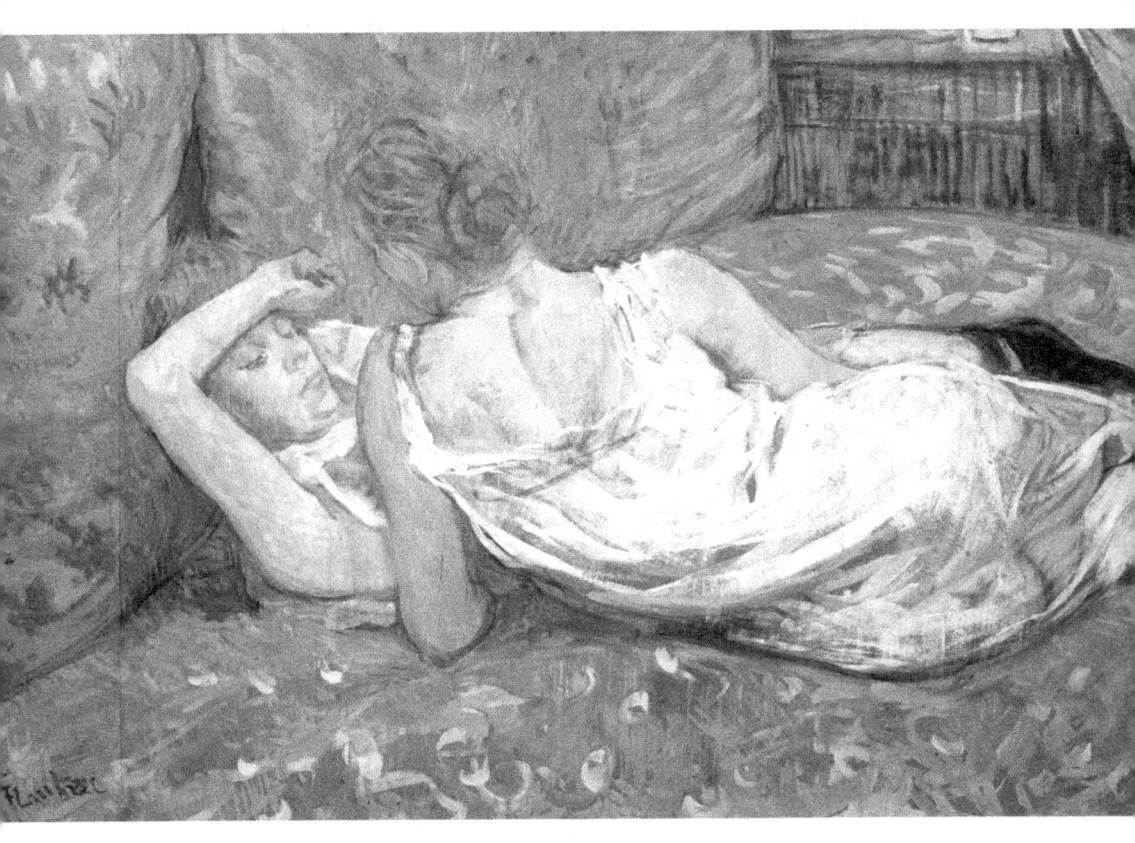

Henri de Toulouse-Lautrec (1864-1901), Two Friends

LESBIAN EROTICISM

Not all feminists agree about the revolutionary potential of lesbianism, if it is a lesbianism that keeps defining itself in terms of patriarchy. Elizabeth Mees reckoned that 'lesbianism, as an attack on hetero-relations, takes (its) place within the structure of the institution of heterosexuality. The lesbian is born of/ in it.'[1] There is no escape, it seems, from patriarchal and heterosexuality: the world is permeated with these ancient structures. As Sheila Jeffreys wrote: '[e]very woman grows up in a heteropatriarchal world',[2] while Ann Barr Snitow remarked in "Mass Market Romance':

> One of our culture's most intense myths, the ideal of an individual who is brave and complete in isolation, is for men only. Women are grounded, enmeshed in civilization, in social connection, in family and in love (a condition a feminist culture might well define as desirable) while all our culture's rich myths of individualism are essentially closed to them.[3]

---

1 E. Mees, in K. Jay & J. Glasgow: *Lesbian Text and Contexts: Radical Revisions*, New York University Press, New York, NY, 1990, 82.
2 S. Jeffreys: "The Censoring of Revolutionary Feminism", in G. Chester, 139.
3 A. Snitow: "Mass Market Romance: Pornography for Women Is Different", *Radical History Review*, no. 20, Spring/Summer, 1979.

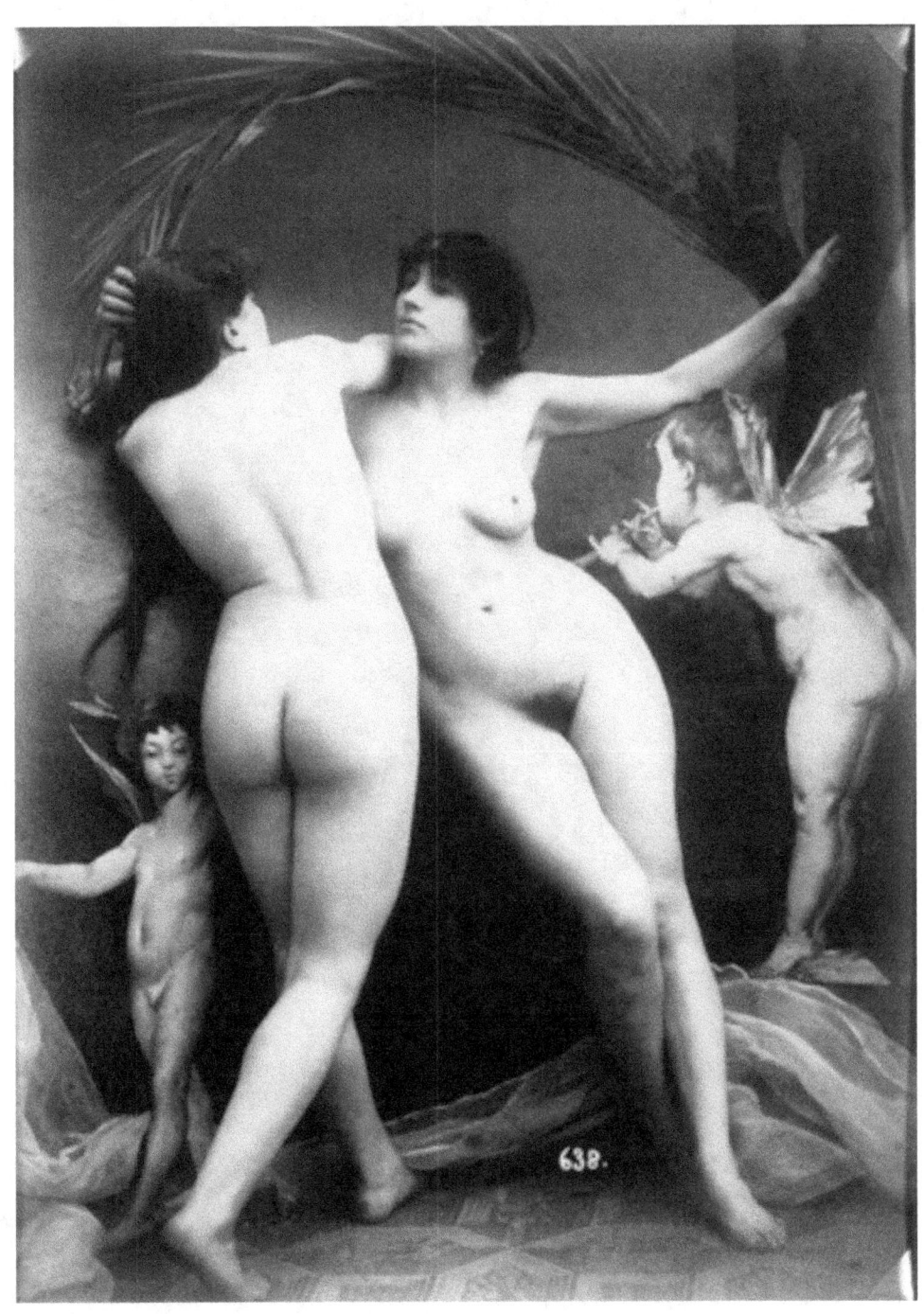

Gaudenzio Marconi (1841-85), Nudes and Angels, 1880s

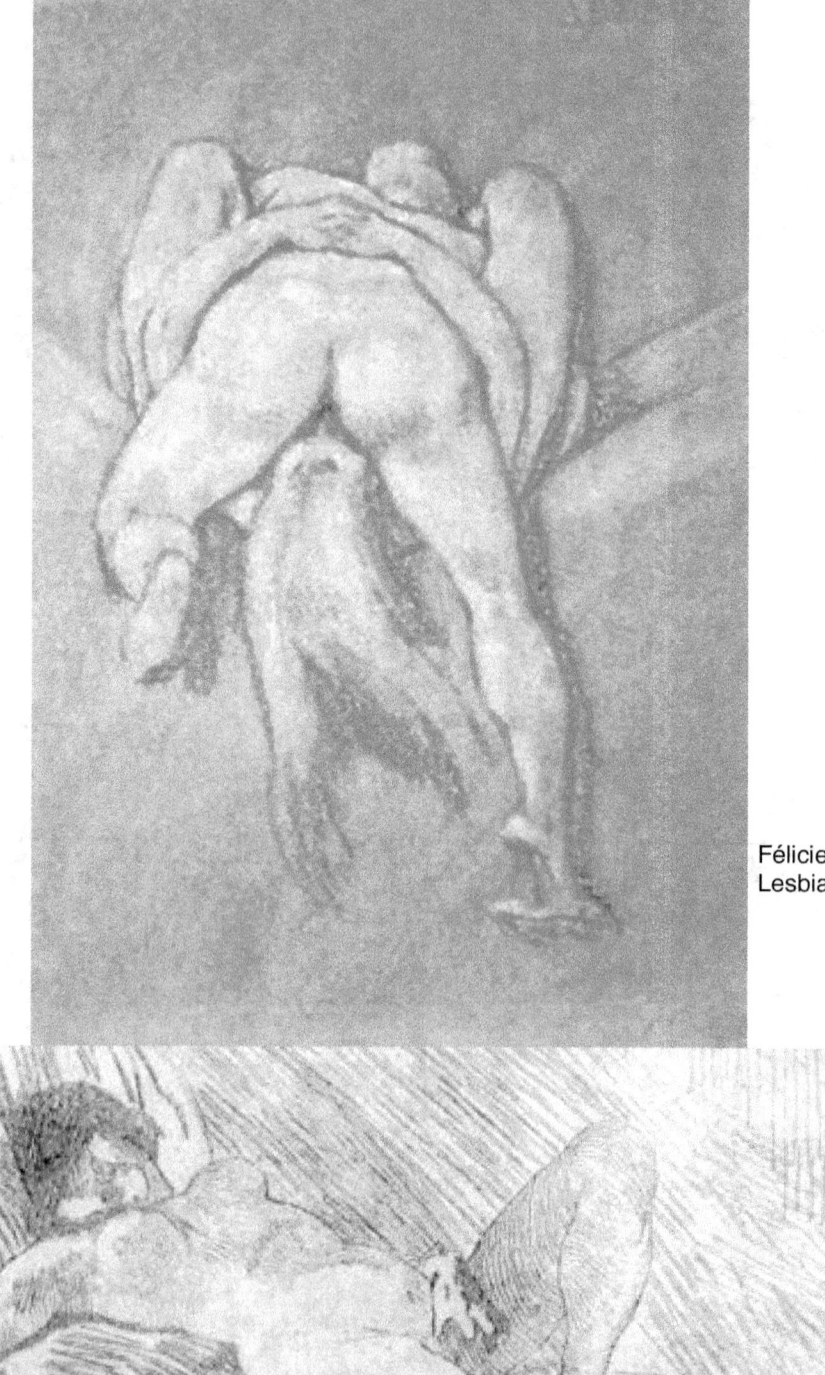

Félicien Rops,
Lesbians (left).

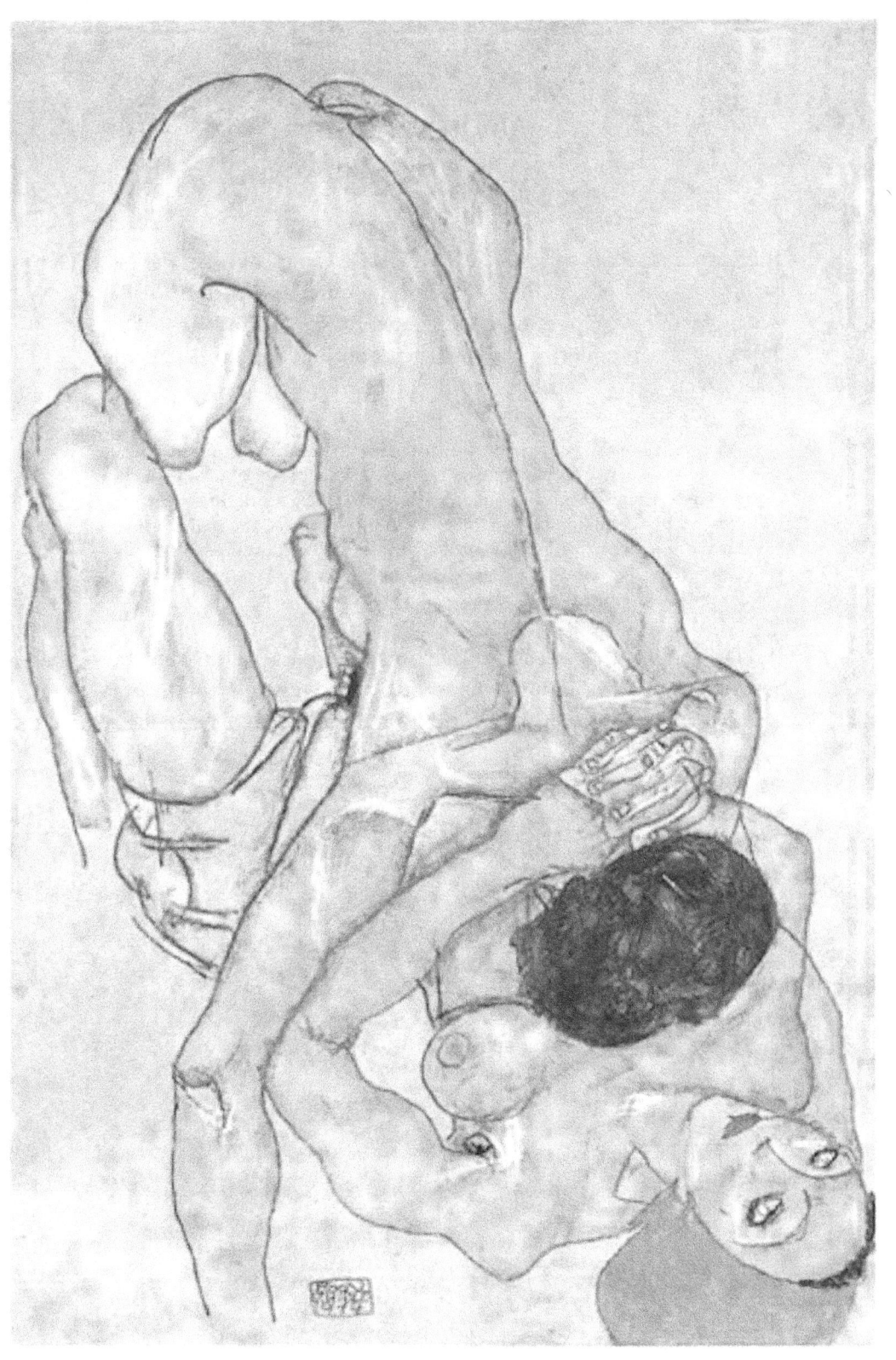

Egon Schiele, Two Women Lovers, 1914

VOYEURISM

The Lacanian Look emphasizes eroticism. Seeing is erotic, the eye becomes a kind of phallus, caressing the obscure object of desire, which it can never 'possess'. As the poet Rainer Maria Rilke wrote '[g]azing is a wonderful thing.'[1] The act of looking eroticizes the object. Jack Zipes describes it thus in *Don't Bet On the Prince*:

> For him [Lacan], seeing is desire, and the eye functions as a kind of phallus. However, the eye cannot clearly see its object of desire, and in the case of male desire, the female object of desire is an illusion created by the male unconscious. Or, in other words, the male desire for woman expressed in the gaze is auto-erotic and involves the male's desire to have his own identity reconfirmed in a mirror image.[2]

The look is an assertion of male power and sexuality. For the gaze is male, and feminists have grappled with the notion of a 'female' gaze, whether there can be such a thing as a 'female' or 'feminine' gaze.[3]

---

1 R. Rilke, letter to Clara Rilke, 8 March 1907, in *Gesammalte Briefe 1892-1926*, Insel Verlag, Leipzig 1940, II, 279f

2 Jack Zipes: *Don't Bet on the Prince: Contemporary Feminist Fairy Tales in North America and England*, Gower, Aldershot 1986, 258

3 Maggie Humm: "Is the gaze feminist? Pornography, film and feminism", *Perspectives on Pornography*, eds G.Day & C. Bloom, Macmillan 1988; Lorraine Gamran & Margaret Marshment, eds: *The Female Gaze*, Women's Press 1988; E.D. Pribram, ed: *Female Spectators: looking at film and television*, Verso, 1988

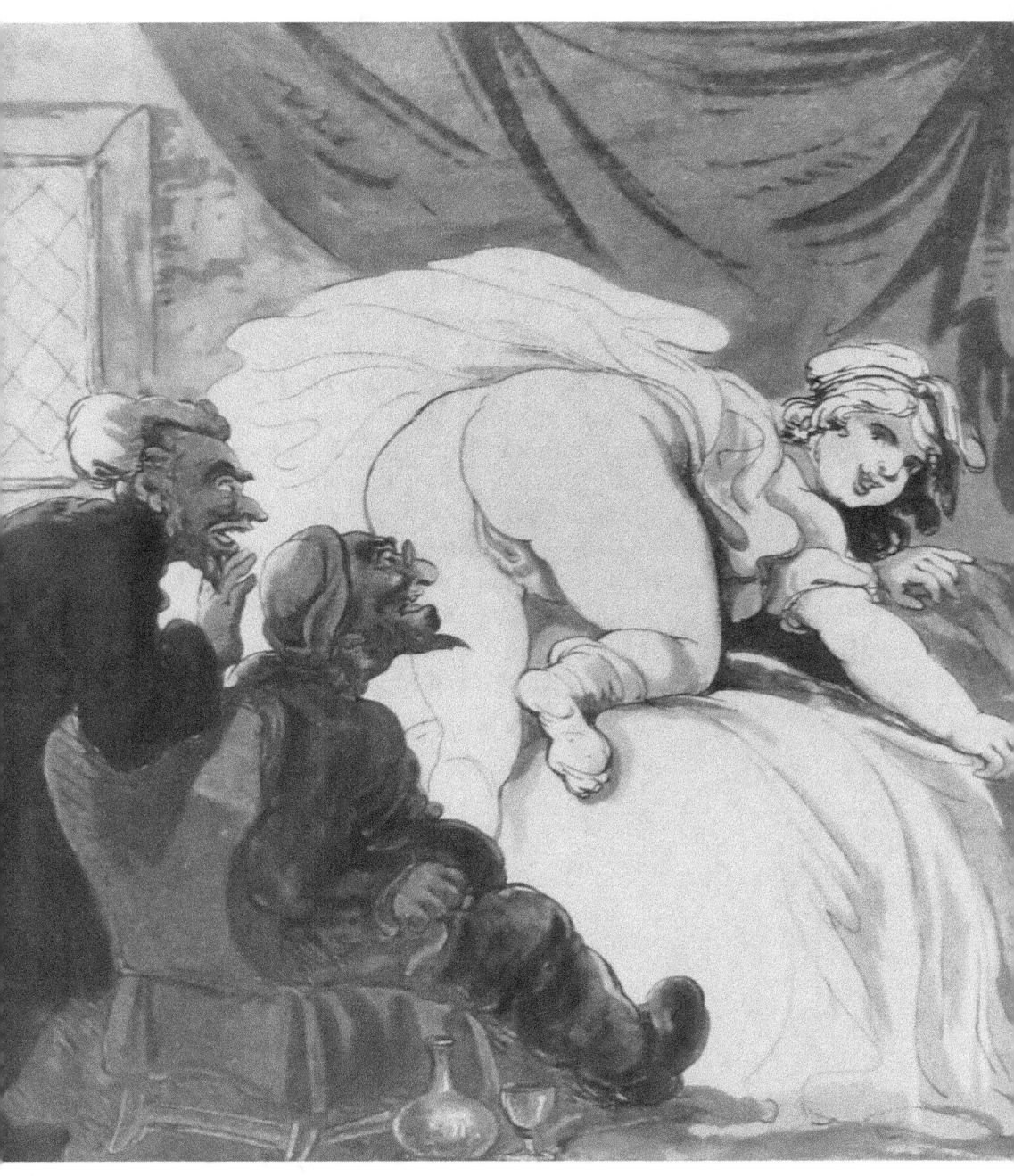

Thomas Rowlandson, Susannah and the Elders, 1820, London

SEX AND DEATH

Pain is good, because it means you are fully alive. This is the Existential view of patriarchal culture. 'Sensual pleasure is agony in the strictest meaning of the word', says C. Mauclair in a Freudian tone.[1] Suffering is holy, in the Christian tradition. The journey from martyrdom to sainthood and beatification is swift. The West exalts pain. Christ *suffered*, say theologians, so he must have been right, he must have lived hard, because he died hard. Death becomes heroic. Death transfigures people. Suicide is even better, if you can manage it. Hence Marilyn Monroe, Vincent van Gogh, Johann Wolfgang von Goethe's Werther, Virginia Woolf. Die young, and become famous (many artists have followed this equation: Egon Schiele, Frédéric Chopin, Wolfgang Amadeus Mozart, Georges Seurat, James Dean, Paula Modersohn-Becker, D.H. Lawrence, Jimmy Hendrix, Jim Morrison, Arthur Rimbaud, Raphael, John Keats, Percy Shelley, and Novalis.

---

1 C. Mauclair: *Magie de l'amour*, 145, quoted in Julius Evola, 84

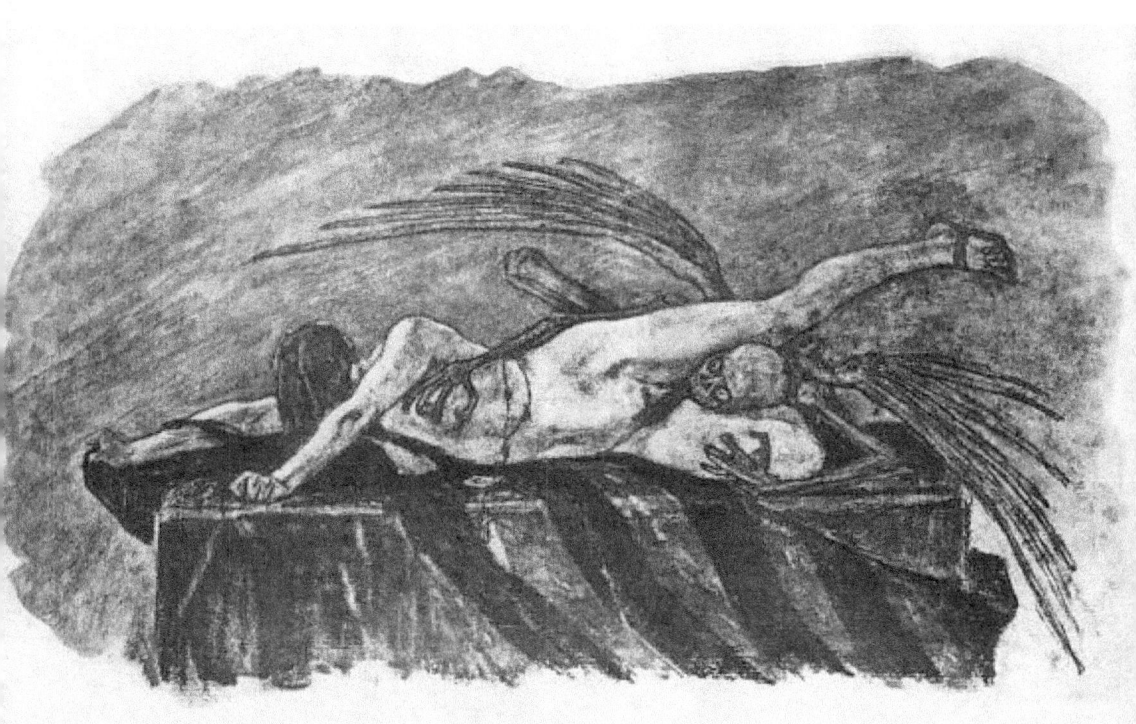

Félicien Rops

Part Two

Erotic Art In the 19th Century

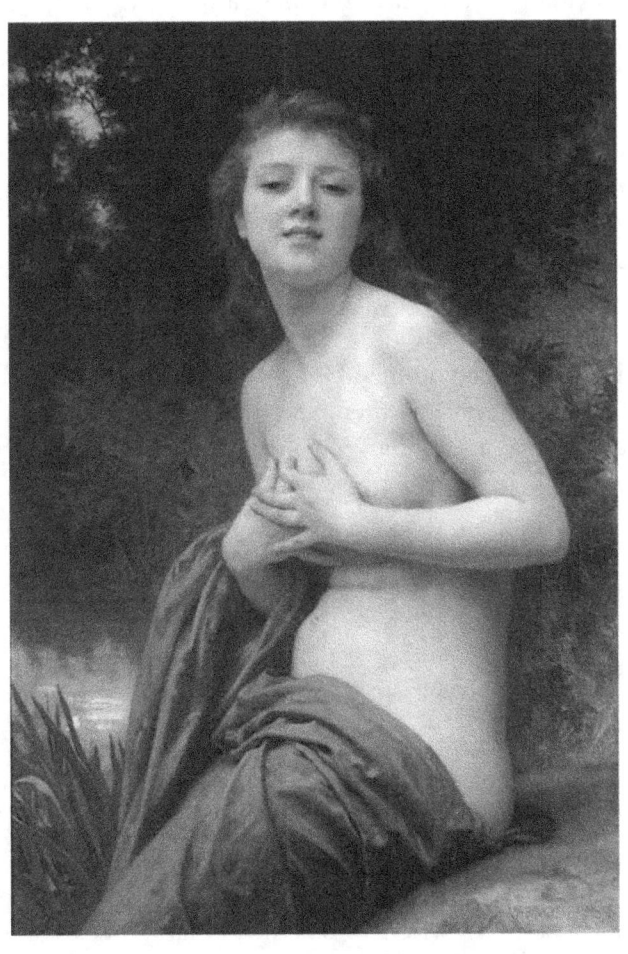

ANIMA

In the Jungian system, Beatrice, Laura, Cleopatra, Isolde, Eurydice, Ariadne and all those women of myth, poetry and legend, are incarnations of the *anima*, which is, as Carl Jung explains, something all males possess: '[e]very man carries with him the eternal image of woman, not the image of this or that particular woman, but a definitive feminine image.'[1] The *anima* is 'a personification of the unconscious in a man, which appears as a woman or a goddess in dreams, visions and creative fantasies', write Emma Jung and Marie-Louise von Franz, glossing Jung's *anima* concept.[2]

Male painters throughout history have depicted their version of the *anima*, it seems. Each (male) painter has a version of the 'inner feminine figure', as Carl Jung calls it.[3] For painters, this idealized *anima* figure seems to be another manifestation of that obscure object of desire, the eroticized woman, a mirror for male lust. The equation is: the more sublime and voluptuous the woman is painted, the more sublime and voluptuous is the artist's desire. The artist's model, then, can be seen as a Jungian *anima*, heavily eroticized, a Lacanian phallic mirror.

1 C. Jung: *The Development of Personality*, vol. 17, Routledge, 1954, 198; Marie-Louise von Franz: *The Psychological Meaning of Redemption Motifs in Fairy Tales*, Inner City Books, Toronto 1980, 39f
2 Emma Jung & Marie-Louise von Franz: *The Grail Legend, tr.* Andrea Dykes, Sigo Press, Boston, Mass., 1980, 64
3 C. Jung: *Memories, Dreams, Reflections*, Collins 1967, 210-1

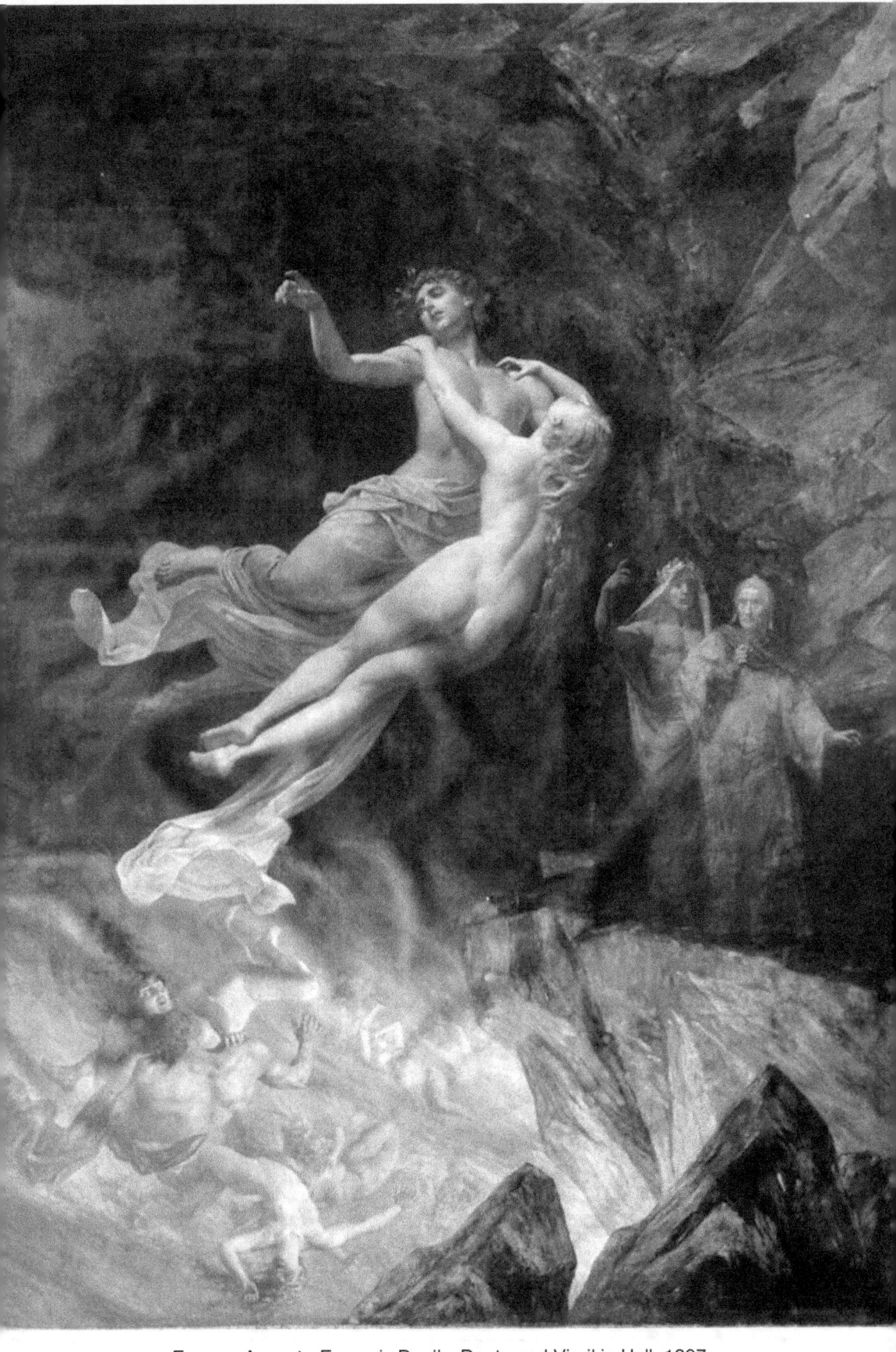

Eugene-Auguste-Francois Deully, Dante and Virgil in Hell, 1897

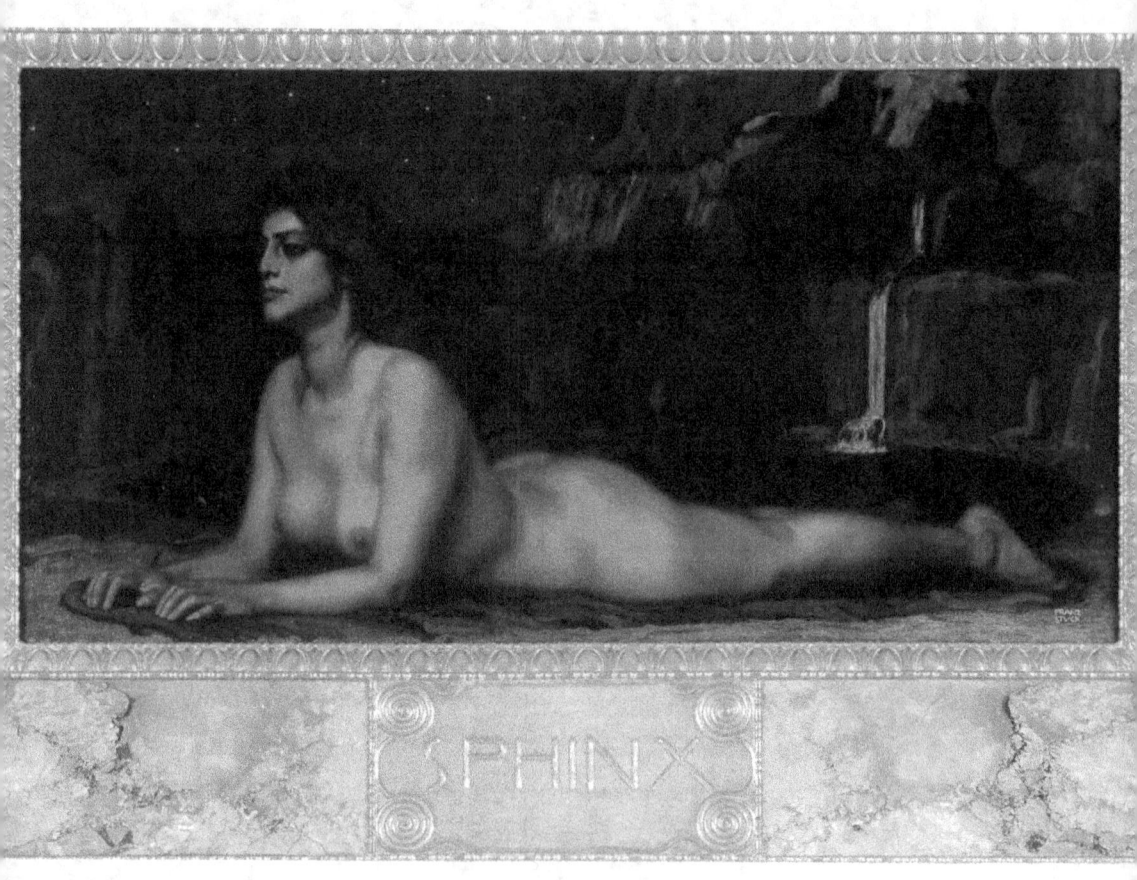

Franz von Stuck, Sphinx

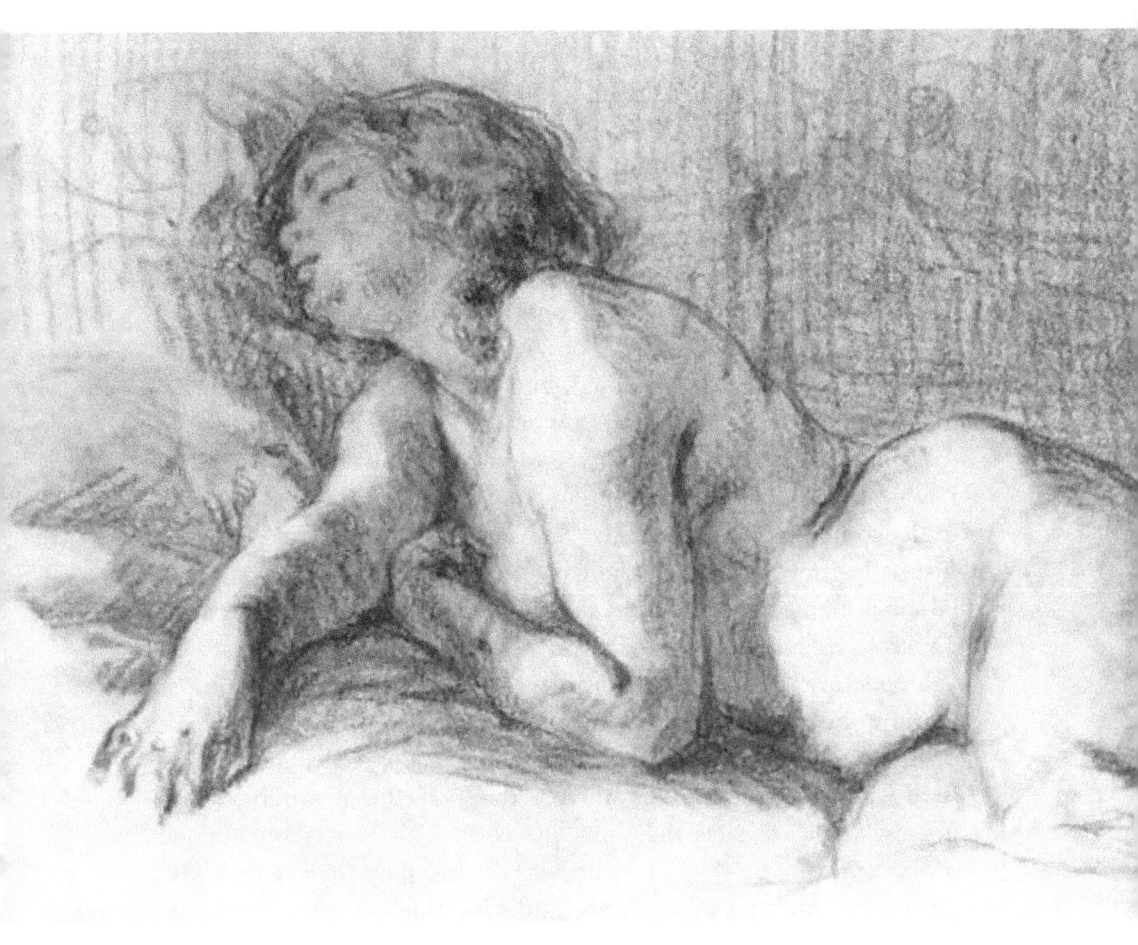

Jean-Françoise Millet

ARTISTS AND MODELS

Seen in Lacanian theory, the female model becomes the 'obscure object of desire' feared and desired, ever unreachable, the manifestation of eternal loss.[1] We can see elements of the Lacanian lack, desire, repression, mirror stage, Symbolic Order and œdipal anxiety in the modern artists who create specifically erotic images. In the output of artists such as Pierre Renoir, Henri Matisse, Jules Pascin, Aristide Maillol, Auguste Rodin, Gustav Klimt, Amedeo Modigliani and Pablo Picasso, one finds loss, desire, repression and anxiety quite clearly. The art they produced is fiercely heterosexual, glorifying women, even as, in some cases (Picasso) the paintings seem to denigrate women. Renoir, in paintings such as *Bather Arranging Her Hair*, Pascin in *The Prodigal Son*, and Lawrence Alma-Tadema in *In the Tepidarium*, produced works that exalt women as sexual objects. The soft flesh is available but also distinctly not available; there is acres of skin, especially in Pascin's painting, but it is not touchable either.[2] These nude paintings remain chimeras, never to be possessed, always to be yearned for. As Nicolas Poussin wrote of painting: '[p]ainting is nothing but an imitation of human actions, which alone are, properly speaking, inimitable'.[3] Poussin recognizes that painting is always an imitation, a mirror; the real thing can never be possessed in art. It is the same in erotic art – indeed, it is most dramatically expressed in erotic art – this paradoxical fear and desire, this simultaneous desire and loss, this ambiguous conflict between possession and dispossession.

1 Toril Moi: *Sexual Textual Politics*, 99f; Anika Lemaire: *Jacques Lacan*, Routledge & Kegan Paul 1977; Elizabeth Wright: *Psychoanalytic Criticism*, Methuen 1984
2 Pierre Renoir: *Bather Arranging Her Hair*, 1885, canvas, 92 x 73cm, Sterling and Francis Clark Institute, Williamstown, Mass.; Lawrence Alma-Tadema: *In the Tepidarium*, 1881, wood, 24 x 33cm, Lady Lever Art Gallery, Port Sunlight; Jules Pascin: *The Prodigal Son*, 1928, oil on board, 15 x 18in, private collection, Switzerland
3 In R. Goldwater, 154.

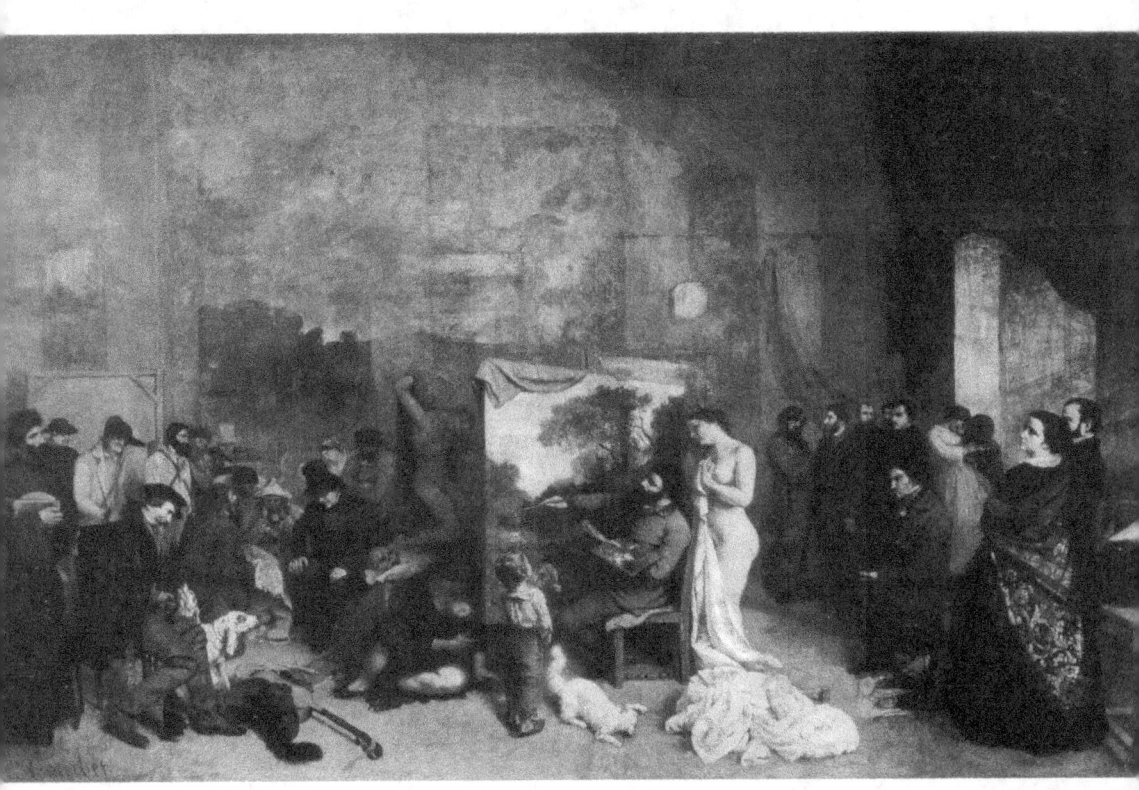

Gustave Courbet, The Studio, 1855, Musée d'Orsay, Paris

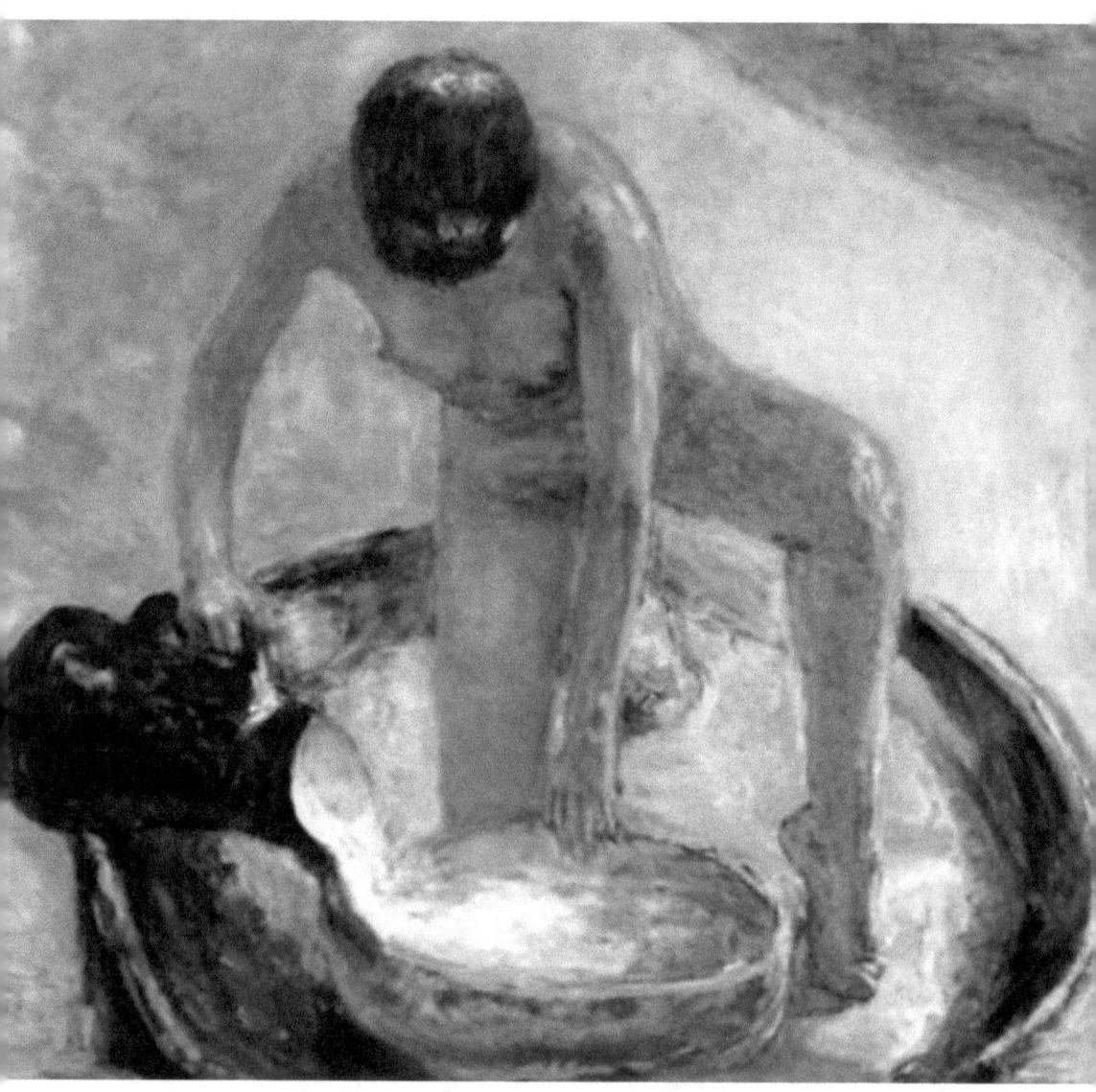

Pierre Bonnard, Nude Crouching In a Tub

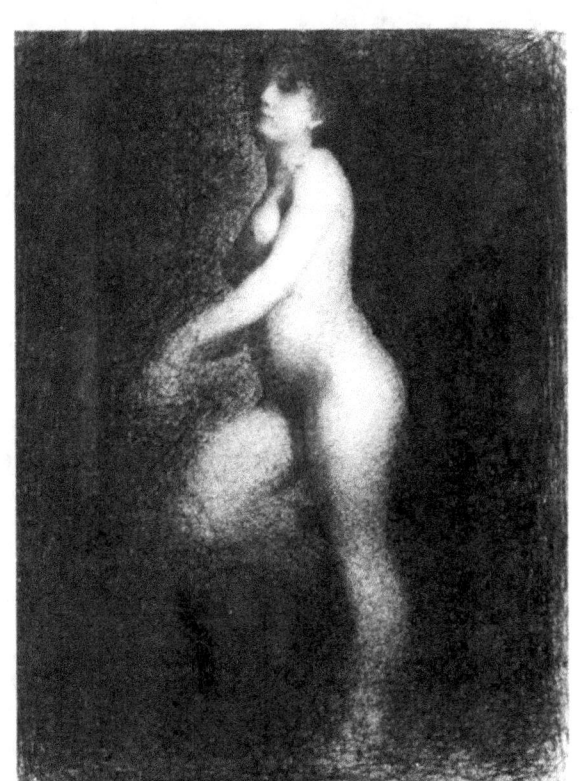

Georges Seurat

THE FEMALE NUDE – 19TH CENTURY

The female nude is the apotheosis of 'high art', yet it constantly wavers around the borderline between art and pornography. The female nude is erotic *and* obscene, in the male system, both desired and loathed, both representable and un-representable.

Lynda Nead writes in *The Female Nude* (71):

> The body is, therefore, central in the formation of individual identity and is the site of the subject's desires and fantasies, actions and behaviour. Once one rejects the perception of the body as a biologically determined and pre-cultural given and moves towards the conception of 'embodied' subjects, the way is opened for feminist interventions within the definition of the female body.

The 19th century saw an enormous increase in the number of nudes being produced in painting, particularly linked to the academies and art schools. This rise in nude painting reflected the social changes of the 19th century, such as the increase in population, the rise of mercantile capitalism, the increase in prostitution, the decline of authoritarian institutions such as organized religion, and the increasing dependence on technology,

William Bouguereau, Evening Mood, 1882

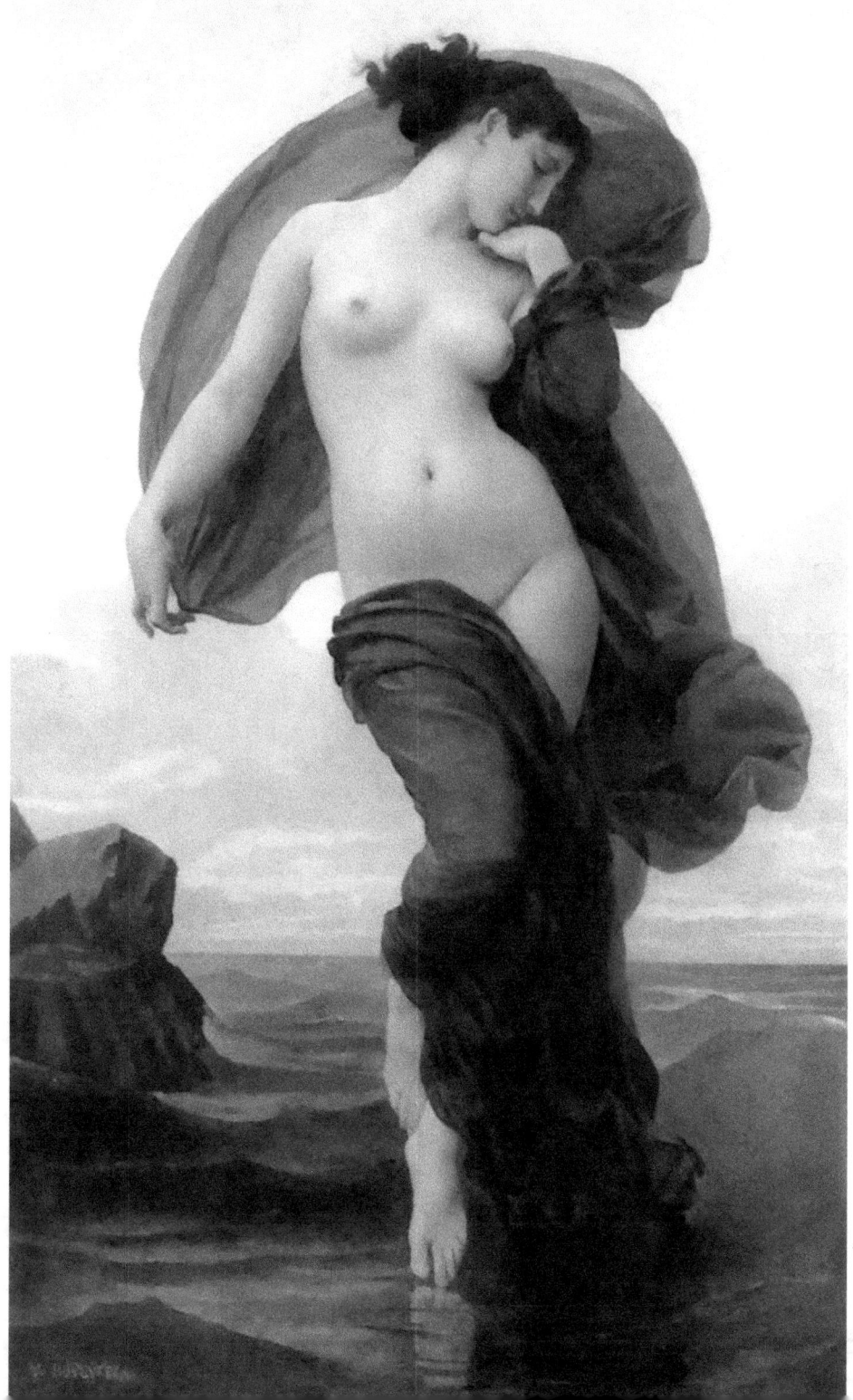

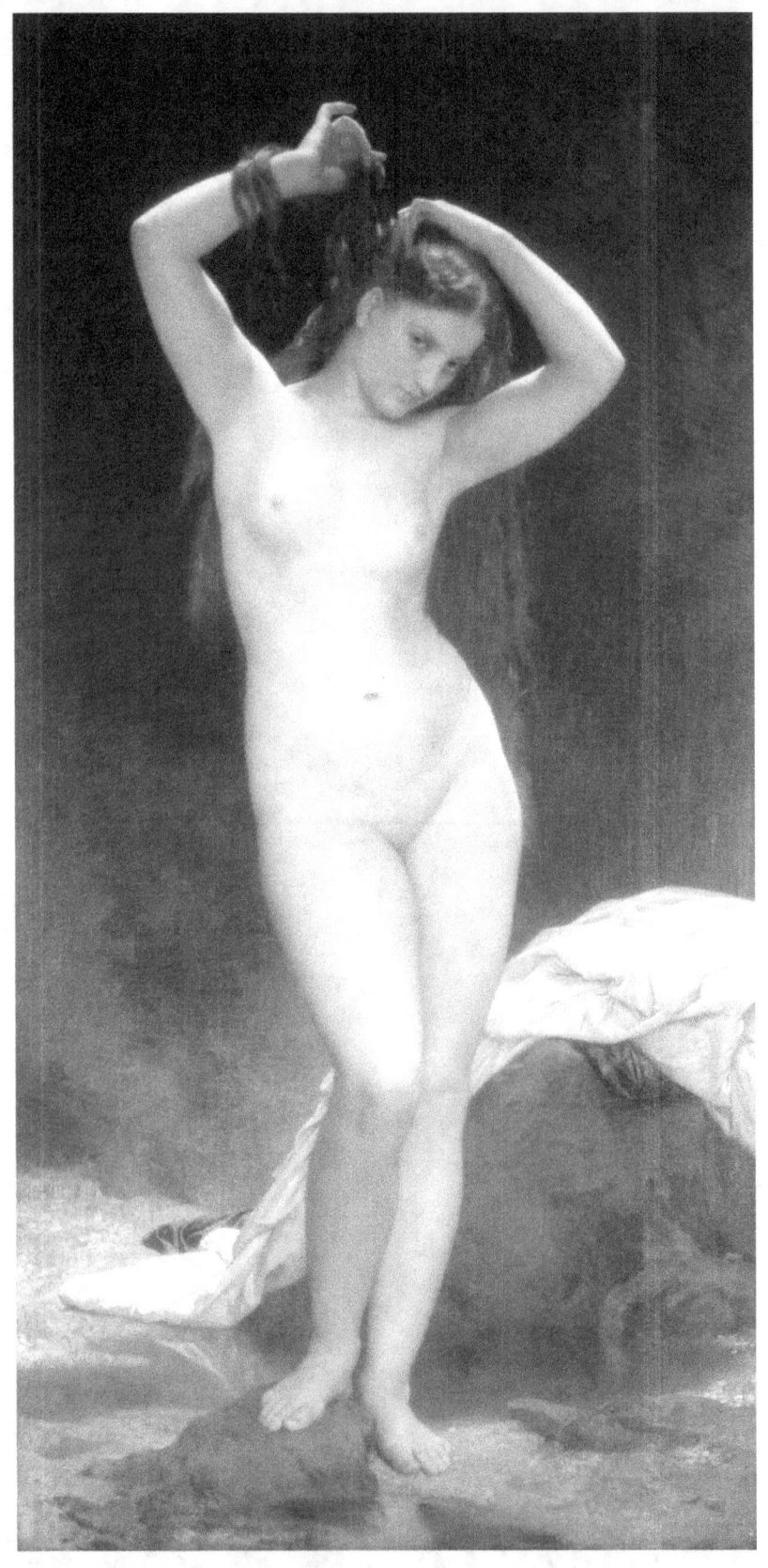

William Bouguereau, The Bather, 1870

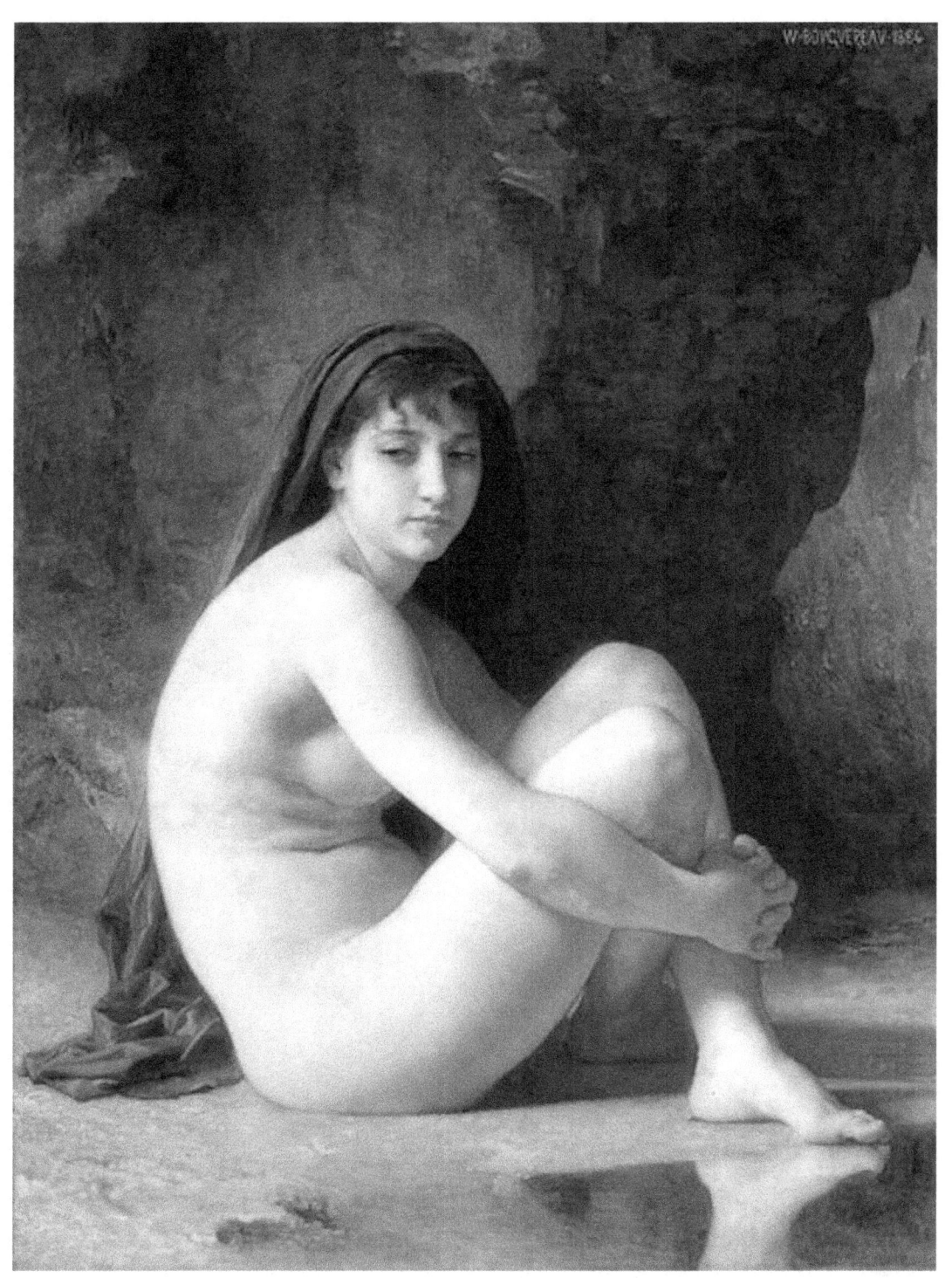

William Bouguereau, Seated Nude, 1884

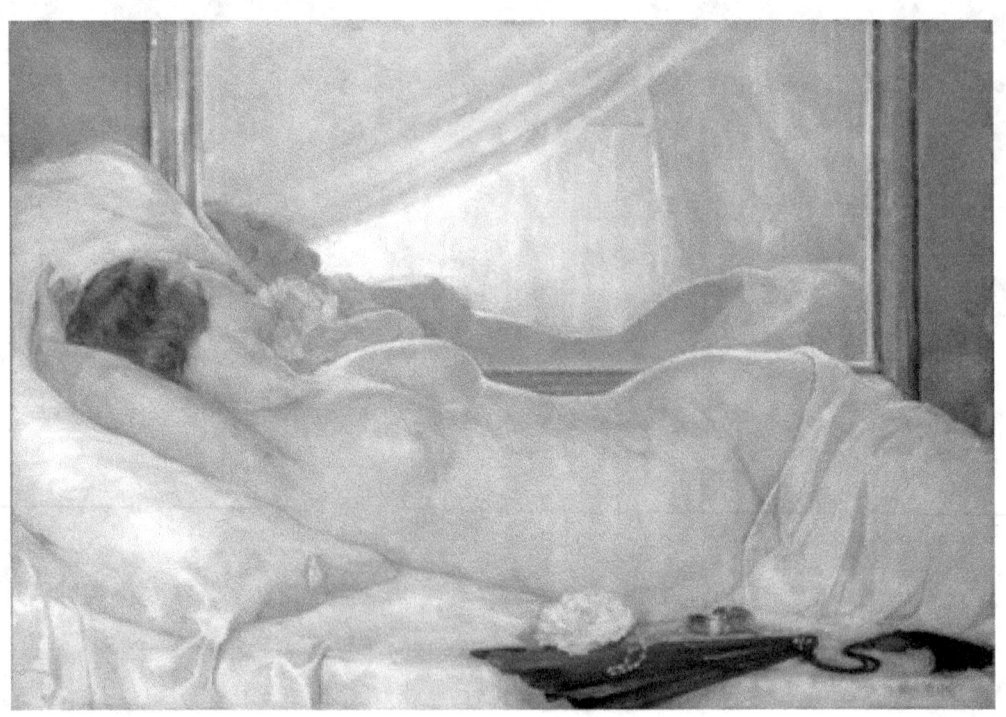

Eugène Huc

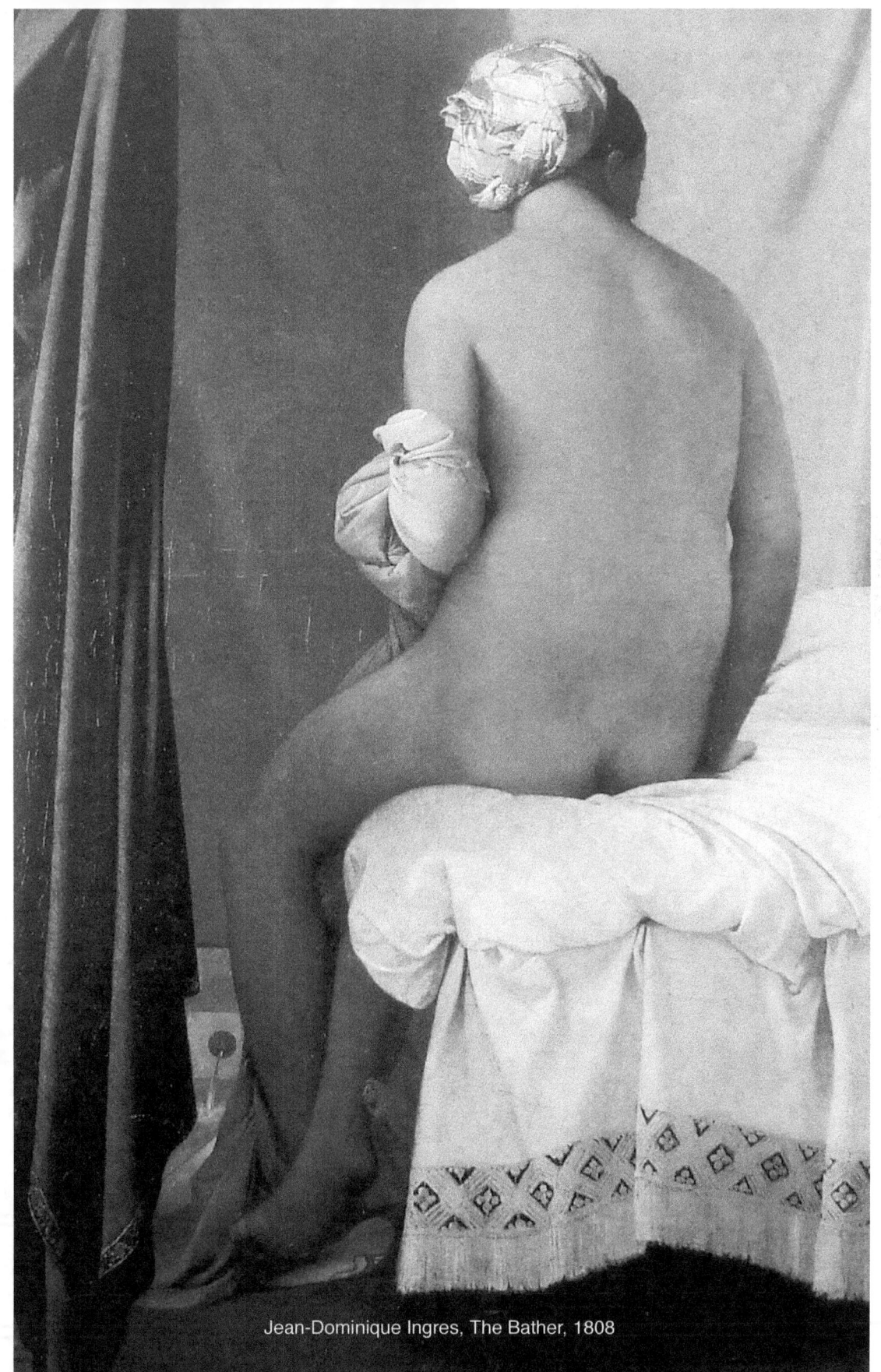

Jean-Dominique Ingres, The Bather, 1808

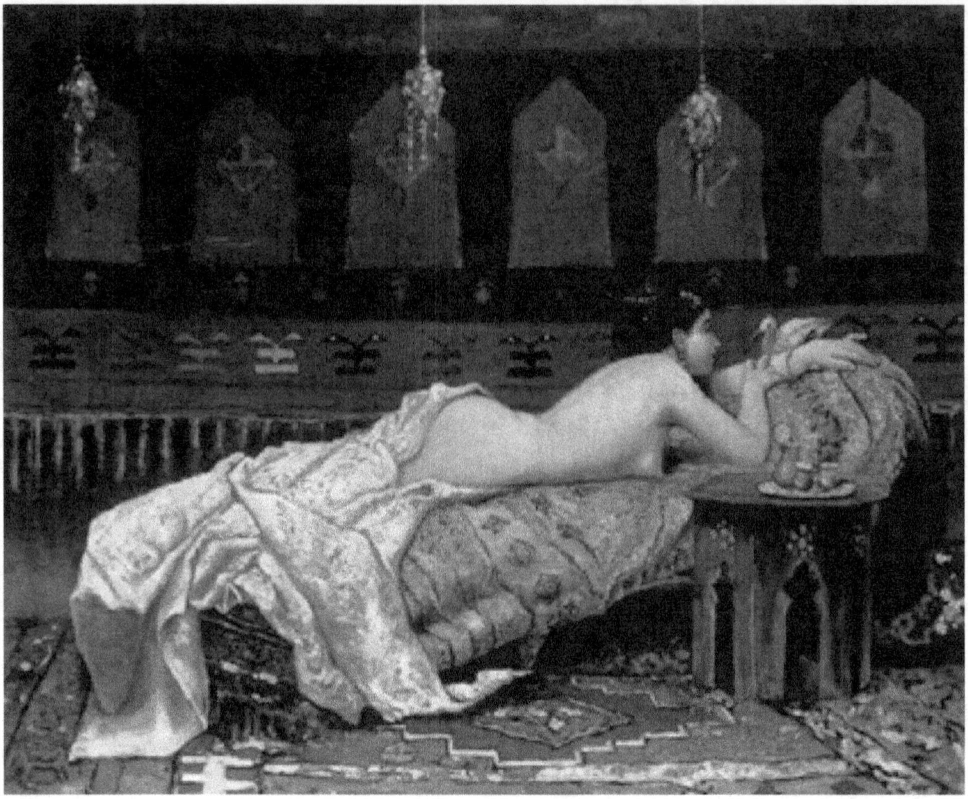

Francesco Paolo Michetti (above).
Paul Bouchard (below).

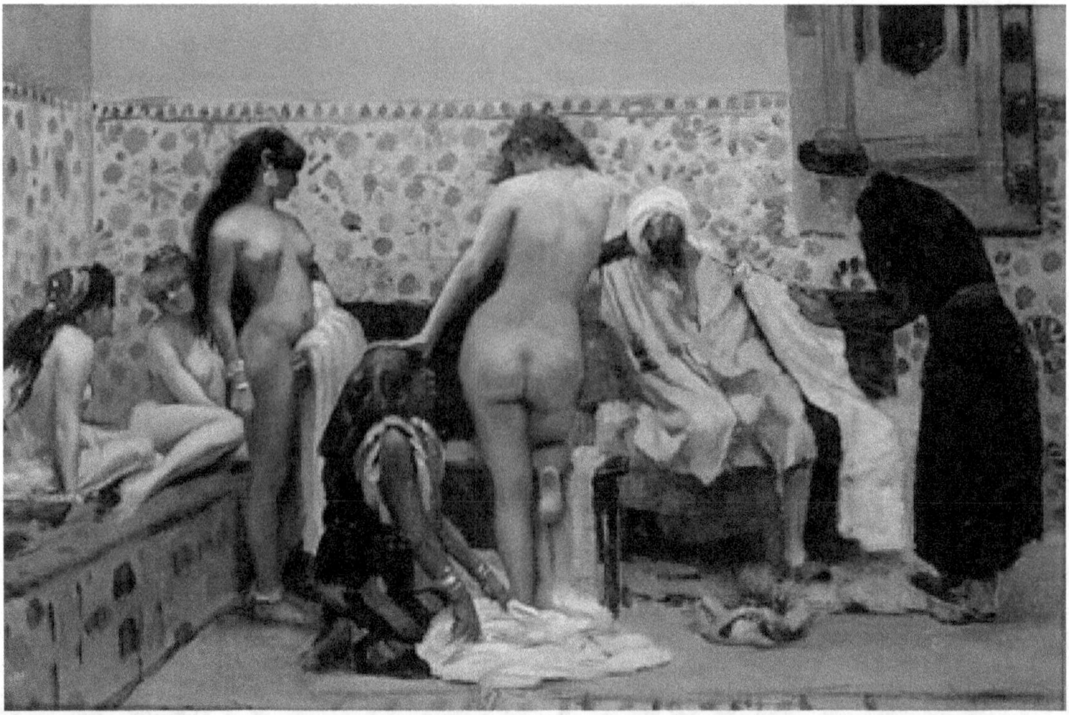

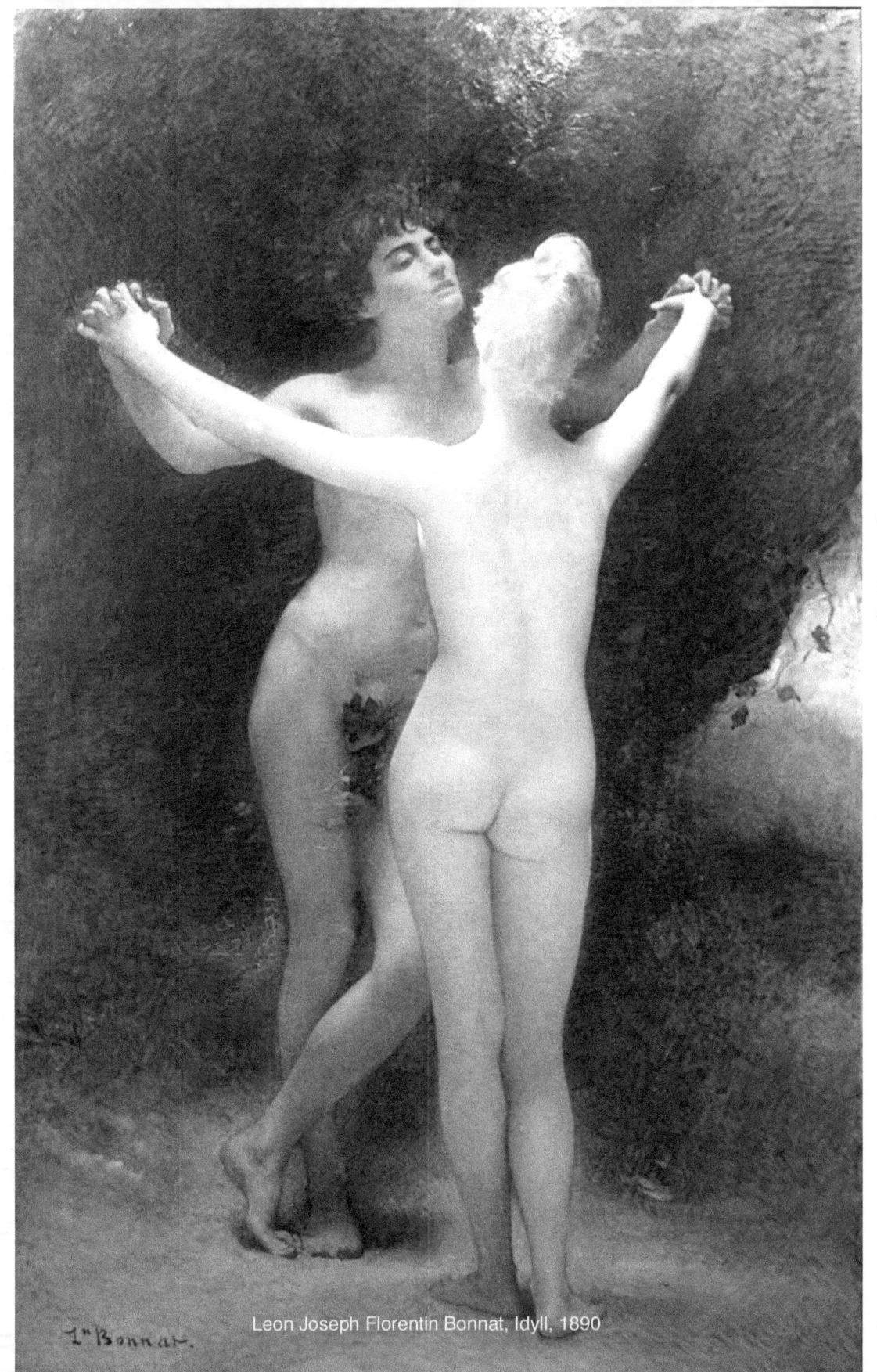

Leon Joseph Florentin Bonnat, Idyll, 1890

CHRISTIANITY AND PORNOGRAPHY

Pornography subverts the laws of Christianity, but it is based on the same laws. Porn comes out of the same world, the same politics, the same culture, as Christianity. Not only is there much of Christianity in pornography, there is much of pornography in Christianity. For instance, Christian history is a catalogue of sadomasochistic events and acts, some really horrific scenes of torture and oppression. More acts of terror have been carried out in the name of God than in the name of 'freedom' or 'truth' or 'honour'.

Painters throughout Western history have reflected the violent acts of Christianity, portraying them as heroic gestures: many painters portrayed St Sebastian full of arrows (Andrea Mantegna, Antonella da Messina, Pietro Perugino, Henrick Terbruggen, and, more recently, Eric Gill and Egon Schiele). In the 19th century, the obsession with portraying the suffering in Catholicism continued.

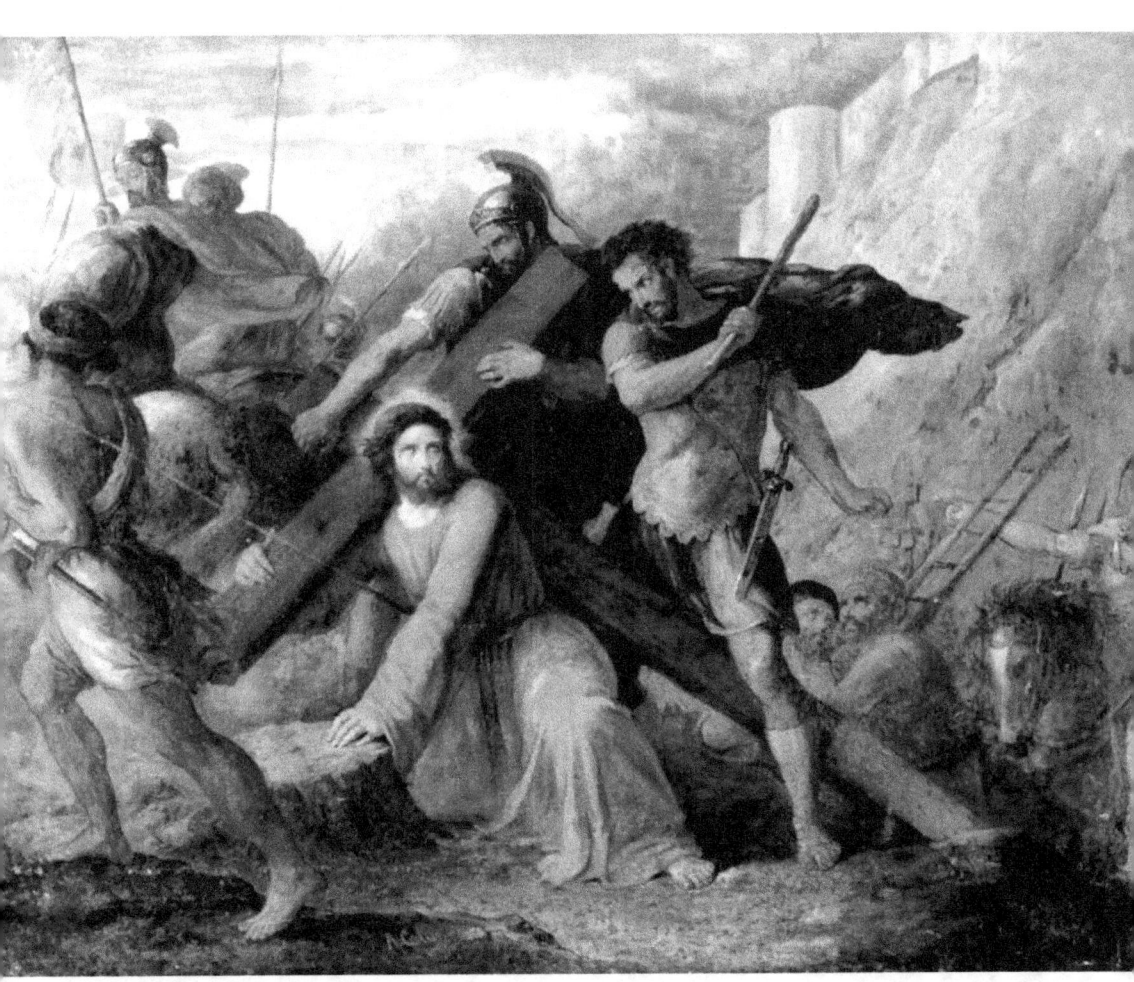

Alexandre-Marie Colin, Christ Falling On the Way To Calvary, 19th century

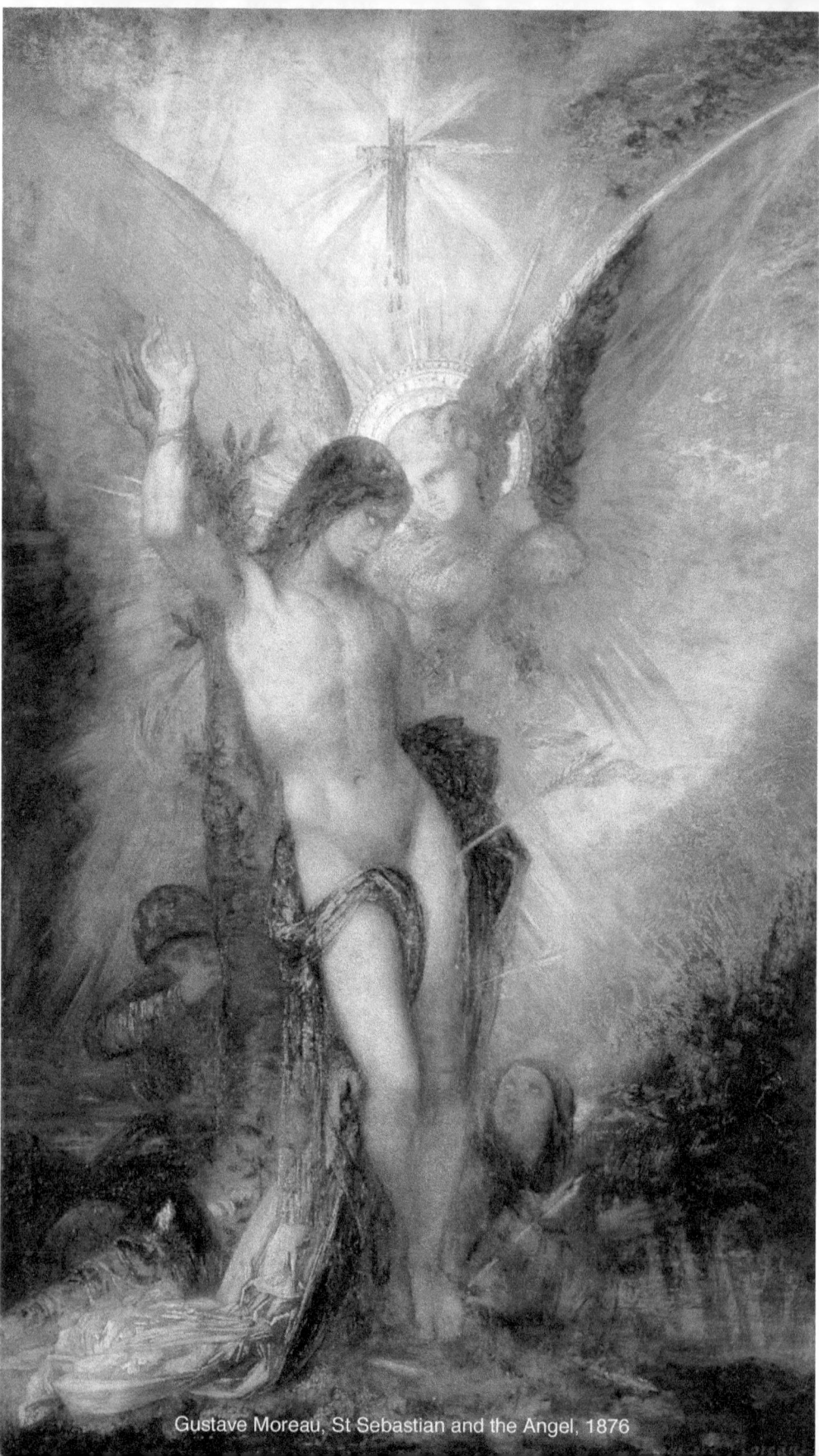

Gustave Moreau, St Sebastian and the Angel, 1876

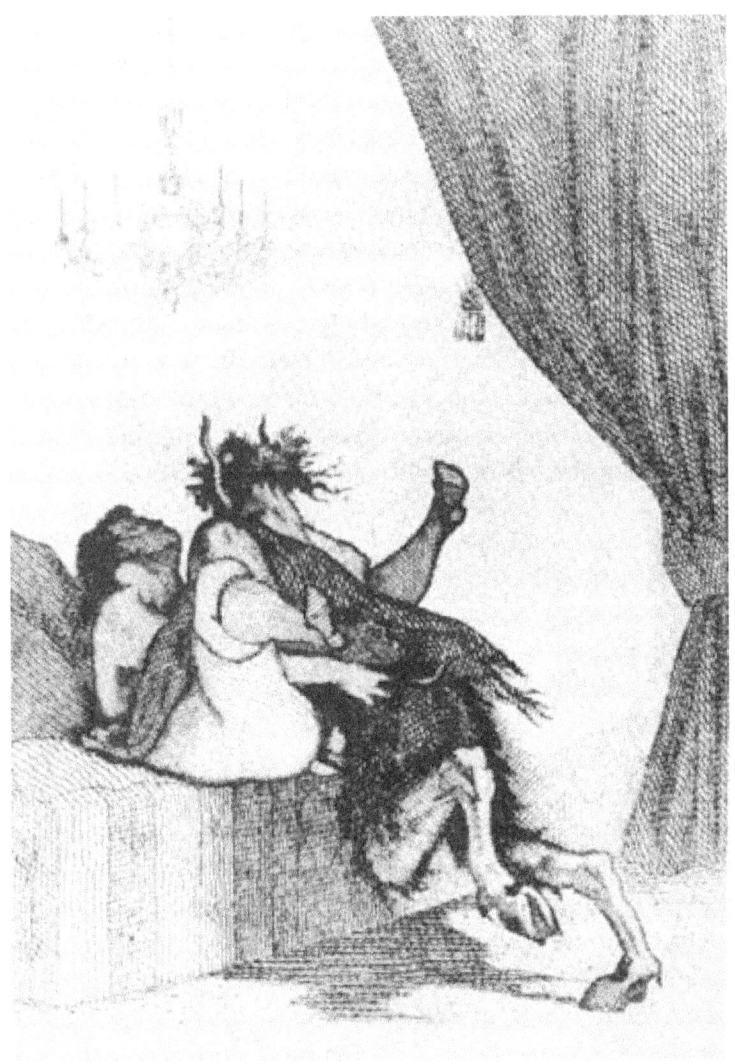

Félicien Rops, from Le Diable du
Corps, by André de Nerciat

CHRISTIANITY

In the patriarchal view, religion is sexy, and sex is religious. Artists in the 19th century often combined sexual and religious imagery (it was another way of exploring eroticism – and could be powerful precisely because the repression and exertion of power in the social realm was so strong). Western art, like pornography, draws on of the Judæo-Christian insistence on sin, death, vice, fornication, dirt and suppression. The father of Christianity is not Jesus but St Paul. Jesus wrote nothing; St Paul wrote everything, setting down the views of Christianity in that fanatical prose in the *Corinthians* and *Galatians* and *Romans*, which gets so many things wrong about flesh and spirit and marriage. Michael Foucault writes of some of the strictures of Christianity:

> Christianity associated it ['the sexual act'] with evil, sin, the Fall, and death, whereas antiquity invested it with positive symbolic values.[1]

In Christianity, women are the 'gateway to Hell' as the early theologian Tertullian poetically put it; women are evil, sinful, lustful ('the Devil is a woman' is a common theme in mediæval philosophy as well as pop songs). From Eve in the *Old Testament* to the Virgin and Magdalene in the *New Testament*, women are definitely second class citizens in the eyes of Western religion. Women-hating is startling in its violent manifestations – not just in wife-beating, which occurs everywhere and, one supposes, at every moment of human history, but also in the mass movements, such as the fight against witchcraft in the Middle Ages and later, when, armed with the *Malleus Maleficarum*, the Witchfinder Generals hunted down and tortured and killed hundreds or thousands, some say millions, of women.

---

1 M. Foucault: *The Use of Pleasure*, 14

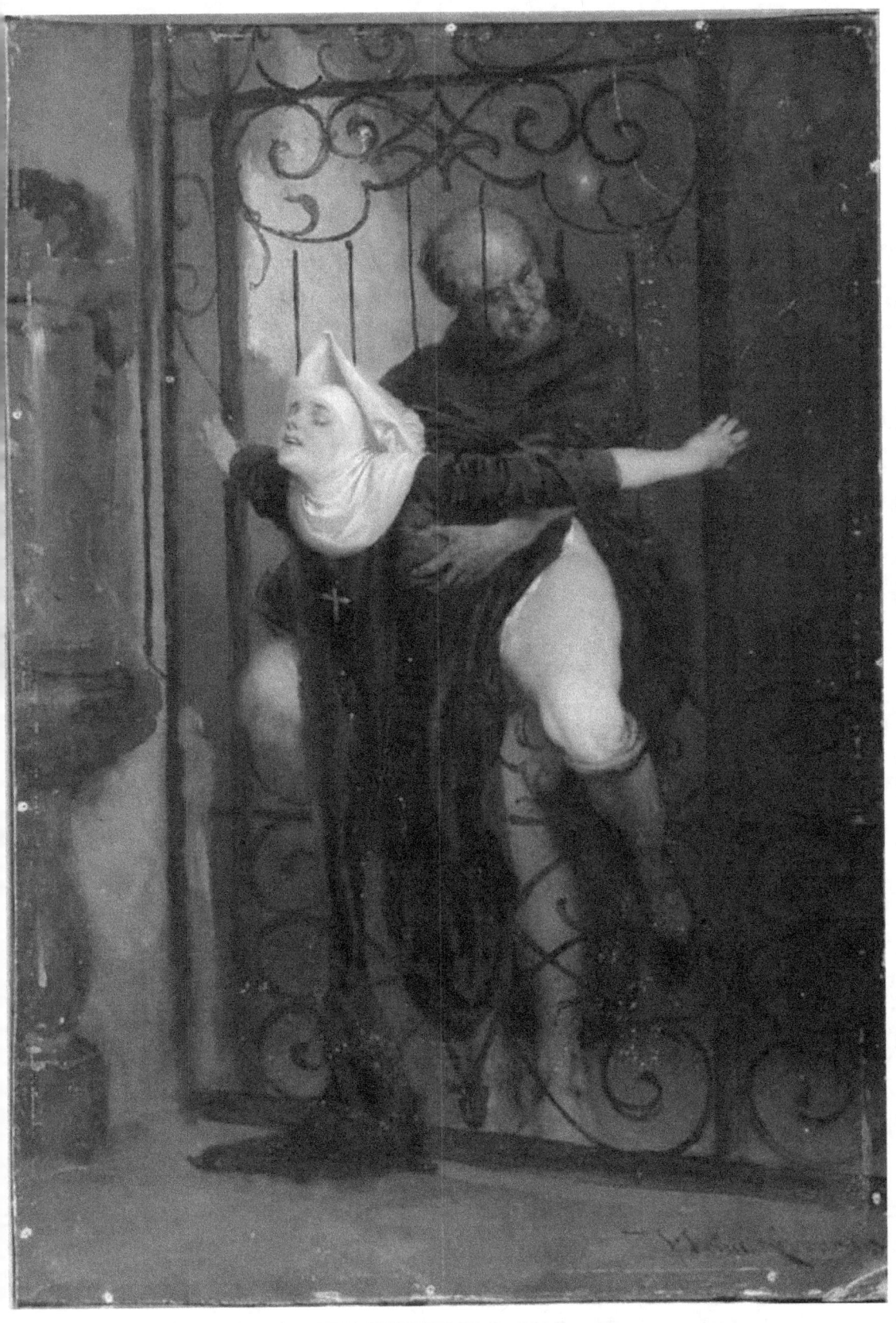

Heinrich Lossow, The Sin, 1880

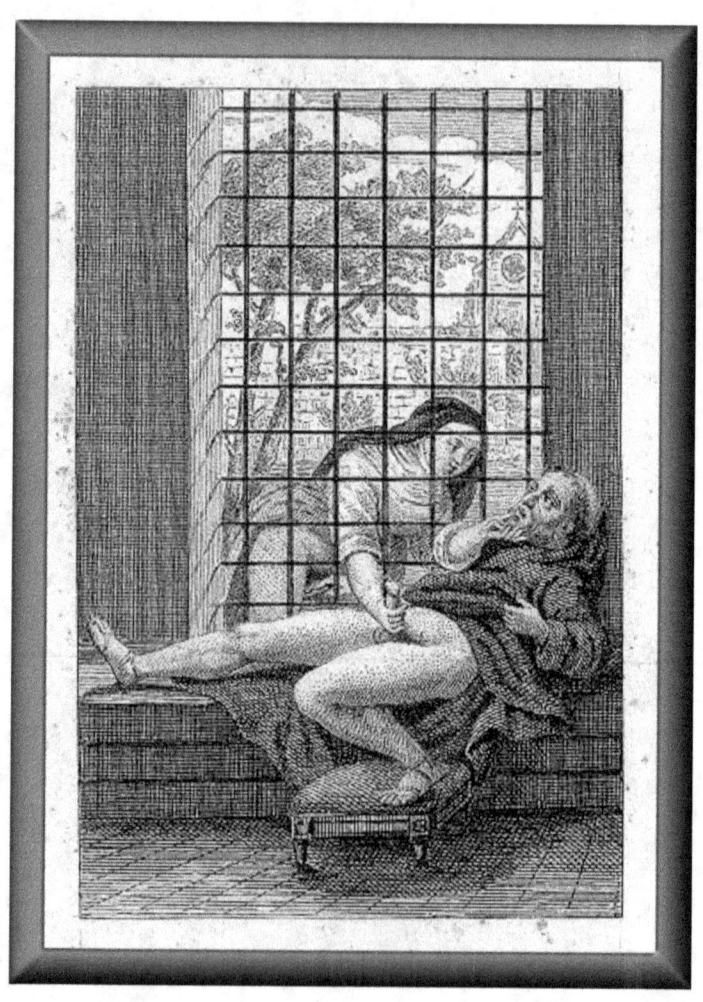

Anonymous, early 19th century

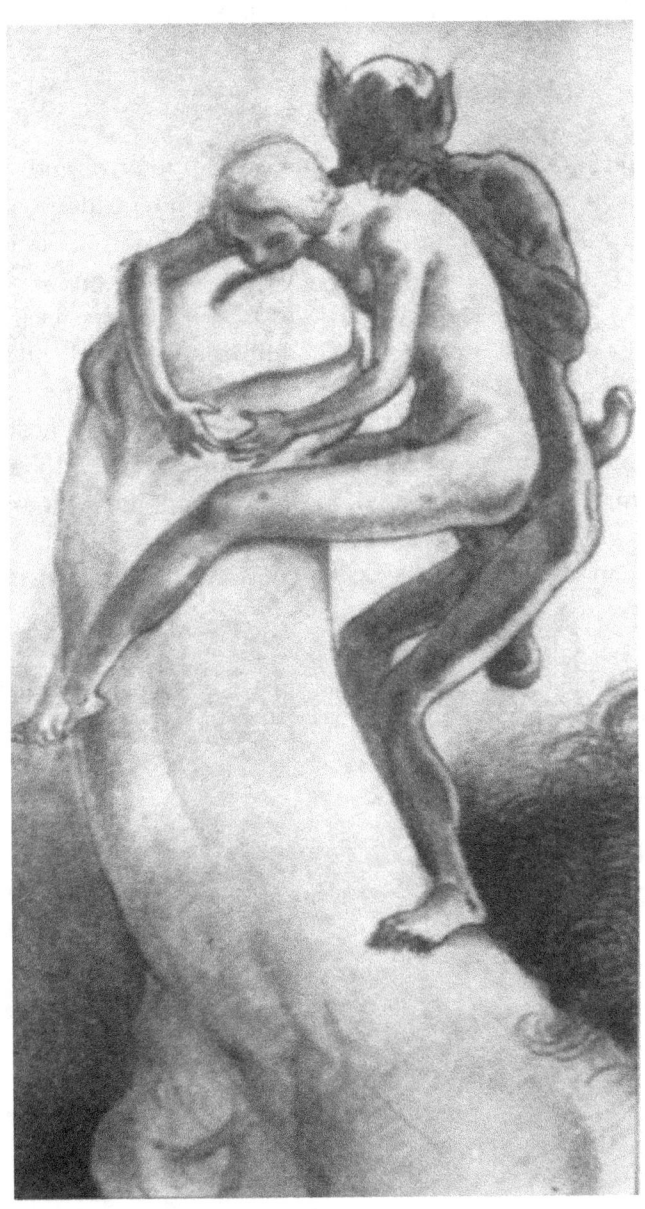

Anonymous, 19th century

EROTIC ART AND PORNOGRAPHY

The establishment art historical view of erotic art and pornography is that true erotic or high art engenders quiet contemplation, a detached ravishing of the senses, a meditation on
Platonic, Aristotlean and Kantian ideas of 'beauty' and æsthetics.
'High art', which is legitimate art, art which justifies itself by its
'genius' or obvious 'greatness', is about distance and disinterested
pleasure. The high art nude, in painting or sculpture, in the
patriarchal view, justifies its existence by the brilliance of its
production, the sumptuousness of its colour and form, the marvel
of its human touches, the grandeur of its design, the loftiness of its
ambition, the dynamism of its structures, and so on. As that
producer of exquisite bodies, French Neo-Classical artist J.A.D.
Ingres, wrote:

> There are not two arts, there is only one: it is the one which has as its
> foundation the beautiful, which is eternal and natural.[1]

---

1 Ingres, quoted in Goldwater, 216

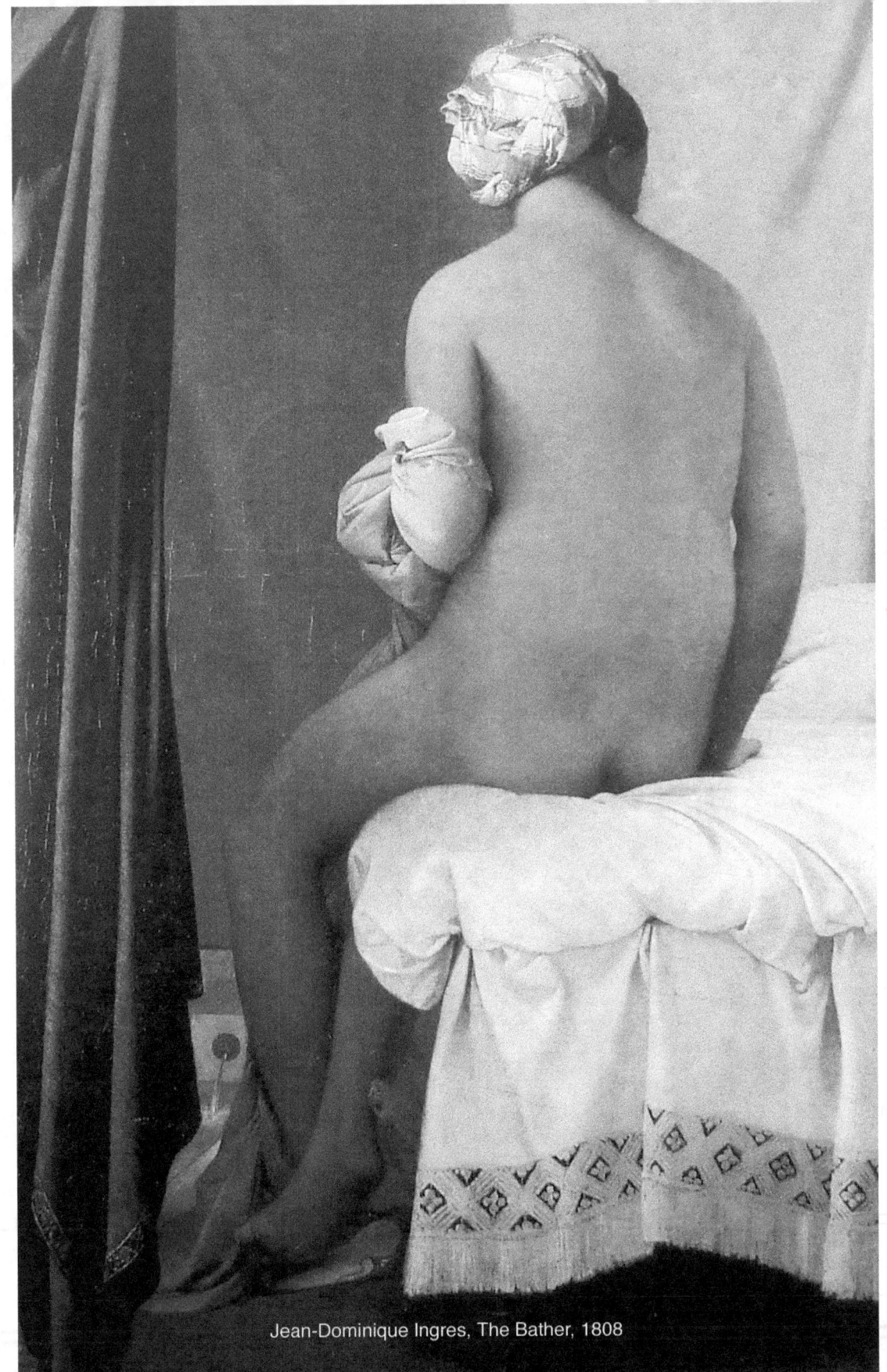

Jean-Dominique Ingres, The Bather, 1808

FEMME FATALES

The *femme fatale* type neatly melds sex and death, desire and fear, contact and loss, for the (male) artist. She appears in Medusa, Salomé, Delilah, Jezebel, Judith, Lilith, Ninuë (the lover of Merlin), Venus, Helen of Troy, La Belle Dame Sans Merci, and Cleopatra. These female 'types' combined beauty with death, immense power and all manner of sadistic, masochistic and fetishistic fantasies. These are the women who will whip you to death, if you wish, as in Leopold Sacher-Masoch's *Venus in Furs*. Figures such as Cleopatra provided the longed for combination of socio-political, religious sovereignty, wild eroticism, intrigue, magnificent settings and gory love-deaths. As Max Lake informs us:

> The amatory skills of Cleopatra passed into legend while she lived. Apart from the rapid seduction of both Julius Caesar and Mark Antony, she is reported to have fellated one hundred noblemen in a single evening. Her Greek nickname was *meriochane*, 'she who parts wide for a thousand men.'[1]

---

1 Max Lake: *Scents and Sensuality: The Essence of Excitement*, John Murray 1989, 58

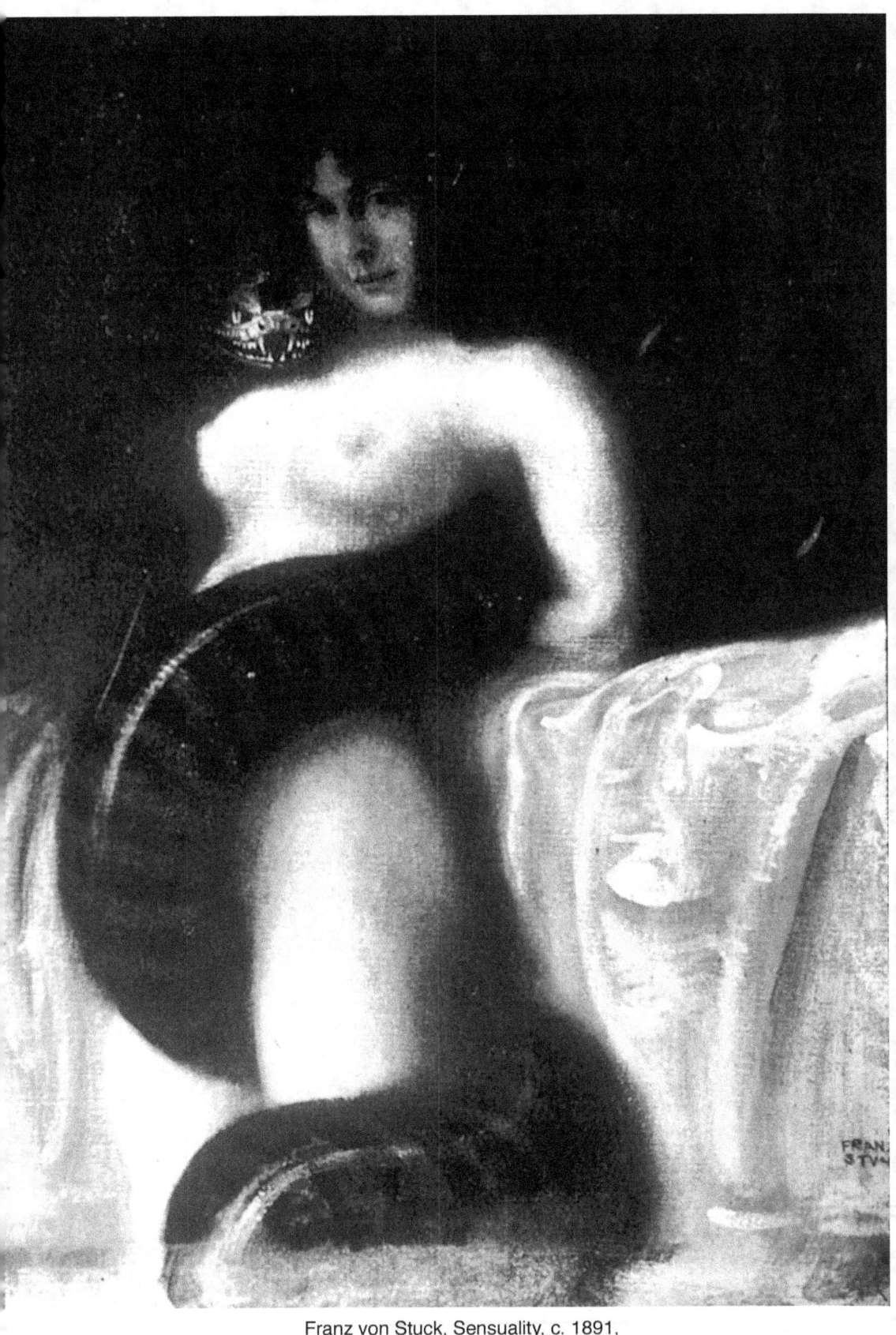

Franz von Stuck, Sensuality, c. 1891,
collection: Abraham Somer, Los Angeles

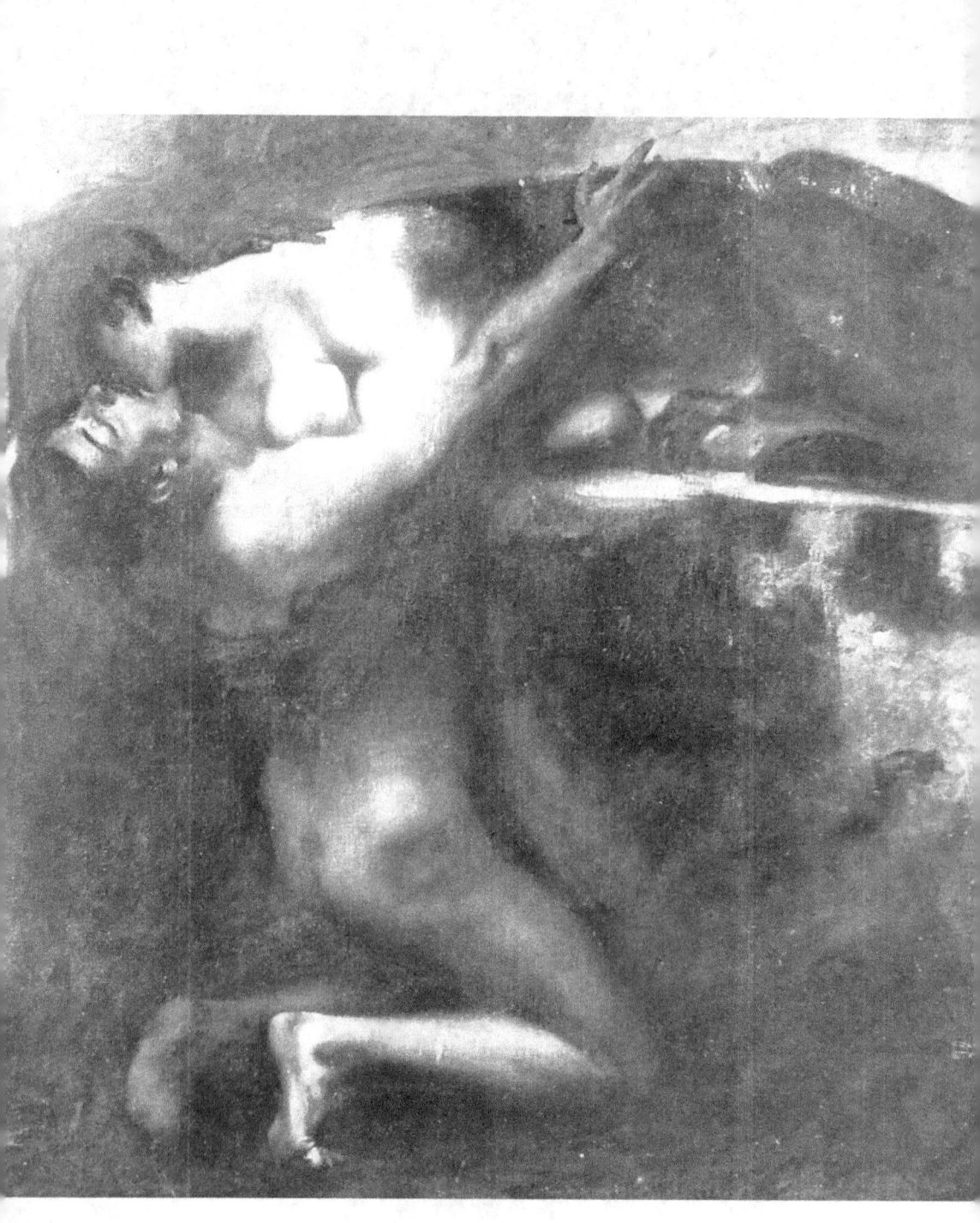

Franz von Stuck, Sphinx

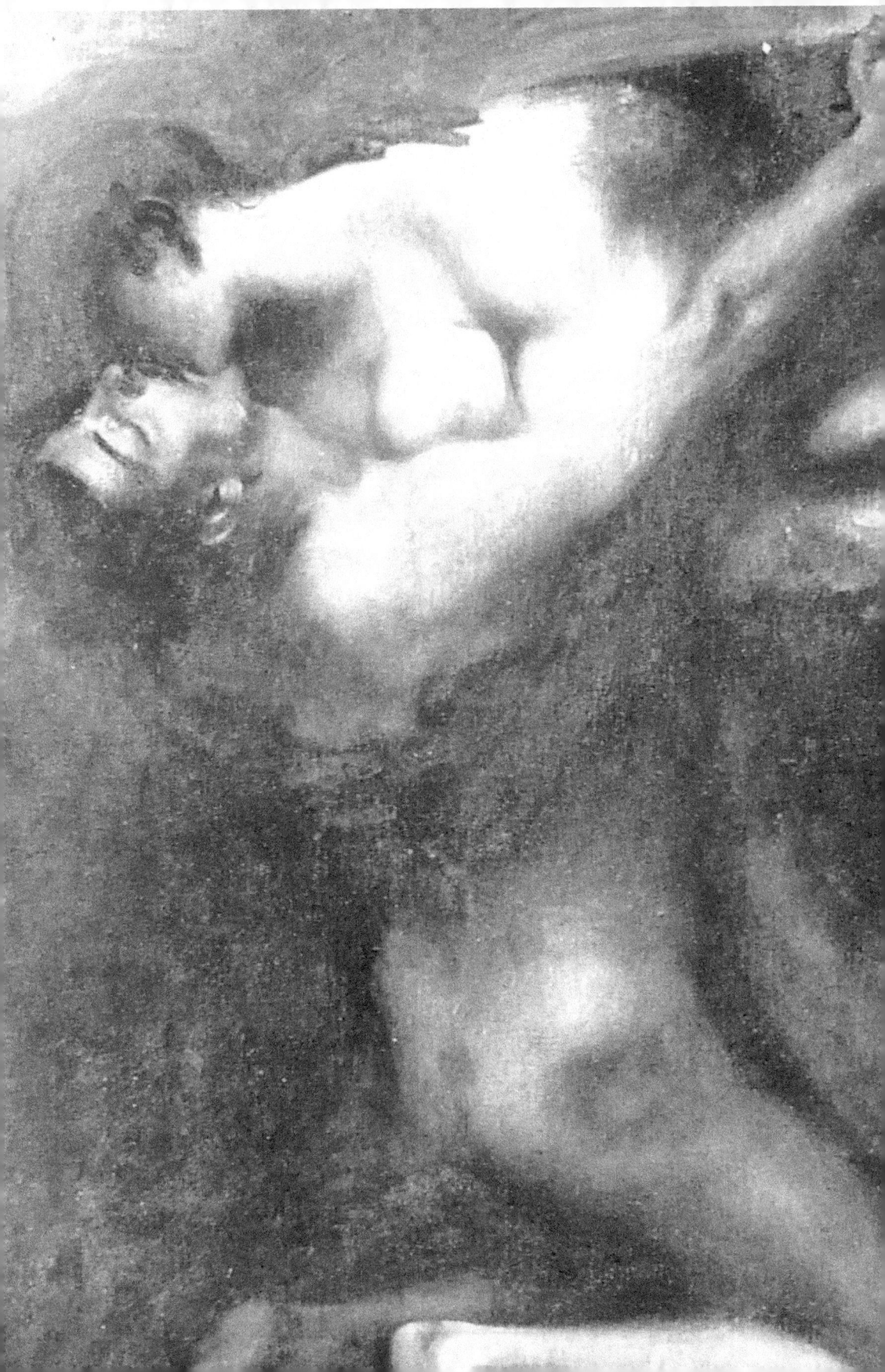

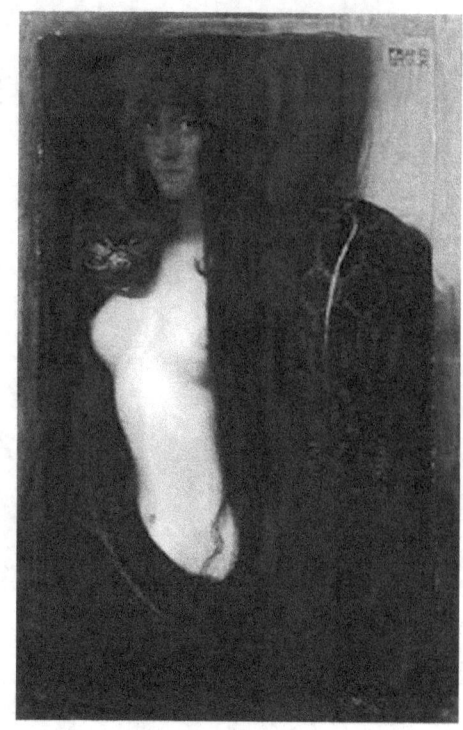

Franz von Stuck,
Wounded Amazon (below).

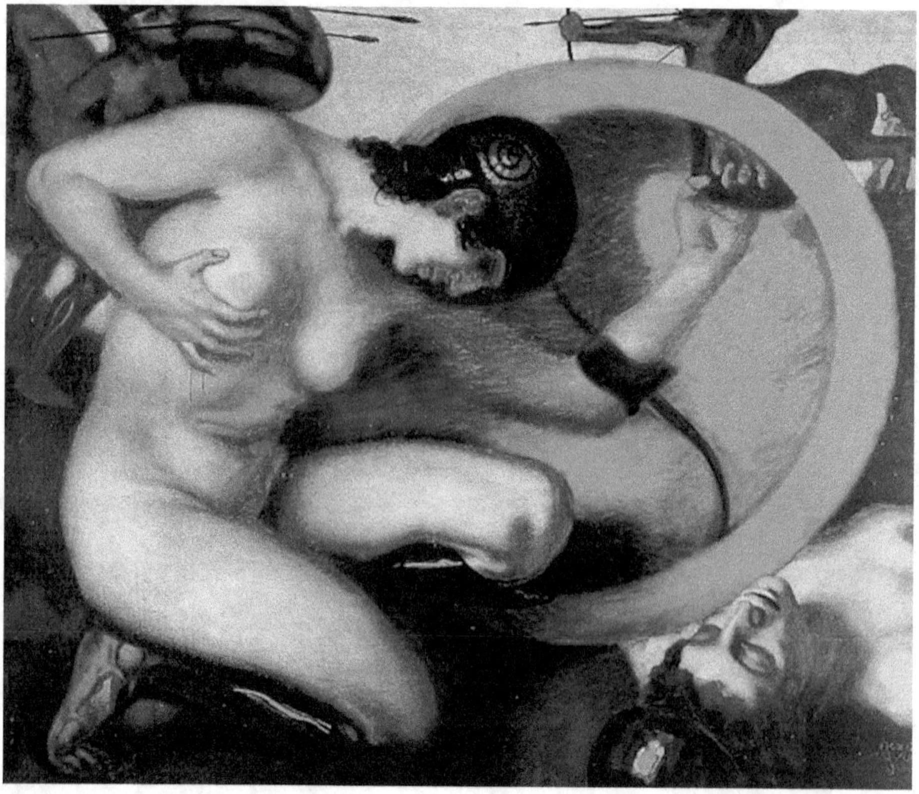

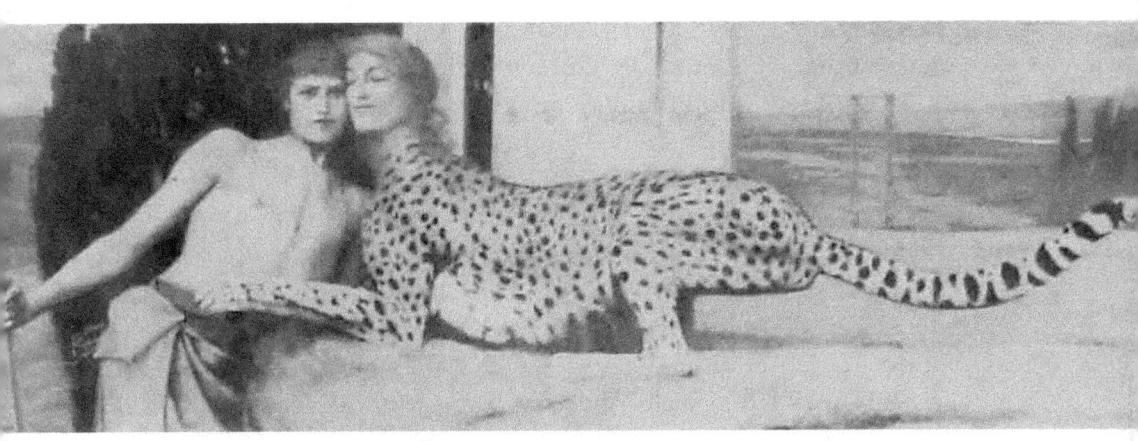

Fernand Knopff, The Caresses of the Sphinx, 1896, Brussels

SYMBOLIST AND DECADENT ART

Symbolist art, Decadent art, *fin-de-siècle* art, whatever you want to call it, is the most pornographic of 'high art'. Other art movements that followed Symbolism – Surrealism, for instance, or Pop Art – simply improvize on the excesses of Symbolist art. For in artists such as Gustave Moreau, Edvard Munch, Félicien Rops, Odilon Redon, Jean Deville and Franz von Stuck – one discovers figurative art at its most excessive. The high priest of the Symbolist era is undoubtedly Gustave Moreau. His images make the Pre-Raphaelites in Britain seem positively watered-down, and the Pre-Raphaelites themselves are as contrived, luxuriant, and mythical as any group of artists.

The Symbolist and Decadent age is marked by 'gory exoticism', as Mario Praz puts it (289), by mysticism and black magic, the macabre, the æstheticism of 'beauty', opulence and indulgence, where the key phrase is from Paul Verlaine: 'Je suis l'Empire à la fin de la décadence'.[1] The Symbolist age was summed up by works of literature such as Arthur Rimbaud's *Une Saison en Enfer*, Lautréamont's *Chansons de Maldoror*, Edgar Allan Poe's horror stories, and Charles Baudelaire's *Flowers of Evil*. Other works which characterize the epoch include: *Salambô*, J.-K. Huysmans' *A Rebours*, Péladan's *Le Vice suprême, Parsifal*. Some of the key artists of the Decadent and Symbolist age include Richard Wagner, Honoré de Balzac, J.-K. Huysmans, Walter Pater, Gustave Flaubert, Gustave Moreau, Oscar Wilde, Arnold Böcklin, and Stéphane Mallarmé. Rimbaud argued for a 'rational derange-ment of all the senses', and showed how marvellous poetry could be when it was unfettered and wild, in his *Les Illuminations*. Rimbaud's tenets, of the 'seer' poet, of madness, of magic, of rebellion, provide the basic ground for many art 'movements', from Symbolism through Surrealism to Pop Art (and rock music).

---

1 Verlaine: *Selected Poems*, tr Joanna Richardson, Penguin 1974, 180

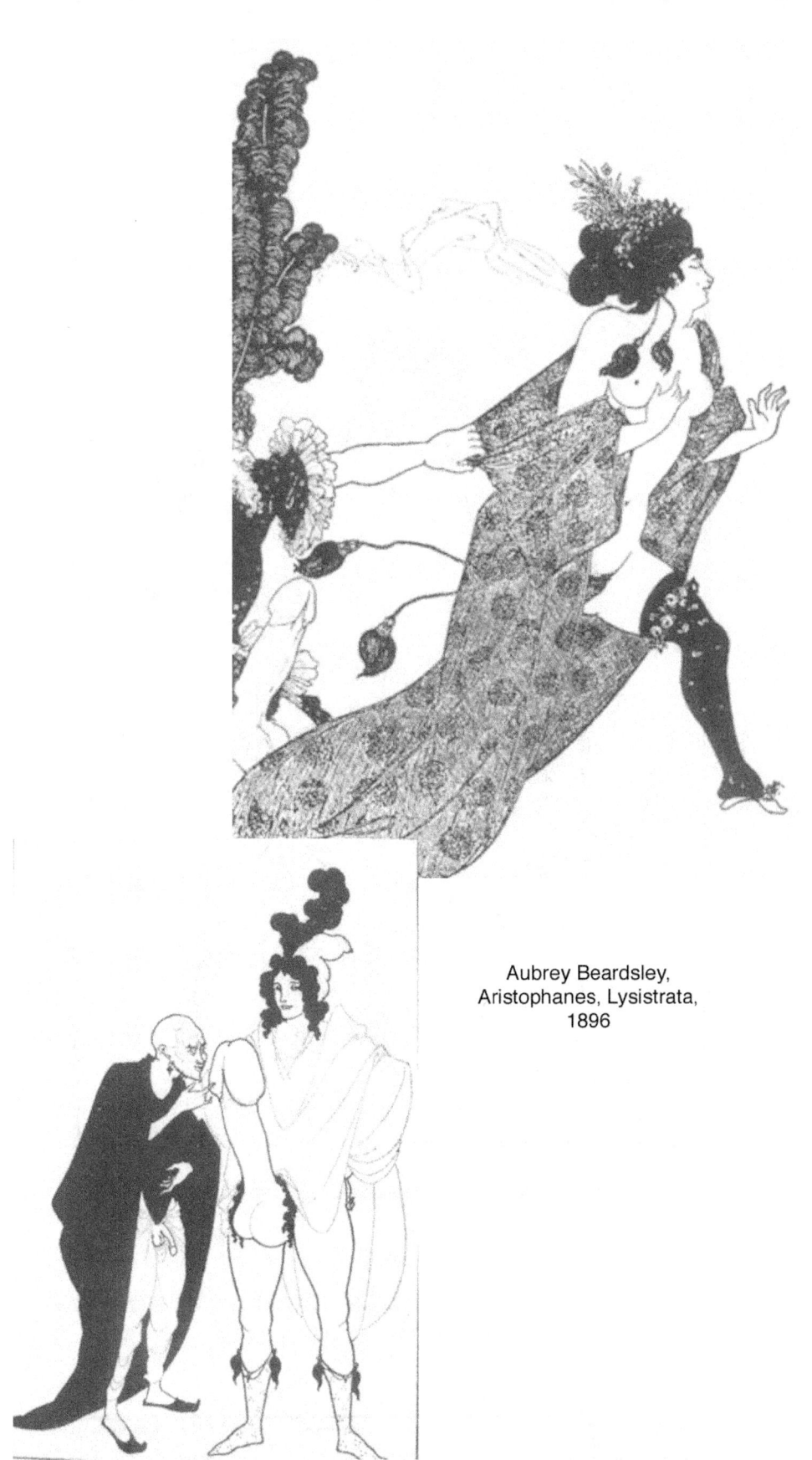

Aubrey Beardsley,
Aristophanes, Lysistrata,
1896

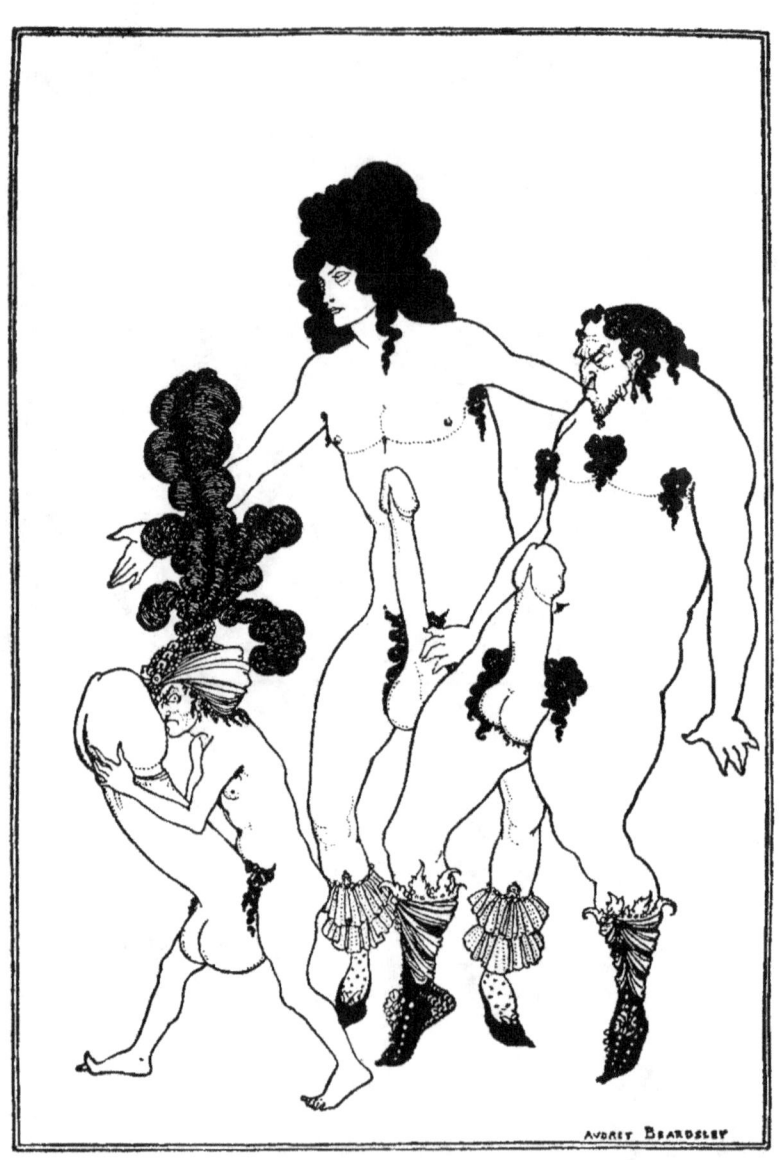

Aubrey Beardsley, Aristophanes, Lysistrata, 1896

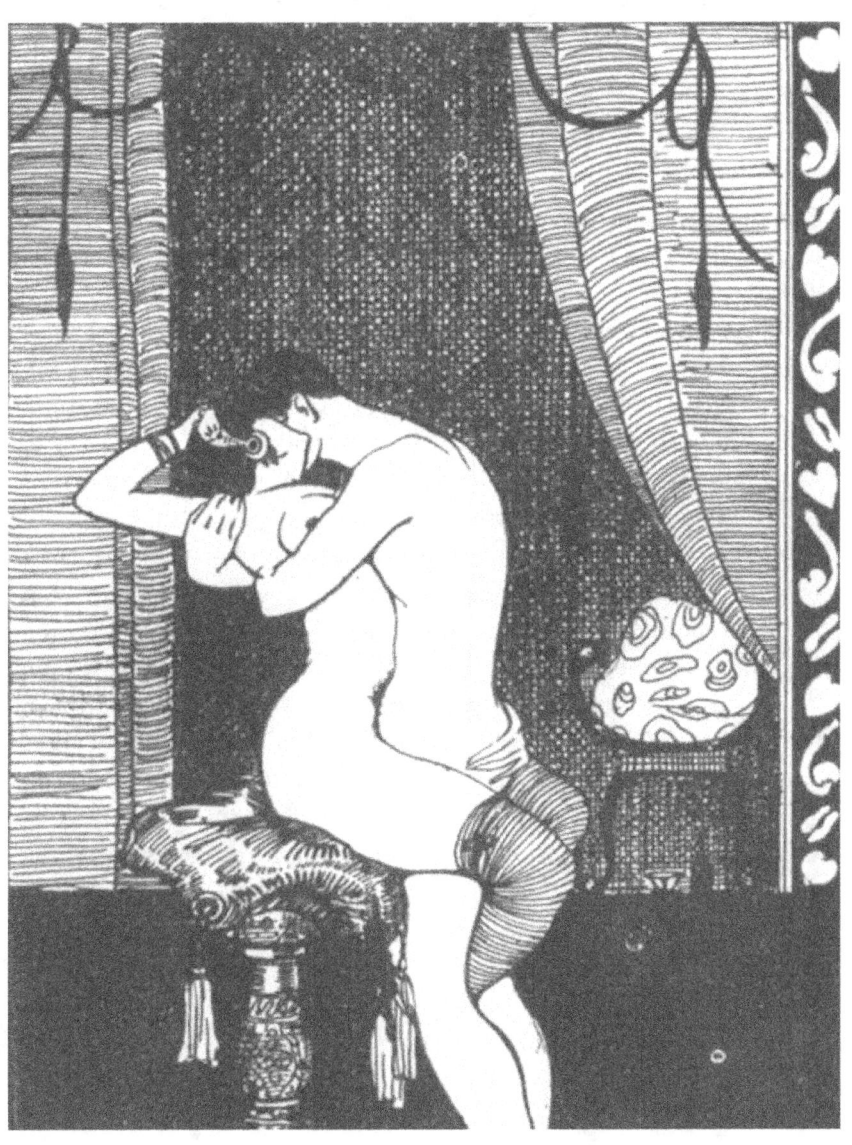

Anonymous, from Fanny Hill by John Cleland, 1889

SYMBOLIST AND DECADENT ART

The representation of women is central to Symbolist and Decadent art, as it is to 19th century art as a whole. The result is a misogynism which is often fierce and vicious. Edward Burne-Jones, the most celebrated of the Pre-Raphaelites, wrote: '[t]iresome the modern woman is. I like women when they're good and kind and pretty – agreeable objects in the landscape of existence – give life to it'.[1] This is a typical sexist comment of the Victorian age. John Burgan, a professor of divinity at Oxford, said: '[w]oman's strength lies in her essential weakness'.[2]

Some late 19th century paintings appropriate women's mysteries, such as childbirth, as in Giovanni Segantini's *The Evil Mothers*, which depicts women tied to trees by their own hair in a wilderness, punished for rejecting motherhood.[3] Many images of the 19th century do nothing more than objectify women sexually, depicting them as sex objects: many artists did not hide their lust; their women are openly displayed, legs akimbo, spines arched, heads thrown to one side, as in standard pornography. The women in many images of 19th century art pose in a porno-graphic fashion: in Henri Gervex's *Rolla*, in many works by Félix Vallotton, in Auguste Rodin's' frenetic sculptures of kisses, in the artworks of Félicien Rops, Gustave Moreau, Jean Delville, etc.[4]

1 Burne-Jones: "Conversations", in Kestner, 107
2 Burgan, 1884, in Joan Burstyn: *Victorian Education and the Ideal of Womanhood*, Croom Helm 1980, 33.
3 Segantini: *The Evil Mothers*, 1894, oil on canvas, 120 x 225cm, Kunsthistorisches Museum, Vienna
4 Gervex: *Rola*, 1878, oil on canvas, 175 x 220cm, Musée des Beaux-Arts, Bordeaux; Félix Vallotton: *The Spring*, 1897, oil on board, 48 x 60cm, Musée du petit Palais, Geneva

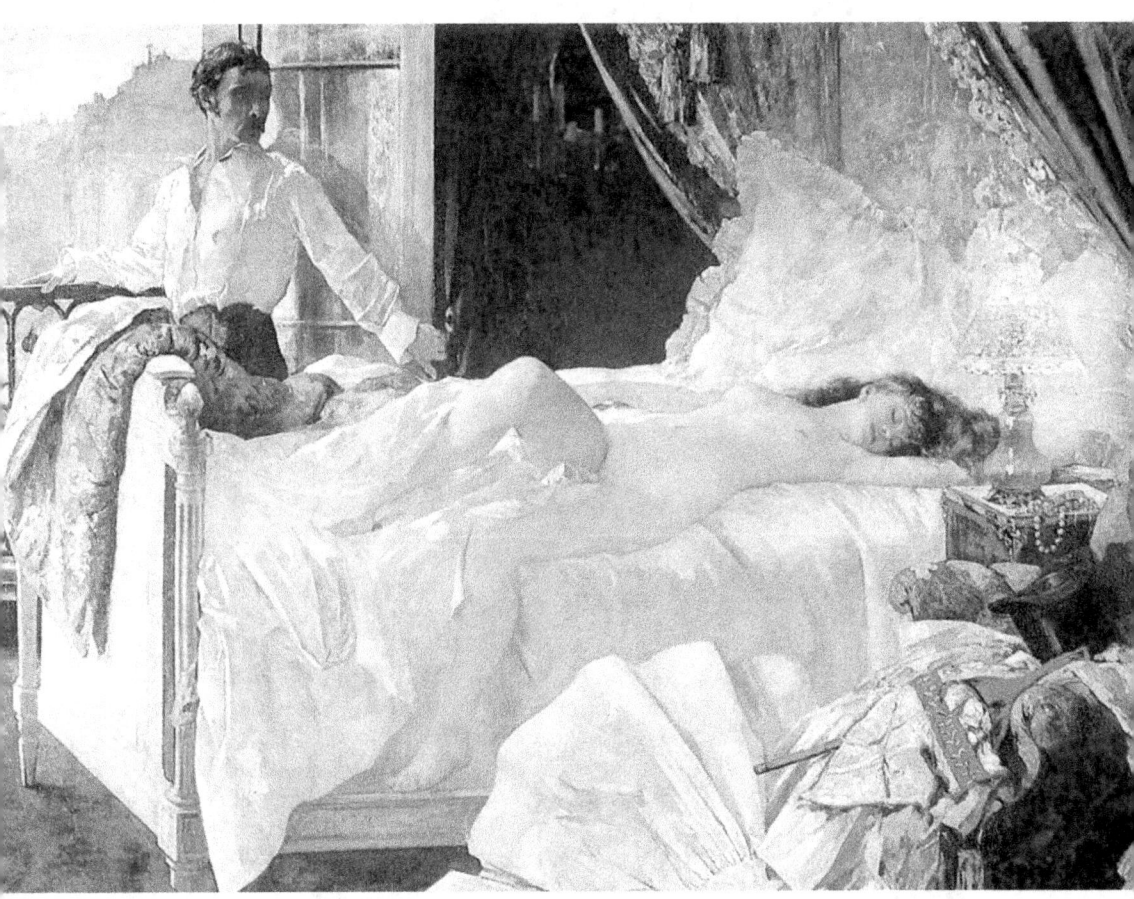

Henri Gervex Rolla, 1878

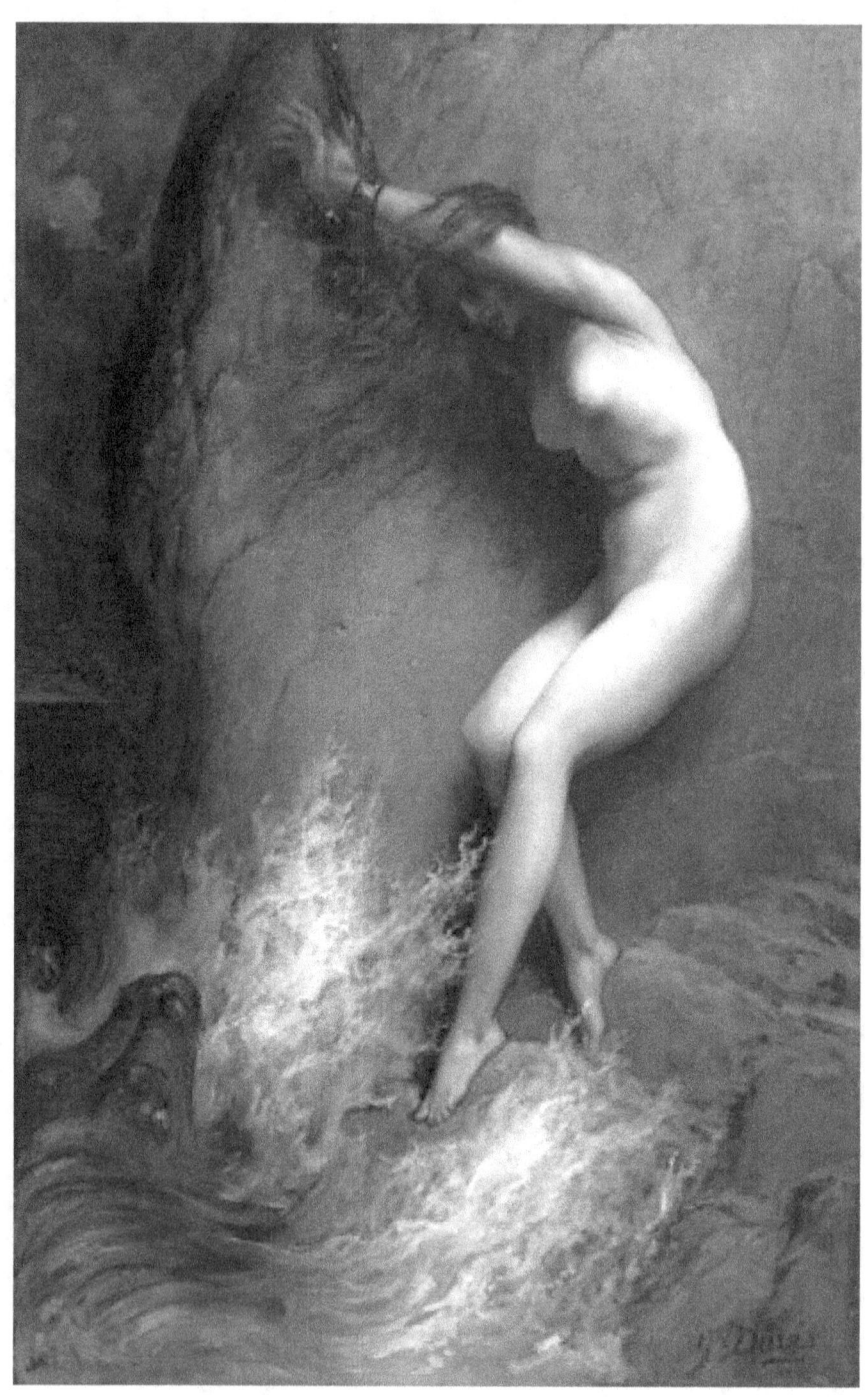

Gustave Doré

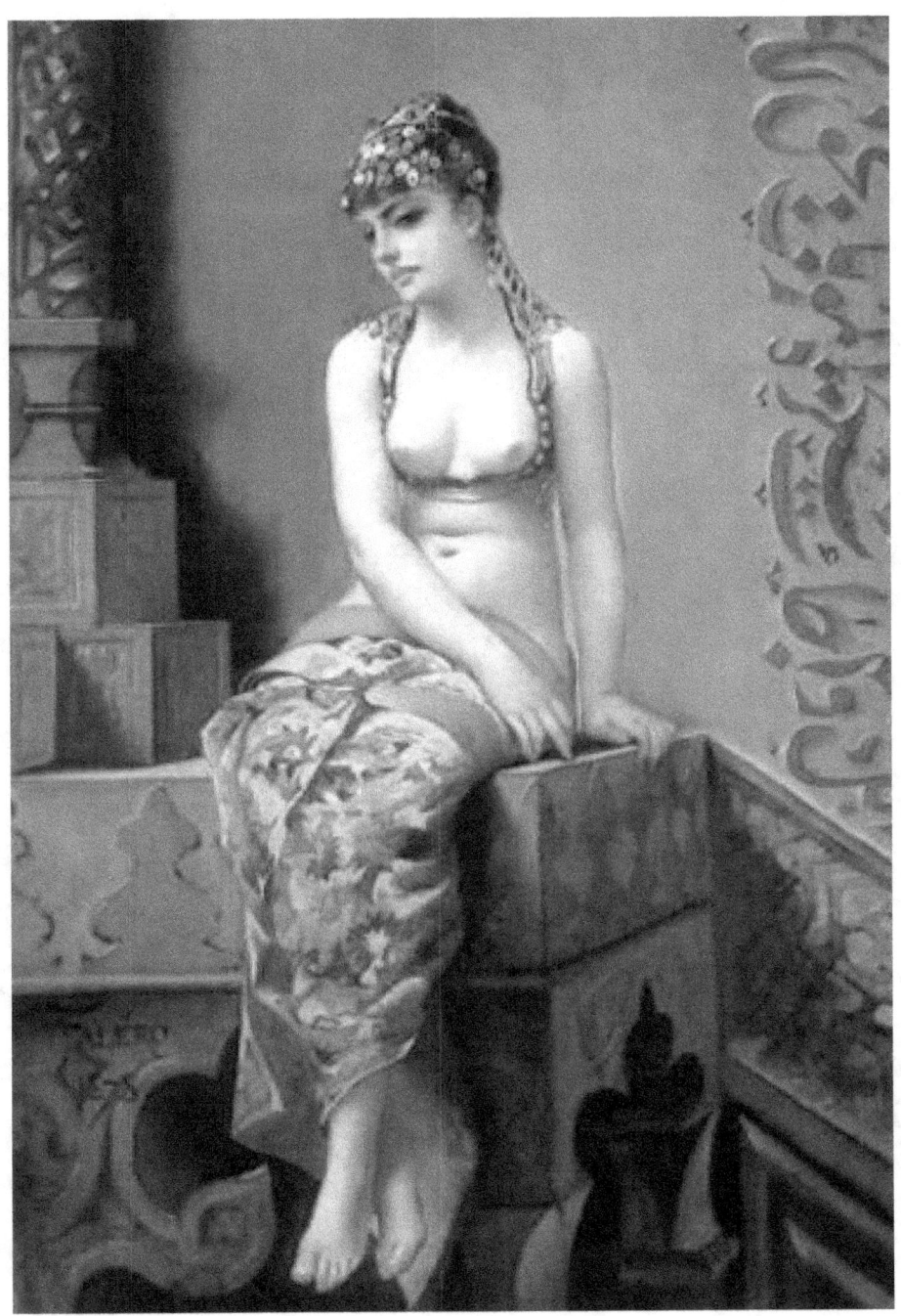

Luis Ricardo Falero

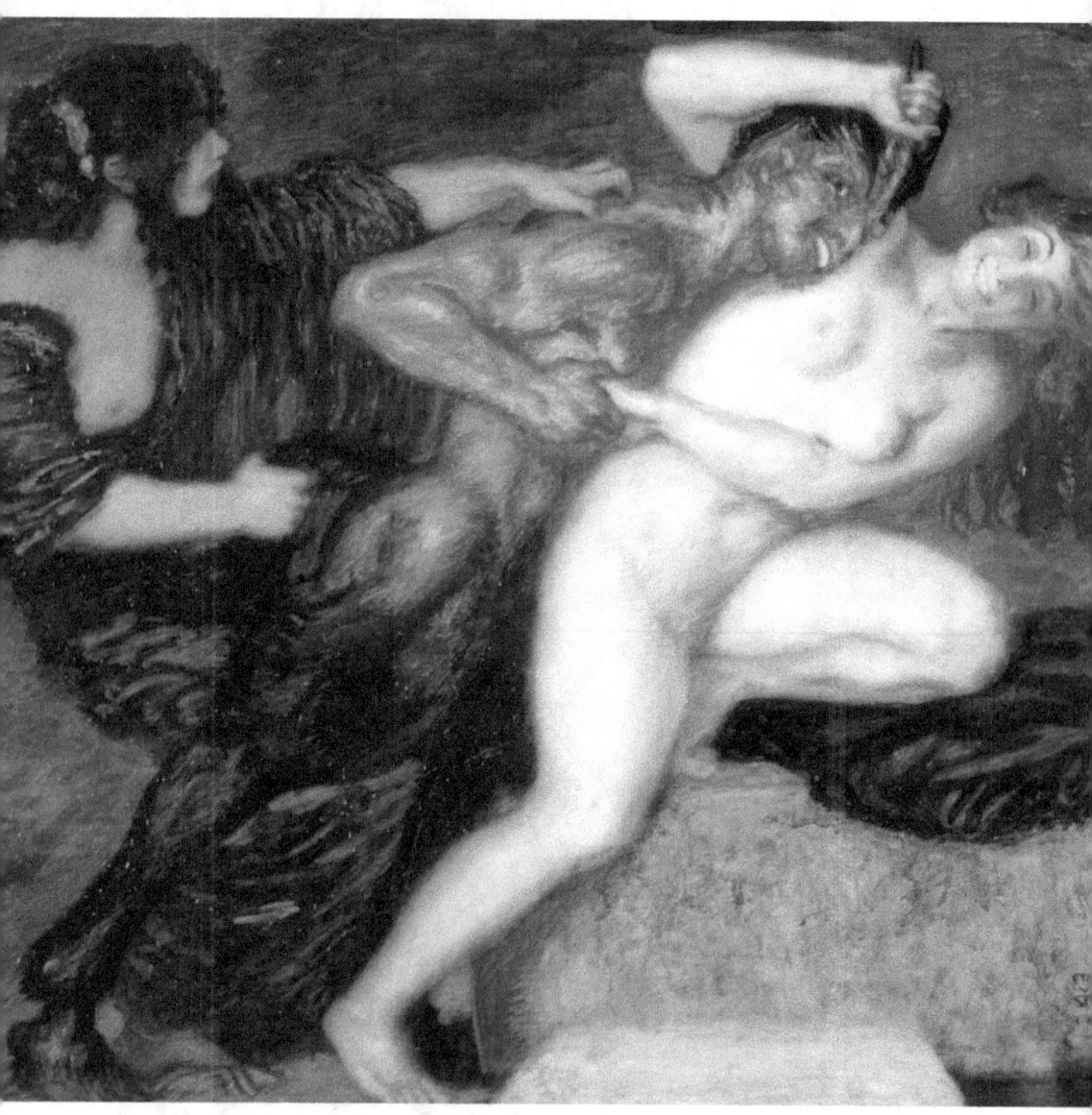

Franz von Stuck, Scherzo

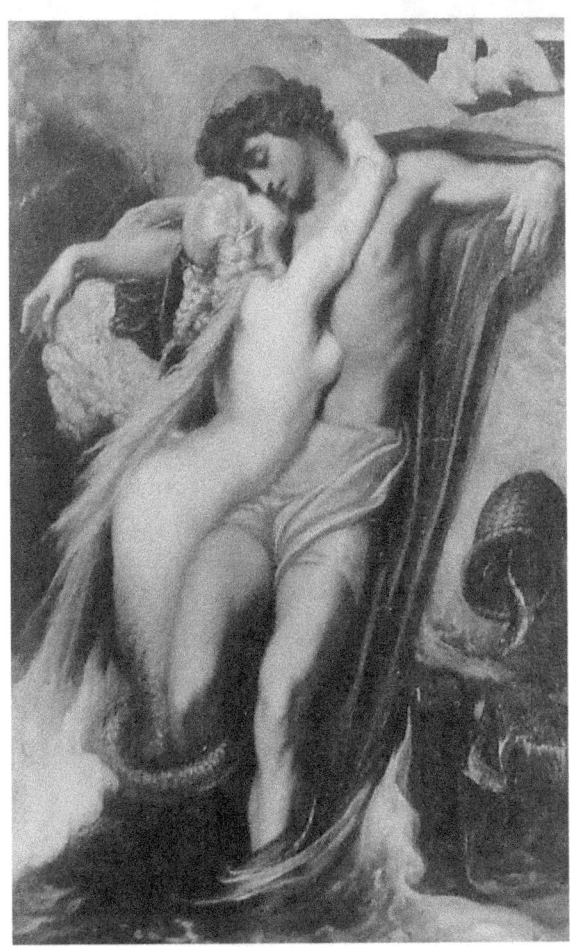

Classic Victorian nude imagery, by Lord Leighton: The Fisherman and the Siren, 1858, Bristol, above; and Actaea, the Nymph of the Shore, 1868, Ottawa, below.

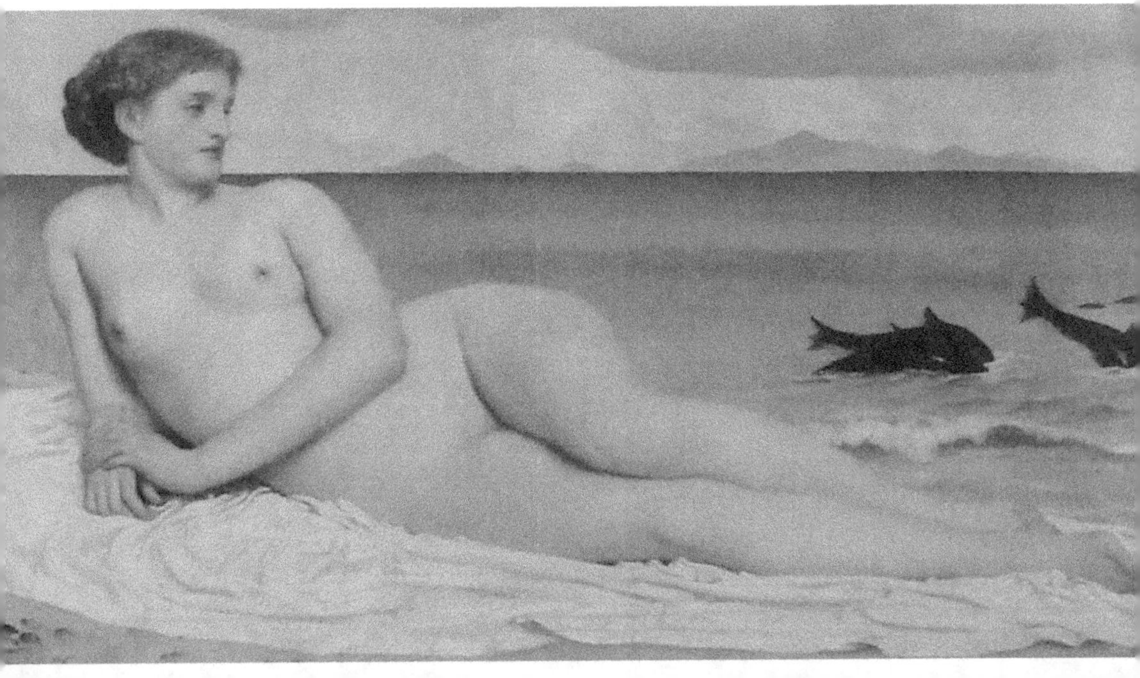

OTTO GRENIER: *THE DEVIL SHOWING WOMAN TO THE PEOPLE*

The depictions of women as mythical beings in Symbolist and Decadent are sometimes misogynistic, occasionally extremely so. If the 'holy whore', whether Aphrodite, Cleopatra or the Sphinx is the Queen or Goddess of Symbolist, Satan is undoubtedly the hero, which is only right for a culture founded on the Marquis de Sade and Charles Baudelaire. Women and death are merged throughout Western art. In many Symbolist pictures, for instance, the figure of death with the sickle is a woman,[1] while in Otto Greiner's *The Devil Showing Woman to the People*, Satan holds up a woman, naked of course, in stockings, of course, as a sex object.[2] Indeed, much of Symbolist art, and modern art, can be seen as 'the Devil showing woman to the people'. The Devil is the artist, showing women in various forms of sexual objectification, from 'high art' nudes to hardcore pornography.

---

1 in Odilon Redon's *Death: My Irony Surpasses All Others*, 1889, lithograph, 26 x 19cm (from Flaubert's *The Temptation of St. Anthony*, another key work of the Symbolist/Decadent era), Bibliothéque Nationale, Paris; Félicien Rops: *Mors Syphilitica*, Bibliothéque Nationale, Paris; Alfred Kubin: *The Best Medicine*, 1901-2, pen and India ink, 17 x 29cm, private collection; Gauguin: *Madame La Mort*, 1899, charcoal and India ink, 24 x 29cm, Musée d'Orsay
2 Otto Greiner: *The Devil Showing Woman to the People*, 1897, chalk on paper, 39 x 29cm, Art Gallery of Ontario, Toronto

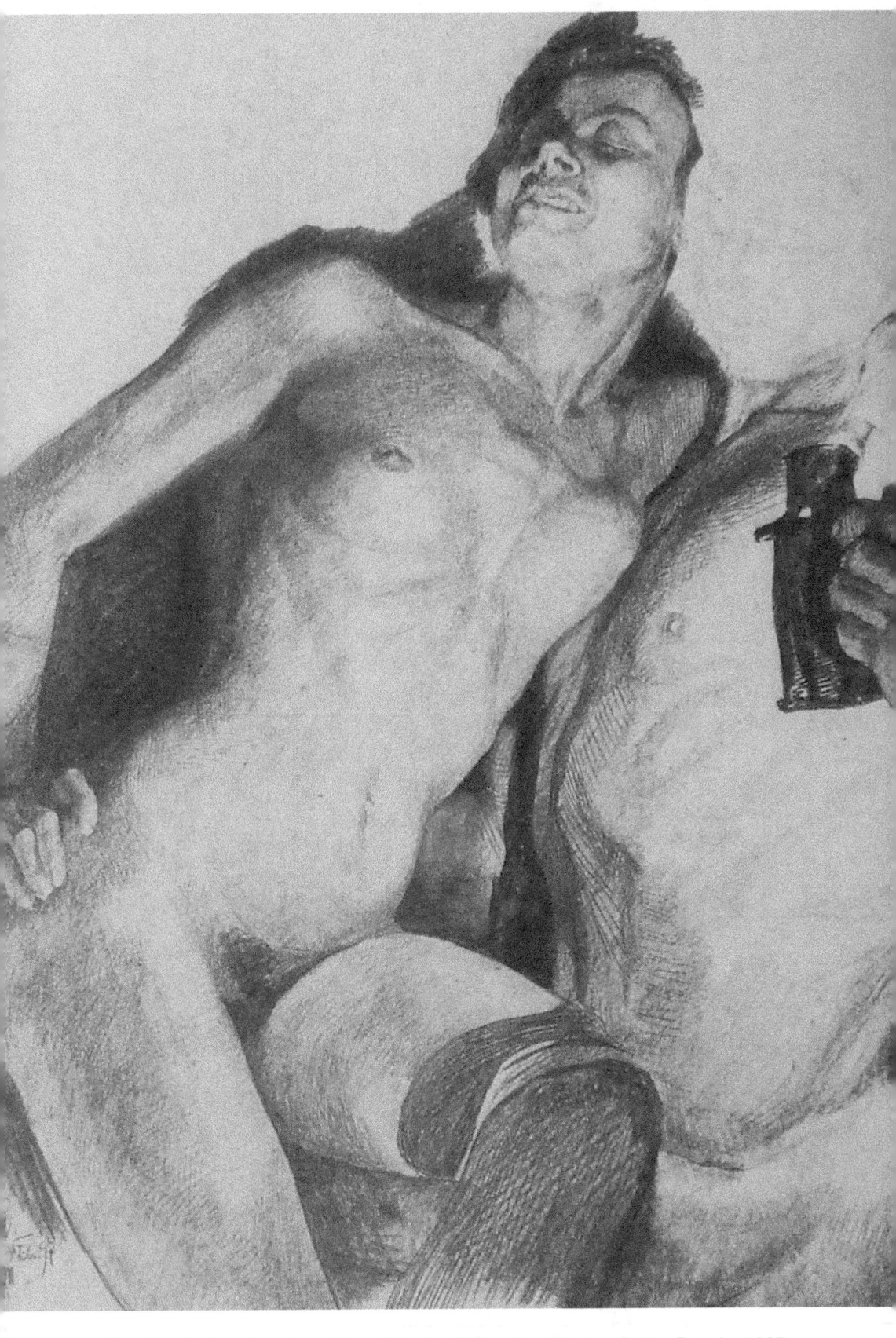

Otto Grenier's truly extraordinary The Devil Showing Woman To the People, 1897

GUSTAVE MOREAU

Gustave Moreau's world is supremely heterosexist. Women conform to stereotypes, to whores, witches, virgins, maidens, etc. Semele swoons over the radiance of the god Jupiter. Moreau's painting is the apotheosis of the religious cult of Symbolism and Decadence, which makes a religion of æsthetic depictions of sex and death and decadence. The word, *decadence*, from Paul Verlaine, connotes profuse amounts of eroticism, debauchery, declining state power, Imperialism and 'perversions'.

Gustave Moreau's is the poet's painter, the painter of 'poetic' visions, someone whom J.-K. Huysmans praised in the Bible of the Decadent era, *À Rebours* (*Against Nature*). Moreau is the painter of pure emotion: 'I only believe what I do not see and uniquely what I feel', he remarked.[1] Moreau's art brings together all the crucial elements of Symbolist art; the mysticism, eroticism, nostalgia (for Byzantium, Greece, Rome), Imperialism, romanticism, decadence, occultism and dreams.

---

1 G. Moreau, quoted in J. Paladilhe, 134

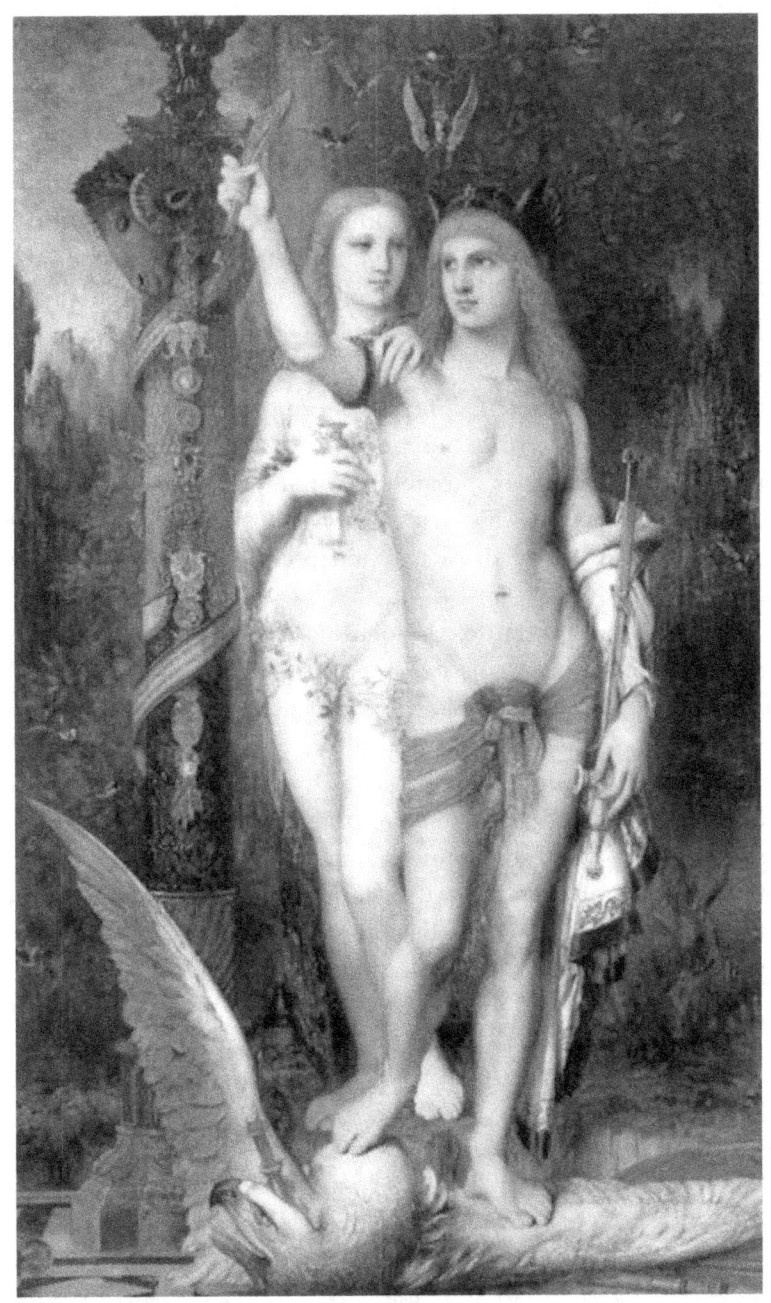

Gustave Moreau, Jason and Medea

GUSTAVE MOREAU

Gustave Moreau's paintings are soaked in dream imagery – not the hallucinatory sort that people think can only be obtained from by use of LSD – but by the visions of poets have in their dreams. Dreams of ancient and timeless worlds, where rituals or mysterious scenes, such as Salomé dancing, or Hercules amongst Thespius' daughters, occur endlessly and statically.[1] Moreau's world is of an eternal Orphic dreaming: he painted Orpheus' head on the lyre, as did Odilon Redon, who is even dreamier than Moreau, if that is possible.[2] Moreau's people seem to be asleep, when they are not wide awake with religious enlightenment. Salomé in many drawings and paintings dances with eyes closed.[3]

The half-asleep figures emphasize the passivity and interiority of Gustave Moreau's mythopoeic world. There is little confrontation, although there is anguish and pain aplenty. Salomé dominates his art. She is the ultimate castrating force. For Freudians, Salomé in Moreau's art is the return of the castrating mother. Moreau's famous *The Apparition* orchestrates in the most decorative and stylized manner, more mannered than Mannerist art, more baroque than Baroque art, more romantic than Romantic art, the anguish of fear and desire, the fear of rejection and loss, the craving for contact and sublimation.[4]

1 G. Moreau: *Salomé Dancing Before Herod (Tattooed Salomé)*, 1876, oil on canvas, 92 x 60cm, Gustave Moreau Museum, Paris; *Hercules Among the Daughters of Thespius*, begun 1852, oil on canvas, 258 x 255cm, Gustave Moreau, Paris
2 Odilon Redon: *Orpheus*, c. 1913-6, pastel, 70 x 57cm, Cleveland Museum of Art; Moreau: *Thracian Girl Carrying the Head of Orpheus*, 1866, oil on canvas, 154 x 99.5cm, Louvre, Paris
3 G. Moreau: *Salomé Carrying the Head of St John the Baptist*, pencil and ink, 30 x 19cm, Gustave Moreau Museum, Paris; *Salomé*, study, oil on wood, 23 x 33cm, Gustave Moreau Museum, Paris; *Salomé*, pencil, 60 x 36cm, Gustave Moreau Museum, Paris
4 G. Moreau: *The Apparition*, 1876, watercolour on paper, 106 x 72cm, Louvre, Paris

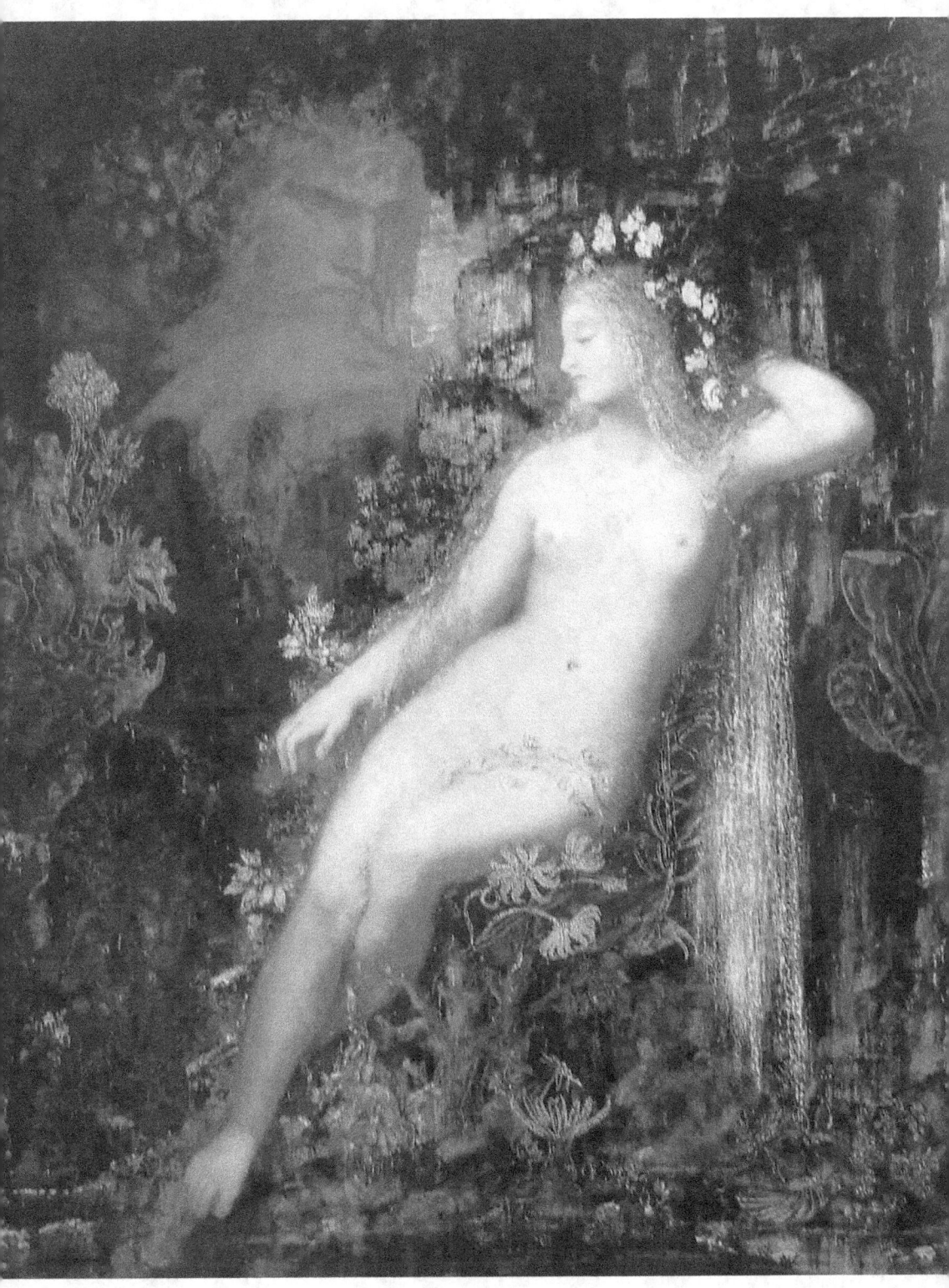

Gustave Moreau, Galatea, 1880

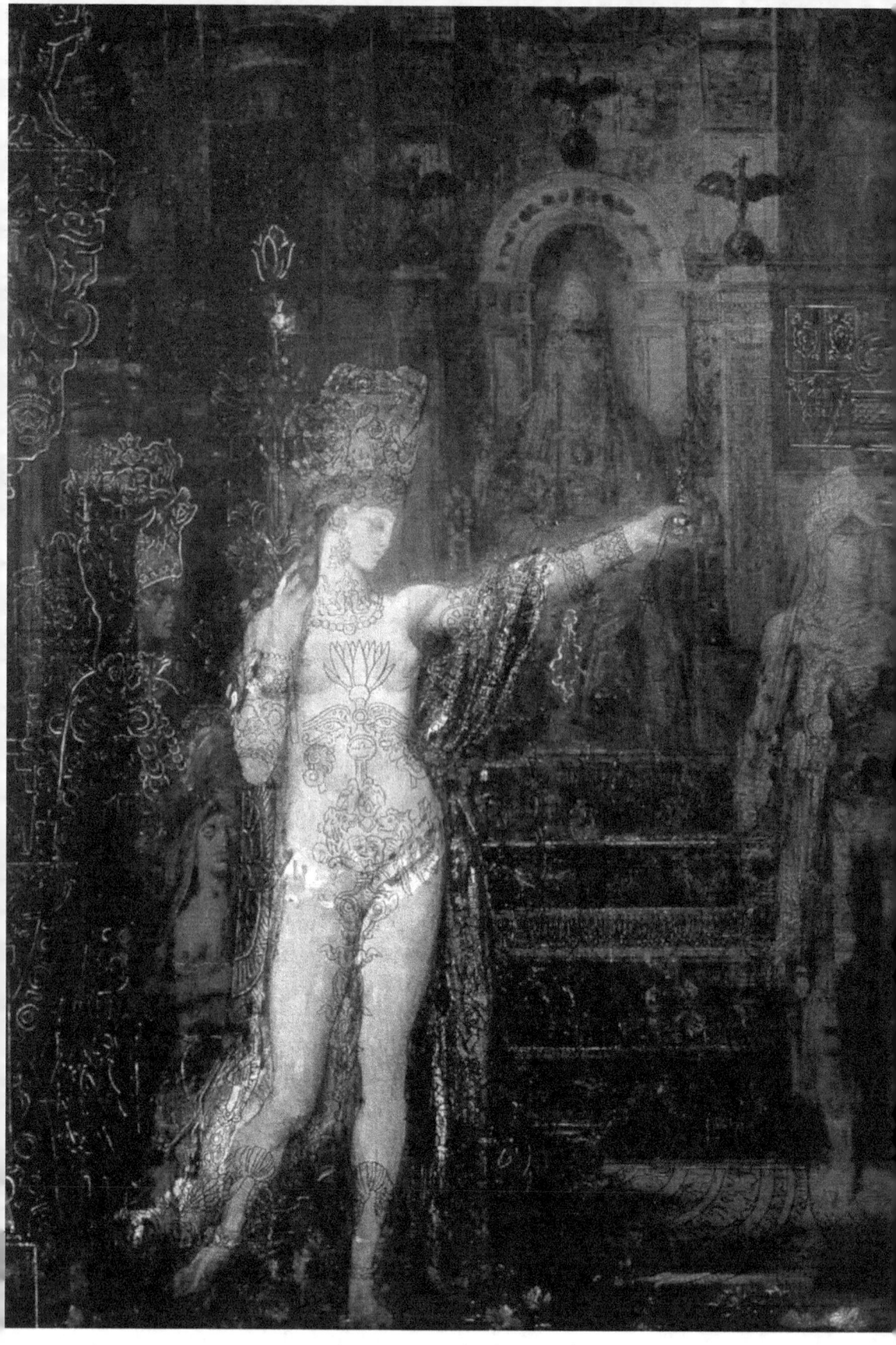

Gustave Moreau, Salomé, 1876

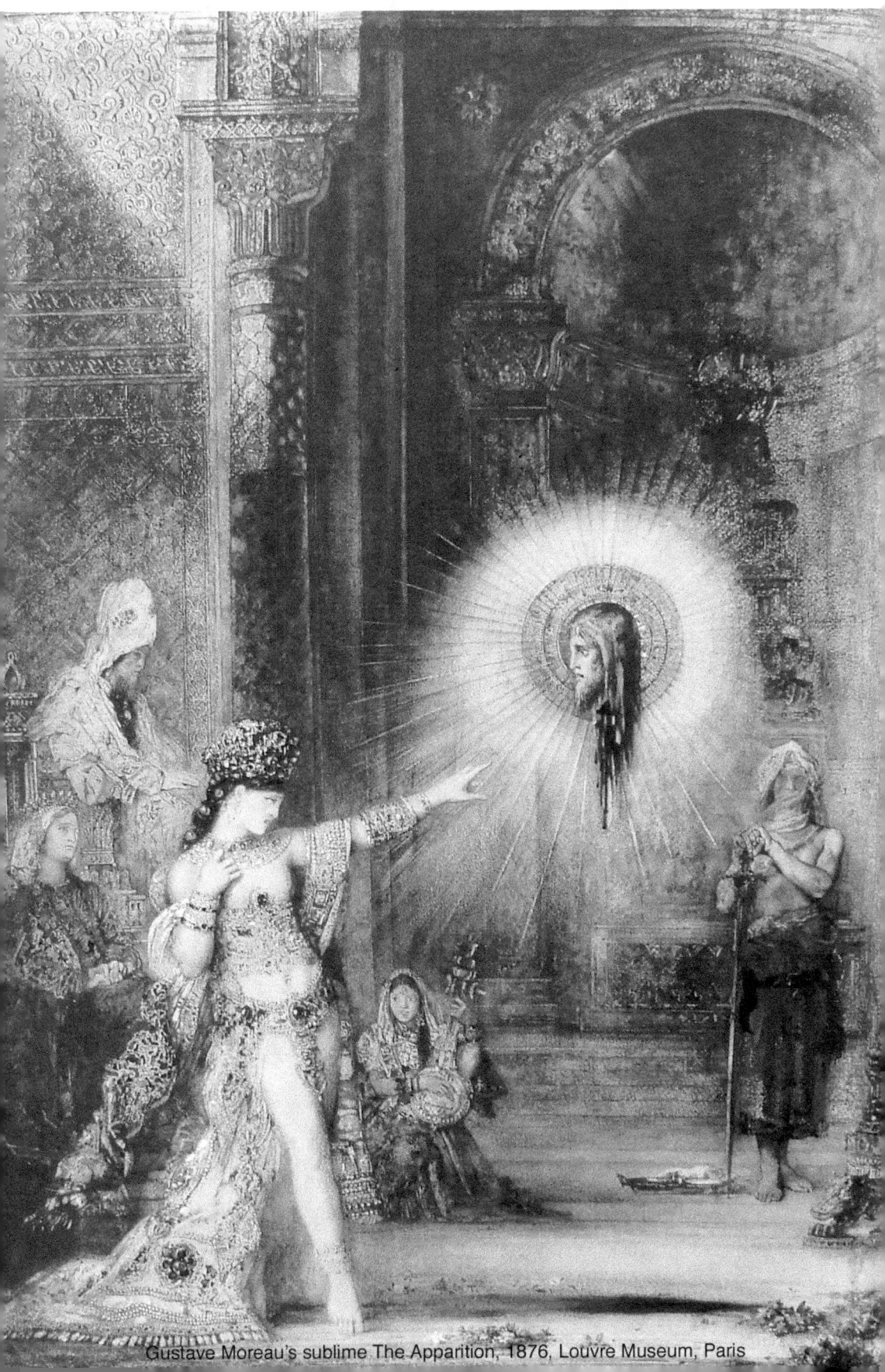

Gustave Moreau's sublime The Apparition, 1876, Louvre Museum, Paris

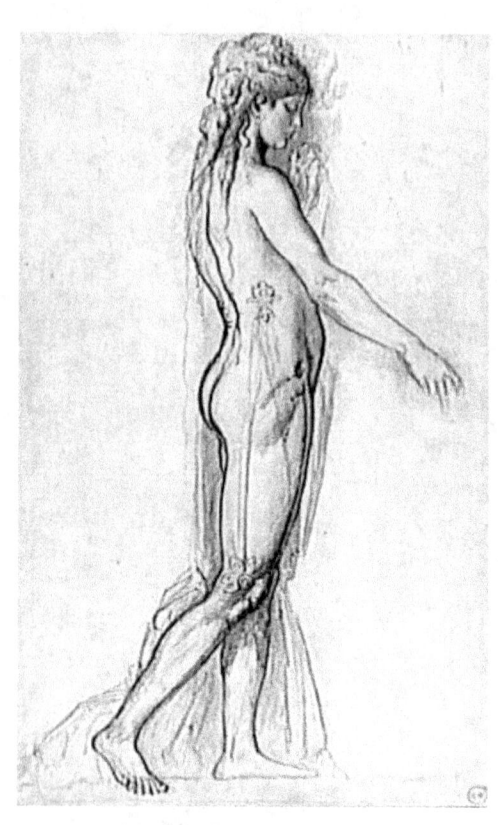

Gustave Moreau, Study for
Salomé (above)

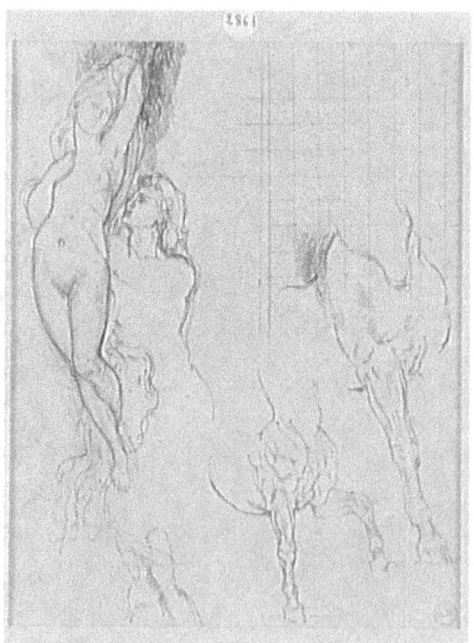

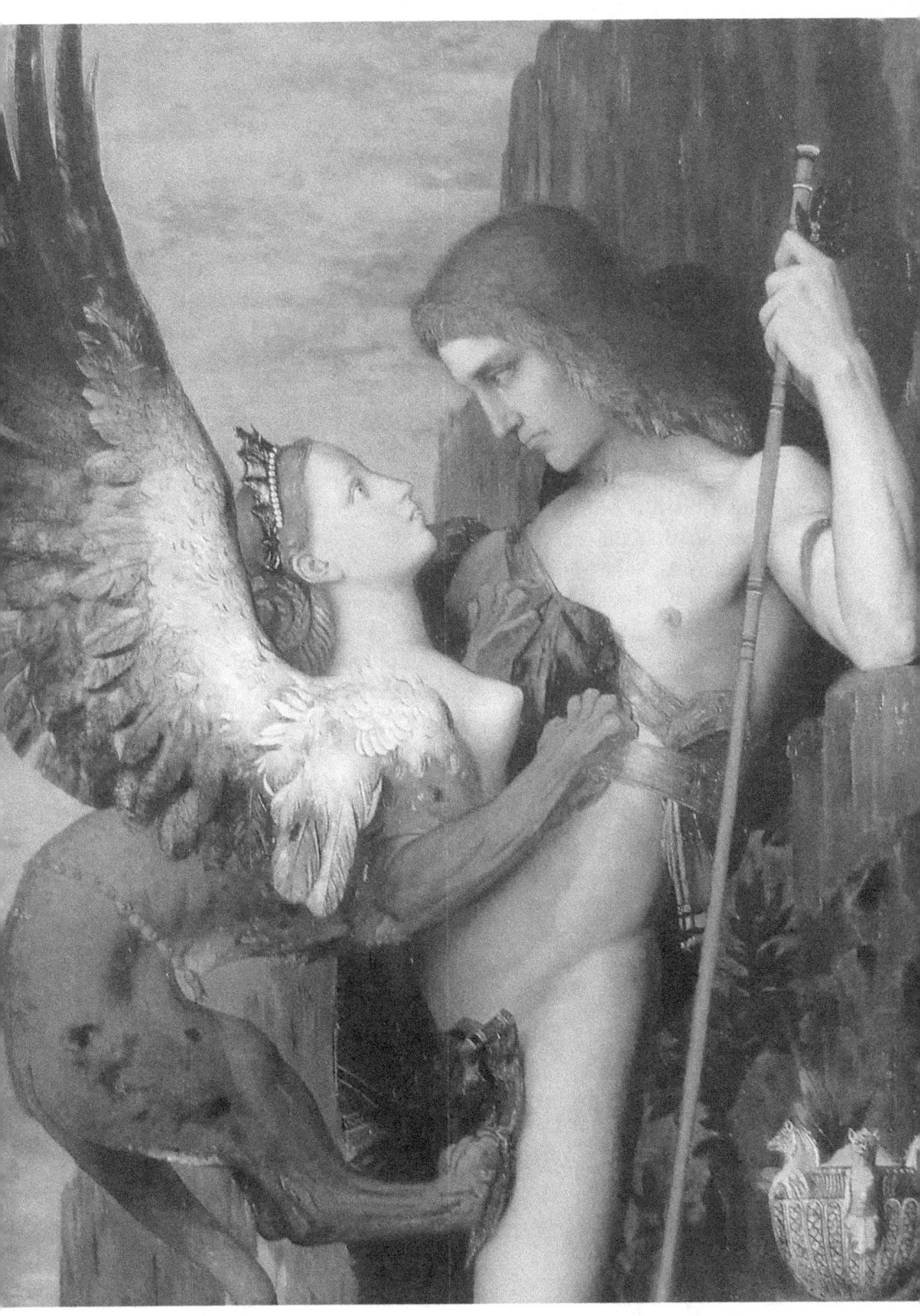

Gustave Moreau, The Sphinx

GUSTAVE MOREAU

However astonishing the fantastical but realist paintings of the Pre-Raphaelites or any 19th century artist may be, those of the French master Gustave Moreau outdo them all. He is the supreme champion of 'fantasy art', of any kind. His paintings are the richest imaginable, in terms both of content – in the exotic, Byzantine architecture, the incredibly ornate costumes, the flamboyant gestures – and of physicality and technique.

For Gustave Moreau's paintings, when he finished them, are extraordinarily densely painted. Layers of oil are laid upon each other, so that the surface of the amazing *Jupiter and Semele* is actually jewel-like.[1] *Jupiter and Semele* is an image of pure sex: it is manufactured deliberately to be an orgasmic and orgiastic feast for the eye, where the pleasure of looking causes multiple orgasms. Moreau's painting is as voluptuous as painting can get. It is a multiple voluptuousness, because the form and the content breed continuously, creating myriad pleasures. The painterly technique, the drawing, the colours and the forms combine with the images of Greek, Byzantine, Roman and Oriental architecture to create a marvellous vision of phallic power. For Jupiter (Zeus) is the supreme phallic god of antiquity – he lusts after and rapes just about every Goddess he can. Sitting on his throne, Jupiter in Moreau's last completed painting is a phallus, adored by the woman swooning in bliss beside him.

---

1 Gustave Moreau: *Jupiter and Semele*, 1896, oil on canvas, 213 x 118cm, Musée Gustave Moreau, Paris

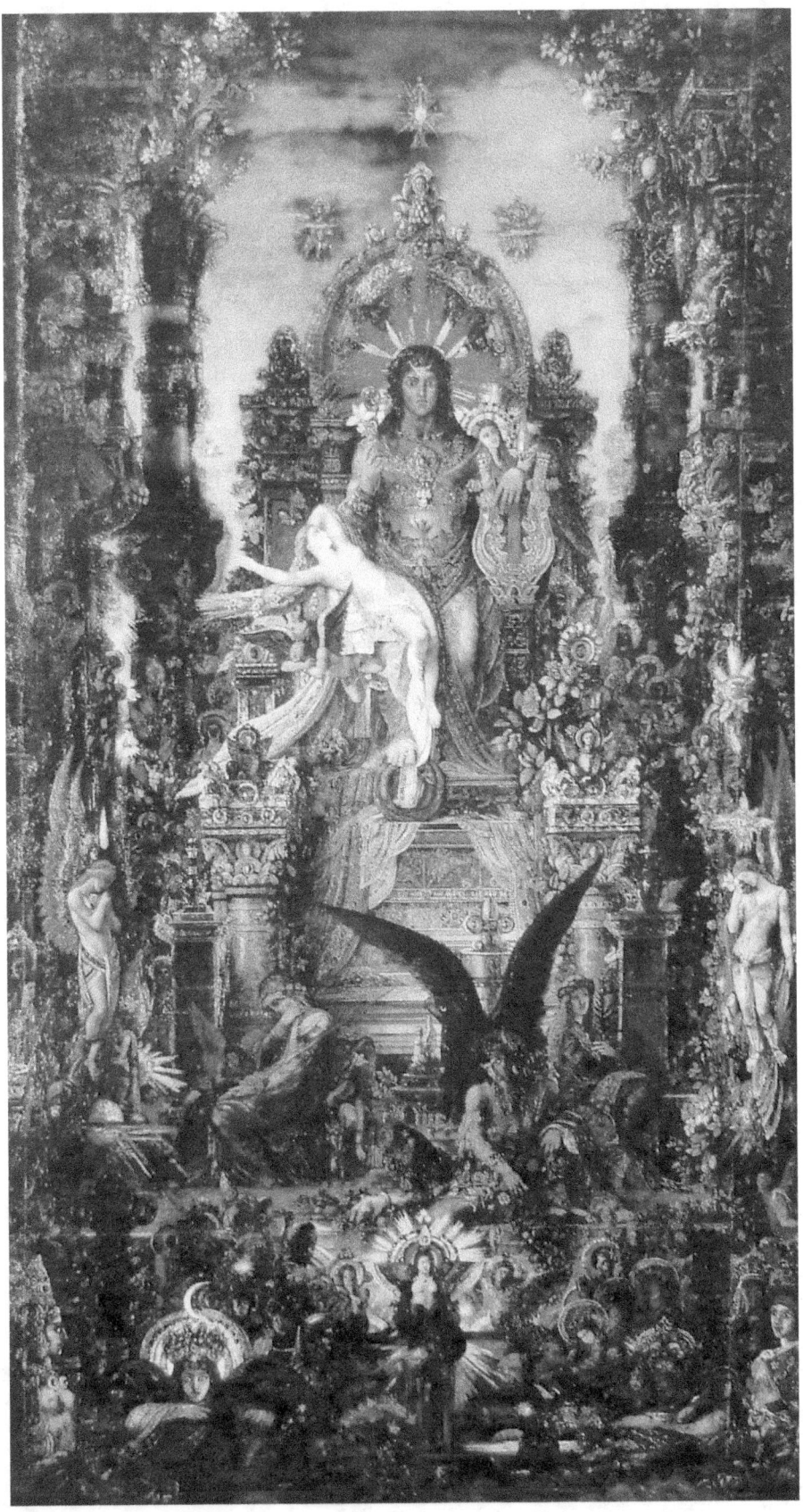

One of Gustave Moreau's masterpieces: Jupiter and Semele, 1896, Paris

JEAN DELVILLE

Only Jean Delville, with the exception of Félicien Rops, comes closest to Gustave Moreau's extravagant vision. Painters such as William Blake, Henry Fuseli and John Martin had depicted phantasma-gorical vistas, but Moreau's art is the apotheosis of visionary art. Delville, like Odilon Redon and Moreau, painted Orpheus' head, and emphasized the dreaming nature of art (floating heads were popular in Symbolist art).[1] It was Deville who created that archetypical image of *fin-de-siècle* occultism, the bizarre portrait of the wife of the Symbolist poet Stuart Merrill.[2] Like Fernand Khnopff's *I Lock the Door Upon Myself*, Delville's image is marked by haunted eyes, weirdly bright eyes which stare at the viewer.[3] These eyes are possessed, perhaps by spirits, born from some ectoplasmic Spiritualist evening session in Paris.

It is Deville who provides the wildest depiction of the King of late 19th century art, Satan, in *Trésor de Satan*, where the fiery archangel dances manically over a flow of nude bodies writhing in a Rubens-like manner at the bottom of the sea.[4] More writhing nude bodies occur in Delville's *L'Amour des Ames*, where the lovers are rising amidst swirls of fire and light above the sea. It is a cosmic image, with its stars and planets in the background, reminiscent of theosophical imagery, the pictures done under hypnosis, like those of A.E. Waite and the Golden Dawn artists.[5] But Delville's most powerful image is that of the extraordinary Goddess in the aptly titled *Idol of Perversity*, which is a phrase that could apply to much of Symbolist and Decadent art, which made idols out of perversity.[6]

1 Jean Deville: *Orpheus*, 1893, oil on canvas, 79 x 99cm, collection: Mme Gilléon-Growet, Brussels
2 J. Deville: *Portrait of Madame Stuart Merrill*, 1892, coloured chalk, collection: E. Jannss-Junior
3 F. Khnopff: *I Lock the Door Upon Myself*, 1891, oil on canvas, 72 x 140cm, Neue Pinakothek, Munich
4 J. Deville: *Trésor de Satan*, Musées Royaux des Beaux-Arts, Brussels
5 J. Deville: *L'Amour des Ames*, lithograph, Bibliothéque d'Art et d'Archélogie, Paris
6 J. Deville: *Idol of Perversity*, 1891, private collection

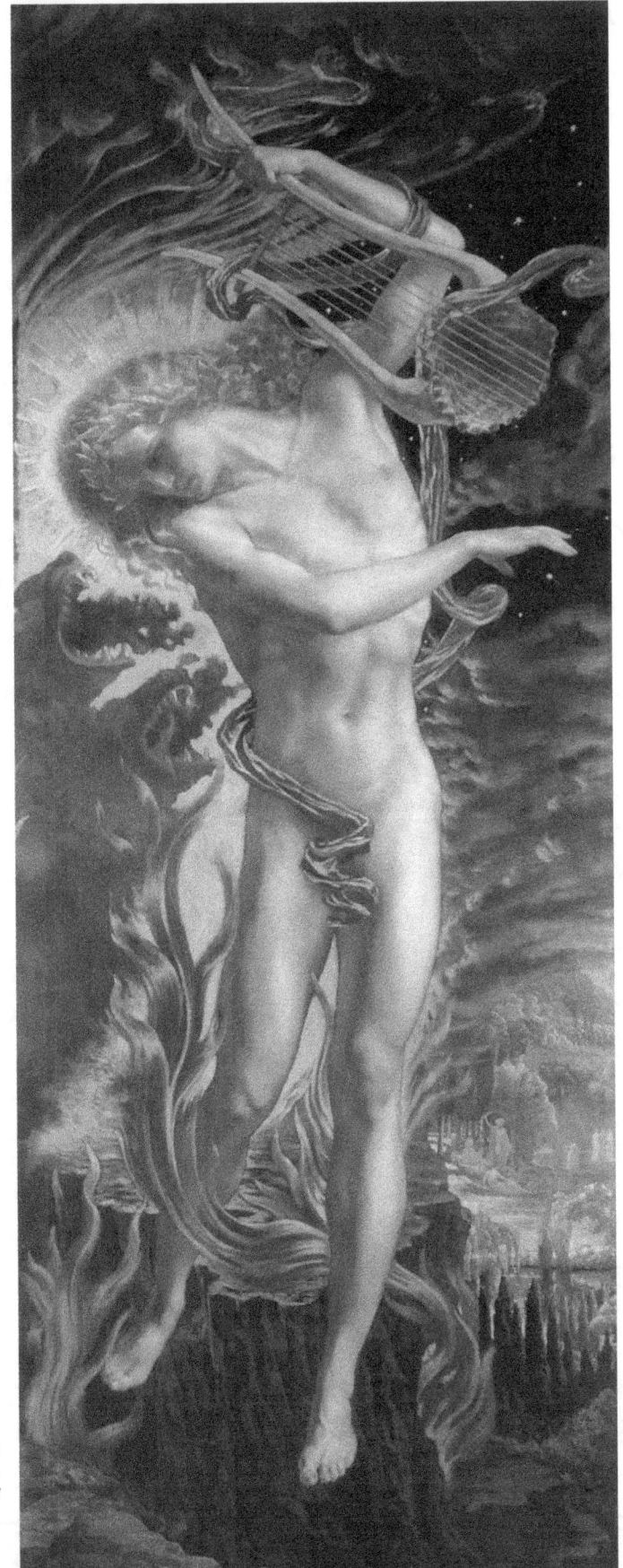

Jean Delville,
Orpheus,
late 19th century

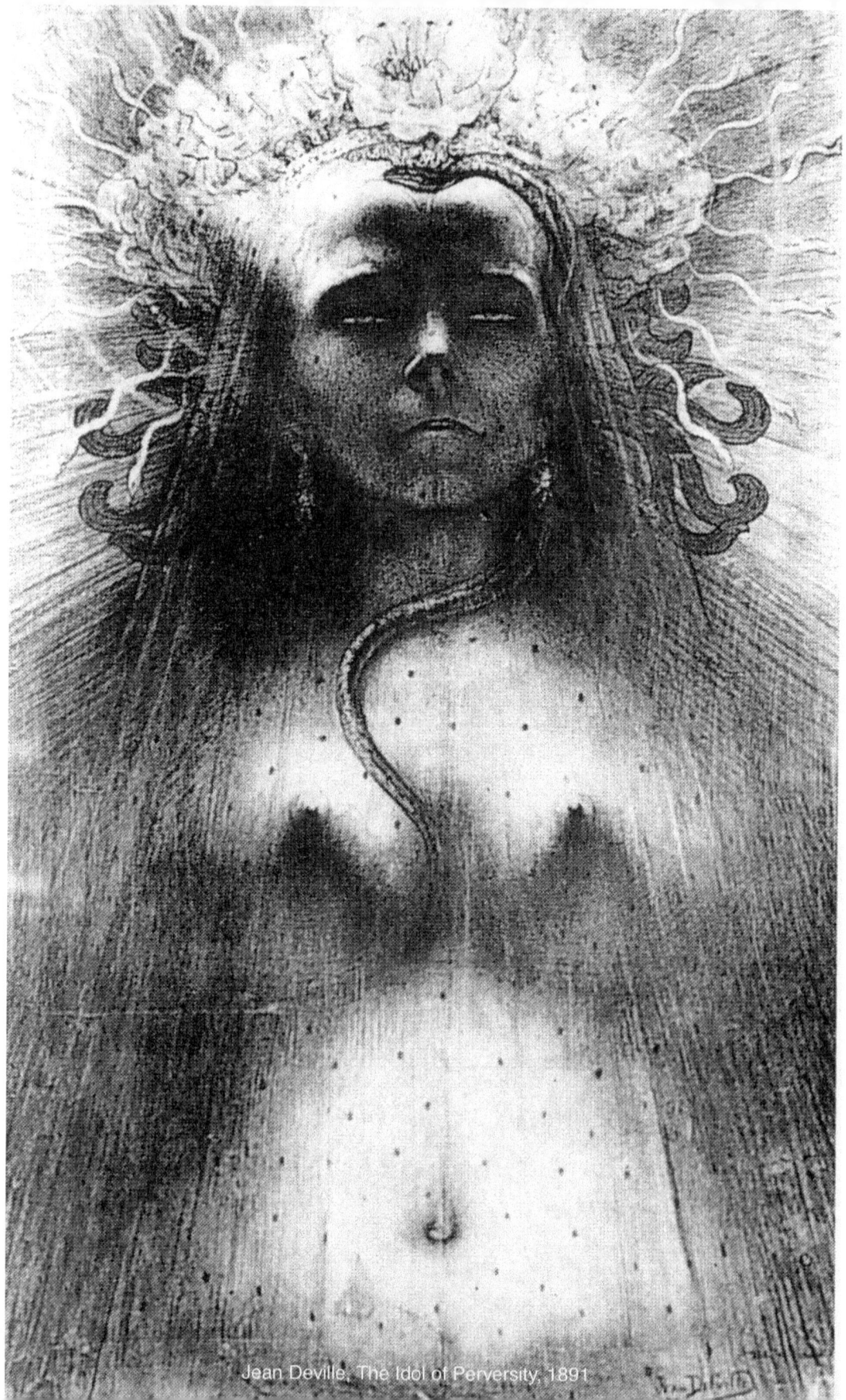

Jean Deville, The Idol of Perversity, 1891

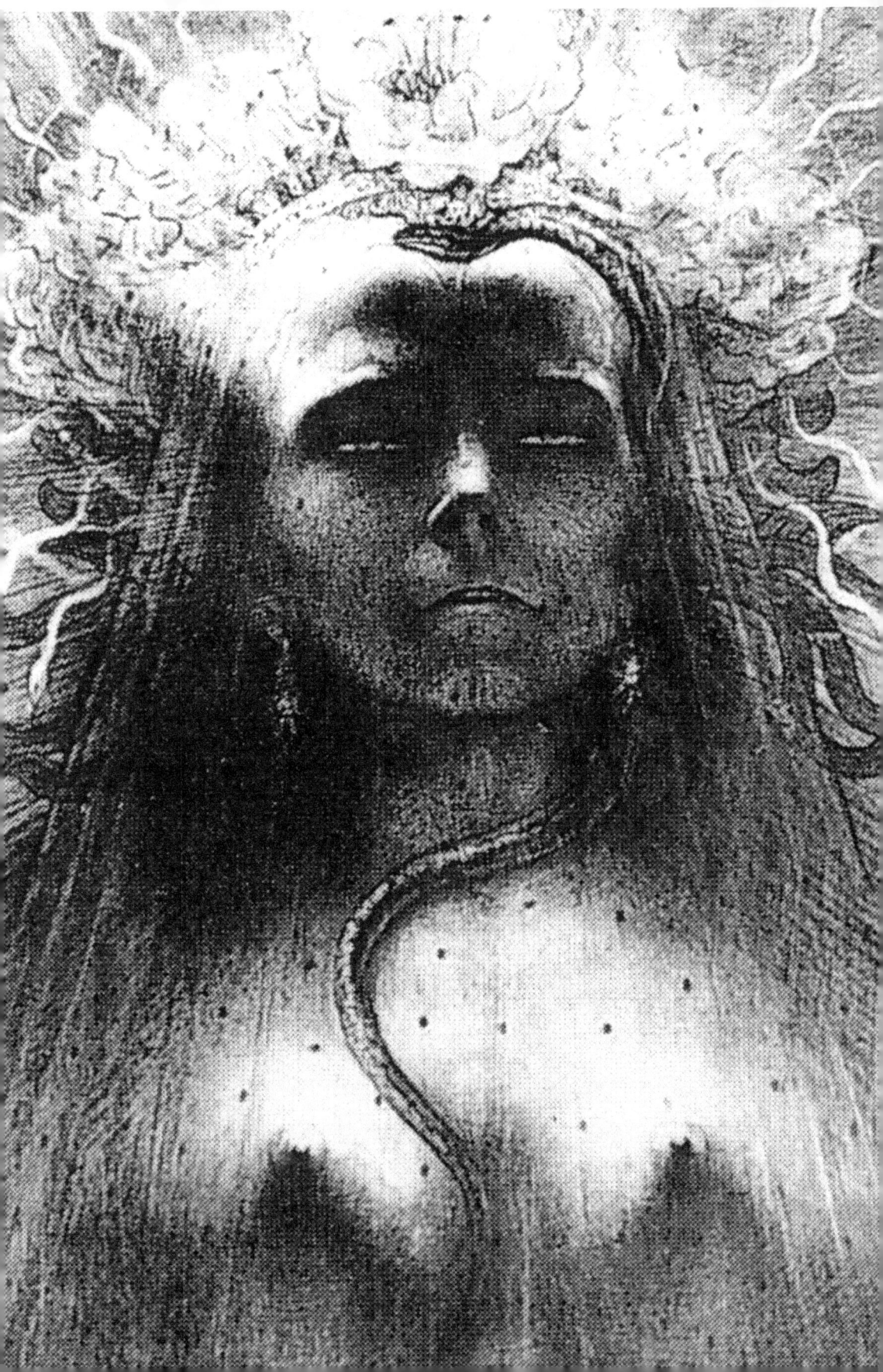

FÉLICIEN ROPS

In Félicien Rops' (1833-98) art, Satan appears as an ithyphallic wraith, like Pan gone Gothic, brandishing his erect penis as an image of terror. Erotic art centres on desire – psychologically and politically as well as physically. In *Les Sataniques*, a series of fantastical etchings, Rops fuses sex and death and religion: Satan is shown on the Cross, a blasphemous image in itself, for nowhere else in Western high art do we see Satan on Christ's Cross. Satan is strangling a woman (naked of course) with her own hair.

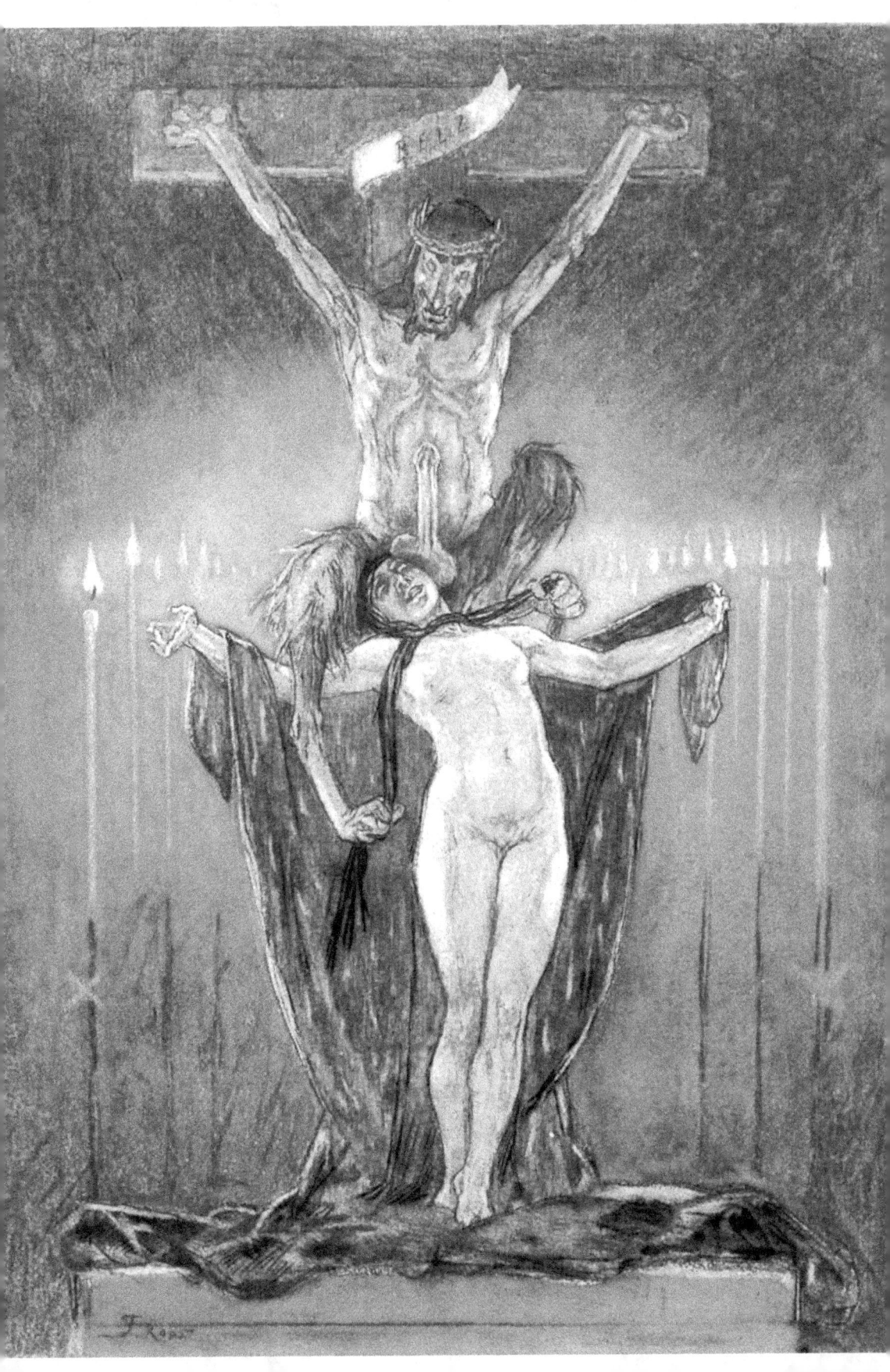

FÉLICIEN ROPS

Félicien Rops' images of torture and eroticism (erotic torture, or torturous eroticism) are also ridiculous. His image of Mary Magdalene masturbating in front of a little wooden cross upon which a phallus is crucified is hilarious.[1] She stares up at the crucified prick as she rubs herself between her legs. Great fun.

1 Rops: *Mary Magdalene*, c. 1885, collection: Simon Wilson, London

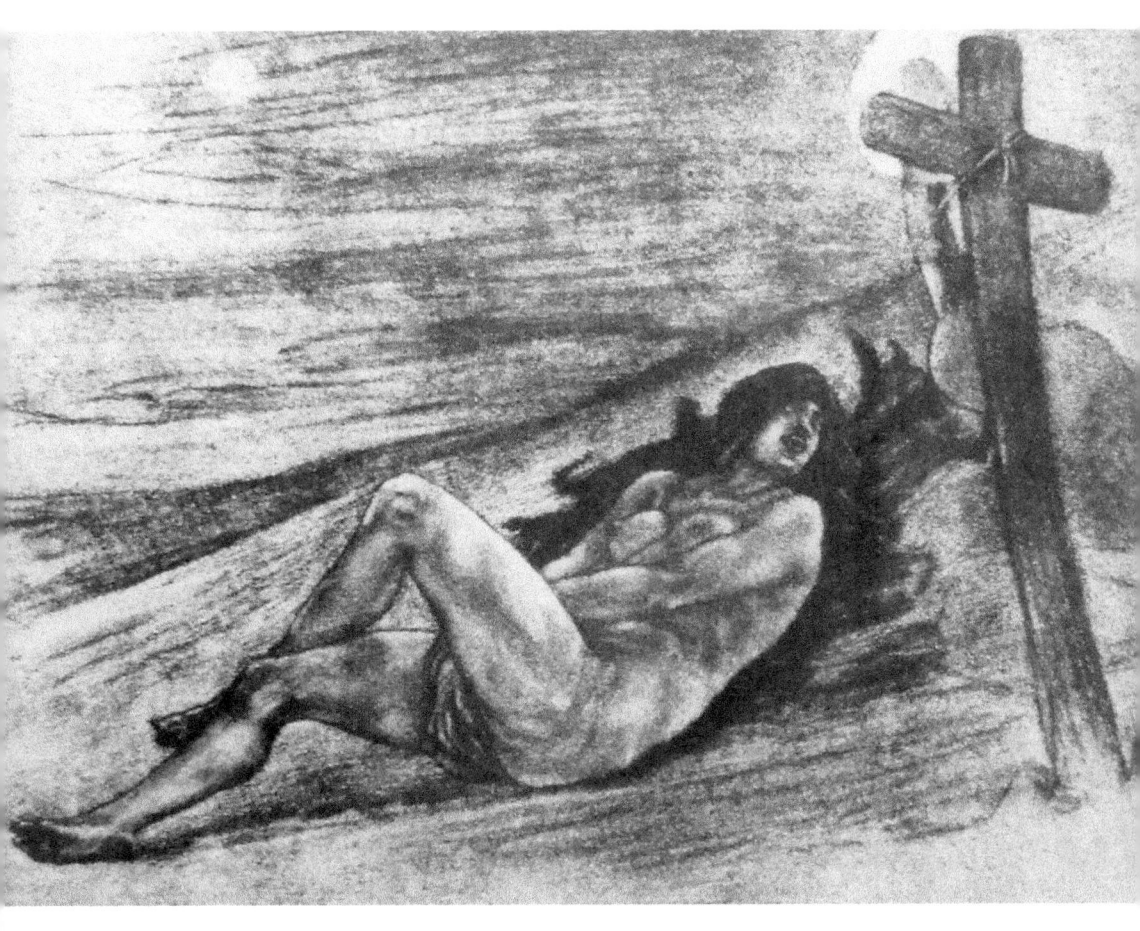

Felicien Rops, Mary Magdalene

FÉLICIEN ROPS

Félicien Rops' etchings are all cock, all phallic energy gone wild. A woman impales herself on the phallus of a statue of a crazily grinning Pan or Satan, flanked on each side by bizarre dwarf-like beasts, each holding up six foot erect penises. In another image, Satan appears as a ram's skull, a familiar motif (deriving again from Pan, perhaps). The phallus this time is a massive snake-like thing which curls downwards and enters a woman, who's naked of course.[1] The phallus becomes a ridiculous motif or image all too quickly. Many people have noted how silly it looks. Hence it is so heavily censored in the modern era, although we do see many phallic metaphors and equivalents – the thrusting red sports car, the articulated lorry, the tank, the missile, the jet plane, the atomic bomb, the gun, the knife, the skyscraper, the computer, all those 'tools' of modern life.

---

1 Rops: *Les Sataniques*, 1884, Piccadilly Gallery, London

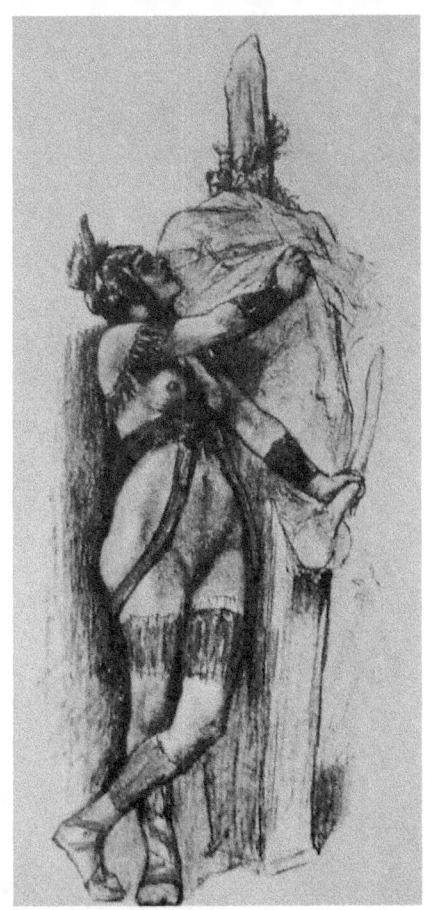

The inimitable Félicien Rops, French fin-de-siècle Decadence at its most extreme.

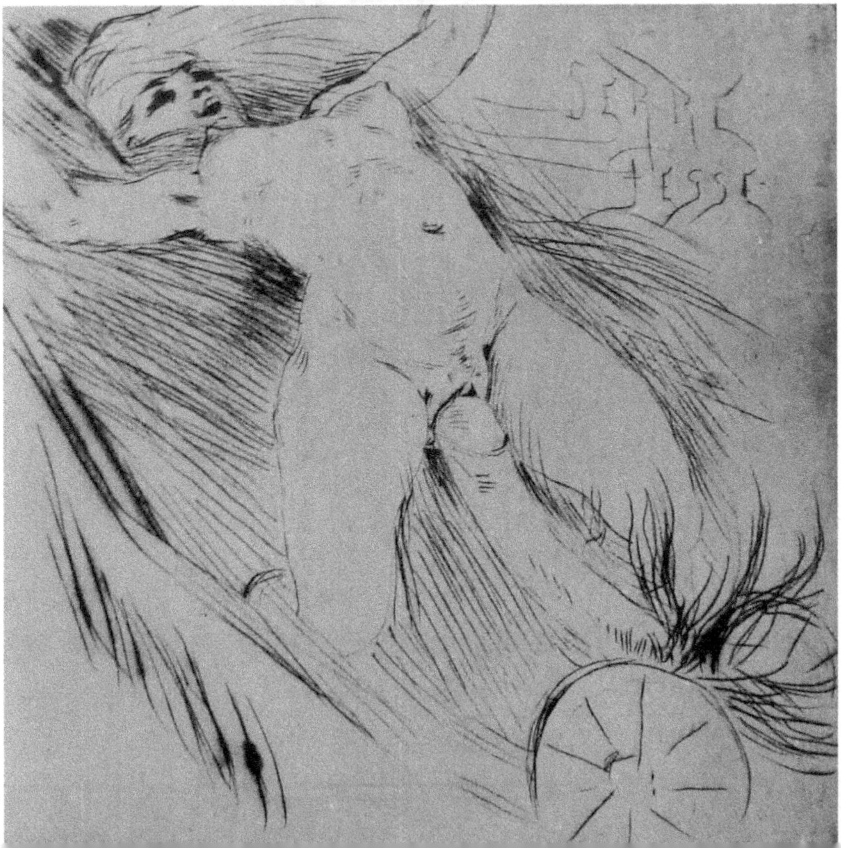

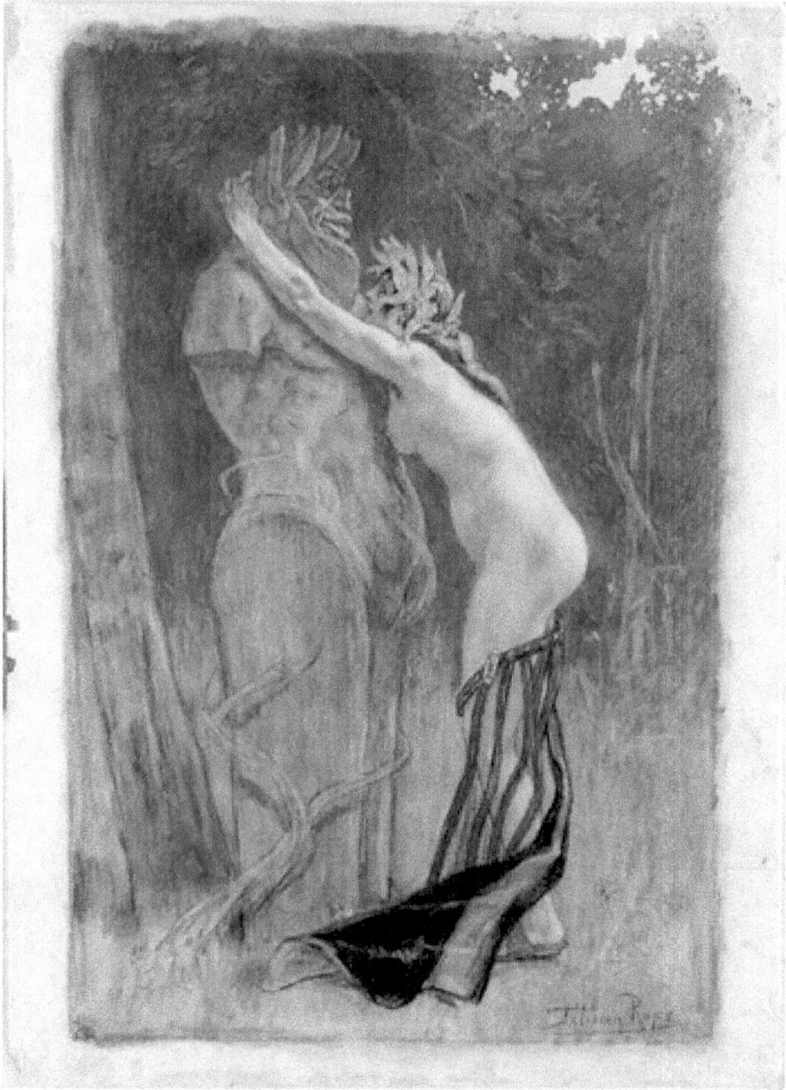

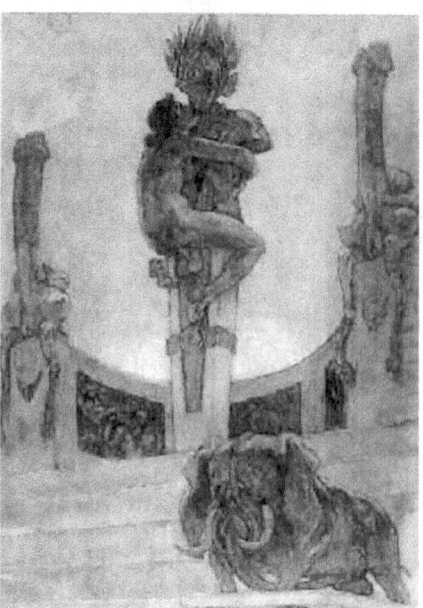

Félicien Rops, Hommage
To Pan (above)

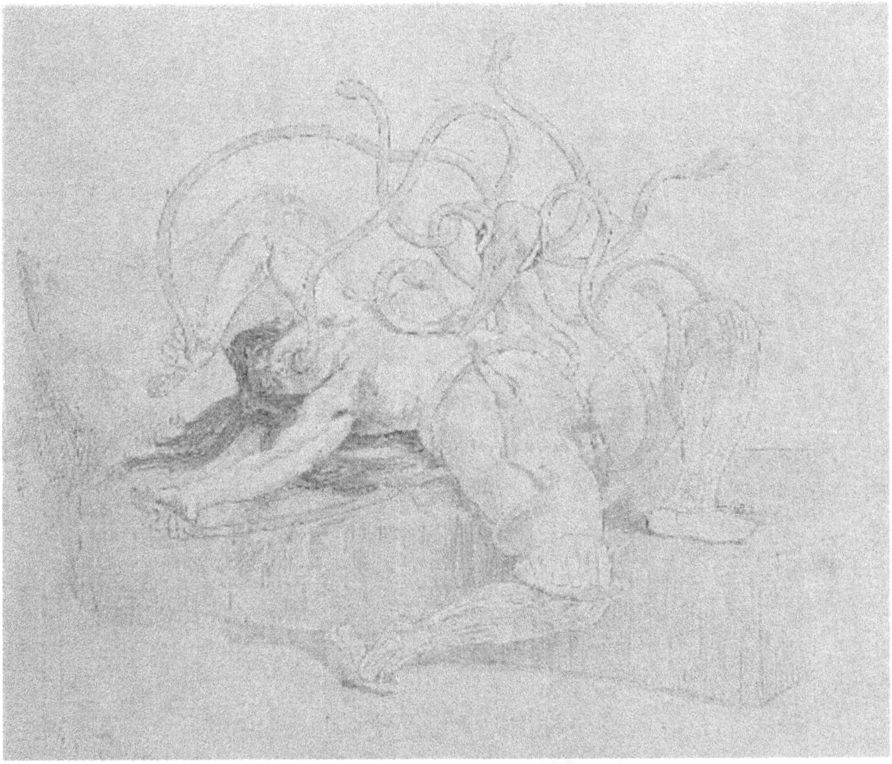

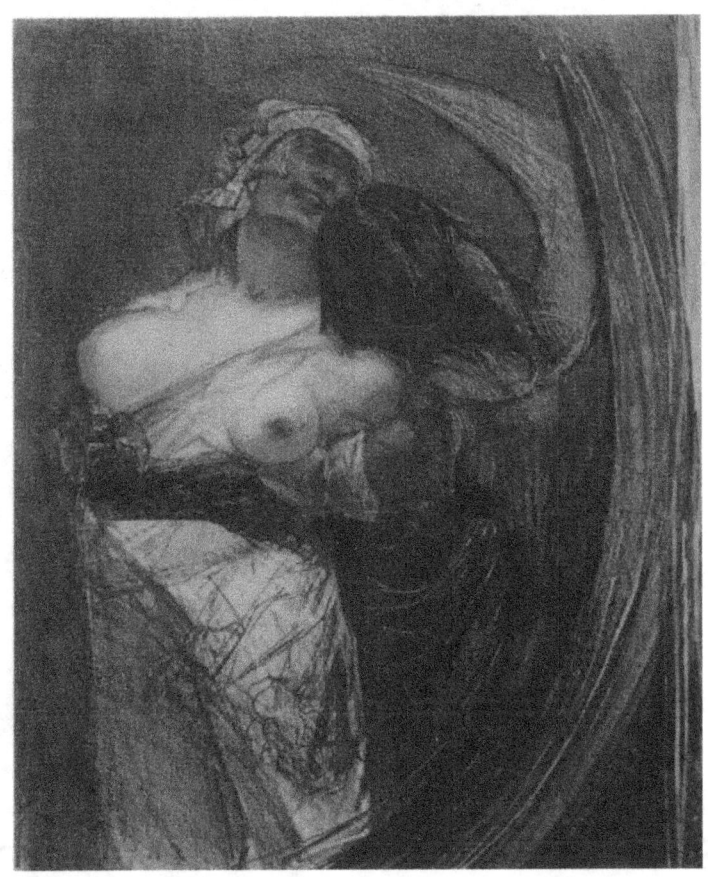

Félicien Rops, The Cold Devils, c 1860 (below).

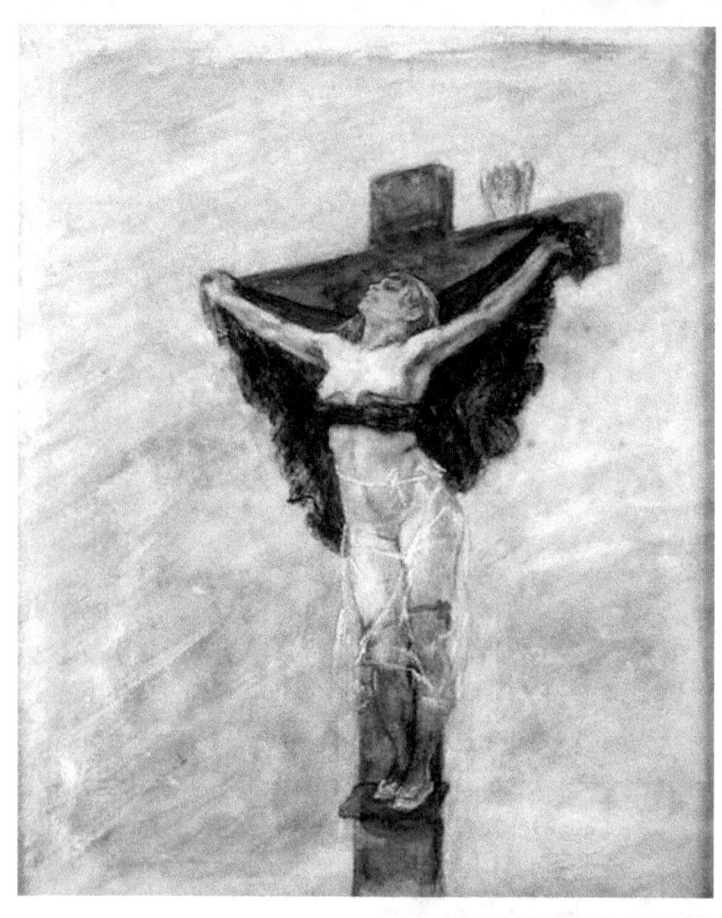

Félicien Rops

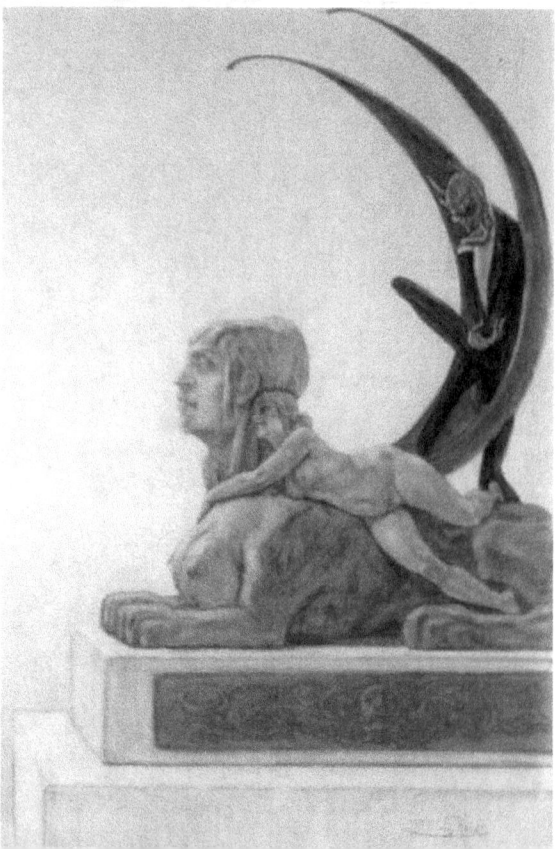

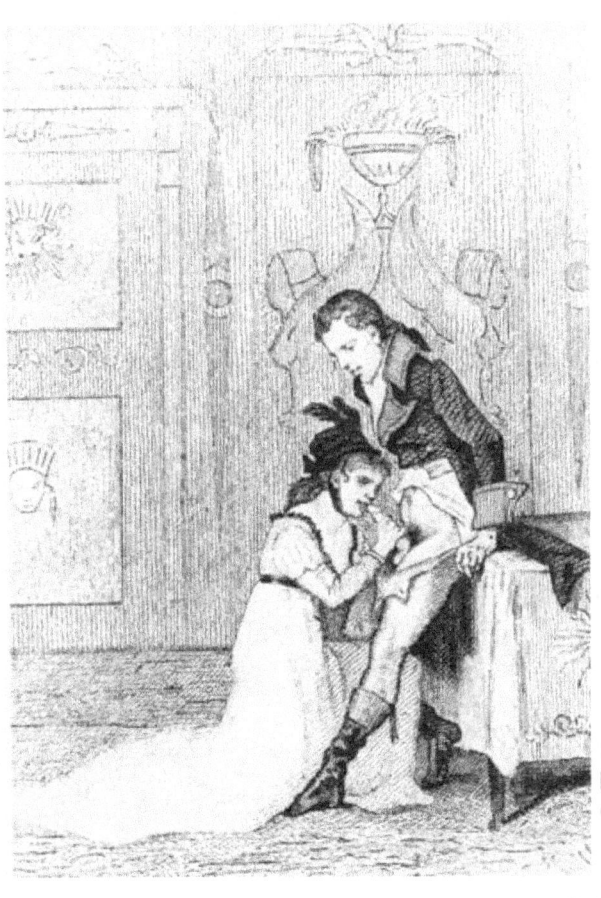

Félicien Rops, from Le Diable du Corps by André-Robert Andréa de Nerciat (1739-1800)

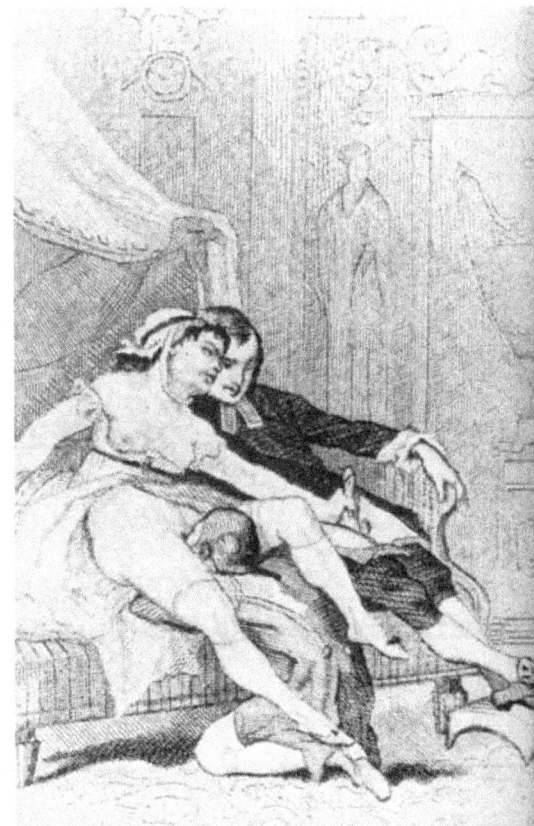

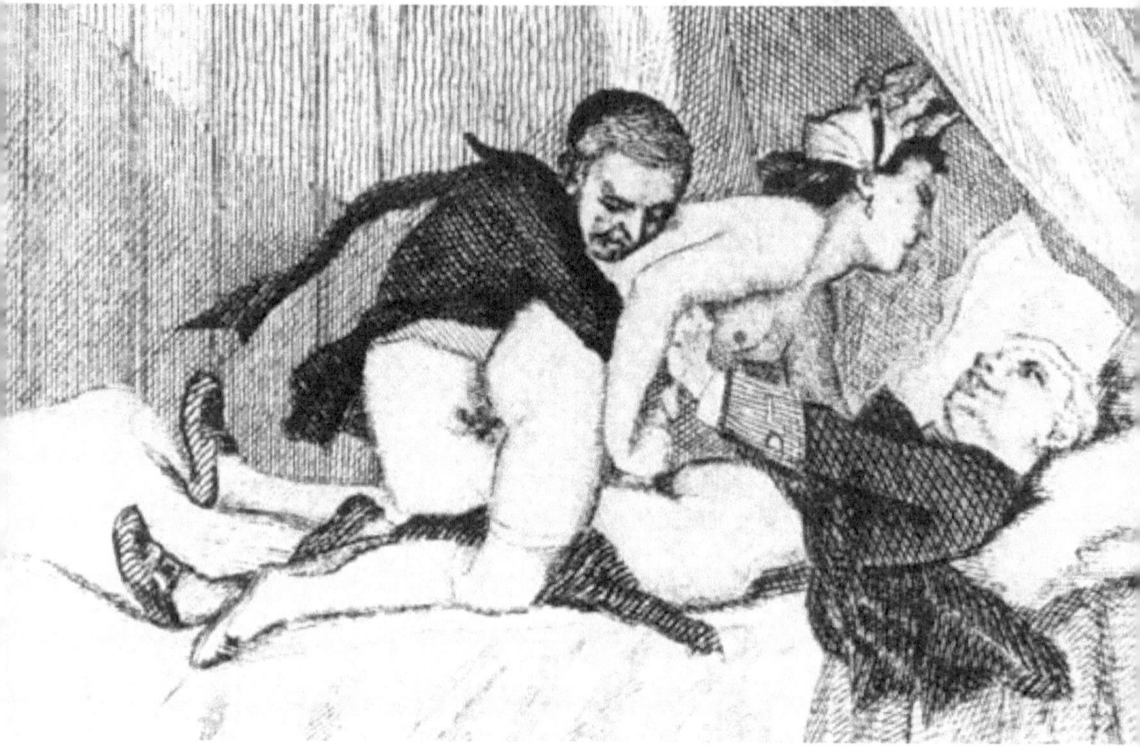

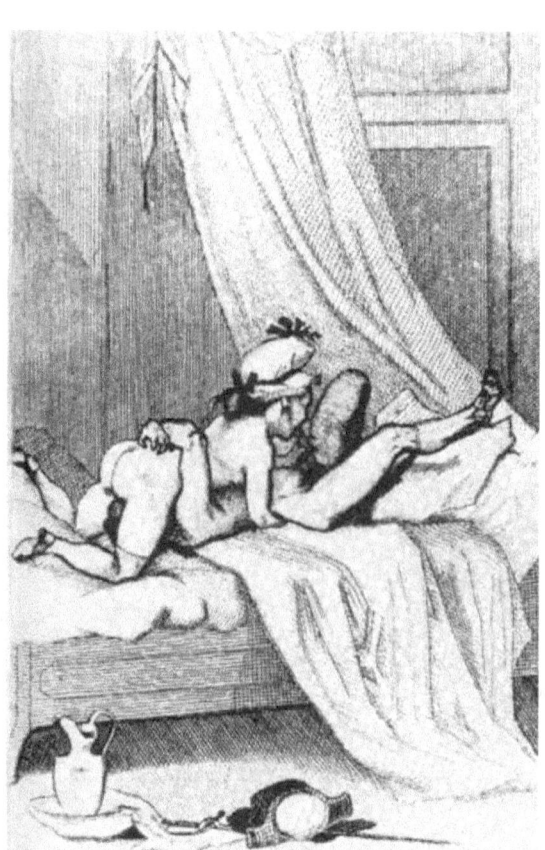

Félicien Rops,
Le Diable du Corps

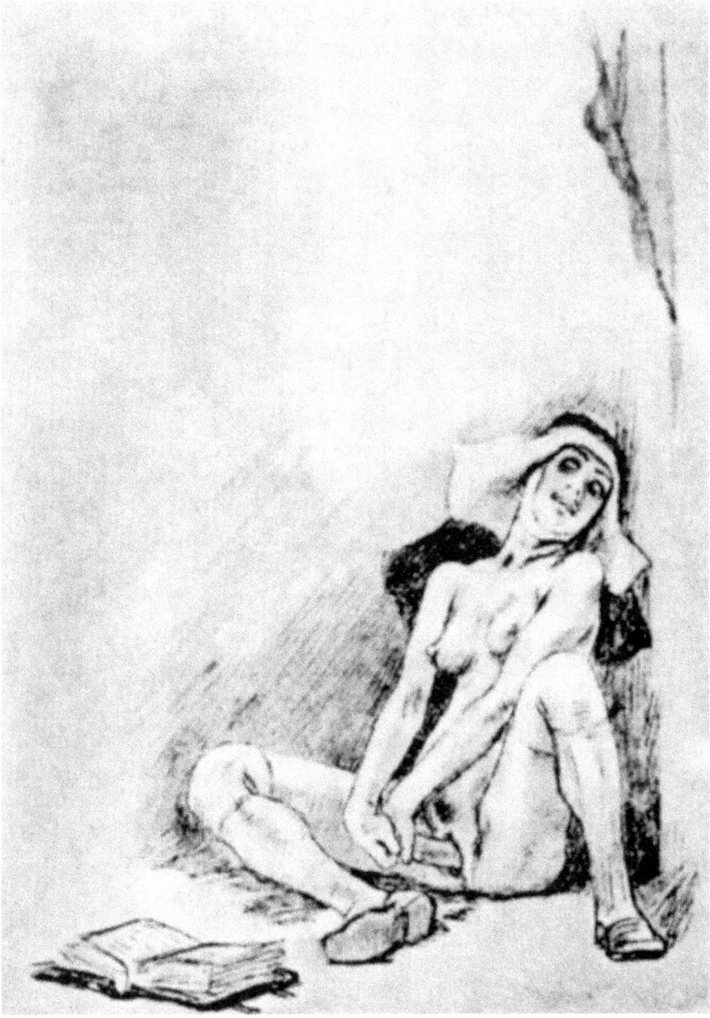

Félicien Rops, Sainte Thérèse (left).

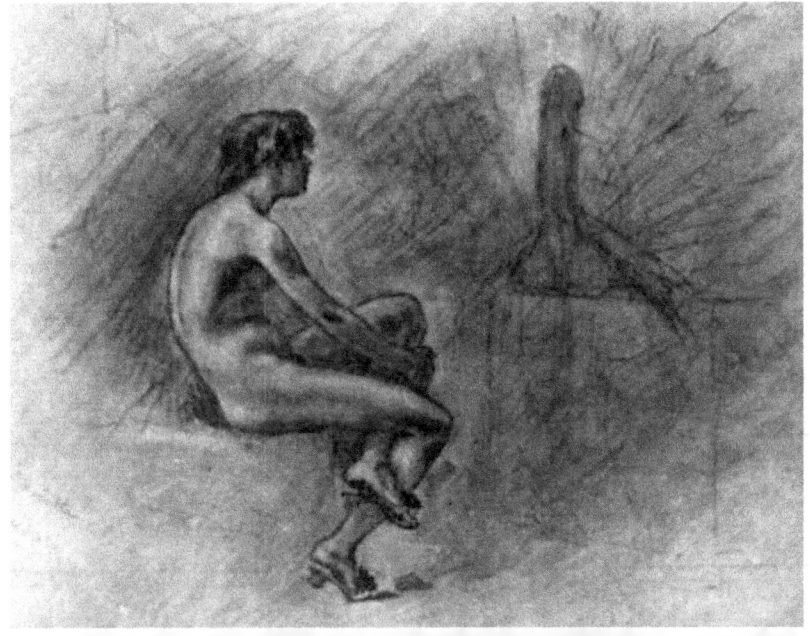

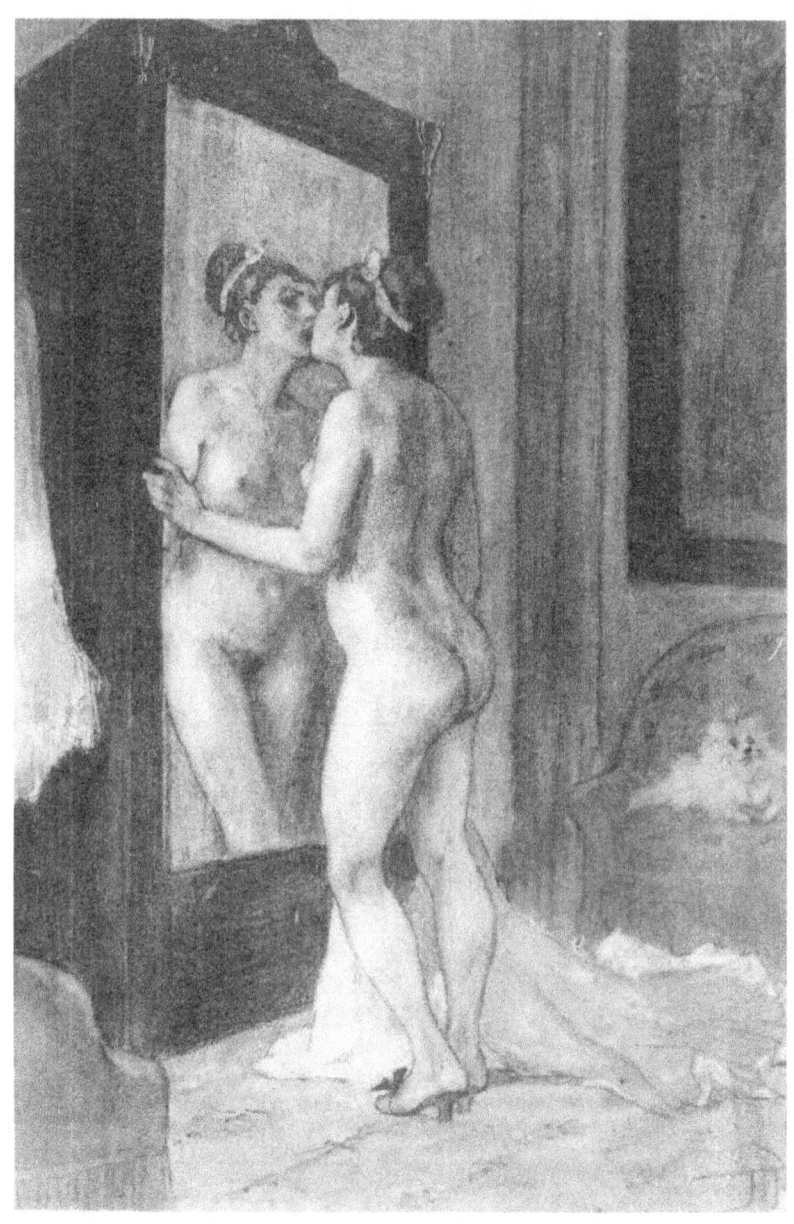

Felicien Rops, Selbstverliebt (between 1878 and 1881)

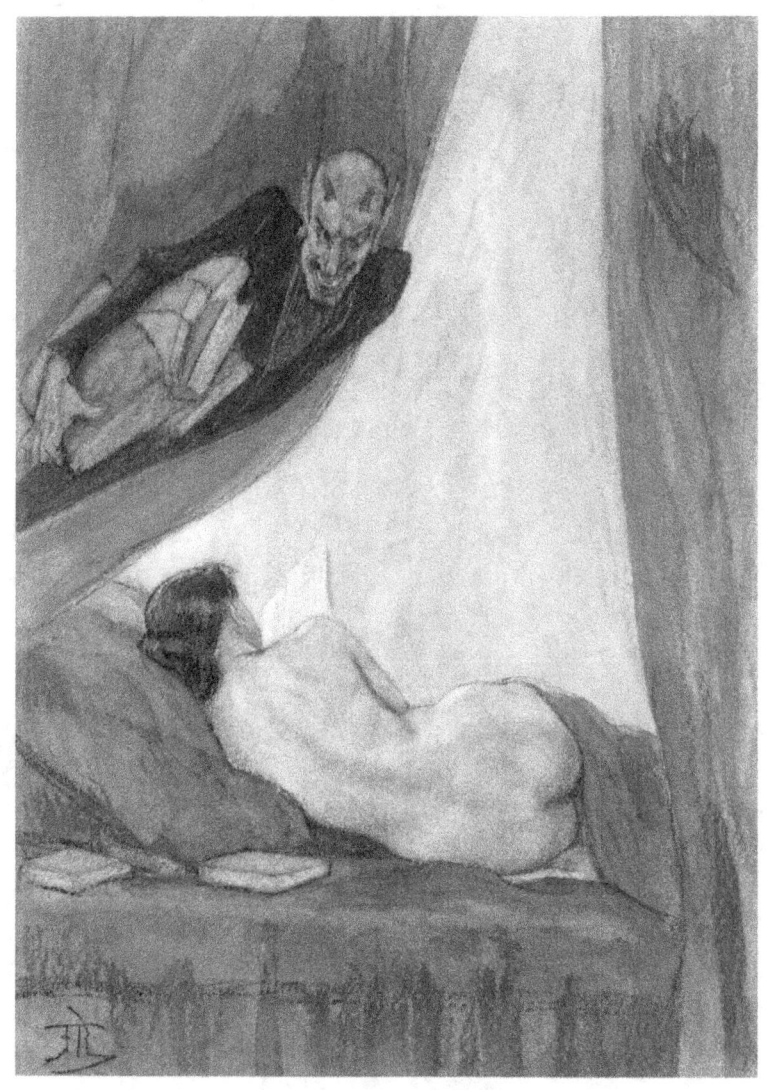

Félicien Rops, Le Bibliothécaire, 1878

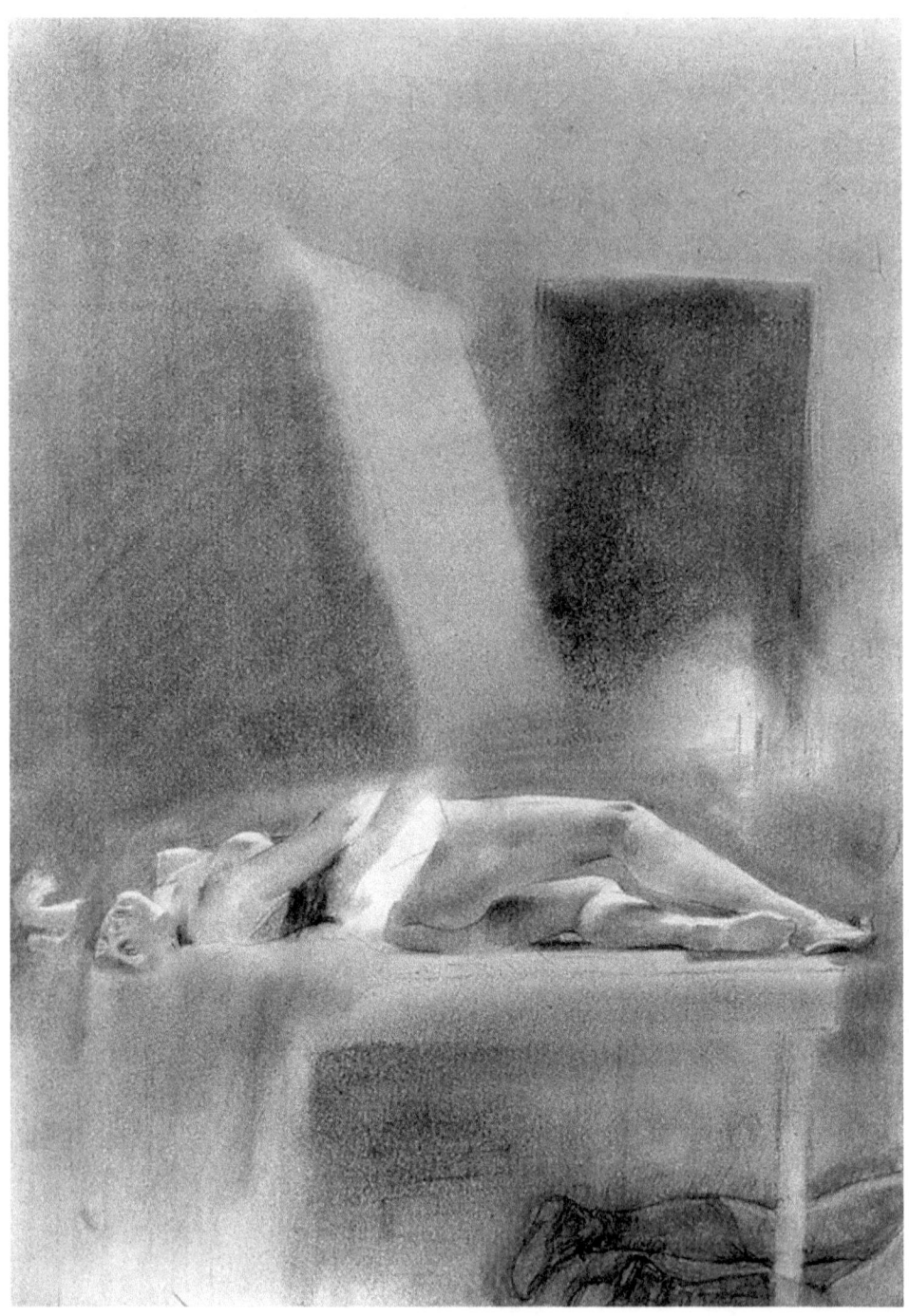

This page and over: illustrations by Félicien Rops
for Diaboliques de Jules Barbey d'Aurevilly.

Above: À un dîner d'athées.

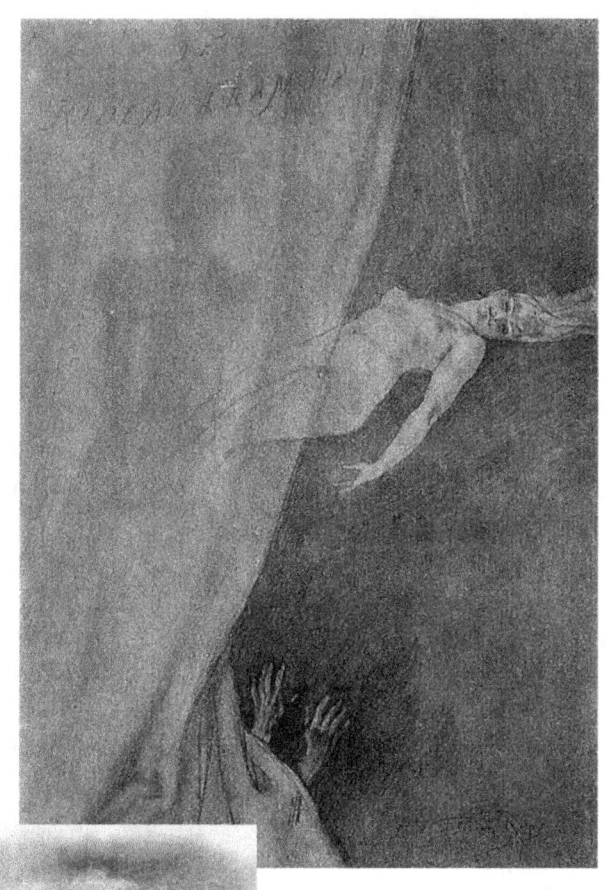

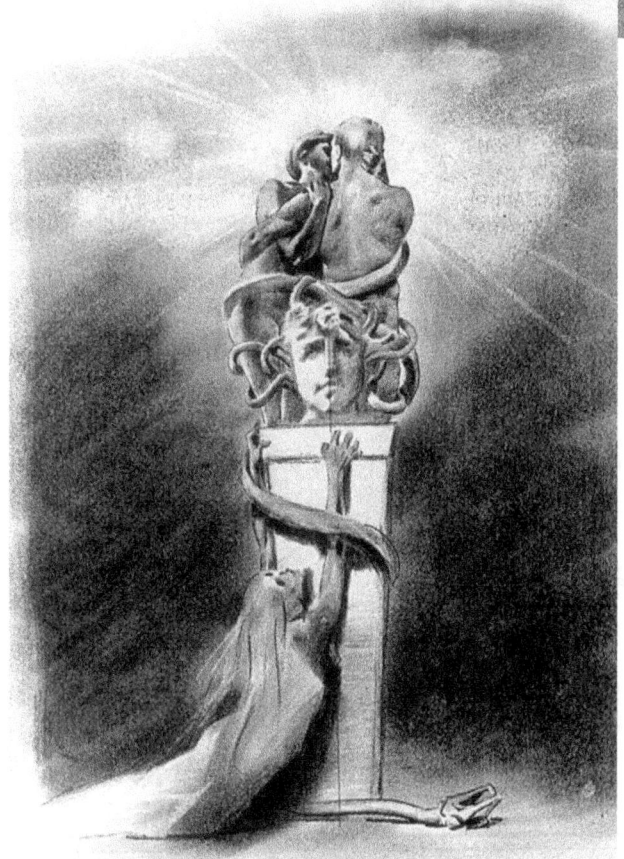

Félicien Rops:
Le Rideau Cramoisi (above).
Le Bonheur Dans Le Crime (left)

MERMAIDS

There is deep sexism in the Judæo-Christian Fall, for it is the woman who picks the apple and offers it to Adam. From the beginning, in the Judæo-Christian tradition, it is the woman who makes men 'fall'. In some depictions, the sexism is doubled, by having the serpent shown as a snake-woman – the torso of a woman, the legs, like those of a mermaid, as in Michelangelo Buonarroti's *Temptation and Expulsion* (1508-12).[1]

The symbol of the half-woman/ half-fish, still in use today,[2] is another manifestation of patriarchal people's projection of their sexual fears onto women, so that what lies 'below the waist' is feared and objectified as something slimy and fishlike, something dark, from the depths of the unconscious, which is the sea. The mermaid appears sculpted on mediæval churches, some of the mermaids expose their genitals, like the *sheila-na-gig* figure, which again fuses sacred and profane, spiritual and sexual, desire and fear.[3] The mermaid appears in much of Victorian art, as an image of men's ambivalent views of female sexuality – in E.M. Hale's *Mermaid's Rock* (1894), for instance, or John William Waterhouse's Pre-Raphaelite *A Mermaid* (1901).[4]

1 Michelangelo: *Temptation and Expulsion*, 1508-12, fresco, Sistine Chapel, Vatican, Rome
2 See the depiction of the Mary Magdalene in the wilderness sequence of Universal's film *The Last Temptation of Christ* (1988, USA)
3 See Anthony Weir & James Jerman: *Images of Lust: Sexual Carvings on Mediæval Churches*, B. T. Batsford, 1986, 48ff
4 John William Waterhouse: *A Mermaid*, 1901, 38.5 x 36.3in, Royal Academy of Arts, London; Edward Matthew Hale: *Mermaid's Rock*, 1894, 48 x 78in, City Art Gallery, Leeds

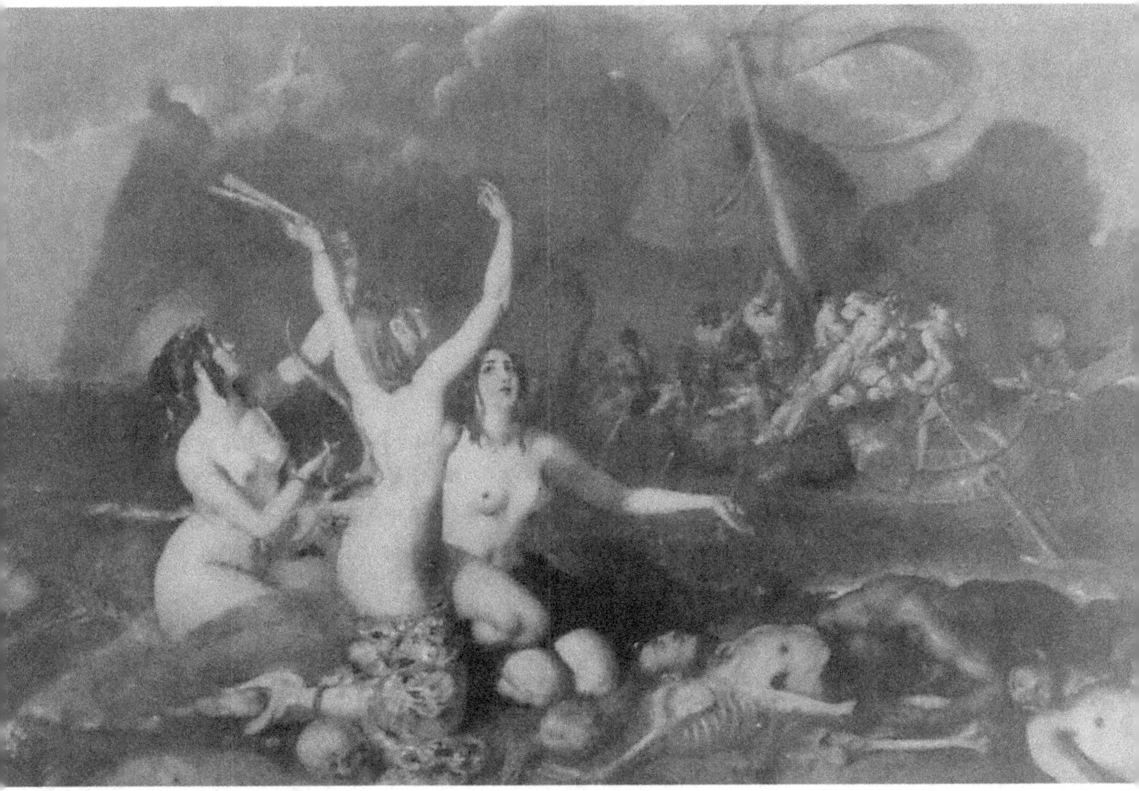

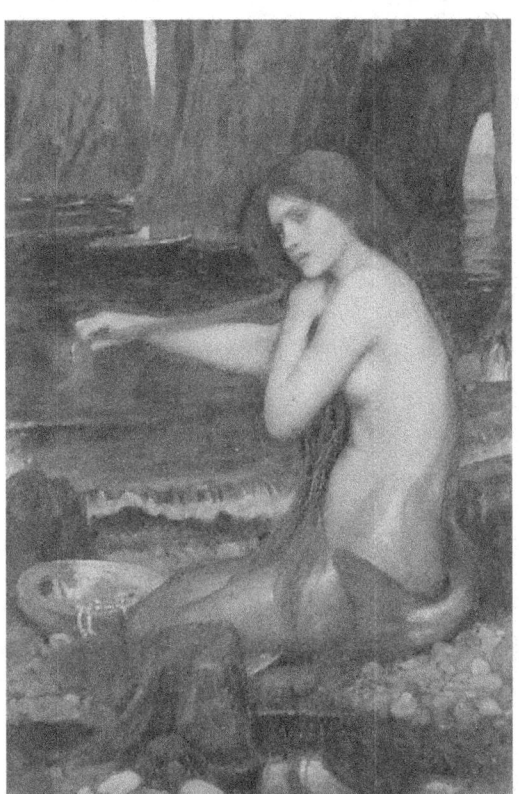

A favourite theme in 19th century painting: sex, death, nudity and the sea.
William Etty's The Sirens and Ulysses, 1837, Manchester. above.

J.W. Waterhouse,
A Mermaid, 1901, Royal Academy, London, below.

PRE-RAPHAELITES

Pre-Raphaelite art hides its gender bias under a surface of mediævalism, Gothic imagery, Arthurian motifs and a breathless romanticism. But the images of women are often stereotypical, reductive, eroticized: there is the purer-than-pure woman, with her unreal, pale skin, who bends wistfully like the Madonnas in Renaissance *Annunciations* (in Edward Burne-Jones' *The Baleful Head*)[1] or they are conniving, nefarious witches (as in the *Morgan Le Fay* painting of Frederick Sandys).[2]

British 19th century painters sometimes rival even Gustave Moreau, the most exotic of figurative visionaries, in the depiction of really bizarre and potentially sexist scenes. Frederic Leighton, for instance, painted a very voluptuous mermaid coiling her tail around a drowned sailor. It is a variation on the theme, depicted by Félicien Rops, Eric Gill and Auguste Rodin, among others, of a nude, long-haired woman, a Mary Magdalene figure, embracing a swooned, seemingly passive male.[3] Frederick Sandys' *Danaë* portrays a dreamy Goddess raising her arm to reveal her body. This painting is clearly pornography, right down to the thin dress she wears, revealing her breasts in a manner similar to women's wet Tee shirt contests.[4]

1 Edward Burne-Jones: *The Baleful Head*, 1885-7, oil on canvas, 155 x 130cm, Staatsgalerie, Stuttgart
2 Frederick Sandys: *Morgan Le Fay*, 1864, oil, Birmingham Art Gallery
3 Frederic Leighton: *The Fisherman and the Syren*, 1858, 26.5 x 18.5in, Bristol Art Gallery
4 Frederick Sandys: *Danaë in the Brazen Chamber*, 1867, chalk on paper, 26 x 17in, Bradford Art Gallery

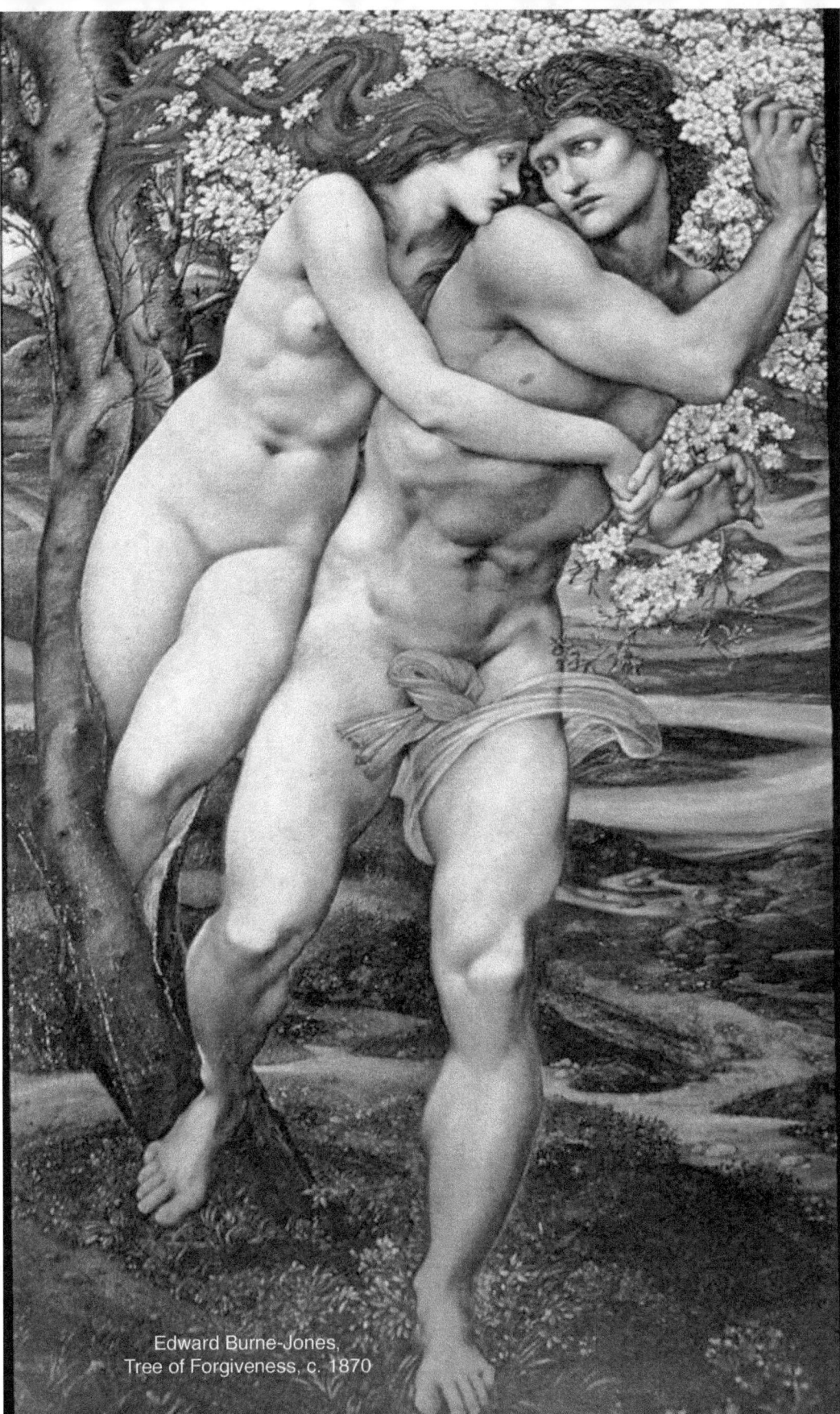

Edward Burne-Jones,
Tree of Forgiveness, c. 1870

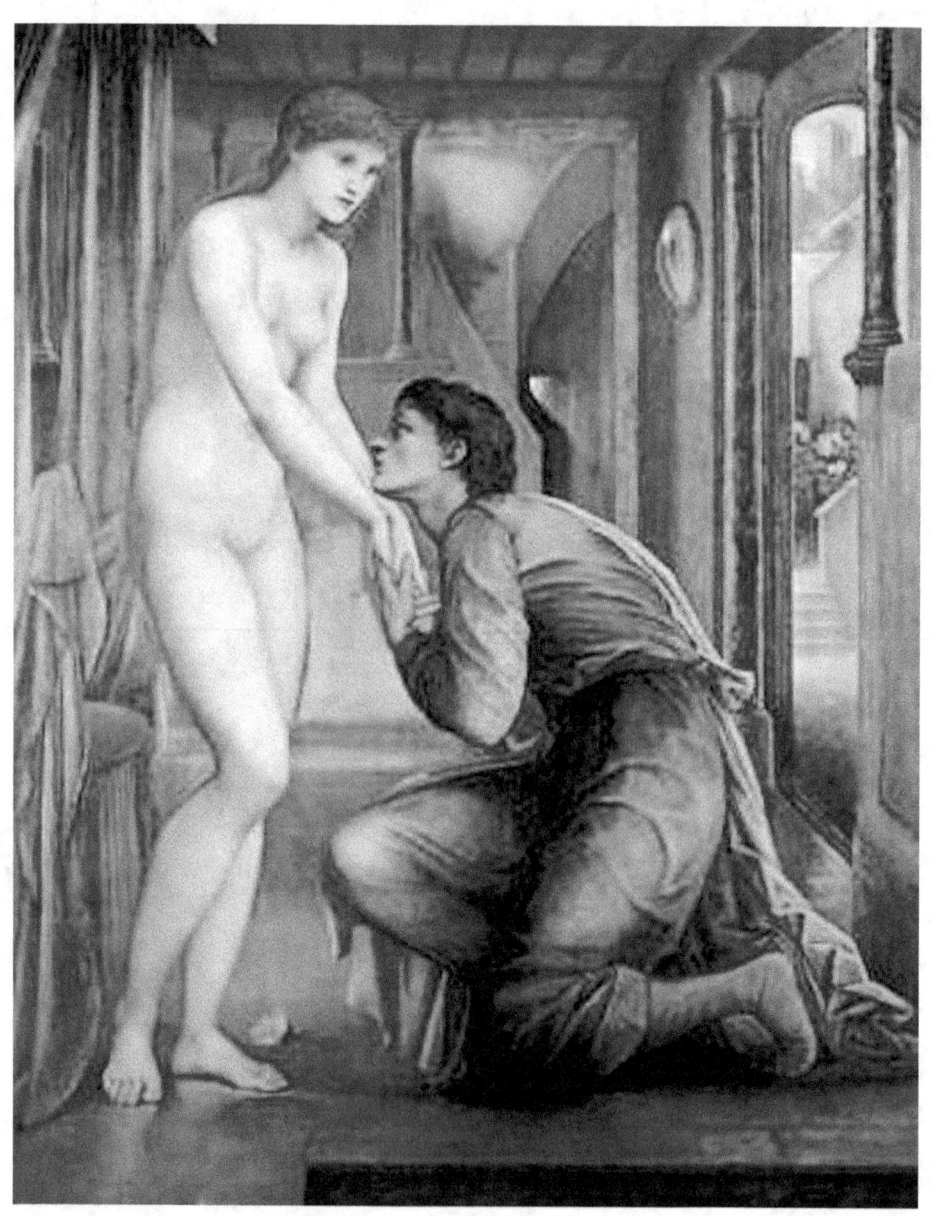

Edward Burne-Jones, Pygmalion, 1878, Birmingham, England

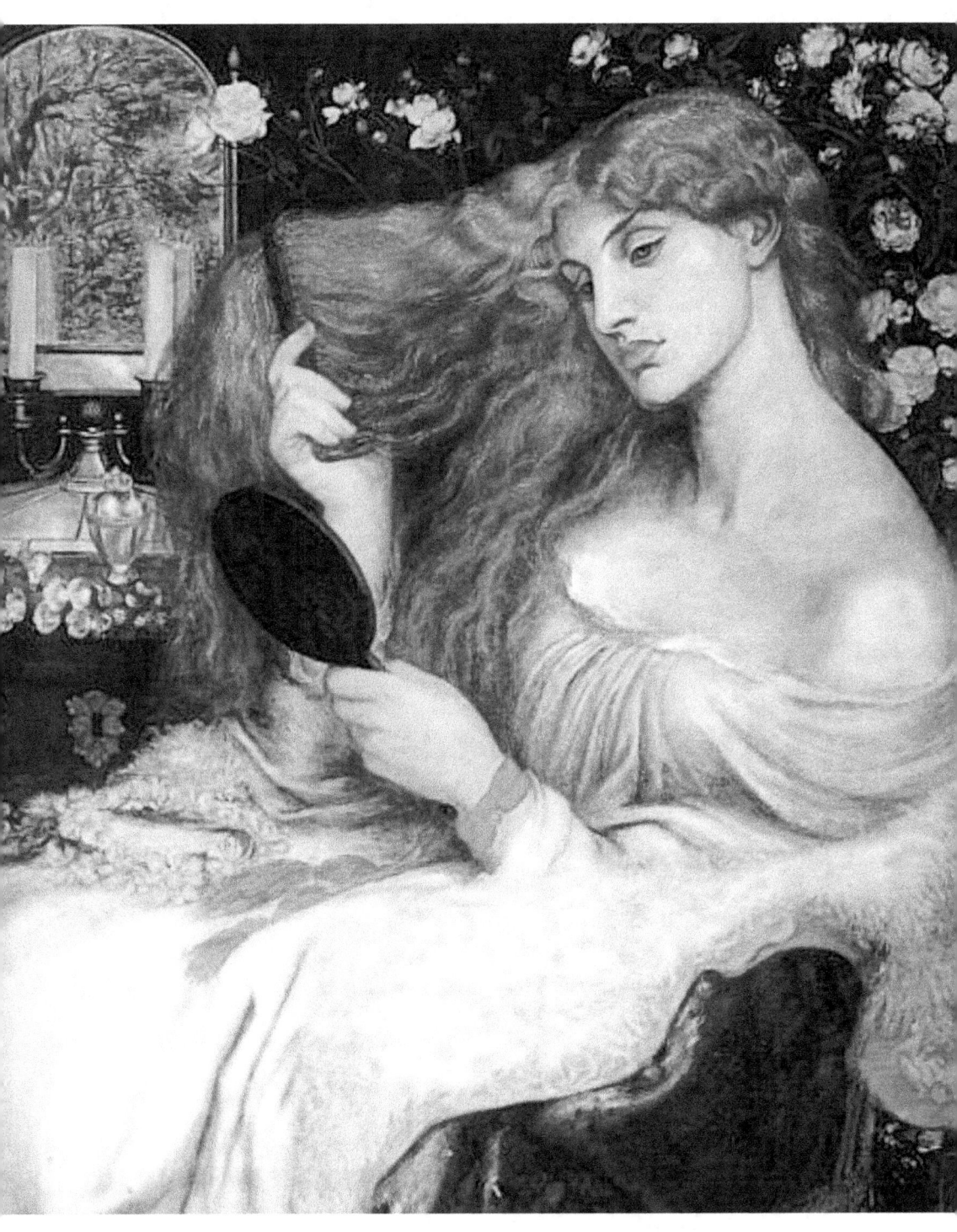

Dante Gabriel Rossetti, Lady Lilith, 1866-68, Delaware Art Museum

THOMAS ROWLANDSON

Thomas Rowlandson (1756-1827) is one of the great social commentators among British artists, capturing in a sprawling, vivacious and often humorous manner the variety of life in early modern Britain. His erotica is well-known, and a clear ancestor of saucy British postcard humour, of *Carry On* movies, of the nudge-nudge, wink-wink, *Monty Python* style of British comedy.

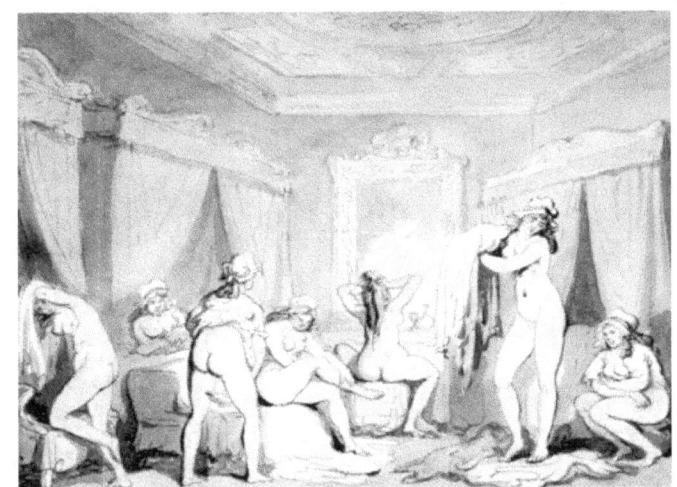

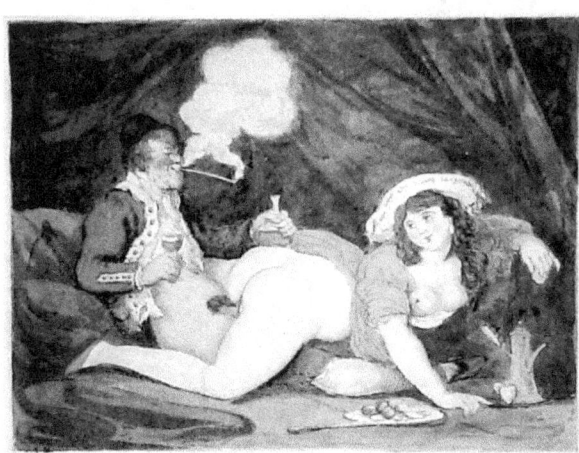

Thomas Rowlandson.
This page and following pages

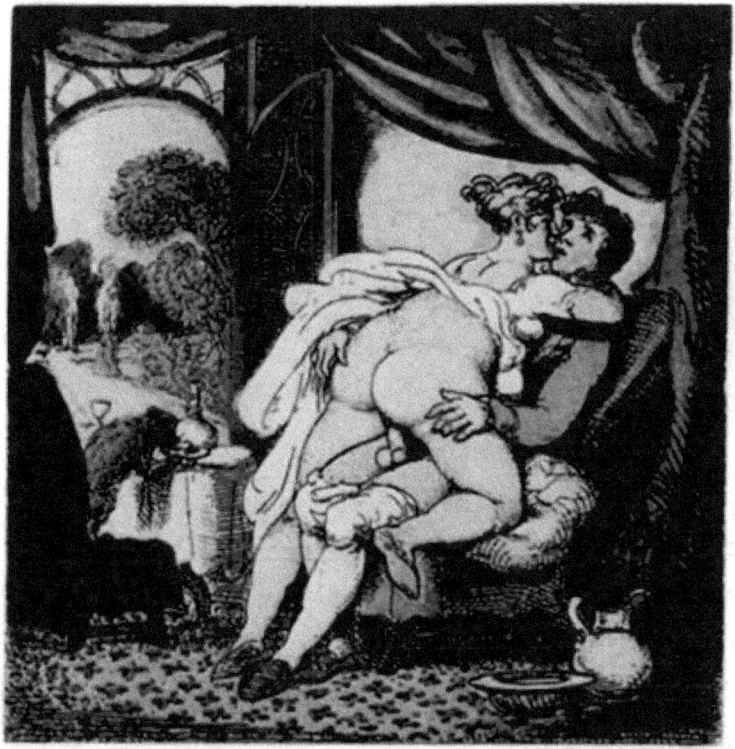

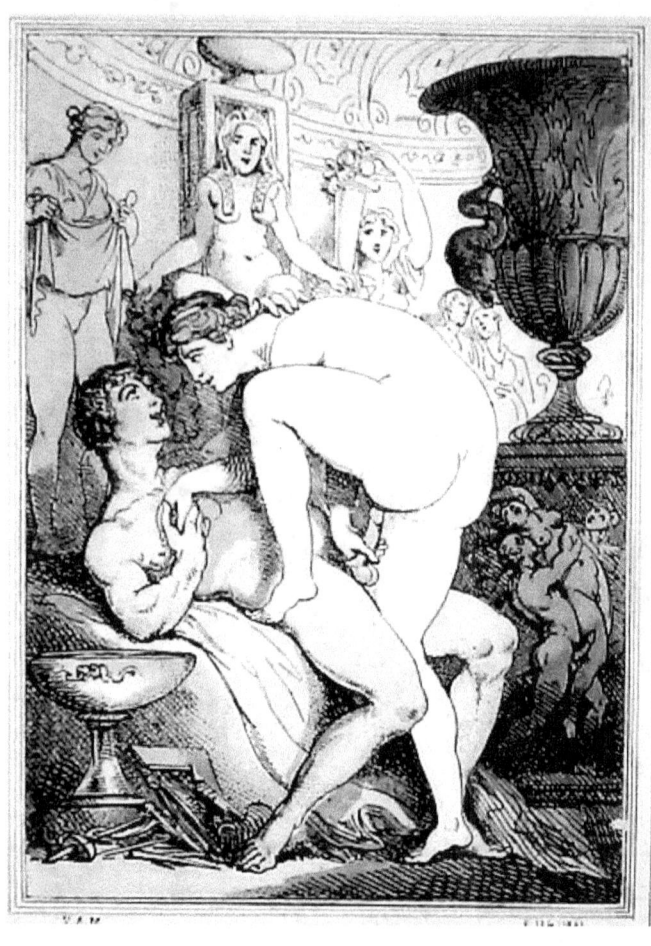

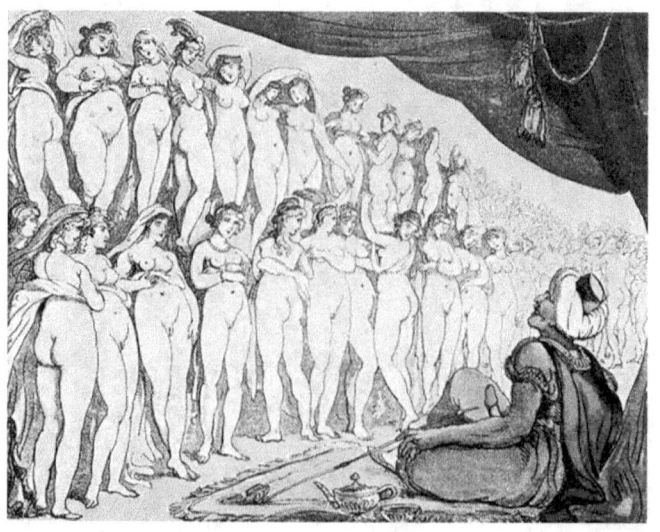

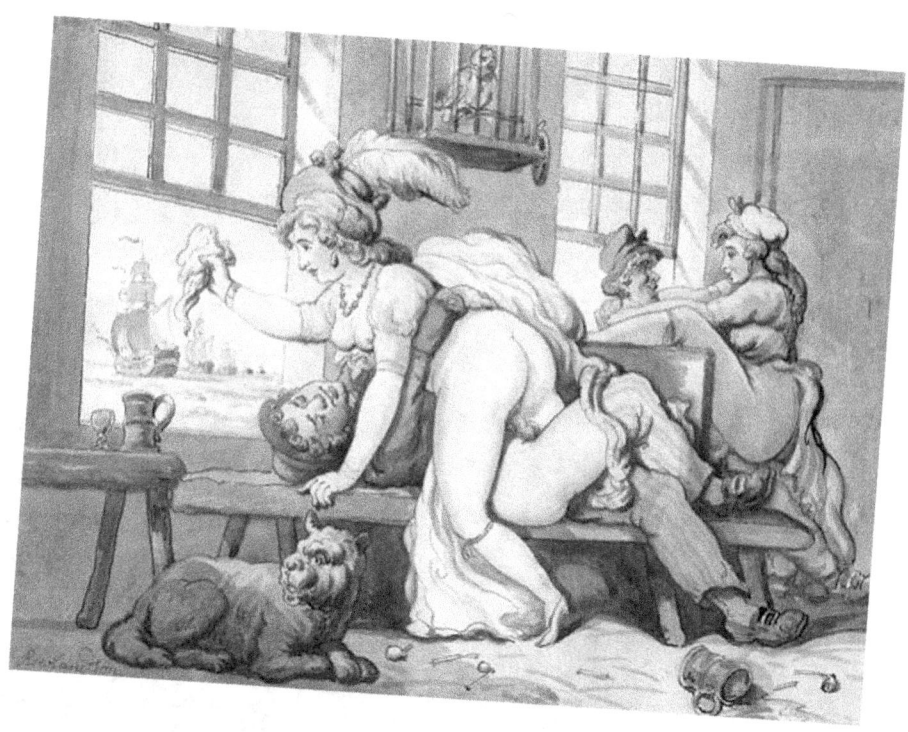

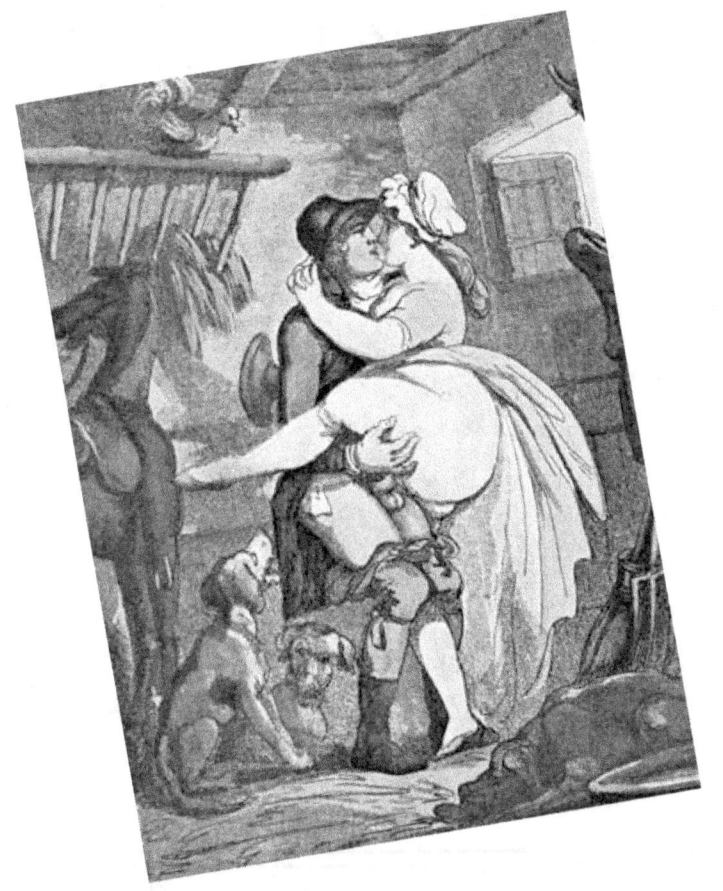

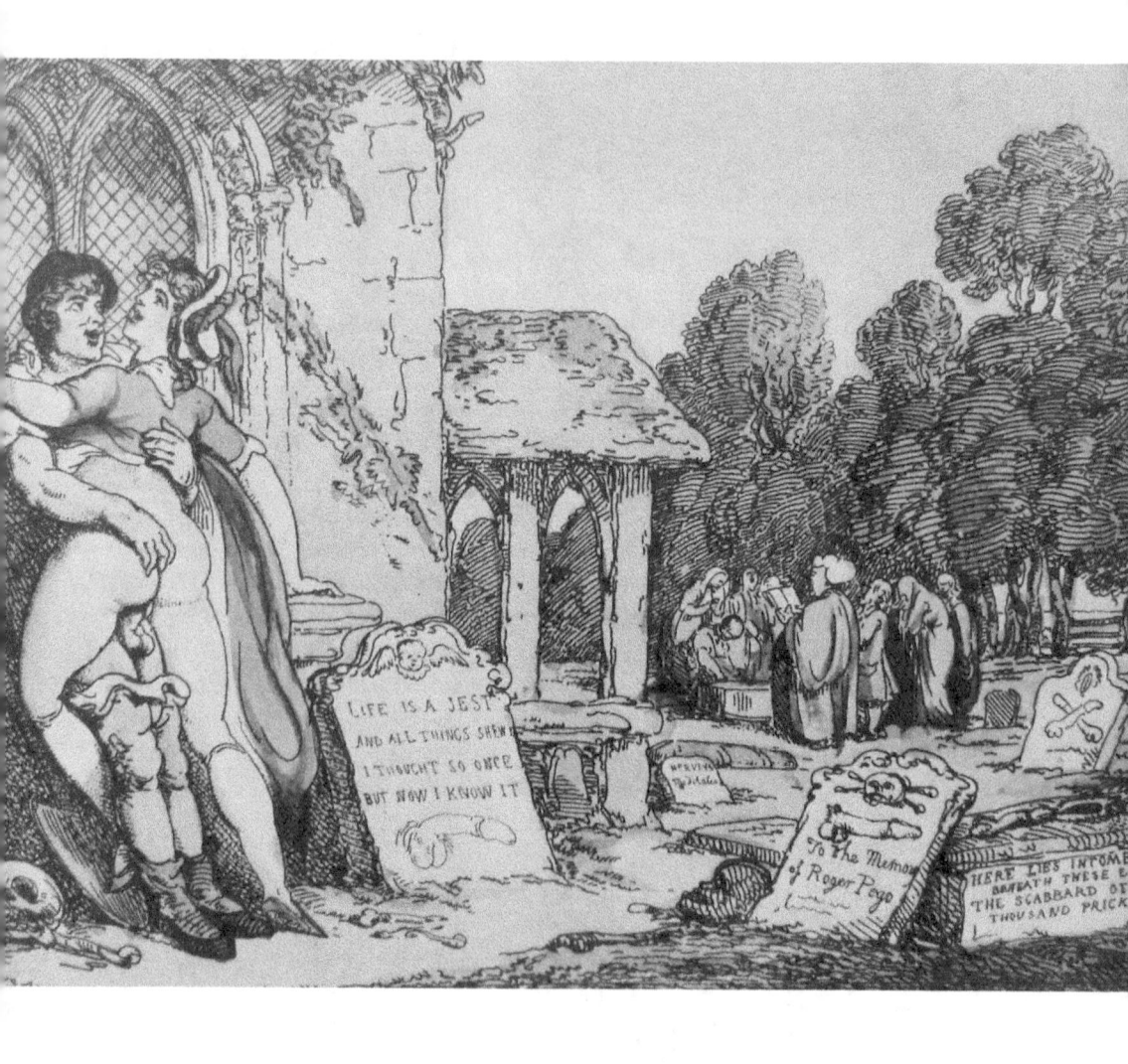

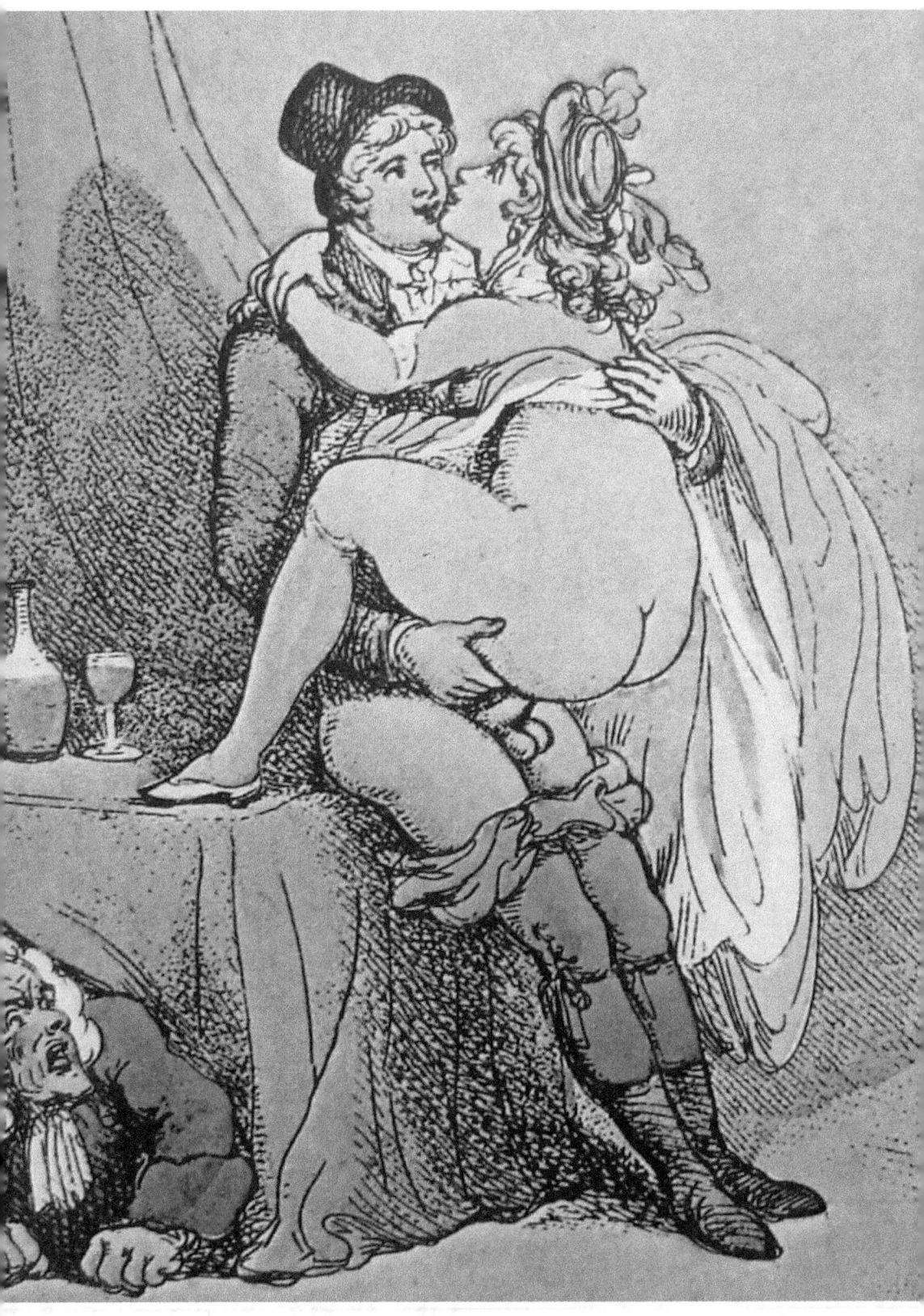

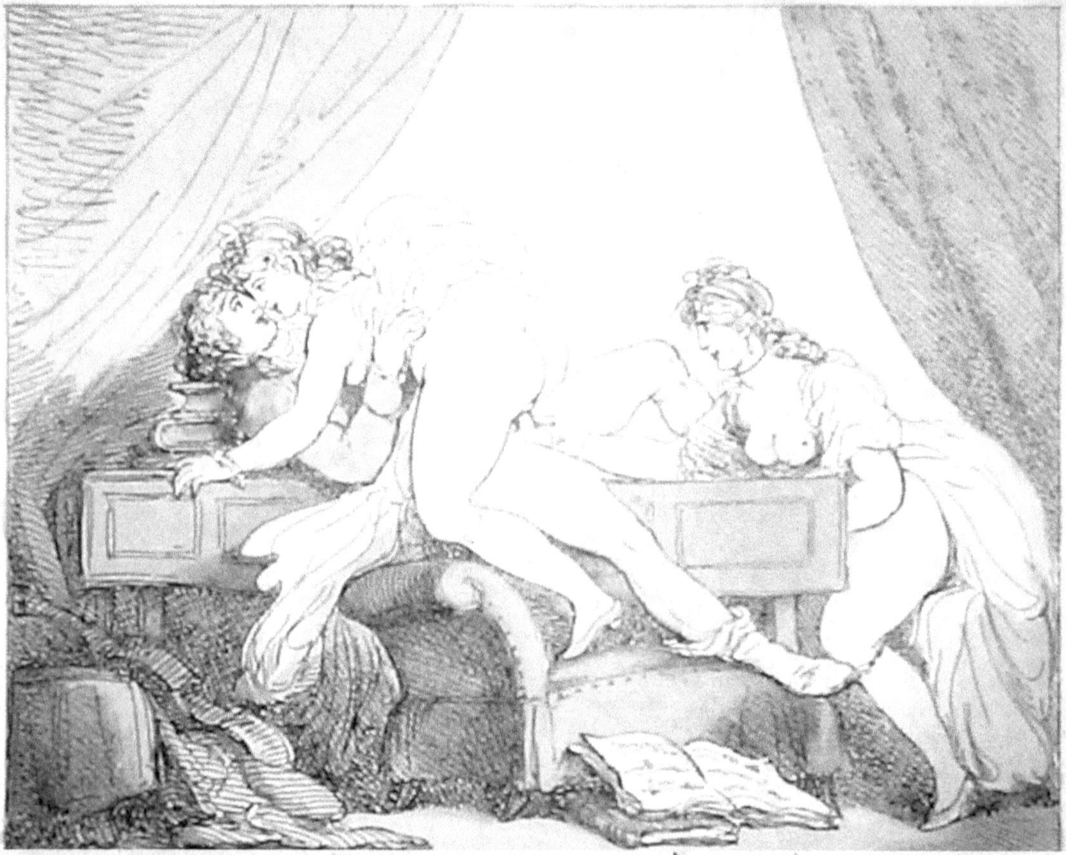

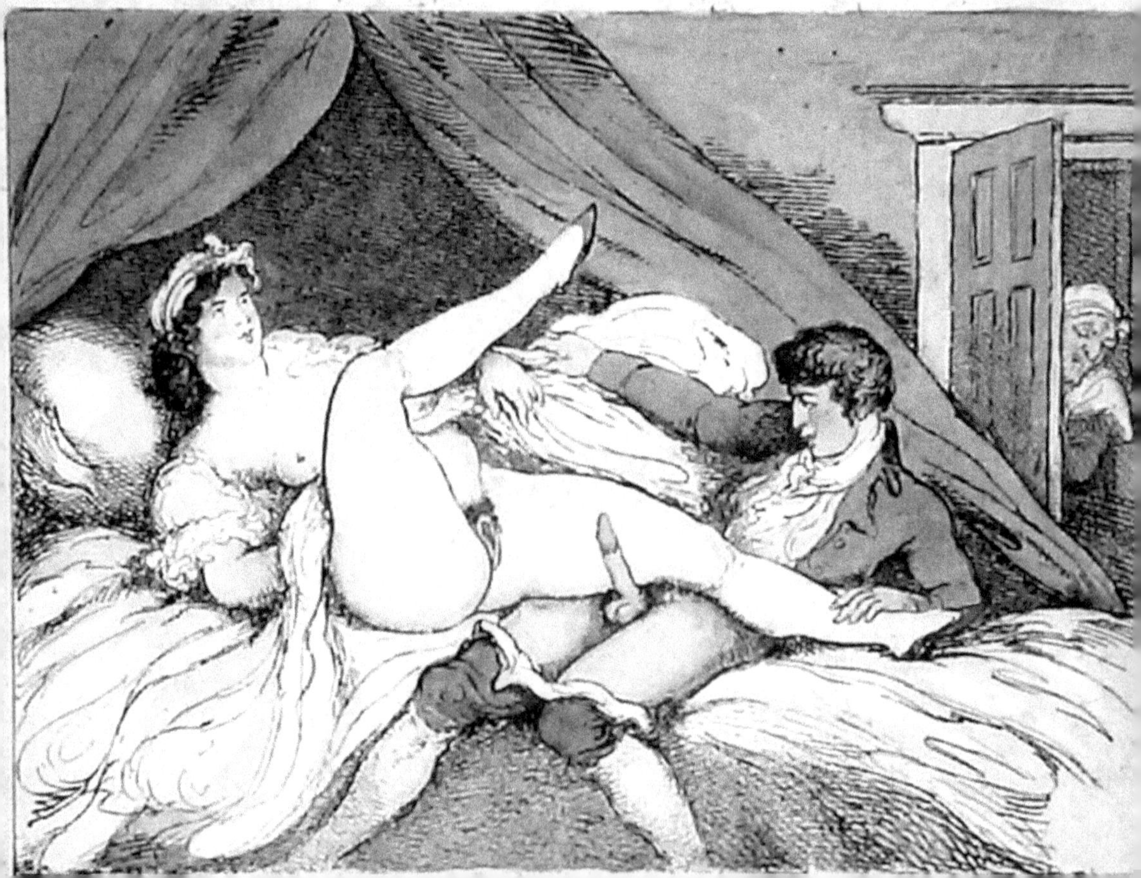

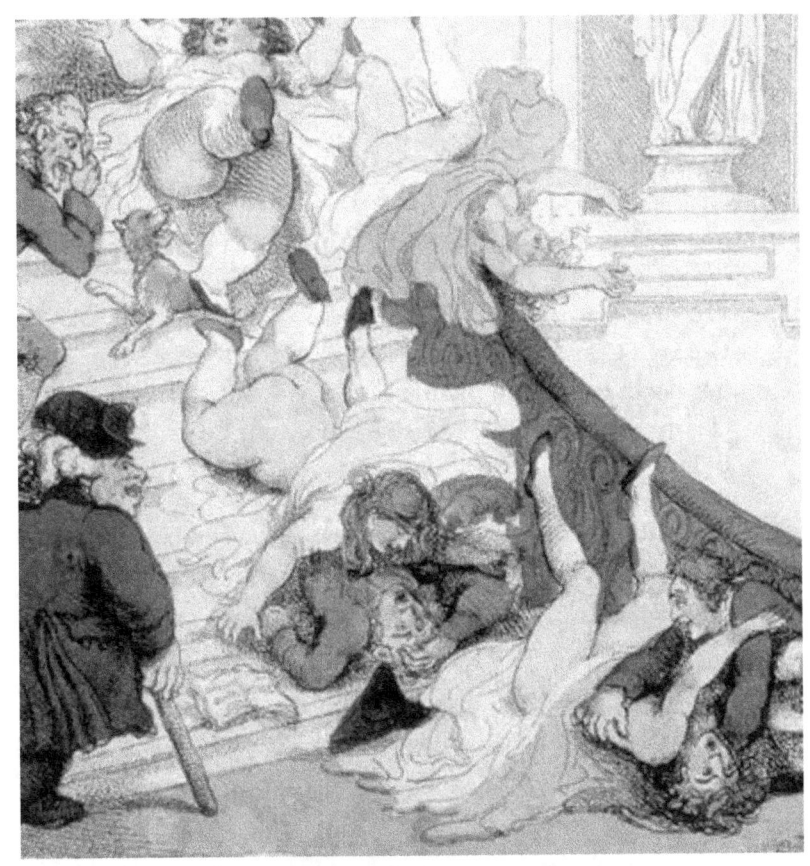

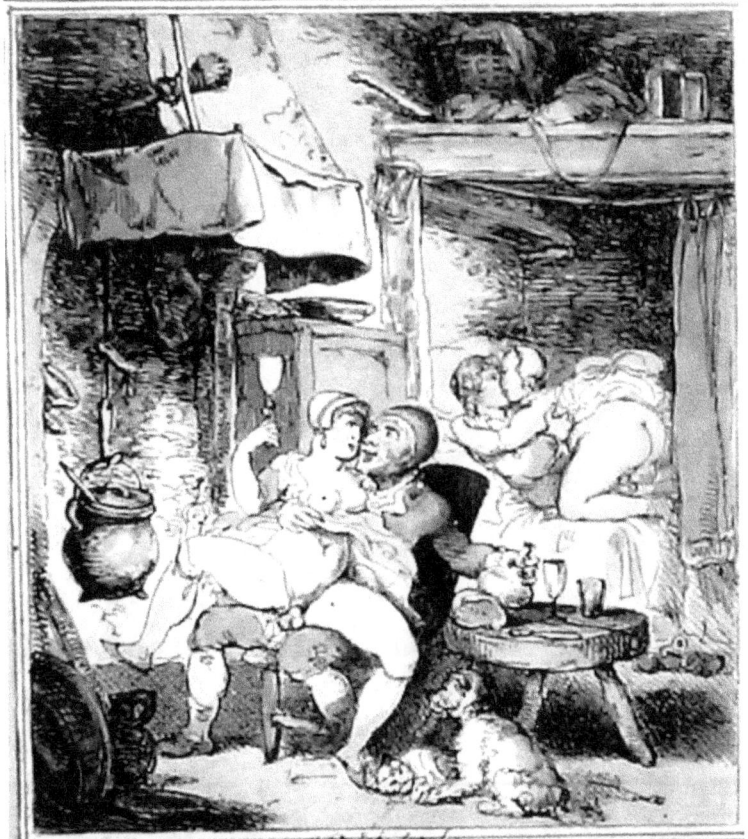

GUSTAVE COURBET:
ORIGIN OF THE WORLD

Gustave Courbet painted a woman's torso, seen from below. With her legs spread, the picture is really a close-up of a vagina, and is clearly pornographic. Maxime Du Camp described how Courbet's painting presented pornography as 'high art':

> In the dressing room of this foreign personage [the Turkish collector Khalil Bey] one sees a small picture hidden under a green veil. When one draws aside the veil one remains stupefied to perceive a woman, lifesize, seen from the front, moved and convulsed, remarkably executed, reproduced *con amore*, as the Italians say, providing the last word in realism. But, by some inconceivable forgetfulness, the artist, who copied his model from nature, had neglected to represent the feet, the legs, the thighs, the stomach, the hips, the chest, the hands, the arms, the shoulders, the neck, and the head.[1]

It has cosmic aspirations, for the title is *The Origin of the World*, again echoing the mythology of the Goddess, and woman as the site of all time and space.[2] For a long time the painting's whereabouts were apparently unknown: now it's on public view in the Musée d'Orsay in Paris.

---

1 Maxime Du Camp: *Les Convulsions de Paris*, Hachette, Paris 1889, II, 189-190
2 G. Courbet: *The Origin of the World*, 1867, Musée d'Orsay, Paris.

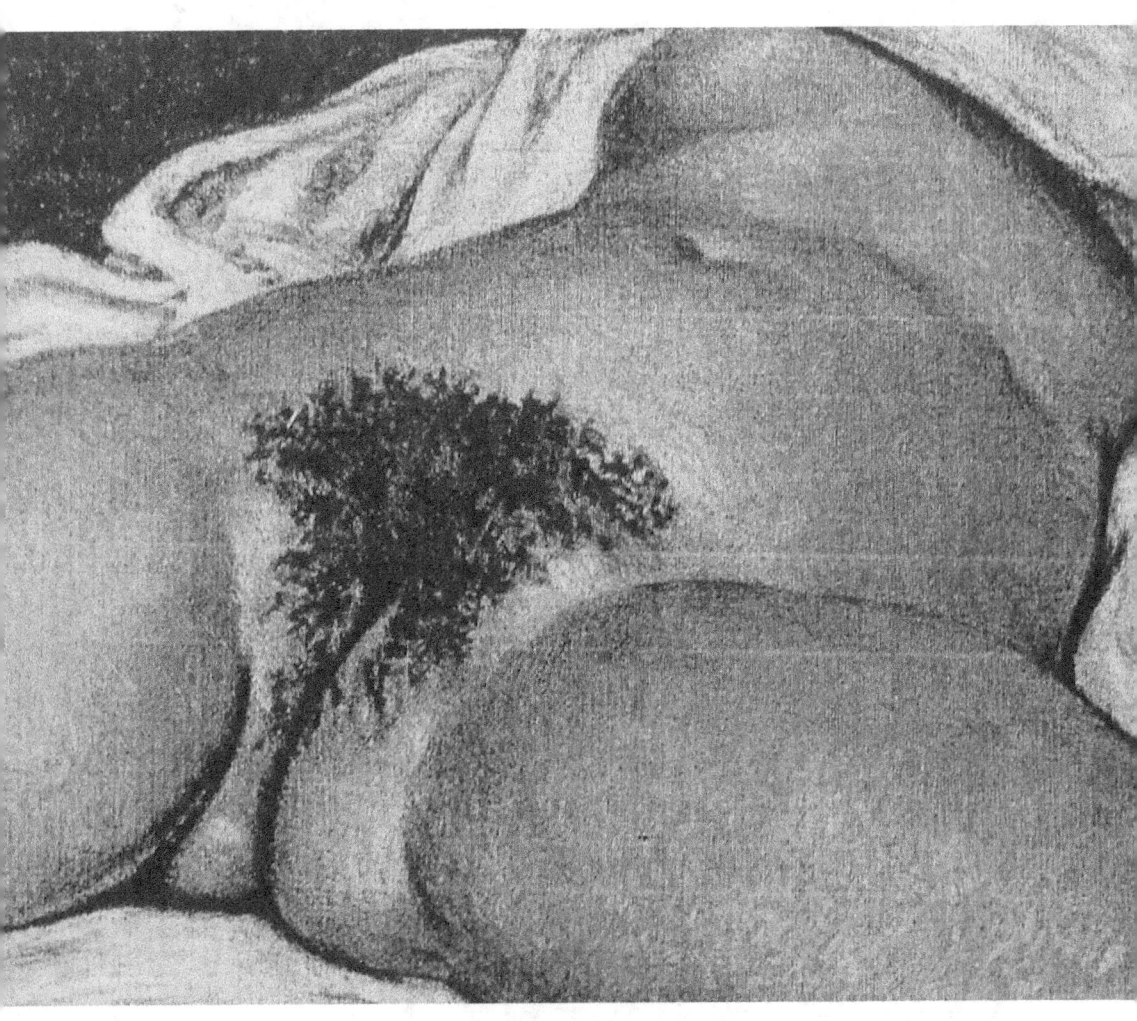

Gustave Courbet, The Creation of the World

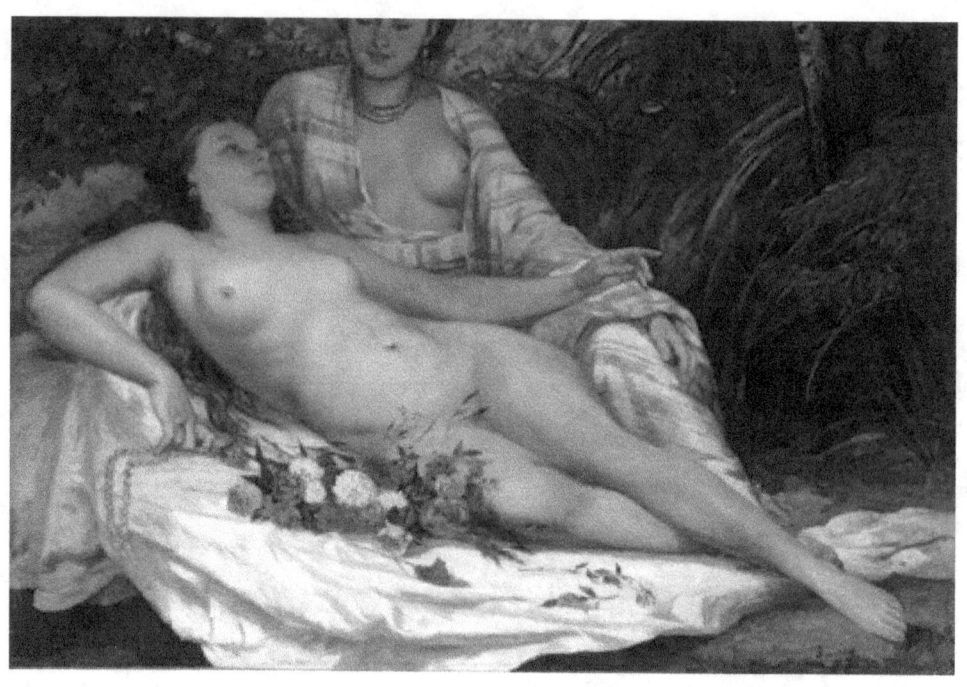

Gustave Courbet, Two Bathers (above).
Woman Lying Down, 1862.

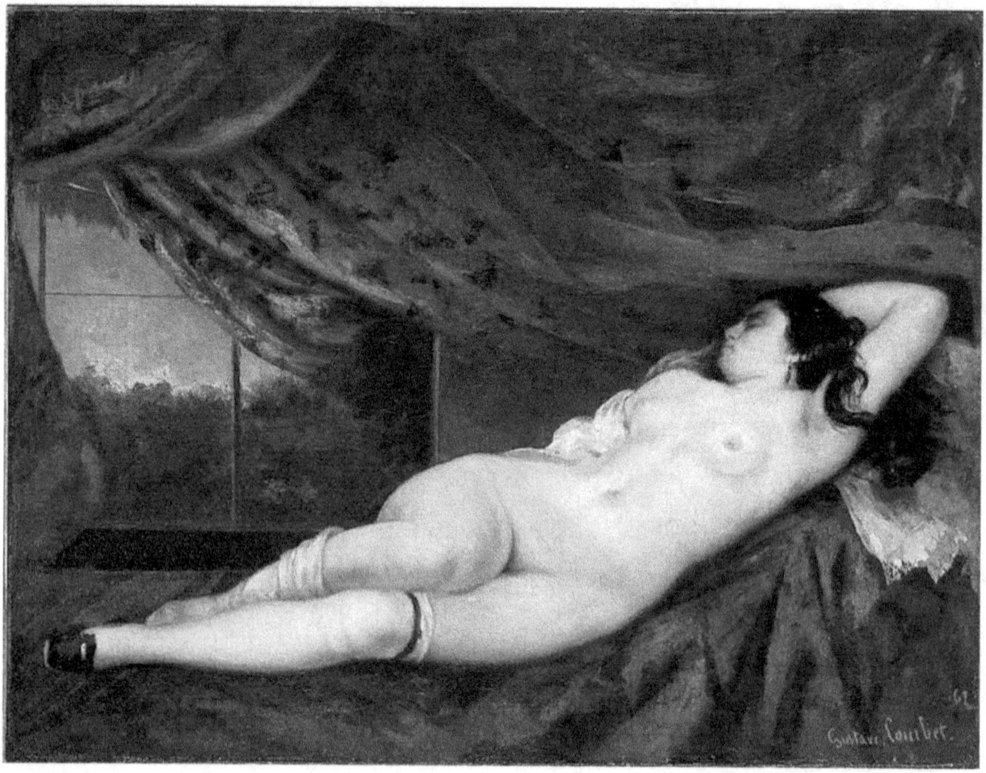

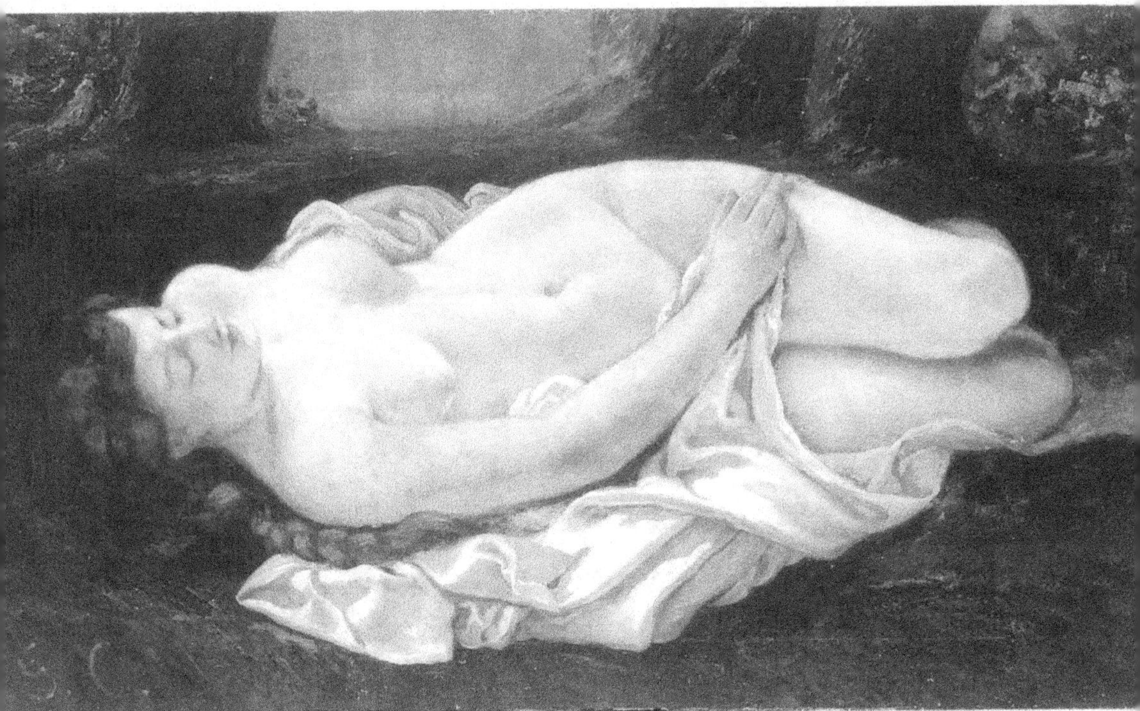

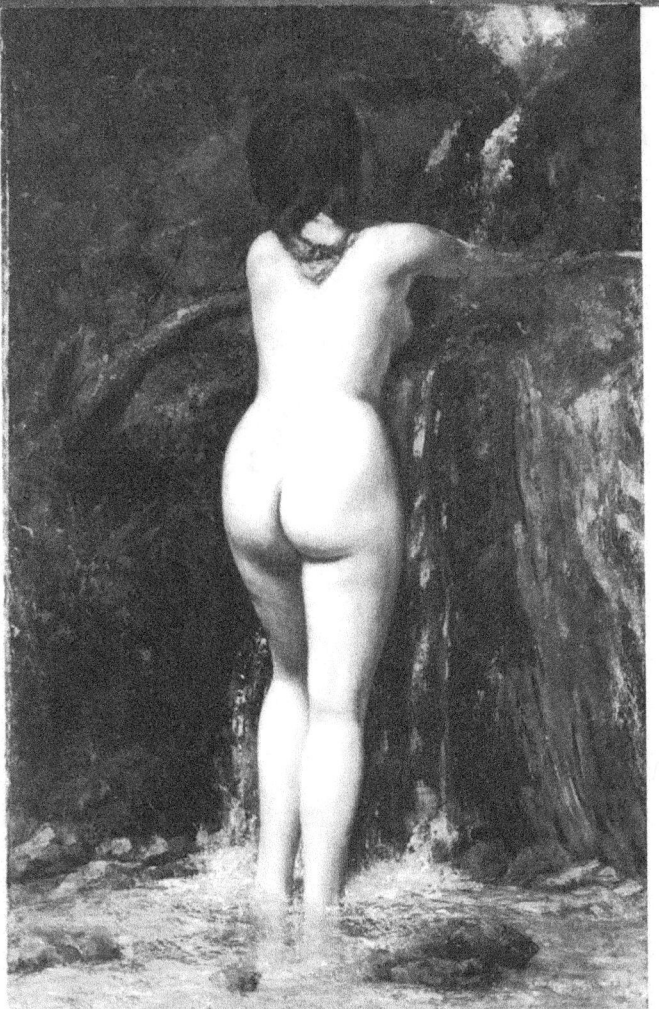

Gustave Courbet, Source, 1862
(left). Reclining Woman (above).

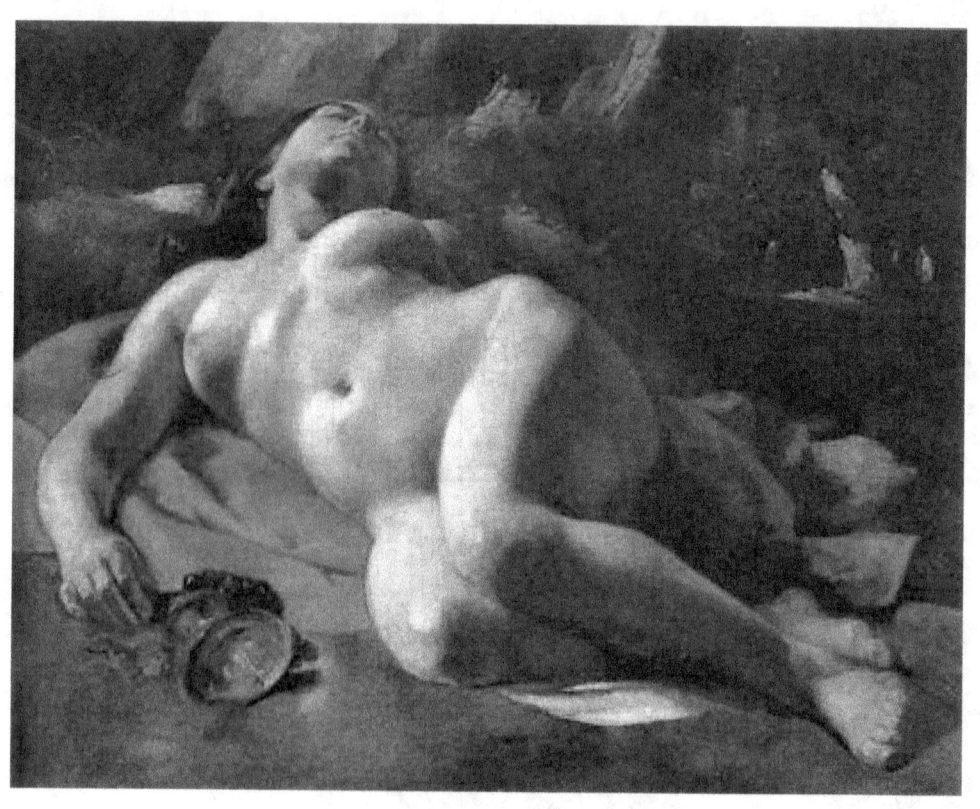

Gustave Courbet, La Bachante, 1844-47

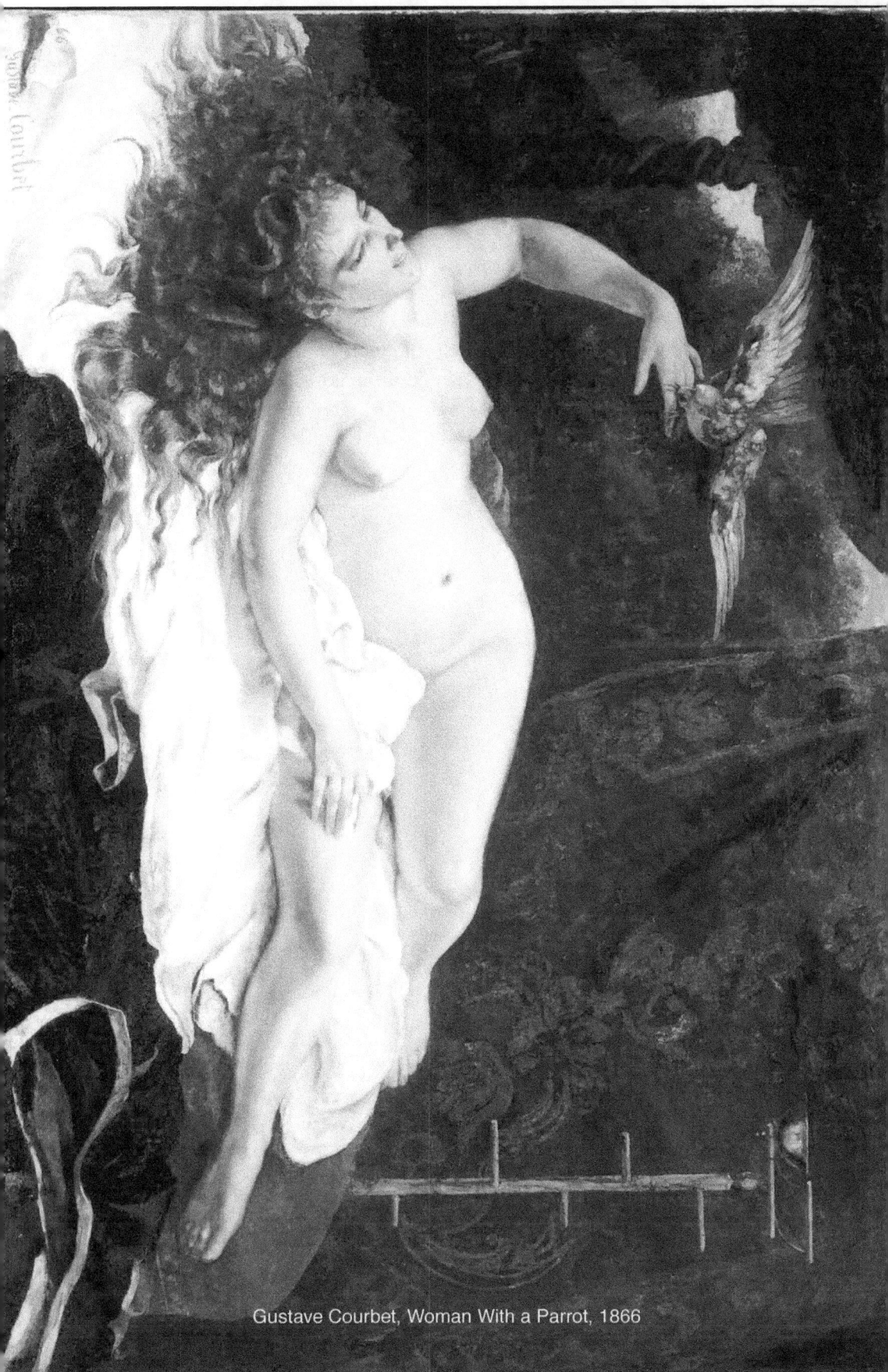

Gustave Courbet, Woman With a Parrot, 1866

J.M.W. TURNER

Many major artists have produced erotic art, from Titan to J.M.W. Turner. Titian drew in charcoal and chalk two people having sex, the woman (as ever) underneath, the man on top (as ever), while Turner made a (rare) sketch of people making love – the people are anonymous and faceless, while the genitals, as in all good erotica, are emphasized.[1]

1 J.M.W. Turner: *Sheet of erotic drawings*, c. 1820s, pencil & wash, 10.5 x 14.5in, British Museum, London; Titian: *A Couple in Embrace*, c. 1750, charcoal & white & black chalk on blue paper, 25.1 x 26cm, Fitzwilliam Museum, Cambridge

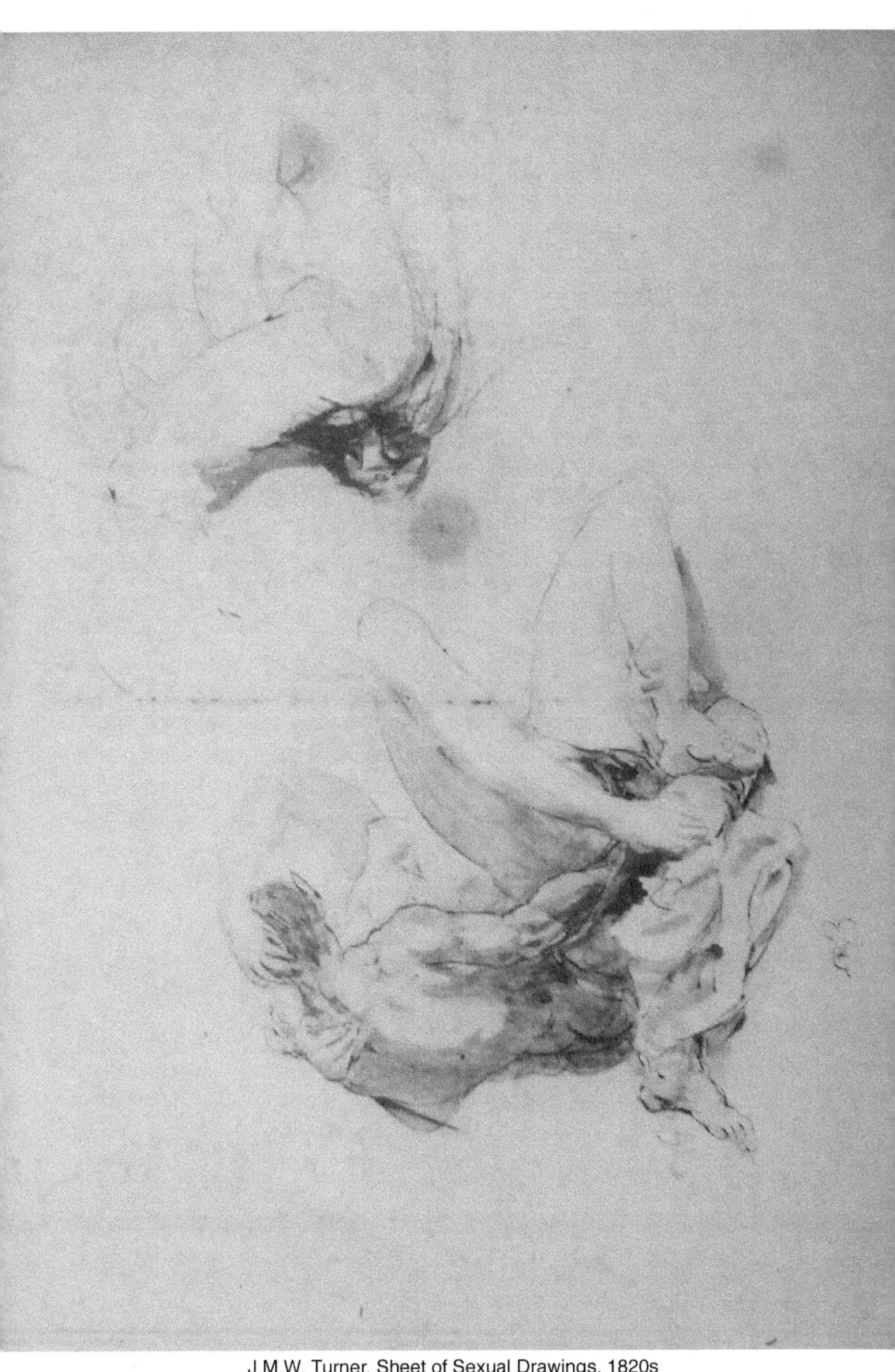

J.M.W. Turner, Sheet of Sexual Drawings, 1820s

THE MARQUIS DE SADE

The Marquis de Sade is quite astonishing. De Sade is the high priest of metaphysical eroticism, as championed by the European artistic élite, such as Charles Baudelaire, Jean Cocteau, the Surrealists, Algernon Swinburne, Lautréamont, Fyodor Dostoievsky and John Cowper Powys. Among visual artists, the inheritors of the Sadeian pornographic ethic include Pablo Picasso, Hans Bellmer, Jean Cocteau, Max Ernst, Allen Jones, and David Salle. Many artists have had a go at illustrating de Sade's work.

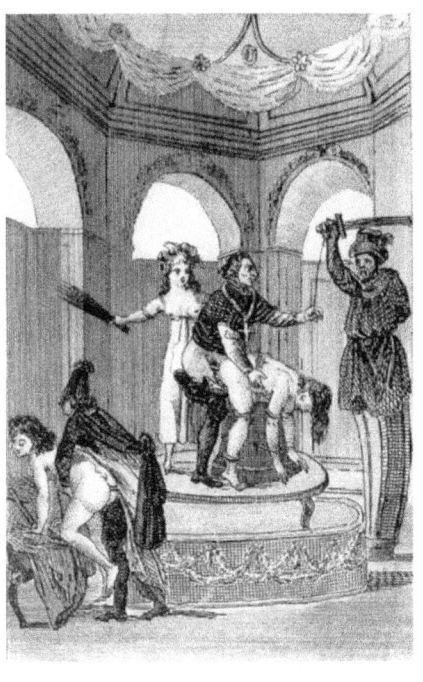

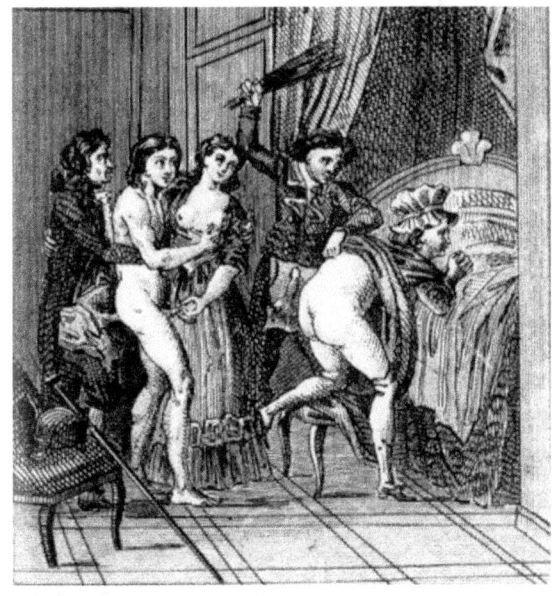

Illustrations from Justine,
late 18th century

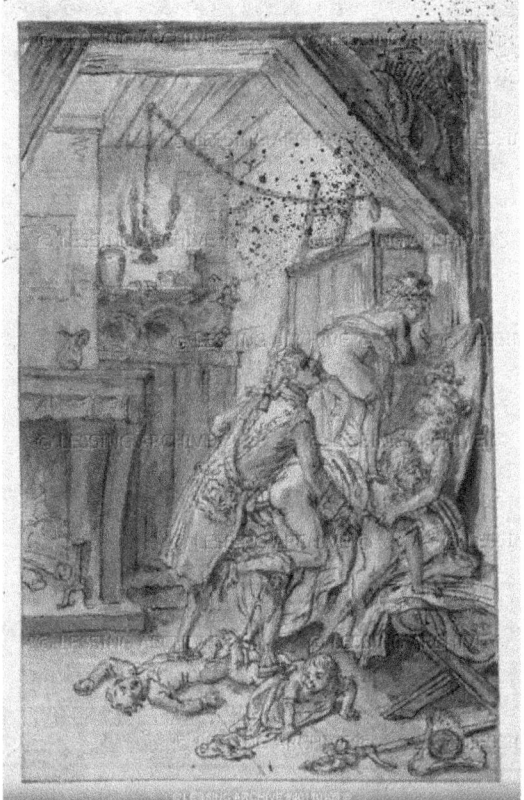

EDGAR DEGAS

Pierre Bonnard's paintings mythicize the intimate day-to-day activities of his beloved, as art has always done, so that drying the body after a bath becomes a religious ritual. The same thing happens in the art of Edgar Degas. In both Degas' and Bonnard's works, the voyeur is built into the image. One is always aware of looking. One is always aware that the image is constructed for the pleasure of the artist. The viewer is a voyeur in Degas' art, in so much of art. As Degas said: '[i]t is as if you looked through a keyhole.'[1] This is emphasized in Degas' art by the studied indifference to the viewer, when the women turn their backs to the viewer, and in Bonnard's art one often looks through doorways or mirrors or frames of some kind. Both artists, as in late Picasso, emphasize the act of looking, the pleasure of seeing.

Edgar Degas' nudes, with their gorgeous pastel colours, spatial flatness, ritualized poses and gestures are brilliant graphic orchestrations, and seem at first to be simply formal explorations, as the poet Paul Valéry maintained.[2] These are the images, of nude bathing women, that Degas is famous for.[3] In fact, Degas' nudes have much to do with voyeurism, with scopophilia, with framing the obscure object of desire, so that the woman retains her 'looked-at-ness', to use Laura Mulvey's term from her key essay on visual pleasure.[4]

---

1 Quoted in P.A. Lemoine: *Degas et son œuvre*, Paris, 1946-9, I, 107
2 'All his life, Degas sought in the Nude, observed from all sides, in an unbelievable quantity of poses… the unique system of lines that would formulate any given moment of the body with the utmost precision and the utmost generality", wrote Paul Valéry (*Degas Danse Dessin*, Gallimard, Paris 1938, 59).
3 Egdar Degas: *Woman Drying Herself*, c. 1890-5, pastel, National Gallery of Scotland, Edinburgh; *The Tub*, c. 1885, pastel and gouache, 71.1 x 71.1cm, Hillstead Museum, Farmington, Connecticut
4 Laura Mulvey: "Visual Pleasure and Narrative Cinema", *Screen*, 16, 3, 1975

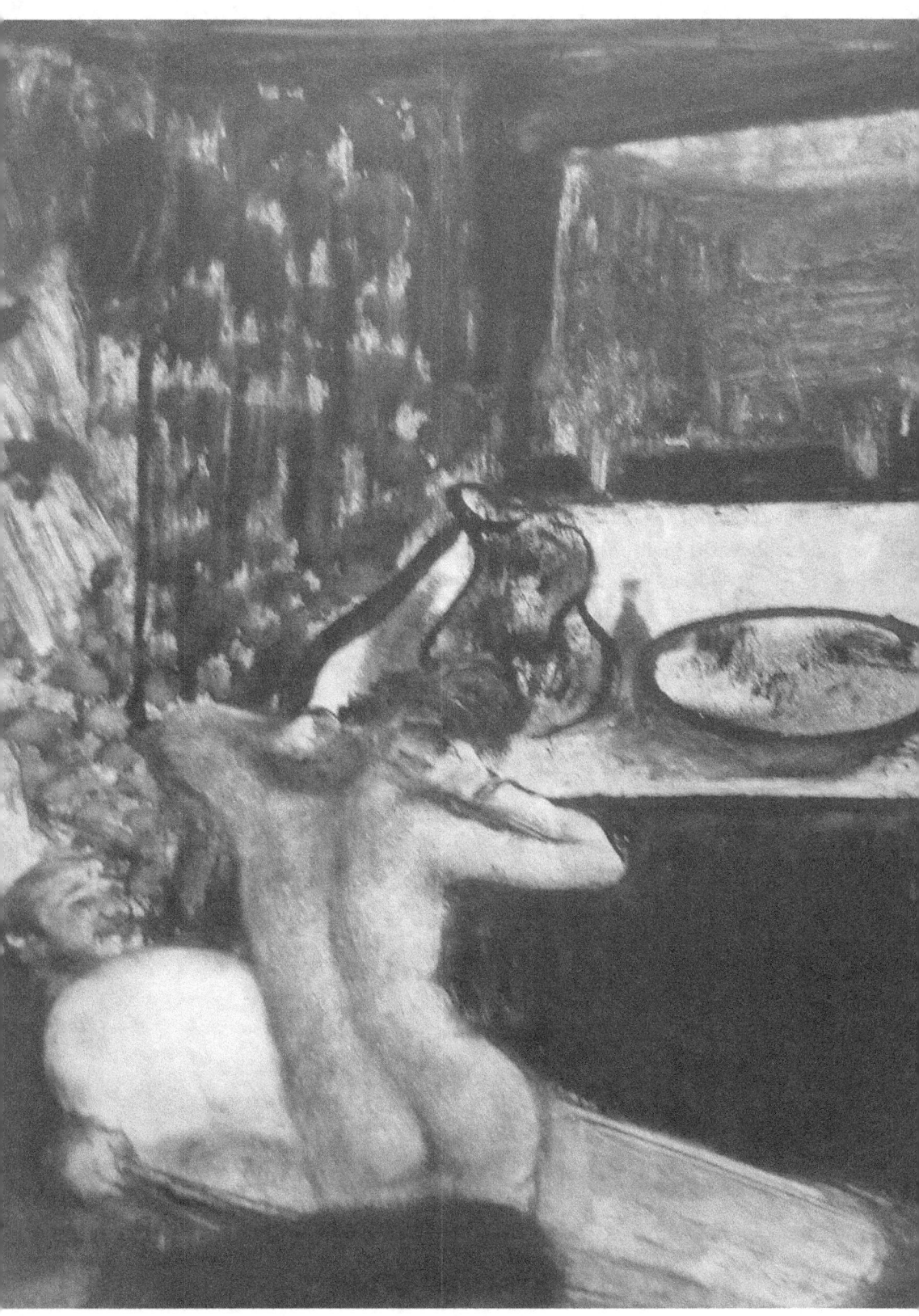

Edgar Degas, The Bath

EDGAR DEGAS

Edgar Degas' tender, sensual and tightly-controlled images try to erase the artist's viewpoint. Degas would like us to believe that he wasn't really there, drawing those women crouching on bathroom floors. They turn away from the artist, and Degas denies his interest in them, which is obviously erotic. But Degas cannot erase his erotic looking, his pleasure in brushing over with pastels every inch of skin of these anonymous women. For instance, Degas so often draws the hips, buttocks and back, and the women, bent over, are like the women of erotica, who always show off their bodies, and often their butts and hips.[1]

Although Edgar Degas' nudes can be seen as detached and aiming for a cool objectivity, Degas is drawing, time after time, nude women, who go about their tasks of cleaning and washing, and sit, like cats, self-absorbed. Degas heavily invests in his subjects, in these nude women. He is very interested in them, it seems, despite his professed detachment. His interest has an erotic component which if *he* can deny it, his art cannot deny it. Degas' nudes, then, can be seen as celebrations of the female nude, which turn out to be formulaic.

1 See Edgar Degas' *The Tub*, c. 1891, pastel on paper, Burrell Collection, Glasgow; *Aprés le Bain*, charcoal on paper, Victoria & Albert Museum

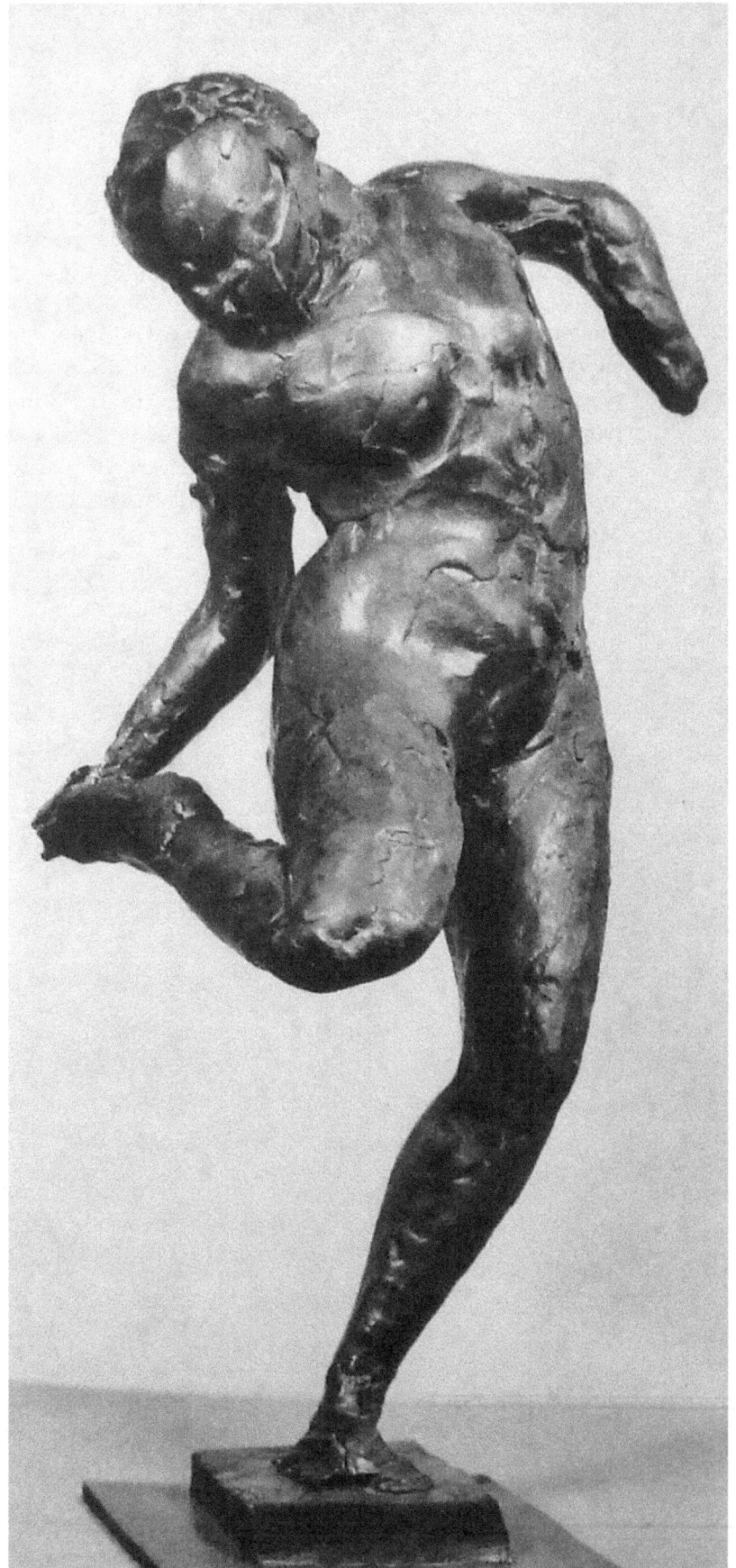

Edgar Degas,
Dancer Looking At
the Sole of Her
Right Foot, 1882-95,
New York

EUGÈNE DELACROIX

Eugène Delacroix is one of France's great Romantic artists. His signature work is *The Death of Sardanapalus* of 1827, with its image of a voluptuous slave being murdered in the foreground, a haunting image of the Romantic fusion of sex and death, which lingers on everywhere in Western erotic art. By the way, if you are ever in Paris, I highly recommend a visit to the Delacroix Museum.

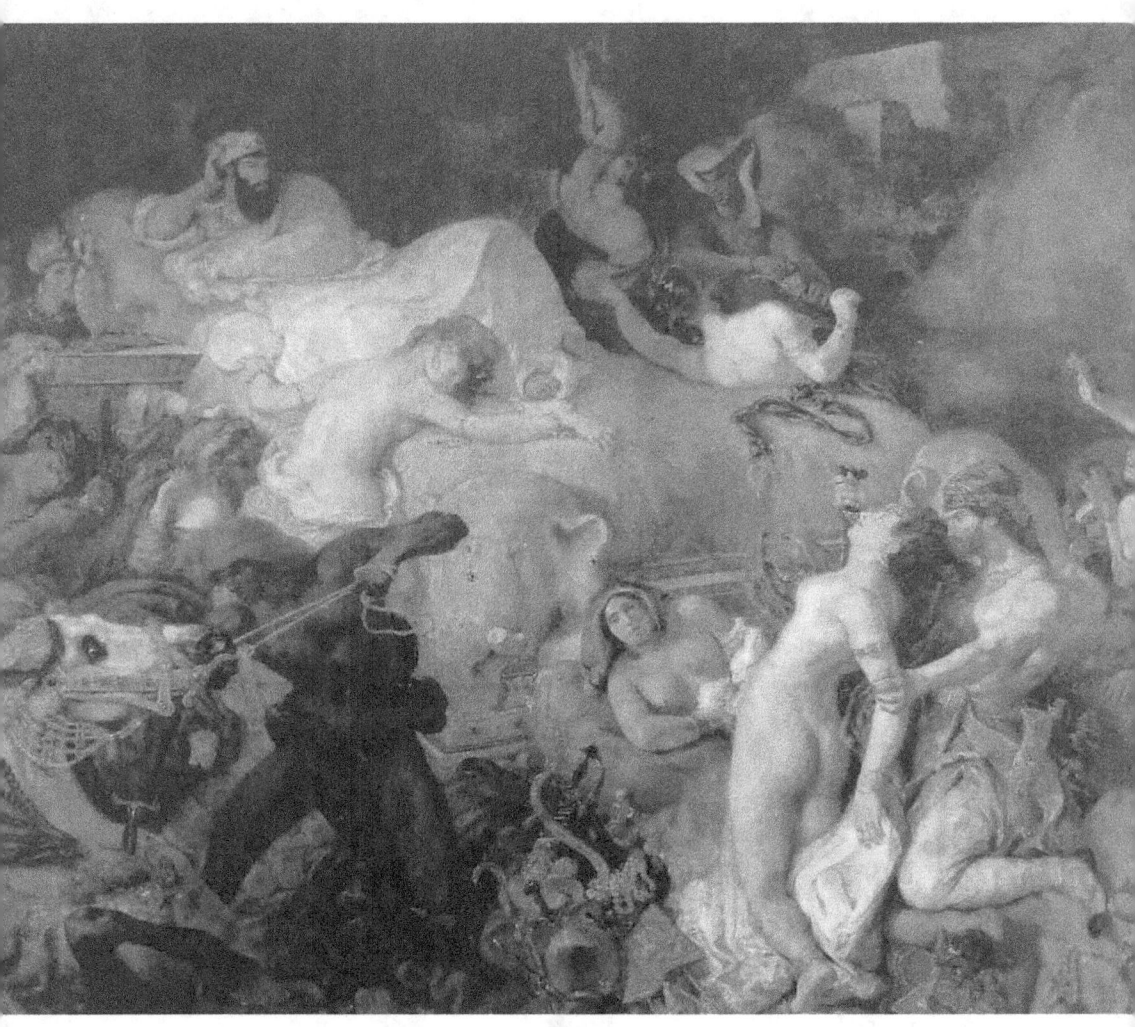

Eugene Delacroix, The Death of Sardanapalus, 1827

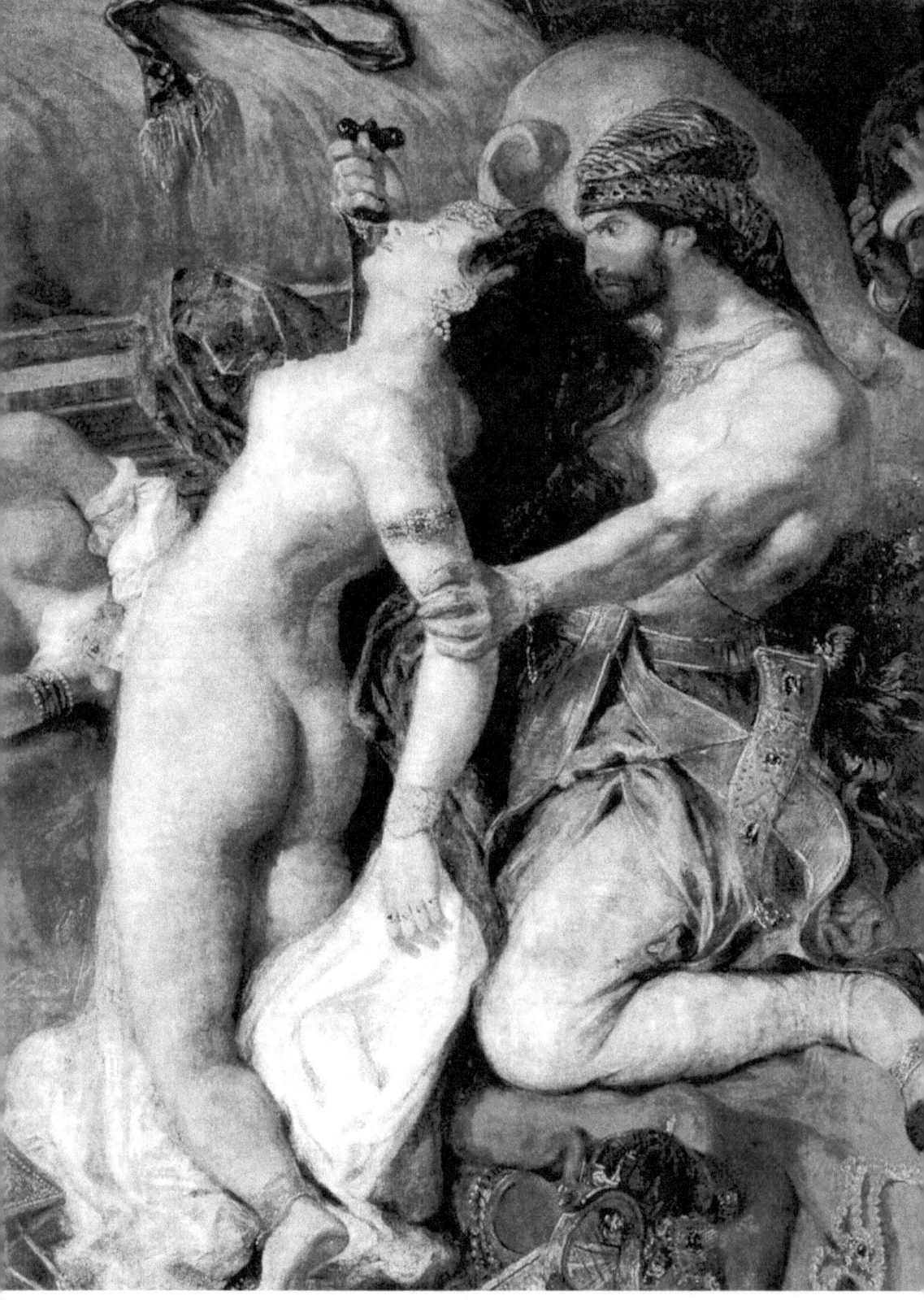

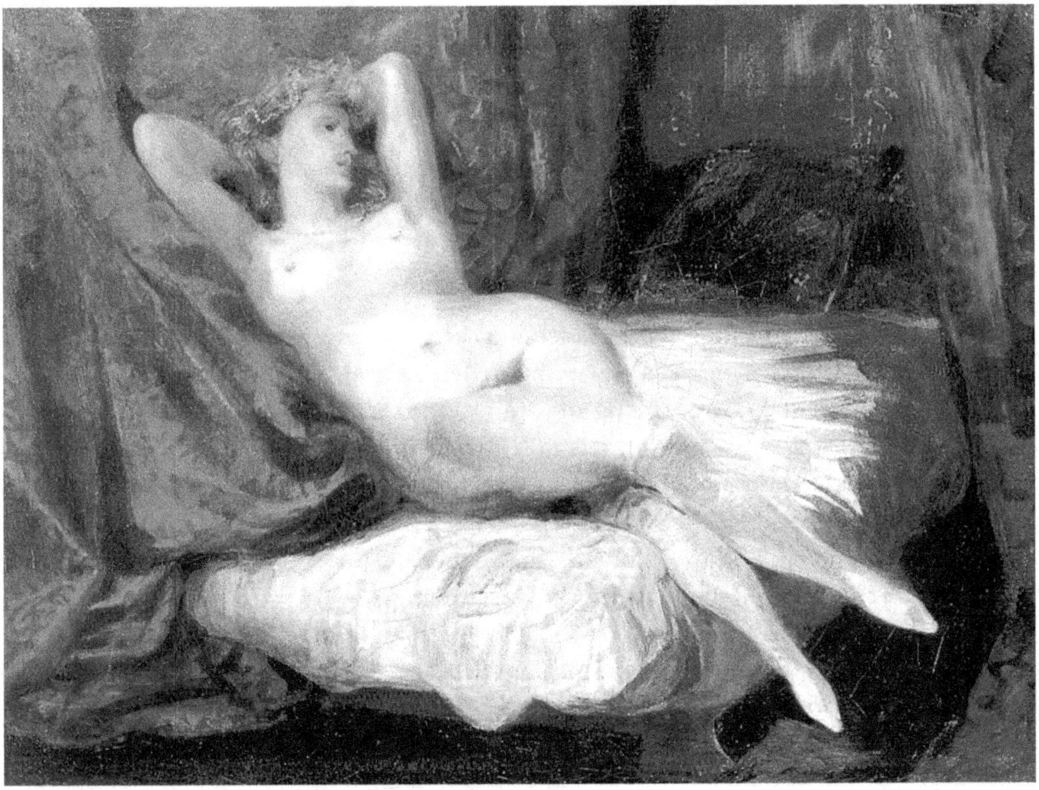

Eugène Delacroix

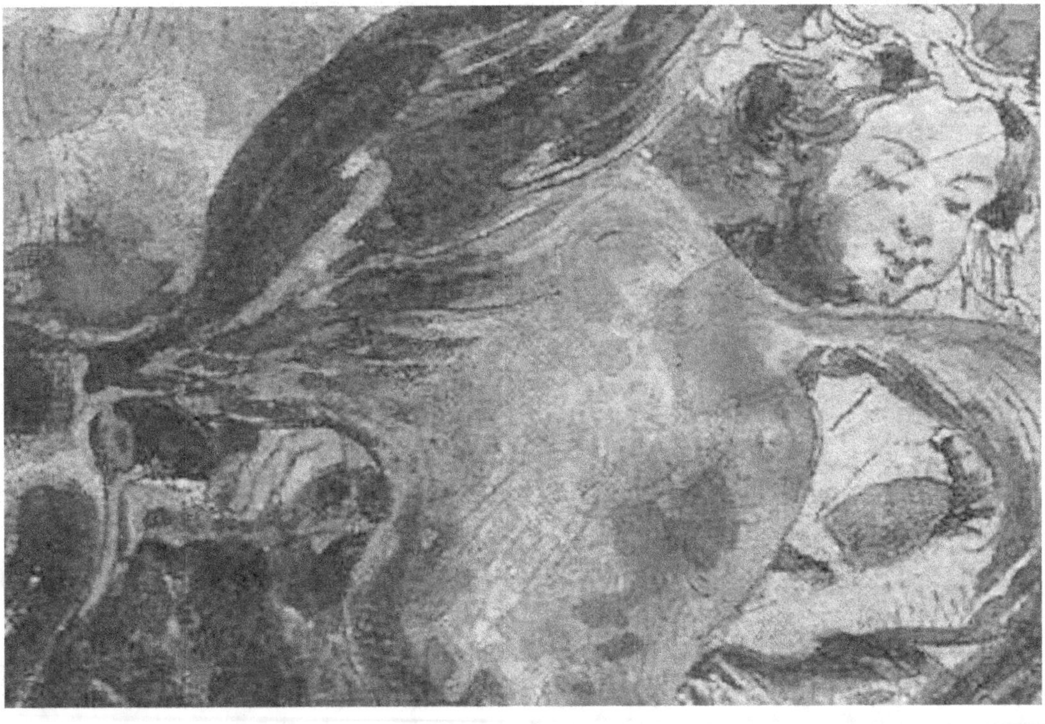

PIERRE RENOIR

Many artists love their subjects. Their paintings are acts of love. As Alfred Sisley says, speaking of landscape, but his notion also applies to the human figure: '[e]very picture shows a spot with which the artist himself has fallen in love'.[1] On canvas, they try to recreate their love of their subject. We see this especially in the nude, whether the male or female nude. Artists such as Pierre Renoir said they painted with their penis. The paintbrush becomes a phallus, gilding and caressing the (obscure) object of desire. The painter creates the Jungian *anima*, the beloved woman, the soul-mate on the canvas.

---

1 In R. Goldwater, 309.

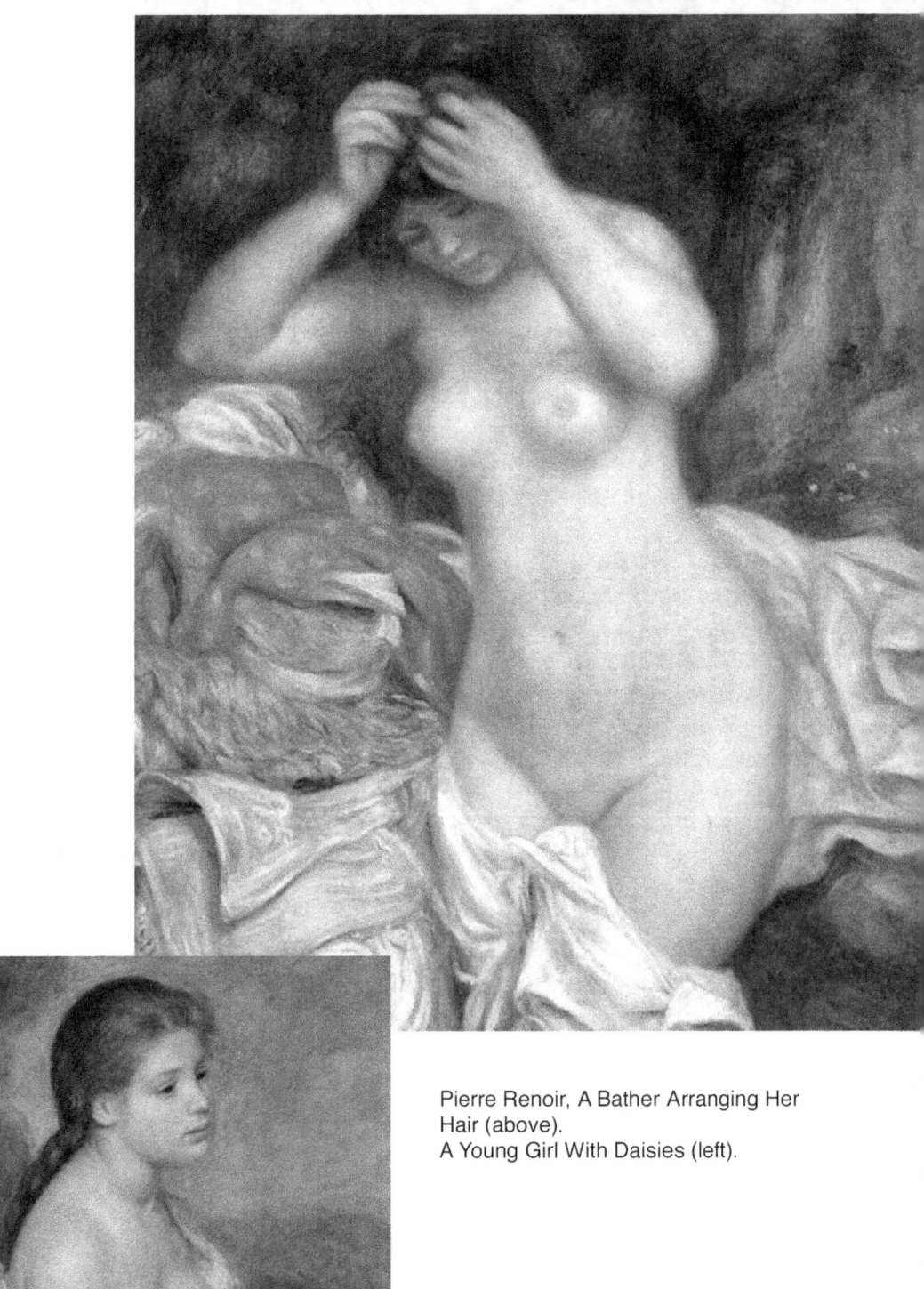

Pierre Renoir, A Bather Arranging Her
Hair (above).
A Young Girl With Daisies (left).

ÉDOUARD MANET

Personal, private erotic art became increasingly public. Thus, Édouard Manet's *Déjeuner sur l'Herbe* (1863) puts the nude into a contemporary setting.[1] The picture is not idealized, the woman is not on a pedestal, the intention is not to be timeless and ethereal, as in so many nudes. Manet's approach is to be direct, to move towards naturalism, as in his infamous *Olympia* (1863).[2]

Édouard Manet is often described as the founder of modern art, and one can see why, for in the art of Manet the seamlessness of the picture surface breaks down, and painting becomes increasingly a matter of marks on a canvas. The naturalism/realism, the everyday subject matter, the indifference to the painting-viewer relation, make Manet 'modern'. A case could be made for many other painters – such as J.M.W. Turner, or Eugène Delacroix, or Jacques-Louis David, or Titian, or Giotto – as being the 'founder' of modern art. It doesn't really matter. But Manet's straightforward treatment of sexuality is powerful. Not necessarily 'new', but new in Western painting. Manet's *Olympia* broke and reworked the traditional relations between female sexuality, representation, 'high' art, and consumption.[3]

1 E. Manet: *Déjeuner sur l'Herbe*, 1863, Louvre, Paris
2 E. Manet: *Olympia*, 1863, Louvre, Paris
3 See T.J. Clark: "Preliminaries to a Possible Treatment of *Olympia* in 1865", *Screen*, 21:1, Spring 1980, 18-41, and T.J. Clark: *The Painting of Modern Life: Paris in the Art of Manet and His Followers*, Thames & Hudson 1985, 79-146

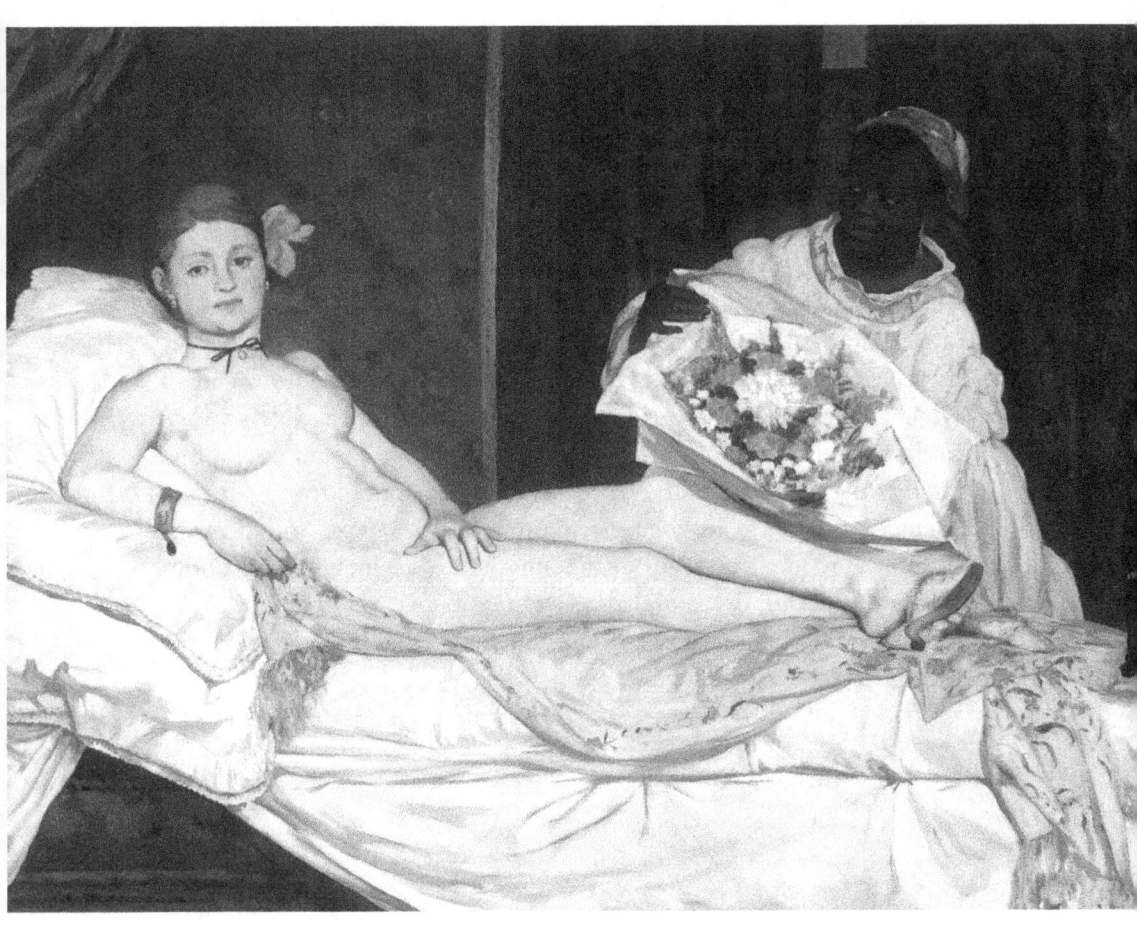

Edouard Manet, Olympia, Musée d'Orsay, Paris

VELÁSQUEZ AND GOYA

Two of the most famous female nudes in the whole history of art, Diego Velásquez' *Venus* and Francisco de Goya's *Naked Maja*, offer views of women as voluptuous sites of pleasure.[1] These are images of pure desire, pure wish-fulfilment, pure pleasure, which are also pornographic. There is no doubt that the painted 'high art' female nude, as an image, is very like the pornographic image, which offers women as sexualized objects of male lust. They are part of a continuum of representation. What different-iates 'high culture' nudes from the nudes in pornography is largely to do with context, with the sociopolitical environment in which the nudes are consumed. You can put Goya's *Naked Maja* into a soft core pornographic context and it would send only a few conflicting signals with the rest of the photography there. Fashions change – in costume, hair, make-up, pose and props – but it is startling how similar the female nude is in art. The funda-mental relation, of sexualized women being offered up to be looked at and lusted over by desirous males is remarkably similar the world over, and through history.

1 Diego Velásquez: *The Rokeby Venus*, 1649-50, oil on canvas, 122.5 x 177cm, National Gallery, London; Francisco de Goya: *Naked Maya*, 1800-5

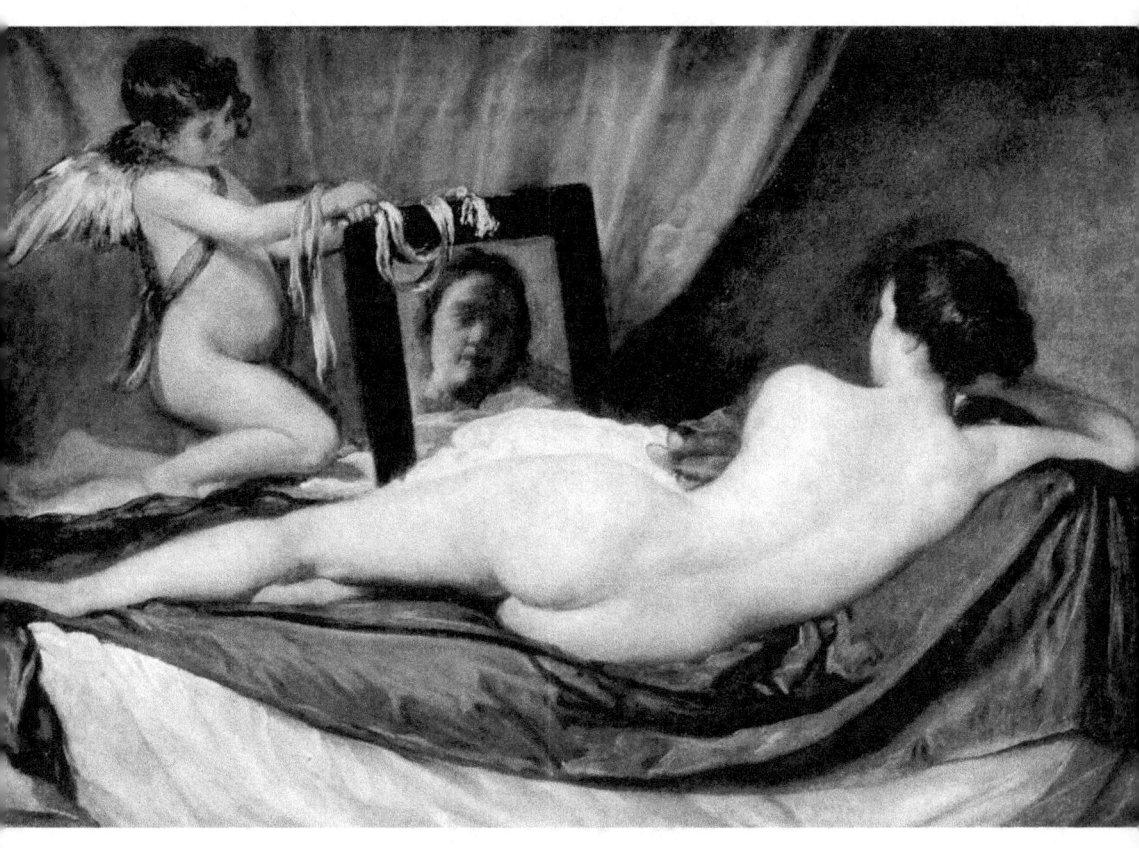

Diego Velásquez, Rockeby Venus, 1649-51,
National Gallery, London

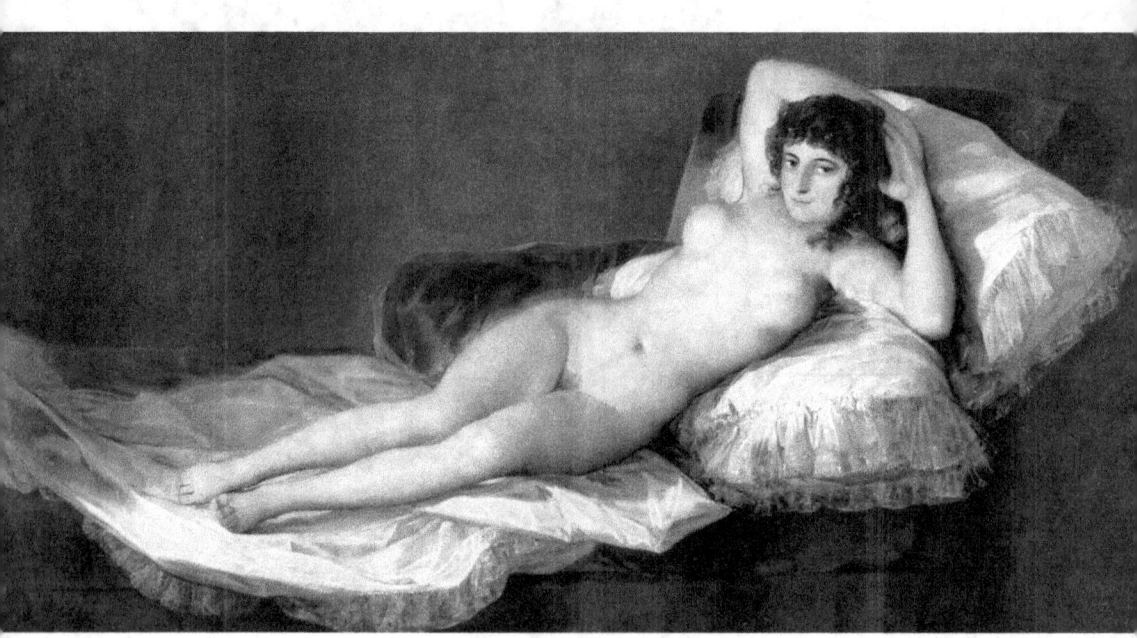

Francisco de Goya, Naked Maja, c. 1801, Prado, Madrid

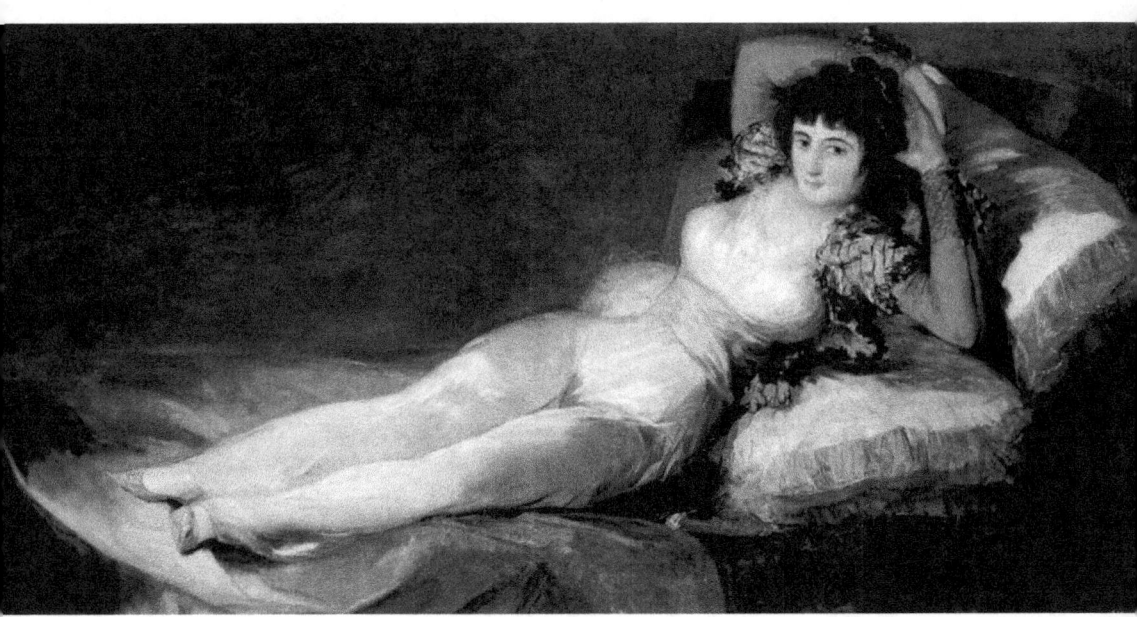

Francisco de Goya, Clothed Maya, 1801

APPENDICES

Extra illustrations, including from the following artists:

Henry Fuseli (1741-1825), a Swiss artist.

•

Peter Fendi (1796-1842), from a collection of 40 erotic prints published in 1910.

•

André de Nerciat, from *Le Diable* (1803).

•

Antoine Borel (1743-1810).

•

Heinrich Lossow (1843-97), from the *Metamorphoses, The Triumph of Cupid.*

•

Johann Nepomuk Geiger (1805-80), a painter and lithographer from Vienna.

•

Otto Schoff (1888-1938), a German graphic artist, from *Loose Engravings* (1920).

•

Mihály Zichy (1827-1906), a Hungarian born artist, from *Liebe* (1911).

•

Martin van Maële (October 12, 1863-September 5, 1926), a French illustrator, including some images from *La Grande Danse Macabre des Vifs.*

•

Ernest Gerhard, a German artist, from *Die Laterne* (1925).

•

F. Christophe, from *Die Verfuhrung*, 1925.

-

Achille Jacques-Jean-Marie Devéria (February 6, 1800-December 23, 1857), French painter and lithographer, from *Diabolico Foutro Manie* (1835).

-

Almery Lobel Riche (1880-1950).

-

William Bouguereau (1825-1905), a French painter known for his academic paintings of female figures.

-

Gustav Klimt (1862-1918).

-

Egon Schiele (1890-1918).

-

Plus a selection of more images from the history of erotic art.

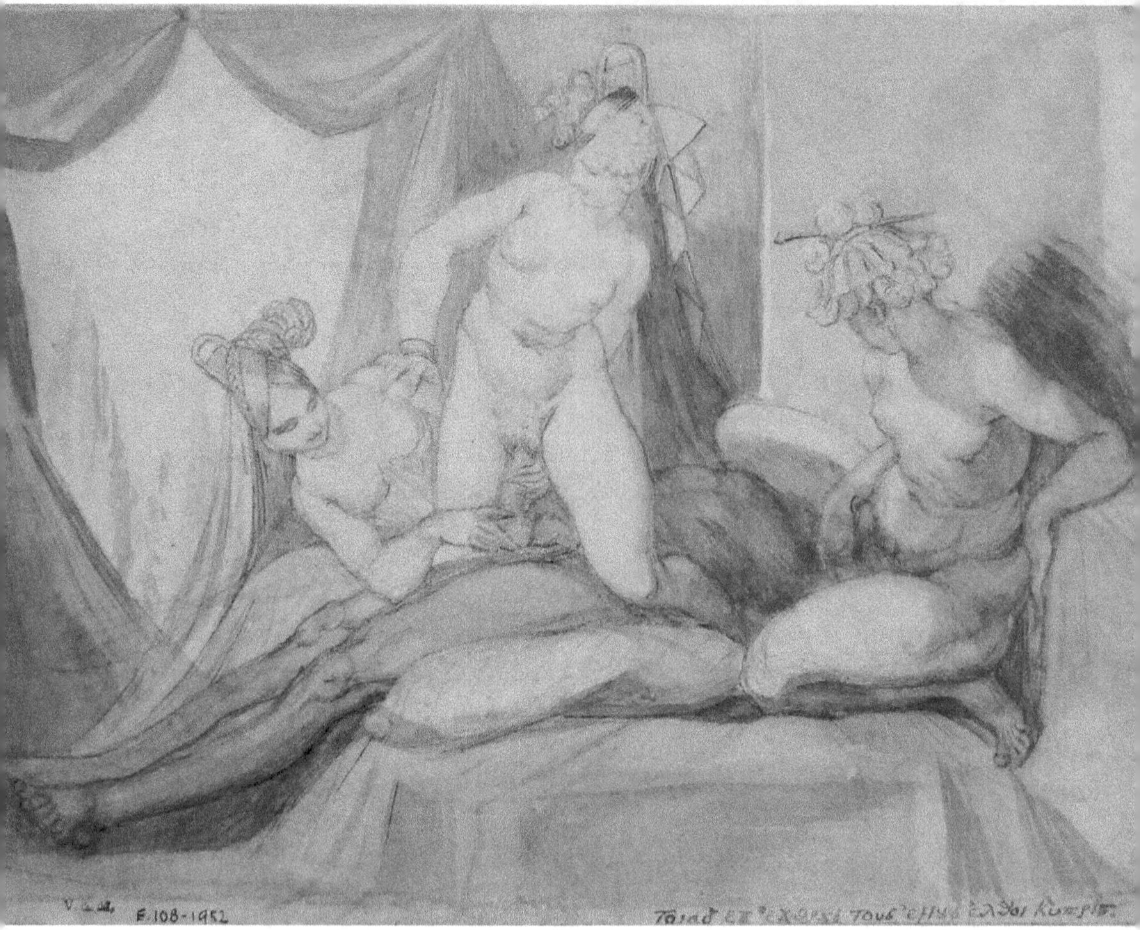

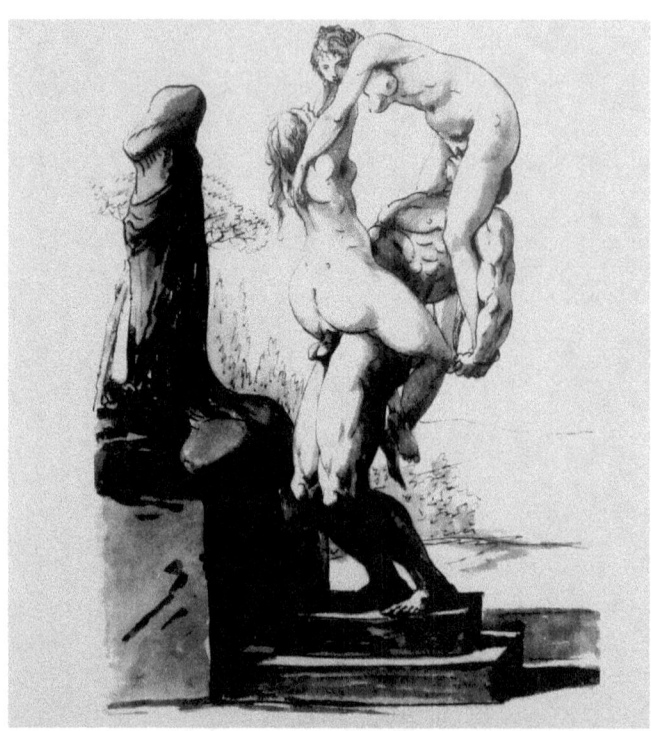

V. add. F.108-1952 Τοιαδ ετ εχθραι τους εχμα ελθοι κωπριτ.

Henry Fuseli, Orgy Scene, 1809-10, Victoria & Albert Museum, London, above.

Jean-Baptiste Regnault, left.

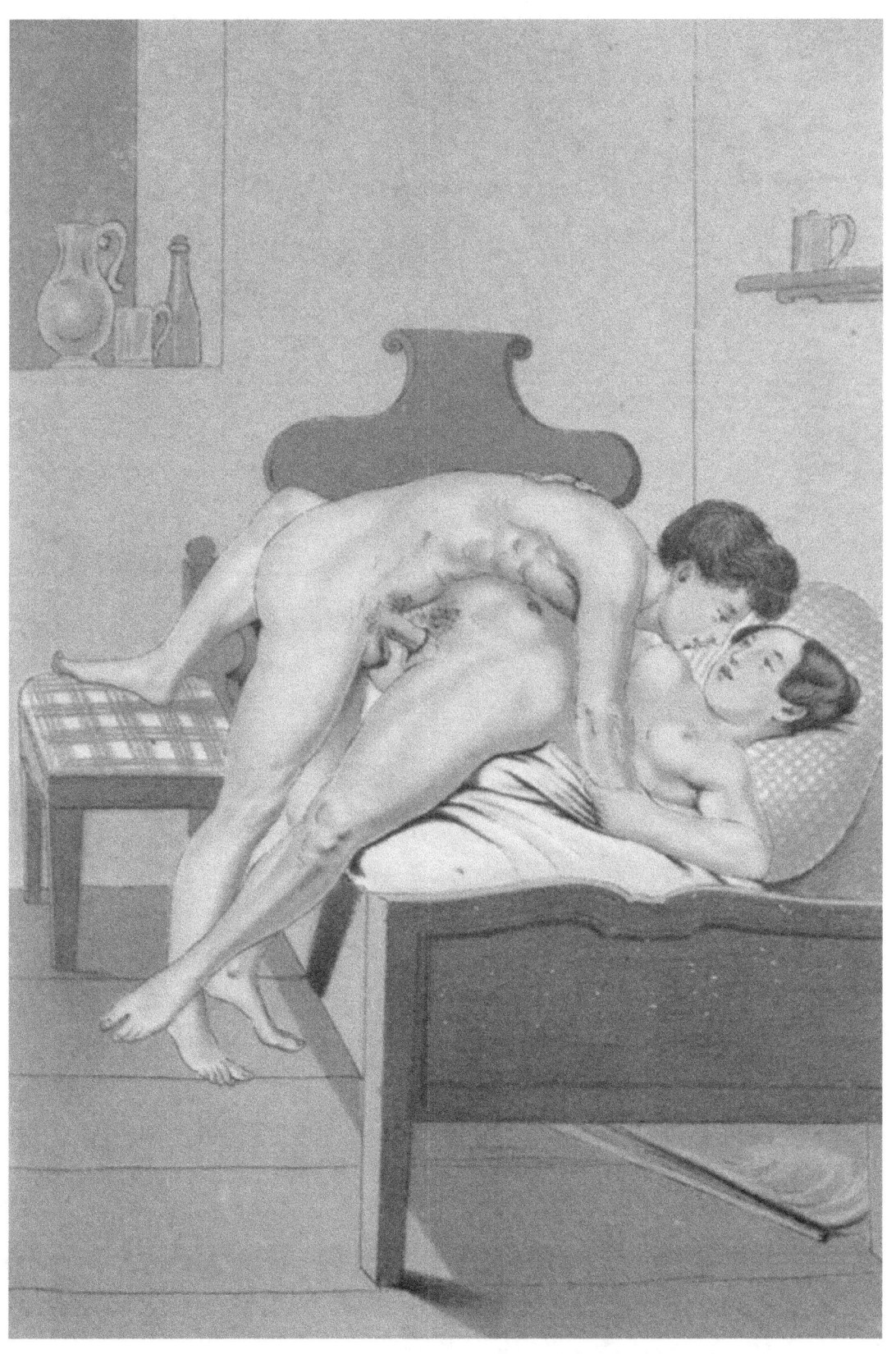

Peter Fendi, this page and following pages

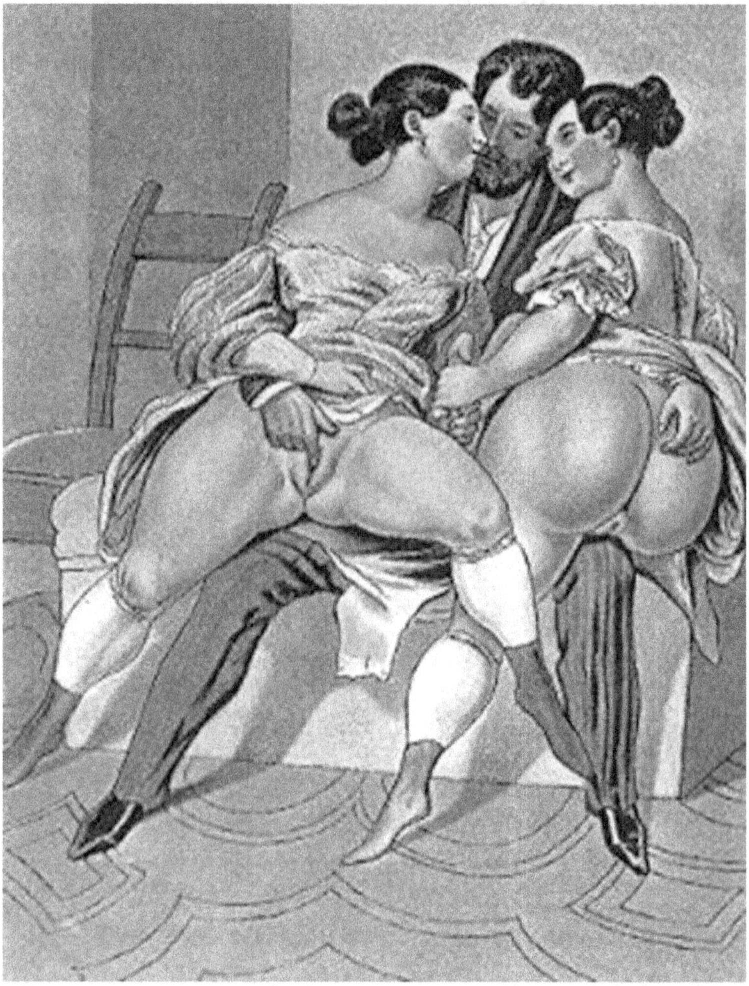

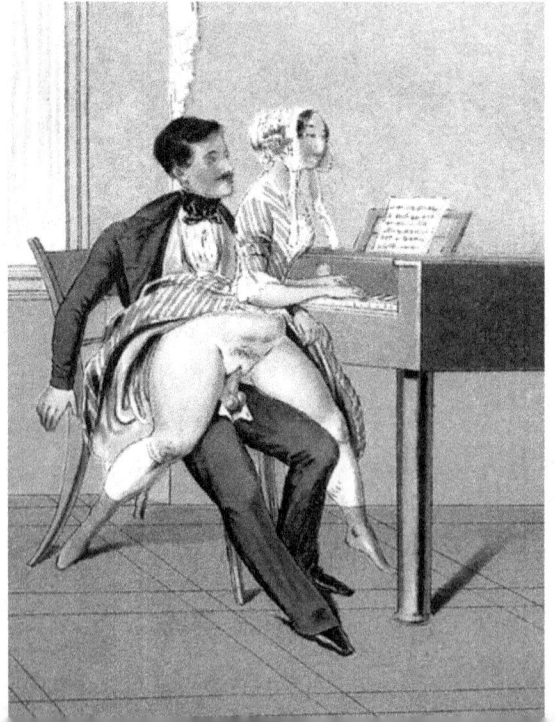

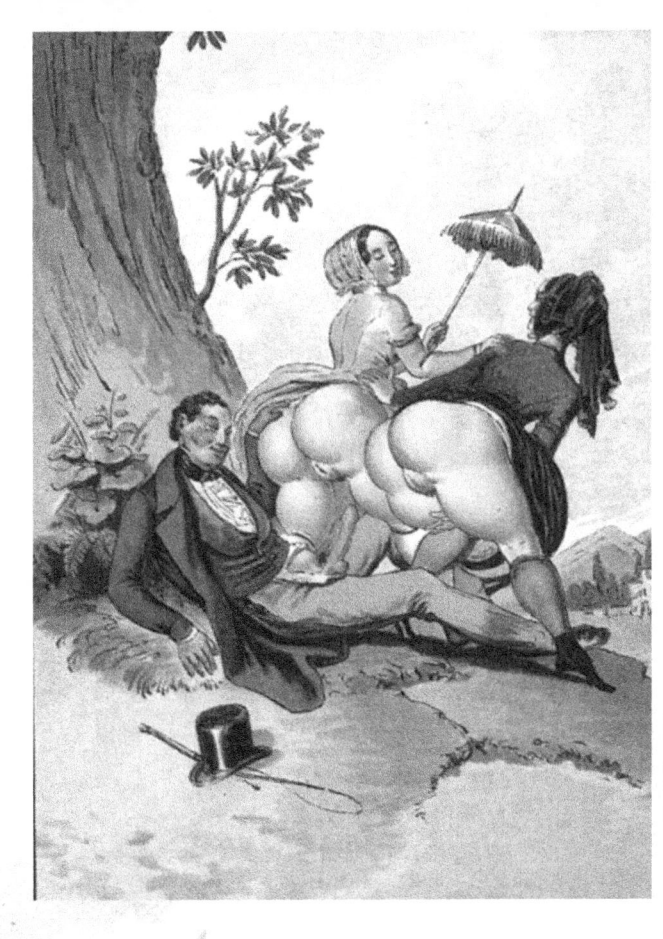

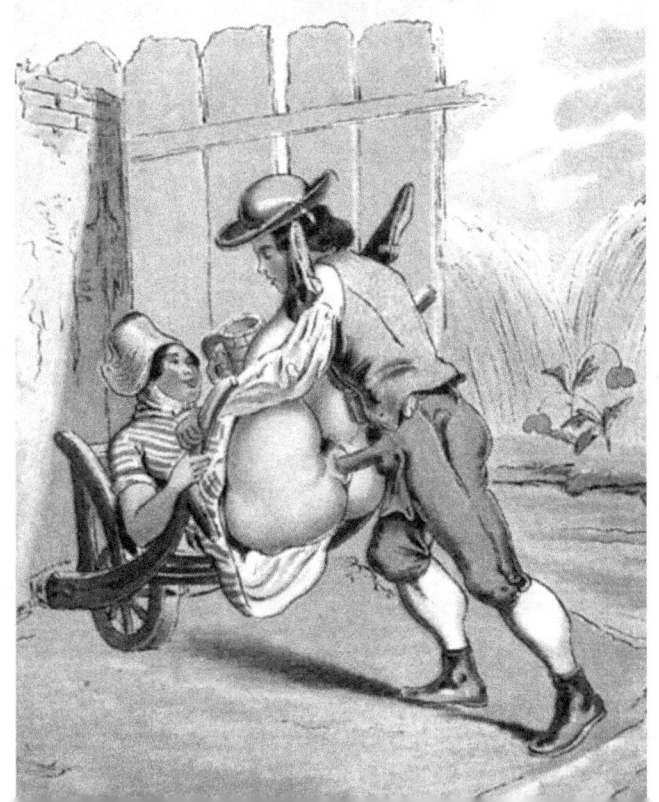

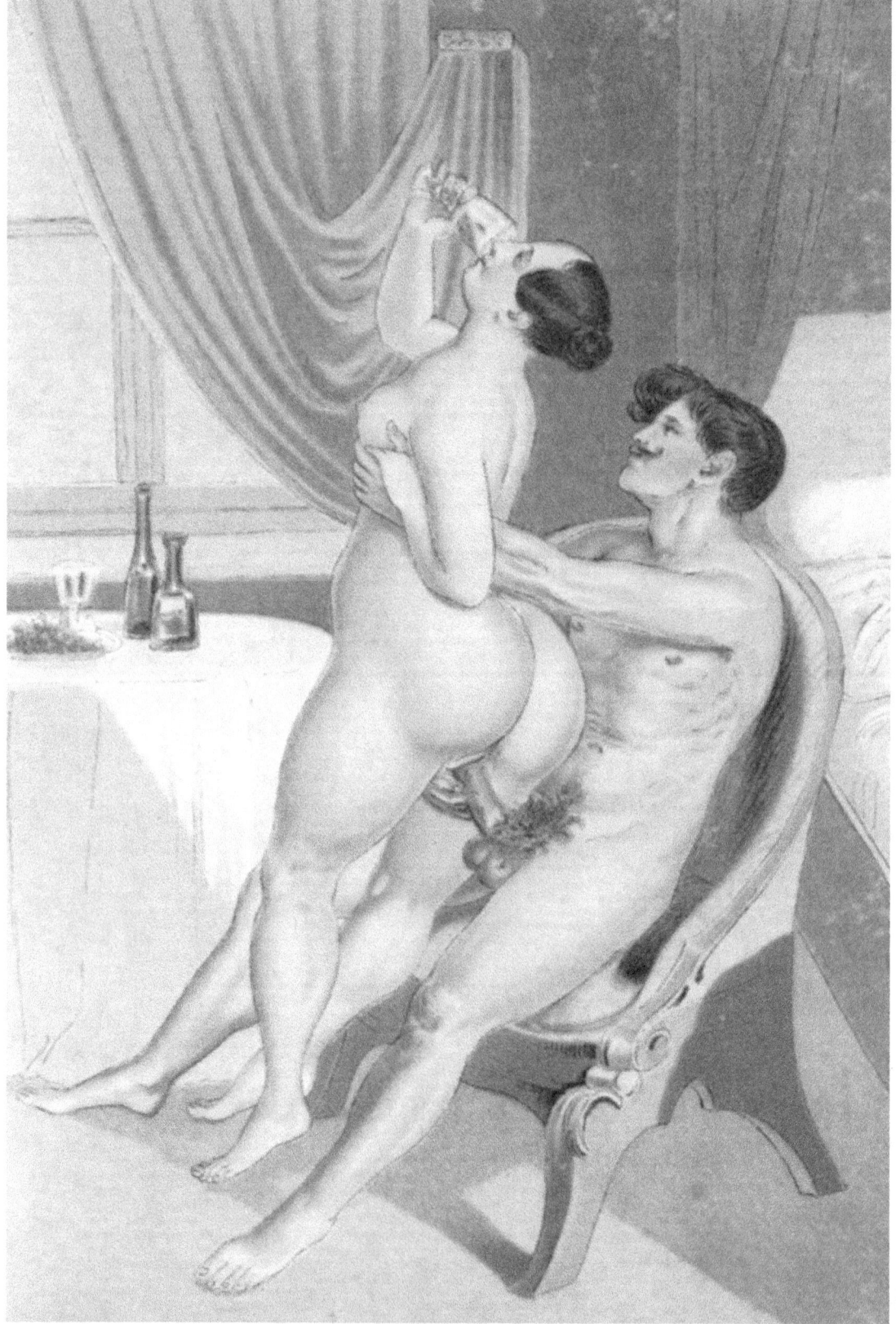

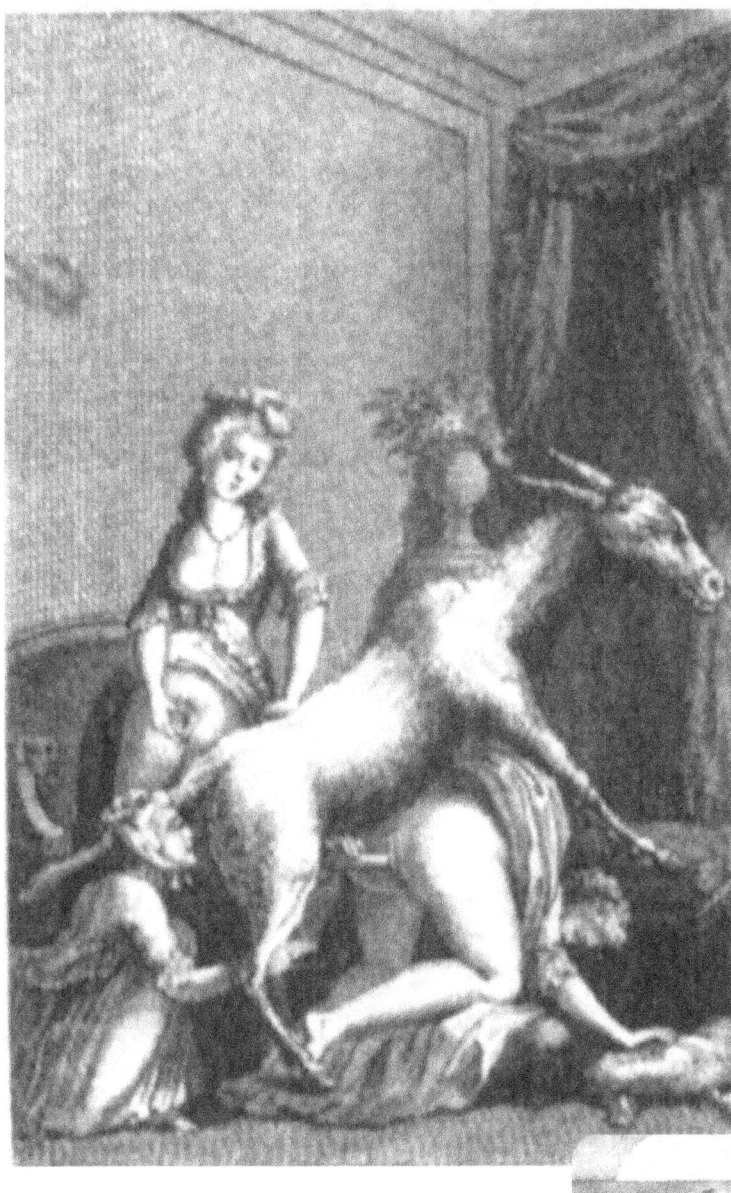

From Le DIable du corps,
by André-Robert Andréa de Nerciat, 1786
this page and following pages.

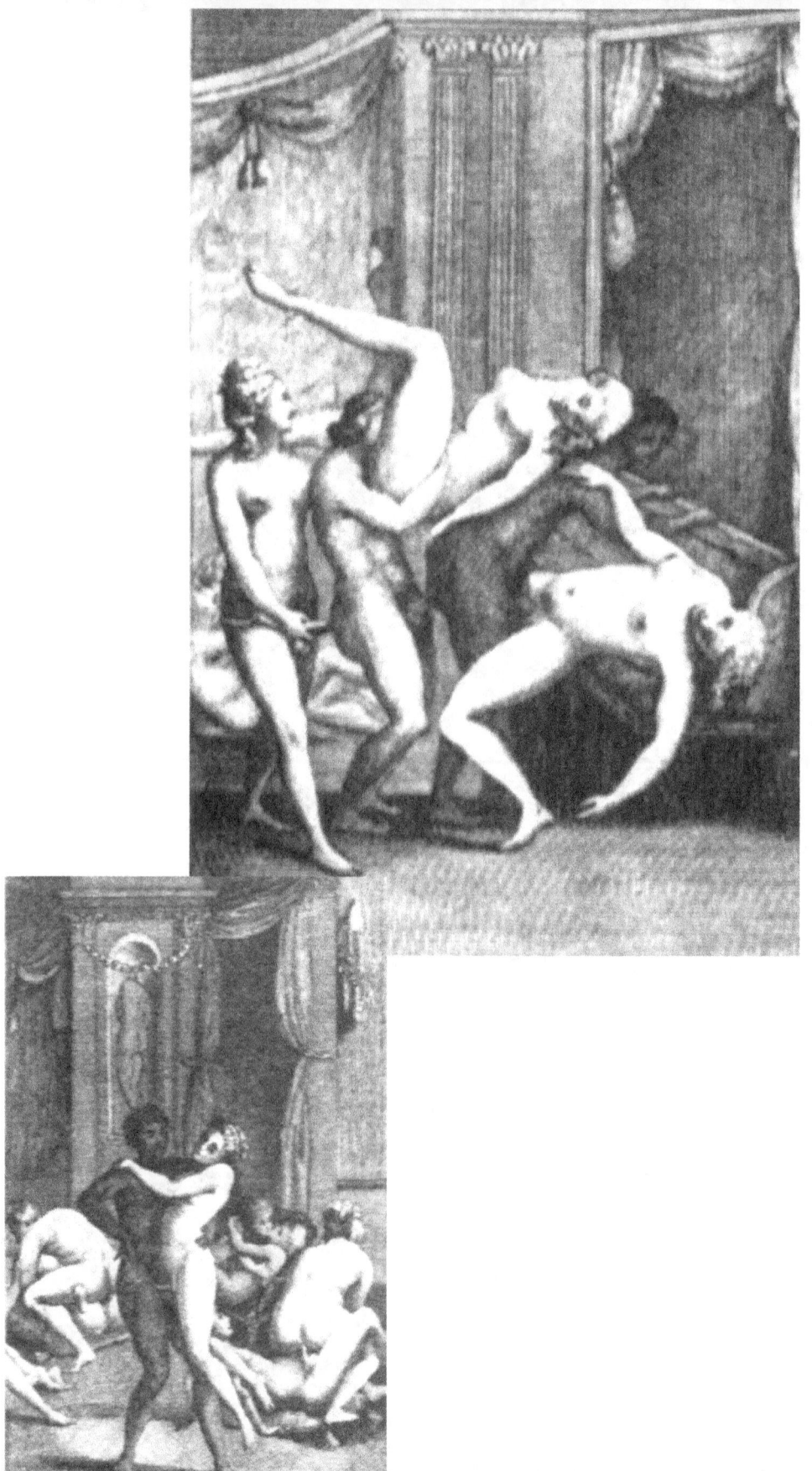

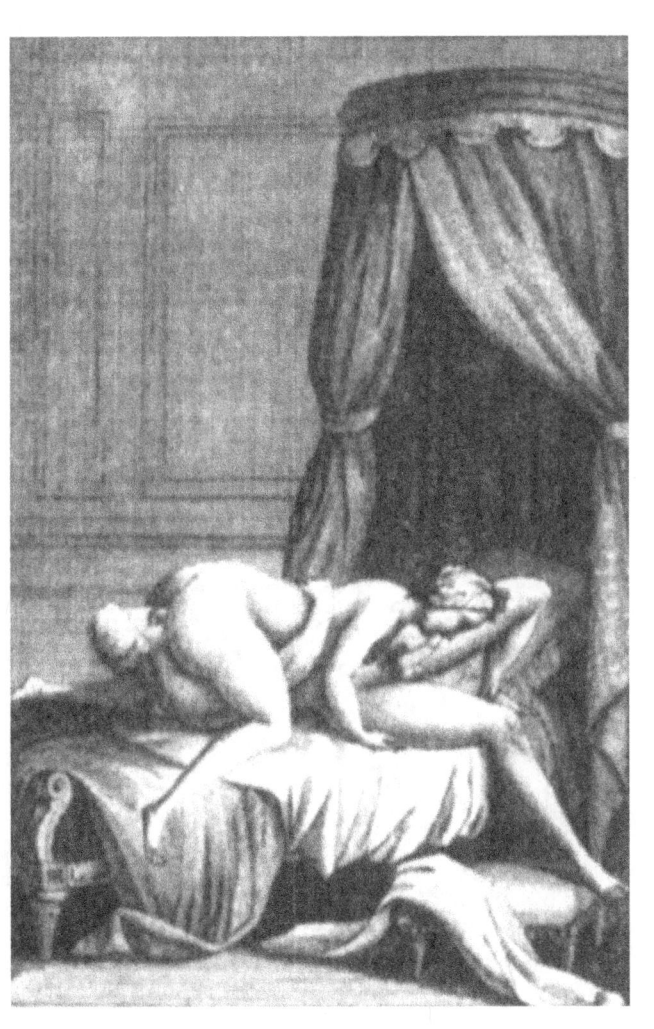

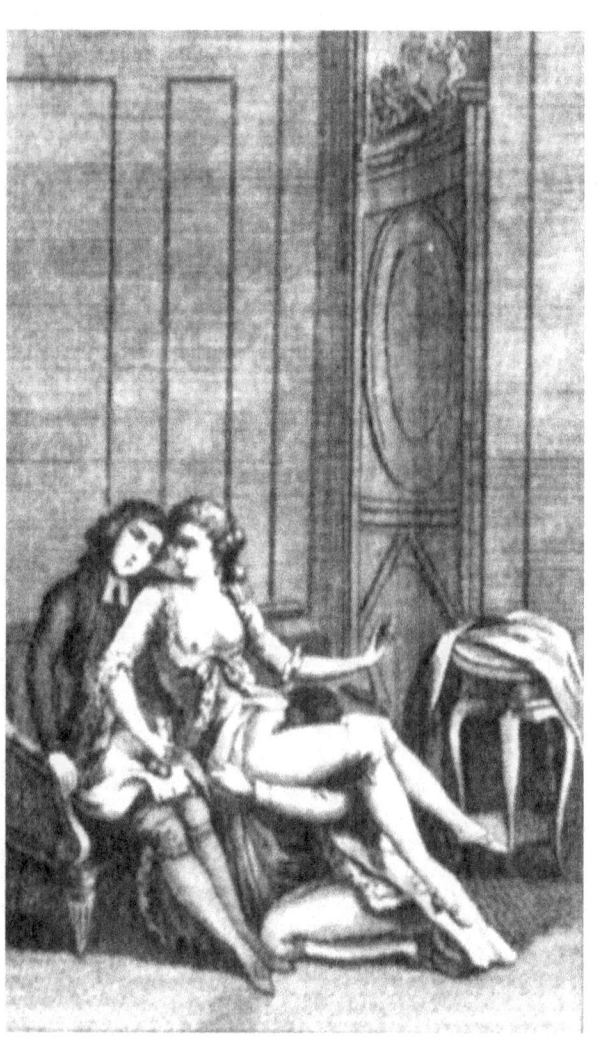

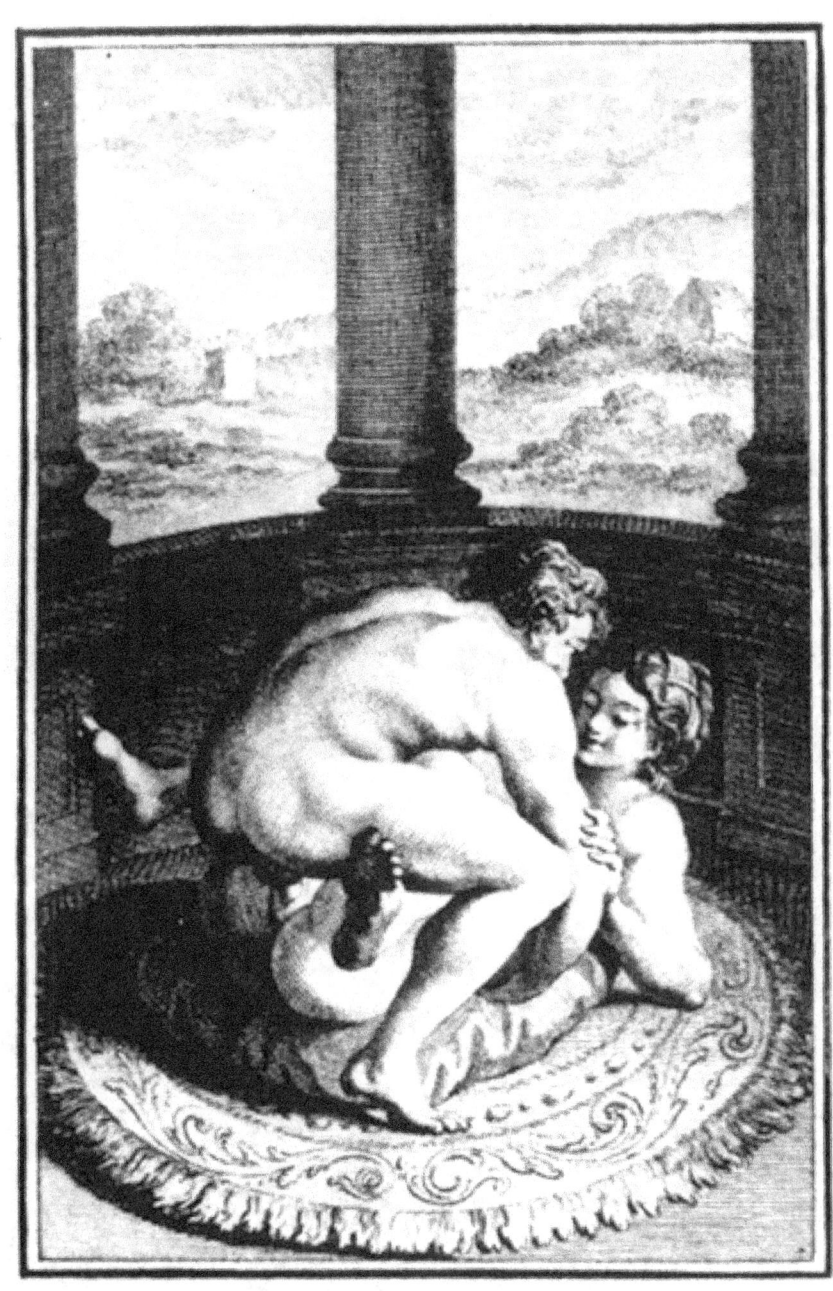

Antoine Borel, this page and following pages

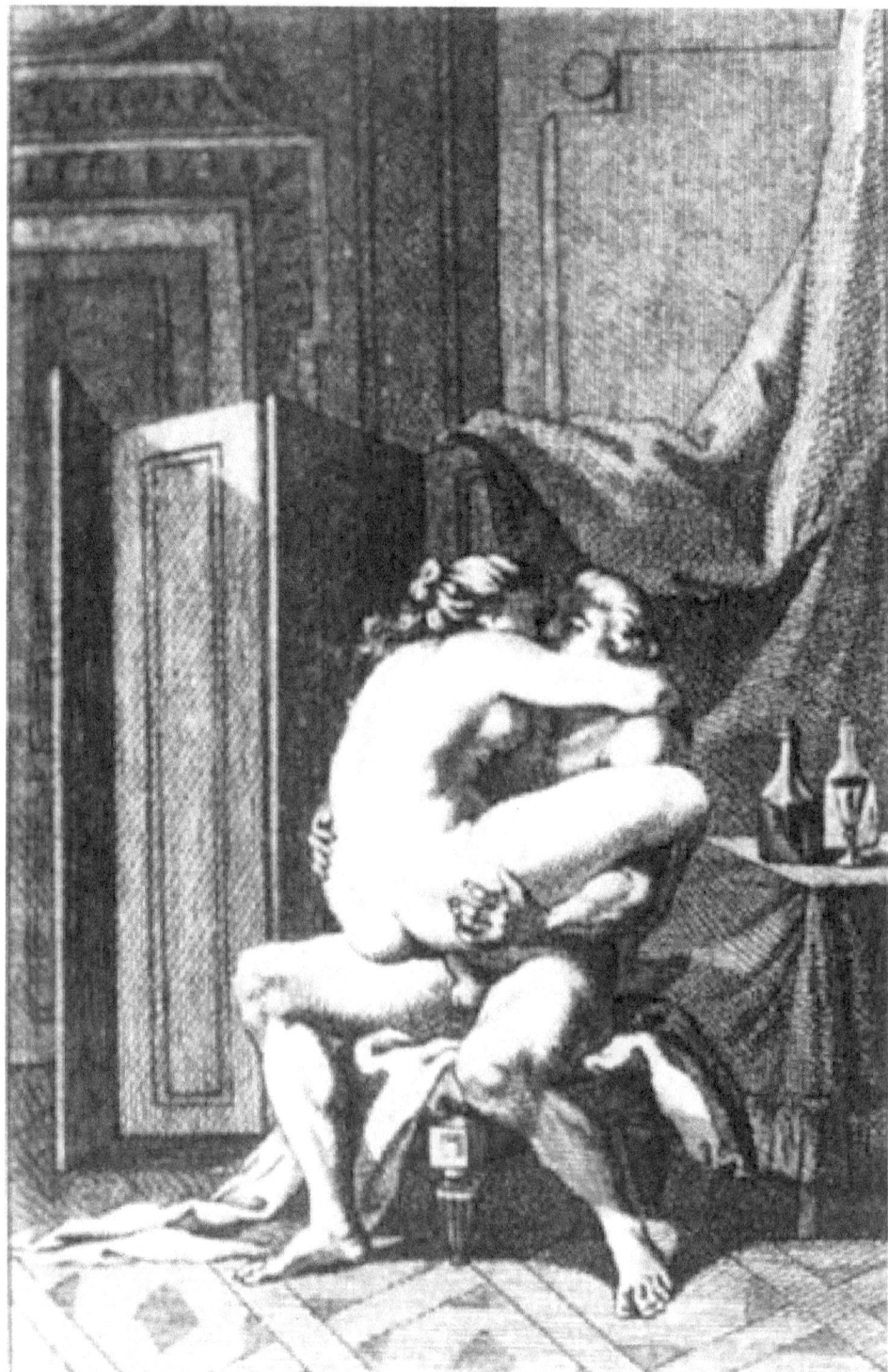

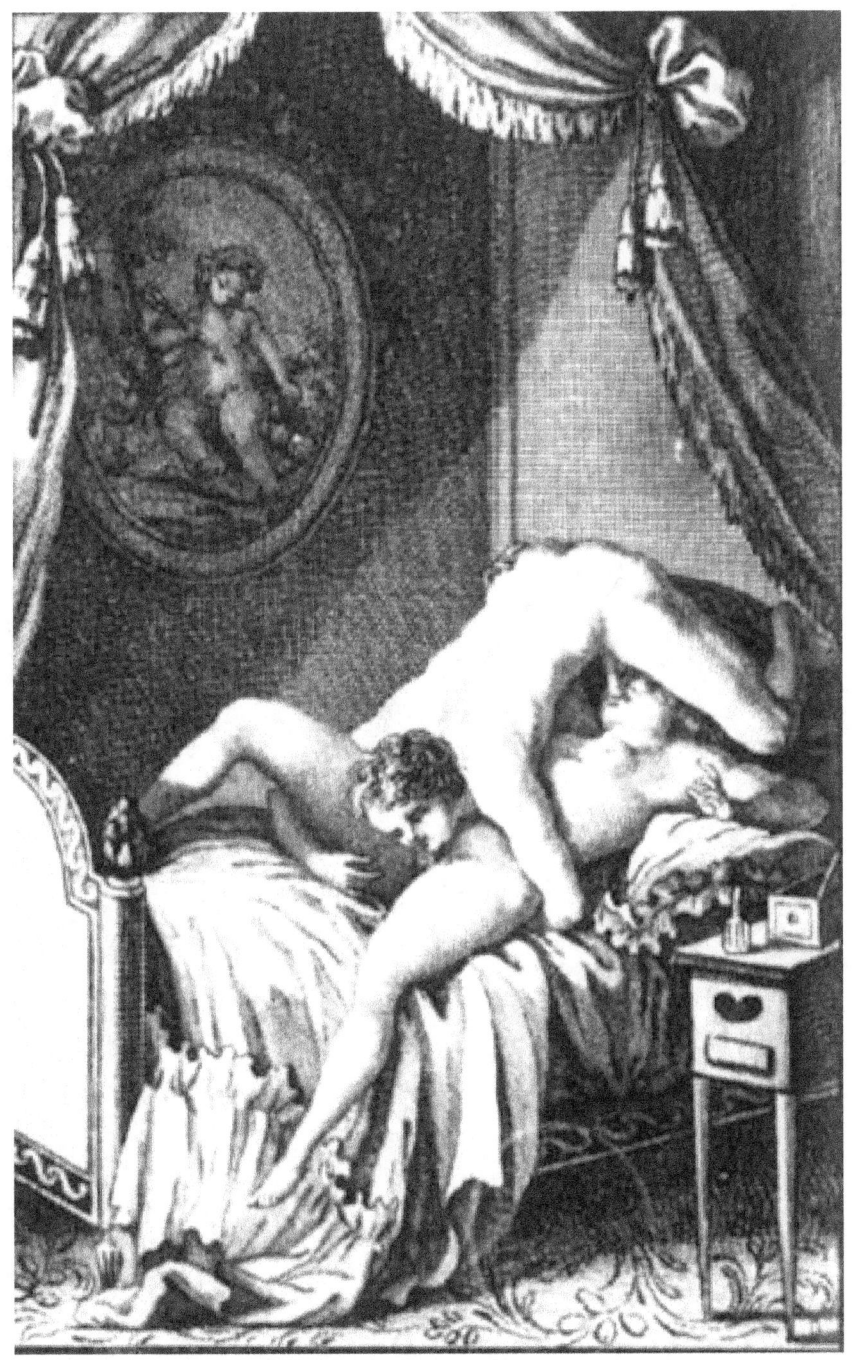

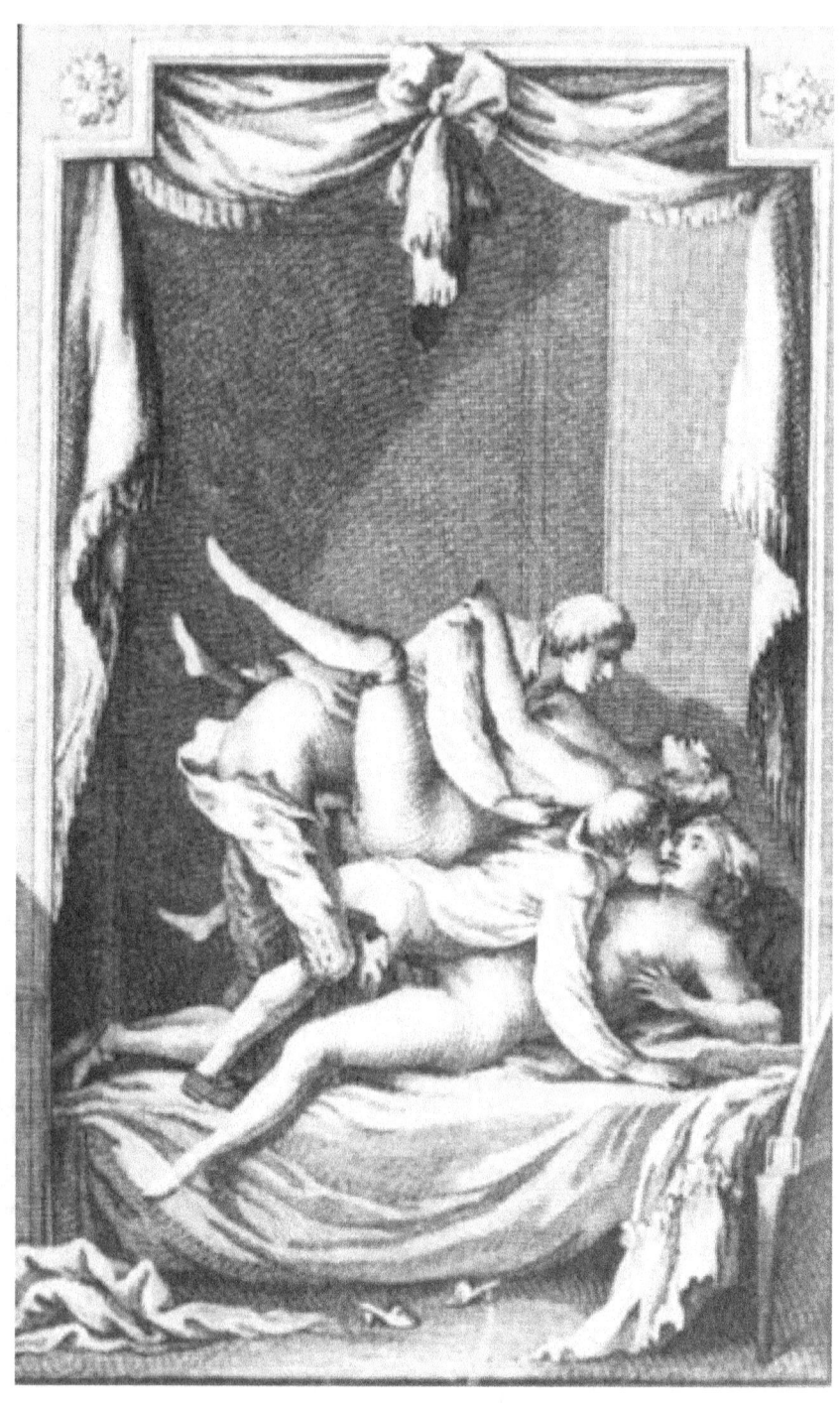

Antoine Borel, illustration for Mémoires de Saturnin,
by Jean-Charles Gervaise, 1787

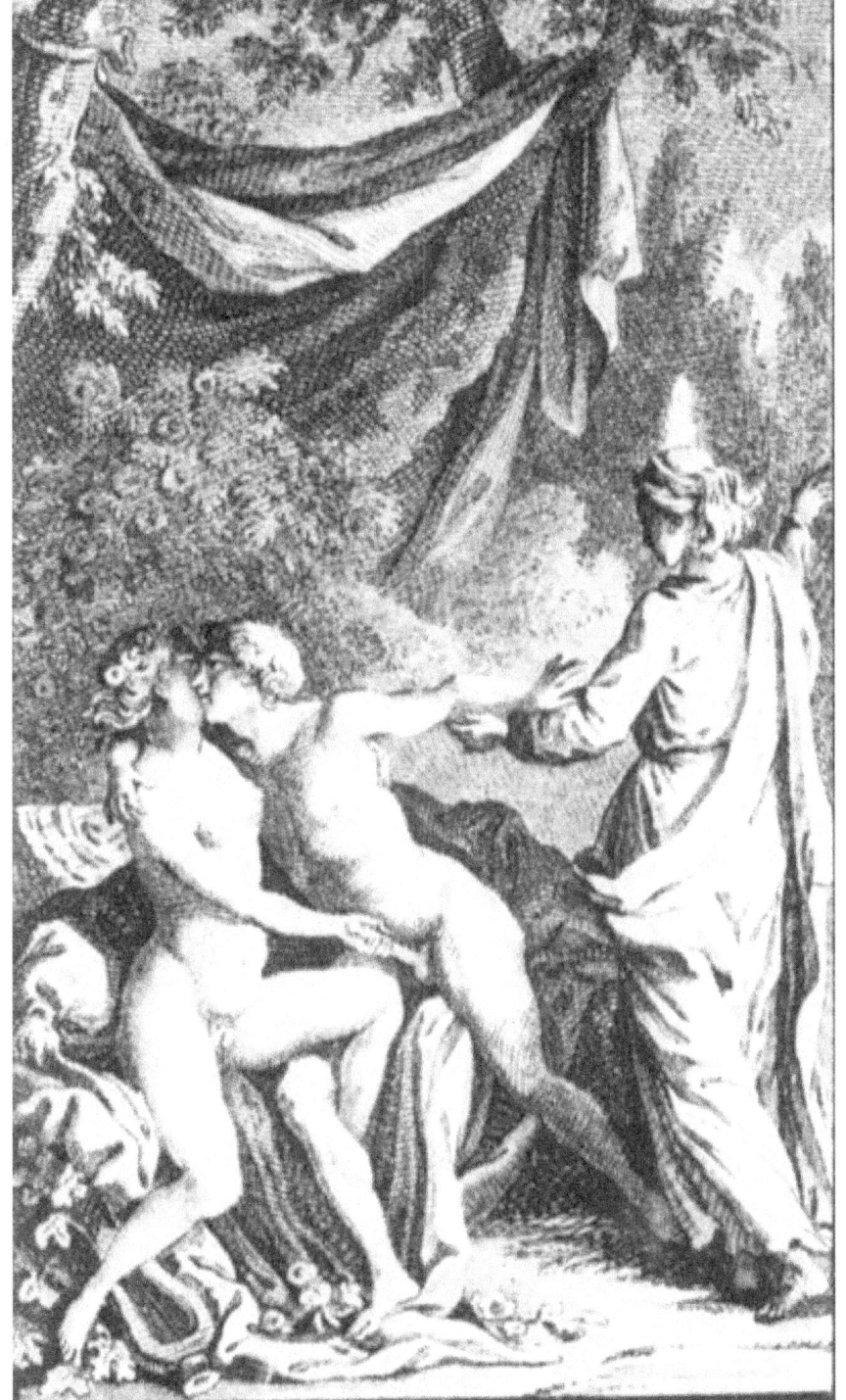

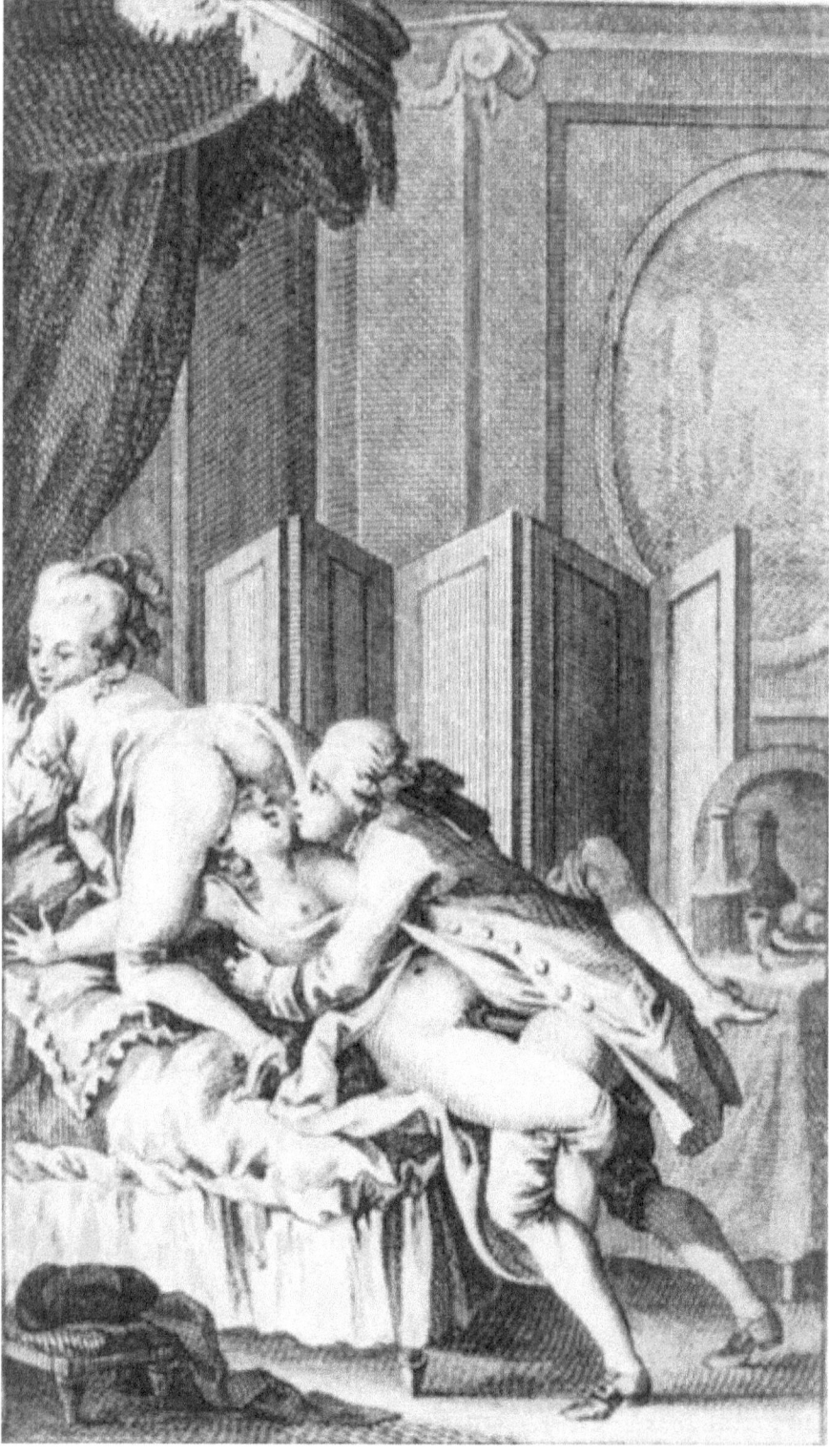

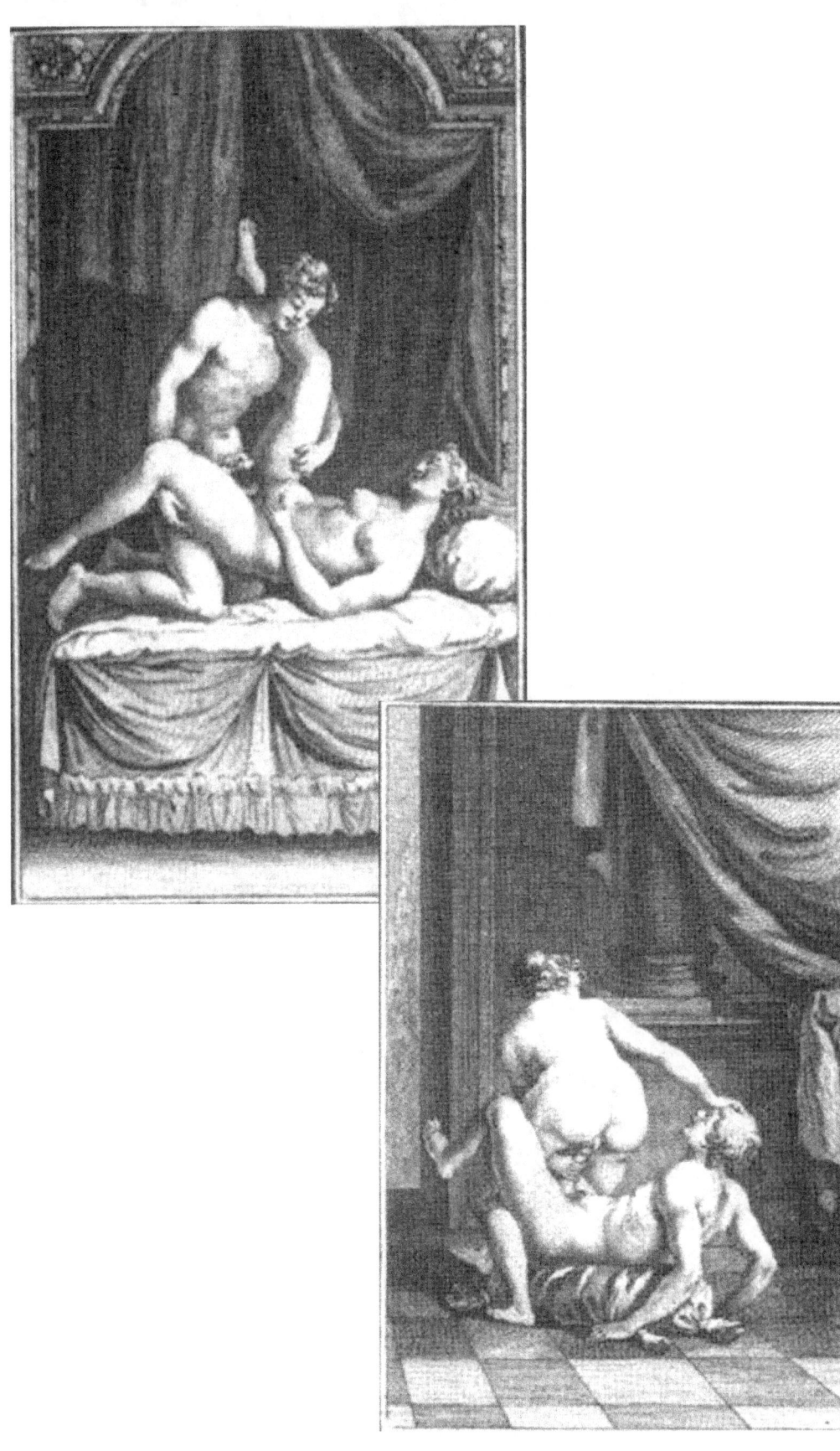

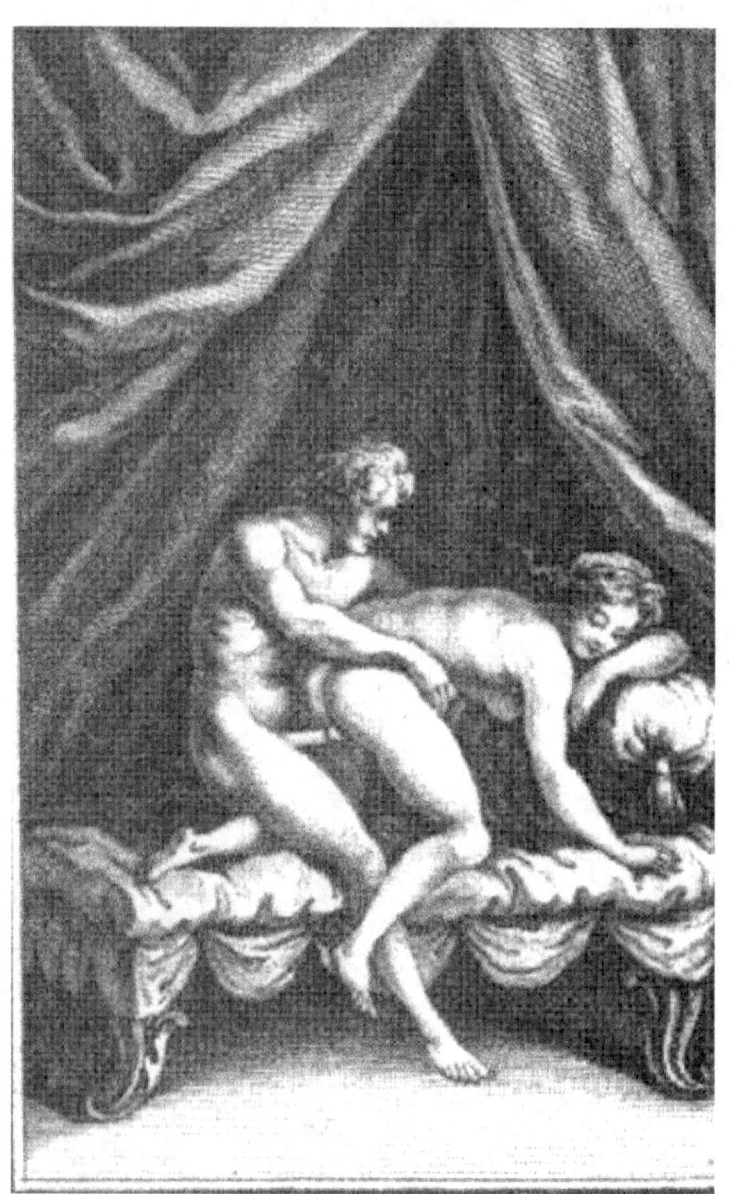

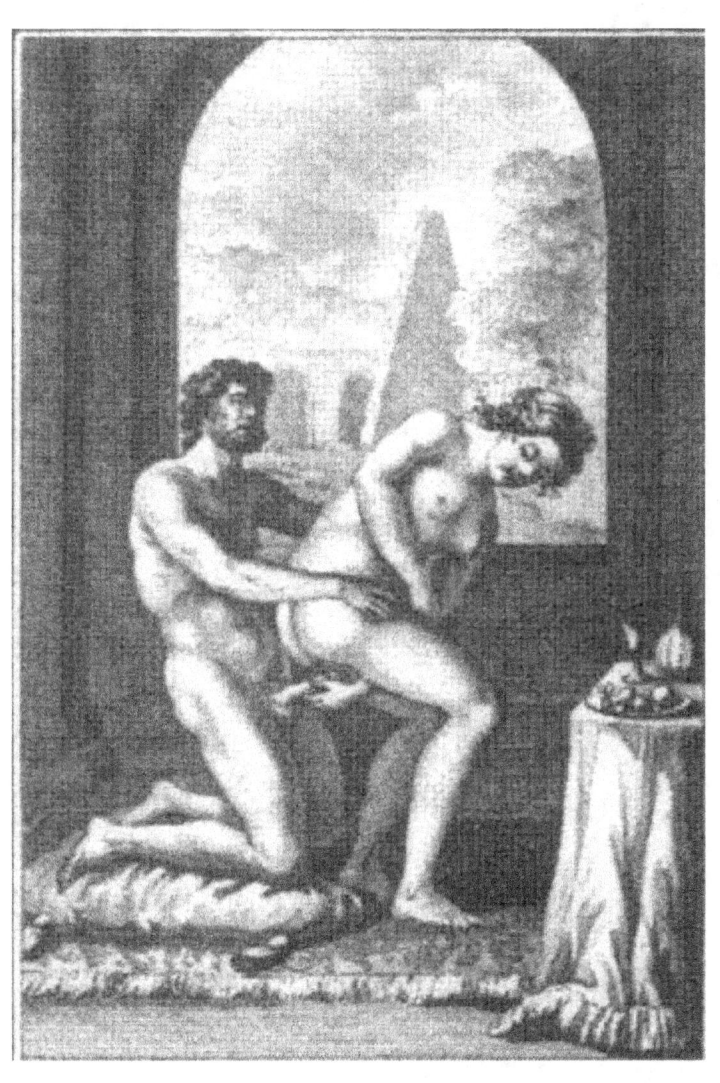

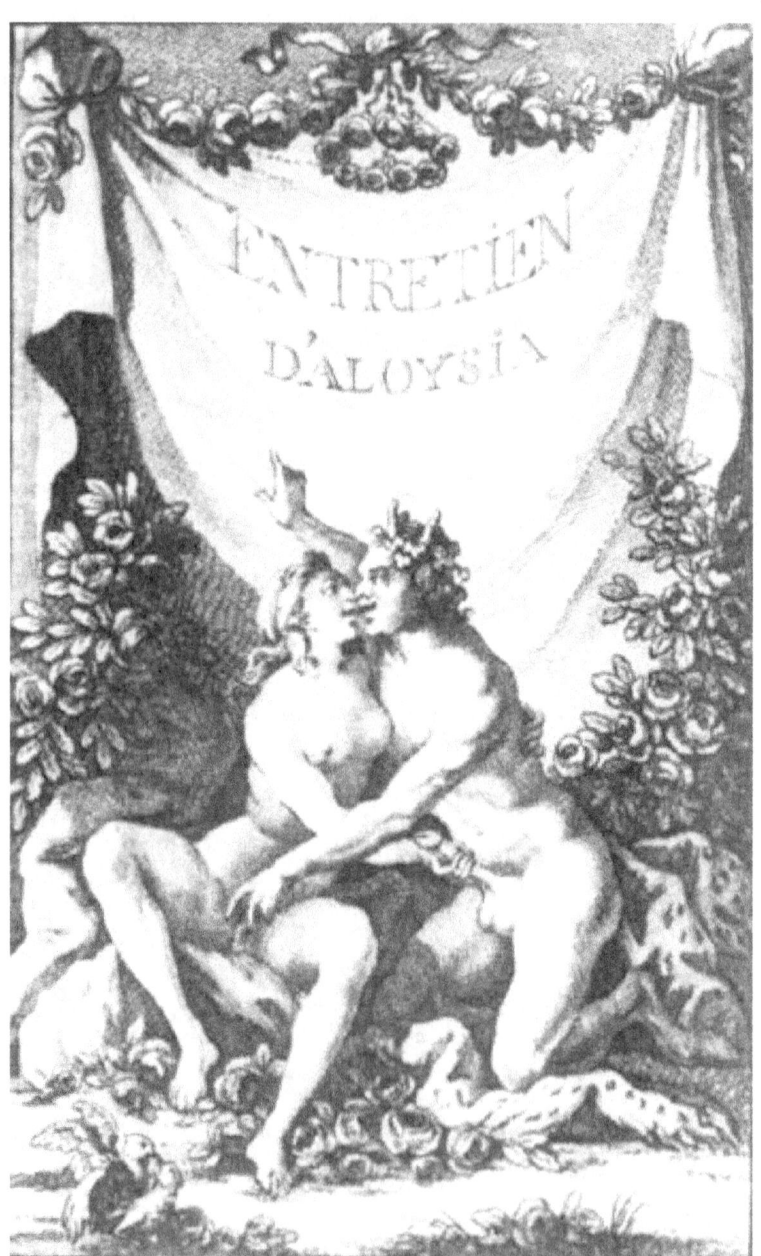

ENTRETIEN

D'ALOYSIA

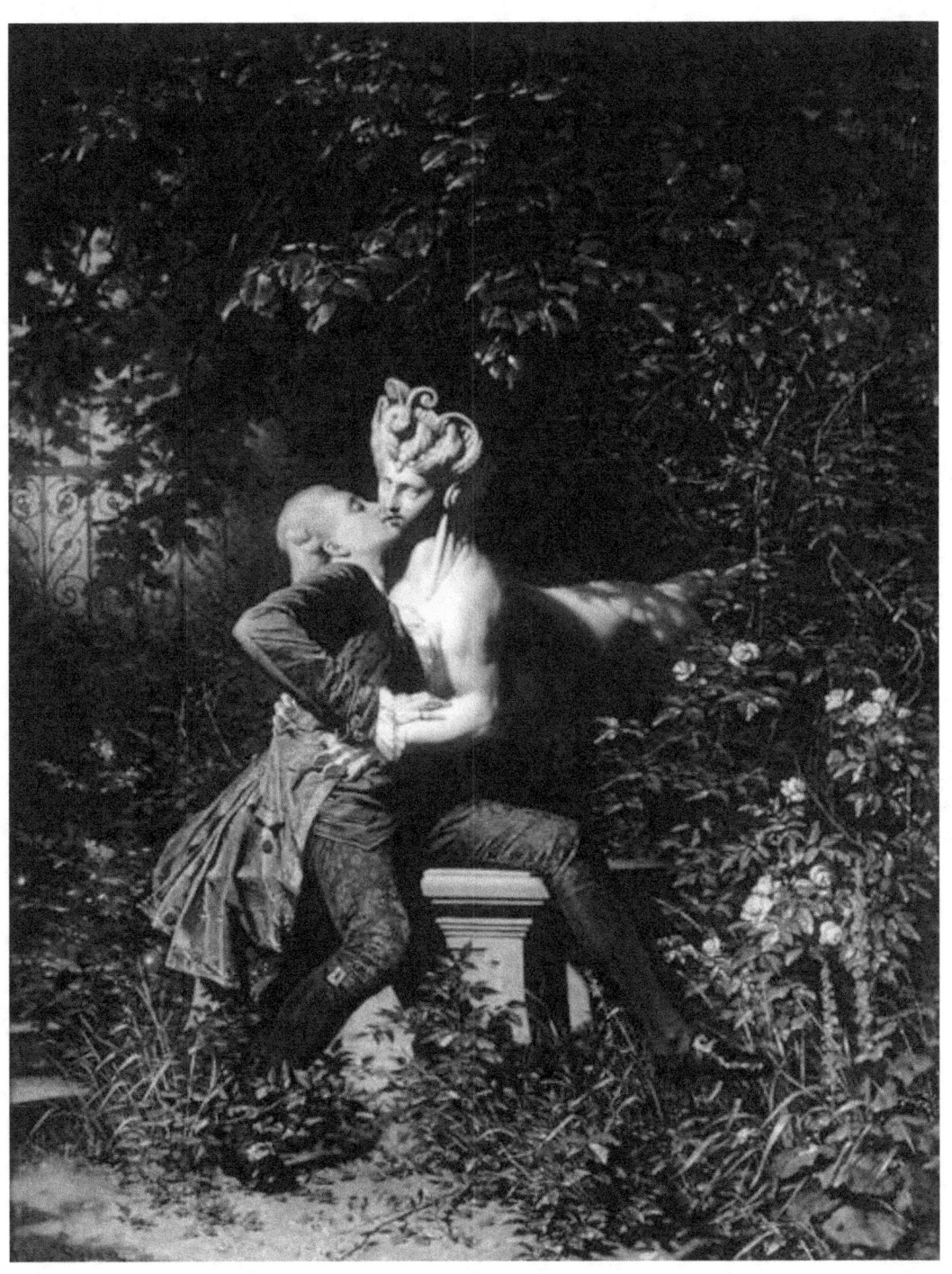

Heinrich Lossow, The Enchantress, 1868

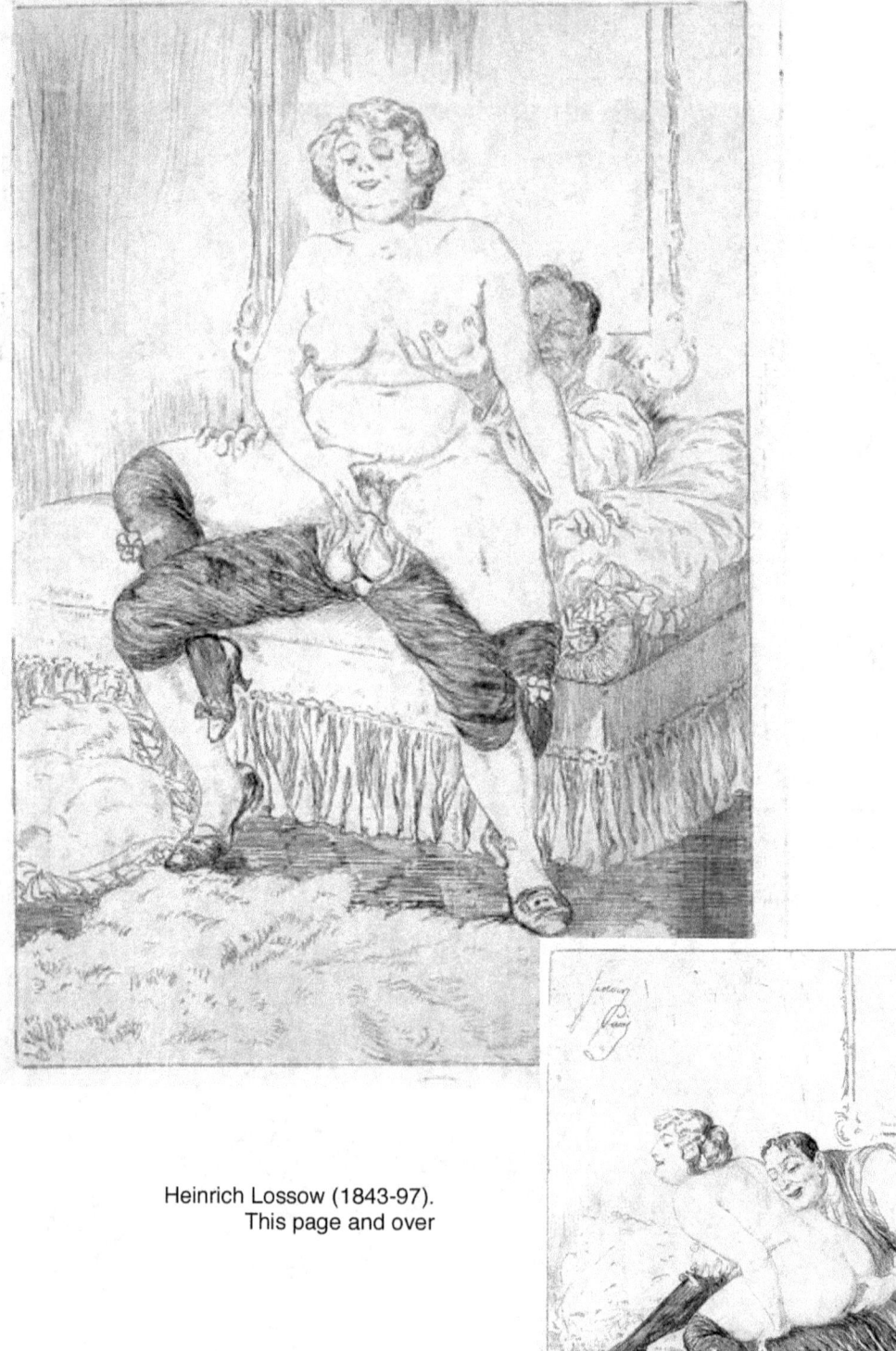

Heinrich Lossow (1843-97).
This page and over

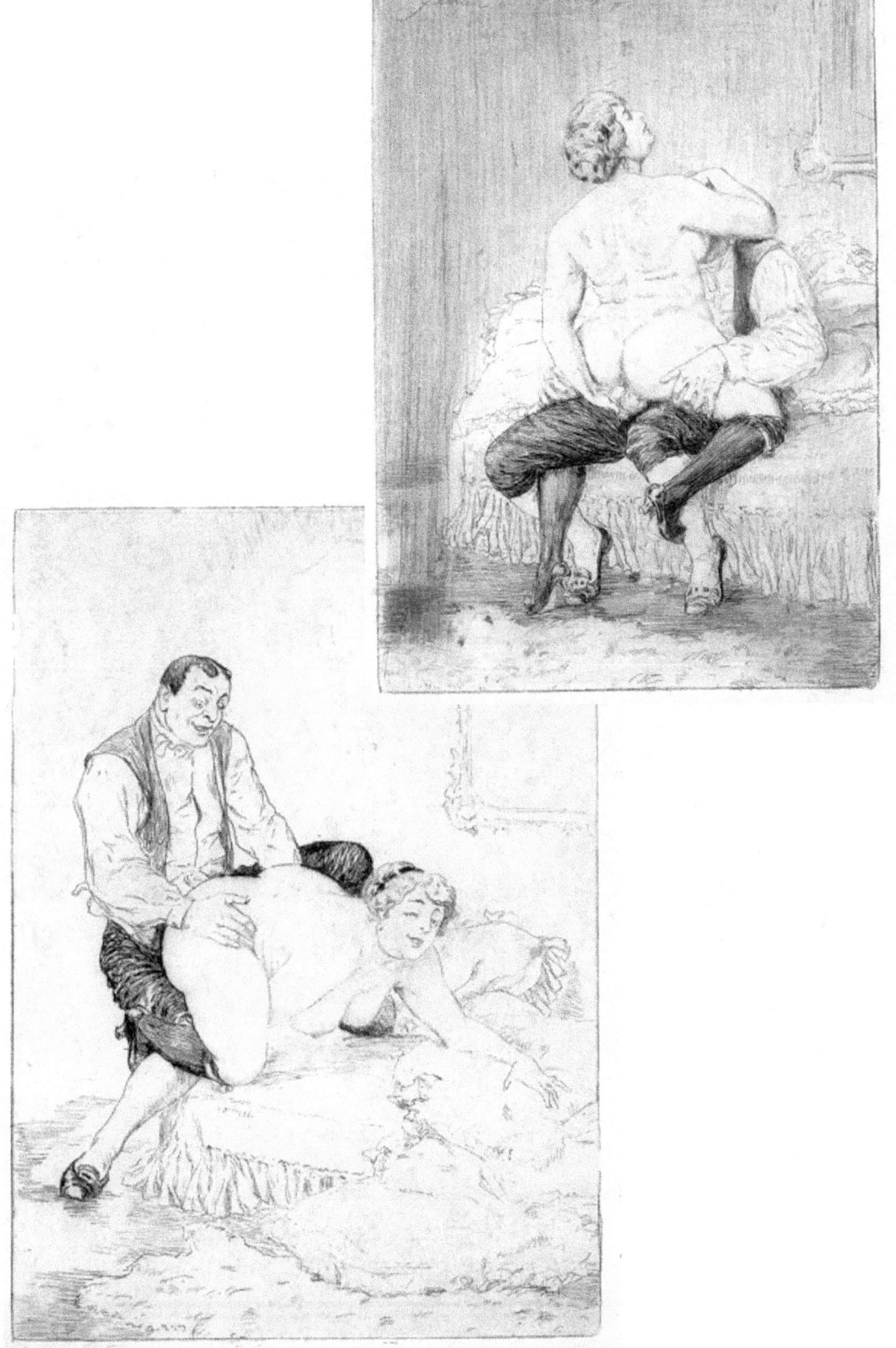

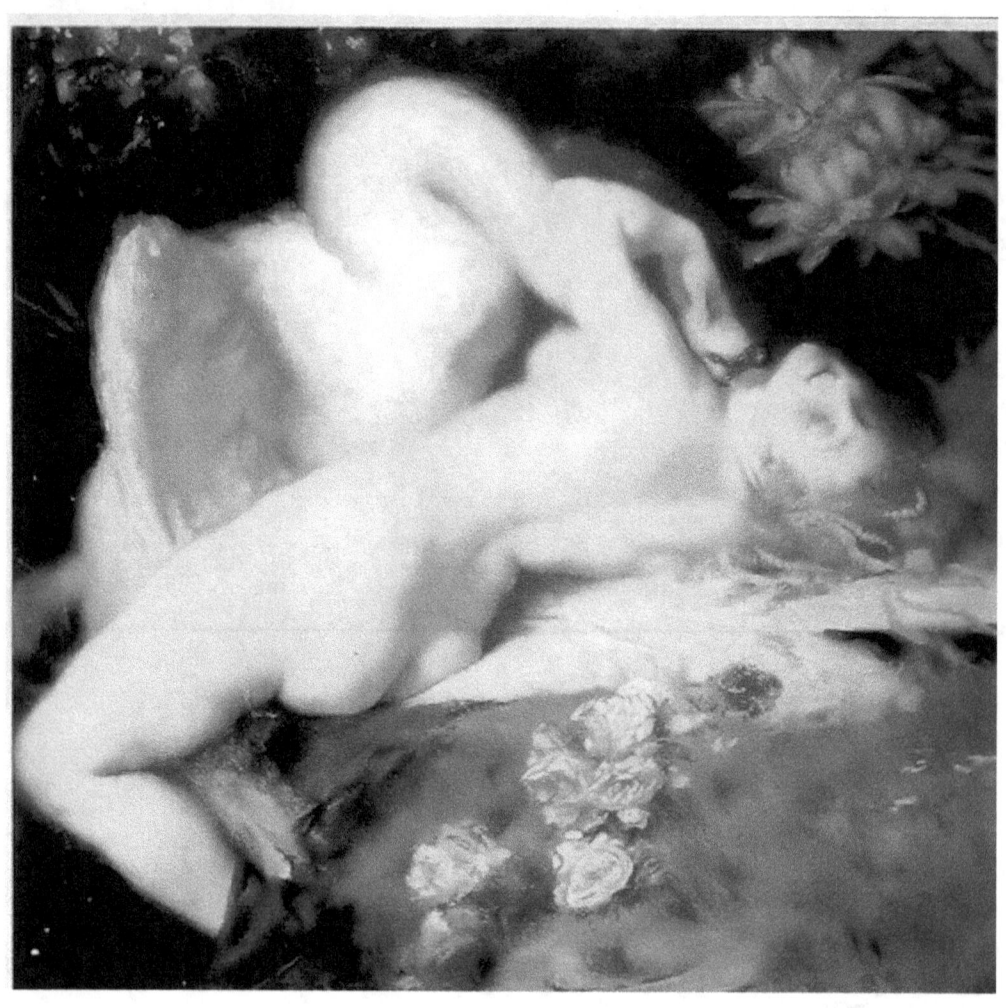

Heinrich Lossow, Leda and the Swan

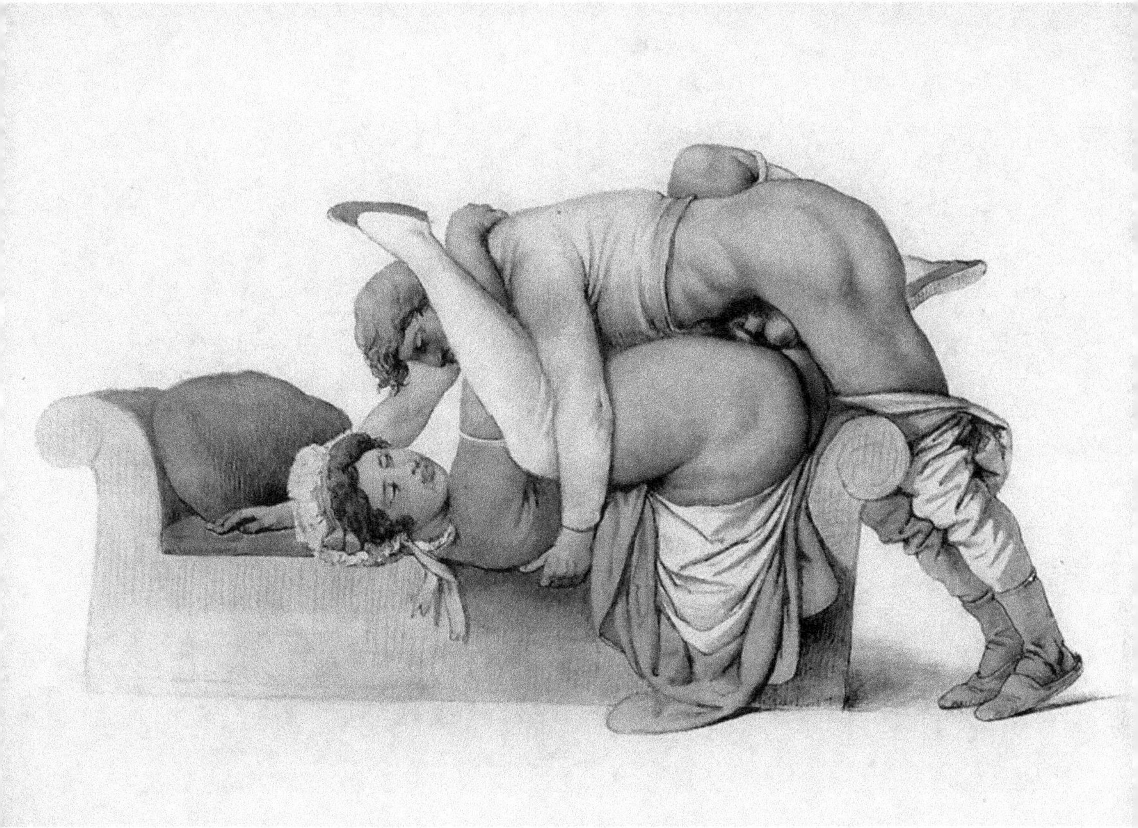

Johann Nepomuk Geiger, this page and the following pages.

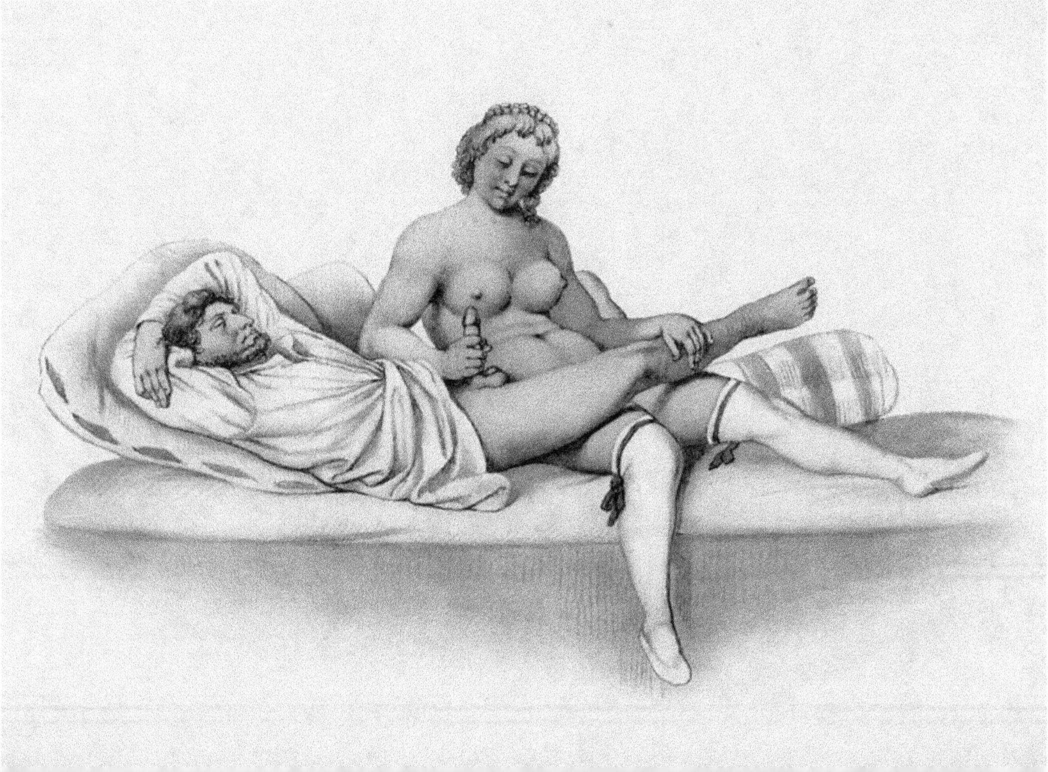

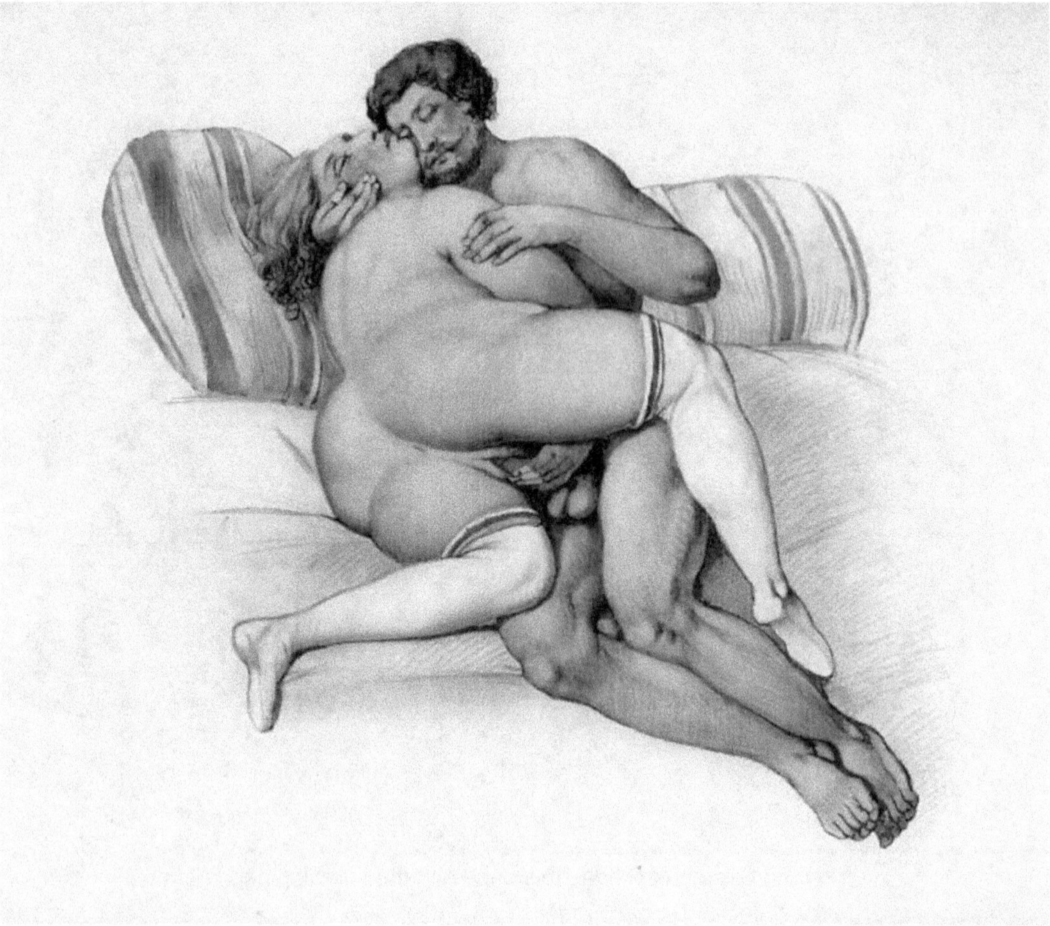

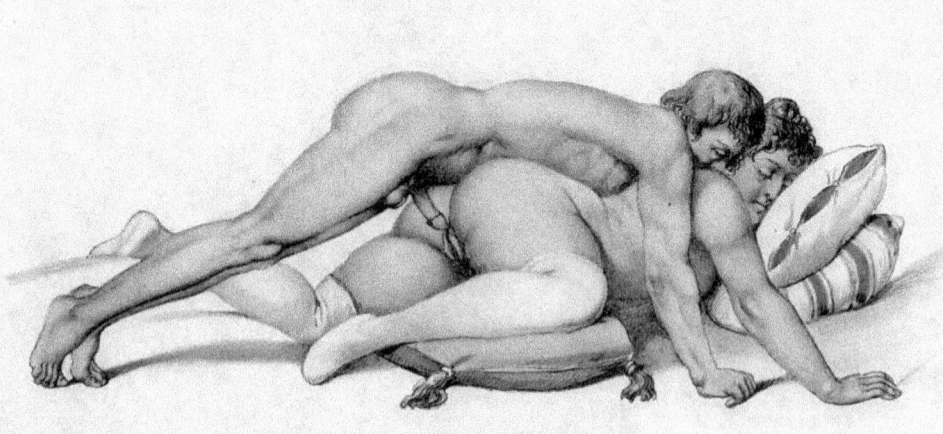

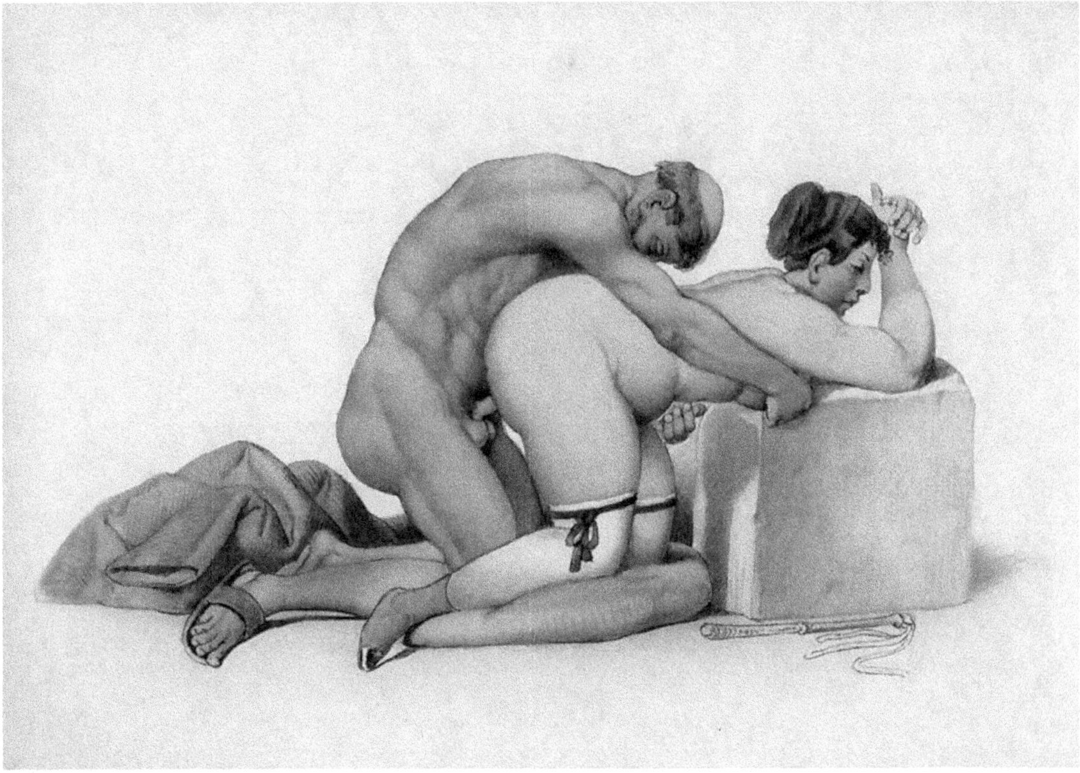

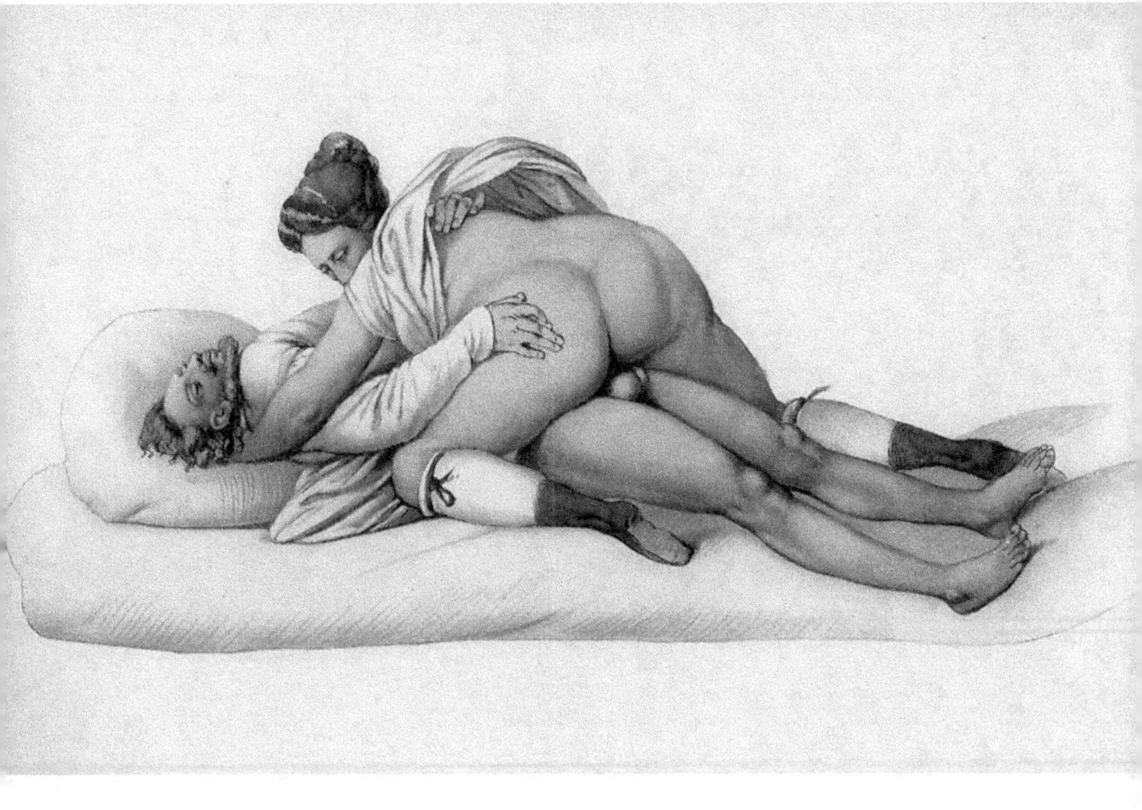

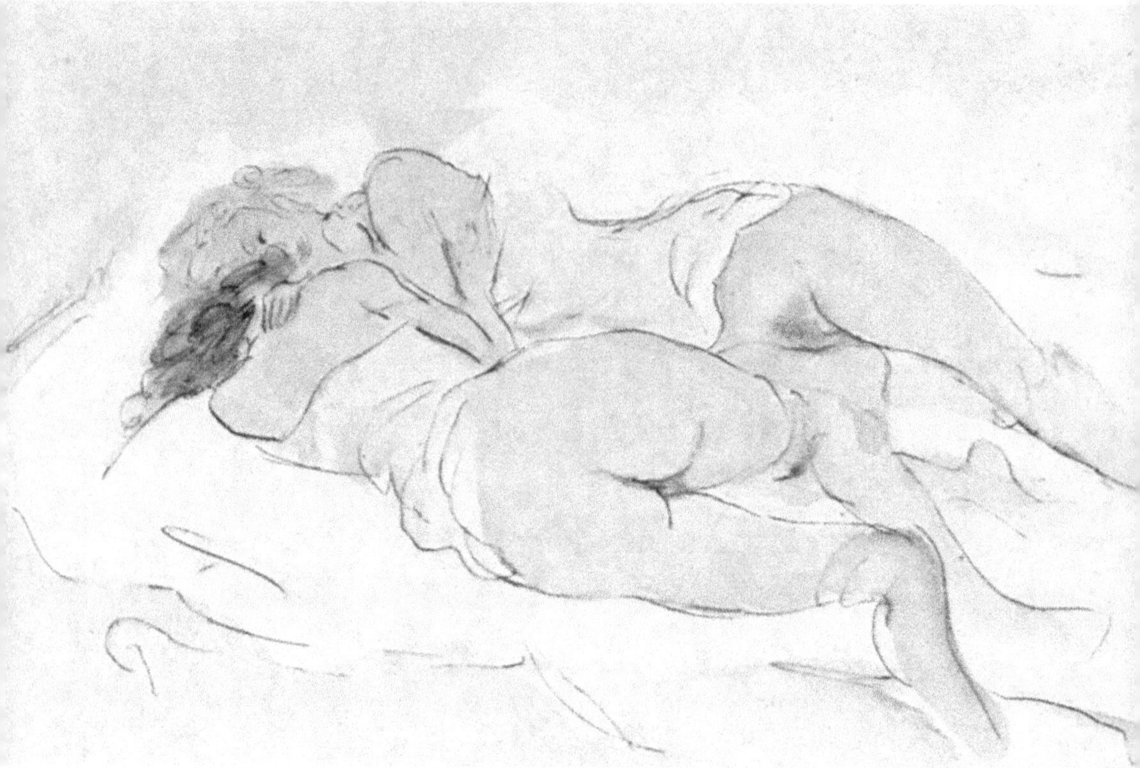

Otto Schoff, this page and following pages

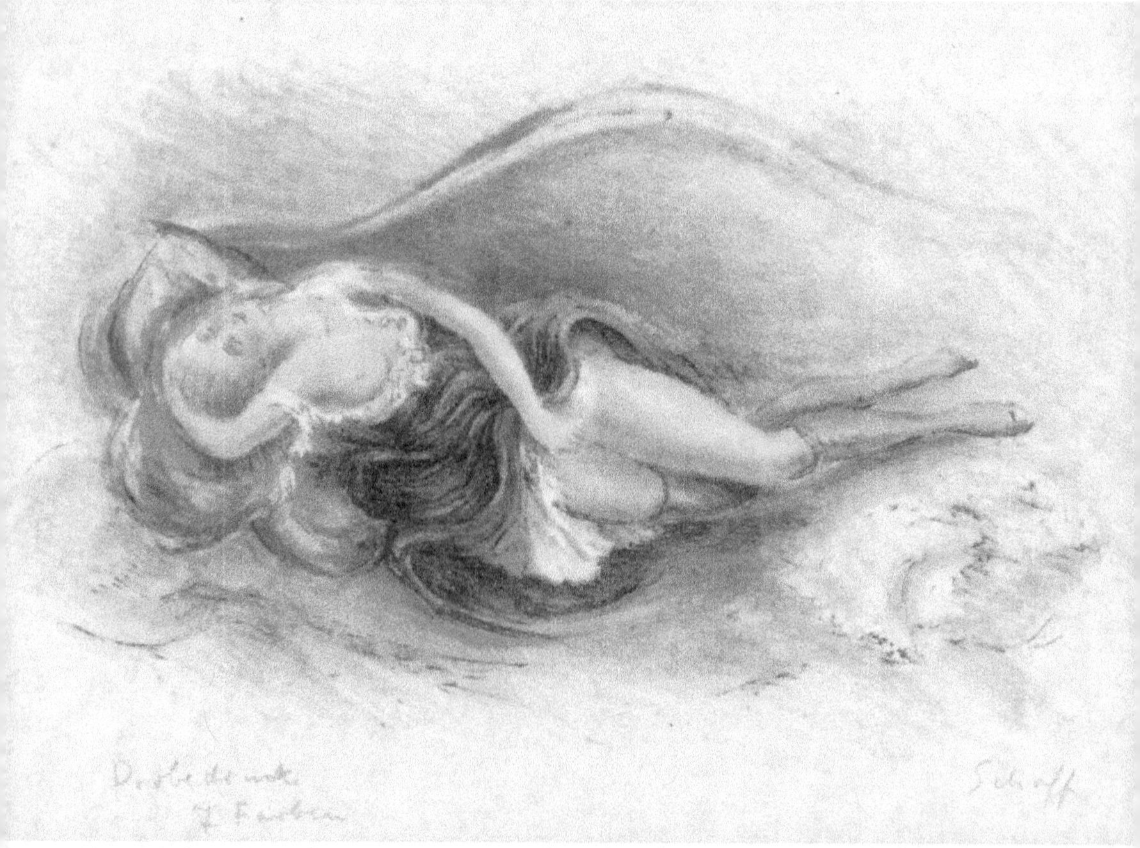

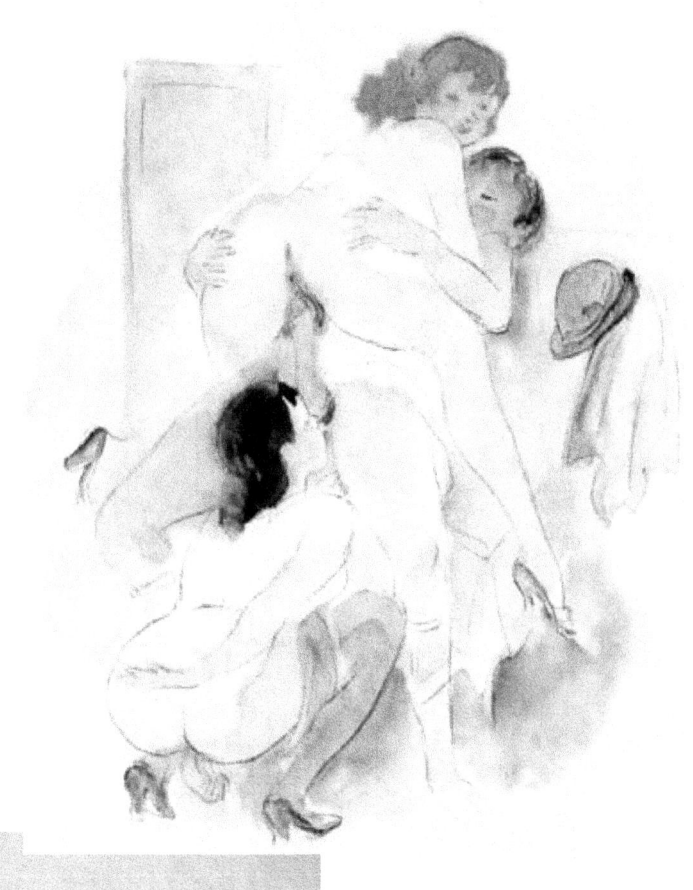

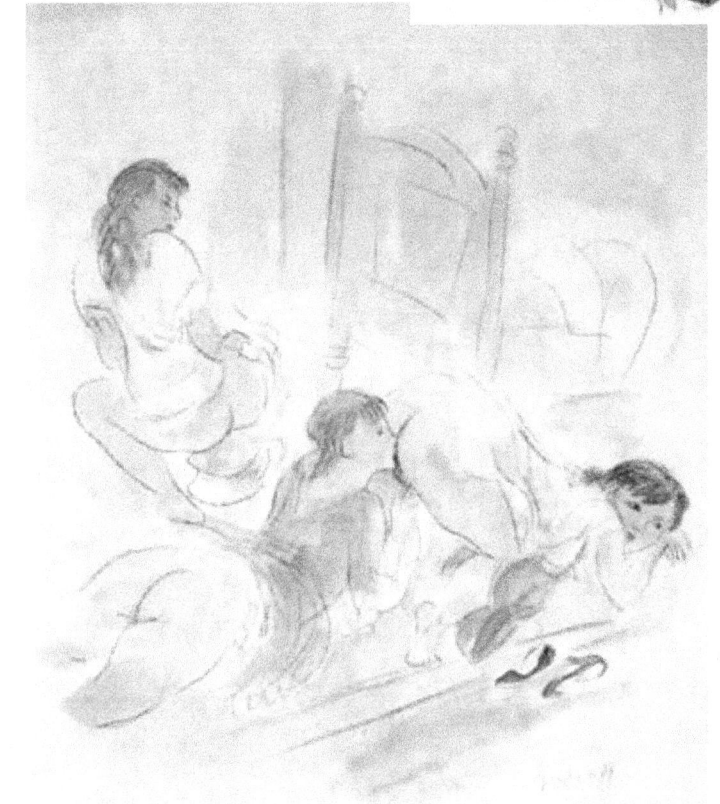

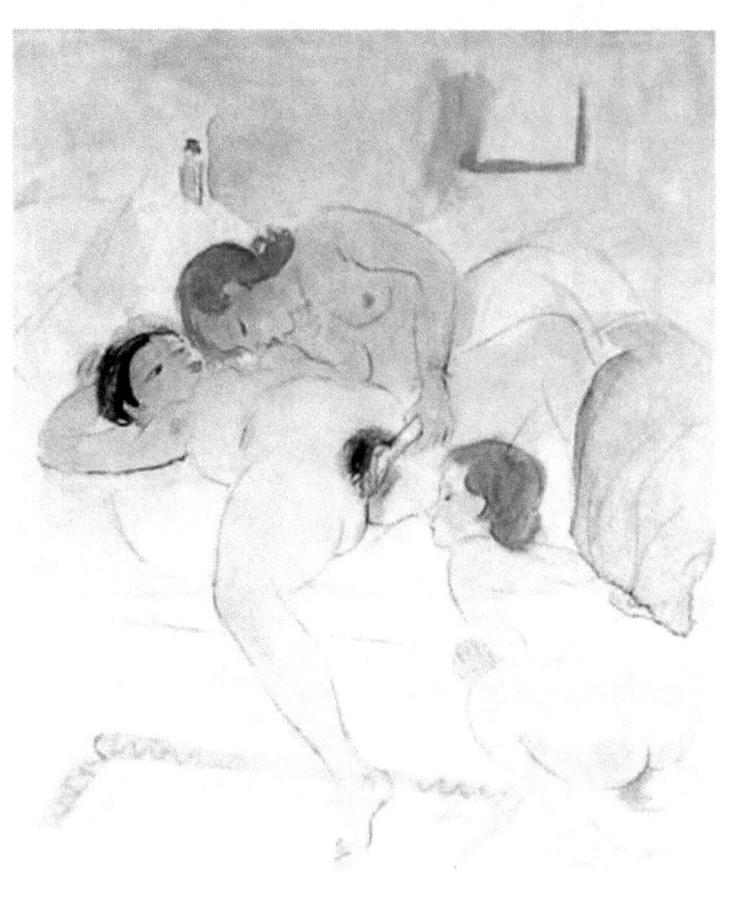

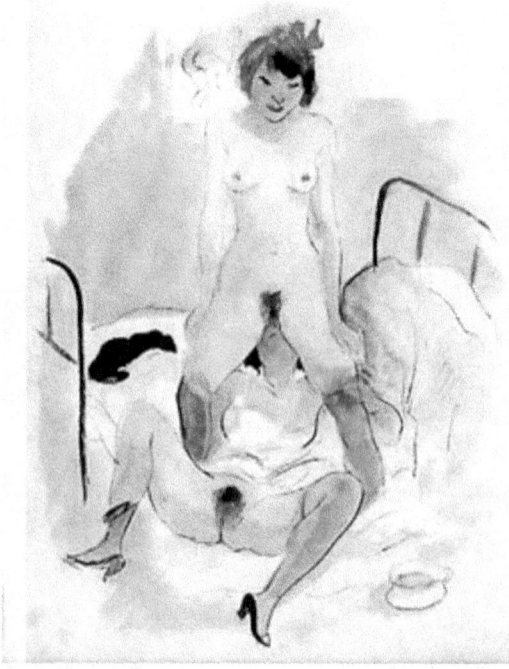

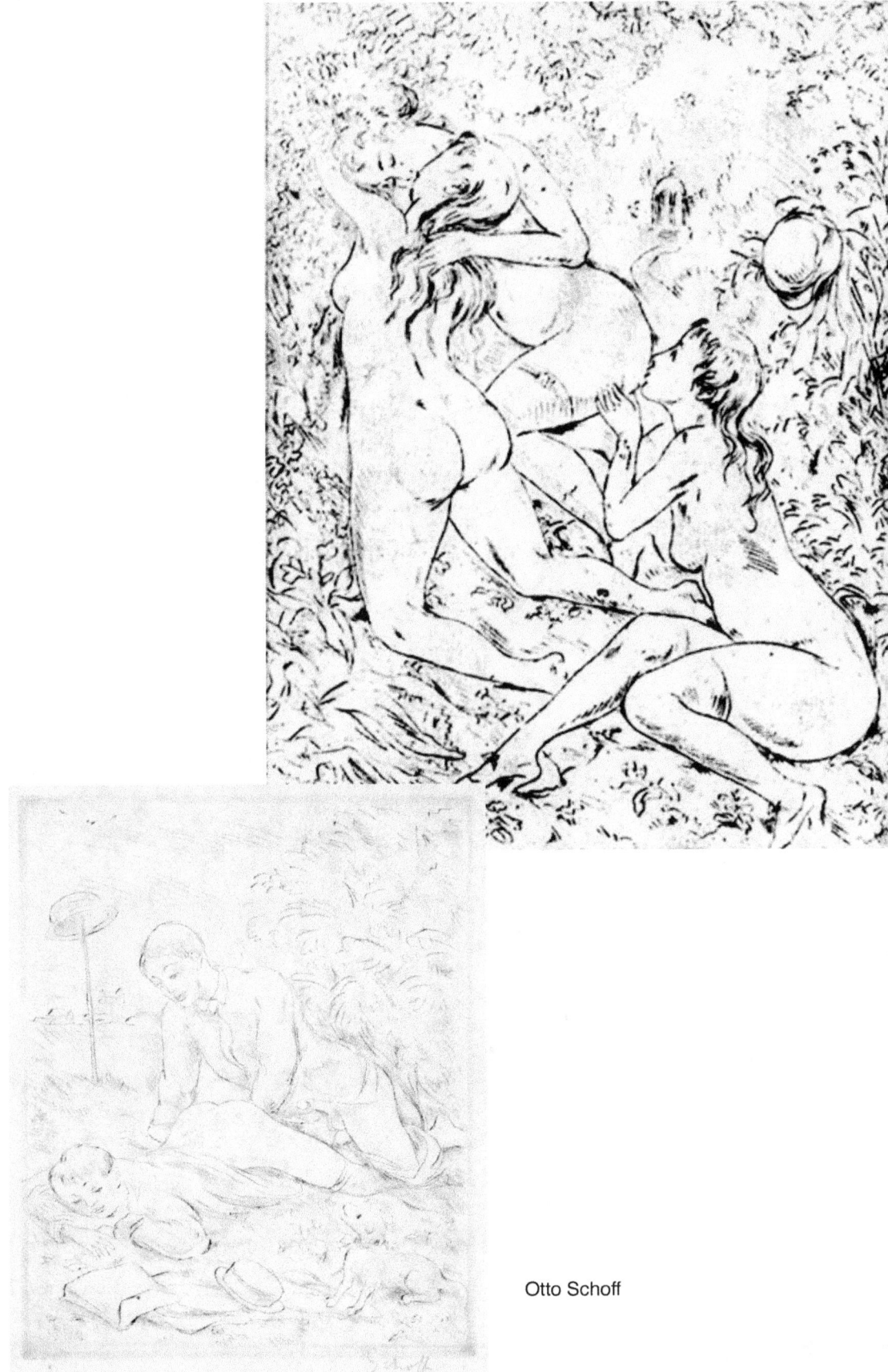

Otto Schoff

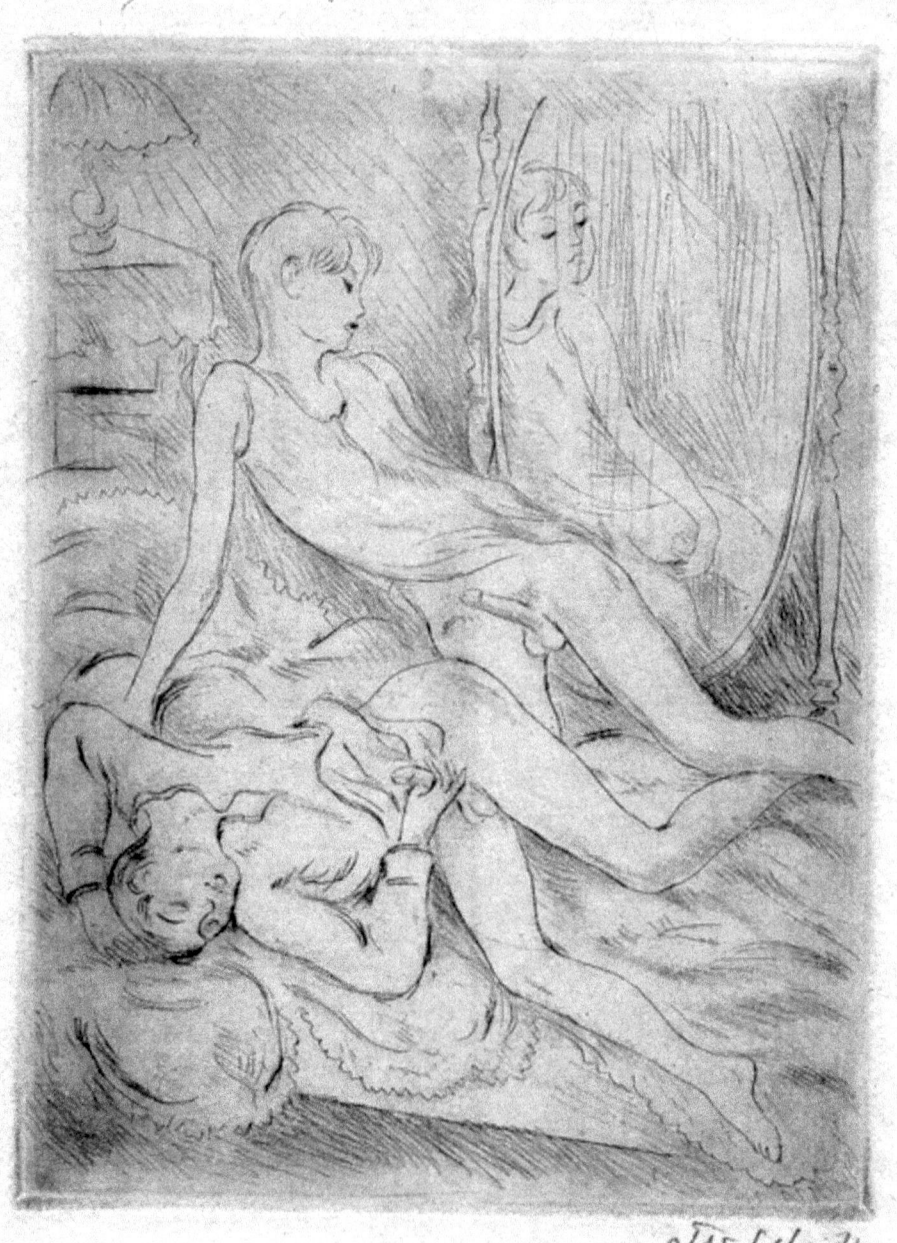

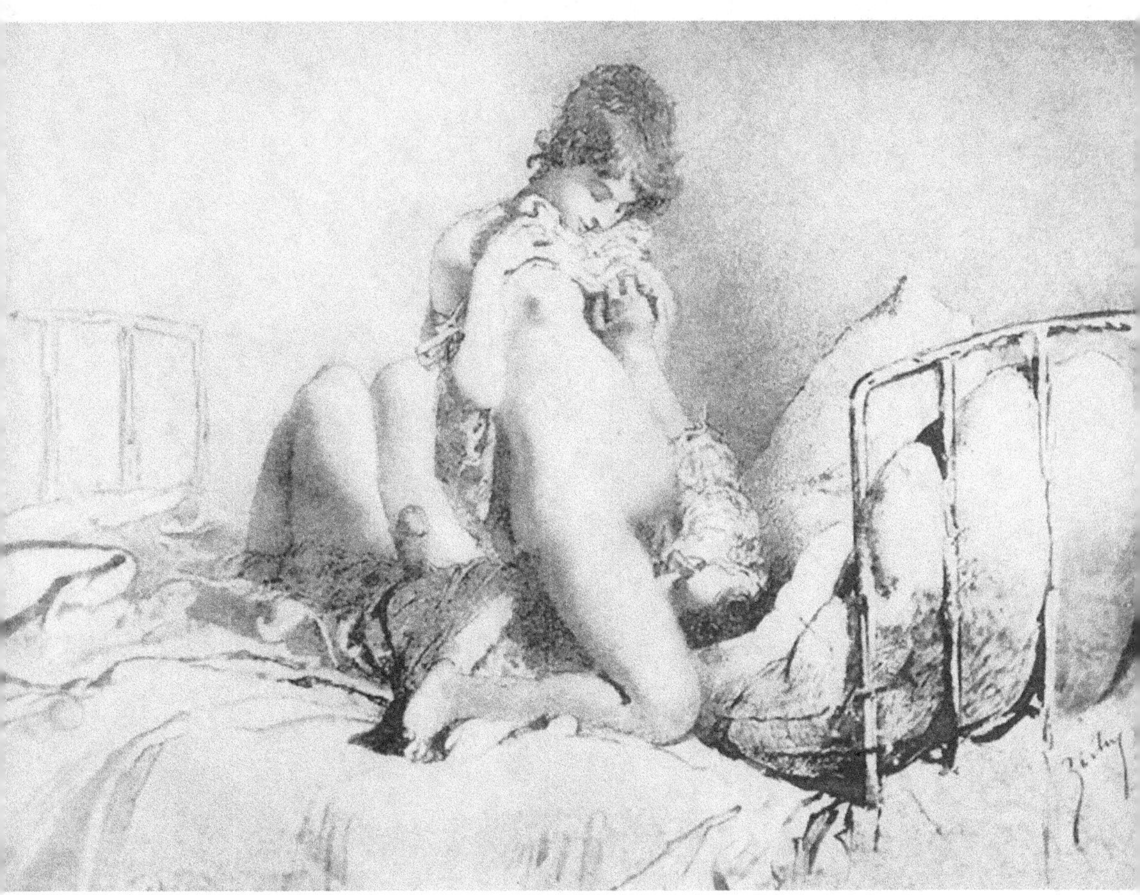

Mihály Zichy (1827-1906), from Liebe, 1911. This page and following pages

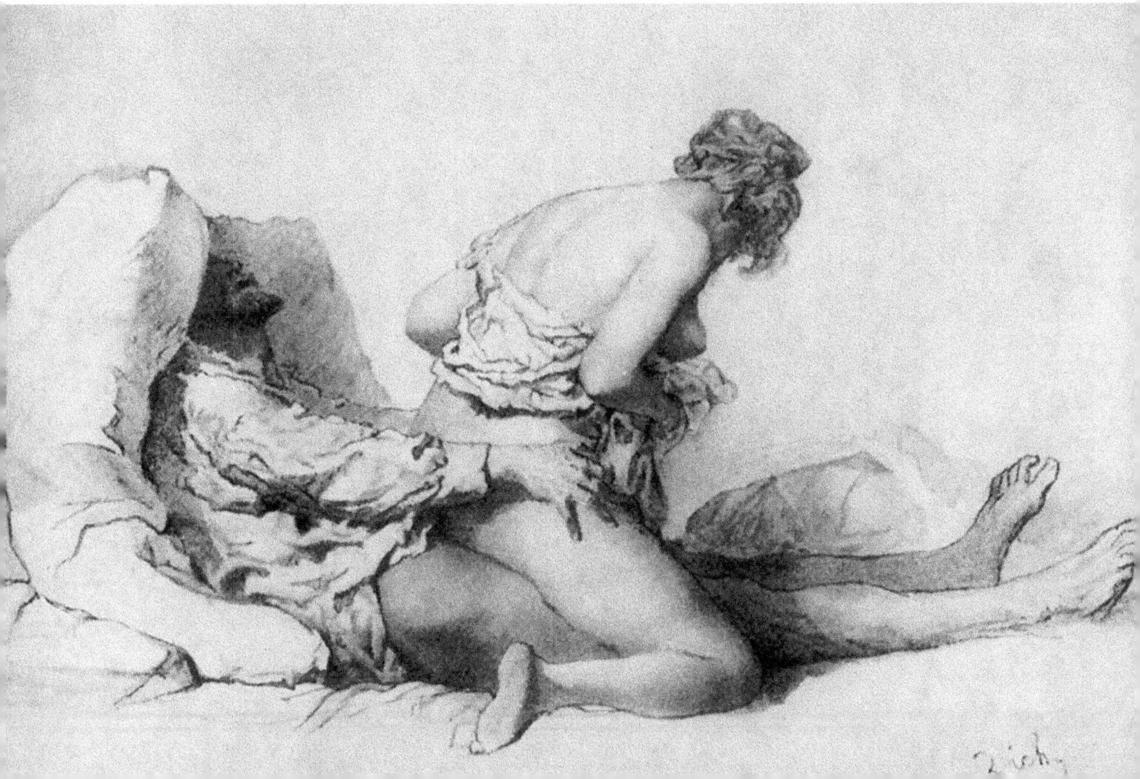

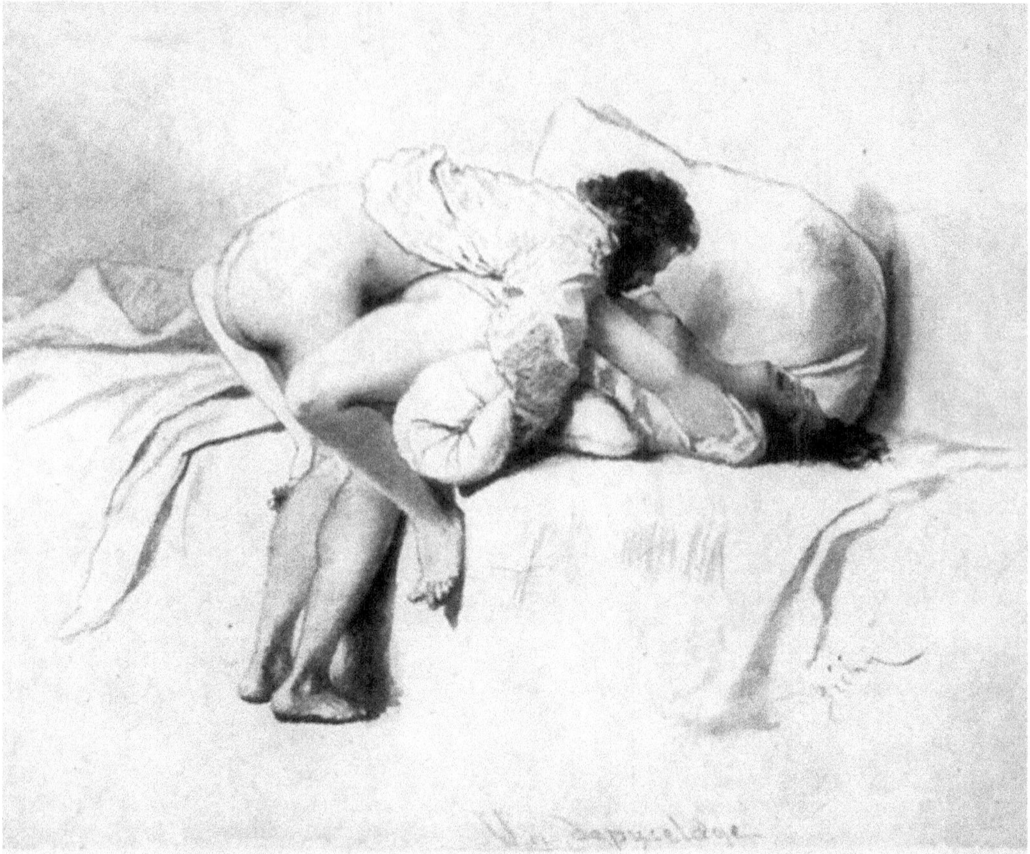

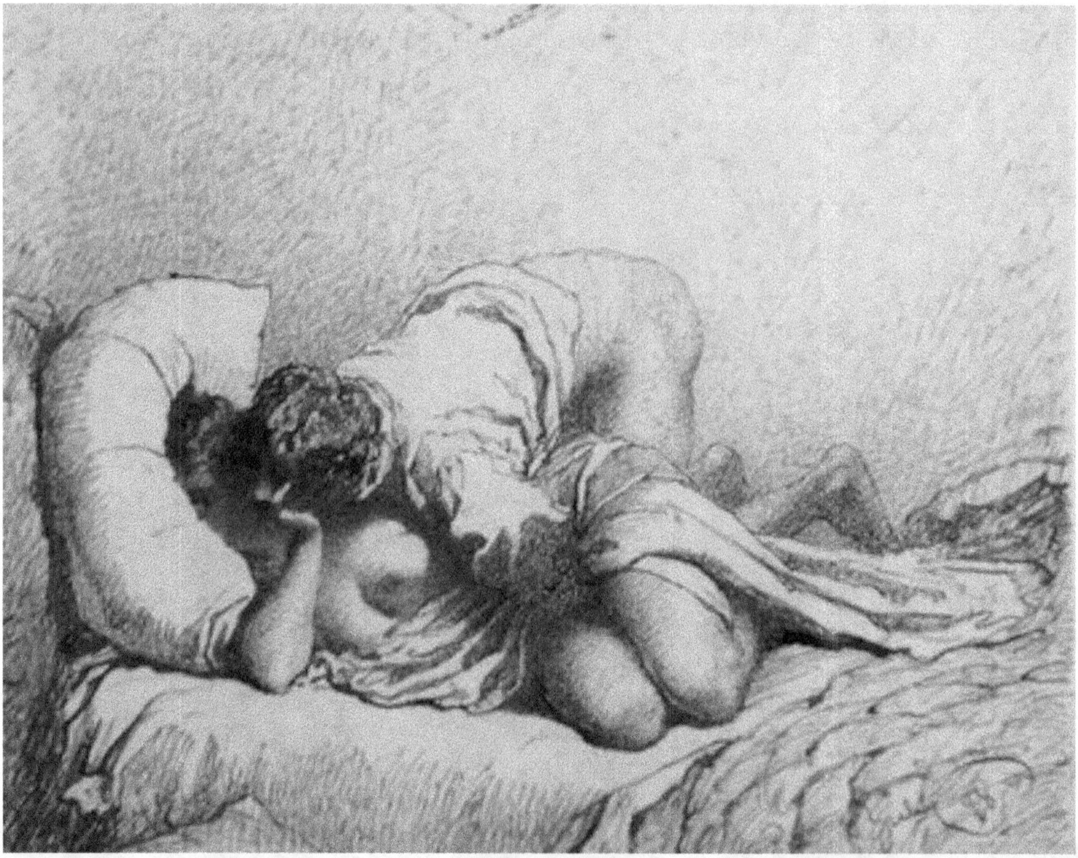

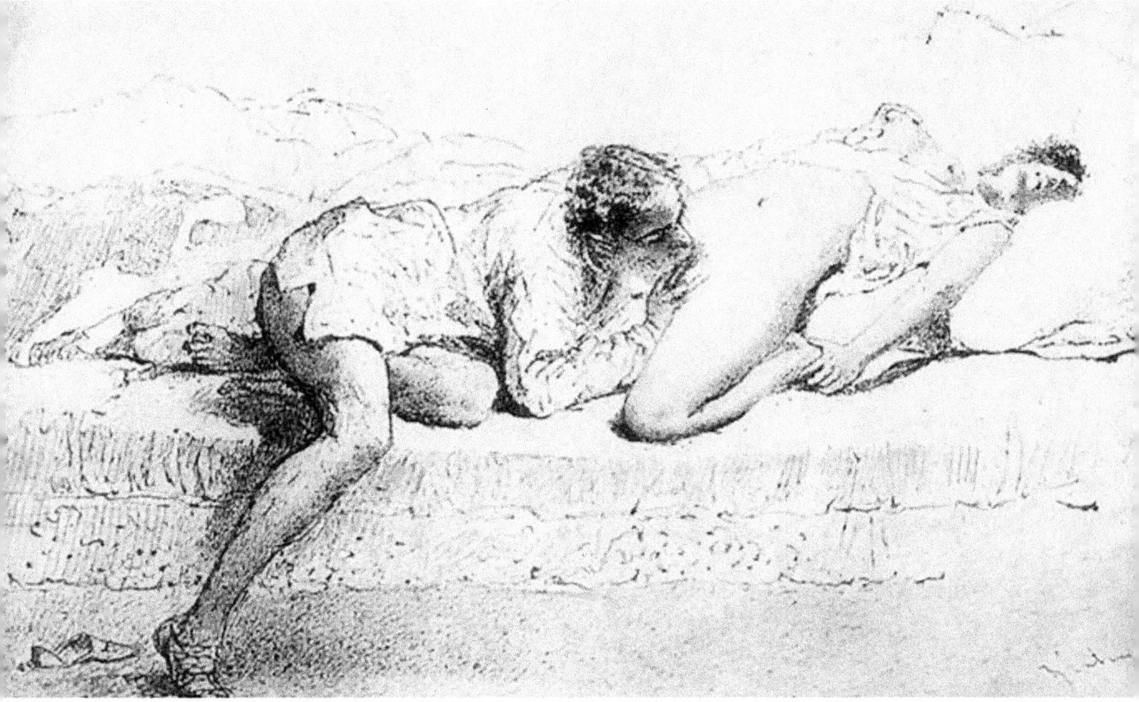

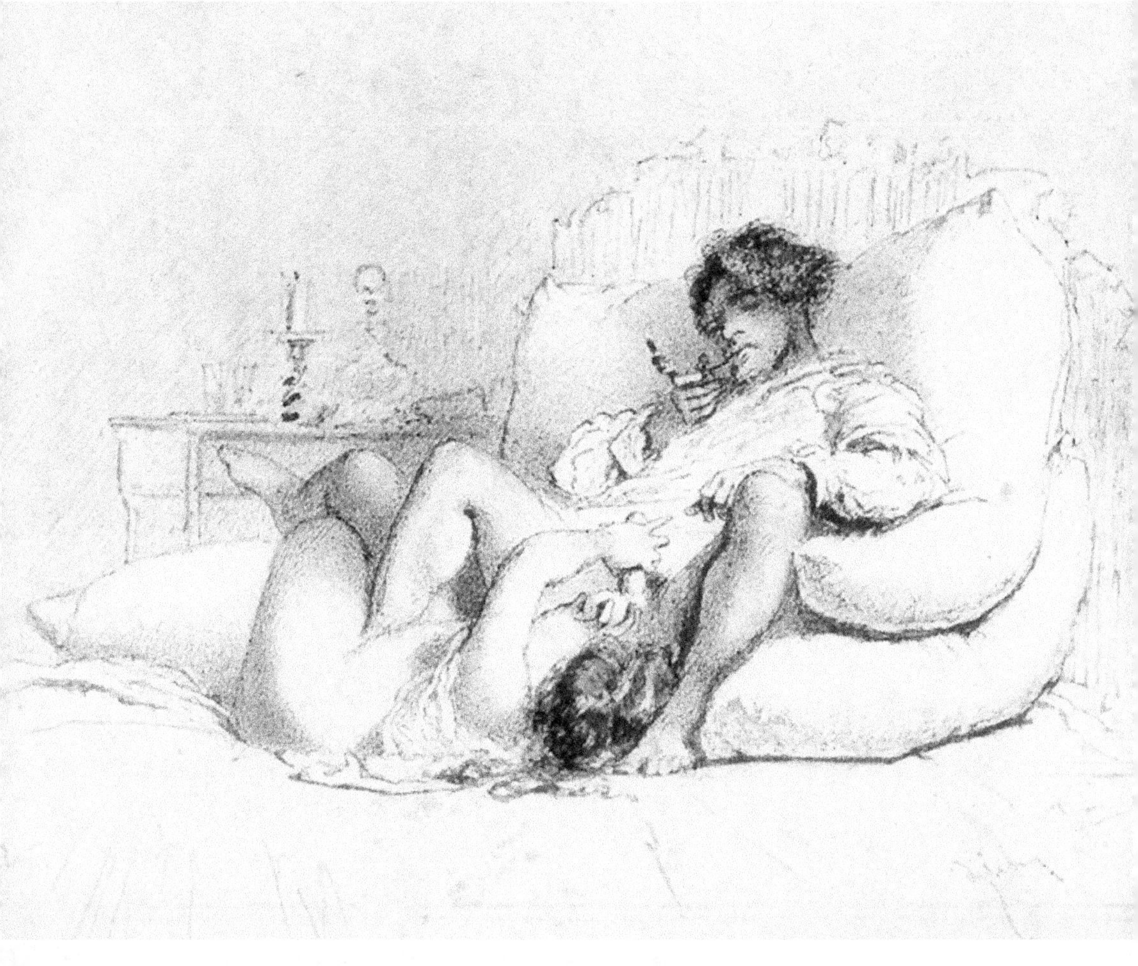

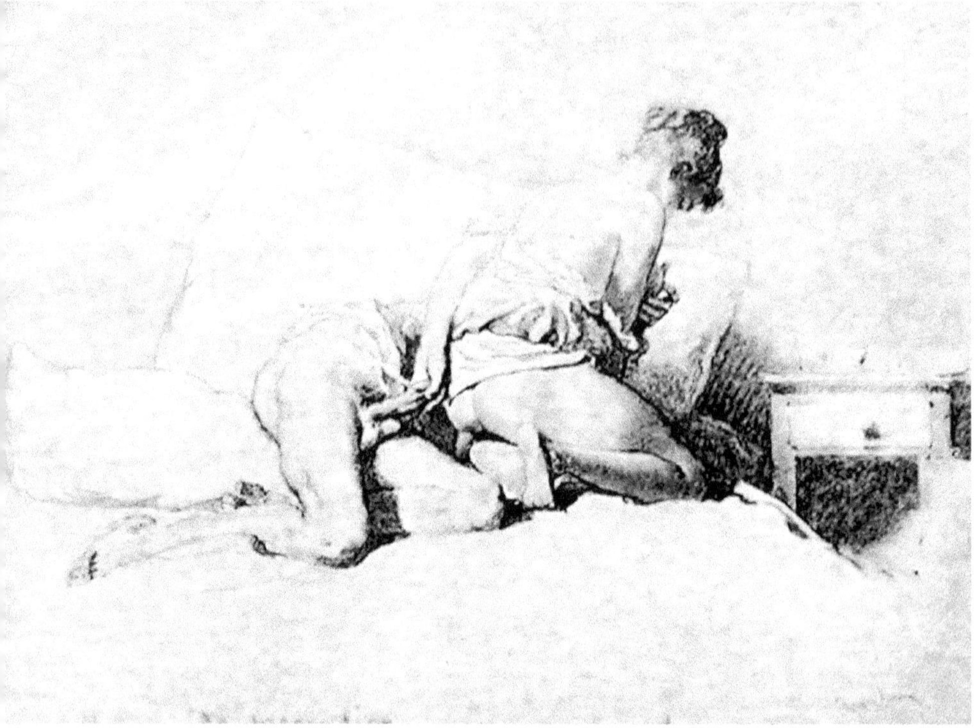

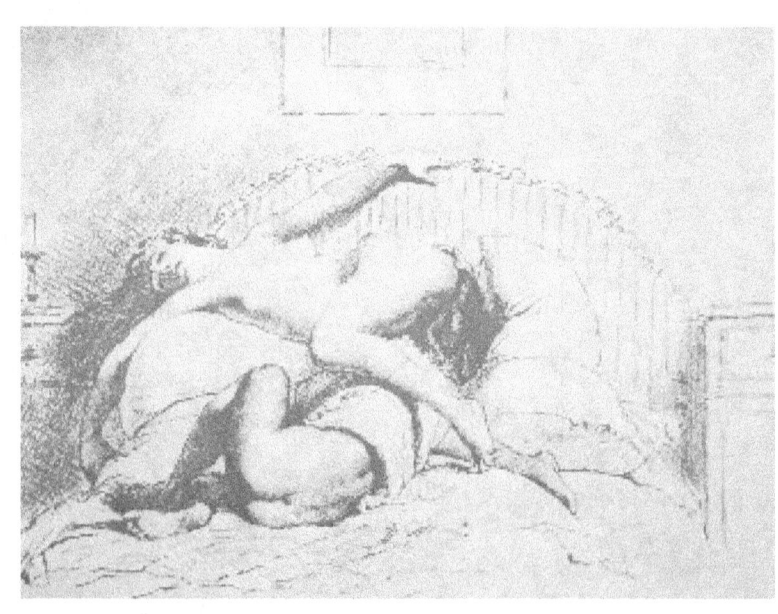

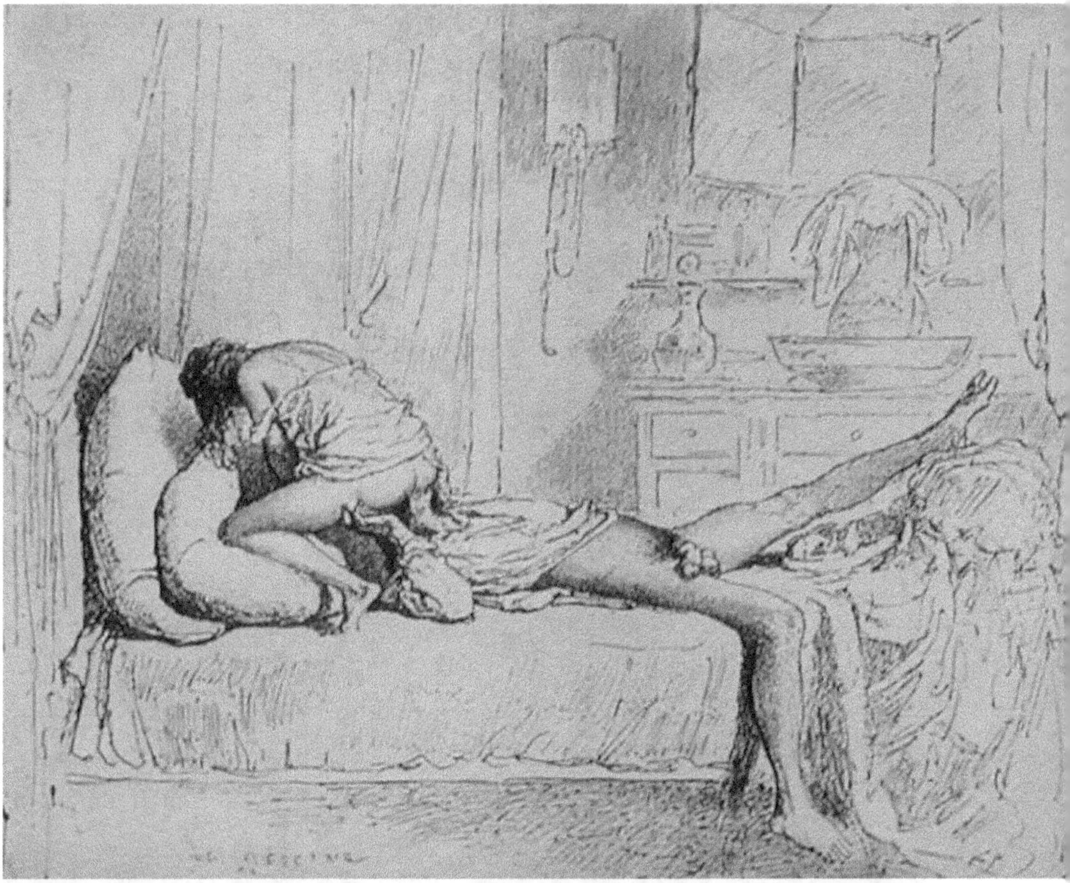

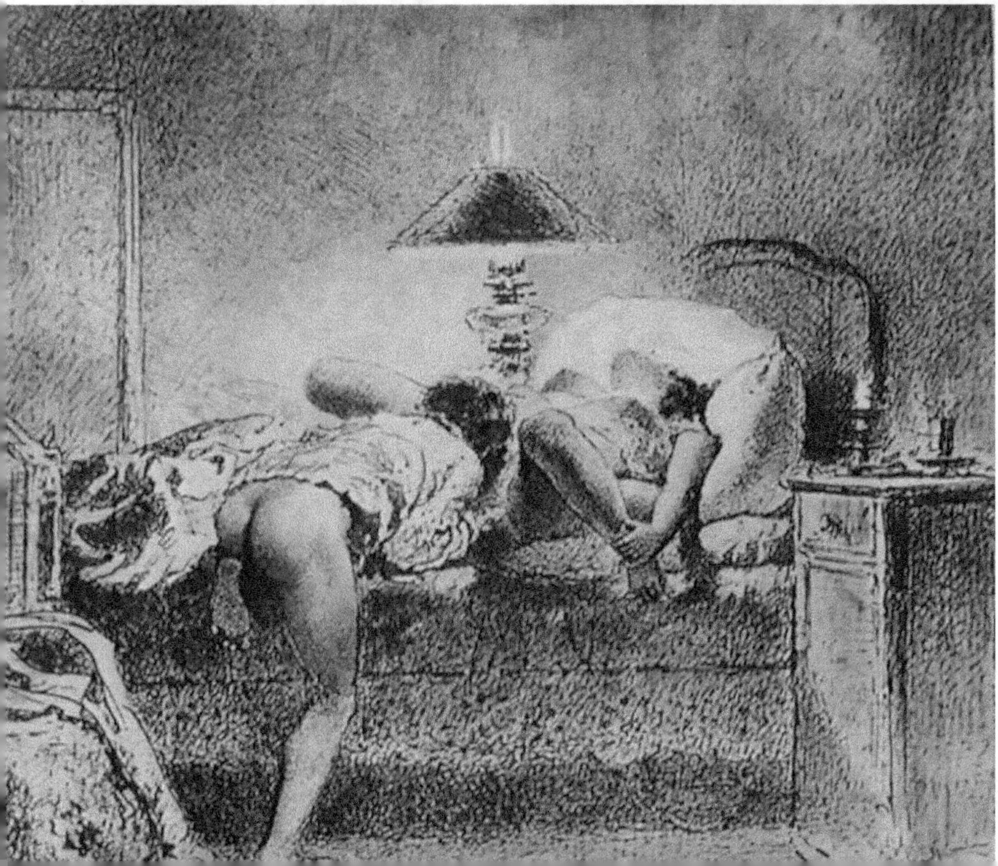

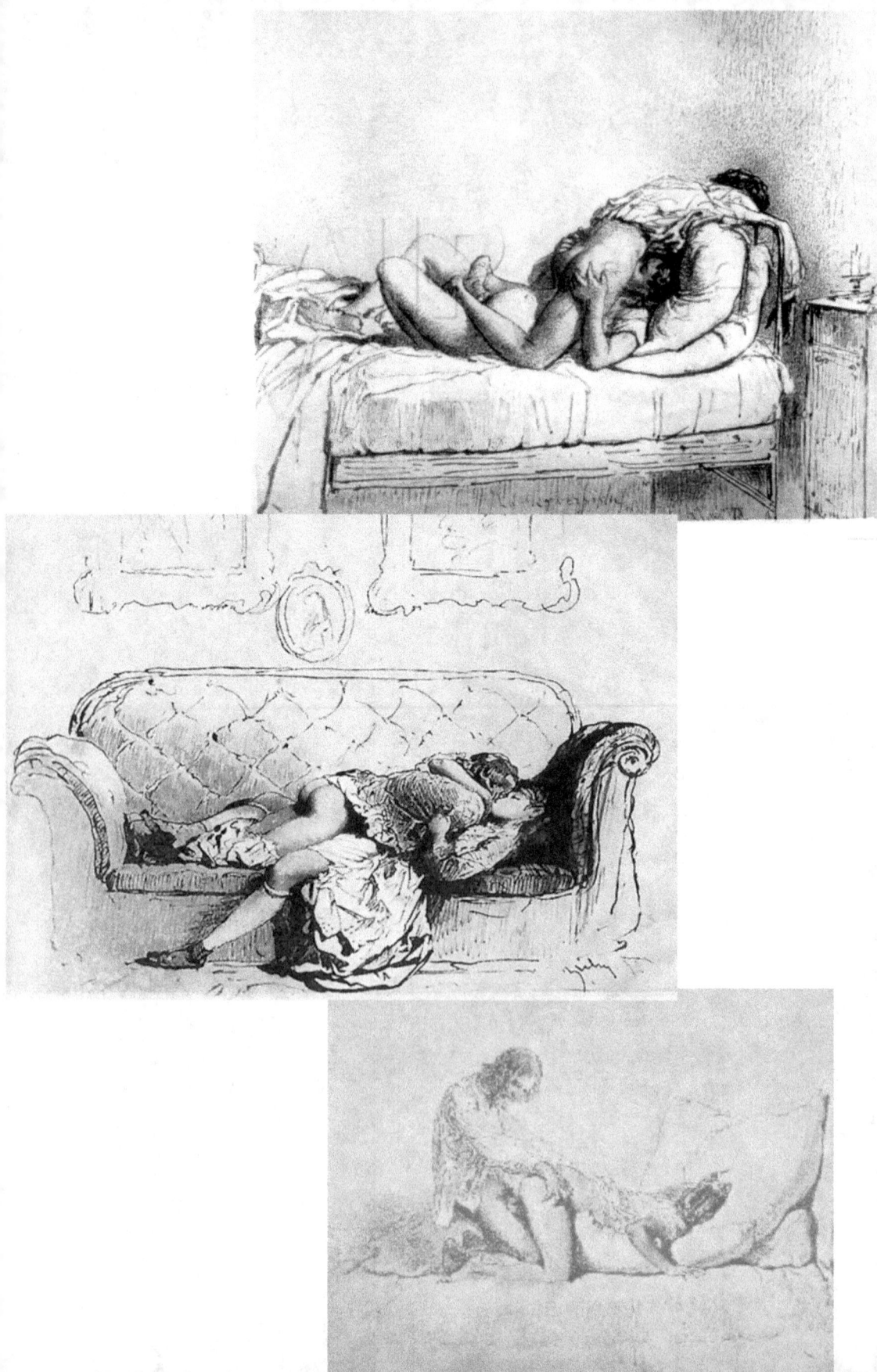

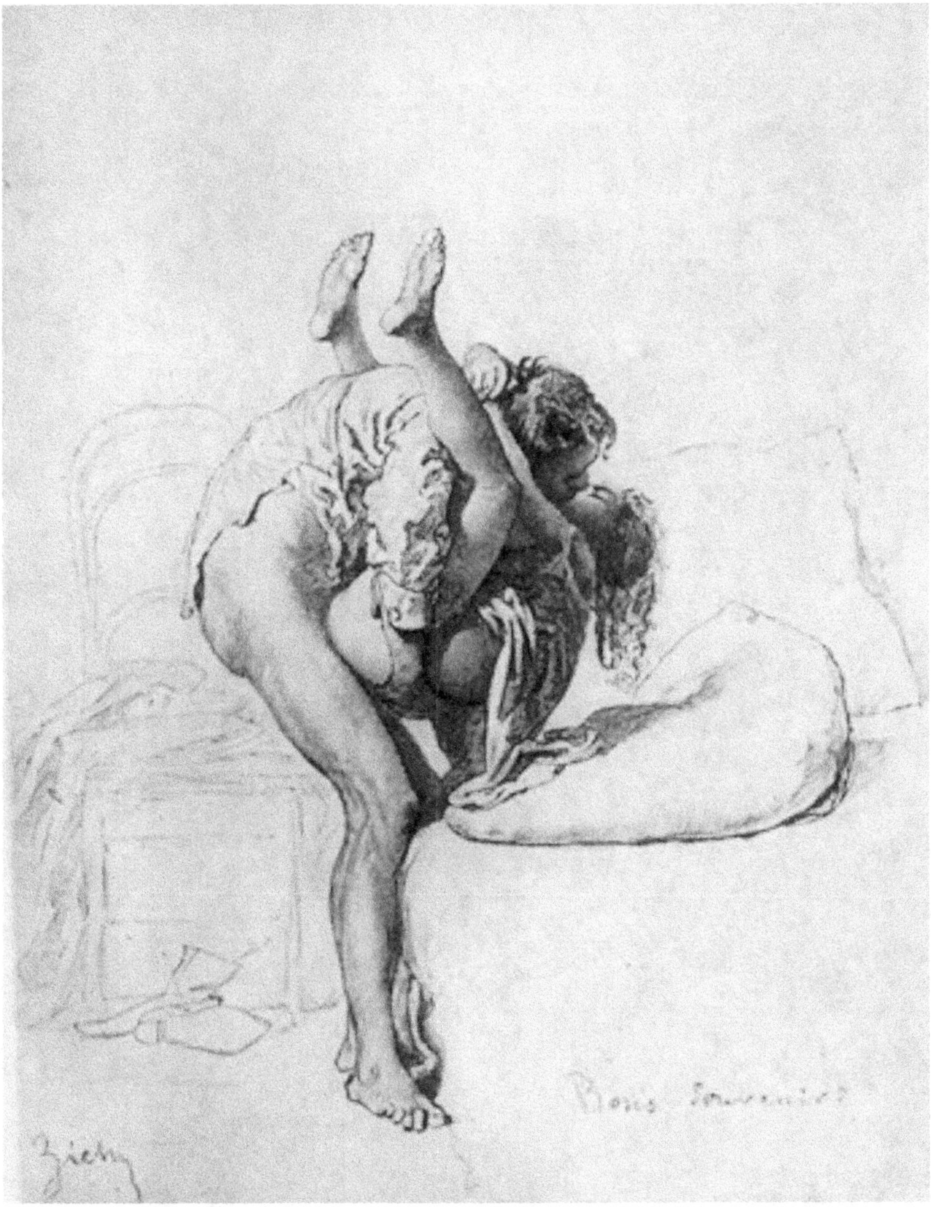

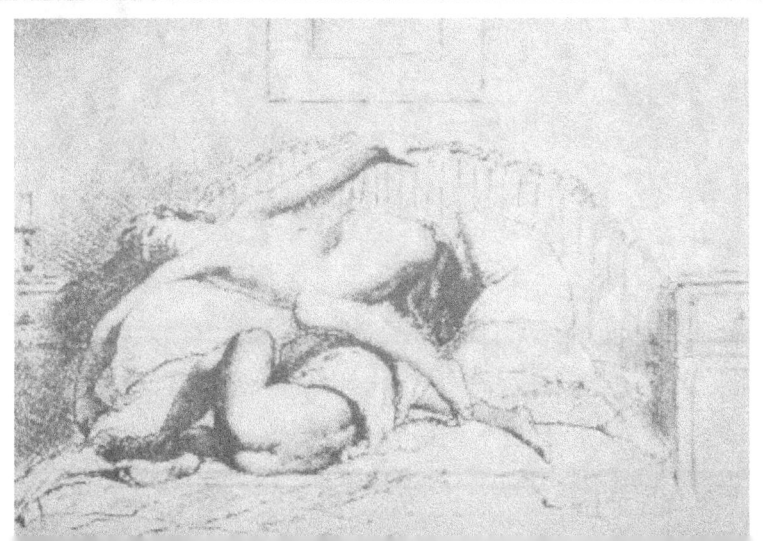

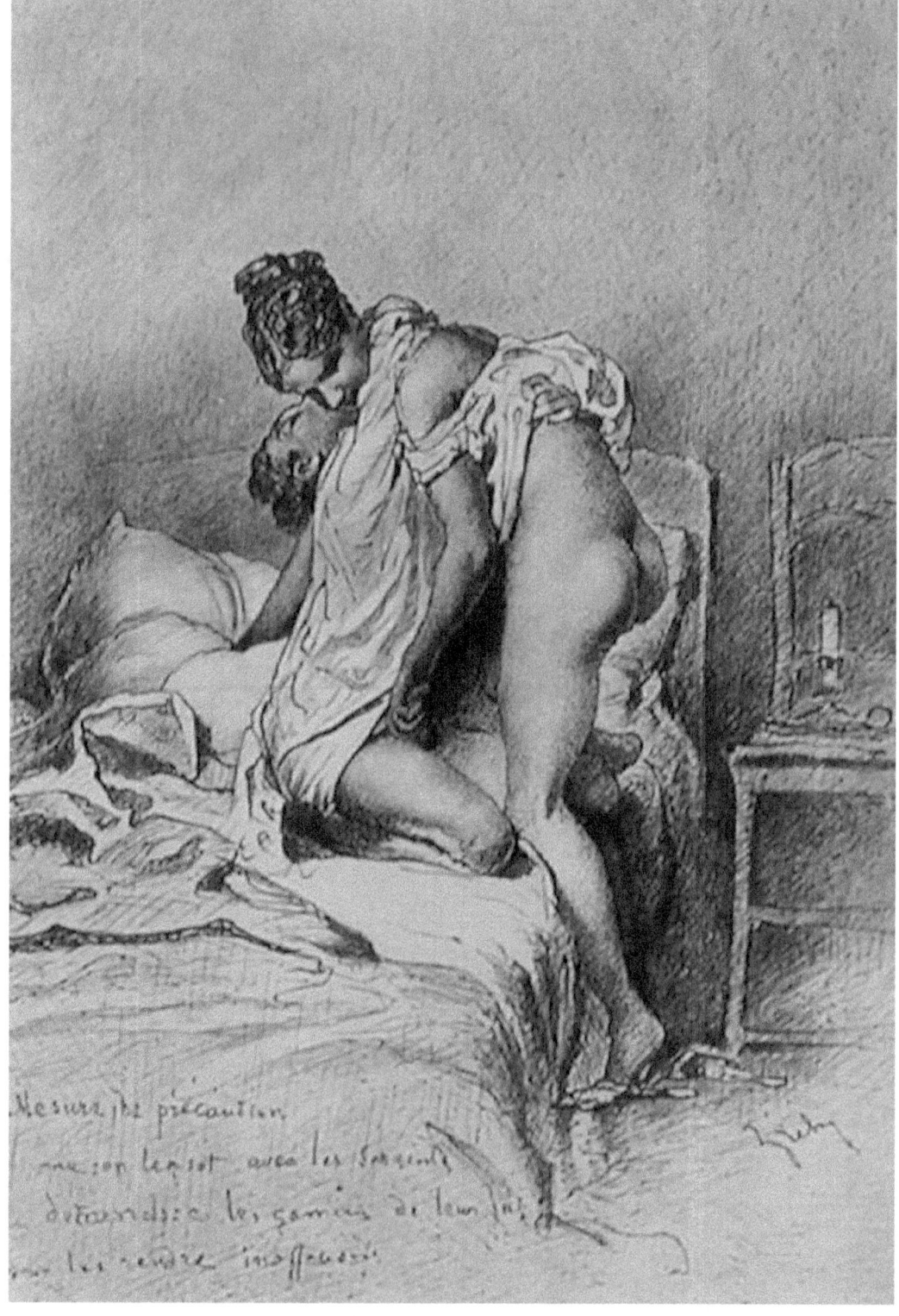

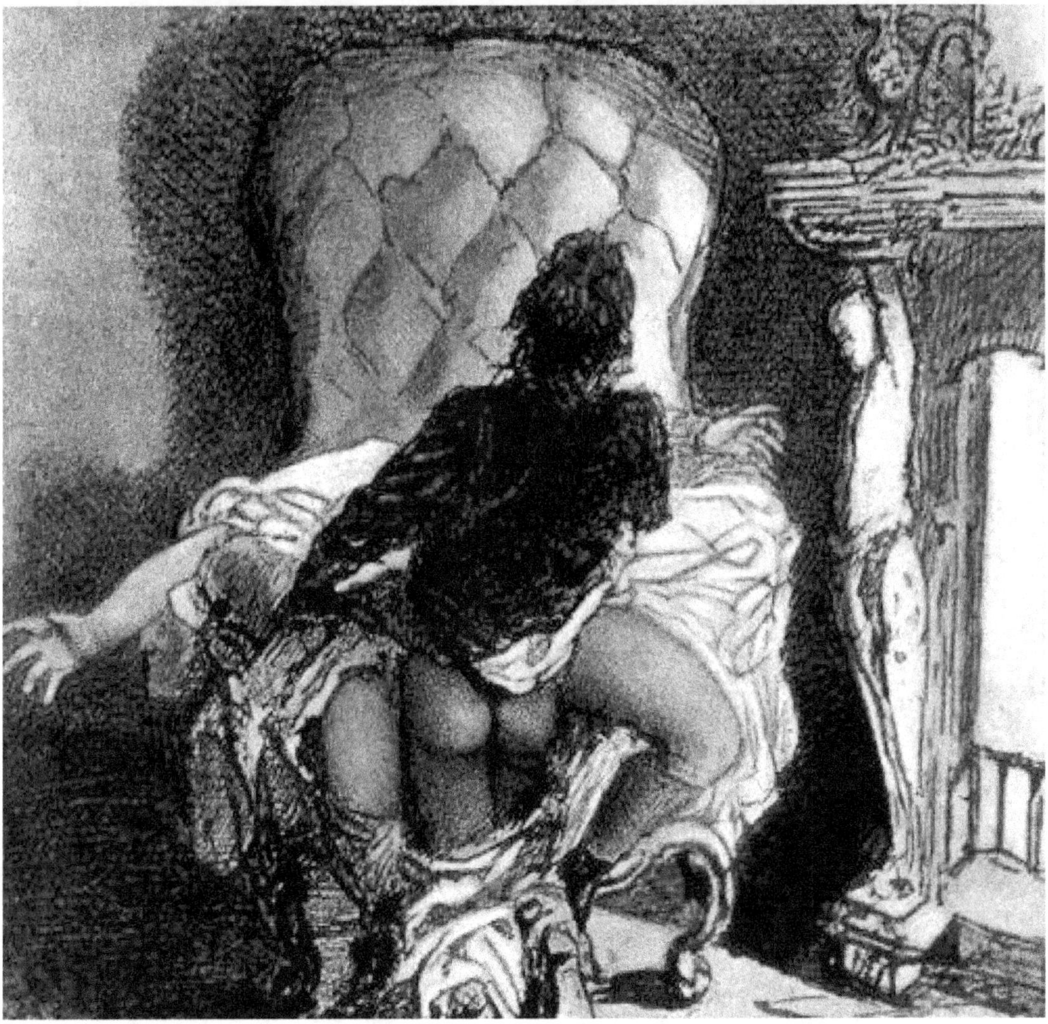

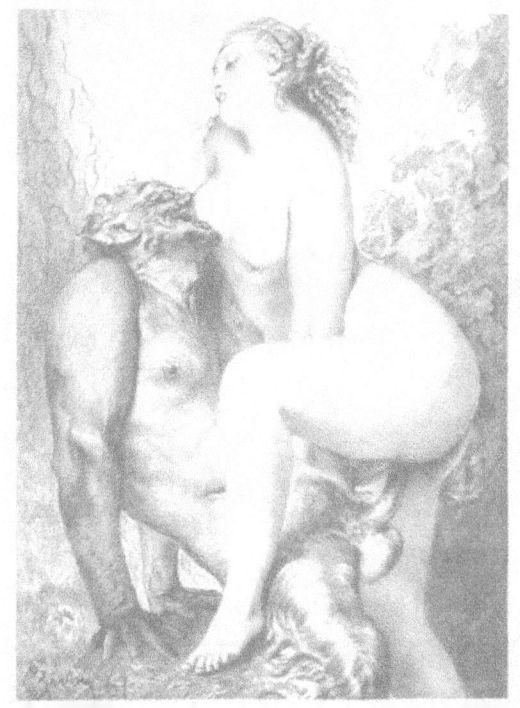

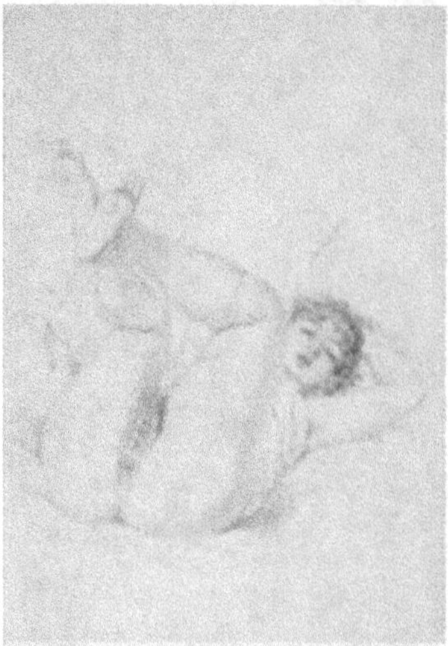

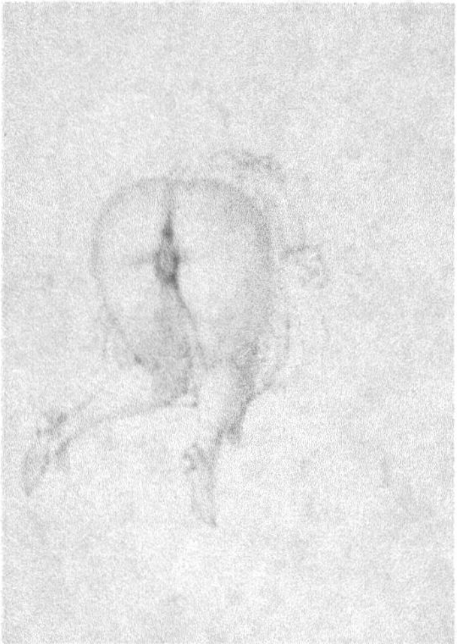

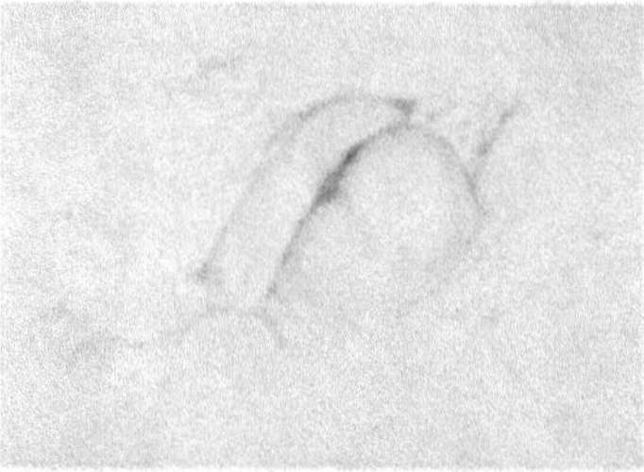

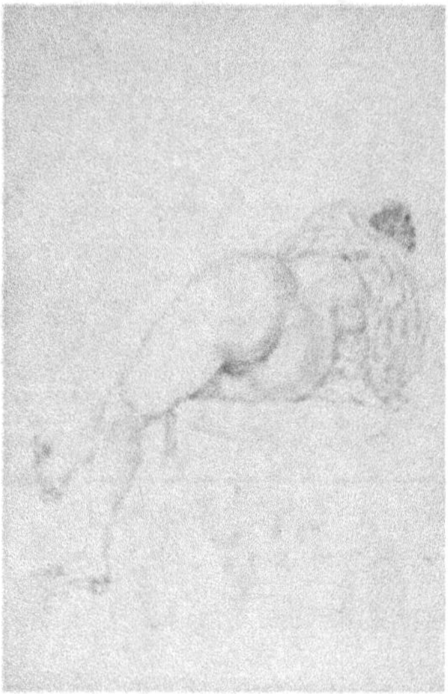

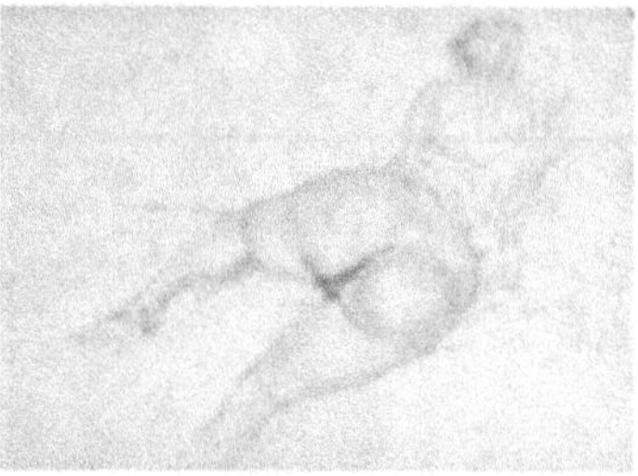

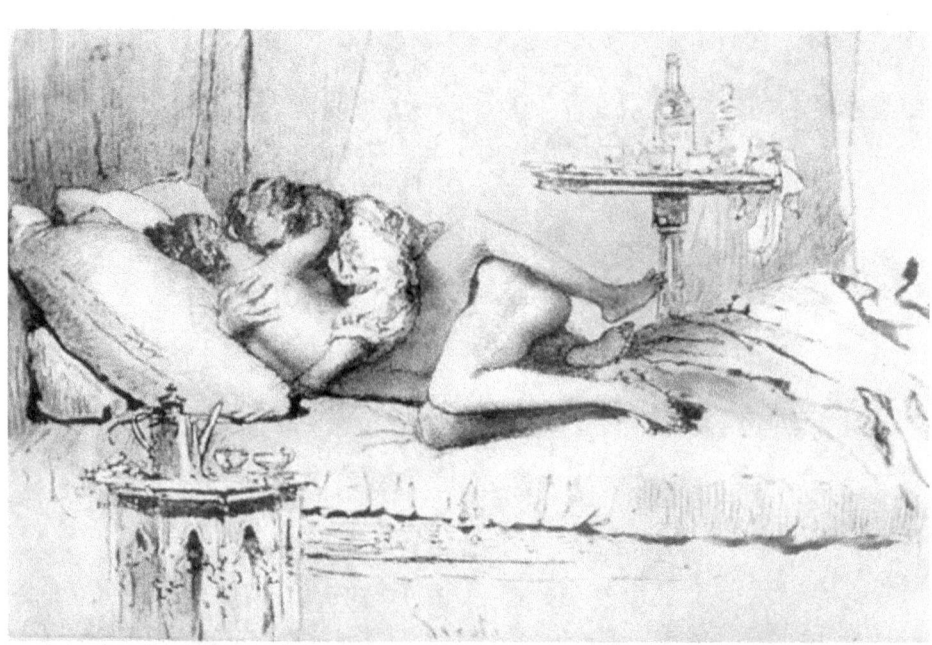

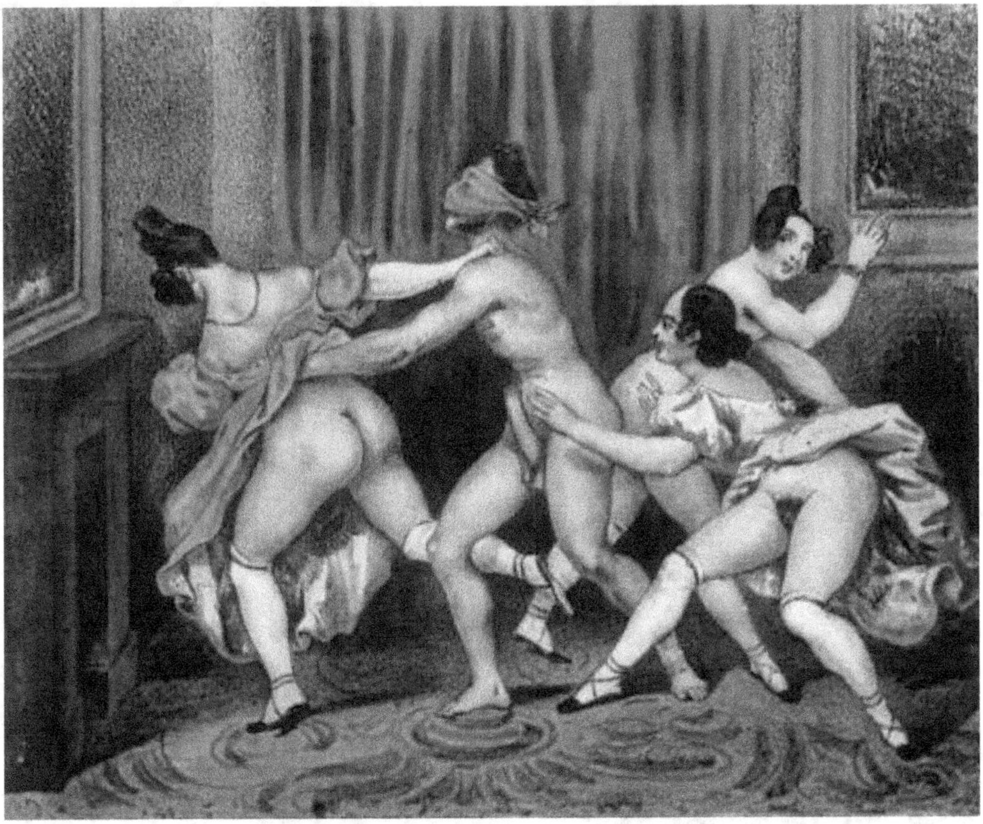

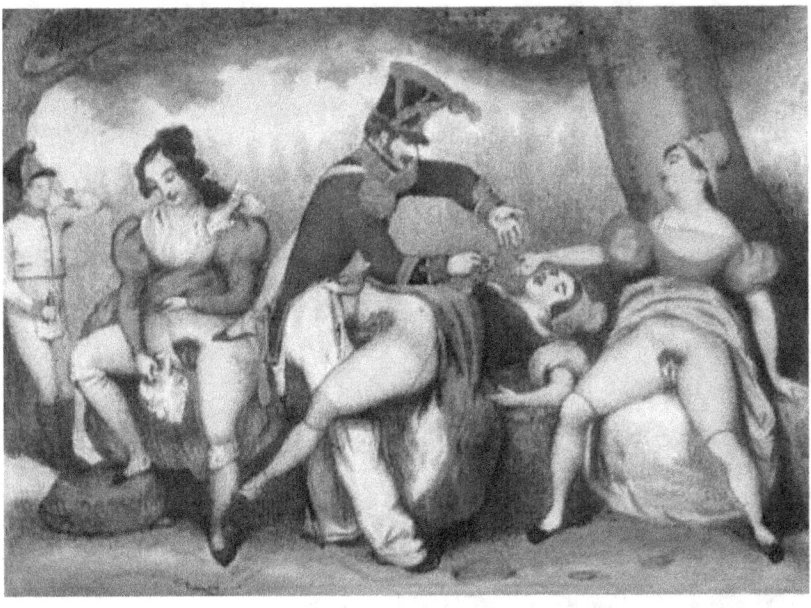

Achille Deveria (1800-1857), this page and following pages

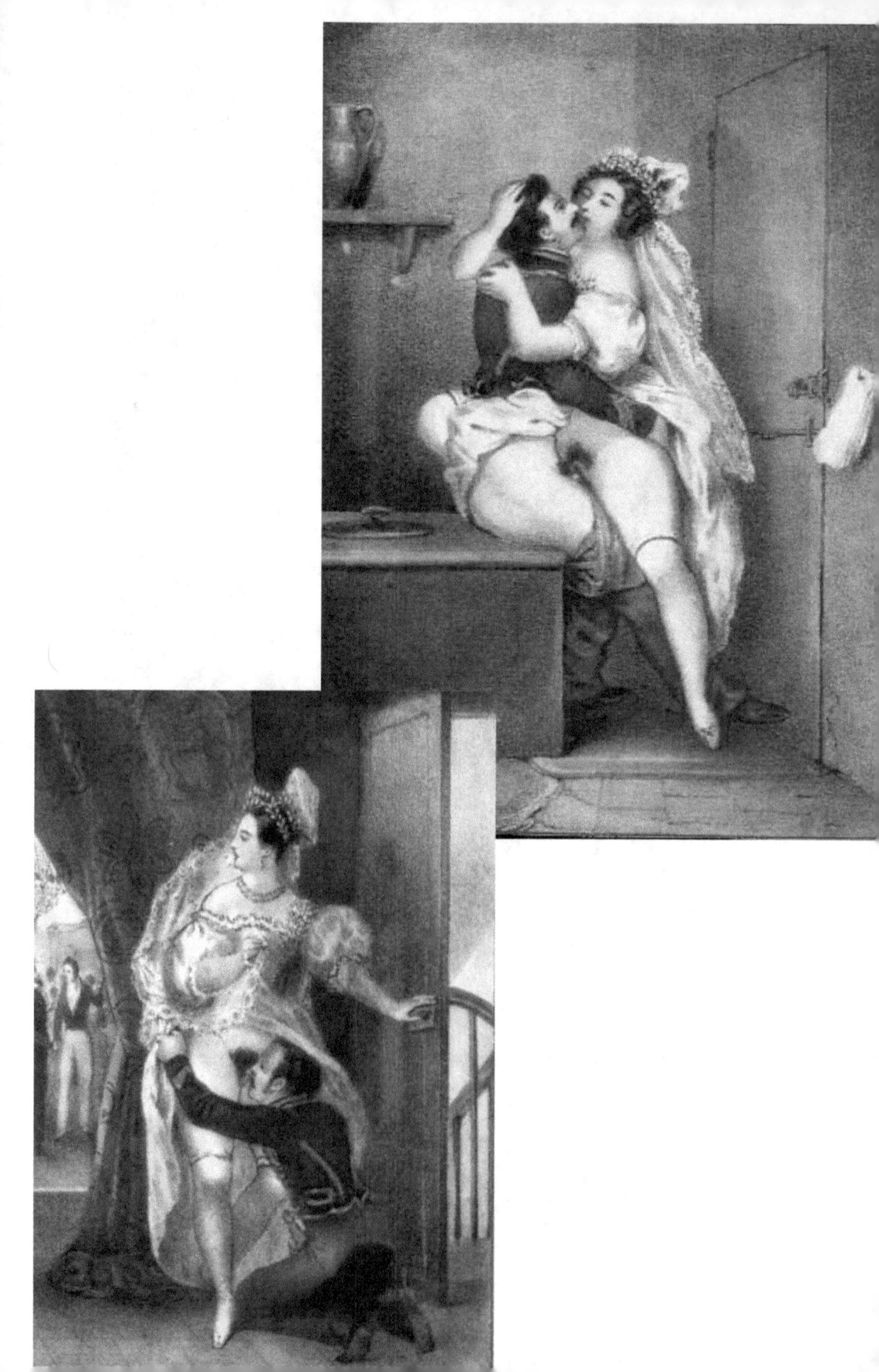

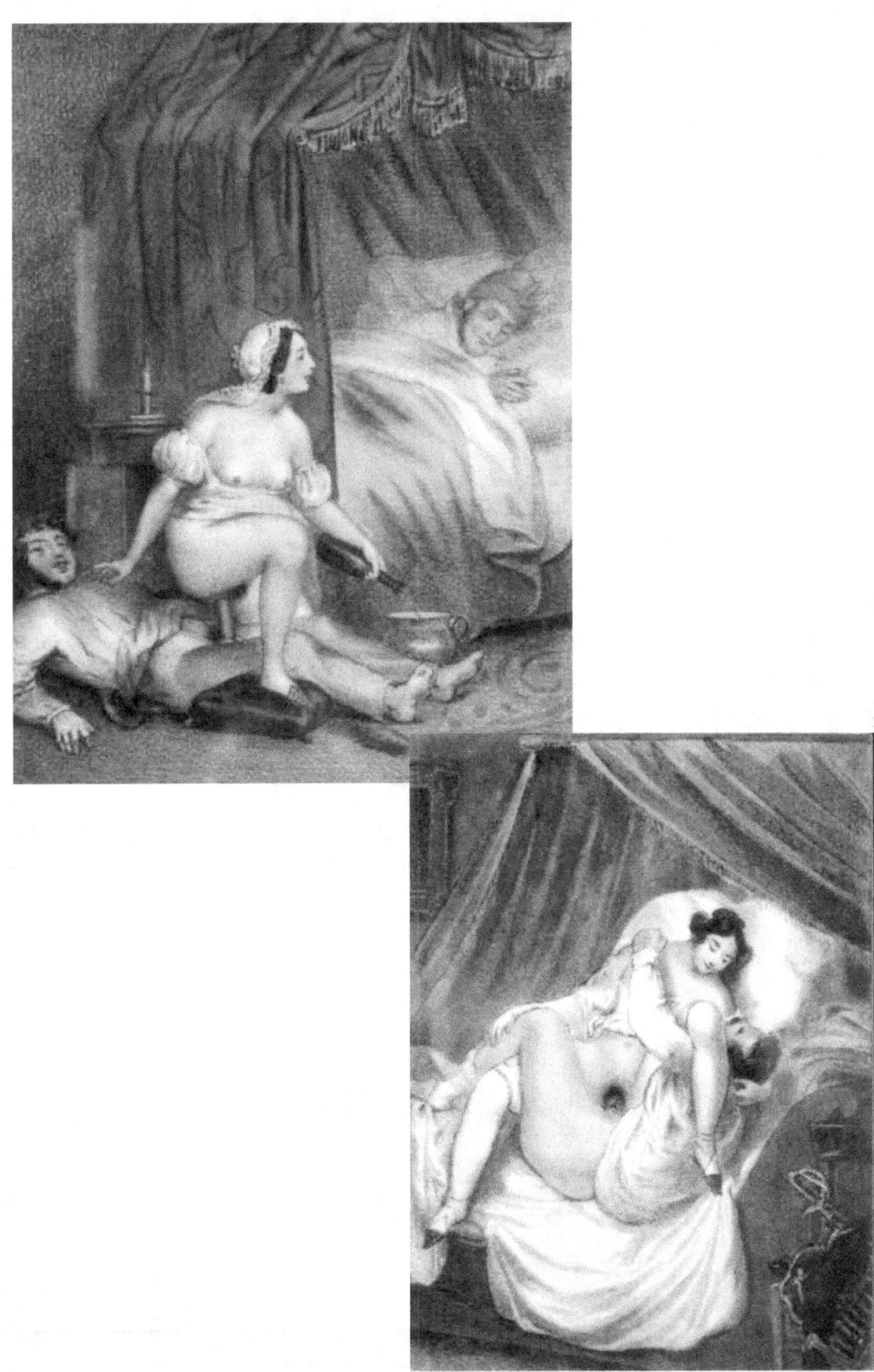

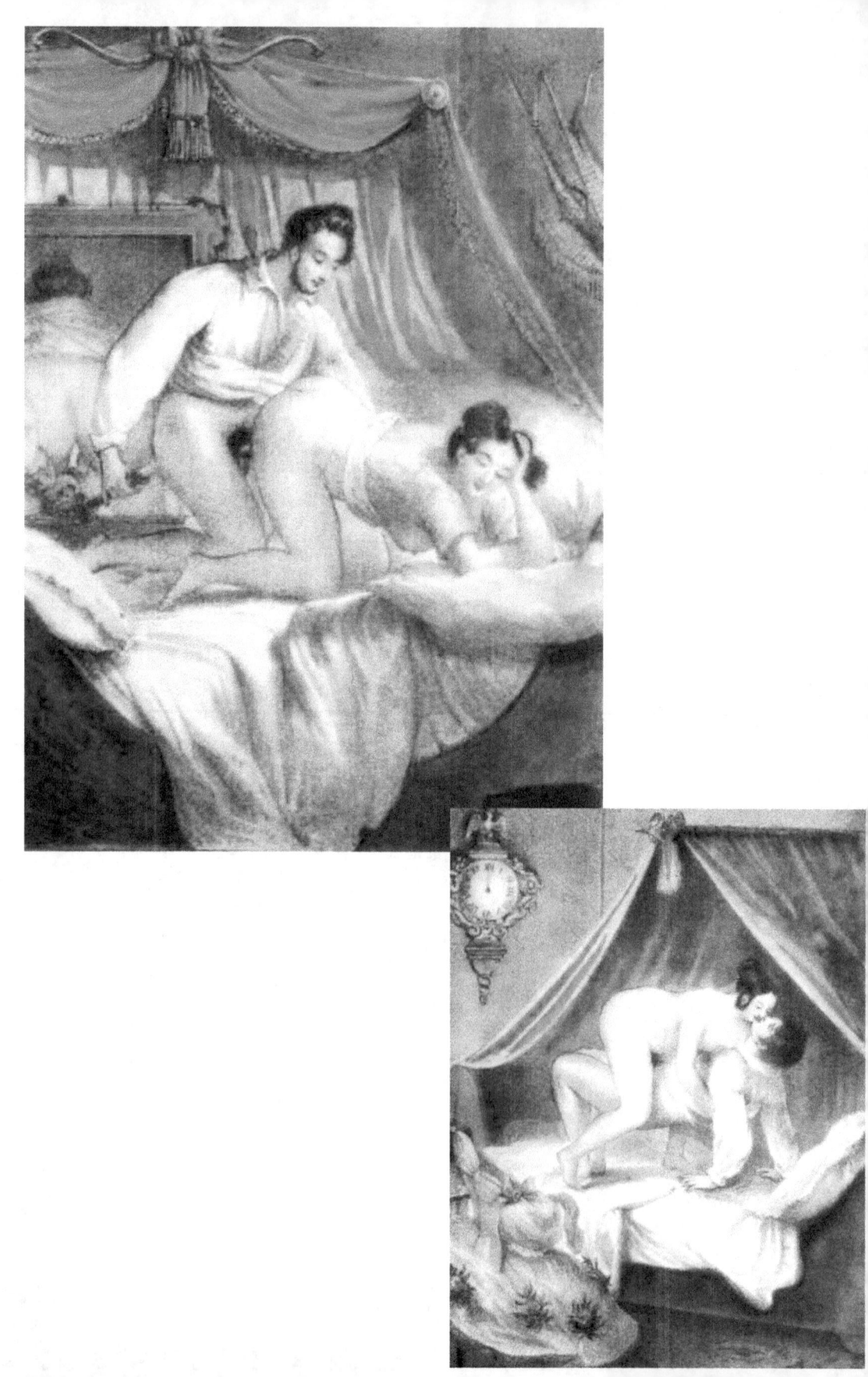

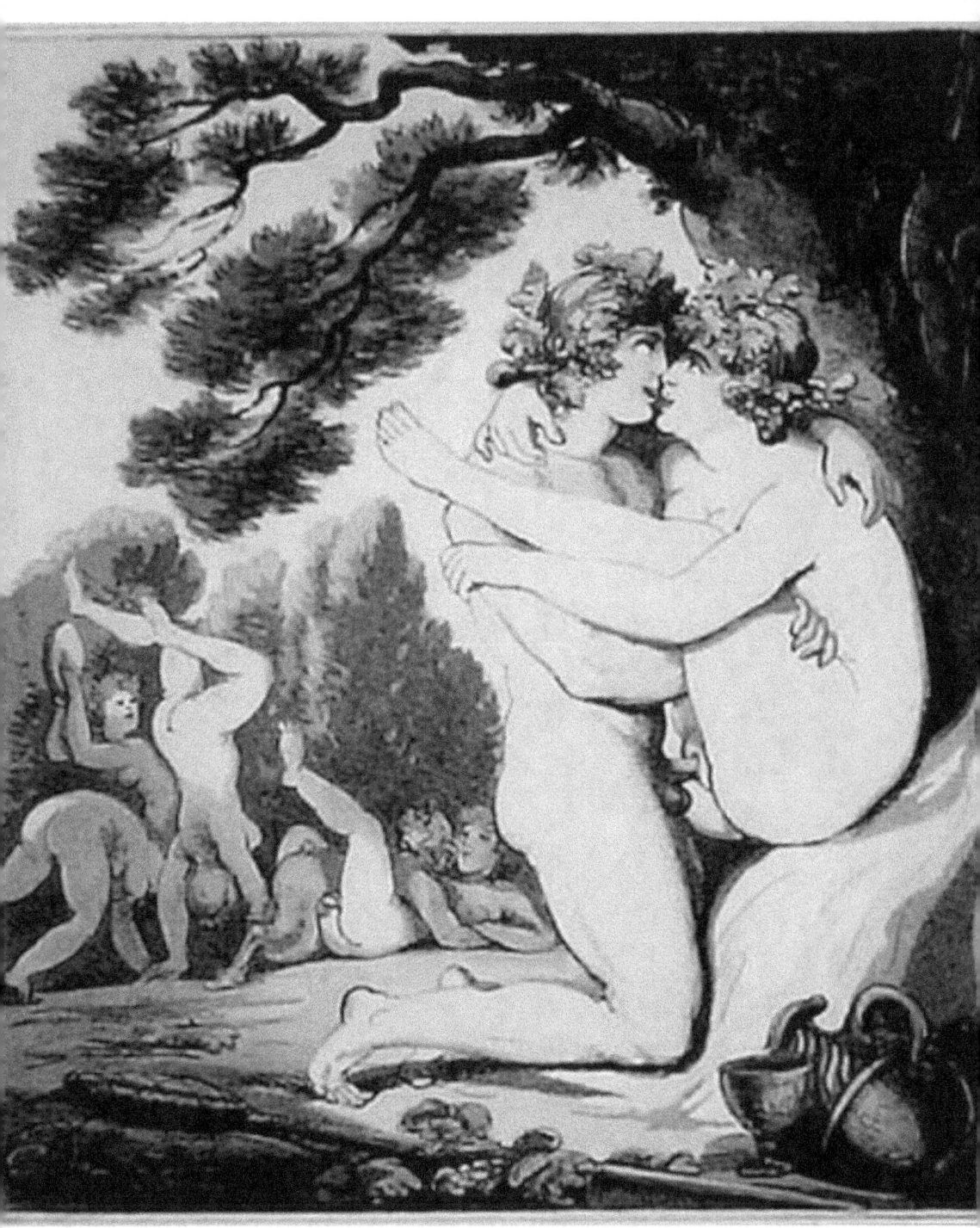

Thomas Rowlandson

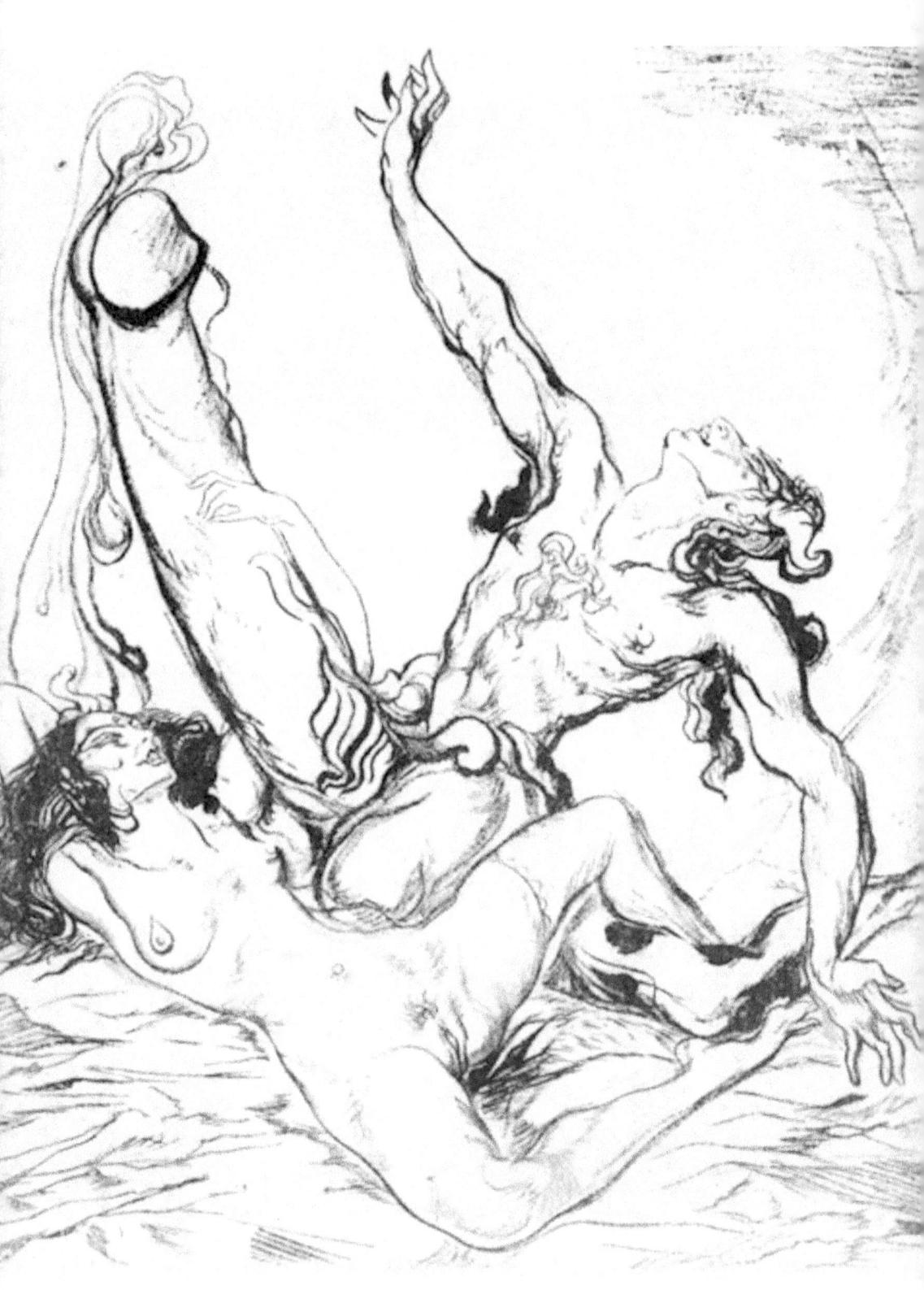

Nicolas Sternberg, from Les orfe vres a la Saint-Éloi (1430), Paris, 1930

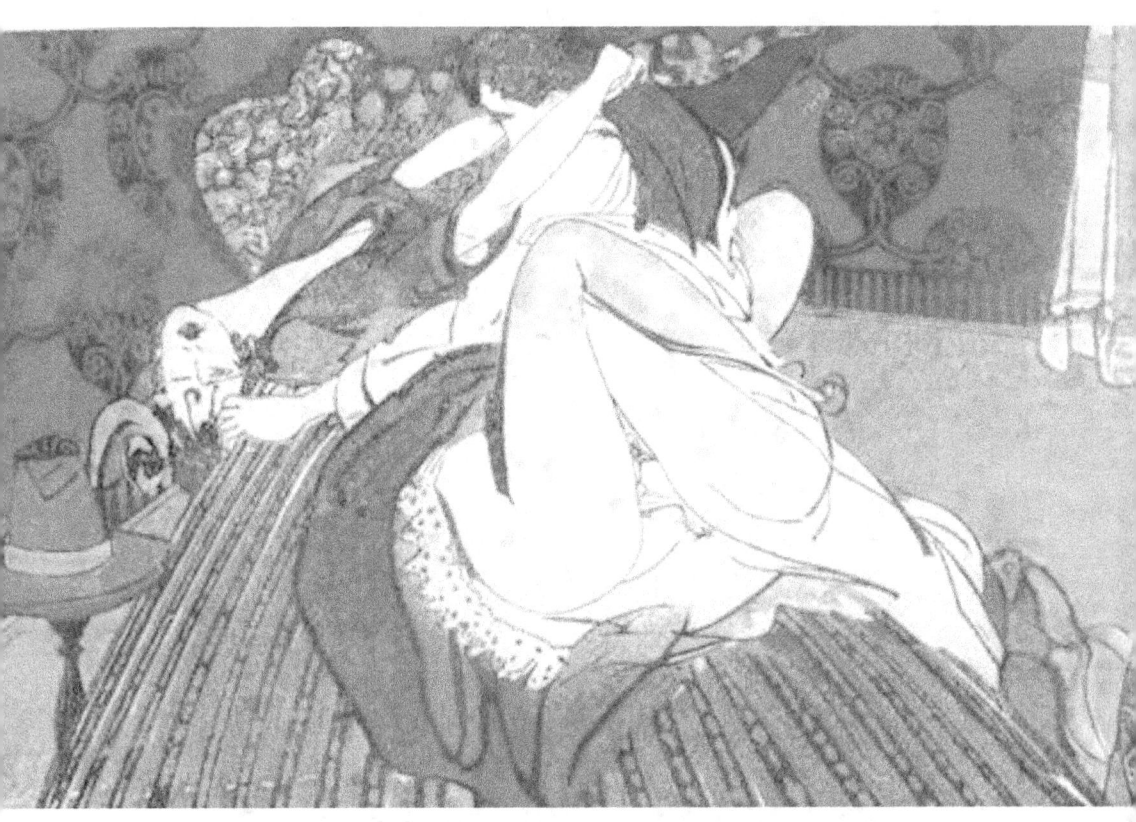

Albert Weisgerber (1878-1915), Passion

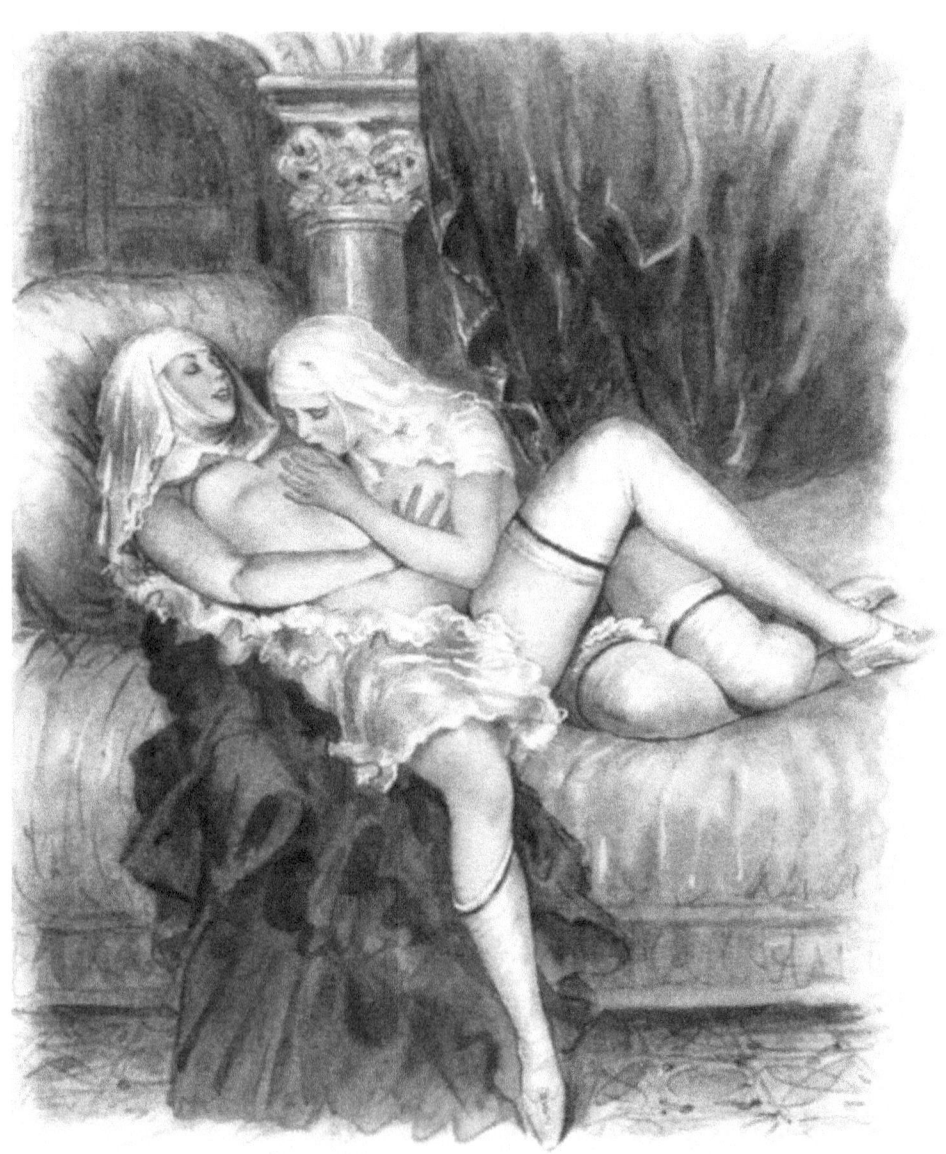

Paul-Émile Bécat,illustration for
Les Ragionamenti by Pietro Arentino (1534)

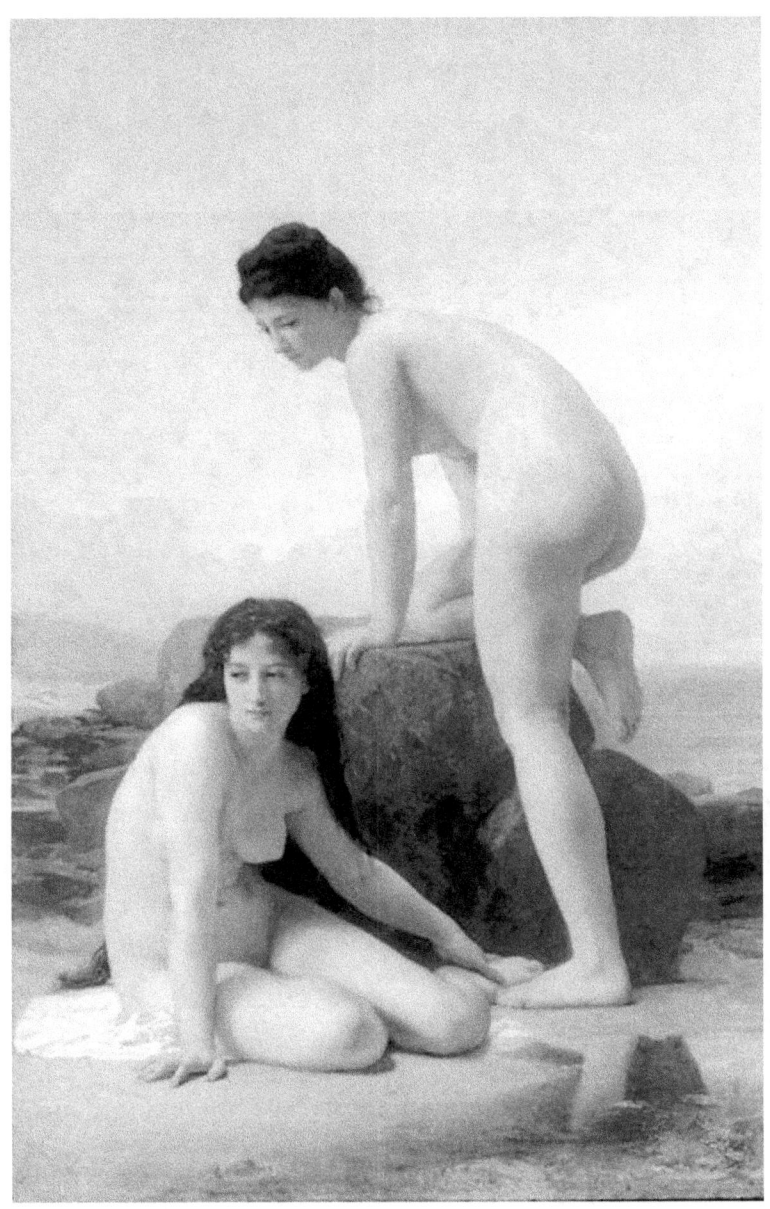

William Bouguereau, Les Deux Baigneuses, 1884

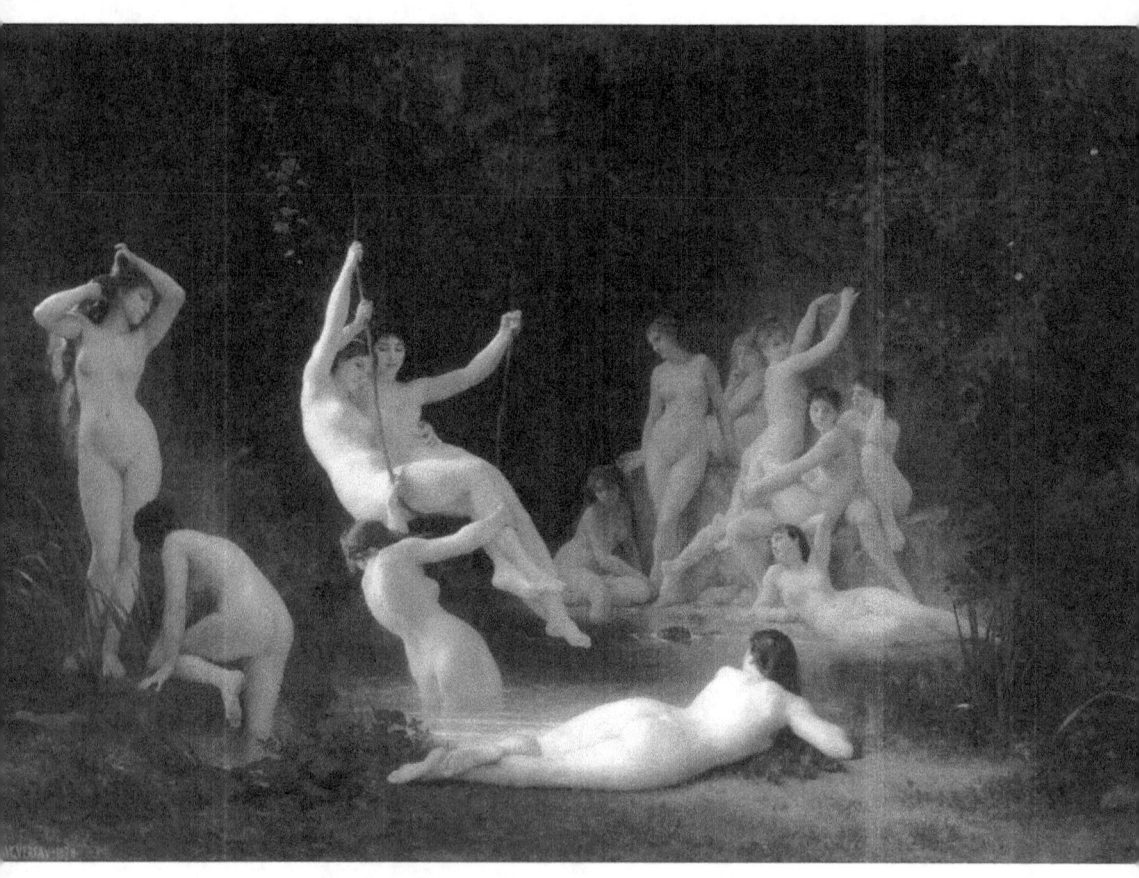

William Bouguereau, The Nymphaeum

BIBLIOGRAPHY

E. de Antonio & M. Tuchman: *Painters Painting,* Abbeville Press, New York, NY, 1984

C.G. Argan: *The Renaissance,* Thames & Hudson, London, 1969

I. Armstrong, ed. *New Feminist Discourses: Critical Essays on Theories and Texts,* Routledge, London, 1992

J. Atkins: *Sex in Literature,* volume 2: *The Classical Experience of the Sexual Impulse,* Calder & Boyars, London, 1973

P. Bade: *Femme Fatale: Images of evil and fascinating women,* Ash & Grant 1979

M. Baxandall: *Painting and Experience in 15th Century Italy,* Oxford University Press 1988

—. *Patterns of Intention: On the Historical Explanation of Pictures,* Yale University Press 1985

G. Bazin: *A Concise History of World Sculpture,* David & Charles, Newton Abbot 1981

J. Beck: *Italian Renaissance Painting,* Harper & Row, New York, NY, 1981

B. Berenson: *The Italian Painters of the Renaissance,* Phaidon, London, 1952

—. *Looking at Pictures with Bernard Berenson,* selected by Hann Kiel, Abrahams, New York, NY, 1974

B. Bernard: *The Queen of Heaven: A Selection of Painting the Virgin from the Twelfth to the Eighteenth Centuries,* Macdonald/ Orbis, London, 1987

—. *The Bible and Its Painters,* Orbis, London, 1983

F. Bonner *et al,* eds. *Imagining Women Cultural Representations and Gender,* Polity Press, Cambridge 1992

S. Bramly: *Leonardo: The Artist and the Man,* Michael Joseph 1992

A. Brahama: *Italian Renaissance Painters of the Sixteenth Century,* National Gallery 1985

J. Burckhardt: *The Altarpiece in Renaissance Italy,* Phaidon, London, 1988

T. Burckhardt: *Sacred Art in East and West,* Perennial Book, Middlesex 1967

W. Chadwick: *Women, Art, and Society,* Thames & Hudson, London, 1990

—. *Women Artists and the Surrealist Movement,* Thames & Hudson, London, 1991

A. Chastel: *Art of the Italian Renaissance,* tr. P. & L. Murray, Alpine Fine Arts Collection, London, 1985

—. *The Studios and Styles of the Renaissance, Italy 1460-1500,* tr. Griffin, Thames & Hudson, London, 1966

G. Chester & J. Dickey, ed. *Feminism and Censorship: The Current Debate,* Prism Press, Bridport, Dorset 1988

H.B. Chipp, ed. *Theories of Modern Art*, University Press of California, Los Angeles, 1968

J.E. Cirlot: *A Dictionary of Symbols*, Routledge, London, 1981

Kenneth Clark. *The Nude*, Pantheon Books, 1957

B. Cole: *The Renaissance Artist at Work*, John Murray, London, 1983

J.C. Cooper: *An Illustrated Dictionary of Traditional Symbols*, Thames & Hudson, London, 1978

L. Dresen-Coenders, ed. *Saints and She-Devils: Images of Women in the 15th and 16th Centuries*, Rubicon Press 1987

W. Dube: *The Expressionists*, Thames & Hudson, London, 1972

S.C. Dubin: *Arresting Images: Impolitic Art and Uncivil Actions*, Routledge, London, 1992

G. Duby & M. Perrot: *Power and Beauty: Images of Women in Art*, Tauris Parke Books,

A. Dworkin. *Intercourse*, Arrow, London, 1988

—. *Pornography: Men Possessing Women*, Women's Press, London, 1984

C. Eisler: *Early Netherlandish Painting: The Thyssen-Bornemisza Collection*, Sotheby's Publications, London, 1989

A. Elsen: *Modern European Sculpture 1918-45*, New York, NY, 1979

J. Evans, ed. *The Flowering of the Middle Ages*, Thames & Hudson, London, 1966

J. Evola: *The Metaphysics of Sex*, East-West Publications, London, 1985

M. Foucault: *The History of Sexuality*, Penguin, London, 1981

—. *The Use of Pleasure: The History of Sexuality*, vol. 2, Penguin, London, 1987

S.J. Freedberg: *Painting of the High Renaissance in Rome and Florence*, Harper & Row, New York, NY, 1972

S. Freud: *Leonardo da Vinci*, tr. A. Tyson, Penguin, London, 1963

E. Gadon: *The Once and Future Goddess*, Aquarian Press 1990

Fred Gettings: *The Hidden Art: A Study of the Occult Symbolism in Art*, Studio Vista, London, 1978

P. Gibson & R. Gibson, ed. *Dirty Looks: Women, Pornography, Power*, British Film Institute, London, 1993

M. Gimbutas: *The Language of the Goddess*, Thames & Hudson, London, 1989

R. Goldwater & M. Treves, eds. *Artists On Art*, John Murray, London, 1975

E.H. Gombrich: *Norm and Form: Studies in the Renaissance I*, Phaidon, London, 1985

—. *Symbolic Images, Renaissance Studies II*, Phaidon, London, 1985

S. Griffin: *Pornography and Silence: Culture's Revenge Against Nature*, Women's Press, London, 1981

J. Hale: *Italian Renaissance Painting*, Phaidon, London, 1977

J. Hall: *A Dictionary of Subjects and Symbols in Art*, John Murray, London, 1984

M. Esther Harding: *Women's Mysteries*, Rider, London, 1989

F. Hartt: *History of Italian Renaissance Art: Painting, Sculpture, Architecture*, Thames & Hudson, London, 1987

N.G. Heller: *Women Artists: An Illustrated History*, Virago, London, 1987

J. Hobhouse: *The Bride Stripped Bare: The Artist and the Nude in the Twentieth Century*, Cape, London, 1988

A. Hollander: *Seeing Through Clothes*, Viking Press, New York, NY, 1980

M. Humm: *Feminisms: A Reader*, Harvester Wheatsheaf, 1992

—. ed. *The Dictionary of Feminist Theory*, Harvester Wheatsheaf 1989

M. Jacobs: *A Guide to European Painting*, David & Charles 1980

—. *Mythological Painting*, Phaidon 1979

P. Julian: *Dreamers of Decadence: Symbolist Painters of the 1890s*, tr. R. Baldick, Pall Mall Press, London, 1971

S. Kappeler: *The Pornography of Representation*, Polity Press, Cambridge 1986

D. Kelder: *Pageant of the Renaissance*, Pall Mall Press, London, 1969

J.A. Kestner: *Mythology and Misogyny: The Social Discourse of Nineteenth-Century British Classical-Subject Painting*, University of Wisconsin Press, Madison 1989

C. Kramarae & P.A. Treichler, eds. *A Feminist Dictionary*, Pandora Press, London, 1987

J. Kristeva: *The Kristeva Reader*, ed. Toril Moi, Blackwell 1986

—. *Desire in Language: A Semiotic Approach to Literature and Art*, ed. L. Roudiez, tr. T. Gora *et al*, Blackwell 1982

J. Lacan and the *Ecole Freudienne: Feminine Sexuality*, eds. J. Mitchell and J. Rose, Macmillan, London, 1982

A. Le Normand-Romain *et al. Sculpture: The Adventure of Modern Sculpture in the Nineteenth and Twentieth Centuries*, Skira, Geneva, 1986

L. da Vinci: *The Drawings of Leonardo da Vinci*, introduction A.E. Popham, Cape, London, 1964

M. Levey: *High Renaissance*, Penguin, London, 1975

—. *Early Renaissance*, Penguin, London, 1967

F. Licht: *Sculpture, 19th and 20th Centuries*, Michael Joseph, London, 1967

L. Lippard: *From the Center: feminist essays on women's art*, Dutton, New York, NY, 1976

—. *Six Years: The Dematerialization of the Art Object from 1966 to 1972*, Praeger, New York, NY, 1973

E. Lucie-Smith: *Symbolist Art*, Thames & Hudson, London, 1972

—. *Sexuality in Western Art*, Thames & Hudson, London, 1991

F. MacCarthy: *Eric Gill*, Faber, London, 1989

E. Marks & I. de Courtivron, eds. *New French Feminisms: an Anthology*, Harvester Wheatsheaf 1981

J.C.J. Metford: *Dictionary of Christian Lore and Legend*, Thames & Hudson, London, 1983

Michelangelo: *The Complete Paintings*, Granada, London, 1980

E. Mitsch: *The Art of Egon Schiele*, Phaidon 1975

T. Moi: *Sexual/Textual Politics: Feminist Literary Theory*, Routledge, London, 1988

E. Mullins: *The Painted Witch: Female Body, Male Art*, Secker & Warburg, London, 1985

L. Mulvey: *Visual and Other Pleasures*, Macmillan, London, 1989

S. Munt, ed. *New Lesbian Criticism: Literary and Cultural Readings*, Harvester Wheatsheaf, London, 1992

P. & L. Murray: *The Penguin Dictionary of Art and Artists*, Penguin, London, 1976

L. Murray: *High Renaissance*, Thames & Hudson, London, 1977

L. Nead: *Female Nude: Art, Obscenity and Sexuality*, Routledge, London, 1992

E. Neumann: *The Great Mother*, Princeton University Press, NJ 1972

S. Nicholson, ed. *The Goddess Re-awakening: The Goddess Principle Today*, Theosophical Publishing House, New York, NY, 1989

J. Paladilhe. *Gustave Moreau*, Thames & Hudson, London,1972

E. Panofsky: *Studies in Iconology*, Harper & Row, New York, NY, 1972

—. *Early Netherlandish Painting*, Harvard University Press, Mass., 1953

R. Parker & G. Pollock. *Old Mistresses: Women, Art an Ideology*, Routledge & Kegan Paul, London, 1981

W. Pater: *The Renaissance*, Oxford University Press 1980

R. Payne: *Leonardo da Vinci*, Robert Hale, London, 1979

K. Petersen & J.J. Wilson: *Women Artists: Recognition and Reappraisal from the Early Middle Ages to the Twentieth Century* Women's Press, London, 1978

G. Pollock: *Vision and Difference: femininity, feminism and histories of art*, Routledge, London, 1988

M. Praz: *The Romantic Agony*, tr. Davidson, Oxford University Press 1933

Peter Redgrove. *The Black Goddess and the Sixth Sense, Bloomsbury, London, 1987*

F. Roh: *German Art in the Twentieth Century: Painting, Sculpture, Architecture*, Thames & Hudson, London, 1968

M. Roskill: *What is Art History?*, Thames & Hudson, London, 1976

G. Saunders. *The Nude: a new perspective*, Herbert Press, London, 1989

P. Selz. *German Expressionist Painting*, University of California Press, Berkely, CA, 1974

—. *Art in Our Times: A Pictorial History 1890-1980*, Thames & Hudson, London, 1982

E. Showalter, ed. *The New Feminist Criticism*, Virago, London, 1986

Penelope Shuttle & Peter Redgrove. *The Wise Wound,* Paladin/ Grafton, 1978/86

M. Sjöö & B. Mor: *The Great Cosmic Mother*, Harper & Row, San Francisco 1987

F. Stella. *Working Space*, Harvard University Press, Cambridge, MA, 1986

—. *Frank Stella*, Madrid, 1995

K. Stiles & P. Selz, eds. *Theories & Documents of Contemporary Art: A Sourcebook of Artists' Writings*, University of California Press, Berkeley, CA, 1996

V.I. Stoichita: *Leonardo da Vinci*, Abbey Library, London, 1978

S. Rubin Suleiman, ed. *The Female Body in Western Culture: Contemporary Perspectives*, Harvard University Press, Cambridge, Mass., 1986

William Thompson. *The Time Falling Bodies Take to Light: Mythology, Sexuality and the Origins of Culture,* St Martin's Press, New York, NY, 1981

A. Tilly: *Erotic Drawings*, Phaidon 1986

P. Trevor-Roper: *The world blunted through sight: An inquiry into the influence of defective vision on art and character*, Thames & Hudson, London, 1970

W. Tucker. *The Language of Sculpture*, Thames & Hudson, London, 1974

L. Venturi: *Renaissance Painting, from Leonardo to Dürer,* Skira/ Macmillan 1979

—. *Italian Paintings,* Zwemmer, London, 1950

P. Vergo: *Art in Vienna: 1898-1918: Klimt, Kokoschka, Schiele and Their Contemporaries*, Phaidon 1975

G. de Vries, ed. *On Art: Artists' Writings on the Changed Notion of Art After, 1965*, Cologne, 1974

B. Walker: *Body Magic*, Paladin, London, 1979

—. *Tantrism: Its Secret Principles and Practices*, Aquarian Press, Wellingborough 1982

Marina Warner. *Alone Of All Her Sex: The Myth and Cult of the Virgin Mary*, Picador, London, 1985

—. *Monuments and Maidens*, Weidenfeld & Nicolson, London, 1985

Valerie Wayne, ed. *The Matter of Difference: Materialist Feminist Criticism of Shakespeare*, Harvester Wheatsheaf, Hemel Hempstead, 1991

P. Webb: *The Erotic Arts*, Secker & Warburg, London, 1983

D. Wheeler: *Art Since Mid-Century: 1945 to the Present*, Thames & Hudson, London, 1991

F. Whitford: *Egon Schiele*, Thames & Hudson, London, 1981

L. Williams: *Hard Core*: Power, Pleasure, and the 'Frenzy of the Visible', Pandora, London, 1990

C. Wilson: *The Sexual Misfits: A Study of Sexual Outsiders*, Collins, London, 1989

H. Wolfflin: *Classic Art*, Phaidon 1952/80

M. Wudram: *Art of the Renaissance*, Weidenfeld & Nicolson, London, 1985

WEBSITES

eroticbibliophile.com
eroti-cart.com
deltaofvenus.com
erotomane.org

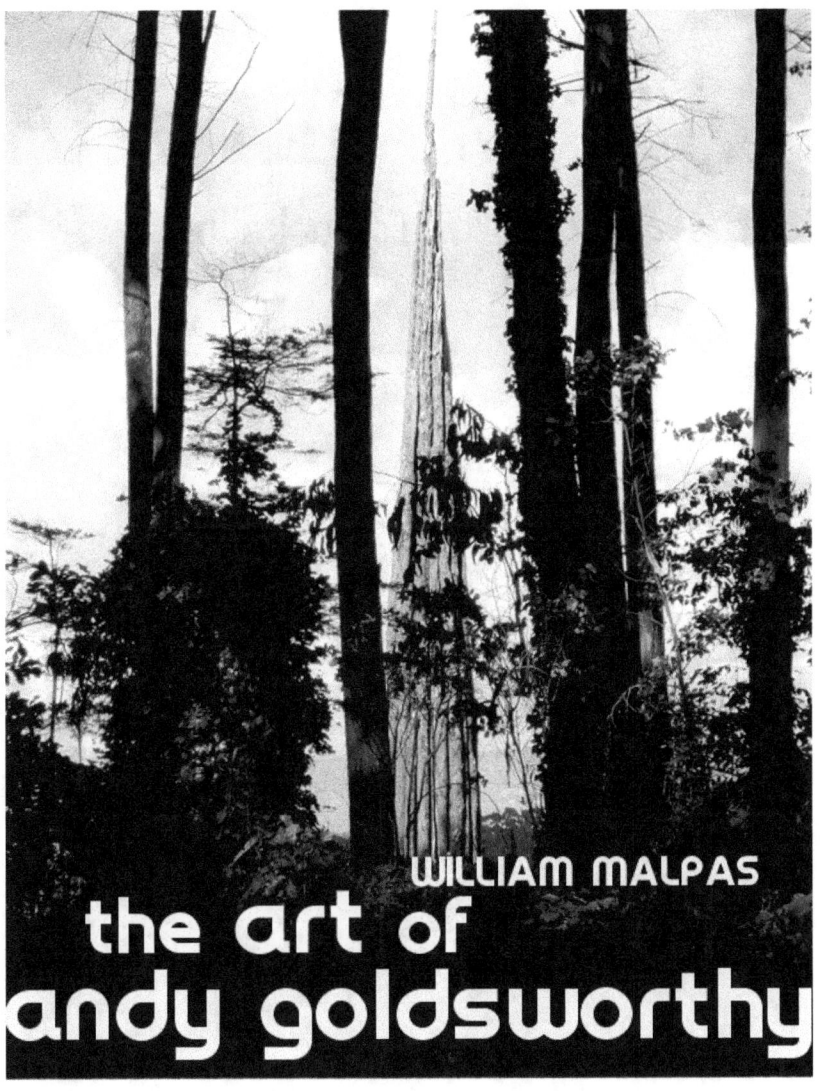

WILLIAM MALPAS
the art of
andy goldsworthy

This is the most comprehensive and detailed account of the art of Andy Goldsworthy available.

This study of Andy Goldsworthy discusses all of Goldsworthy's major exhibitions, books and projects, including the *Sheepfolds* project; *Garden of Stones* in New York; TV and dance collaborations; and the books *Wood, Stone, Time* and *Passage*. William Malpas surveys all of Goldsworthy's output, and analyzes his relation with other land artists such as Robert Smithson, the Christos, Walter de Maria, Chris Drury, Richard Long and David Nash; women sculptors; sculpture in the modern era; and Goldsworthy's place in the contemporary British art scene.

The book has been updated and revised for this new edition.

ISBN 9781861714107 Pbk   ISBN 9781861714114 Hbk
Fully illustrated   www.crmoon.com

MAURICE SENDAK

& the art of children's book illustration

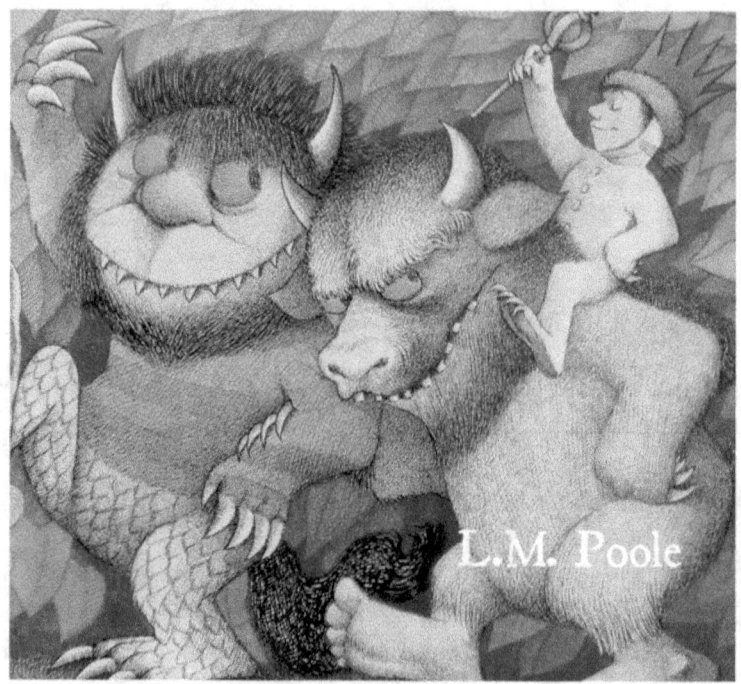

L.M. Poole

Maurice Sendak is the widely acclaimed American children's book author and illustrator. This critical study focuses on his famous trilogy, *Where the Wild Things Are*, *In the Night Kitchen* and *Outside Over There*, as well as the early works and Sendak's superb depictions of the Grimm Brothers' fairy tales in *The Juniper Tree*. L.M. Poole begins with a chapter on children's book illustration, in particular the treatment of fairy tales. Sendak's work is situated within the history of children's book illustration, and he is compared with many contemporary authors.

Fully illustrated. The book has been revised and updated for this edition.
ISBN 9781861714282 Pbk   ISBN 9781861713469 Hbk

Beauties, Beasts, and Enchantment

CLASSIC FRENCH FAIRY TALES

Translated and with an Introduction
by Jack Zipes

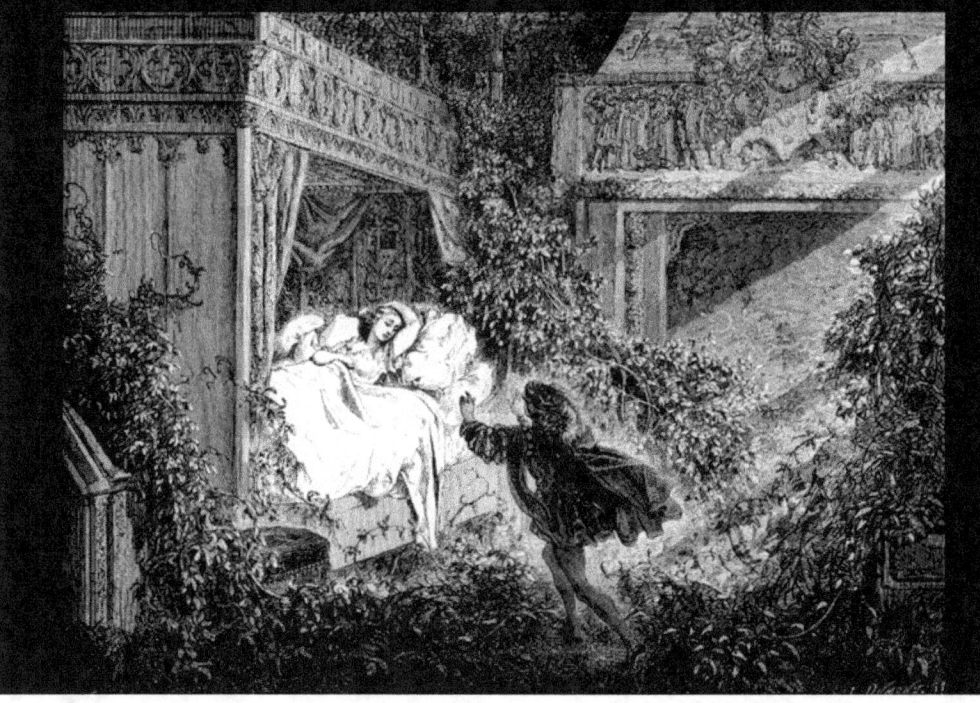

A collection of 36 classic French fairy tales translated by renowned writer Jack Zipes.
Cinderella, Beauty and the Beast, Sleeping Beauty and *Little Red Riding Hood* are among the
classic fairy tales in this amazing book.
Includes illustrations from fairy tale collections.
Jack Zipes has written and published widely on fairy tales.

'Terrific... a succulent array of 17th and 18th century 'salon' fairy tales'
- *The New York Times Book Review*

'These tales are adventurous, thrilling in a way fairy tales are meant to be... The translation
from the French is modern, happily free of archaic and hyperbolic language... a fine and
sophisticated collection' - *New York Tribune*

'Enjoyable to read... a unique collection of French regional folklore' - *Library Journal*

'Charming stories accompanied by attractive pen-and-ink drawings' - *Chattanooga Times*

Introduction and illustrations   612pp.   ISBN 9781861712510 Pbk   ISBN 9781861713193 Hbk

CRESCENT MOON PUBLISHING

web: www.crmoon.com e-mail: cresmopub@yahoo.co.uk

ARTS, PAINTING, SCULPTURE

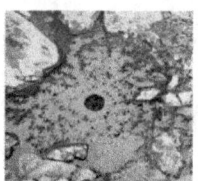

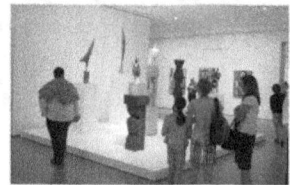

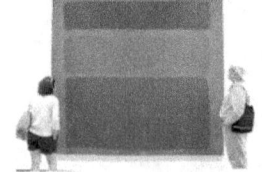

The Art of Andy Goldsworthy
Andy Goldsworthy: Touching Nature
Andy Goldsworthy in Close-Up
Andy Goldsworthy: Pocket Guide
Andy Goldsworthy In America
Land Art: A Complete Guide
The Art of Richard Long
Richard Long: Pocket Guide
Land Art In the UK
Land Art in Close-Up
Land Art In the U.S.A.
Land Art: Pocket Guide
Installation Art in Close-Up
Minimal Art and Artists In the 1960s and After
Colourfield Painting
Land Art DVD, TV documentary
Andy Goldsworthy DVD, TV documentary
The Erotic Object: Sexuality in Sculpture From Prehistory to the Present Day
Sex in Art: Pornography and Pleasure in Painting and Sculpture
Postwar Art
Sacred Gardens: The Garden in Myth, Religion and Art
Glorification: Religious Abstraction in Renaissance and 20th Century Art
Early Netherlandish Painting
Leonardo da Vinci
Piero della Francesca
Giovanni Bellini
Fra Angelico: Art and Religion in the Renaissance
Mark Rothko: The Art of Transcendence
Frank Stella: American Abstract Artist
Jasper Johns
Brice Marden
Alison Wilding: The Embrace of Sculpture
Vincent van Gogh: Visionary Landscapes
Eric Gill: Nuptials of God
Constantin Brancusi: Sculpting the Essence of Things
Max Beckmann
Caravaggio
Gustave Moreau
Egon Schiele: Sex and Death In Purple Stockings
Delizioso Fotografico Fervore: Works In Process 1
Sacro Cuore: Works In Process 2
The Light Eternal: J.M.W. Turner
The Madonna Glorified: Karen Arthurs

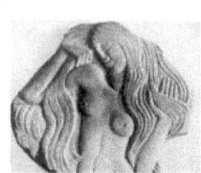

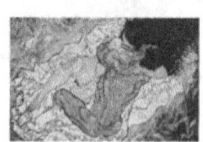

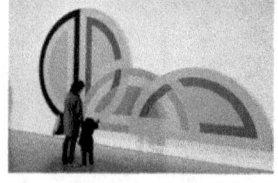

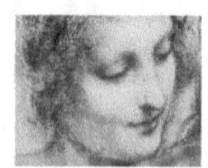

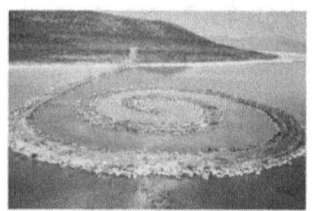

LITERATURE

J.R.R. Tolkien: The Books, The Films, The Whole Cultural Phenomenon
J.R.R. Tolkien: Pocket Guide
Tolkien's Heroic Quest
The *Earthsea* Books of Ursula Le Guin
Beauties, Beasts and Enchantment: Classic French Fairy Tales
German Popular Stories by the Brothers Grimm
Philip Pullman and *His Dark Materials*
Sexing Hardy: Thomas Hardy and Feminism
Thomas Hardy's *Tess of the d'Urbervilles*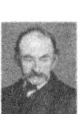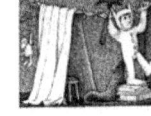
Thomas Hardy's *Jude the Obscure*
Thomas Hardy: The Tragic Novels
Love and Tragedy: Thomas Hardy
The Poetry of Landscape in Hardy
Wessex Revisited: Thomas Hardy and John Cowper Powys
Wolfgang Iser: Essays and Interviews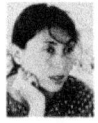
Petrarch, Dante and the Troubadours
Maurice Sendak and the Art of Children's Book Illustration
Andrea Dworkin
Cixous, Irigaray, Kristeva: The *Jouissance* of French Feminism
Julia Kristeva: Art, Love, Melancholy, Philosophy, Semiotics and Psychoanalysis
Hélène Cixous I Love You: The *Jouissance* of Writing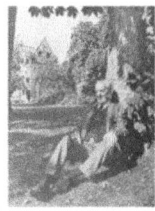
Luce Irigaray: Lips, Kissing, and the Politics of Sexual Difference
Peter Redgrove: Here Comes the Flood
Peter Redgrove: Sex-Magic-Poetry-Cornwall
Lawrence Durrell: Between Love and Death, East and West
Love, Culture & Poetry: Lawrence Durrell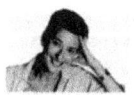
Cavafy: Anatomy of a Soul
German Romantic Poetry: Goethe, Novalis, Heine, Hölderlin
Feminism and Shakespeare
Shakespeare: Love, Poetry & Magic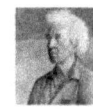
The Passion of D.H. Lawrence
D.H. Lawrence: Symbolic Landscapes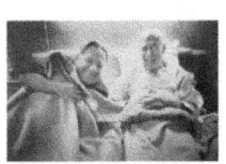
D.H. Lawrence: Infinite Sensual Violence
Rimbaud: Arthur Rimbaud and the Magic of Poetry
The Ecstasies of John Cowper Powys
Sensualism and Mythology: The Wessex Novels of John Cowper Powys
Amorous Life: John Cowper Powys and the Manifestation of Affectivity (H.W. Fawkner)
Postmodern Powys: New Essays on John Cowper Powys (Joe Boulter)
Rethinking Powys: Critical Essays on John Cowper Powys
Paul Bowles & Bernardo Bertolucci
Rainer Maria Rilke
Joseph Conrad: *Heart of Darkness*
In the Dim Void: Samuel Beckett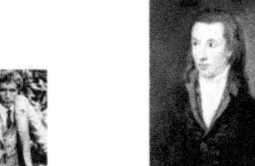
Samuel Beckett Goes into the Silence
André Gide: Fiction and Fervour
Jackie Collins and the Blockbuster Novel
Blinded By Her Light: The Love-Poetry of Robert Graves
The Passion of Colours: Travels In Mediterranean Lands
Poetic Forms

POETRY

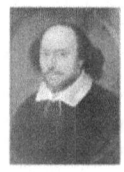
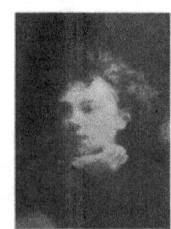

Ursula Le Guin: Walking In Cornwall
Peter Redgrove: Here Comes The Flood
Peter Redgrove: Sex-Magic-Poetry-Cornwall
Dante: Selections From the Vita Nuova
Petrarch, Dante and the Troubadours
William Shakespeare: Sonnets
William Shakespeare: Complete Poems
Blinded By Her Light: The Love-Poetry of Robert Graves
Emily Dickinson: Selected Poems
Emily Brontë: Poems
Thomas Hardy: Selected Poems

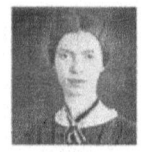

Percy Bysshe Shelley: Poems
John Keats: Selected Poems
Joh n Keats: Poems of 1820
D.H. Lawrence: Selected Poems

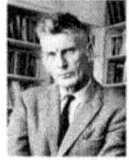
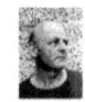

Edmund Spenser: Poems
Edmund Spenser: Amoretti
John Donne: Poems

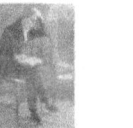
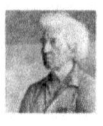

Henry Vaughan: Poems
Sir Thomas Wyatt: Poems
Robert Herrick: Selected Poems
Rilke: Space, Essence and Angels in the Poetry of Rainer Maria Rilke

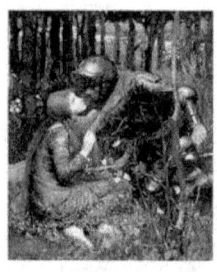

Rainer Maria Rilke: Selected Poems
Friedrich Hölderlin: Selected Poems
Arseny Tarkovsky: Selected Poems
Arthur Rimbaud: Selected Poems

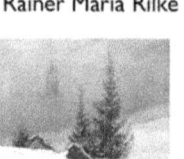

Arthur Rimbaud: A Season in Hell
Arthur Rimbaud and the Magic of Poetry
Novalis: Hymns To the Night
German Romantic Poetry
Paul Verlaine: Selected Poems
Elizaethan Sonnet Cycles

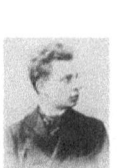
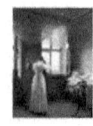

D.J. Enright: By-Blows
Jeremy Reed: Brigitte's Blue Heart
Jeremy Reed: Claudia Schiffer's Red Shoes
Gorgeous Little Orpheus
Radiance: New Poems
Crescent Moon Book of Nature Poetry
Crescent Moon Book of Love Poetry

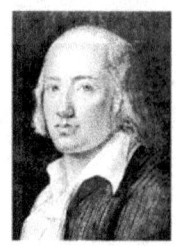

Crescent Moon Book of Mystical Poetry
Crescent Moon Book of Elizabethan Love Poetry
Crescent Moon Book of Metaphysical Poetry
Crescent Moon Book of Romantic Poetry
Pagan America: New American Poetry

MEDIA, CINEMA, FEMINISM and CULTURAL STUDIES

J.R.R. Tolkien: The Books, The Films, The Whole Cultural Phenomenon
J.R.R. Tolkien: Pocket Guide
The *Lord of the Rings* Movies: Pocket Guide
The Cinema of Hayao Miyazaki
Hayao Miyazaki: *Princess Mononoke*: Pocket Movie Guide
Hayao Miyazaki: *Spirited Away*: Pocket Movie Guide
Tim Burton : Hallowe'en For Hollywood
Ken Russell
Ken Russell: *Tommy*: Pocket Movie Guide
The Ghost Dance: The Origins of Religion
The Peyote Cult

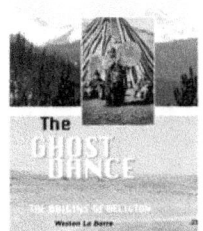
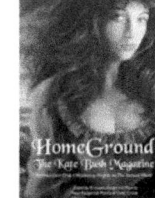

Cixous, Irigaray, Kristeva: The *Jouissance* of French Feminism
Julia Kristeva: Art, Love, Melancholy, Philosophy, Semiotics and Psychoanalysis
Luce Irigaray: Lips, Kissing, and the Politics of Sexual Difference
Hélène Cixous I Love You: The *Jouissance* of Writing
Andrea Dworkin
'Cosmo Woman': The World of Women's Magazines
Women in Pop Music
HomeGround: The Kate Bush Anthology
Discovering the Goddess (Geoffrey Ashe)
The Poetry of Cinema
The Sacred Cinema of Andrei Tarkovsky
Andrei Tarkovsky: Pocket Guide
Andrei Tarkovsky: *Mirror*: Pocket Movie Guide
Andrei Tarkovsky: *The Sacrifice*: Pocket Movie Guide
Walerian Borowczyk: Cinema of Erotic Dreams
Jean-Luc Godard: The Passion of Cinema
Jean-Luc Godard: *Hail Mary*: Pocket Movie Guide
Jean-Luc Godard: *Contempt*: Pocket Movie Guide
Jean-Luc Godard: *Pierrot le Fou*: Pocket Movie Guide
John Hughes and Eighties Cinema
Ferris Bueller's Day Off: Pocket Movie Guide
Jean-Luc Godard: Pocket Guide
The Cinema of Richard Linklater
Liv Tyler: Star In Ascendance
Blade Runner and the Films of Philip K. Dick
Paul Bowles and Bernardo Bertolucci
Media Hell: Radio, TV and the Press
An Open Letter to the BBC
Detonation Britain: Nuclear War in the UK
Feminism and Shakespeare
Wild Zones: Pornography, Art and Feminism
Sex in Art: Pornography and Pleasure in Painting and Sculpture
Sexing Hardy: Thomas Hardy and Feminism

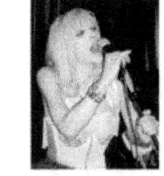
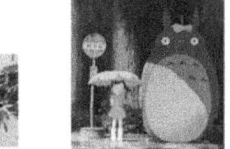
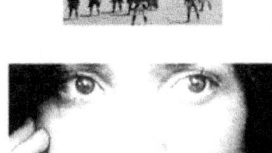

The Light Eternal is a model monograph, an exemplary job. The subject matter of the book is beautifully organised and dead on beam. (Lawrence Durrell)
It is amazing for me to see my work treated with such passion and respect. (Andrea Dworkin)

CRESCENT MOON PUBLISHING
P.O. Box 1312, Maidstone, Kent, ME14 5XU, Great Britain. www.crmoon.com

cresmopub@yahoo.co.uk   www.crescentmoon.org.uk

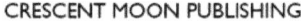